The
Barrier
and the
Javelin

302

H. P. Willmott

The
Barrier
and the
Javelin

Japanese and Allied
Pacific Strategies
February to June 1942

Naval Institute Press
Annapolis, Maryland

DEER PARK PUBLIC LIBRARY
44 LAKE AVENUE
DEER PARK, N. Y. 11729

RECEIVED APR 16 1984

Copyright © 1983
by H. P. Willmott

All rights reserved.
No part of this book may be reproduced without
written permission from the publisher.

Library of Congress Cataloging in Publication Data

Willmott, H. P.
    The barrier and the javelin.

    Second vol. of a trilogy that began with Empires in
the balance.   022779
    Bibliography: p.   24.95
    Includes index.
    1. World War, 1939–1945—Japan.   2. Coral Sea, Battle
of the, 1942.   3. Midway, Battle of, 1942.   4. Japan—
History—1912–1945.   I. Title.
D767.2.W537   1982   940.54'26   83-17218
ISBN 0-87021-092-0

All photographs courtesy of the U.S. Navy.

To
My Parents

Contents

Maps

Preface

The Barrier and the Javelin is the second volume of a trilogy on the Pacific war, the first volume of which, *Empires in the Balance*, attempts to explain the circumstances that led to the outbreak of the war and the course of its first five months. *Empires* offers an explanation of why in 1941 Japan chose to go to war with Britain, the Netherlands and the United States, and it also sets out the strategy she adopted both in the short term for the campaign in Southeast Asia and in the long term for the defense of her intended area of conquest.

Empires in the Balance closes with the Doolittle Raid of April 1942 and an examination of the options facing the Japanese high command in that first spring of the Pacific war. *The Barrier and the Javelin* was originally intended to carry the story forward until December 1942, thereby covering the period that forms the watershed of the Pacific war, when the Japanese and their enemies fought for the strategic initiative in a series of ferocious exchanges in the southwest and central Pacific. This period opened with the Japanese seeking to consolidate and expand their area of conquest while at the same time planning to bring an inferior enemy fleet to battle; it ended with the Japanese forced to admit defeat around Gona, Buna and Wau in eastern New Guinea and on, above and around Guadalcanal in the Solomons. This phase of the war was decisively resolved in favor of the Allies. In the course of increasingly ineffective efforts both in the Solomons and on New Guinea the Japanese exhausted themselves, losing men and material at a rate beyond their replacement capacity. The losses suffered by the Allies in this period were hardly less severe than those incurred by the Japanese, but because the resources of the Allied nations were so much greater than those of Japan, the latter was fought to a standstill by forces that imposed their initiative upon her to growing effect after 1943. By that time the Allies, unlike Japan, had made good their losses of the first year of the war.

But events in the Solomons and on New Guinea are too large and complicated to be incorporated in a single-volume history beginning with an examination of the first two carrier battles in history, the Coral Sea and Midway. Any account that covers all these actions is certain to be exhausting long before it is exhaustive. Moreover, there is good reason to draw a distinction between the events that came to a climax at Midway in June 1942 and those that followed. Before June 1942, in the Indian Ocean, in the Coral Sea and off Midway, the Japanese were on the offensive, and they held a superiority of numbers not only in these theaters of operation but in the Pacific as a whole. Their defeats in the Coral Sea and off Midway brought about a rough balance of power in the Pacific, with the result that the subsequent campaigns, particularly the air and naval struggles for Guadalcanal, were fought by well-matched opponents, neither of whom was able to secure the upper hand until the very end of 1942.

The diversity of this subject matter is evident, but that it cannot be done justice within the pages of a single volume was only one of several considerations that conspired to limit the scope of *The Barrier and the Javelin* to the battles of the Coral Sea and Midway. The initial consideration was the slow and reluctant realization of the extent to which factual errors, particularly relating to matters Japanese, invariably litter Western accounts of these battles. If certain histories are to be believed, the final stages of both the Coral Sea and Midway actions were fought by air formations which in actuality had been destroyed earlier in the battles. Orders of battle and statements of strengths and losses more often than not fail to tally correctly, and those accounts where inconsistencies have been eliminated are more often than not those that have ignored orders of battle, strengths and losses in the first place. For example, one account of Midway manages the not inconsiderable feat of telling the story of the battle without relating Japanese air strength either at its outset or at its end. Another account gives an order of battle and a statement of losses that cannot be reconciled, and a text that contradicts both.

Such comments are intended not to denigrate the efforts of others, merely to indicate that an awareness of weaknesses in existing histories was a factor in prescribing the scope of *The Barrier and the Javelin*. But this factor carried relatively little weight when set alongside the problems of incomprehension and interpretation that beset any Westerner attempting to set down the record of these battles.

The element of incomprehension stems from a lack of coherence in Japanese policymaking before the battle of the Coral Sea. At least to this writer, Japanese deliberations appear flawed on several counts, of which only two need detain us at this point. First, many of the problems the Japanese encountered after May were the direct result of their need to improvise with inadequately prepared plans drawn up for immediate im-

plementation. Japan went to war in December 1941 with nothing more
than a plan of campaign intended to carry her through the next five months.
The Japanese high command was divided on the aims to be pursued
thereafter, and not suprisingly it had no idea of how its undefined goals
might be realized. All it knew for certain was that the needs of the civil
population could not be met after April 1942 if the military kept all the
shipping it had acquired for the first operational phase. The military was to
"lose" some 1,100,000 tons of shipping from a total of 3,900,700 tons at the
very time its own needs had never been greater and were growing with the
demands of the garrisons in Japan's newly acquired possessions. At best,
Japanese strategy was little more than a number of overlapping plans of
campaign drawn up with little or no reference to available resources and the
strength of the opposition. Second, Japanese naval doctrine traditionally
eschewed the concept of command of the sea, yet in common with the
American and British navies of the interwar period the Imperial Navy was
wedded to the idea of fighting a decisive battle. It is impossible to discern
for what purpose such a battle would be fought except as the means of
securing command of the sea. In fact, the Imperial Navy, drawing on its
experiences of the battle of the Yalu and off Tsushima, was obsessed with
battle. Other navies anticipated fighting another Jutland—this time a Jutland that would be recognizably decisive in both strategic and tactical
terms—but none did so in such comprehensive and painstaking a manner as
the Japanese. In the interwar period the Imperial Navy produced a *tactical
concept of battle* that was elaborate, thorough and, inevitably, obsolescent by
the time it was implemented as the *strategic policy* that was to bring the
Pacific war to a successful conclusion in the second half of 1942.

What also limited the scope of *The Barrier and the Javelin* was the recognition that at least three aspects of the Coral Sea and Midway, which are
crucial to any understanding of the battles and of Japanese failure, seem to
have been consistently overlooked by historians. First, in both actions the
Japanese possessed a pronounced superiority of numbers in the general
theater of operations, but their enemy possessed numerical superiority at
the point of contact. In the case of the Coral Sea the American advantage
was marginal; at Midway it was more substantial. Surprisingly, neither
battle was won by the Americans against the odds—at least not in terms of
numbers. That the Japanese failed twice within a single month to emerge
victorious when they had unused numerical superiority raises obvious
questions about their planning arrangements and their conduct of operations.

Second, at Midway the Japanese put virtually every one of their available fleet units into the battle, and yet in five days of fighting they attacked
only one enemy ship. The desultory action around Unalaska excluded,
virtually the whole of the Combined Fleet contrived to attack nothing more

than the carrier *Yorktown*. (The *Hammann* was sunk in the course of the battle, but only as a result of being hit by a torpedo aimed at the *Yorktown*.) That such an otherwise inconceivable situation arose indicates there was something very wrong with Japanese tactical arrangements.

Third, these errors in planning, deployment and operational procedure place the failure of Japanese reconnaissance to find the enemy on the morning of 4 June in its proper perspective. The delay of the one seaplane tasked to search the sector where the American carrier forces were positioned has been deemed by many historians to have been a crucial factor contributing to the Japanese defeat at Midway. The Japanese were indeed unfortunate in this respect, but any explanation of defeat in terms of this single failure is spurious. Even if Japanese reconnaissance had proved completely effective, there is no reason to suppose that their subsequent losses could have been avoided—though those of the enemy might conceivably have been greater than proved to be the case. The cause of Japanese failure at Midway was not a delayed seaplane but a plan that called for a division of force, an attempt to do too much with too little against underrated opponents. The Japanese failure at Midway owed less to poor conduct of operations or individual shortcomings, important though these were, than to basic errors in planning, deployment and aim.

The problem of interpreting these events has to do in large part with the difficulty of placing the Coral Sea and Midway into the overall picture of Japanese defeat in the Pacific war. Two conclusions must be drawn from any assertion that the defeat of Japan was assured because she was industrially, financially and demographically inferior to the enemies she raised against herself. If Japan could not win a war in the Pacific, then her only chance of avoiding defeat was through a German victory in Europe or an Axis victory, in some theater other than Europe and the Pacific, that would cause a global realignment of power and thereby ease Japanese problems in the war against the Americans. Moreover, if Japan could not win a war in the Pacific, if material inferiority condemned her to long-term defeat, then her failure in one single battle can hardly have been decisive. The element of inevitability precludes decisiveness, and individual defeats are milestones along the way rather than signposts that mark the parting of the ways. Midway's result did not decide the outcome of the war in the Pacific.

All final hope of dealing with events in the Solomons and on New Guinea in *The Barrier and the Javelin* was abandoned when the question arose of why the war came to these particular operational theaters in the first place. These were areas that before December 1941 had never figured in American calculations, yet within three months of the start of the Pacific war U.S. armed forces were committed to their defense. The key to understanding how such a widening American commitment was accepted after Pearl Harbor and the reaffirmation of the "Germany-first" principle is the absence from the Allied orders of battle at the Coral Sea and Midway of any substantial force provided by America's allies. The United States had to accept an ever-deepening commitment to the southwest Pacific because of the manifest inability of its allies to defend themselves in the first half of 1942. Such a situation can be deemed sufficient cause to treat these nations with scant regard or none at all, but any account of the Coral Sea and Midway that seeks to be comprehensive must examine the sequence of events that left the lesser Allied powers unable to fend for themselves and the United States in a position to assume responsibilities undreamed of even as late as November 1941. It is not enough to note that the Royal Navy was unable to provide units (except from the Australian service) for the Allied effort in the Coral Sea and off Midway: it is important to explain why what still remained one of the three most powerful navies in the world proved incapable of helping its only major ally in the most crucial phase of the latter's war.

The Barrier and the Javelin is an attempt to explain the events of just five months, February to June 1942, toward the end of which were fought two of the more significant naval actions of the Second World War. The book is an attempt to explain the deliberations on both sides that led to the confrontations first in the Coral Sea in May and then off Midway in June. It is an attempt to set down, as accurately as the record will allow, a complete account of these battles, the decisions that preceded them and the results that flowed from them.

In trying to fulfill these various aims I received much needed and greatly appreciated assistance from colleagues and friends. A number of fellow lecturers from the Department of War Studies and International Affairs, Regal Military Academy Sandhurst, who helped to frame the terms of reference and basic structure for *Empires in the Balance* helped again with *The Barrier and the Javelin*. For their discussion of a paper on the subject and for their commentary on many other occasions, I wish to thank Mr. D. G. Chandler, Dr. C. J. Duffy, Dr. P. G. Griffith, Mr. M. J. Orr, Major R. d'A. Ryan (Ret.), Lieutenant Commander A. G. Thomas, RN (Ret.), and Major P. R. Thomas, RAEC. Similarly, I would like to express my appreciation for the trenchant critical analysis provided by members of the British Military History Commission who attended the naval symposium at Greenwich in November 1982, when I presented what almost amounted to the final product for their consideration.

I would also like to acknowledge my debt to various others who either served as editors for various chapters or found themselves involved in the preparation of this book as their best ideas were acquired and incorporated. For their efforts I wish to thank Mr. E. Grove of the Department of Strategic Studies and International Affairs, Britannia Royal Naval College, and five staff members from the Royal Military Academy, Sandhurst—Dr.

A. H. le Q. Clayton and Major A. Danchev of the Department of Political and Social Studies; Mr. N. C. de Lee and Dr. E. R. Holmes of the Department of War Studies and International Affairs; and Mr. B. T. Jones, the academic registrar. To these I would add Professor Kanji Akagi of the Military History Department, the National Defense College, Tokyo; Lieutenant Colonel T. Sakamaki, presently attending the Staff College at Camberley; and Major H. L. Zwitzer of the Military History Department of the Dutch General Staff. All three provided me with translations and material dealing with both the well-known and some of the more obscure aspects of my subject. In addition I would like to thank Lieutenant General Sir Ian Jacob, assistant military secretary to the war cabinet between 1939 and 1946, for guidance and information relating to combined planning and British perspectives about the Pacific war.

It is always invidious to single out certain individuals for special recognition when others not so treated may appear slighted. But with no offense intended to all who have helped me, I must record the special debt I owe to the three people without whose help *The Barrier and the Javelin* could never have been completed. First, I have to acknowledge my gratitude to John B. Lundstrom, author of that excellent study, *The First South Pacific Campaign*. At a time when I encountered mounting difficulties because of records that could not be reconciled, he helped guide me through the maze and gave me access to the information he had gleaned from a decade of research. For his generosity I can only express my deepest appreciation. Second, I freely acknowledge my debt to Jon Wenzel of the Imperial War Museum, London. He and his unpublished paper, "The Japanese Decision for War and the Genesis of the Three-Phase Operational Concept," provided invaluable information about the events that led to the Japanese foray into the Indian Ocean in April 1942. Third, I am deeply indebted to Lieutenant Commander Akihiko Yoshida, JMSDF, recently of the Military History Department at the National Defense College, for his help in checking Japanese sources and the text against the official Japanese record. Whatever value *The Barrier and the Javelin* possesses is in large part the result of the efforts of these men, but neither they nor anyone else who assisted in the preparation of the text are answerable in any way for errors of omission and commission, which remain the exclusive responsibility of the author.

My thanks also extend to the staffs of the various libraries in which I have worked or with whom I have been in contact: the Admiralty Library; the British Museum; the Center of Military History, Department of the Army; the Imperial War Museum; the Institute of Historical Research; the National Maritime Museum; the Naval Historical Center, Department of the Navy; the Royal United Services Institute; and the School of Oriental and African Studies, University of London. My greatest thanks are owed to the staffs of the libraries on home ground, namely those of the Royal Military Academy and the Staff College.

Final thanks are due to my former agent, Mr. Aubrey Davis, and to the Naval Institute Press for having the confidence in me after *Empires in the Balance* to go ahead with *The Barrier and the Javelin*. I am grateful for all the help given me by the staff at Annapolis who so seldom get the formal acknowledgment that their efforts merit. I would like to thank Dick Hobbs, Susan Artigiani and Beverly Baum; Moira Megargee for her work on the maps; and particularly Connie Buchanan, a long-suffering editor who smoothed away the rough edges with a tolerance, cheerfulness and grace that on occasions must have come very close to the breaking point. And, of course, the last of all debts is to those most immediately affected by the writing life: I hope that my family will consider the demands that the manuscript made upon them to have been justified by the end result.

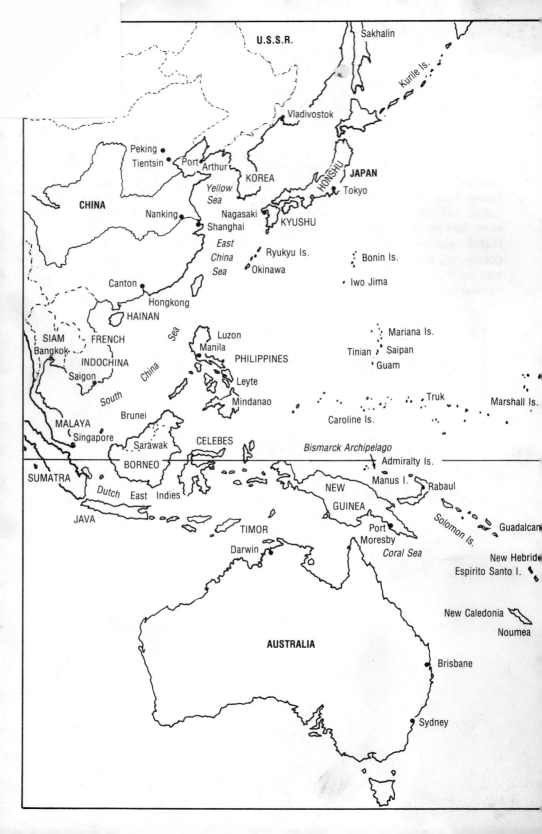

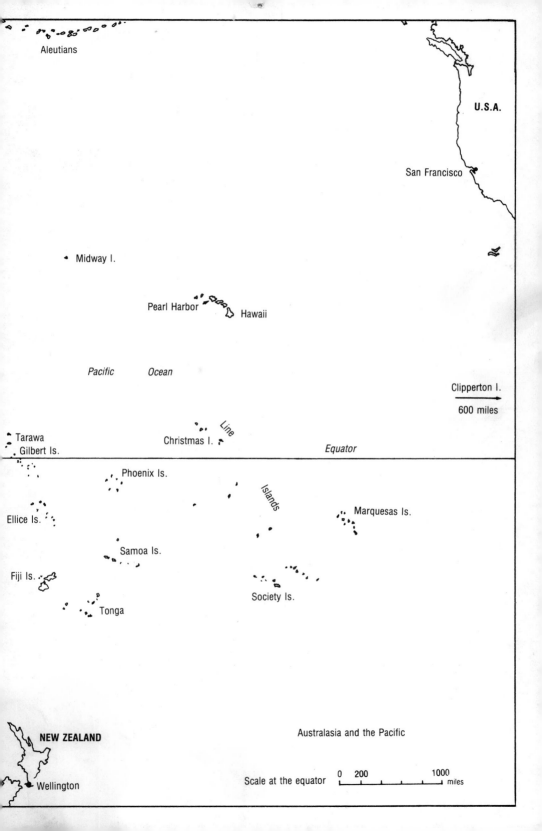

Aleutians

U.S.A.

San Francisco

Midway I.

Pearl Harbor 　Hawaii

Pacific　Ocean

Clipperton I.

→
600 miles

Tarawa
Gilbert Is.

Christmas I.

Line

Equator

Phoenix Is.

Islands

Marquesas Is.

Ellice Is.

Samoa Is.

Fiji Is.

Society Is.

Tonga

NEW ZEALAND

Australasia and the Pacific

Wellington

Scale at the equator　0　200　1000 miles

PART I

The Japanese Situation

CHAPTER 1

The Barrier or . . .

If Clausewitz is to be believed, "the first, the grandest, and most decisive act of judgement which the Statesman and General exercises is rightly to understand [the nature of] the War in which he engages, not to take it for something, or to wish to make of it something, which . . . it is impossible for it to be."[1]

Perhaps the abiding paradox of the Second World War is that of all the major combatants, Japan alone did not aspire to final victory but nevertheless fought with a totality and finality unequaled by countries intent on securing the unconditional surrender of their enemies. All the warring nations had units and formations that fought to the last man and the last round at times, but only the Japanese armed forces saw such sacrifice as the normal and not the occasional method of waging war. For all the ferocity of her effort, however, Japan's goal was to secure a negotiated peace by limiting and winning the conflict she began in the Pacific in 1941. She aimed to force her enemies to come to terms with the gains she intended to make in the opening months of the war.

In the four months that followed the start of the Pacific war there were many indications that Japan's leadership had gauged correctly the nature of the conflict it had unleashed. The British had been humbled with contemptuous ease in Malaya and Singapore. The Dutch had been broken, with scarcely any effort, in the Indies. In the southwest Pacific the Japanese had recorded gains in the Bismarcks, in the Gilberts and on New Guinea without undue trouble. Admittedly, the initial attempt to secure Wake had proved a fiasco, but the island had been pocketed the second time around. Guam had not posed any problems at all. And on Luzon in the Philippines, the Americans had proved obstinate and their resistance to Japanese arms had been prolonged, but this opposition did not make any real inroads into the Japanese timetable, and there was no doubt about the outcome of operations. American forces on Bataan and on the lesser islands of the Philippines were doomed.

Around their various conquests in Southeast Asia the Japanese intended to form a protective cordon along which would be fought a defensive war that would exhaust their enemies. The Japanese calculated that their foes would tire of war if they were shown that any attempt to carry the conflict to the Japanese homeland would be bloodily indecisive. In such circumstances the enemy would accept peace, just as the Chinese and Russians, in their wars with the island empire around the turn of the century, had come to terms when they realized they could not carry the fighting to Japan herself.

But even in the midst of victory there were certain disquieting signs. The most obvious, though perhaps the least appreciated at the time, was that Pearl Harbor had been attacked and the enmity of the United States provoked without the Japanese having registered either of the two objectives they considered essential to long-term success. Their attack had mauled but not devastated the U.S. Pacific Fleet, and it had not shattered American morale. The Pacific Fleet in fact emerged from the attack with remarkably few losses, while the effect of the attack on American public opinion was completely unexpected.* Moreover, within a month of Pearl Harbor Japan's enemies served notice on her that the war she had begun would not necessarily be fought to rules of her making. The Declaration of the United Nations, signed by twenty-six nations on 1 January 1942, did not set out the demand for "unconditional surrender"—that contentious formula had to await the Casablanca Conference of 1943 to find expression—but the meaning of the declaration was nevertheless quite unmistakable: Japan's foes harbored no thought of accepting any form of compromise with her.

In many instances there is, of course, a difference between a declaration of intention and an ability to put that intention into practice. The Declaration of the United Nations was only a declaration, and as far as Southeast Asia in the first quarter of 1942 was concerned, declarations of intention seemed the limit of the power of Japan's enemies. But for the Japanese leadership the moral to be drawn was obvious: it had to examine how to bring about a negotiated settlement with enemies who had announced their refusal to negotiate. The Japanese leaders would have to review their options once the initial phase of conquest was complete, and quite clearly they had to consider putting aside the idea of fighting a defensive campaign

---

*Of course, so did the attacking Japanese themselves. Their naval leadership had anticipated losses of perhaps one-third of their strike force, and a total disaster was expected by not a few high-ranking officers of the Imperial Navy.[2] In the event, only twenty-nine aircraft were lost at Pearl Harbor against eighteen American warships either sunk or damaged.[3]

behind a secured perimeter in favor of an offensive campaign designed to force the enemy to the conference table.

Few Japanese commanders could have appreciated the various ironies of the situation in which they found themselves during the initial weeks of victory. Japan had been plunged into war with Britain, the Netherlands and the United States primarily as a result of her determination to acquire the resources of Southeast Asia, particularly the Dutch East Indies. Without them she could not survive as a great power. Without them, Japan believed, she would never possess the wherewithal to withstand American threats and, at the same time, to bring the seemingly interminable war with China, waged since 1931, to a satisfactory end. To reduce China Japan needed British and Dutch possessions in Southeast Asia, and to secure the latter she chose to go to war with the United States, despite the fact that no treaty of alliance or mutual assistance existed between any combination of the Americans, British, Chinese and Dutch. Even by the least exacting standard, the manner in which the Japanese ranged a combination of these four peoples against them hardly speaks highly of their leaders' acumen and political sagacity. Indeed, of all the Japanese failings in the Second World War this was the most critical. Though the Japanese believed when they began the war that they had judged its nature correctly, that they were not attempting to make it into something it was not and never could be, this was precisely what they did. But the important point is that in 1941 the Japanese saw no alternative to going to war with the Americans.

It was her duty, Japan believed, to free Asia from the rule of white imperialists, and it was her destiny to be the leader of an east Asian league that would embrace the area between Siberia and Australasia. The name she gave to this area reflected a sincere if misguided Japanese conviction that what she offered the peoples of Asia was partnership in a new international order in the Far East. The "Greater East Asia Co-Prosperity Sphere" was not simply a name invented to disguise the rapaciousness of Japanese ambitions; it referred to a vision of Japanese leadership in east Asia during a difficult transitional period, after which the enlightened self-interest of the sphere's members would ensure their cooperation and mutual benefit. There was no room to accommodate American and European imperialists in this Japanese design. If Japan was to realize these aspirations, if she was to take control of her destiny, then a clash with the white imperialist powers was inevitable.

In 1941 the prospect of a war with the British (and Dutch) did not make the Japanese hesitate overmuch. Britain was clearly in so desperate a position in the Atlantic and Mediterranean that she posed no immediate danger to the realization of Japanese ambitions, though not a few Japanese were wary of embarking on war before a final German victory in Europe was consummated. Many influential Japanese, particularly those of the

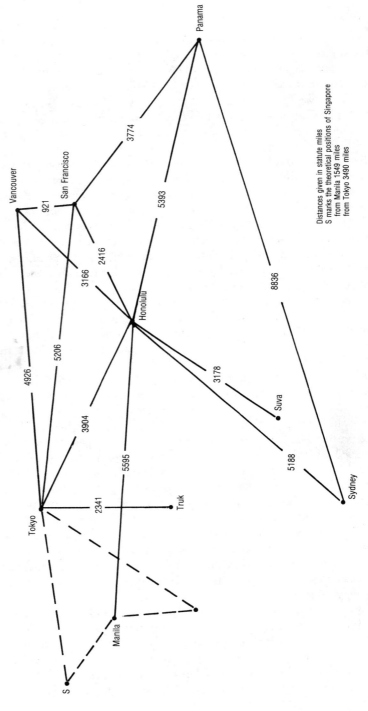

Panama

San Francisco

Vancouver

3774

5393

921

2416

8836

3166

Honolulu

5206

3178

4926

Suva

3904

5188

5595

Sydney

Tokyo

2341

Truk

Manila

S

Distances given in statute miles
S marks the theoretical positions of Singapore
from Manila 1549 miles
from Tokyo 3490 miles

Distances in the Pacific

older generation, were aware of Britain's enviable reputation of losing every battle but the one that mattered—the last one.[4] But caution was misplaced in the Japan of 1941. The Japanese knew that the Europeans in Southeast Asia had never been and would likely never be weaker than they were then. They knew that British power in the Far East was more illusory than real and that the Dutch military presence in the Indies was insignificant.

The possibility of a war with the Americans, on the other hand, was an entirely different matter. By 1941 at least two decades had elapsed since the Imperial Navy, for the first time, singled out the U.S. Navy as its most likely enemy in the event of war. But more than twenty years of familiarity with the idea of a war with the Americans had not made such a prospect any less daunting. The Imperial Navy was conscious of the strength and professionalism of the U.S. Navy, and it was aware that the latter was backed by immense industrial strength. Exchanging blows with the Americans was not a matter that the Imperial Navy entertained lightly, because it knew that in a drawn-out struggle the disparity of national resources would strongly favor the Americans.

But it was this very disparity that in 1941 prompted the Japanese to settle for war as the only means by which they could possibly become secure and self-sufficient. By 1941 Japan was in the dangerous position of knowing that her strength was at or near its peak, and that as the years marched on the odds against her would mount. To use a modern phrase, in 1941 the Japanese saw that "the window of opportunity" was gradually being closed upon them.

Japan's temptation arose from two factors: first, the territories she coveted were all but undefended by their owners, and second, the Americans, though increasingly committed to the British cause in the Atlantic, had neither an alliance with Britain and the Netherlands with regard to Southeast Asia nor the means to counter any Japanese attempt to secure the area in 1941. But the Japanese leadership also knew that the latter situation would change, rapidly, once the process of American rearmament was in full flow. Even though Japan had a head start in the rearmament business, the Americans were certain to overtake her in an arms race with relatively little difficulty. Japan had begun to rearm as soon as she was free of the limitations imposed by international treaties. Her initial construction program of March 1937, called the Third Replenishment Program, consisted of orders for two 18.11-in-gun battleships, the *Yamato* and the *Musashi*; two fleet carriers, the *Shokaku* and the *Zuikaku*; fifteen destroyers; fourteen submarines; and thirty-four other warships and auxiliaries.* The program

---

*The Third Replenishment Program was so named because it was the third major construction program adopted by the Imperial Navy after the Washington Naval Treaty. The reason it is referred to as Japan's initial construction program is that the first and second

was to be spread over five years and was scheduled for completion in either late 1941 or early 1942. During the same period as the program the naval air arm was to double in size. The Fourth Replenishment Program, introduced in 1939 in response to foreign programs, called for the building of two more battleships, one fleet carrier, five cruisers, twenty-two destroyers, twenty-five submarines and twenty-two other warships and auxiliaries. This far-from-modest increase from one program to the next was to be repeated with the projected Fifth Replenishment Program, scheduled for 1942. By mid-1941 the Imperial Navy had penciled in three battleships, two battle cruisers, three fleet carriers, five cruisers, thirty-two destroyers, forty-five submarines and seventy other warships and auxiliaries for this new program. What is more, just as the Japanese had opted for qualitative improvement in battleship armament by settling upon the 18.11-in gun for their 1937 battleships, so with the last two battleships of the Fifth Replenishment Program they decided to go one step further with the introduction of the 19.7-in gun.[5]

By mid-1941, however, even these unprecedented efforts—the cost of building the facilities needed to construct 18.11-in guns and their turrets alone was ten million dollars—were still not enough to give the Imperial Navy any degree of long-term effectiveness relative to the Americans.[6] At that time the Japanese calculated that they were being outbuilt three-to-one, and in order to counter even the existing American programs the Imperial Navy estimated that it would have to double the projected provisions of the Fifth Replenishment Program. By that time, however, the navy knew that meeting the terms of the Fourth Replenishment Program would overtax Japan's resources.

The root of Japan's problems lay not so much in the provisions of America's annual programs, increasingly heavy though these were, but in the terms of the Two-Ocean Naval Expansion Act. Passed by the U.S. Congress in June 1940, at the time when France went down to defeat before the German *blitzkrieg*, this measure allocated four billion dollars for the construction of 7 battleships, 18 fleet carriers, 27 cruisers, 115 destroyers and 43 submarines, to add to the 130 major units already being built.[7] With 358 major units already in service, the Japanese were not slow to appreciate that whereas in 1941 and early 1942 they would stand at a 70 to 75 percent strength relative to the Americans, this would fall to about 65 percent in late 1942, to 50 percent in 1943 and to a disastrous 30 percent by 1944.[8] Thus a position of clear superiority over the Pacific Fleet in 1941 would be wiped out within three years. The situation would become even graver for the

---

programs had not dealt with capital ships, the construction of which was controlled under the terms of the Washington and London treaties. The third was in effect the first program under which the Japanese were free to build capital ships.

Japanese in 1946–48, when the provisions of the Two-Ocean Act would be fully realized.

Since 1907, when the Japanese inaugurated their National Defense Policy, the navy had adhered to the notion that Japan's security needs demanded the maintenance of fleet strength at a level of 70 percent of that of the U.S. Navy. The Japanese navy, in common with other navies, accepted the principle that an attacking fleet needed to be 50 percent stronger than its enemy. Because the Japanese envisaged their being on the defensive in any war in the Pacific, maintenance of 70 percent strength relative to the strongest power in the Pacific bestowed security. This figure, which in 1907 had only been a tentative one, became enshrined over the years as an indispensable requirement. It was calculated that as long as the Japanese maintained themselves at such a level of strength, the Americans would have to check any desire they might have to test their arms against those of Japan. By the standards of the day the Japanese were correct. They concurred in the general belief that a fleet lost 10 percent of its effectiveness for every thousand miles that it advanced from its base, and that 2,000 miles was about the maximum radius of action for a fleet. These calculations explain why various naval limitation treaties to which Japan had been a party in the interwar period were so unpopular within the Imperial Navy. In the capital ship category, Japan was afforded 60 percent of the strength allowed the British and Americans; the latter two each had a 66 percent margin of superiority over the Japanese. Thus treaty provisions were said to seriously jeopardize Japanese national security. The 10 percent margin between what the Imperial Navy wanted and what the British and Americans were prepared to allow it was generally regarded as the critical difference between insufficiency and sufficiency in waging a successful defensive campaign against a more powerful American fleet. This was precisely why the Americans were so insistent on the lower percentage for Japan in the first place.[9]

Thus the Japanese prospects that emerged in 1941 were bleak. Relegation to a 30 percent strength ratio within three years of implementation of the Two-Ocean Naval Expansion Act was certain to end any chance of Japan's ever realizing her ambition to dominate east Asia and exclude the Americans from the area. Once the provisions of the Two-Ocean Act were fulfilled Japan's freedom of action would be destroyed and the country would be reduced to the status of third- or fourth-class irrelevance off the Asian mainland, at the beck and call of Washington.

By 1941, then, the eclipse of Japan was foreshadowed, but such a situation could have been foreseen two decades before, as, indeed, in a sense it was. The 60 percent ratio had been accepted at Washington in 1922 by such leaders as Admiral Tomosaburo Kato precisely because they knew that an arms race between Japan and the United States could only end in the hopeless compromising of Japanese security. Kato knew that Japan lacked the power to challenge the Americans to an arms race, and he was personally convinced of the Japanese need to work with the Americans and do everything possible to avoid a conflict with them. As Kato saw things, Japan's best interests would be served by treaties that imposed restraint on both countries. In fact by 1936, when the various treaties of limitation lapsed, the policy of mutual limitation had served Japan well: rather than standing at 60 or even 70 percent of American strength, Japan stood at nearly 80 percent, because she had built up to the limits allowed her under treaty while the United States had not. Nonetheless, the treaties remained unpopular with the Imperial Navy, and long before 1936 it had decided to oppose any attempt to persist with limitation treaties when the present ones expired. The caution and perceptiveness of Kato did not long survive the admiral's untimely death in 1923, and Japan, for a variety of reasons, settled on a policy of societal regimentation at home and expansion abroad.[10]

By 1941 the Japanese leadership thus found itself in the nightmare situation that Kato, through his careful diplomacy and his tight control of the officer corps within the navy, had managed to avoid. The naval limitation treaties had ended. Japan had begun an arms race, despite the fact that the treaties had bestowed upon her a greater degree of security than she could ever secure in an unrestricted arms race with the United States. But by 1941 Japan was well on the way to losing the race as the Americans, perhaps belatedly, began to react to a situation brought about by powers that appeared not to know the meaning of the phrase "voluntary restraint." With more than half of Japan's national budget being lavished on the armed services, there was no slack within her economy that could be picked up to meet the new situation caused by American rearmament, which was clearly intended to curtail Japanese ambitions. In response to the thinly disguised Japanese occupation of French Indochina in July 1941, the Americans froze all Japanese assets in the United States and imposed a total embargo on trade with Japan. Subsequent negotiations revealed that the price America demanded of Japan for a resumption of normal commercial relations was total relinquishment of the gains she had recorded on the Asian mainland over the previous decade.

In this situation the Americans made the fundamental error of assuming that the Japanese leaders were rational men who would look at the balance of power and resources, discern its implications and react by an appropriate adjustment of policy. American leaders failed to realize that their moves pushed Japan into a corner with virtually no choice other than to fight or accept total humiliation. Very few nations, and certainly not the Japan of the interwar period, would have accepted a diktat of the kind the Americans tried to force upon the Japanese in 1941, especially when the corollary to

THE BARRIER OR . . .

supine acceptance of American terms was almost certain to be social upheaval and revolution inside Japan.

Though the primary responsibility for the circumstances in which Japan found herself in mid-1941 lay with the Japanese themselves, particularly with the Imperial Navy, whose strident policies finally placed Japan in a "no-win" situation, the Japanese still retained certain limited options when they decided in favor of war as the cure for their problems. It was generally agreed that there was no alternative to war, but there was fundamental disagreement on the secondary question of whom Japan should fight.

The question was resolved in the course of a series of staff discussions and war games and an imperial conference that took place between the second and thirteenth of September in Tokyo.[11] Months of argument within the Japanese hierarchy had to be and were resolved during these exchanges. The Japanese had agonized for months over the choices open to them—whether to conciliate or oppose the United States; whether to try to use their links with Germany and Italy as a lever against the Americans or throw off the Axis connection in an effort to come to some sort of deal with the United States; whether to honor or break their recent nonaggression treaty with the Soviets; whether in the event of moving into Southeast Asia they moved against one or all of the imperialist powers. September 1941 saw these various conflicts settled as the Japanese military command decided upon war with Britain, the Netherlands and the United States, even though a very considerable body of opinion, led by Admiral Osami Nagano, chief of the Naval General Staff, initially opposed going to war with the Americans. There was no disputing the need to go to war with Britain and the Netherlands—these two countries had colonial territories that Japan had to secure if she was to be self-sufficient—but Nagano and like-minded colleagues could point to the American public's isolationist sentiment, traditional anti-imperialist feelings and resistance to President Franklin D. Roosevelt's policy of support for Britain as reason enough not to become embroiled in a war with the United States. To many Japanese commanders it seemed more than a little unlikely that Roosevelt would be able to convince his countrymen of the need for war with Japan in defense of Southeast Asia, unless the Japanese themselves provided the pretext by attacking American territory. For the American president to maneuver his country into war in defense of British and Dutch possessions in Southeast Asia seemed inconceivable.

Nagano and those who doubted the wisdom of precipitating a war with the United States lost this strategic argument, which was indeed the critical one as far as the Japanese were concerned. The decision was in effect taken by the military after the senior officer in the Imperial Navy was effectively overruled by his subordinates and by the army—a reflection of the manner

Admiral Osami Nagano

in which the Japanese settled policy. Nagano and his like-minded colleagues were overruled by their peers within the Japanese high command because it was generally believed that war with the Americans was inevitable and therefore should be induced rather than postponed.

None of the commanders who settled their country's fate in the second half of 1941 could help but be aware of the difficulties that had characterized American-Japanese relations for most of the century. America's immigration policy and her move to block the principle of racial equality in the Covenant of the League of Nations were but the more obvious examples of insensitivity towards Japan. Denigration of Japan, as a nation and a people, were keynotes of the American press, and while some comment, particularly with regard to Japan's economic capacity to wage war, was perceptive, most was ill-informed and deeply insulting.[12] To this constant source of friction were added the clash of interest throughout the Far East and the question of naval rearmament. By mid-1941 the last consideration was the crucial one, because the whole issue of Japanese security and the provisions of the 1937 and 1939 programs had been predicated on the belief that the Americans would not accelerate their building.[13] By this time the assumption had been proved wrong. The Americans were not prepared to accept restraint indefinitely while the Japanese showed none at all. But the Japanese also knew that their advantage in lead time gave them one and perhaps even two years of clear superiority over the Americans in the Pacific.

It was this consideration of lead time that enabled those who doubted the wisdom of provoking a clash with the Americans to go along with the majority feeling that it was in Japan's interest to force rather than delay a recourse to arms. But below this level of geopolitical and economic argument in favor of war with the United States lay other considerations. The Japanese wanted the Indies for oil and raw materials, but there were three fundamental objections to any attempt to secure these islands without a war against the United States. First, it made no sense to leave exposed across the whole width of the Pacific an open flank that could be assaulted by the Americans at a time of their own choosing. The Indies straddled the equator: Japan lay well to the north. The American fleet at Pearl Harbor rested in latitudes between the two. It was hardly logical for the Japanese to leave an alert and intact enemy no farther from Japan than she would be from her intended conquests. Second, leaving the Philippines unreduced in the rear of an advance to the south would be folly. It was not fear of what the Americans presently had in the Philippines that concerned the Japanese. In December 1941 the U.S. Asiatic Fleet, based at Manila, was no more than a paper force. It had one heavy and two light cruisers, thirteen destroyers, two seaplane tenders, six gunboats and twenty-nine submarines, as well as various other auxiliaries and support ships.[14] This posed no problem to the Japanese; the problem would be a future one. The Japanese could not remain indifferent to the prospect of the Americans building up their forces, particularly heavy bomber forces, in a position to cut Japanese lines of communication to Southeast Asia. Third, the Japanese were concerned about the American line of communication between the Philippines and Pearl Harbor, via Guam and Wake, which lay across their own lines to the southeast. Even if Guam was vulnerable and Wake was isolated, even if the Japanese lines of communication, by virtue of Japan's possession of the Marianas, Carolines and Marshalls, were stronger than those of the Americans, the Japanese could not ignore the threat the American presence represented.

The combination of wider economic considerations, a belief in war's inevitability and calculations of operational necessity proved decisive in favoring those who argued that a war for Southeast Asia had to encompass a war against the Americans. This had long been an article of faith for the navy; it was the army that maintained that it would be possible to drive a wedge between Britain and the United States, and that a war against both should be avoided. But the navy had never prepared separate war plans, indeed it had never developed any plans at all for a war against Britain except as part of those for a general war in the Pacific. According to conventional naval beliefs, the Americans would fight to deny the Japanese

Southeast Asia, while Japan needed Southeast Asia to fight the United States successfully. Nagano in fact hoped to reverse the whole basis of the navy's strategic thinking and planning in the interwar period when he tried to champion the idea of a war in Southeast Asia that would not involve the Americans.[15] He had to contend not only with this deeply ingrained strategic belief but with a much more powerful set of immediate arguments which were available to those who, like Admiral Isoroku Yamamoto, commander in chief of the Combined Fleet, insisted that war with the Americans was essential if Southeast Asia was to be secured and held. Three arguments supported such a view. First, an attack on the Indies had to be staged through and not around the Southern Philippines. Second, the American fleet had to be neutralized at the outset of war—just as the Russian squadron at Port Arthur had been neutralized at the start of the Russo-Japanese war in 1904—in order for Japan to overrun Southeast Asia without the Americans falling on her flank and rear. Third, if crushed at the outset of war, the U.S. Pacific Fleet would be able only to wage a broken-backed campaign, and new construction, rather than add to strength, would merely replace losses. If the Japanese managed to inflict significant damage on the Pacific Fleet in an initial attack, then it was possible that the worst threats posed by the provisions of the Two-Ocean Naval Expansion Act would be turned aside and that Japan would gain a large measure of long-term security.

There were certain salient features of these conclusions. First, the logic that pointed to an attack on the Americans ruled out the possibility of an operation designed to secure any or all of the Hawaiian Islands. Japanese aims relative to the United States not only had to be limited, but the bulk of Japanese strength had to be concentrated against Southeast Asia. This point was accepted as a result of the staff deliberations of the sixth and seventh of September 1941, although it was to be the subject of heated debate in another six months.[16] Moreover, the rationale behind the plan to attack Pearl Harbor was divided between the desire to break enemy morale—hence Yamamoto's initial selection of enemy battleships, the symbols of naval power,[17] as the principal target—and the buying of time.[18] These vital considerations were part of an overall strategic and tactical doctrine that the Imperial Navy had distilled over the years in anticipation of a war with the United States.

Once the principle of going to war with the Americans had been accepted within the navy, the notion of a preemptive strike against the American main force in the Pacific had followed logically. Yet by March 1942 it was clear that Southeast Asia would be secured without either of the two basic premises deemed by the "Yamamoto faction" to be prerequisites for success being realized. Southeast Asia had been, or would be, conquered without the Pacific Fleet being destroyed; the Philippines had not been reduced before the Indies had been overrun. In a sense the events of the first four months of the war proved that Nagano had been correct: the Japanese could have conquered Southeast Asia without beginning their campaign with an attack on the Americans. Japan had partially staged her attacks on the Indies through the southern Philippines, and what American air and naval power escaped destruction was withdrawn from the Philippines at the end of December 1941, but neither possession of the southern Philippines nor the breaking of American power had proved absolute requirements for success. Southeast Asia had been secured by the Japanese with minimal loss. The Imperial Navy had lost five destroyers, three patrol boats, seven minesweepers, one minelayer and seven submarines after four months of war. At the end of this phase of conquest the Japanese had to face the bitter irony implicit in their position: how to defend their conquests against the Americans, the only people who could threaten Japan and her gains and whose involvement in the war against her Japan might well have provoked needlessly.

This was the nub of Japan's strategic problem in the first four months of 1942 as the planning staffs, after seeing success achieved with a speed and economy that surprised them, began to turn their attention to the consolidation of their victories. Paradoxically the staffs had both overplanned and underprepared for this second phase of operations.

This was the result of a whole host of factors, but only those of immediate concern should be mentioned at this stage. On the one hand, the Japanese plan of campaign, drawn up in the last months of peace, had called for the occupation or neutralization "as speedily as operational conditions permit" of eastern New Guinea, New Britain, Fiji, Samoa, the Aleutians, Midway and "strategic points in the Australian area."[19] When the Japanese went to war this vague directive was about the sum of their considered strategic intentions after the initial phase of conquest. On the other hand, this phase of hostilities had been considered carefully by the Imperial Navy for the whole of the interwar period, so much so indeed that what emerged was, in effect, not a reasoned strategy but a substitute for one.

This substitute took the form of an elaborate battle doctrine which evolved over the years as the formula for success against odds. The emphasis of interwar thinking, planning, training and construction had been placed so heavily upon an impending clash of fleets that the Japanese neglected other aspects of naval warfare—such as the protection of merchant shipping—that were no less important for their being more defensive. The Imperial Navy was built, trained and committed to battle, and this involved a degree of strategic, tactical, weapons and building integration the extent of which was probably unparalleled by any other navy—not even by the *Kriegsmarine* with its "Z Plan" and its intention to wage tonnage warfare.[20]

Japanese naval doctrine was a strange synthesis of feudal mythology, recent Japanese historical experience, the most intensive application of advanced technology, and both Eastern and Western concepts of warfare.[21] Nevertheless, it largely rejected Western ideas and practices. Perhaps the most striking feature of Japanese doctrine was that it eschewed interest in the concept of command of the sea. In occidental theories of naval warfare this notion had always held a central position; it had long been accepted by Westerners that anything that aimed at less than securing command of the sea was doomed to defeat.[22] To the Japanese the concept of commanding the vast Pacific was totally unrealistic, particularly because, they believed, neither they nor the Americans had the means of destroying the other's fleet. In Western terms the Japanese sought not command of the sea but "sea control," which aimed to prevent effective enemy interference with land-based operations. Herein lay the key to the emphasis of the Imperial Navy. It was a deterrent force, one that was subordinate to the army in a country that was primarily continental rather than maritime.[23] The orientation of the Imperial Navy was towards support of operations on the Asian mainland.[24] Thus Japanese naval doctrine was essentially defensive, even though it appeared to be extremely aggressive, having evolved in response to certain specific circumstances.

The degree of caution and limitation imposed on naval objectives stemmed in part from an awareness of the scarcity of national resources, but it also traced its origins back to the well-established strategic tradition, firmly entrenched in both Sino-Korean and Japanese military thinking, of the preservation of main battle strength whenever and wherever possible. Main force units, because there were so few of them, were far too valuable to be risked in anything short of the most dire national emergency or the most favorable of circumstances. But this unwillingness to expose strength unnecessarily meant that the aim of battle was primarily defensive; the maintenance of one's own strength was more important than the destruction of the enemy's forces. The frustration of enemy plans and intentions held priority over the annihilation of the enemy. In this respect it is worth recalling that while many considerations shaped the decision to begin the war with an attack on the Pacific Fleet in its base at Pearl Harbor, one of the main considerations was that if such an attack was successful it would destroy the capacity of the Americans to interfere with Japanese operations in Southeast Asia. Annihilation was not seen as the most effective manner of frustrating the enemy. Annihilation as the means of securing command of the sea, axiomatic in Anglo-American naval doctrine, had no place in Japanese strategic doctrine; both annihilation and command of the sea were ideas contrary to Japanese military culture and values.* To the Japanese,

---

*As nations that at different times sought and secured command of the sea, Britain and the United States felt that supremacy was secured by and based on battle. Other nations saw

breaking the enemy's will by constantly upsetting his plans, while at the same time exposing oneself to minimum risk, was the primary objective of operations.[25]

The connection between these basic tenets of doctrine and the Japanese plan of campaign for 1941–42 is obvious, just as the connection between the same tenets and the Japanese conduct of naval operations in the Sino-Japanese and Russo-Japanese wars can be easily located by the student of military history. The strategic parentage of the 1941–42 plan can be readily identified. Still, any Western observer will note that somewhere between the 1941–42 operations and Japan's earlier conflicts there is a missing link. Whereas in all their wars—with the Manchu empire of China, the Romanov dynasty of Russia and the United States—the Japanese aimed at limiting the scope of conflict, there were two fundamental differences between, on the one hand, the wars with China in 1894 and Russia in 1904, and on the other, a war with the United States (and Britain) in 1941.

What each of Japan's enemies had in common, on paper at least, was military superiority over Japan. But Japan beat both China and Russia, and her success in these wars explains in part the calm with which many Japanese contemplated war in 1941. Apprehension was not absent from Japanese calculations, but it would have been much stronger had the Japanese realized the full extent of the differences between wars against two decaying dynasties, each more fearful of social revolution than of foreign defeat, and a war against a roused democracy that would not accept anything short of total victory (or total defeat) in a global war. Equally serious—and on this point Japanese intentions were to part company with reality—was that in 1941 Japan planned to limit the scope of a future war as she had been able to limit her two earlier wars. In her wars against China and Russia, however, Japan had pitted herself against continental powers, and she had been able to limit these wars because of her naval supremacy. In 1941 Japan chose to go to war with the two most powerful maritime nations in the world, and her intention was to control the extent of the conflict by naval means.[26] Herein lay the crux of her error in 1941. Japan's leaders failed to recognize where their country's potential to make war stopped, and they failed to understand the political and military strength of the nations they had so casually and willfully ranged against themselves. They failed to understand that politics did not exist to serve war making, and that force was not the only means by which the fortunes of nations were resolved. To this was added another error, namely that of believing that none of their enemies was capable of waging a protracted war in the face of Japanese martial prowess and superiority.

---

matters differently, particularly with regard to the example of Britain in the days of sail. The general European view was not that British supremacy was based on success in battle but that success in battle was the result of an existing supremacy.

The missing link that would enable Japan to limit the extent of a naval war against superior sea powers was provided by the battle doctrine that the Imperial Navy devised in the interwar period in preparation for a possible war with the United States. It was based on the reasonable premise that in case of war the U.S. Pacific Fleet would move into the western Pacific to challenge the Japanese to battle. The idea was generally shared by the Americans, whose press frequently bandied about the notion of "two weeks to Tokyo." More seriously, U.S. Marine Corps planning in the interwar period envisaged a progressive advance across the western Pacific, and the whole drift of U.S. naval planning had been for the army to fight a holding action in the Philippines while the navy battled its way westwards.[27] This basic outline for a plan of campaign was known to the Imperial Navy. In 1920 it had acquired American draft proposals for a naval war against Japan and had planned accordingly.[28]

The central problem confronting the formulation of a coherent riposte to American intentions was that the Imperial Navy was certain to be inferior to its opponent in numbers. But American superiority would in part be offset by the enemy's moving into the western Pacific, away from his own bases and into an area relatively near Japanese dockyards and repair facilities. For most of the interwar period Japanese thinking was geared to the acceptance of battle in the western Pacific, either amidst the Marianas and Carolines or to the north. Accordingly, in 1934 the Japanese set about providing the two island groups with certain base facilities; in 1939 these were increased and the zone of operations was extended to include the Marshalls.[29] Amongst this web of Japanese islands the Imperial Navy intended to meet an American challenge—relatively near its own bases but far from Pearl Harbor, and in this respect it is worth remembering that until 1940 the home base for the Pacific Fleet was not in the Hawaiian Islands but at San Diego.[30]

Nevertheless considerations of time, distance and geographical location could not compensate for too severe a material deficit. This the Japanese knew only too well. To counter the numerical advantage an American fleet advancing into the western Pacific was certain to possess, the Japanese planned to use space, to mobilize national determination and to implement a coherent strategic doctrine devised by the navy. They would further balance the books with their military prowess and their qualitative superiority, which they calculated could offset quantitative inferiority.

The Japanese calculated that as long as they could maintain themselves at a 50 percent ratio of strength relative to the Americans, they had every chance of fighting the Americans to a standstill in the western Pacific. They believed that in war the relative effectiveness of fleets was dependent on the squares of their strength. A 70 percent ratio, by this token, left them at a 2.04:1 disadvantage; the 60 percent ratio afforded them by the Washington treaties would have left them in a 2.78:1 position—hence the Japanese displeasure with the treaties. But 50 percent was the level below which the Japanese believed they dare not fall, the minimum level at which they believed they could conduct operations with any hope of success.[31] This ratio meant an apparently suicidal inferiority of 4:1 in war; certainly few nations would consider it sensible to fight a defensive campaign on the basis of such inferiority.

Most nations assess national power in terms of production, consumption, trading capacity and similar such criteria. Military power, by such reckoning, is measured by reference to trained manpower, reserves, weaponry and logistical support. The Japanese were not unaware that these were realistic yardsticks of national power, and before the war they figured that the American war capacity was more than ten times that of Japan.[32] But the Japanese tempered their assessment of national strength with considerations other than the indices of production and the number of troops under arms. Their assessment had evolved along peculiarly Japanese lines, which stressed the subordination, or perhaps more accurately, the dependence, of materiel on moral factors. To the Japanese, since war was a political phenomenon, the political manifestations of conflict and not the material ones were the decisive elements in the conduct and resolution of war.

Japan relied primarily on human resources to make up for her material weakness. The most easily tapped resource was the loyalty, discipline and self-sacrifice of an obedient population. Social cohesion was vitally important in giving the Japanese leadership confidence to face up to the prospect of a war with the Americans. This cohesion and the Japanese ethic of obedience had its roots in a national mythology that told of Japan's divine origins and the protection she was offered by the gods. Her people were members in a semidivine elect ruled over by an emperor who was himself the direct descendent of the greatest of the deities. Death in his service was the minimum obligation imposed by the mandate of the gods. Translated into practical terms, this meant, on the civilian side, absolute and unquestioning support for a war effort; on the military side, devoted professionalism and an acceptance of death. As one eminent British soldier has noted, it was a tenacity to the death that made the Imperial Army, regardless of its condition, so frighteningly formidable.[33] In Japanese songs, Johnny did not come marching home again—he went marching away to die.[34] This national mystique lay at the heart of the Japanese belief that they could wear down the Americans in a series of rearguard actions, thereby convincing them of the futility of operations that would be protracted, costly and indecisive. With the blessing of heaven, there could be no question of Japanese failure, of the Americans prevailing. When a people base their actions on the belief that they are divine instruments, such mundane matters as conventional morality, foreign opinion and regard for enemy resolve are no more than self-imposed burdens, and the Japanese had no inclination to thus burden themselves. Moreover, such a national belief shows why the Japanese regarded the breaking of enemy will as important.

Men willing to fight to the death—indeed, to die in order to fight— proved the one and only clear-cut advantage the Japanese held over their enemies throughout the war, but it should not obscure the extremely high standard of training that obtained throughout the Imperial Navy, particularly in its aviation branch. Many arms of the navy had gained combat experience in the conflict with China. The grisly realism of navy training frequently claimed a hundred lives during a single routine exercise in the stormy waters of the northern Pacific, and the training of the aircrew involved in the Pearl Harbor attack broke virtually every safety rule in the manuals. In almost all aspects of fighting, and notably in the most hazardous aspect of naval warfare, night fighting, the Japanese were at least the equal of their enemies.

The second factor on which the Japanese relied as compensation for their numerical inferiority was a qualitative superiority that took many forms— extremely high speed in all types of warships; the provision of main and secondary armament on a scale that left many ships overgunned and unstable; fearsomely effective torpedoes; and a whole range of impressive equipment, pyrotechnic, optical, electronic. The Imperial Navy was critically weak, however, in radar development.

Inevitably the new heavy ships of the day, the battleships *Yamato* and *Musashi*, have been regarded as the best examples of this deliberate policy of stressing quality at the expense of quantity. But all Japanese battleships were rebuilt in the interwar period on a scale quite unparalleled in the West, and even these two new super-battleships were, as we have seen, only an interim class to be superseded by the projected 1942 battleships, with their 19.7-in main armament.[35] This aside, the Japanese achievement with their 1937 class was impressive enough. With their high flared bows, clean lines and depressed forward turrets, the *Yamato* and the *Musashi* were built to be superior to any warship capable of passing through the Panama Canal. The Japanese calculation was that warships displacing more than 63,000 tons could not use this waterway, and that on such a displacement the Americans could not do better than a main armament of ten 16-in guns and a top speed of 23 knots.[36] The Japanese believed that moving from a 16-in to an 18-in gun would be so problematic that the Americans would not adopt the larger bore; they went to this gun despite complications in order to secure an assured qualitative superiority over the Americans. The Japanese reasoning was faulty on technical grounds. In theory they should have had a crushing advantage over any enemy battle line, in terms either of range or weight of broadside. The American 16-in shell, for example, came in two versions: a 2,240-lb version with a range of 40,200 yards, and a 2,700-lb variant with a 37,000-yard range. The American 14-in shell weighed 1,500 pounds and had a maximum range of 43,300 yards. The Japanese battleships therefore had a 28,800-lb broadside to broadsides of 18,000–24,300 pounds on the American side, but this advantage did not actually materialize. Postwar analysis revealed that the gun and shell were no better than the American heavy 16-in shell and gun. The point that emerges from this analysis is that the Japanese effort to secure a definite qualitative advantage by accepting the technical problems involved in building the 18.11-in gun was not justified. If the Japanese wanted to build super-battleships they should have abandoned the development of a new gun (at hideous expense) and built around their existing 16-in gun. A 60,000-ton battleship with twelve 16-in guns and a speed of 30 to 32 knots would have served the Japanese far better than the *Yamato* and the *Musashi* served them. But at the time, being armored on the all-or-nothing principle, and with a speed of 27 knots, the 71,000-ton *Yamato*-class battleships were elegant and intended to be in a class of their own.

In fact, overall quality within the Imperial Navy was impressively high. In carrier design and technique the Japanese matched the Americans. The *Akagi* and the *Kaga* were the equals of their contemporaries, the *Lexington* and the *Saratoga*, while the two carriers nearing completion in mid-1941, the *Shokaku* and the *Zuikaku*, matched the *Yorktown*-class and probably remained as good, if not better, than any carrier in American service until late 1943. Japanese cruisers, whether heavy or light, proved savage fighting units, capable of sustaining and inflicting fearful punishment. The Japanese destroyers possessed features unequaled by their Western counterparts until late in the war. The 3.9-in armament, adopted for destroyers under the terms of the 1939 program, had a rate of fire and range superior to that of the contemporary American 5-in gun,[37] while more than a decade earlier the Imperial Navy had led the world with the development of enclosed dual-purpose main armament for destroyers.[38] By 1941 the Japanese had produced a series of remarkably effective aircraft whose value was all the greater for the refusal of Western powers to credit the Japanese with the ability to build aircraft at least the equal of their own. With the Zeke Japan possessed perhaps the most devastatingly successful fighter of the war, though after a short period of rampant superiority its effectiveness rapidly decreased when it was retained in front-line service for want of a suitable replacement.[39] In short, the quality of materiel matched the quality of personnel, and even though the Imperial Navy suffered from certain grave weaknesses it is hard to resist the conclusion that, ship-for-ship and man-for-man, it was second to none when it went to war.

This search for qualitative superiority was very deliberate. It was not merely an instinctive reaction to numerical inferiority—it was part of a systematic attempt to incorporate superior design features into all types of warships to enable them to perform certain tasks and operate in a specific manner in a set-piece battle. High speed, for example, was always a priority for the Japanese because it provided the means to concentrate strength against any part of a slower enemy line and to break off or decline action.[40] The latter was an important consideration for a navy that traditionally saw its primary task as the support of invasion forces rather than the destruction of the enemy.[41] The *Yamato* had been ordered for 32 knots, a demand that was cut back to 30 knots before the final designs accepted 27 knots—some 6 knots faster than the existing American battle line could achieve.[42] To counter American heavy cruisers and the battle cruisers believed to be under consideration by the American naval command, the Japanese planned to build 40-knot battle cruisers of their own. This was reduced to a 33-knot requirement under the terms of the projected 1942 program, but the two ships scheduled for construction, armed with either 12-in or 14-in weapons, were never laid down.[43] Similarly, Japanese heavy cruisers and destroyers were exceptionally fast. The first two members of the 1931 *Mogami* class were endowed with 37 knots, though this had to be reduced as a result of modifications made to counteract stability problems.[44] To accompany such fast cruisers the Japanese planned 40-knot destroyers. Such high speeds were not simply a response to the great distances that had to be covered in the enormous Pacific theater. In a general fleet action superior speed alone would allow light formations to secure the all-important position ahead of the enemy in order to launch torpedoes across his line of advance. Because the chances of securing hits on an enemy line with attacks from astern or abeam were infinitesimal, light forces had to be endowed with high speed to secure the optimum position for carrying out the important part they had been given in the Japanese scheme of battle.

Gunnery, too, figured highly in their calculations. The Japanese had led the world with the introduction of the 14-in gun (with the *Kongo* class) and the 16-in gun (with the *Nagato* class).[45] The introduction of the 18-in gun was part of their continuing attempt to maintain a lead, however small or short-lived, in offensive power, which in capital ship design tended to be stressed (along with speed) at the expense of armor. Japanese ships were generally underprotected compared with their British or American counterparts. The Japanese, however, opted for a high rate of fire from as many guns as possible in order to smother, demoralize and incapacitate an enemy. This was deemed more important than sinking an enemy, especially if the Japanese ships involved in an action were detailed as covering forces. The repulse of the enemy was victory in itself; anything beyond that was a bonus, and on many occasions the Japanese showed a marked reluctance to follow up successful encounters with all-out action. Overwhelming quickly and then breaking off action was preferable to a more deliberate stand-off action in which ships would be exposed to counterfire and risks would be divided between the two sides.[46]

In dealing with the gunnery-speed-armor formula the Japanese were no different from any other navy. When they sought qualitative improvements in gunnery and speed the Japanese faced the same problems that the Americans, British, French, Germans and Italians encountered, and their solutions would have been recognized by the others to be but one of several possibilities. But the Imperial Navy had long since ceased to be an imitative navy, and in torpedo development Japanese innovation produced a range of weapons unmatched by Western navies until the sixties.

The impetus to Japanese torpedo development was provided by the combination of the lessons drawn from the First World War and the provisions of the Washington treaties. From their staff studies the Japanese realized that during the battle of Jutland destroyers and torpedo boats had had to close to suicidally short ranges in order to have any chance to record a hit, and even then success was rare. Only one British battleship, the *Marlborough*, was hit by a torpedo in battle, and of the capital ships on both sides only the predreadnought *Pommern* was sunk by torpedo attack. To the Japanese the experience of Jutland in this respect was serious: like many of the second-rank navies, the Imperial Navy regarded the torpedo as the shortcut to first-class status. It was the poor man's weapon, which could cancel the advantages held by superior navies with their greater number of capital ships.[47] Because results at Jutland had been so indifferent, examination of the battle pointed the Japanese in a new direction in torpedo development. Attacks by destroyers and torpedo boats had to be made from beyond the range of effective enemy gunfire; thus torpedoes had be both fast and long-range if they were to be effective and not expose their user to unnecessary risks. The development of torpedoes powered by compressed oxygen and kerosene, a combination of fuels that provided high speed and endurance, followed in the interwar period. The important point about torpedo development, however, was that the Imperial Navy, having developed some formidable weapons, realized that the best hope of ensuring both the safety and success of their forces lay in conducting massed attacks by light forces at night—hence the proficiency of Japanese cruiser and destroyer forces in night fighting.*

---

*In the early thirties the Japanese developed three different torpedoes: the 18-in Type 91, the 24-in Type 93 and the 21-in Type 95. Of these, the first was an air-launched weapon and was conventionally fueled; the other two, the Type 93 (the Long Lance) deployed on surface units and the Type 95 on submarines, were fueled by enriched oxygen. The Type 91 was built because the Imperial Navy did not consider the development of "oxygen"-propelled torpedoes for aircraft worthwhile. (Aircraft launched torpedoes at very short ranges, and handling facilities for aerial torpedoes were expensive.) The Type 93 had a range of 24 miles at 39 knots or 12 miles at 49 knots. It had a warhead of 1,100 pounds. The Type 95 had a range of 5.5 miles at 49 knots and a warhead of 880 pounds. By comparison, the British had a 21-in torpedo in two versions, one for surface units and the other for submarines. Both carried a warhead of about 700 pounds and had a range of about 2 miles at 46 knots or about 6 miles at 30 knots. American torpedoes were roughly similar to those of the British.

It was the way the Japanese built their ships around the torpedo in order to operate in this specific manner that is significant, for it illustrates how Japanese design evolved to meet the demands of their battle doctrine. Except for battleships and carriers, all fleet units of the Imperial Navy carried torpedoes, though obviously the greater part of torpedo strength was concentrated in the destroyer force. Between the two world wars the number of tubes and torpedoes carried by Japanese destroyers steadily increased as the emphasis of the destroyer's function shifted from defense of the battle line to attacks on the enemy. At the end of the First World War Japan was building units with either four or six 21-inch tubes, located in double or triple mountings, with no reloads. By the middle of the interwar period, however, the Japanese had moved up to the 24-in weapon, and ships of the *Fubuki* class carried nine tubes in triple mountings, with reloads. In 1939 the Japanese went further when they opted for a heavy fleet destroyer—in effect a light cruiser—with three quintuple mountings, one of which carried reloads. The *Shimakaze*, with six 5-in guns and a speed of 40 knots, was ordered as the prototype for two sixteen-ship flotillas, but she alone was completed. The best example of this trend toward an evermore powerful offensive armament for light forces was the rearmament of the light cruisers *Oi* and *Kitakami*. Unlike most light cruisers, which had a relatively modest torpedo armament because they were intended to operate as flotilla leaders, the *Oi* and the *Kitakami* were rearmed in 1941 as fleet scouts with no fewer than forty 24-in tubes in ten quadruple mountings, with reloads. The desire for increased offensive power could hardly have gone to greater lengths than it did with these two ships, but the rearmament of the two cruisers must be seen in its proper context: it formed one part of a much wider effort to acquire at relatively small cost a punch at night that would be the equivalent of the punch of the battle squadrons by day. In this way the Japanese planned to counter the capital ship superiority of her only possible enemies, and it was precisely Japanese inferiority in this field that had prompted the development of torpedoes and destroyer tactics in the first place. In these areas the Japanese were the leaders, not the led; their developments were uniquely Japanese.[48]

Complementing such innovations was a parallel evolution of Japanese submarines which, like the light surface forces, were intended to operate against the enemy battle line. The relatively small Type K6 or *Kaisho* submarines were developed for the specific purpose of the local defense of the islands of the western Pacific, but all other Japanese submarines built in the interwar period were given high speed so that they could take part in a fleet action. All could make 18 knots, and the more modern ones, built after the Japanese dispensed with foreign designs and machines and began to build to a specific tactical requirement, were considerably faster.[49] The best of the Japanese units could make more than 23 knots. The Japanese believed such high speed was essential if their units were to scout and fight effectively. In the vast Pacific, concentration against an enemy fleet was possible only by high-speed cruising to the scene of action, and once in contact submarines, according to Japanese doctrine, were to mount successive attacks on enemy forces. This was possible only if their submarines had a higher surface speed than the economical cruising speed of enemy main forces. Since most Japanese submarines carried one set of torpedoes and two reloads, only a speed superior to that of the surface forces would enable them to attack, withdraw in front of an advancing enemy and then move in for further attacks.[50]

But the development of fast attack submarines formed only one strand of a fourfold specialization of role within the fleet submarine service that was intended to overcome the two main tactical problems of the branch: locating the enemy and bringing units against him. To aid the process of finding the enemy the Type B1 submarine, with a single reconnaissance seaplane, was developed. The seaplane, the E14Y1 Glen, should have been the eyes of the submarine force, but in reality it proved incapable of operating except on the smoothest of seas.[51] To supplement the Type B1 submarines and their Glens the Japanese adapted four old Type KRS submarines, originally built as minelayers, to operate as refueling submarines for flying boats. Because it would be impossible to send carriers, tenders and seaplanes into distant waters where reconnaissance was necessary, the Japanese calculated that such submarines could be employed as midocean fueling depots for long-range flying boats in seas controlled by enemy surface and air forces. To direct these various efforts and to exercise command and control of subsequent operations against the enemy, Type A1 submarines were built. These were headquarters submarines, designed for long-range cruising and provided with extensive communications systems. (To complement the Type A1s the Japanese planned to build a class of nine light cruisers for the same purpose, but in the end, just as only three Type A1 submarines were built, so only one of the proposed seaplane-submarine liaison cruisers, the *Oyodo*, was built.) The remaining development in the submarine service was the evolution of the standard attack submarine, the Type KD6, into the orthodox Type KD7 and the less than orthodox Type C1. The latter was an attack submarine modified to carry a Type A midget submarine. In fact the Type B1 and Type C1 submarines were so similar that on occasion they carried one another's "passengers."[52]

Many nations built midget submarines for operations against enemy bases and the ships that might be in them, but it seems that the Germans and Japanese were alone in building such submarines for use at sea. The Germans, however, only cast their midget submarines in a defensive coastal role; the Japanese midget submarines were intended for a far more significant activity.[53] Though Type C1 submarines carried midget submarines for the attack on Pearl Harbor and later for raids on Diego Suarez and Sydney, the Type A was developed not for raids on enemy bases or for the defense of Japan's coasts but for operations on the high seas against enemy main forces, and to this end the Japanese built three mother ships, the *Chiyoda*, *Chitose* and *Mizuho*, and later added a fourth, the *Nisshin*, to carry the midgets to the scene of battle. It was the task of the parents to lay their brood across the known path of an advancing enemy force. In this way the Type A submarines would join the conventional submarines, destroyers and cruisers in attacks on the enemy as he advanced to contact Japanese main forces.

What marked these developments as significant was not merely the precision with which they dovetailed into a defined pattern but the relatively late hour at which they appeared. The Type 91 torpedo was developed in 1931, the Type 93 two years later. The Type 95 torpedo was developed in 1935. The Type A submarine was designed in 1933 but only went into production in 1938. The Type A1, Type B1 and Type C1 submarines were ordered in the Third Replenishment Program of 1937, the same year as the Glen was authorized. The *Mizuho*, built to carry Type A submarines, was laid down in 1937, but the *Chiyoda* and the *Chitose* were not converted to carry these midgets until 1941. The *Nisshin* had to wait until 1942 for similar conversion. All these developments indicate the parameters of Japanese tactical thinking; the construction of these new ships and weapons systems reflected the prevailing belief that naval action would take the form of traditional fleet action. These various developments had been intended to supplement the gun, to pave the way for Japan success in an artillery duel in fleet action. Even as late as the period 1939–41 the Japanese were thinking in terms of battle as something that took place between lines, in exactly the same manner as Tsu-shima and Jutland had been fought; for the Japanese only the influx of new and more sophisticated equipment marked the passing of time.

The heart of Japanese strategic and tactical doctrine reflected these two great naval battles, but the doctrine was not so simple as to be thus easily described. Japanese concepts were nothing if not elaborate and complicated. Any examination of Japanese torpedo, destroyer and submarine development in the interwar period naturally leads into a discussion of the strategy of attrition, prior to battle, that the Japanese intended to put into effect against an aggressive and superior enemy fleet. The whole purpose of Japanese light force construction was to ensure that the Americans, as they moved into the western Pacific, would be weakened by successive attacks from the Imperial Navy's light forces before being met by an overwhelming concentration of fire power that would scatter them and complete their destruction.[54]

The concept of attrition followed by battle had its origins in the Russo-Japanese war, the doctrine and plans of that conflict having been refined and amended to accommodate the different technical and geographical factors that had to be considered in planning for a war against the Americans. It is important, therefore, that our account of technical progressions be set aside to look briefly at this, Japan's first major naval war. It was a war in which the infantry Imperial Navy had to face three enemy forces: the squadrons that were at Port Arthur and Vladivostok, and the Baltic Fleet. The latter, after an epic voyage from European waters, was to arrive in the Far East to bring relief to the hard-pressed czarist forces in southern Manchuria.

Throughout this war the Japanese sought to contain the squadron at Port Arthur and the one at Vladivostok, thus preventing any challenge to Japanese control of local waters and support of their land forces. Japanese dealings with these squadrons were defensive and, after the loss of two battleships on mines outside Port Arthur, cautious. On the few occasions when battle was joined the Japanese refused to press action, being content to parry Japanese sorties and to ensure that the enemy could not develop actions that would interfere with their own supporting operations for the army.[55] Similarly, Japanese planning for the arrival of the Baltic Fleet in the Far East was defensive, but for different reasons and with different results. The Baltic Fleet was numerically superior to the fleet that the Japanese could send against it, and it possessed a marked superiority in heavy guns.* Yet Russian superiority of numbers had not prevented the annihilation of the Baltic Fleet at the battle of Tsu-shima in May 1905. In that conflict the Japanese, for the loss of three torpedo boats, 110 dead and 590 wounded, had enjoyed one of the most overwhelming victories in naval history. Only three of the thirty-four warships and auxiliaries that made up the Baltic Fleet had survived to make their way to Vladivostok. One auxiliary had survived by withdrawing (to Madagascar of all places) and the other three cruisers and two auxiliaries that had escaped either destruction or capture had done so by flight and internment in neutral countries. Given the disparity of strength between the two sides at this battle, it is hardly surprising that the Japanese had seen their victory as the result of the advantages they had held over the Russians in terms of individual ship design, tactics, morale and training.†

---

*At Tsu-shima the Russians had twelve battleships and nine cruisers; the Japanese had four battleships and eleven cruisers of various descriptions.

†The Russian superiority in numbers of guns was wasted because so many guns were built into the hulls of their ships. With the Russian ships low in the water—they were forced to carry extra coal—few of these guns were of much value in the choppy seas encountered off Tsu-shima. The Japanese had fewer guns but carried them higher.

Equally important, the Japanese realized that the basic plan of campaign for dealing with the Baltic Fleet had had its validity confirmed by events even though, ironically, the plan had never been implemented. Drawn up by Commander Saneyuki Akiyama, the plan had envisaged the Russians being found and immediately attacked by Japanese light forces. As the enemy came into the main combat zone, nearer the Japanese homeland, he was to be subjected to successive attacks by light units before a general fleet action was joined in daylight. For the general action Japanese plans stressed the "wheeling attack." In this attack Japanese forces, by virtue of their superior speed, would maneuver and, by approaching from an oblique angle, bring concentrated fire power against part of the enemy line.[56] The favored ploy was to concentrate on the enemy's bow and pulverize the head of the line.* At night battle would be continued by replenished light units. The Japanese heavy forces, because they were so important and valuable on account of their small numbers, were to be withdrawn from the combat area as darkness set in. In the final stages of the battle all ships were to mop up or drive escaping Russian units northwards to Vladivostok (Port Arthur having fallen earlier) and the minefields that awaited them outside that harbor. These had been laid as much to stop reinforcements getting through to Vladivostok as to keep those forces already there from getting to sea.[57]

The battle of Tsu-shima did not go according to plan—a point that the Imperial Navy would have been well advised to consider carefully in light of the conclusions it had drawn and later tried to apply—mainly because of the incompetence of the Russians. The Baltic Fleet was not so much badly commanded as not commanded at all. Its shiphandling and tactical ability was so bad that the Japanese did much as they pleased. In the aftermath of the battle, however, the Imperial Navy decided that the special circumstances of the battle did not overrule the basic soundness of the aim of attrition before battle. On the tactical and technical sides, the manner in which the Japanese had been able to choose the range, maneuver for position and concentrate crushing fire power against the enemy line confirmed the value of certain tactical concepts (such as the need for high speed and rapid gunfire) that were to become enshrined in Japanese battle doctrine.

In planning to deal with the Americans the same basic pattern was adopted, but on a greater scale in terms of both distance and forces. Initially the Japanese envisaged action in the area bound by the Marianas, Carolines, Philippines and Japan, but as the range and speed of warships and aircraft increased between the wars, so the area of operations was extended, to include first the Marshalls and then the Hawaiian Islands.[58] Growing range

*This was almost the same as "crossing the T" since the "wheeling attack" came obliquely across the line of the enemy advance.

and speed meant greater depth to the battle zone, and the Japanese planned to make full use of that depth as the enemy came westwards towards the Philippines. The Type B1 scouting submarines, supplemented by Mavis flying boats, were to locate the enemy in Hawaiian waters. As a result of the contacts thus obtained, the American movement westwards would be harassed all the way by submarines brought to the scene of action and later, when the enemy came within range of the Japanese islands of the western Pacific, by naval aircraft from the bases that were being prepared for just this eventuality. By 1941 the cutting edge of the land-based air effort was to be provided by Nell and Betty medium bombers. In their respective times both aircraft had the best performance of any land-based naval bomber in the world,[59] and their extreme long range and high speed were considered vital in making good their lack of numbers.[60] (In fact, when the Japanese were discussing the war option in mid-1941 one disadvantage they had to accept was that the navy had only 52 percent of its medium bomber requirement in service.)[61] The Imperial Navy thought it possible and indeed essential in the initial phase of battle to reduce the fighting capacity of the enemy by 30 percent.[62] Submarines were expected to inflict half of the enemy's losses in the attrition phase,[63] their primary targets being first carriers and then battleships.[64]

The Japanese envisaged fighting initially with forces they regarded as expendable; submarines and aircraft were considered cheap craft, capable of relatively quick and easy replacement.[65] Heavy losses would be accepted as the price for wearing down the enemy, physically and morally. This had to be achieved if the Japanese battle force was to join battle on the basis of either equality or superiority.

Once the Americans had been softened up by Japanese light forces, main forces would engage the enemy in two distinct waves. The first wave was to consist of a fast task force or advance guard made up of the high-speed battleships, cruisers and destroyers. This task force, which might include as much as half the destroyer strength of the navy and certainly the bulk of its most modern and powerful destroyers, would come into contact with the enemy late in the day and engage him during the night. In a reversal of the normal state of affairs, the battleships and cruisers would be escorts to the destroyers. The Japanese relied on the torpedoes of the destroyers to reap a rich harvest in the course of two, possibly three, night attacks. The Japanese anticipated reasonable results with massed numbers of destroyers and heavy torpedo armament. They believed that as many as one in four of their torpedoes might find their mark, and they planned to conduct full flotilla attacks with at least 150 torpedoes being launched in any single assault. The battleships and cruisers, in this phase of the battle, would be on hand to sweep aside the enemy's screening forces, thereby protecting their own destroyers and improving their chances of making successful attacks on the enemy line. Between 1933 and 1940 Japan's four battle cruisers, the *Haruna*, *Kirishima*, *Kongo* and *Hiei*, were rebuilt as fast battleships to enable them to perform this specific function.[66]

After the night attacks the Japanese would join battle with their carrier forces at dawn. Before the outbreak of the Pacific war the Imperial Navy concurred in the conventional wisdom of the day, which denied carrier aviation an independent or potentially decisive role. The Japanese saw carrier aircraft as supplementary to the gun; they tasked aircraft to secure air superiority over the battle line, to scout, to spot and, when circumstances allowed, to attack an enemy in flight with a view to his being slowed and then brought to battle by pursuing surface units—as the British had done at Matapan and in the hunt for the *Bismarck*. In common with other navies the Imperial Navy realized that carrier aviation could be decisive in one sense: a fleet without control of the air might never be able to win a fleet action. In these calculations the Japanese were no different from the British and the Americans, but whereas all wanted to ensure air control as a minimal requirement, the Japanese wanted to join battle with their dive-bombers carrying out attacks intended to put the enemy flight decks out of action. If the Japanese were successful, the advancing American forces would be blinded and left unable to counter the series of blows the Japanese would rain down on them during the remainder of the day.[67] The Japanese planned to disperse their carrier divisions in order to prevent an enemy attack from accounting for more than one part of their carrier force. After 1936 the Japanese devised elaborate plans for the use of their carriers in support of the battle divisions. Their carriers would be in separate formations rather like the horns of a bull, the flanking divisions—about 300 miles apart and some 200 miles or so from the main central force—sweeping around an advancing enemy force in a double envelopment. Thus would be set up "the most favorable of circumstances" that would enable the battle forces to administer the coup de grâce.

As their skirmishing carrier divisions moved around the flanks of the advancing enemy, the Japanese main forces would close from directly ahead. With contact imminent, the midget submarines were to be released from their mother ships. Then the advance guard, hovering on the flank after its nocturnal activities, would come into action again, once more engaging with torpedoes. By attacking the enemy from the flank with the advance guard and from ahead with the Type A submarines, the Japanese would subject the enemy to a "scissors attack" whereby any attempt of his to comb one set of torpedoes would leave him broadside to the other set. In this way the midget submarines would add to the chaos and damage that by this time should be engulfing the enemy battle line.

While these exchanges were taking place the battle force was to maneuver into a position favorable to its entering the fray. First to engage would

be the *Yamato* and the *Musashi*. With a main armament that could hurl a
3,200-lb shell nearly 25 miles, these two battleships were built for this very
moment. No other battleships in the world were designed to withstand
18-in shells, and the Japanese calculation was that the two ships could stand
at almost maximum range and shoot the enemy to pieces with impunity.
The Japanese battleships would join battle at 37,500 yards, and with a
six-knot advantage over American battleships they would be able to pick
their own range and position and then pour an irresistible volume of fire
into the enemy line without any fear of retribution. Under the cover
provided by the fire of the *Yamato* and the *Musashi*, the other Japanese
battleships would enter the line, first the slow division—the *Mutsu*, *Nagato*,
Fuso, *Yamashiro*, *Ise* and *Hyuga*—and then the fast division. The latter was
unfit to enter the line unless the enemy had been first shaken and his
fighting power reduced.

One cannot help but be awestruck by the clockwork precision of this
planning and the attention to detail. Every element of construction had
been considered to fulfill a specific task in battle. The Japanese did not
expect everything to go completely according to plan, but the comprehen-
siveness of their arrangements was evidence of an intention to cover as
many eventualities as possible. They appear to have anticipated a 50
percent success, and this they calculated would put the Americans back
two years. That was the amount of time the Japanese estimated the Americans would need to make good their losses; whether the Americans would
recover their nerve for battle, equipped with ships that even after these two
years would still be too weak to fight and too slow to run away, was quite
another matter. It is clear, however, that the estimate of a 50 percent
success was cautious. If battle was joined anywhere in the region of the
Marianas, Carolines and Philippines, there would be little chance of damaged American ships escaping to safety. Any withdrawal would have to be
attempted in the face of attacks by land-based bombers, the same sort of
attacks the Americans had encountered when they made their outward
passage. If these land-based aircraft had already registered the success that
was expected of them during their first attacks, then it is rather difficult to
see how this withdrawal phase could end in anything other than an American rout, the consummation of the battle of annihilation. The Japanese
themselves referred to this intended engagement as the decisive battle and
believed that if it resulted in a victory of Tsu-shima proportions, the
American cause would be set back ten years. In that case, the Japanese
reasoned, the Americans were more than likely to come to the negotiating
table.[68]

Such were the main elements of policy and doctrine with which the
Imperial Navy went to war. For all the stress on battle and offensive action,
and notwithstanding the operations at the start of the war, Japanese policy

and strategic thinking were primarily defensive. The Imperial Navy saw itself as the barrier that would stand between Japanese conquests and Allied hopes of wresting back Southeast Asia; it saw itself as Japan's shield, as the bulwark of the nation.[69] Yet there were obvious inconsistencies and weaknesses in Japanese concepts. The navy's strategic reserve included three million barrels of oil set aside for "a single major sea battle," and that the Imperial Navy could consider a naval war in terms of "the big battle" was the clearest possible indication that it had little idea of the nature of the war it had to fight.[70] When Emperor Hirohito asked whether or not the navy anticipated a great victory like Tsu-shima he was told by Nagano that such a success would not be possible.[71] It was an answer that in retrospect seems to have made a mockery of all the planning and construction of the decade before the start of the Pacific war. And, of course, the Japanese themselves were to go on to pioneer a form of naval warfare that showed the superiority of the tactical offensive over the strategic defensive. Aircraft, whether land based or carrier borne, proved the ability of the offensive to project concentrated and overwhelming fire power directly into sea areas hitherto regarded as inviolate and controlled by surface units. High-speed torpedoes running to unparalleled ranges with greater warheads than ever before, guns of unequaled size and range, ships with speeds of 35 knots and more—none of these could outrun aircraft. The majestic clockwork of Japanese battle doctrine was invalidated by the navy's own actions, but the inconsistency between theory and practice went unrealized by most people at the time. Commanders such as Vice Admiral Shigeyoshi Inoue saw the paradox and argued that the carrier had superseded the battleship as the arbiter of naval warfare, that the type of battle the navy was planning to fight was anachronistic nonsense. But Inoue and his views of air power were regarded as dangerously unsound, especially when these opinions were allied with his often-expressed conviction that war with the United States should be avoided.

However, the Japanese could see the need to persist with offensive action in the first months of 1942, not because of obsolescent doctrine but for sound political and strategic reasons. Japanese planning staffs, when they came to consider second-phase operations, knew that to cede the initiative and go over to the defense was unsound on both counts, even though this had been Japan's original intention. The initiative was Japan's only real and immediate compensation for her potential numerical weakness, and reflective members of the Japanese high command realized that it was clearly in Japan's interest to try to continue to dictate the tempo and direction of operations as the war entered a new and more difficult phase. To have no plan of campaign other than the improvisation of responses to emerging counterattacks was an invitation to defeat.

Nagano and Yamamoto, though they differed in many respects over the strategic direction of the Japanese war effort, were in basic agreement on one matter. Service as naval attachés in Washington had familiarized both men with the realities of American industrial power, and both were convinced that Japan was certain to be defeated in a protracted war. Nagano believed that Japan had the means to sustain herself for two years in a war with the Americans but that "thereafter conflict will tend to be unprofitable"—an observation that must rank highly amongst the understatements of this or any other war. [72] Yamamoto believed that Japan had less time than that: he allowed between six months and one year before the tide turned against her. [73] Both agreed that the issue had to be forced to a conclusion if Japan was to have any chance of avoiding defeat. However, to Yamamoto, who by the spring of 1942 had moved into the position of being the arbiter of Japanese naval policy, it was not the case that in the second phase of the war it would be in Japan's interests to continue to dictate the pace and direction of operations: to continue to dictate them was the *only* means by which Japanese strategic interests would be served. Offensive action alone promised to be the means of bringing about a favorable end to the war.

Since Japan's enemies had already declared their intention not to negotiate with her, there was no alternative to persisting with offensive operations. The knockout blow that had eluded the Japanese at Pearl Harbor continued to elude them in the first four months of the war, which only added to the urgency on this matter. In the first fifteen weeks of the war the Japanese destroyed seven enemy capital ships, one light carrier, one seaplane tender, four heavy cruisers and about twenty light cruisers and destroyers, but there was no fleet action, and there was little sign of success in waging the campaign of attrition against the Americans at the forward edge of the battle zone. The Japanese believed that one of their submarines, the *I-6*, had accounted for the *Lexington* on 11 January off Johnson Island, but even this (overstated) success represented a poor return for all the effort they had put into their submarine service. Clearly, therefore, Japan would have to provoke and win "a decisive battle" if she was to be secure. This meant undertaking further offensive action and registering the kind of success she had missed at Pearl Harbor on 7 December.

Yet translating the desire for offensive action into the real thing proved to be extraordinarily difficult for the Japanese. Before mid-April few members of the high command shared Yamamoto's overwhelming sense of urgency. But this was only one factor amongst many that served to confuse the direction of the Japanese war effort at this time. Just as detrimental to the orderly and clear formulation of strategic policy were three other factors—the high command's lack of a properly constituted and defined policymaking authority, which resulted in further divisions within its ranks; the momentum of events already in hand; and the overbearing assumption that Japanese success could be perpetuated. It is possible that it was the latter, the prevalence within the armed forces of the phenomenon later diagnosed as "victory disease," that proved most inimical to the Japanese cause.[74]

"Victory disease" was born of triumph being piled upon triumph with staggering speed. Enemies hitherto regarded by Japan if not with respect then with a certain awe were swept aside, and from success the victors developed an overweening confidence in the seemingly irresistible ability of Japanese martial prowess (*nihon seishin*) to carry all before it. Such confidence had always been a part of the national character, but before the war it had been held in check. Undreamed-of success in weeks rather than months could only bring this confidence to the surface with disastrous results. It was an incentive to persist with offensive action, but in such a way as to blur perspective on two counts. First, it encouraged the belief that the form of initial operations—action across a wide surface area with its characteristic dispersal of resources and slender administrative margins—could be continued in the second phase of operations. Second, it encouraged the Japanese to think that the enemy, who had been forced to conform to Japanese actions in the first phase of the war, could be forced to conform in the future by further offensive action. In short, "victory disease" reinforced the notion that Japan could wage a limited war and continue a mode of operations that had worked against unprepared enemies. This was the very time Japan should have been seeking a fresh tactical approach to the problems posed by the prospect of further operations against enemies who were now stronger and better prepared than at any previous stage of the conflict.

CHAPTER 2

. . . the Javelin?

Even if the need to recast strategic and tactical doctrine to meet changing conditions had been realized, the Japanese high command could not have risen to this challenge because it was incapable of implementing change quickly and effectively. In part such incapacity stemmed from Japan's economic frailty, which precluded the rapid industrial expansion required by the increased demands of a war prosecuted over vast areas at great distances from the homeland. But equally important in accounting for Japan's disability was that the structure of the high command did not lend itself to orderly, rapid and coherent decision making.

In theory power in Japan was vested in a sovereign head of state, but in reality the divine emperor was excluded from its exercise. His was a ceremonial and symbolic role, and real power was wielded by a prime minister and cabinet responsible to a democratically elected legislature. This, however, had become no more than a legal fiction. The representative process had been emasculated in the interwar period, and the Imperial Diet exercised no control over the executive. But the authority of the administration itself had been fatally compromised by the existence of various organizations with which it was forced to share power. Over the decades many advisory bodies had developed which, drawing their members from retired public figures, should have acted as a buttress to governmental authority. In reality, however, they undermined it. Bodies such as the Privy Council, the Diplomatic Advisory Council and the Supreme Military Council became powerful and quasi-independent parts of the decision-making process. Their existence diminished rather than enhanced the prestige of the government. As if this were not enough, governmental authority had been deliberately and remorselessly eroded in the interwar period by the armed services. These had used what amounted to the power of veto to bend successive governments to their will. Governments could not be formed—

nor could they stay in office—without ministers for the armed forces. These posts had to be filled by active-duty officers, and by refusing to provide them, or by withdrawing one of their number, each service had the power to prevent the formation of an administration or to bring it down if service demands were not met. In the thirties the armed services used this power to become the arbiters of government and policy.

Exacerbating the situation were the lack of agreement between the army and navy in regard to long-term aims and the deep internal divisions both services suffered. To make matters worse, the troubled interwar period had seen increasing recourse to direct action on the part of middle-ranking and junior officers intent on implementing militant policies. For a variety of complicated reasons little effort was made by the upper ranks of the armed services to enforce discipline and check the drift towards insubordinate extremism that led, in the end, to "government by assassination."[1] The tendency towards extremism was directly related to the fragmentation and diffusion of power, and it made the expression of militant nationalism incoherent. It never congealed into a single political movement under one leader, and it never exhibited the tight discipline that characterized European fascism.[2]

What had happened in the thirties and what was so important in defining the future direction of the Japanese war effort was a weakening of authority throughout the high command, with the upper echelons either unwilling or unable to enforce discipline on the lower ranks. The hierarchy of command at the highest levels became blurred. Policy should have been settled by the prime minister, and by extension the cabinet, working through the Imperial General Headquarters—Government Liaison Conference. The latter was a permanent consultative body consisting of the premier, the foreign and service ministers, and the two chiefs of staff. The very order of the names in the organization's title indicated where the power of decision lay. Imperial General Headquarters, not the government, had the decisive word on policy, yet it was itself little more than institutionalized antagonism. It consisted of two sections, staffs for both services that dealt with planning, operations, administration and logistics, but no proper means of deciding policy and supervising its implementation existed. The rivalry between the two services was open and notorious,[3] and their operational interests lay in diametrically opposed directions.[4] The army always thought in continental terms; it would conduct its business on the Asian mainland. The navy's concern was always for the western Pacific and Southeast Asia. Since the formulation of the 1936 statement of imperial defense policy, which had specified the Soviets as the army's most likely enemy and the Americans as the most likely foe of the navy, the two services had been investing their efforts in different areas, and there was little attempt by either service to understand the problems and thinking of the other.⁵ The two services agreed on war in 1941 only because they both felt it was inevitable and the only way out of the difficulties in which Japan found herself. The merging of views in mid-1941, however, could not hide the long-term disagreement over the prosecution of the war once the initial conquest of Southeast Asia was accomplished. The army wanted to disengage from the Pacific as rapidly as possible. It anticipated the defeat of the Soviets, and it wanted to preserve the strength and freedom of action necessary to take advantage of the German victory it believed would be achieved in the course of 1942.⁶ The nonaggression pact the navy had wanted to secure its northern flank against the Soviets as it overran Southeast Asia did not jell; the army refused to pull back its units from the Soviet border. The army believed that the account with the Soviets had only been postponed for the duration of the drive through Southeast Asia, and it was not prepared to enter into any major or long-term military commitment away from the Asian mainland.⁷ The navy, on the other hand, needed the support of the army. It could not hope to garrison Southeast Asia and the central Pacific without military assistance. The navy would have liked army troops and aircraft to supplement its own, but given the division of interests and bad relations that generally existed at all levels between the services, there was little prospect of the army providing the navy with the support that would be essential to Japanese hopes of success in 1942. In many ways the services treated one another, rather than the Americans, British, Chinese and Dutch, as the real enemy.

Thus at the highest level there was a fundamental divergence of attitudes about the conduct of the national war effort, and Imperial General Headquarters and the Liaison Conference, rather than being the agencies that settled policy and reconciled differences, were forums for dispute where the two services fought one another for the acceptance of their own particular points of view. At best policy evolved not from choice but from compromise and exhaustion, but it was always weighted in favor of the army. The navy needed the army far more than the army ever needed the navy, and the army, with its power to frustrate the plans, hopes and intentions of its sister service, had secured a position of preeminence within Imperial General Headquarters.

Similar divisions were reproduced within the Imperial Navy itself. The chief of the naval general staff, Nagano, was *ex officio* head of the Naval Section of Imperial General Headquarters, but just as he was *minor inter pares* when he dealt with his army counterpart, so he was never more than *primus inter pares*—and perhaps not even that—when it came to dealing with the higher command of his own service. The Imperial Navy was not immune to the compromised authority and blurred chain of command that beset all state institutions, and Nagano and his deputy, Vice Admiral Seiichi Ito, were little more than arbiters in the disputes of their subordi-

nates, particularly those between Rear Admiral Shigeru Fukudome's First
(Operations) Section of the Naval General Staff and Yamamoto's Combined Fleet staff. Nagano and Ito did not take the initiative in matters of
strategic policy by enforcing their views on their subordinates. Rather they
were content to express themselves only on proposals set before them, like
inverted Macawbers always waiting for things to turn down.[8] In the first
months of 1942, partly because there were many ideas being put forward
by various interested parties, there was no clear indication of what might be
the best policy for the navy to pursue over the next few months. Because of
its lack of organization, the reticence of Nagano and Ito in formulating
policy and the sheer complexity of the issues facing the Imperial Navy at
this time, chaos gripped the higher levels of the service as it tried to order its
(strategic) priorities. In the absence of decisive leadership, policy was to be
decided as much by accident as design, as much by responding to events as
by controlling them.

In theory the initiative for strategic planning should have come from the
Plans Division of Fukudome's First Section, but in reality the initiative for
the strategic planning had been largely usurped by Yamamoto and the staff
of the Combined Fleet, and for three reasons. First, the status of the
Combined Fleet was unique and in a sense overwhelming. Because it was a
single-ocean organization it had both administrative and operational func-
tions, and it was the largest single naval force in the world. Yamamoto,
therefore, was in an extremely strong position.[9] Second, he had considerable personal prestige and authority of long standing. Yamamoto was
widely regarded as the best possible commander of the Combined Fleet,
and on this count alone his replacement was not an option open to Nagano
and the staff. Such worthies as Mineichi Koga and Soemu Toyoda would
step into Yamamoto's shoes should anything happen to him, but they were
replacements, not rivals. Third, Yamamoto enjoyed unequaled power
because of his command's success in war. In the first weeks of the Pacific
conflict the Combined Fleet moved from one victory to another. This could
not but strengthen Yamamoto's position relative to the Naval General
Staff, which had opposed the plan to attack Pearl Harbor and had harbored
doubts about various aspects of the plan of campaign in Southeast Asia. On
most matters the opening exchanges proved Yamamoto right and the more
cautious staff wrong, and this had the inevitable effect of undermining the
authority of the staff when it came to dealings with the Combined Fleet.
Success confirmed the latter in its view that on matters of strategic policy it
was better for it to go its own way than be bound by the dictates of an
overcautious staff. The Combined Fleet came to regard itself as the proper
source of planning and execution, and the arrogance of its assumption
provoked much hostility from the First Section.[10]

Admiral Isoroku Yamamoto

These various matters converged in the first weeks of 1942 as success was achieved throughout Southeast Asia. The high command of the Imperial Navy found itself faced with five separate options as it tried to piece together a rational and coherent strategy for the future. Of these options one was to call a temporary halt to operations to prepare for an eventual clash that would decide the outcome of the war. Rear Admiral Ryunosuke Kusaka, chief of staff to the all-important carrier force, favored this defensive course of action, since Japanese air losses in the opening weeks of the war were heavy and time was needed to train and integrate air crews. The weakness of this option, however, was obvious. Japanese opinion was hardening in favor of a continuation of offensive operations, and Kusaka's option could not provide any answer to Japan's immediate difficulty. Moreover, Kusaka himself did not command much personal authority. He had opposed the Pearl Harbor attack, and when it had been carried out he had turned down the demands for a second strike which alone might have achieved significant results for the Japanese.

The defensive option never had any chance of being accepted. This left four offensive options available to the Imperial Navy, the first of which concerned Australia. Clear signs that the Americans intended to concentrate in Australia foreshadowed an eventual buildup of strength in that country for the purpose of mounting operations that would "roll back" the tide of Japanese conquest. Such a possibility had been considered by the Imperial Navy even before the war, and the plan to secure Rabaul and its immediate neighborhood after acquiring various island groups in the central Pacific had been inspired by the need to defend Truk and the Indies against an American attack launched from Australia. Events during the first weeks of the war caused the Japanese to think in terms of a preemptive operation to prevent Australia from becoming the springboard from which the Americans would attempt the reconquest of Southeast Asia and the southwest Pacific.

In studying the Australia option the Japanese had to consider the occupation of either northern Australia or the whole of the continent. Both courses strongly recommended themselves to the Plans Division of the Naval General Staff. The Australia option was in many ways the brainchild of the division's commanding officer, Captain Sadatoshi Tomoika. Tomoika has been portrayed as a vain man, and perhaps he was, but there was no doubting his ability. He was the son of the chief of the First (Operations) Section at the time of the Russo-Japanese War, and he had graduated at the top of his year from the Naval War College.[11] His was one of the finest brains in the Imperial Navy, and his idea of an attack on Australia was not as incredible as it might first appear. Both in terms of inhabited area and population the country was (and is) extremely small. Tomoika's designs on Australia enjoyed support from Inoue, commander of the Fourth Fleet, and from his chief of staff, Rear Admiral Shikazo Yano. Inoue commanded the Mandates Fleet or, in its operational form, the South Seas Force, the formation tasked with protection of the southwest Pacific against enemy incursions. Its area of interest naturally extended to Australia, and the South Seas Force would be the naval command on which would fall the responsibility of meeting any American offensive in the area.[12]

The second offensive option, important in its own right, was really an offshoot of the Australia proposal. It was the suggestion to expand Japanese operations into the southwest Pacific, the objective being to isolate and neutralize Australia by securing the islands that stood across the American line of communication that ran between Pearl Harbor and eastern Australia. The Plans Division and the South Seas Force would take up this alternative only in the event of their failure to win acceptance of the plan to occupy Australia.

The next option was to extend operations into the Indian Ocean, the maximum objective being to link up with Japan's European allies somewhere in the Middle East. The immediate aim of such an effort was to secure Ceylon and to destroy the British fleet, which in January 1942 was being built up in the Indian Ocean after the previous month's disasters. Japanese planning against Britain had been more than tentative before

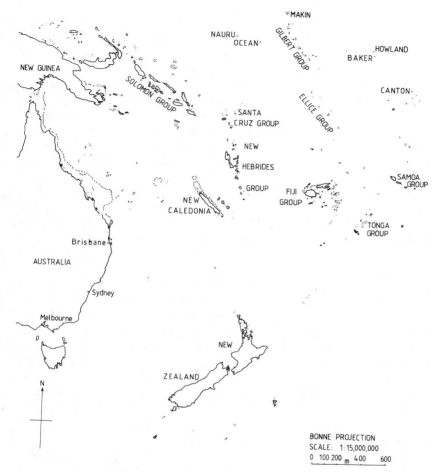

The Southwest Pacific Theater

1941, and even in February 1939 the guideline instructions for a war with Britain had allowed for nothing more than the conquest of British possessions in the Far East and for Japanese forces thereafter "to await the probable expedition of the British fleet through the Suez Canal to the east." Then the Japanese planned to destroy it.[13] Such a resolve remained the basis of Japanese policy with regard to the Indian Ocean until January 1942, when the balance of intentions began to shift from the defensive to the offensive. Success in Malaya in part accounted for the changing attitude, but the real impetus for a forward strategy west of Singapore came from the signing of the Tripartite Pact by Germany, Italy and Japan on 19 January. The idea of the three nations joining hands across half the globe was one loudly championed by the tightly controlled Japanese press at this time, and it was one that commanded strong support from the many admirers of Nazi Germany in the imperial armed forces.[14] But the idea of an offensive into the Indian Ocean predated the signing of the pact because either Yamamoto or his chief of staff, Rear Admiral Matome Ugaki, had already proposed that such an operation be carried out once the conquest of Southeast Asia was completed. After the proposal had been broached, Ugaki turned over formal examination of the option to the Combined Fleet's operations officer, Captain Kameto Kuroshima.[15]

The final option was for Japan to turn her attention towards the one theater of operations that in September 1941 had been dismissed from calculations as being both too large and too far away from the main theaters for the Japanese to have any chance of mounting a successful operation in it. The development of an offensive into the central Pacific was the option, and it adhered to the traditional Japanese notion of dealing with the main enemy, the United States. The 1942 proposal envisaged offensive and not defensive operations. This was the option that attracted Yamamoto and Ugaki, though both realized that an offensive into the central Pacific had more than its share of problems. Before the war any number of objections had been raised against the possibility of the navy developing an offensive into the Hawaiian Islands, and these basic objections had not been overcome by the unfolding of more favorable events. Yamamoto himself seems to have been uncertain about how to proceed with the central Pacific option, and Ugaki was no more than lukewarm about it at first.[16] But the idea began to take shape once the critical decision was made to exclude Oahu from the scope of any immediate operations that might be mounted in the Hawaiian Islands. The calculation that three divisions would be needed to take Oahu had been at the heart of the Imperial Navy's concern over operations in the central Pacific. The navy could never have coaxed three divisions from the army for such an enterprise. A directive issued by Yamamoto on 14 January ordered his staff to study the feasibility of an operation designed to secure Midway instead.[17] This proposal suggested securing Midway and then Johnson as outposts from which an assault on Oahu could be staged.

Support for this option was to come from Vice Admiral Moshiro Hosogaya, commander of the Fifth Fleet. This formation, a paper force, watched the northern approaches to Japan. Less enthusiastic backing came from Vice Admiral Nishizo Tsukahara, commander of the Eleventh Air Fleet, which consisted of the navy's shore-based aviation. But Tsukahara's support did not count for very much: his own command could not become involved in any central Pacific operation on a significant scale.[18]

The endorsement that all five options received from different sectors of the navy pointed to the difficulties it was certain to encounter in trying to sort out its priorities. The alternatives were, or should have been, mutually exclusive. There could be no question of the Japanese having either the resources or the time to mount all four operations concurrently or in any combination. It also seems unlikely that the Japanese would have had the means to implement these operations consecutively. They had to make a definitive choice, and what made this so difficult was the fact that proponents and detractors of all the options could juggle strong arguments in support of their views. Each plan of action carried with it substantial risks, but equally each offered the prospect of considerable gain. Between January and early April the Japanese high command faced a delicate and awkward "option of difficulties," but at least by the end of February three alternatives had been eliminated. As we have noted, the notion of switching to the defensive while strength was built up was a nonstarter: the Japanese had to force the pace while the initiative remained in their hands. In addition, the southward drive against Australia and the offensive westwards into the Indian Ocean had been dismissed from serious consideration. Both these moves, which appeared grandiose to the point of folly, shared the common fate of being rejected more or less out of hand by the Army Section of Imperial General Headquarters.

The army's rejection of the Australia option was to prove far more emphatic than its refusal to contribute to the Indian Ocean effort, and it was the Australian proposal that was the first to be destroyed by the outright opposition of Lieutenant General Shinichi Tanaka, Fukudome's counterpart on the Army General Staff. The First (Operations) Bureau killed the proposal, and there was never any question of its being revived successfully,[19] even though in July, after the battles of the Coral Sea and Midway, the prospect of occupying northern Australia was again resurrected by the Naval General Staff.[20]

Tanaka's case was undoubtedly strong. When the Army Section was informed in January of the drift within the navy's Plans Division, its response was immediate. The army had deliberately sought to minimize its involvement in the south and southeast Pacific in the opening months of the war, and it had absolutely no intention of entering into an open-ended commitment far beyond the line of the Malay Barrier. It was only with reluctance that the army had sanctioned the navy's arguments in favor of taking Rabaul in New Britain, and the navy had had to fight for military endorsement of its plans to secure other islands in the southwest Pacific that would complete a chain of air bases through which combat aircraft could be staged to meet any emerging threat in the area. The army hesitantly agreed to help strengthen Rabaul with a series of small operations in the south and southeast, but the ten or twelve divisions that would be needed to secure an indefensible Australia were withheld. Though not blind to the political, economic and strategic advantages that would flow from conquering Australia, the army asserted that neither the troops nor the transports and logistics for such a major undertaking were available.[21] Moreover, in the army's view the navy lacked the means to sustain so large an expeditionary force at so great a distance from the homeland.[22]

The objections of the army were unanswerable on any logical basis, but it was rather late in the day for such a show of rationalism on the part of the military. As the army so rightly observed, the navy was already overextended by its existing commitments; this was the army's justification for its belief that these should not be increased. But there was little if anything to be gained by keeping within the rigidly prescribed limits of existing responsibilities if these could not discharged, and overextension was a positive inducement to further overextension as the only means by which an impossible strategic dilemma might be resolved. Recent events provided three more precedents as well for widening the scope of war as an answer to strategic dilemmas. First, there had been the progressive expansion of the war in China after 1937, which had been undertaken in an effort to gain the final victory over Chiang Kai-shek's regime. Second, there had been the decision to start the Pacific war. Third, there had been the switch away from defensive policy, from the tactic of "rolling with the punch" and then battling with the bulk of the Combined Fleet in the western Pacific. The new policy—throwing a defensive cordon around Japan's conquests, hardening up its outer crust and relying on an unyielding defense at the point of contact in order to wear down the enemy preparatory to main battle—was made without any corresponding increase of the logistics and support services that alone could have made the proposition a practical one. If the truth were told, Japanese strategic policy was already nonsense, and the army's attempt to apply logic to the situation in which it found itself was a belated one.

But such tortuous reasoning in favor of further overextension as the solution to Japan's strategic problems was beyond the Naval General Staff and would never have been accepted by the Army Section of Imperial General Headquarters. By the end of January the Australia option was dead, though it was not until the Liaison Conference of 7 March that the army formally vetoed it. Somewhat surprisingly, the Germans were told that "The Southern Operation" had been cancelled because it would leave the Japanese too weak to cover the Bering Sea.[23] If the Germans believed that they would have believed anything. But despite the army and the lies, the concern with Australia on account of the American interest and presence there was inevitable, and it would be important in Japanese strategic discussions over the coming weeks.

The Indian Ocean option was an even bolder concept than Tomioka's because it broke with all the basic tenets of interwar strategic planning. It would have involved a voluntary curtailing of success before the process of

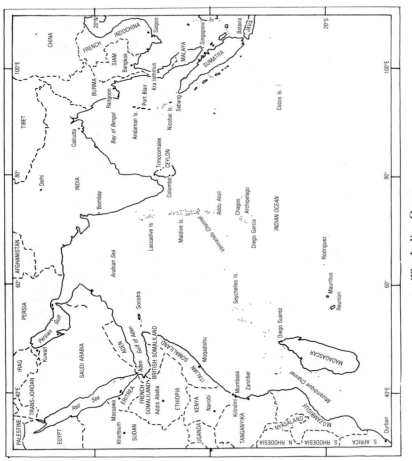

The Indian Ocean

conquest and consolidation was properly completed, and it would have stretched Japanese resources to the breaking point by opening up an entirely new theater of operations at a time when the Japanese capacity to wage war was being severely tested by the demands of the Pacific war. Mounting an offensive in the Indian Ocean would have required a complete overhaul of strategic policy. Yet this was precisely what the Japanese Navy at one stage planned to do.

Or rather, it was what certain individuals within the navy high command hoped to do—and on two separate occasions. Just as the northern Australia option resurfaced after the battles of the Coral Sea and Midway, no doubt as compensation for failure, so the Indian Ocean option was resurrected in July. But it was the Kuroshima proposals of January and February that became important as they were subjected by him and his superiors to further examination. Yamamoto and Ugaki at this time had several matters under consideration, and while they clearly favored the central Pacific option, during January they warmed to the Indian Ocean option. Ugaki was not unsympathetic to the initial suggestion, and even while he had to pursue other questions he continued to support Kuroshima as the plan evolved.[24]

The Kuroshima proposals were sufficiently developed by 5 February for the Combined Fleet to invite representatives from both general staffs to the new fleet flagship, the *Yamato*, to play a series of war games on the theme of a major undertaking in the Indian Ocean. These deliberations began on the twentieth and lasted three days before the various staffs dispersed, leaving the Combined Fleet with the feeling that things had gone well. The Naval General Staff and the Combined Fleet were in unusual accord, and even the army seemed impressed.

Circumstances certainly favored the Indian Ocean option. Singapore had fallen five days before the start of the staff discussion; much of the fleet was already in the south, and with the Indian Ocean option already penciled in for late April as the means of rounding off the first phase of conquest, the time for sanctioning a much more serious endeavor in the Indian Ocean was never more propitious. There was a widespread assumption in Japan that she would provide one arm of a gigantic pincer movement that would shatter Allied power in the one area where two of the three major Allied powers shared a land frontier. Indeed, on 18 February the German naval attaché in Tokyo reported back to his superiors that the Japanese had sounded him out on the matter of a joint German-Japanese move to secure Madagascar, after German pressure on Vichy had made the French amenable to the "suggestion." This report came one day after the General Operations Division of the German Navy had passed on to the Japanese all the information it had about possible landing sites on Ceylon.[25]

But the terms of the Tripartite Pact made no arrangements for a joint offensive into the Middle East, the Gulf and the western Indian Ocean, which had done much to cool the enthusiasm in Japanese circles for a linkup of the swastika and the rising sun. It was clear to Japan that Hitler did not regard the pact as affecting his freedom of action in any way, and many members of the Japanese high command were similarly disinclined to see their country tied to a course of action even as part of an effort intended to benefit both states. Despite their assurances on 1 February to the Germans that the intended attack on Ceylon was designed to draw Anglo-American resources away from Germany, Japan relied on Germany to tie down or defeat Britain and the Soviets, thereby ensuring the division of American power between the Atlantic and Pacific. This reliance was not part of any reciprocal arrangement as far as the Japanese were concerned. The Japanese had no good reason to break the power of the various European empires, the Americans or perhaps even the Soviets in order to facilitate the rise of the Teutonic *Übermenschen*. Their status as honorary Aryans could hardly have appealed to the Japanese. The Tripartite Pact was made up of members who eyed one another suspiciously. To its members it was never anything more than a statement of the obvious: that its signatories would conquer or be conquered together. It did not bind them to common policies or aims, and it dampened rather than spurred any thought of military cooperation.

However disappointing the lack of commitment to joint military action under the terms of the pact might have been to certain individuals who were keen admirers of Nazi Germany, the Japanese were not blind to the strategic advantages of unilateral Japanese action in the Indian Ocean. As proposals were examined and refined, it became clear that the suggestion to occupy Ceylon with two divisions and to secure an advanced base in the Chagos Archipelago in the central Indian Ocean offered exciting possibilities. Least amongst these would be the security that might be obtained for the western approaches to the Greater East Asia Co-Prosperity Sphere; more substantial would be the prospect of inflicting more and perhaps conclusive defeats on the British.

No one in the Japanese high command was unaware of the delicacy and importance to Britain of her position in India. India was the anchor of the British war effort in both the Middle and Far East, yet given the state of nationalist opinion within India, and the British loss of Malaya and Singapore and her defeats in southern Burma, there was every chance that further British reverses might well result in the collapse of her authority on the subcontinent. An offensive against Ceylon could easily have gained victory *en passant* with regard to India and rolled up the whole of the British position on the Persian Gulf, in Arabia and north and east Africa. Indeed, it is hard to see how British authority in the area could have survived another defeat. This was a point Yamamoto made to Kuroshima in the course of examining the plan. The collapse of British authority in India was the expected result of an offensive into the Indian Ocean.

Moreover, no one in the Imperial Navy could fail to be attracted by the prospect of securing another victory over what had been, until a few short weeks before, the most prestigious of the world's navies. Yet at stake in the Indian Ocean was more than mere prestige. The Imperial Navy could not remain indifferent to the British buildup in the Indian Ocean, which in the opening weeks of 1942 began to assume quite significant proportions. Before the outbreak of the Pacific war the British planned to have a major fleet assembled in eastern waters by April 1942, and notwithstanding the untimely start of hostilities, the loss of first the *Repulse* and the *Prince of Wales* and then Singapore, this concentration went ahead.* By the third week of March the British had assembled an Eastern Fleet with two modern fleet carriers and one old light carrier that was quite useless; one modernized and four old battleships; two heavy and five light cruisers; sixteen destroyers, seven submarines and various auxiliaries.[26] Both in terms of quality and numbers this force was no match for the Japanese, but that the British could gather together a fleet of any description at this perilous juncture augered ill for the Japanese in the long run. When the Japanese were considering their Indian Ocean options the exact composition of the Eastern Fleet was unknown to them, but they needed no second warning that it was in their interests to crush the British before the latter had time to reemerge as a serious threat. Furthermore, the Japanese could not be unaware of the possibility of the Royal Navy taking refuge in American waters if Britain was forced out of the war by Germany. In such a situation the Royal Navy might enter the Pacific, perhaps with disastrous results for Japan. Hence there was good reason for the Imperial Navy to carry out a major offensive operation in the Indian Ocean in the spring of 1942.

It has been suggested that Japan's defeat in the Second World War was assured by her refusal to risk everything on an all-out offensive in the Indian Ocean in the spring of 1942. At first sight such an assertion seems exaggerated, but the passing of time has obscured the critical importance of the Indian Ocean theater to the Allies in the summer of 1942. Indeed, there are good grounds for the claim that it was the pivotal area of global strategy, that the ability of the Allies to stave off defeat depended on their maintaining the physical separation of Japan and the European Axis powers. Had the Japanese made a sustained effort to sever Allied lines of communication in the western Indian Ocean, the lynchpin of the Allied global position

---

*Under the terms of its 24 December directive dealing with the assembly of the Eastern Fleet, the Admiralty set out its intention to develop fleet bases at Addu Atoll, Freemantle, and Sydney for a fleet of one light and three fleet carriers, nine old battleships, ten cruisers, twenty-four destroyers, ten submarines, sixteen fleet minesweepers and various auxiliaries.[27]

would have been destroyed. The anchor of the Soviet front in southern Russia and central southwest Asia, the means by which the British sustained themselves in North Africa, the vital line of communication to the Middle East from Australasia, and the Allied supply route to the Soviets via Iran—which for two years after June 1942 carried much more traffic than the Arctic route—would have been shattered by a major Japanese offensive in the Indian Ocean in the spring of 1942. As a token of the importance of this area to the Allies, and as an offering to historical speculation, it is worth considering what would have happened had the British line of supply to Egypt been cut, if only for one or two months, in the second quarter of 1942.

It is unclear why the Japanese did not commit themselves to a major offensive in the Indian Ocean. When the discussions in the *Yamato* broke up, the staff of the Combined Fleet was left with the impression that the army and navy staffs were favorably disposed towards the idea of an offensive into the Indian Ocean in mid-1942. In the two weeks after the discussions, however, the Indian Ocean option went the same way as its Australian rival. Many have asserted that the navy's belated insight could not have been imposed on the Army Section of Imperial General Headquarters because the naval plan of campaign, despite its strategic acumen, called upon no fewer than five divisions to be made available to support the proposed offensive.[28] As with the Australia option, the army's case was that the troops and transports needed for this operation were simply not available.

This explanation was as inadequate as the reasons the army paraded in opposition to the Indian Ocean option. The army view was that the proposed thrust into the Indian Ocean was "premature," but without any definition of what constituted timeliness this seems to have been no more than a device used to disguise a wider disinterest. Reluctance to endorse the Indian Ocean option was not justified on the basis of a lack of troops and transports, a point that will be examined a little later, but if the army planners had second thoughts about this operation once they escaped the lavish hospitality of the *Yamato*, so, too, did the various naval planners. Just four days after the end of the Yamato games, on the twenty-sixth, a liaison conference of staff and fleet representatives did not even discuss the Indian Ocean option, indication that even by that stage the euphoria had worn off and an element of sensible caution had reasserted itself. Even before the army showed itself opposed to the idea of a full-blooded offensive in the Indian Ocean, the navy itself, it seems, had backtracked on its initial enthusiasm.

Why the navy should have reversed its position so soon after the games is not clear; what is clear is that the games themselves were notably disorganized and produced mixed results that hardly encouraged the navy to go ahead with its proposals. Staff examination of the proposals revealed that the Eleventh Air Fleet would encounter considerable difficulty if it tried to support the Combined Fleet from bases in southern Burma and the Andaman Islands. Moreover, the Japanese did not expect to record a decisive victory over the British. At best they anticipated a partial victory; the major part of any British fleet encountered in battle, they believed, would escape. What was worse, unacceptably high Japanese losses were foreseen. The Japanese substantially overestimated the strength and effectiveness of British air formations on Ceylon, and they also exaggerated British submarine strength in the Indian Ocean. As a result they expected to meet ten British submarines and even to come under air attack at a range of 800 miles from Ceylon. The Japanese expected to lose one, perhaps two, of their carriers to enemy air and submarine action, but on this matter their estimates of enemy strength and capabilities were wildly inaccurate, and they admitted as such in the latter stages of the *Yamato* games. The extent of the disorganization that plagued these games and staff discussions can be measured by the Japanese anticipation that they might encounter three British carriers— and that they would sink all seven of them.[29] Aside from the question of arithmetic, the question of where in 1942 the British were to secure seven carriers for the Indian Ocean and how their destruction could be regarded as only a partial victory hardly suggest that the Japanese were taking much care in their staff analyses.

But even if some element of confusion arose during the staff games and discussions, there was no doubting that in one vital assumption about an Indian Ocean sortie the Japanese were correct. According to the plans that Kuroshima put forward Japan would commit the whole of the Combined Fleet to the Indian Ocean. In fact, the Kuroshima plan envisaged an operation in the Indian Ocean that was grander than the one put into effect at Midway. Even the First Fleet was to take part in this operation. The Japanese believed that their battleships had a better chance of seeing action against the British than against the Americans, and they also wanted to revive morale amongst the battle divisions after months of inaction. But the Japanese estimation was that the Americans might take advantage of the deployment of the Combined Fleet into the Indian Ocean by launching perhaps as many as two carrier raids on Tokyo. This was a perceptive analysis, and it may well have been one of the major reasons the idea of a major offensive in the Indian Ocean was set aside in favor of the plan for a short-duration raid. The security of the homeland was the central responsibility of the navy, and one likely reason the Kuroshima plan failed to gain acceptance was that it ignored the cardinal rule of war—the preservation of a reserve.

If this was indeed the case, then other considerations can be said to have contributed to the shelving of Kuroshima's proposals. First, long before the winter was over it had become evident that the Germans had no intention of undertaking a major offensive in the eastern Mediterranean and the Middle East to destroy the Allied position between two advances. However much the parties to the Tripartite Pact distrusted one another and avoided entangling commitments, the German decision not to contribute to an offensive had to weaken the rationale behind the proposed operation. The Army Section of Imperial General Headquarters appears to have used German reluctance as excuse enough to throw out the whole plan of campaign. But on this occasion the army's refusal to cooperate in a naval venture did not prevent the navy from going ahead with their plans for a strictly limited offensive, first suggested as early as the previous December. In reality, the navy would have been better advised to cut its losses altogether and not to persist with an operation that could not hope to achieve any worthwhile strategic success in its truncated form.

But there was a real difference between the army's refusal to go along with the Australia option and its decision not to support an offensive in the Indian Ocean. Its opposition to the former was natural and proper. In the final analysis the navy could not take umbrage at the army's opposition to its proposals. But in the case of the Indian Ocean option at least some of the troops and transports that it was claimed could not be released were on hand. Indeed the two divisions required for a descent on Ceylon could have easily been put at the navy's disposal—both were immediately available. To add insult to injury, at the very time that the navy went ahead with its modified offensive in the Indian Ocean, the unavailable troops in their equally unavailable transports were actually at sea—in the Indian Ocean. The Eighteenth and Fifty-sixth Infantry Divisions, plus the First and Fourteenth Tank Regiments, had been placed under the command of Lieutenant General Shojiro Iida's Fifteenth Army as of 4 March.[30] The main troop movements to Rangoon were carried out between 25 March and 19 April with the veteran Eighteenth Infantry Division, fresh from the Malayan campaign, making the sea passage from Singapore between the second and seventh of April.[31] This was exactly the time the navy's carriers made their first attack on Ceylon. So it was not a question of the army not having the troops to support Operation C: it was simply that the army chose not to make forces available. Rather than provide troops for an expedition to Ceylon, the army decided to move forces into Burma, and whether these had more than a marginal effect on the outcome of the campaign in that country is doubtful. A Japanese victory in Burma had been assured from the time that the British had been broken in February on the Sittang, and the forces that arrived in Burma just before the monsoon broke had little impact. They may have speeded up the success of the Fifteenth Army as it encountered stiffening resistance in central and upper Burma from the Chinese forces that had entered the country, but this did not really amount to very much. In Ceylon these formations might well have proved invaluable to the Japanese cause, perhaps even changing the course of the war. It was not that there was very much in Ceylon to withstand an attack, though the defenders were far more formidable and numerous than the Japanese had expected. By the end of March the British had two brigades from the Thirty-fourth Indian Division on the island, along with a local Ceylonese and the Sixteenth British, Sixteenth and Seventeenth Australian and Twenty-first East African Brigades.[32] Such a garrison could not hope to hold an enemy of equal size who was backed by air and naval superiority, but had the Japanese landed on Ceylon in April it is likely that they would have encountered a more effective resistance than anything that they had met thus far in Southeast Asia.

Thus by the first week of March the navy found that two of its possible courses of action had been ruled out of further consideration, mostly but not entirely because of the army's reluctance to consider the Australia and Ceylon options. Yet by this time the navy had managed to get itself into quite a predicament. It had gone to war with the intention of conducting a three-phase campaign. It had no plan worthy of the name for its second-phase operations, yet in January in consultations within Imperial General Headquarters it accepted 1 April as the date for the inauguration of this second operational phase.[33] By the end of the first week of March the navy still had no idea what policy was to be implemented at the close of the month. All the navy had in the pipeline was a plan to attack Ceylon at the beginning of April, a plan that had been floated in December as the finale of the first operational phase. After the various discussions of February and March the plan, like Japanese planning overall, was in limbo.

But that was not how things appeared to the Naval General Staff at the time. The Plans Division, its hopes for Australia and then Ceylon shattered, had been working on the possibility of an offensive into the southwest Pacific. It planned to extend the scope of operations already in hand there, and in this effort it was encountering success. Having broken the navy's hopes with regard to Australia and Ceylon and kept itself from being caught with an open-ended commitment to these theaters, the army was now prepared to back the idea of a naval offensive in the southwest Pacific. The Army Section of Imperial General Headquarters endorsed the suggestion of the First Section, and on 13 March the Liaison Conference sanctioned an offensive into the southwest Pacific. The idea was to develop an offensive against New Caledonia, Fiji and Samoa that would throw the enemy on the defensive and ensure that he stayed there.[34] But unbeknownst to the Plans Division and Imperial General Headquarters, the staff of the Combined Fleet was preparing its own proposals for an offensive. Not surprisingly, these proposals ran counter to those that the Liaison Conference sanctioned on the thirteenth. The Naval General Staff and the

Combined Fleet, therefore, were pulling in different directions, and exacerbating the situation once their conflicting proposals emerged in open competition with one another, American operations began to exert an additional influence on Japanese deliberations—with, as it transpired, dire long-term consequences.

Before the start of the war the navy had given careful consideration to the question of what it should attempt to secure in the southwest Pacific. Its central concern was for the security of its main fleet anchorage in the south, the atoll of Truk in the Carolines. The importance of the atoll had grown considerably as a result of the 1939 decision to form a forward defensive perimeter to the east of the line of the Marianas, into the area of the Gilbert, Ellice and Marshall islands. Because of the need to hold the approaches to Truk from the southeast, the navy had decided upon securing Rabaul, an Australian seaplane base for most of the interwar period, and taking Lae and Salamaua, two small settlements on the northern coast of (Australian) New Guinea. Tulagi, a small island in the southern Solomons—their admisistrative "capital" and the site of another Australian seaplane base— was also marked down for occupation. The navy believed that by securing Lae, Salamaua and Tulagi it could give depth to the main position that it intended to establish at Rabaul. This was essential if, as the Japanese calculated, the Americans made their effort to "roll back" the tide of Japanese conquest in the sea area around eastern New Guinea and the Bismarcks.[35]

The navy had encountered opposition from the army to even these relatively modest proposals before the start of the war. For exactly the same reasons that it opposed the Australia and Ceylon options between January and March 1942, the army had refused in the autumn of 1941 to take troops off the Asian mainland on the scale needed to secure the positions that the navy believed had to be taken. The army's desire to be in a position to take advantage of the anticipated collapse of the Soviet Union kept it from providing any more than one regimental group, built around the 144th Infantry Regiment (from the Fifty-fifth Infantry Division), to supplement the naval troops in the western and southwest Pacific. As a result of the army's parsimony, first-phase operations in these areas could embrace only Guam, Wake, Makin (in the Gilberts) and then Rabaul. Guam and Makin were occupied on 10 December 1941, Wake on the twenty-third. Rabaul and Kavieng were taken one month later, on 23 January.

But long before the fall of Rabaul both the Plans Division and the Combined Fleet had begun to consider future action, and the concern of the former was to tidy up the unfinished business of the southwest Pacific theater. After issuing formal instructions to the South Seas Force to secure Rabaul on 4 January, the Naval General Staff found that its growing interest in the area had been anticipated by the local commander. Inoue asked permission to expand the scope of his planned operations to include Lae and Salamaua.[36]

On 29 January, with Rabaul secured, Imperial General Headquarters instructed the navy to secure first Lae and Salamaua and then Tulagi. It also instructed the army and navy to pool their efforts and secure Port Moresby on New Guinea's southeast coast.[37] Later, on 27 February, Imperial General Headquarters instructed Inoue to prepare to secure the islands of Nauru and Ocean.[38]

At first no major problems were entailed in complying with these instructions. The Japanese forces in the area were small, but those of Japan's enemies were smaller. Apart from an awkward first assault on Wake, the Japanese had suffered no undue difficulty in fulfilling their initial objectives, and no good reason existed to suppose that this situation would change. Except for its support of four fleet carriers during the Rabaul operation, the Combined Fleet had not had to support the South Seas Force, and there was no apparent need for it to become involved with Inoue's command in the future. Despite the fact that Japanese forces in the area were not of sufficient strength to do what was expected of them, they were considered capable of achieving their objectives. Indeed, Imperial General Headquarters made this perfectly clear: planning and execution were left to the local commanders. These were Inoue, who commanded the South Seas Force, and the army's Major General Tomitaro Horii, who headed up the South Seas Detachment, the 144th Infantry Regiment in its operational guise.[39]

Inoue was able to comply with the terms of the 29 January directive by 16 February, when his staff completed a plan whereby Lae and Salamaua were to be secured in early March and Tulagi and Port Moresby in early April. When he received the 27 February directive Inoue decided to wait until the latter two objectives had been secured before moving against Nauru and Ocean.[40] Inoue calculated that the forces he had at hand would be enough to secure these two islands: small and isolated, they were certain to be lightly defended. Thus there seemed to be no immediate obstacle to carrying out the instructions that Inoue himself had wanted to receive.

Appearances were deceptive. The isolation of Nauru and Ocean, the only islands in the 20 degrees of longitude between Rabaul and the Gilberts, made them important. If they were in Japanese hands any enemy attempt to move inside the arc of the Gilberts could be countered. But access to the islands was difficult for both sides, and for the Japanese their occupation would require more than a simple hop from one island to another under the assured cover of land-based aircraft. To secure Nauru and Ocean the Japanese would have to move beyond cover, just as they had in the case of the first Wake offensive. The same was true, or at least partly true, of the proposed operation against Port Moresby. Japanese naval forces would have to move around the southeast tip of New Guinea and then negotiate waters controlled by enemy aircraft in northern Australia and at the objective itself. Lae and Salamaua had to be secured—this would allow the Japanese to bring their airstrips into service and neutralize Allied air power at Port Moresby before the start of any amphibious operation to secure the town.

Securing Port Moresby had been the rationale of Inoue's original proposals. He had been amongst the first to recognize that in Allied hands Port Moresby could soon become a major thorn in the Japanese side.[41] Allied heavy bombers there could roam as far north as Truk, and Inoue, as noted earlier, saw that Port Moresby and northern Australia could easily develop into a springboard for enemy attacks westwards into the Indies, northwards into the Carolines or towards the northeast and the Marshalls and Gilberts. But in Japanese hands Port Moresby could become the base for air operations against northern Australia and deep into the Coral Sea; Rabaul and Tulagi would thereby be covered in the one direction from which an enemy counterattack might materialize. Moreover, once in Japanese hands Port Moresby would complete the air ferry route from Singapore and the Philippines via the Indies and New Guinea to Rabaul. Thus the Japanese, by taking Port Moresby and covering Lae and Salamaua, would have a mesh of mutually supporting air bases that could be used to concentrate overwhelming numbers of land-based aircraft against any Allied naval force that dared challenge Japanese gains along the southern perimeter of the Greater East Asia Co-Prosperity Sphere.

It is not hard to see why and how the ideas of Inoue coincided with the opinions of Tomioka and the Plans Division. Inoue would dearly have loved it if Japan secured the eastern seaboard of Australia, since that would have removed the most serious threats to his position. When the chance to gain the seaboard was denied him, Inoue's concern turned to certain limited but still vitally important objectives. Tomioka's same concern had led him to advocate the Australia option, but once this was rejected the logic of the situation and the momentum of events already in hand encouraged the Plans Division to consider widening the scope of existing operations. This would include the objectives outlined in those vague draft plans for the second operational phase—Fiji, Samoa and other targets in the "Australia area." What the army's power of veto forced the navy to consider for the first time was upgrading the second string of the southern option, the offensive into the southwest Pacific. This idea came to involve a detailed proposal to isolate and neutralize Australia by using those islands designated to be Inoue's final objectives as the starting points for a full-scale offensive. Such a proposal, set out by Tomioka's division, was the one accepted by Imperial General Headquarters on 13 March.

This coincidence was neat, but by the time the Naval General Staff came to consider the implications of operations in the southwest Pacific in detail, the situation had changed dramatically. A series of events had revealed that the main assumption underpinning the whole concept of Japanese operations was flawed. The assumption, as we have seen, was that the Japanese would be able to dictate the operational pattern of the war and that in the future the enemy would have to conform to it just as he had in the past. The events that proved the Japanese wrong were a series of raids conducted by American carrier task forces against targets in the Marshalls and Gilberts on 1 February, an abortive mission against Rabaul on 20 February, the attacks on Wake on 24 February and on Marcus on 4 March, and most significant of all, the raid of 10 March.

The initial raids amounted to no more than pinpricks. On the first occasion the *Enterprise* and her escorts attacked Wotje, Roi-Kwajalein and Taroa-Maloelap in the Marshalls, while the *Yorktown* and her consorts tried to neutralize Jaluit, Mili and Makin in the Gilberts. Then, some three weeks later, the *Enterprise* and her escorts moved against Wake.[42] In all these raids Japanese losses were light and could be absorbed without much trouble; that their losses were light because they did not have the strength to garrison any of the bases properly should have been the lesson drawn from these events. What the American raids did do was induce a surprising element of caution into Japanese planning. After 1 February the Naval General Staff detached the Fifth Carrier Division, consisting of the *Shokaku* and the *Zuikaku*, from the all-conquering Carrier Striking Force so it could patrol the approaches to Japan. The two carriers were to cover the exposed Pacific flank while Vice Admiral Chuichi Nagumo led his remaining carriers on a series of operations in the Indies south of Java and against northern Australia.[43]

More important than these events, however, was the attempted raid on Rabaul by the *Lexington*, part of the "tip-and-run" strategy employed by the U.S. Pacific Fleet at this stage of the war. Vice Admiral Wilson Brown had intended to take his task force against Rabaul on 21 February. But during his approach his task force was detected by Mavis flying boats operating from Rabaul. Fighters accounted for two of the flying boats that found and reported the *Lexington*, but Brown, his presence now known to the enemy, felt that there was no alternative to abandoning his mission. To keep the Japanese guessing and to retain what element of surprise remained to him, he decided to maintain his course during the remaining hours of daylight and then turn away under cover of dark. Brown failed to take account of the naturally aggressive reaction of the Japanese to their discovery of the *Lexington*. The naval bombers at Rabaul had no intention of foregoing the first contact that the naval air force had had with an American carrier thus far in the war.

Rabaul sent seventeen Betty bombers against the *Lexington*. The action that followed was much more than a simple battle between rival air squadrons. Few could have realized the full significance of the events that were to unfold: the concept of perimeter defense, in which the Japanese had placed their trust, was about to be put to the test for the first time. The Japanese strategic intention was for local forces to wear down the enemy by aggressive action at the point of contact, and the clash of 20 February was in effect a test case for attrition.

The encounter was a disaster for the Japanese. Few engagements during the war show the gap between their aspirations and performance better than this action, which took place at a time when the Japanese were at the peak of their strength and effectiveness. To garrison Rabaul and use it as the focus of defense in the southwest Pacific, the naval air force had allocated two air groups from the Twenty-fourth Air Flotilla (the Eleventh Air Fleet) to Vunakanau air base. It planned to operate twenty-four long-range flying boats out of Rabaul on reconnaissance patrols and to hold twenty-seven fighters and thirty-six bombers as the base's teeth. Thus provisioned, Rabaul was to be the most important Japanese base in the southwest Pacific.[44] The flying boats were to be provided by the Yokohama Air Group, the fighters and bombers were to come from the Fourth Air Group.[45]

The force, with less total fighting strength than an air group from a carrier, could hardly prove effective against an enemy that was certain to possess numerical superiority if and when he chose to move against Rabaul. Perimeter defense could have a chance of working only with great strength, otherwise the result was certain to be weakness everywhere. Because the Japanese lacked an adequate pool on which to draw for their island air garrisons in the first place, they were condemned to attempt too much with too little over too great an area; individual bases were no more than hostages to fortune, since there was never a chance of making the all-important first contact with the enemy on a basis remotely approaching equality.[46] Such was the theoretical situation: the reality was worse. Japanese losses in the opening weeks of the war had been so heavy and production and delivery of replacements so sluggish that even four weeks after Rabaul's fall its new owners had only eighteen Betty bombers on station. Moreover, Rabaul still did not have a supply of torpedoes for antiship operations.[47] What was significant about this situation was that Rabaul was a high-priority base that was supposed to be strong and well supplied by Japanese standards. However Rabaul performed, other bases were certain to do less well.

Japanese aggressiveness and impetuosity in sending bombers to attack an enemy carrier beyond the range of escorting fighters met with entirely predictable results. In the melee over the *Lexington* the Americans lost two of their Wildcats but in return accounted for no fewer than fifteen of the attackers. For the Japanese this was an ominous exchange. Before this encounter the Betty, owing to the shape of its fuselage, had been known as the Cigar; it was later to become known as the Flying Lighter because of a tendency to crumple and ignite under fire. On 20 February, just one day after Betty bombers had joined carrier aircraft in the razing of Darwin, the airplane lived up to her second and unflattering nickname with unenviable ease.

The magnitude of Japanese losses on 20 February revealed another weakness in their preparations. Long-term planning had envisaged waging defensive warfare along a perimeter cordon, and to do so effectively the Japanese needed strong concentrations of fighters and powerful strike forces. Yet the short-term requirement was for offensive action, and the construction of Japanese aircraft had reflected this. The demands of offensive action were for high speed, good maneuverability, long range and heavy payload; the demands of defensive warfare were for ruggedness of construction, the ability to take punishment, armor and heavy fire power. Defensive needs had been sacrificed to secure optimum performance in the attack. The Betty bomber was structurally ill suited to take punishment and fight defensively. This was the case for all first-line Japanese naval aircraft, including the Zeke fighter. But in the end defensive power had to depend on fighters; they had to prove as effective in the battle of attrition as the bombers of 1941 and 1942 had proved in the strike role. Events were to show, however, that such effectiveness was beyond Japanese fighters.

The action of 20 February constituted a bad defeat for the Imperial Navy, even though the Americans had no means of appreciating the full extent of their victory at the time. The *Lexington* destroyed Rabaul's effectiveness as a base. The numbers involved in this affray were so small that such words as *battle*, *victory* and *defeat* cannot describe it, but the Japanese themselves saw in the confrontation a need to revise their operational timetable. The proposed occupation of Lae and Salamaua had to be postponed for five days (until 8 March) while the losses suffered by Rabaul, and also those sustained by Wake on the twenty-fourth, were made good. From both Tinian (in the Marianas) and the Marshalls came nine bombers to replace Rabaul's losses; the Marshalls were also called upon to make up the losses suffered on Wake.[48] The restocking of Rabaul—and it was significant that the Japanese could only replace its losses, not bring the base up to its authorized strength—was essential if it was to provide support for the forthcoming operations against Lae, Salamaua, Tulagi and Port Moresby.

While replacement aircraft were arriving at Rabaul Inoue began to mount a series of raids over New Guinea. The aim of the attacks was to soften up enemy positions and gain air superiority over targets to be attacked by amphibious forces in the near future. This effort began to assume serious proportions on and after 4 March, when Japanese aircraft struck at Port Moresby, Salamaua, Lae, Wau and Bulolo, but overall these raids were conducted with forces too small and over a period too short to make permanent or significant inroads into Allied strength.[49] The Japanese lacked the strength to conduct operations on the scale and with the intensity needed to neutralize Allied air power before the invasion forces bound for Lae and Salamaua sailed from Rabaul on 5 March.[50] The landings, Operation SR, called for two transports, the *Yokohamamaru* and the *Chinamaru*, to carry a battalion group from the South Seas Detachment—the 2nd/144th Infantry plus a mountain battery and supporting troops—to Salamaua. Four transports were to take the Maizuru Second Special Naval Landing Force, plus a 400-strong naval construction battalion, to Lae. Also bound for Huon Gulf with the two front-line units was a 1,500-strong naval base unit that was to garrison Lae and Salamaua once the assault forces were withdrawn.[51]

The transports sailed in the company of the minesweeper *Tsugaru*, operating as flagship; the auxiliary minesweepers *Tamamaru* and *Tamamaru No. 2*; the armed merchant cruiser *Kongomaru*; the seaplane tender *Kiyokawamaru*; the light cruiser *Yubari*; and six members of the Sixth Destroyer Division, the *Mutsuki*, *Yayoi* and *Mochizuki*, and the *Oite*, *Asanagi* and *Yunagi*. In support of these units were four heavy cruisers, the *Aoba*, *Kinugasa*, *Kako* and *Furutaka*, from the Sixth Cruiser Division, and the light cruisers *Tenryu* and *Tatsuta* from the Eighteenth Cruiser Division. The cruisers were to operate as a covering force for the New Guinea–bound forces and were in company for two days, until on the seventh of March they doubled back to carry out a landing on Buka Island at Queen Carola Inlet the following morning. This was a token landing, the Japanese main concern being to mark the inlet with navigational aids in preparation for the arrival of construction troops, which were to build an airstrip on the island.[52] In addition, the Japanese intended to use the inlet as a permanent anchorage.[53] In the meantime, the Lae-Salamaua forces arrived off their objectives late on the seventh and went ashore the following morning. Brushing aside slight Australian resistance, the landing parties brought the Lae airstrip back into service on the ninth and then hopped around the coast to secure Finschhafen on the tenth.[54]

Unbeknownst to the Japanese, however, the Americans, for the first time in the war, were in a position to interfere with one of their landings. Brown, after the episode of 20 February, urged his superiors to sanction another effort against Rabaul, and on 25 February it was decided to concentrate the *Lexington* and the *Yorktown* for offensive operations in the southwest Pacific. On 2 March Brown received instructions to attack Japanese positions in the Solomons and New Britain area on 10 March or thereabouts.[55]

Brown's initial intention was to mount the first American two-carrier strike of the war against Rabaul: there was no other target worthy of such attention. But when reports of the Japanese landings on Huon Gulf were received, he decided to test his luck and try to catch the enemy off the invasion beaches before he had time either to disperse his ships or to take effective countermeasures.[56] Shedding liaison officers to fly to Townsville in Queensland and coordinate the carriers' operations with those of shore-based aircraft, Brown took his combined task force almost within sight of New Guinea before flying off his aircraft on the morning of 10 March.[57] Though the staff of the Pacific Fleet was to doubt the wisdom of his choice and the value of the results that were claimed, Brown's luck held with credible results. He and his staff had calculated that the enemy would not expect an attack by carrier aircraft that came from out of the Solomon Sea after negotiating the towering Owen Stanley Range. This calculation and not the one made by the Pacific Fleet proved correct.

Four heavy cruisers and six destroyers, mostly drawn from the *Yorktown*'s screen of Task Force Seventeen, formed a distant covering force while four more cruisers and twelve destroyers, mostly drawn from the *Lexington*'s original formation, Task Force Eleven, screened the *Yorktown* and the *Lexington* as they flew off a total of 104 aircraft against Lae and Salamaua. The carriers committed eighteen Wildcats, sixty Dauntless dive-bombers and twenty-five Devastators to the attack. Of the latter, thirteen were from the *Lexington* and were armed with torpedoes; those from the *Yorktown* operated in the high-level role. Both Devastator squadrons were to attack Salamaua, as were the two squadrons of Dauntless bombers. The two squadrons of Dauntless scouts were tasked to attack Lae. The fighters from the *Lexington* were divided between Lae and Salamaua, but the Wildcats from the *Yorktown* were to concentrate their efforts over Salamaua.

Because of the payloads of the Devastators, the American aircraft were forced to fly through a 7,500-ft pass in order to get through the Owen Stanleys. One Dauntless, piloted by Commander William B. Ault, commander of the *Lexington*'s air group, took up a position ahead of the two groups and led them through the mountains before they swept down on their targets from seaward. Surprise was complete, with the aircraft from the *Lexington* attacking both Lae and Salamaua more or less together at about 0922. The *Yorktown*'s aircraft formed a second attacking wave that hit the objectives about thirty minutes later.

Though the attack by the *Yorktown*'s Devastators proved something of a disappointment, the collective results of the raids were not. Two Dave seaplanes were destroyed at Lae, and overall the various attacks accounted for the *Kongomaru* (though she took her time in sinking and was lost with just one fatality), the *Tamamaru No. 2*, and the transports *Tenyomaru* and

Yokohamamaru. The destroyer *Oite* was strafed, and the *Kiyokawamaru* and the *Chinamaru* sustained only slight damage. More extensively damaged were the *Yubari*, *Asanagi*, *Yunagi*, *Tsugaru* and *Tamamaru*, and the transport *Kokaimaru*. At Lae and Salamaua the Americans did better than they realized at the time; they rendered the South Seas Force incapable of continuing the operations designed to secure Tulagi and Port Moresby. Incomplete returns show that the Japanese loss amounted to 112 killed and 247 wounded. With no base facilities within easy reach, the badly damaged ships were forced to return to Japan for repair.[58]

The war diary of the U.S. Pacific Fleet recorded on 11 March that "it is doubtful if [*sic*] the enemy will be greatly retarded" as a result of the losses he had sustained.[59] But since Inoue was forced to run his campaign on a shoestring and had no option but to use the same warships, transports, auxiliaries and troops time after time as his plan of campaign unfolded, this assessment could not have been wider of the mark. Japanese losses were serious because they could not be covered by local resources. There was consolation of a sort in the fact that none of the covering cruisers had been damaged, but this could not gloss over another fact—that at Lae and Salamaua the Japanese suffered their worst setback of the war to date. Admittedly, the Japanese had taken losses at Wake, Balikpapan and Bantam Bay, but the losses at Huon Gulf were heavier and rather different. At Lae and Salamaua the Americans did better than they realized at the time because they rendered the South Seas Force unable to continue the operations to secure Tulagi and Port Moresby; an inability to continue operations had not resulted from Japanese losses on any previous occasion. Nevertheless, Inoue and his command were not the only losers. Brown assessed the effect of the raid more accurately than the staff of the Pacific Fleet when he observed in his action report that the attacks on Rabaul and Huon Gulf would cause the Japanese to proceed with caution in the future. But the soundness of this comment did not prevent his losing his command in what was a curious upshot to the Lae-Salamaua raid. With just one raid to the credit of Task Force Eleven after nearly two months at sea, Brown was removed from his command when he returned to Pearl Harbor.[60] His dismissal, ordered by Admiral Ernest J. King, was one of the latter's first actions after his appointment as chief of naval operations on 12 March.[61] King had suspected that Brown lacked drive and felt that the results obtained at Lae and Salamaua were somewhat less than impressive. But, curiously, Roosevelt's summary of the raid, written to Churchill on 18 March, claimed that two enemy heavy cruisers had been sunk; one light cruiser was believed to have been sunk; and one destroyer and one minelayer were classed as "probables." Two other destroyers were "badly damaged and probably sunk," while another two were equally damaged but only "possibly sunk." Five transports were either sunk or badly damaged, and two patrol boats were "possibles." One seaplane tender was deemed to have been "seriously damaged." [62] These results could not justify the removal of Brown or the Pacific Fleet's negative assessment of the situation on 11 March.

The real significance of the raid, however, had nothing to do with the personal misfortunes of opposing commanders; it was the result, which Brown had predicted, that counted. Coming as it did on top of the attacks of 1 and 20 February, the raid on Lae and Salamaua clearly revealed that the period of easy and virtually unopposed Japanese success was coming to an end. But the Japanese still had time to carry out a number of small-scale operations free from American interference. On 30 March Kessa and Buka were secured, and on the following day Shortland was occupied by the Japanese. For these operations, at the northern end of the Solomon chain, the Japanese used a company of marines and a close support group consisting of the minelayer *Soya*, three destroyers and two auxiliary gunboats. The four heavy and two light cruisers of the original covering force, plus the four destroyers that had escaped damage at Huon Gulf on 10 March, stood cover for these operations, which tied up the loose ends of the seventh and eighth. Hundreds of miles to the west, Japanese forces in the central Indies also began to extend the area of Japanese conquest in the direction of eastern New Guinea and the Admiralties by securing islands and bases on the western approaches of New Guinea before and at the same time as they secured a number of objectives on the Vogelkop and on the northern coast of the island. With an escort provided by the seaplane tender *Chitose*, the light cruiser *Kinu*, two destroyers, six escorts and three auxiliary gunboats, one marine unit in two transports embarked on a series of minor operations that resulted in the securing of Boela on 31 March, Fak Fak the next day, Babo on 2 April, Sorong on the fourth, Ternate (the island off Halmahera) on the seventh, Manokwari on the twelfth, Moemi on the fifteenth, Seroei (on Japen Island) on the seventeenth, Nabire the following day and both Sarmi and Hollandia on the nineteenth. [63] At the same time minor units from Rabaul moved to secure Lorengau on Manus Island, its occupation being completed on 8 April. [64] But these operations, important though they might have been in helping to establish a net of air bases on New Guinea, were not the critical ones as far as the Naval General Staff and Inoue were concerned.* The operations that counted were the ones that would go beyond the line of the Louisades and into the central and southern Solomons. These moves could no longer be improvised, nor could they be seen through to success with the forces that were left to Inoue after 10 March.

*Subsequent operations allowed the Japanese to secure a line of air bases to be brought into service in the course of 1943. Bases at Madang and Wewak were commissioned in December 1942, and Hollandia was brought into service in February 1943. This completed the line from the Philippines to Rabaul, but not before the end of the Guadalcanal campaign.

Indeed, after this date there was even some risk involved in the operations that were taking place in the northern Solomons. The raid by the *Lexington* and the *Yorktown* on Huon Gulf meant that future Japanese operations in the southwest Pacific would have to be very deliberate affairs if losses on the scale of 10 March were to be avoided. This, in its turn, meant that more substantial air support than was previously committed to the southwest Pacific would have to be made available to Inoue, and the implication of events was that land-based air support would not be enough to lessen Japanese vulnerability. The carrier forces would have to be committed to this theater of operations.

The revelation of Inoue's manifest inability to carry out his mission in the face of enemy carrier activity therefore had the effect of raising the question of future operations in the southwest Pacific from a matter purely of local concern to one of national attention. As long as Inoue had seemed capable of taking his objectives in the Solomons and on New Guinea without making demands on the main forces, there was no great importance attached to operations in what was until that time clearly a secondary theater of operations. But if Inoue needed carrier support—and the scale of the 10 March attack, which revealed the presence of two enemy carriers in the southwest Pacific, indicated that he did—then the whole question of how, when and where Japan was to make her main effort in 1942 had to be rethought. The fleet carriers were so few in number and so vital in function that their employment was a matter of national importance. Rightly or wrongly, naval strategy revolved about them. They could not be wasted on peripheral operations. Inoue's request for carrier support in the aftermath of the 10 March raid therefore raised the question of the direction of the Japanese war effort in this second operational phase. If the carriers were to be committed to Inoue's support, then it was inevitable that the Japanese effort in the southwest Pacific would have to be a major one, perhaps the major one for 1942.

In the wake of Inoue's request for support, the air officer on the staff of the Combined Fleet, Captain Yoshitake Miwa, made the flight down to Truk to confer with Inoue about the unexpected and unwelcome turn of recent events. This meeting could easily have been disastrous, for Inoue, a man of strong views, had a rasping contempt for the staff officers of the Combined Fleet. "The Young Turks" who surrounded Yamamoto were unpopular with everyone except themselves, and Inoue was not a person who hid his opinions. He had openly opposed the drift to war before 1941, he scorned the army, and he was infuriated by the lack of discipline within the navy. At every stage of a stormy but outstanding career he had made enemies and been threatened with assassination, but force of personality and undoubted ability had saved him from his adversaries.[65] He was generally regarded as the best head of aviation the Imperial Navy had ever had, and he was a firm and unwavering believer in the primacy of air power. He openly disdained the gunnery school and the notion of "the decisive battle." He envisaged naval warfare being fought by masses of aircraft on which the surface forces were totally dependent.

On this occasion Inoue had to check his personal feelings, for he needed to win the support of Miwa. If Inoue was to pry the carriers from the grip of Yamamoto—with whom he had had close relations before the war, when they had served together in the Navy Ministry—he had to convince Miwa of the merits of his case. In the event, this did not prove too difficult. Both he and Miwa were in agreement on the one point that really mattered. They accepted that if operations in the south were to be continued, two carriers would have to come into the theater in support of the South Seas Force. Given the gradual but perceptible increase in enemy air activity over New Guinea and the lurking possibility of enemy carrier forces reappearing in the southwest Pacific, nothing less than a full carrier division would be enough to support the operations that had been planned for Tulagi and Port Moresby. The problem, however, was that no such carrier division was immediately available.

With the carrier force then in the Indies and poised to begin the emasculated operation against Ceylon, there was no chance of Inoue receiving carrier support for about two months. But in the course of their conversations Miwa, who stood high in Yamamoto's estimation and might have been privy to the thinking of the commander in chief and his staff on this matter, informed Inoue that the Combined Fleet's main effort was to be made in the southwest Pacific. He also told Inoue and his staff that the Eleventh Air Fleet would be concentrated to support the operations that were to be mounted in this theater.[66] Accordingly, Inoue and his Fourth Fleet staff drew up provisional proposals to take account of this general indication of commitment. In settling on a timetable for operations, the Fourth Fleet had to take two facts into consideration. First, the carrier operations then in hand would have to be seen through to their conclusion, and the carriers themselves would have to be restocked and quickly refitted before they could start operations in the southwest Pacific. With the truncated operation in the Indian Ocean starting from Starling Bay at Kendari on 26 March, the carriers could not return to Japan for overhaul until the second half of April. Second, the extra flotillas of the Eleventh Air Fleet could not begin to assemble at Rabaul until about that same time. Several more weeks would have to elapse before the preparations for an offensive could be completed. Armed with these calculations, Inoue scheduled a move against Port Moresby and Tulagi for late May. In this outline form Inoue's planning blended well with the deliberations of Tomioka's Plans Division, backed as they were by the army, Imperial General Headquarters and the Liaison Conference after the 13 March agreement. The idea of the Plans

Division was to develop an offensive against New Caledonia, Fiji and Samoa in June or July *after* Port Moresby and Tulagi had been secured.[67] With Miwa and Inoue agreeing that carrier support would be needed to secure Port Moresby and Tulagi in the first place, Inoue drawing up a late May schedule, and Miwa suggesting to Inoue that this area of operations would be the scene of the Combined Fleet's main effort, there was no real ground for dispute between the Naval General Staff, the Combined Fleet and the South Seas Force, although innumerable loose ends would obviously have to be tied together.

But by the time Inoue was able to complete and submit his draft proposals on 4 April, they counted for very little.[68] Contrary to what Miwa had told Inoue, the Combined Fleet was not planning to make its main effort in the southwest Pacific. Either by accident or design Miwa totally misled Inoue; Combined Fleet deliberations at this time were already taking Yamamoto and Ugaki in a direction far removed from the southwest Pacific. When Inoue had perfected his plan of campaign and passed it up the chain of command, he found that it was blocked. The real intentions of the Combined Fleet had come to the surface, and the Plans Division and the fleet were already locked in a battle over the strategy to be implemented in the next few months.

The Plans Division could point to American carrier activity in the southwest Pacific as justification for the Imperial Navy making its main effort in the same area, its primary objective being to secure positions from which the isolation and neutralization of Australia might be achieved and to bring the American carriers themselves to battle. American activity in the area suggested the presence there of objectives that the enemy valued and for which he might fight, either out of choice or necessity. The staff hoped and anticipated that any threat to Australia might well provoke the Americans to give the battle that had so far eluded the Japanese.

If one conclusion drawn from the American raids in the southwest Pacific was that they justified the Japanese making their own effort in that area, the consideration of all five American carrier raids in February and March gave rise to quite another conclusion: the enemy carriers that had conducted the raids were the important part of the equation, not where they operated. The real lesson of the raids, it could be argued, was that the enemy's carriers had to be brought to book at the earliest possible opportunity before they had the chance to begin serious operations. Such, indeed, was the conclusion of Yamamoto and Ugaki, and even while they supported the Kuroshima suggestion for operations in the Indian Ocean, they had concurrently begun to formulate proposals for an operation specifically intended to draw the Pacific Fleet into the decisive battle. In the view of its authors this could best be guaranteed by carrying the war beyond the 180th meridian, into the western hemisphere. To Yamamoto and Ugaki the surest way of provoking the enemy into giving battle was to conduct operations against his national territory—everything else, in the final analysis, was negotiable to the Americans. The islands of the southwest Pacific under consideration by the Plans Division as objectives were not in the western hemisphere, and none of the islands, with the exception of Eastern Samoa, belonged to the United States.

By mid-March, at the very time that Imperial General Headquarters agreed over the southwest Pacific option, the Combined Fleet had hardened in its conviction that the central Pacific had to be the main theater of operations and that the Imperial Navy had to force a favorable decision at the earliest possible opportunity. Yet a problem presented itself once this conclusion was reached. In the vast Pacific there was no clearly identifiable target against which the Japanese could conduct sustained and intensive operations of a kind that would force the Americans to give battle under adverse conditions.

The only two targets in the Pacific for which the Americans would definitely fight under any circumstances were the Panama Canal and Pearl Harbor, but neither of them was seen as a realistic objective. Sheer distance ruled out the former. As for the latter, the war had begun with a raid that showed that Pearl Harbor was within range, but the Japanese were well aware that success seldom repeats itself. They knew that on 7 December 1941 they had been more than a little fortunate to escape detection as they approached to a flying-off position well within range of aircraft based on Oahu. Radio intelligence in the opening weeks of the war had revealed that reconnaissance around Oahu greatly increased after the start of hostilities, and a carrier force could not hope to elude American patrols if it again tried to approach Pearl Harbor from the north. With so many land-based aircraft operational on well-dispersed airfields on Oahu, the Japanese had no realistic hope of being able to fight for and then secure air supremacy over Pearl Harbor. Moreover, any attempt to approach Oahu was almost certain to be met by aircraft from two bases that served as outposts to the American position in the northern and central Pacific—the Aleutians to the north and the tiny atoll with its two islets, together known as the Midway Islands.

Midway is almost at the western end of the Hawaiian chain, before the point where the islands link up with the Emperor Seamounts and make their submerged way to the forbidding wastes of Kamchatka. Prewar Japanese planning had recognized that Midway, the location of a twenty-million-dollar seaplane base, would become the first line of American defense in the central Pacific.[69] The Japanese had toyed with the idea of trying to secure the two islets, Eastern and Sand, but dismissed it before the start of the war because of the demands of the campaign in Southeast Asia. Nevertheless Midway remained a possibility for the second operational phase. Once the war was under way the attention of Japanese planners had to return to the huge expanse of sea and sky with scarcely an intervening island between Kamchatka and the Gilberts. It was in this area that the Americans could hope to operate with impunity, as the raid on Marcus showed. With the choice of when and with what strength to mount their operations, the Americans could jab offensively with little fear of being brought to battle, since the Japanese had little or no chance of responding quickly or effectively. Yet as the raid on Marcus on 4 March showed, the Americans could conduct operations well inside the supposed perimeter of Japan and her conquests. Marcus itself was about 1,000 miles from Tokyo, and as Yamamoto knew, the example of Pearl Harbor could be repeated— in reverse.

Yamamoto's inordinate concern to ensure that enemy carriers could not approach to within range of the Japanese homeland is sufficiently well known to need no recounting, but in the spring of 1942 all that the Combined Fleet had in the vastness of the North Pacific was a picket line of converted fishing boats stationed some 700 miles east of Tokyo. Under the command of the Fifth Fleet, these boats were part of an arrangement begun before the war, the Japanese intention being to provide the capital with an early warning system.[70] Midway, which acted as an outpost for Pearl Harbor and as a refueling base for the occasional submarine, appealed to the Combined Fleet planners as the first line of defense for Honshu—and as the forward base for future operations in the Hawaiian Islands. By mid-March Yamamoto and Ugaki had convinced themselves that this small atoll should be the scene of the attempt to provoke the Americans into giving battle. Midway was American national territory, and it was on the right side of the international date line; as such a Japanese attack on Midway was certain to be unacceptable to the Americans. The Combined Fleet's thinking was that the Americans would fight rather than accept Midway's fall. If this line of reasoning was correct, the Combined Fleet would get the battle it had sought since the start of the war.

Thus even when Miwa was assuring Inoue that the main Japanese effort in 1942 would be made in the southwest Pacific, and the Naval General Staff, backed by the army and the Liaison Conference, was working independently on the same assumption, Yamamoto's staff was preparing to carry out the main offensive effort of the year in another direction. There could be no question of reconciling the two views: they were mutually exclusive. As we shall see, the Plans Division believed that the notion of a central Pacific offensive was nonsense, while the Combined Fleet was never prepared to accept the idea of an offensive into the southwest Pacific before and at the expense of the one into the central Pacific. Thus the scene was set for a clash between the Naval General Staff and the Combined Fleet. It took place in Tokyo between the second and the fifth of April.

The case for the Combined Fleet was presented by Commander Yasuji Watanabe, a gunnery officer who was on the fleet's staff as a logistics officer. Like Miwa, he stood high in Yamamoto's estimation, and at this time he was acting as Kuroshima's deputy. The most significant feature of the plan that Watanabe outlined to the leading members of the Naval General Staff was that other operations would be subordinate to it. The proposed attacks on Port Moresby and Tulagi and all points beyond would wait until after the central Pacific offensive had been completed. The plan of campaign, in its most rudimentary form, called for the full strength of the Combined Fleet to be committed against Midway in early June, only two months away. With the Japanese carriers even then only a couple of days off Ceylon, there was no time for any major operation in the southwest Pacific before the start of an offensive into the central Pacific. Any time that might be available had to be used in overhauling the heavily worked carriers.

The tight schedule was to be one of the matters over which Watanabe and representatives of the Naval General Staff clashed during the next four days; indeed, the question of timing was constantly raised in the course of the next four weeks. But much more serious issues were at stake during the first three days of deadlock in Tokyo. Although timing was critically important—the staff assessment was that it could not meet more than 70 percent of the supply needs for a Midway operation in early June—the real objections of the staff to the proposals put forward by Watanabe related to concept, not scheduling.[71]

The case against the Midway proposal was to be argued by Tomioka and his two leading subordinates, Commanders Yuji Yamamoto and Tatsukichi Miyo. Given that so much of the Midway proposal revolved around carrier operations, it was perhaps inevitable that Miyo should be in the forefront of the Plans Division's opposition to the venture. Miyo was one of the few airmen on the Naval General Staff. He had carried out the first night landing made on a Japanese carrier, and his most significant contribution to the war effort to date was his conceiving Operation K, the importance of which will become apparent later.[72] Obviously handling the case against the Midway proposal was different from his past duties, but Miyo proved equal to his task. He put together a careful case based on three objections. These concerned the problems attached to seizing the atoll, its maintenance after capture and the expected results of its being taken.[73]

Miyo's objections were presented in a coherent and sober manner which contrasted sharply with the shallow, facile optimism that characterized the Yamamoto plan. His most compelling argument was his third one challenging the assumption that an assault on Midway would provoke—or, more accurately, was the course of action most likely to provoke—decisive battle and the negotiated peace that an assured victory would bring. Miyo considered this assessment far too sanguine. Moreover, he doubted the assertion that Midway would be much of an asset in support of future operations down the Hawaiian chain. The First Section believed that Midway, in Japanese possession, posed no threat to Pearl Harbor or to the American mainland and that, as a result, its loss would not affect American morale one iota. In formulating this argument Miyo returned to the orthodox staff view that proposed operations in the southwest Pacific were far more likely to achieve significant strategic results than a venture in the central Pacific.[74] Miyo argued that the Americans could not accept the loss of islands in the southwest Pacific that would have to serve as springboards for subsequent operations against Japan. The emphasis of his argument was not that the Americans would fight to deny the Japanese the southwest Pacific but that their attempts to reopen their line of communication between Pearl Harbor and eastern Australia would lead to battle along lines that were certain to be favorable to the Japanese cause. The Imperial Navy would be able to meet any American counterattack in the southwest Pacific with their carriers and land-based aircraft, which could be moved into the area once it had been secured.[75] Moreover, if battle was joined in the southwest Pacific the logistical difficulties of the two sides would be about equal, since both would be forced to operate far from their fleet bases and major repair facilities. Any offensive elsewhere in the Pacific was certain to extend Japanese lines of communication while those of the enemy shrank. In Miyo's view, an offensive via Port Moresby and Tulagi into New Caledonia, Fiji and Samoa offered far better prospects than an operation against an atoll, six miles in diameter, that stood almost in the center of the Pacific. Miyo argued that there was nothing to prevent the Americans from letting Midway fall, because they knew that the Combined Fleet would not be able to stand guard over the atoll forever, waiting for the Pacific Fleet to come and give a battle that it would then conveniently lose. Miyo saw that the Americans might accept the loss of Midway in the sure knowledge that they could "roll with the punch" and regain it without undue trouble at a time of their choice. The Yamamoto plan allowed the Combined Fleet to stay on station for just six days after the capture of Midway; thereafter it would have to head either for Truk or for home, and home was 2,591 miles away. With Pearl Harbor 1,323 miles from Midway, the advantages of time and distance clearly lay with the Americans. This Miyo knew and argued at length. To Miyo and the First Section the attempt to straddle the enemy line of communication between Australia and Oahu promised much better results than any move against Midway.

This consideration of distance lay at the heart of Miyo's second argument, namely that the atoll could not be sustained in the event of capture and a garrison could not function effectively on the base.[76] Miyo directly challenged the Combined Fleet's assumption that Midway would prove a strategic asset. A base on the atoll would be able to operate patrol aircraft that could search sectors that interlocked with those patrolled by aircraft from Wake or from bases to be secured in the Aleutians, but this was a theoretical and not a practical proposition. The extent of any overlap could not be more than a few minutes' flying time for a patrolling flying boat, and in any event the Japanese had so few scouts that they could not hope to carry out more than a single-phase reconnaissance on any given day from the bases that might be acquired.[77] Flying boats on Midway and in the Aleutians would not provide a reconnaissance capability; at best they would be no more than a sieve through which the enemy could pass without hindrance.

But this was not the only objection to be raised against a claim that Midway would provide the Imperial Navy with a vitally important advanced air base. Miyo suspected that the Japanese did not have the number of aircraft needed to provide Midway with an all-round defense and reconnaissance capability, and in any event the Imperial Navy lacked the means to sustain a garrison for any length of time. In piecing together this particular argument Miyo must have knowingly understated his case. With so little merchant shipping available to Japan in the first place, and so much of what there was committed to Southeast Asia and the maintenance of bases in the south, there was never any prospect of the Japanese being able to provide for a Midway base over a protracted period. Simply on the matter of aviation fuel alone the Japanese would have encountered insurmountable problems. In May one of the most skeptical of the officers involved in the operation, Vice Admiral Nobutake Kondo, commander of the Second Fleet, wrung the reluctant admission from Ugaki that it might prove impossible to sustain Midway and that the atoll would probably have to be abandoned in the long run. It was a surprising admission, one that undermined the credibility of the entire operation: if the Japanese could not hold Midway there was little point in trying to take it in the first place. But by the time the fleet chief of staff confirmed Kondo's suspicions that the Midway venture was nonsense it was far too late to check the momentum of events already under way. Certain other matters had intervened to ensure that the operation would go ahead. That did not alter the fact that Miyo's point was well made, and there was no doubting that he was correct when he observed that the aircraft the Combined Fleet planned to base on the atoll would be no more than fuel for potential bonfires. Midway covered less than two square miles, so a dispersal program could not be implemented, and the atoll was well within range of heavy bombers from Oahu.

This concern over Midway's proximity to Oahu and the other islands in the Hawaiian group was the basis of Miyo's first argument against the plan.[78] He pointed out that a Japanese attempt to secure Midway could be met by the enemy with his fleet and with submarines and aircraft based on the eastern Hawaiian Islands. Implicitly if not explicitly, Miyo touched upon the single most glaring inconsistency of the plan to attack Midway when he pointed out that the Combined Fleet, not the Pacific Fleet, would be forced to operate without shore-based air support. What in fact the staff of the Combined Fleet intended was to put into effect a campaign they had spent the whole of the interwar period planning to defeat—and which at that time they believed they would defeat if the Americans were so foolish as to adopt it. As we have seen, Japanese battle doctrine had long antici-pated breaking an American offensive in the western Pacific through suc-cessive attacks by aircraft, submarines and light forces, and finally by fleet action; the final Midway proposal was no more than a role-reversal program with an amended outcome and one other change incorporated to update plans and keep them on nodding terms with at least one element of reality. No longer confined to a limited or defensive role, the carrier was to clear the way for the rest of the fleet: it was to be the javelin, and not the barrier. Such matters made no impression on Miyo. Although he had been an exact contemporary of Watanabe at the naval academy and later at a staff college, he did not share the latter's confidence in Yamamoto's judgment. But unfortunately for Miyo, he had earlier been less than enthusiastic about Yamamoto's plan to attack Pearl Harbor.[79] As far as Miyo and his colleagues of the Plans Division were concerned, the Combined Fleet's proposals were both risky and misdirected. An American counterattack would come in the southwest Pacific because the Americans no longer had any possible base for an offensive into the web of Japanese islands in the western Pacific. Moreover, an American counteroffensive had to come in 1943. The dictates of distance and the need to build up reserves and stockpiles would prevent the Americans from going over to the offensive in the southwest Pacific in 1942.* As far as the Plans Division was concerned, such considerations determined Japan's course of action: she had to launch a preemptive attack in the area in 1942 to destroy the basis of the American threat before it became a real one.[80]

Miyo's views, put forward on 2 April, had no effect on Watanabe. Over this and the next two days Watanabe and representatives of the Naval General Staff simply restated their declared positions without concession, until on the fifth Watanabe broke the opposition by directly involving Yamamoto in the fray. His telephoned intervention—he was in his flagship at Hashirajima—was decisive. When called upon to comment on the assess-ment of the First Section with regard to the southwest Pacific, Yamamoto observed that "the most direct and effective way to achieve [the severing of American lines of communication with Australia] is to destroy the enemy's

---

*Arguably the course of the campaign on and around Guadalcanal in the last quarter of 1942 proved this calculation correct.

carrier forces without which the supply line could not in any case be sustained." It was rather strange to have so orthodox a view about the primacy of force so emphatically expounded and easily accepted when Japanese strategic thought had traditionally stressed the importance of position and distance in modifying the effectiveness of conventional force. Yamamoto continued with the following: " . . . by launching the proposed operation against Midway, we can succeed in drawing out the enemy's carrier strength and destroying it in decisive battle. If, on the other hand, the enemy should avoid our challenge, we shall realize *an important gain by advancing our defensive perimeter to Midway and the western Aleutians* without obstruction." [Italics added][81]

By the time Yamamoto finished speaking two matters were evident. First, having shown his continuing support for an aide who had been shaken by the arguments he had encountered, the commander in chief of the Combined Fleet made it clear that nothing short of dismissal would deflect him from his proposed operation. The Naval General Staff was therefore faced with the choice of giving way and going back on its agreement with the army or insisting on a settled policy even at the price of replacing the senior fleet commander in the navy. The staff had no real choice, and Fukudome, head of the First Section and Tomioka's superior, had already indicated what the choice would be. When Miyo and Watanabe had taken their dispute to him, Fukudome had listened to Watanabe and then told Miyo, without hearing him out, that since Yamamoto was intent on his proposals the Plans Division should try and accept them. From that moment Watanabe had the measure of Miyo and Tomioka, and in a sense the Combined Fleet had always had the measure of the Naval General Staff. The acid test had taken place long before, on 18 October 1941, when Kuroshima had told Tomioka and Miyo that unless the First Section dropped its opposition to the proposed plan to attack Pearl Harbor, Yamamoto and the whole of the staff of the Combined Fleet would resign. Tomioka and Miyo, and after them Fukudome, Ito and Nagano, had given way with a speed that was indecent.[82] Now, on 5 April, there was a repetition of that event. As the whole hierarchy of the Naval General Staff got involved in the argument—or perhaps tried not to get involved— Fukudome suggested to Ito that with Yamamoto evidently determined to have his way the staff should stand aside and let matters take their course. Ito nodded his assent without speaking. Nagano, apparently, said and did nothing. Only Miyo, who seems to have received support from none of his superiors except Tomioka, showed any sign of emotion or dissent.[83]

By any standard, this was a disgraceful way of conducting a business on which could depend the outcome of the war. The collective behavior of Nagano, Ito and Fukudome represented nothing less than an abject and craven shirking of responsibility, a shameful capitulation in light of the second matter that had become evident during the course of Yamamoto's long-distance intervention. Aside from Yamamoto's determination to have his plan come what may, the case for the Midway option was insupportable, and in the course of these discussions the Combined Fleet did not even attempt to argue its merits. Watanabe refused to answer objections, and neither he nor Yamamoto showed themselves willing to consider any reasoned objections to the Combined Fleet proposals. There was merely the statement of opinion and its subsequent repetition as fact, deemed to be beyond discussion and reproach. No attempt was made to reconsider the problems of logistical support in the light of Miyo's observations on the matter. No attempt was made to justify a plan that divided attention and strength between two objectives—seizing an island and tackling an enemy naval force. Instead, there was just a glib assertion that success was assured. To gain acceptance of his plan Yamamoto relied not on reason but on intimidation, and he was prepared to ride roughshod over the Naval General Staff in the sure knowledge that his threat to resign would never be realized.[84]

Of course the problem with all these discussions was an inevitable lack of objectivity. The claims for one theater instead of another were largely speculative and very much a matter of personal preference or prejudice. There was little hard fact on which the litigants could base their cases, though most of what firm evidence was available would seem to have supported the case against Midway. The weakness of Miyo's argument and the Plans Division's case, on the other hand, was that most if not all of the objections raised against the Midway proposal could be raised against the southwest Pacific option. With both cases sharing weaknesses and neither being open to proof, the Combined Fleet merely stood on its stated case and wore down the opposition in a battle of attrition by ignoring its arguments.

The battle of attrition the Combined Fleet won in Tokyo on this occasion was the only such battle it won in the whole of the war, but even though they capitulated in the face of Yamamoto's intransigence it must have been perfectly clear to Nagano, Ito and Fukudome that Miyo's case was sound and that Yamamoto, by producing such a throughly bad plan of campaign, was certain to raise as many problems as he was trying to solve. Nothing made this more obvious than the second argument Yamamoto had used to justify his proposal: that even if it failed to goad the Americans into giving battle there were advantages to be gained by the extension of Japan's defensive perimeter to include Midway and the western Aleutians. This was simply not true, and the assertion had been opposed by Miwa during the deliberations of the Combined Fleet staff.[85] The western Aleutians and Midway could not be regarded as neighbors, able to provide one another with mutual support. At their nearest point they were separated by more than 1,600 miles of desolate ocean, and the main bases of the two island chains were some 2,350 miles apart. An attempt to secure any of the islands of these groups would involve a divergent effort, and the extension of a defensive perimeter beyond the range of the strongest existing base in the area could only involve a diminution of force that the Japanese could ill-afford. A base here, a base there, inadequately supplied and undergarrisoned, beyond the range of effective support—this was not a defense line but a formula for disaster. It would be to repeat the 20 February Rabaul situation on a larger scale. Yet under the terms of Yamamoto's proposals the "front" was to be extended eastwards and the western Aleutians were to be attacked at the same time as Midway. Their inclusion in the plan of campaign appears to have been as casual as the subsequent vow on the part of the Combined Fleet to implement the southwest Pacific option after Midway.[86] This promise was no more than a sop, offered to and accepted by a defeated staff.[87]

Thus on 5 April the Combined Fleet, as it had anticipated, won on the crucial questions of the form and timing of Japanese operations in the Pacific for the remainder of the year. But that very day there was evidence to suggest that it had misjudged the current state of affairs in the southwest Pacific within the New Britain–New Guinea line.

Before the day was out Ugaki issued an order to the Combined Fleet warning of major organizational changes that would be put into effect on 10 April in order to facilitate future operations. Inoue, who the previous day had completed his draft plans for operations in late May against Port Moresby and Tulagi, was now told that between 20 April and 10 May he was to have the services of the *Kaga*, six heavy cruisers and two destroyer flotillas.[88] In addition he was to receive support in the shape of the *Shoho*, hitherto confined to ferrying duties as she worked up to full effectiveness after having entered service in late January. She was now to be activated for combat duty and placed under Inoue's operational command. Two air flotillas were to be allocated to Rabaul for the same period, during which the commander of the South Seas Force was to secure Port Moresby and Tulagi.

Thus at one fell swoop Inoue was instructed to abandon his intention to open operations in about eight weeks' time with two carriers supporting his amphibious forces. Instead he would carry out an operation with what was in effect a 1½-carrier force in the next two to four weeks. With neither of the promised air flotillas in position Inoue, if he complied with the directive, would be forced to undertake an offensive without any prior attempt to secure air supremacy over the battle area. That was asking for trouble, and Inoue's reaction to his orders was an understandably angry one. He must have realized not only that his instructions could not be carried out but that he had been misled by the Combined Fleet from the time that Miwa had given him the nod in mid-March. Later he was to discover that his South

Seas Force was the one tasked to provide logistical support to Midway once the atoll had been taken. Inoue would prove perhaps the most implacable opponent of the Midway operation, and undoubtedly it was this combination of considerations that made him thus. But in the first days of April he had urgent matters to attend to if Tulagi and Port Moresby were to be secured in the course of the next month. His immediate preoccupation was with the provision of only one fleet carrier for what was now dignified as Operation MO. Inoue knew that the raid of 10 March had been carried out by two enemy carriers. The dispatch of the *Kaga* to support him, therefore, was by definition inadequate for the task in hand, and Inoue's initial reaction to his new orders was to request the additional support of the Second Carrier Division.

Inoue's request received serious consideration from the Combined Fleet, but not for any reason that related directly to Inoue and his need. The Army Section of Imperial General Headquarters had grown concerned about the scale of air support that was to be provided for Horii's South Seas Detachment in its operations in the southwest Pacific. In fact, the army was becoming somewhat agitated about the antics of the navy in general. It had backed proposals to develop an offensive into the southwest Pacific only to find that within a month the navy wanted to undertake offensives in the central and northern Pacific. The army opposed the proposal to attack Midway, but since it would be called upon to provide no more than a minimal contribution it found that it had very little say in the matter. Moreover, with the officers of the Naval General Staff doing what they were told whenever the Combined Fleet barked out its orders, the united front provided by the navy ensured that the army had little choice but to give way with as much good grace as it could muster. But the army's worries about Operation MO were quite another matter.[89] The Combined Fleet could not dismiss the army high command with the same cavalier abandon with which it handled the Naval General Staff.

But there was no question of Inoue's receiving the help of the Second Carrier Division in support of Operation MO. Though its two light fleet carriers had relatively small air groups, the Second Carrier Division was generally regarded as the best of the three front-line carrier divisions. As such, the *Hiryu* and the *Soryu* were held to be particularly important to the success of the Midway venture, now known as Operation MI, and as far as the Combined Fleet was concerned they could not be risked on Operation MO. It was not fear of loss or damage that shaped the Combined Fleet's reluctance to part with these two carriers: it was an awareness that over the previous year they had been worked desperately hard. Alone of the capital ships these two had taken part in every carrier operation since the start of the war—Pearl Harbor, Wake, Rabaul, Ambon, Timor, Darwin, Java and now Ceylon—and they had to be overhauled at some time.[90] The reason the

Combined Fleet had singled out the *Kaga* to support Inoue and the South Seas Force was that she alone would not need a short refit or overhaul in the second half of April. On 2 March she had been forced to leave the carrier force with engine trouble, and on the twenty-sixth she had entered dry dock for a quick overhaul.[91] She missed Operation C, but the six carriers that entered the Indian Ocean stood in no less a need of overhaul when they returned to Japan at the end of their raid on Ceylon. None of these carriers could support Operation MO if they were to be made ready in time for Operation MI. Under the circumstances sending the refurbished *Kaga* to the south to support Inoue while preparations for Operation MI went ahead seemed the best possible use of time and resources. It was quite obvious that Ugaki did not attach a great deal of importance to Operation MO at this stage; his decisions regarding the *Kaga* and the *Shoho*, and the timetable for Operation MO, reflected his priorities.

Inoue's request and the army's concern over the question of air support for Operation MO thus presented the Combined Fleet with the problem of how to make available resources it did not have. Some arrangement had to give, and such was the importance of the situation that Yamamoto himself was obliged to decide which reinforcements were to be sent to the south. On 10 April he ruled that the *Kaga* would be retained in home waters. He vetoed the transfer of the Second Carrier Division and ordered Vice Admiral Chuichi Hara's Fifth Carrier Division, consisting of the *Shokaku* and the *Zuikaku*, to take part in Operation MO. The reason for this choice was that the Fifth Carrier Division was not regarded as highly as the other two carrier divisions. It was a new formation, the *Zuikaku* not having been commissioned until 25 September 1941. The four units of the First and Second Carrier Divisions had had between two and seven years to work up to full effectiveness. Such was the newness of the Fifth Carrier Division that at Pearl Harbor its aircraft had been assigned shore targets only and had been regarded as second class in all subsequent operations.[92] Thus when it came to deciding the order of battle for Operation MO the Fifth Carrier Division presented itself as a logical choice for inclusion. A small operation in the southwest Pacific would do it no harm and possibly even some good; it would certainly need some extra practice before the real thing in June. Ugaki therefore issued orders that put Yamamoto's decisions into effect on 12 April. The Fifth Carrier Division plus two destroyer divisions were to go south under the command of Vice Admiral Takeo Takagi, victor of the battle of the Java Sea. All units and formations were to come under Inoue's command on 18 April.[93] This meant that after the Ceylon raid the *Zuikaku* and the *Shokaku* would have to put in at Formosa for resupply; they would not have time to return to Japan and then move south to come under a new command by the eighteenth. It also meant that they would be hard pressed to fit in repairs or an overhaul between the end of Operation MO and the start of Operation MI.

The casualness with which these changes were made in the Combined Fleet's operational schedule belied their significance. In committing the Fifth Carrier Division to Operation MO the Combined Fleet made the execution of the main effort, Operation MI, dependent on the outcome of the secondary effort. This was a cardinal error. At the same time the Combined Fleet gave the Fifth Carrier Division a task that was either beyond or beneath it. If the enemy was not present in the southwest Pacific the commitment of the *Shokaku* and the *Zuikaku* to Operation MO was superfluous. If, on the other hand, American carriers were still operating in the southwest Pacific, and recent events suggested that they were, the provision of two fleet carriers gave the Japanese no margin of assured superiority. With the *Shoho* operating separately, and in any case unfit to be considered front-line material, the Japanese arrangements for Operation MO represented a perilous dispersal of force, an economy of effort well beyond the limits of what was prudent, at a time when the whereabouts and strength of the enemy remained unknown.

By any reckoning it was mandatory that the Fifth Carrier Division take part in Operation MI. As the Japanese knew full well, the Americans had begun the war with seven fleet and light fleet carriers of which one, the *Ranger*, was recognized as unfit for front-line service. One more carrier, mistaken for the *Lexington*, was believed to have been sunk off Johnson Island in January. The Japanese, therefore, thought that they faced a five-carrier enemy, but they had no idea how many American carriers might be in the Atlantic. Common sense had to suggest that the Americans might have all five of their carriers in the Pacific; it was certainly unsafe to assume anything else. In this case the *Shokaku* and the *Zuikaku* represented the bare margin of superiority that the Imperial Navy held over the Pacific Fleet. If the Combined Fleet was to have an assured superiority over the enemy at Operation MI, the *Shokaku* and the *Zuikaku* had to return from Operation MO at full strength and effectiveness. But the Japanese could not guarantee the safe and timely return of their two carriers any more than they could calculate the odds involved either in Operation MO or in Operation MI.

In April it did not seem to be asking too much to have the Fifth Carrier Division return undamaged from the southwest Pacific in time for Operation MI. Despite 10 March everything seemed too easy, there was no real threat, and the experience off Ceylon could only have added to misplaced Japanese confidence. After the war games in February, which had pointed to losses, Operation C proved embarrassingly easy for the Japanese. British bombers did attack the Japanese carriers, but to no effect, and in return nine

British warships and merchantmen were destroyed. When the Fifth Carrier Division was detached there was no good reason to suppose that anything untoward might be in the offing, and after so much success one more victory did not seem beyond even the *Shokaku* and the *Zuikaku*. The Combined Fleet seemed to have time and means enough to indulge itself in one last "limited" offensive before it embarked upon a series of operations that would bring the war to a successful conclusion.

Yet the point was that Japan did not have the time for one last limited operation before the final offensive. The Japanese were not standing on the brink of the war's end—the war was only just beginning and the commitment to Operation MO was irrelevant. Nothing was to be gained by engaging in a minor skirmish in the southwest Pacific or undertaking a minor raid in the Indian Ocean. Without the means to exploit any success that might be registered in these operations, the Japanese were certain to be doomed to frustration in both areas; at the same time the effort made in these two theaters before Operation MI was to be enough to prevent the Combined Fleet from operating with its full strength in any direction at all. In April 1942 the Japanese were in a position similar to that of Germany between December 1914 and December 1917: concern for security at all points and a penchant for local offensives that brought local success resulted in a failure to record decisive success anywhere, and by the time an all-out effort was made the moment for doing so had passed. In the case of the Japanese this situation could have been avoided. In April 1942 the Combined Fleet won the argument over the strategic direction of the war effort. It also enforced its views regarding the timing of operations. Yet having imposed its views on the Naval General Staff, the Combined Fleet committed itself to operations that contradicted the basic argument that had been used to support the case for Operation MI. In the first week of April it contended that with every passing month the task of defeating the Americans was made that much more difficult. Under these circumstances, so the argument ran, the fleet had to make an all-out effort in just one theater, the central Pacific. In the second week of April it was busy organizing an offensive into the southwest Pacific and had already committed a vital part of the carrier force to this theater.

By mid-April the Imperial Navy had settled its policy, but the price of continuous argument and muddled strategic thinking was a plan of campaign riddled with inconsistencies. And there was no way the incoherence could be dispelled: the authors of the plan considered themselves beyond advice and criticism. The Imperial Navy, without realizing the full implications of what it was doing, committed itself to a fragmented effort in three directions across a vast area with no margin of superiority over an enemy whose strength, location and intentions were unknown. Such is the extent of the lack of logic in Japanese planning that the historian is hard pressed to

determine how so great a nation and navy could have placed themselves in
so incongruous and inauspicious a position. That the Japanese managed to
pick what was arguably the wrong course of action every time it was
confronted with a choice is not easily explained. Certain factors such as a
confused chain of command, institutional pressures, the complexity of the
issues and "victory disease" undoubtedly played their parts, but even more
important in pushing the navy into such a disastrous situation in March and
April was a combination of frustration and lack of time. The element of
frustration was directed against the army. On 8 March, the day after the
army had used its power of veto, Miwa recorded the following view:

> We want to invade Ceylon; we are not allowed to! We want to invade Australia;
> we cannot! We want to attack Hawaii; we cannot do that either! All because the
> army will not agree to release the necessary forces. Though it is understandable
> that the army has to retain troops to deal with the Soviet Union, is it that
> impossible to spare us just one or two divisions out of a million men in Manchuria
> and 400,000 in China?[94]

The navy was bitter towards the army after the Liaison Conference of 7
March, when the latter used its powers of obstruction to dispense with two
of the options the navy was keen to pursue. Miwa's reaction was understandable. But the upshot of the army's discarding the navy's "first choices"
was to force the navy back on its contingency planning. As we have seen,
from early January onwards the Combined Fleet was considering two quite
separate options simultaneously. These were the Indian Ocean and central
Pacific alternatives. Meanwhile, the Plans Division was pressing ahead
with the Australia and southwest Pacific options. But when the army ruled
out the pet schemes of both the Plans Division and the Combined Fleet at
one and the same time, it did something more than leave the navy disappointed and foiled—it left them with just three weeks to put together a
policy, any policy, before 1 April and the inauguration of the second
operational phase. When the army used its power of veto on 7 March it
forced the navy to adhere to an impossible deadline, but for this the navy
had only itself to blame. In this context it is worth recalling that the
argument between the staff and the Combined Fleet over strategic policy
actually took place after the new operational phase should have begun. It
may very well be that a lack of time prevented the proper scrutiny of plans
before the final product was stamped with approval.

But if it is bold to suggest a tight timetable as the most important of the
many factors that conspired to make nonsense out of Japanese strategic
deliberations at this time, it is still hard to resist the idea that the Japanese,
with a more liberal schedule, would not have come up with a plan for the
second operational phase that was much different from the one they produced. Such a conclusion leaves the historian with an obvious problem of

interpretation, and only one matter can be stated with any certainty: any confusion on his part is less significant than that of the Japanese high command at this stage of the proceedings. At the highest level of command there was a pervading confusion that contained the ingredients of defeat. Its debilitating presence went unsuspected by armed forces with a sequence of victories so impressive that they could not envisage the prospect of defeat. They could not adjust to the new situation in which they found themselves because they could not see that the war would not be a limited one. They could not recognize the futility of persisting with secondary or limited operations in any theater, nor could they appreciate the irrelevance of planning second-string operations to go alongside preparations for an all-out offensive in one particular theater. The Japanese erred in failing to realize that the alternative to victory in their forthcoming operations was not going to be a setback or temporary reverse: the stark alternative to victory off Midway and in the central and southwest Pacific was devastating defeat which would leave the Combined Fleet's effectiveness impaired on a permanent basis. In a situation where illusion and self-deception abounded, this was the hidden reality.

CHAPTER 3

MORYALMI:
The Schlieffen Plan
of the Pacific War

By careful selection of material a battle of one war can always be made to call to mind a battle of an earlier conflict. There are battles of the Second World War that can be said to be repetitions, even direct parallels, of actions of the First World War. Kursk-Orel has been called the Second World War's Verdun, the fearful battle of attrition in which fire power, tenacity and discipline, rather than leadership, flair and initiative, were the factors that determined its outcome. Germany's "victory offensive" of 1918 and the Ardennes offensive of 1944 bear remarkable similarities. But few aspects of the Second World War so closely resemble any single aspect of the earlier global struggle as the Japanese plan of campaign for the summer of 1942. Like many of the great operations of the First World War, it was the product of much procrastination and argument, but in the end the hypnotic effect that all great plans exert was instrumental in curbing the skeptics, whose caution, protests and incredulity were lost amid the facile optimism of the majority. Though the Japanese plan of 1942 has parallels with many operations of the First World War, Allied and German, it is most reminiscent of one specific part of that war, namely the Schlieffen Plan with which Germany began hostilities. Both failed, narrowly but decisively, and in the aftermath of failure the nations that undertook these operations were condemned to face strategic dilemmas they could not resolve. In each case the plans were hatched in response to the potentially disastrous strategic situations in which their authors found themselves, their own past immoderation having raised a formidable ring of enemies about them.

Before comparisons between the Schlieffen Plan and the Japanese plan of campaign of 1942 are made, the Japanese plan itself must be examined, first in outline, then in detail. The months of April and May 1942 were taken up on the Japanese side with planning and preparation for a series of operations designed to bring an end to the war. As a result of a series of decisions taken between 5 April and 2 May, the Japanese committed themselves initially to a relatively small effort to secure Port Moresby and certain objectives in the Solomons, most notably Tulagi. This was Operation MO, to be completed by 10 May. It was to be followed by Operation RY, the occupation of Nauru and Ocean by some of the forces involved in the earlier operations in the Solomons. This was to be completed by 15 May.

The Japanese were then to embark on their main endeavor, a twin offensive against the Aleutians, Operation AL, and against the western Hawaiian Islands, Operation MI. Their plans scheduled the Combined Fleet forces detailed for this latter operation to be in the central Pacific, in pursuit of victory in the decisive battle, until 13 June, the offensive against Midway Islands having opened on the fourth. Thereafter Japanese planning, predicated on the success of Operation MI, envisaged main force units, less the battle forces, regrouping at Truk between the fifteenth and twentieth of June. Just as many of the formations committed to Operation MI were to form up at Guam and Saipan, since the Marianas had to be the base for operations into the central Pacific, so the selection of Truk as the point of assembly and regrouping after Operation MI had to mean that the Japanese planned to develop an offensive into the southwest Pacific. Their intention was to mount a major offensive during July with the newly raised Seventeenth Army securing New Caledonia, Fiji and Samoa. Thereafter operations were to continue, with attacks on the Australian mainland and then against Johnson Island in August, the main islands of the Hawaiian chain presenting themselves as the obvious target of future operations. Their fall would be assured, as would the fall of the islands of the southwest Pacific, once the Pacific Fleet had been annihilated.

Detailed planning was confined to Operations MO, RY, AL and MI, with the army completing its order of battle and its initial proposals for operations in the southwest Pacific on 4 June. On that date the Army Section of Imperial General Headquarters stamped a seal of approval on its draft, but matters never went beyond that stage. The final form of the various operational plans was as follows: Operation MO, the plan to secure the immediate defensive perimeter around Rabaul before the start of Operations AL and MI, embraced a series of step-by-step operations against divergent objectives by a number of separate but interdependent task forces. The plan that the South Seas Force, in consultation with its subordinate formations, devised in order to take Port Moresby and positions in the Solomons was typically Japanese: it involved the movement of a number of small and, for the most part, relatively weak task forces across a wide area in a tightly synchronized pattern, in part to enhance security, in part to achieve surprise and confusion of the enemy.

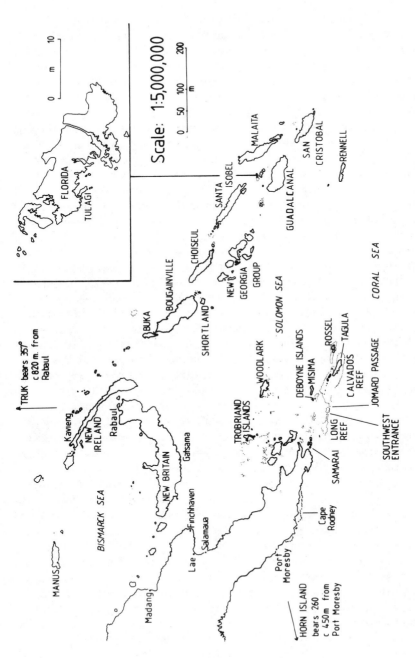

Operation MO Theater

Scale: 1:5,000,000

TRUK bears 357°
c 820 m. from
Rabaul

HORN ISLAND
bears 260
c 450m from
Port Moresby

MANUS

Kavieng

NEW
IRELAND

Rabaul

Gatsama

NEW BRITAIN

Finchhaven

BISMARCK SEA

Lae

Salamaua

Madang

Port
Moresby

Cape
Rodney

SAMARAI

TROBRIAND
ISLANDS

WOODLARK

LONG
REEF

DEBOYNE ISLANDS

MISIMA

SOUTHWEST
ENTRANCE

JOMARD PASSAGE

CALVADOS
REEF

ROSSEL

TAGULA

BUKA

BOUGAINVILLE

SHORTLAND

NEW
GEORGIA
GROUP

CHOISEUL

SOLOMON SEA

CORAL SEA

SANTA
ISOBEL

GUADALCANAL

MALAITA

SAN
CRISTOBAL

RENNELL

FLORIDA

TULAGI

m   0   10

0   50 100 200
          m

To safeguard the main invasion forces during their approach to Port Moresby, the principal objective of Operation MO, the Japanese planned to open their offensive with a series of suboperations in the northern and central Solomons. These were designed to secure bases from which flying boats and seaplanes could conduct reconnaissance missions over the northern and central Coral Sea. The first steps in this process had been completed. As we have seen, during the assault on Lae and Salamaua, the Covering Force had scouted Buka and then, at the end of March, moved to secure Shortland and northern and central Bougainville. Now, as the first part of Operation MO, the Japanese planned to build on earlier results by deploying the 2,562-ton converted gunboat *Nikkaimaru* and the 15,450-ton tanker *Iro* to Shortland. The two ships were to make their separate ways to Shortland, the *Nikkaimaru* being ordered to make its landfall by 28 April, when it was to establish and bring into operation a temporary base for flying boats. The Japanese knew that there was little or no chance of their encountering resistance to this move, and the passage from Rabaul to Shortland and the setting up of a naval air base at Faisi went through without a hitch. Rear Admiral Kuninori Marumo's Support Force was to sail from Rabaul on the twenty-ninth, Rear Admiral Kiyohide Shima's Tulagi Invasion Force the following day. Marumo and Shima were to lead their forces down the Solomons chain, Marumo bound for Santa Isobel, Shima, as the name of his force made clear, on course for Tulagi.

Marumo had under command the light cruisers *Tenryu* and *Tatsuta*, the seaplane tender *Kamikawamaru*, and the gunboats *Keijomaru* and *Seikaimaru*. He was to be joined en route for Santa Isobel by the *Nikkaimaru*, and his force was tasked to secure Santa Isobel and establish a naval air base there on 2 May. Seaplanes that would be flown into the base that same day were to provide Shima with some measure of air support on the following day, when his force moved to secure Tulagi with troops drawn from the Kure Third Special Naval Landing Force. His command consisted of the minelayer *Okinoshima*; the converted minelayer *Keoimaru*; the 7,614-ton transport *Azumasanmaru*; the destroyer-transports *Kikuzuki* and *Yuzuki* from the Sixth Destroyer Squadron; the submarine chasers *Toshimaru No. 3* and *Tamamaru No. 8*; the fleet minesweepers *Wa. 1* and *Wa. 2*; and the converted minesweepers *Hagoromomaru*, *Noshiromaru No. 2* and *Tamamaru*. The base that this force was to establish would be handling Mavis flying boats the following day; this would allow the Japanese to all but complete arrangements to have the Coral Sea and the approaches to Port Moresby covered by reconnaissance units before the main forces involved in Operation MO were committed to passing beyond the line of the Louisades. As the air units moved on to the Tulagi station on 4 May, so units from the Eighth Submarine Squadron were to be on the very last part of their passage to form a patrol line across the southern Coral Sea. The Type B1 submarines

I-21, *I-28* and *I-29*, along with the Type C1 units *I-22* and *I-24*, were ordered to take up position on 5 May, some three days before the date that an Allied reaction to Japanese operations was expected to materialize. In those three days the Japanese planned to regroup and complete the arrangements whereby other forces would move into position to frustrate any enemy attempt to interfere with the Port Moresby operation.

Once Tulagi was secured and the newly established base there made operational, Shima's force was to disperse. The minesweepers were tasked to link up with the main invasion force bound for Port Moresby. The larger units would withdraw to Kavieng in New Ireland and prepare to take forces to Nauru and Ocean. As we have seen, the landings on these two islands, code named Operation RY, were to be completed by 15 May. In the meantime Marumo's force, which was to stand some 60 miles to the west of Tulagi in support of Shima's attack, was to come westwards across the Solomon Sea to establish a seaplane base in the Deboyne Islands on 6 May and another at Cape Rodney two days later.

This part of the operation was but one aspect of the navy's threefold attempt to meet the army's demand for continuous air cover during the passage of the invasion convoy to Port Moresby. The initial effort was to be made by land-based formations operating from Rabaul. Their task was to neutralize enemy air power at Port Moresby, but after the experiences of 10 March the South Seas Detachment was understandably apprehensive about making the long sea journey from Rabaul unless it had the strongest available air support at all times. The Marumo force was therefore tasked to provide some measure of air cover for what was certain to prove the most exposed part of the passage from Rabaul. On its way back from Port Moresby, after the landing operation, the Marumo force was to secure Samarai Island, at the very tip of New Guinea, for use as a seaplane and supply base. This was to be carried out on 12 May. With this move, the Marumo force was to complete a line of advanced air bases around the coast of southeast New Guinea, along the route between what was certain to be the two main Japanese bases in the southwest Pacific.

The South Seas Detachment, however much it might welcome the support of seaplanes from land bases and from the *Kamikawamaru*, took more comfort in the reassuring presence of the carrier *Shoho*, tasked to provide organic air defense for the invasion force. She and her plane guard, the destroyer *Sazanami*, along with the *Aoba*, *Kinugasa*, *Kako* and *Furutaka*, were to operate in a role similar to that of Marumo's force, coming across the Solomon Sea to take close order to the invasion force when it approached the Louisades. This formation, the MO Main Body Support Force, was under the command of Rear Admiral Aritomo Goto. It was to leave Truk on 28 April in order to provide general cover for the Santa Isobel and Tulagi operations. Goto, in tactical command of the whole of Operation MO, was to mark time just to the south of New Georgia after the Tulagi operation. He was then to lead his force across the Solomon Sea to make a rendezvous with the transports and attack forces destined for Port Moresby.

The Transport Group, under the command of Rear Admiral Koso Abe, consisted of eleven transports. Five of the transports, the *Mogamigawamaru*, *Akibasanmaru*, *Chowamaru*, *Goyomaru* and *Syokamaru*, were naval transports. They were detailed to the Third Special Naval Landing Force. Six of the transports, the *Chinamaru*, *Daifukumaru*, *Asakasanmaru*, *Marsuemaru*, *Mitomaru* and *Nichibimaru*, belonged to the army's pool of transports and were detailed to the South Seas Detachment. The transports were to sail on their six-day passage from Rabaul on 4 May, the day Tulagi was to become operational. They were to sail in the company of the minelayer *Tsugaru* and the minesweepers *Wa. 20*, *Fumimaru No. 2* and *Sekimaru No. 3*, with the minesweepers from Shima's force joining up in the Solomon Sea.

In direct support of the Transport Group was the so-called Attack Force. This was to sail from Rabaul on 5 May under the command of Rear Admiral Sadamichi Kaijioka. He was in charge of the landing phase of the operation, scheduled for the tenth. He had with him the bulk of the Sixth Destroyer Division, namely the *Yubari* (with her new skipper) and the destroyers *Uzuki*, *Asanagi*, *Oite*, *Mochizuki*, *Mutsuki* and *Yayoi*. In support of this Port Moresby Invasion Group but sailing with the transports were to be the oiler *Hoyomaru* and the supply ship *Oshima*. The transport *Goyomaru* also doubled as an oiler.

The spearhead of the amphibious assault was to be the South Seas Detachment. Two of its units were tasked to land at the Pearl Mission, the third was to come ashore at Barute. The three battalions were to secure these places as their immediate objectives, then the airfield and finally Port Moresby itself, all on the day of the landings. The Japanese aim was to get the airstrip back into service with the least possible delay. The South Seas Force planned to have units fly into Port Moresby to provide for the air defense of the enterprise as the heavy carriers allocated to Operation MO set course for home and Operation MI. The Port Moresby Invasion Group—the Transport, Attack and Main Body Support Forces, plus the attached units—was to transit the Jomard Passage on 7 May. In doing so, and then in moving around the tip of New Guinea to begin its run to Port Moresby, it would be at its most vulnerable, for these waters were not controlled by Japanese air power. The navy anticipated that its land-based air formations would have secured air superiority over Port Moresby by the time the Invasion Group came through the Louisades, but this could not get around the unpleasant fact that Port Moresby was within range of air cover provided from northern Australia. It was impossible for the Japanese to neutralize Allied air power in Australia. The army insisted that the *Shoho* accompany the transports to counter this threat, and their view was endorsed by Inoue and the South Seas Force.

But it was resisted by the commander whose force was to provide the backbone of Operation MO. Vice Admiral Takeo Takagi would bring the Carrier Striking Force south from Truk and to a position south of the Louisades by 8 May to deal with any enemy carrier force that might put in an appearance. Takagi had under command his own *Myoko* and *Haguro* from the Fifth Cruiser Division; Hara's *Zuikaku* and *Shokaku* from the Fifth Carrier Division; the *Ushio* and the *Akebono* from the Seventh Destroyer Division; and the *Ariake, Yugure, Shigure* and *Shiratsuyu* from the Twenty-seventh Destroyer Division. Attending to the fuel requirements of this force while it was in the Coral Sea was to be the *Tohomaru*.

Originally Hara was given instructions to take his two carriers against airfields in northern Australia in addition to guarding the exposed flank of the Invasion Group as it came through the Louisades. His protests against these orders led to their modification and his being given discretion in the matter. He had absolutely no intention of moving against Australian targets because it was all but certain that any approach to a flying-off position would be compromised and that his carriers would then become involved in an unequal battle. Any doubts on this matter were finally resolved on 29 April, just two days before the Carrier Striking Force was to sail from Truk, when Yamamoto intervened with specific orders to the Fifth Carrier Division not to involve itself in operations against the Australian mainland.

Takagi was to lead his force south from Truk and fly off nine Zekes to reinforce the Rabaul garrison on 2 May. He would refuel the next day and then come around the eastern side of the Solomons before passing between San Cristobal and Rennell to enter the Coral Sea on the fifth. Then he was to lurk in the eastern Coral Sea, hoping to stay beyond the range of enemy reconnaissance but in a position to pounce on any enemy carrier or surface force coming north to contest the Port Moresby landings. Once the operation was complete, Hara was to take the *Zuikaku* and the *Shokaku* straight back to Japan to make ready for Operation MI.

Operations AL and MI, like Operation MO, consisted of a series of suboperations by a number of separate task forces. Each force was to secure objectives according to a rigid timetable to allow the operations as a whole to roll forward. The differences between Operation MO and the other two, however, were many. The most important related to scale. The area across which the Japanese planned to operate in June 1942 was the whole western Pacific, and it required the commitment of the bulk of the Combined Fleet. Some idea of the size and complexity of this venture—Operations AL and MI were in effect two parts of a single endeavor—can be gauged from the fact that no fewer than twenty-eight admirals and not less than eighty-four captains were employed in command and major staff positions on the

Japanese side. Moreover, in the course of this single effort the Imperial
Navy logged more miles and used more oil than it had previously recorded
in any single year of its existence.

Operation MI was to open with a two-part reconnaissance, one conducted by flying boats over Pearl Harbor, the other by submarines operating between Oahu and Midway. Under the terms of a suboperation,
Operation K, flying boats from Jaluit and Wotje in the Marshalls were to
conduct a series of reconnaissance missions over Pearl Harbor beginning on
30 May. The aim of these flights was to establish the whereabouts and
strength of the U.S. Pacific Fleet before the main part of Operation MI
began to unfold.

The difficulty that Operation K encountered was that even the impressive products of the Kawanishi factories, the Emily and Mavis flying boats,
did not have the range to make the round trip from the Marshalls to Pearl
Harbor. To get around this problem the Japanese therefore resorted to an
expedient that had enabled them to mount a reconnaissance-strike mission
against Pearl Harbor on 3–4 March. On that night two units from the
Yokohama Naval Air Group had carried out a desultory mission after
staging through French Frigate Shoals in the central Hawaiian group.
There they had been met by one of the Type KRS refueling submarines,
and after refueling they had been able to reach Oahu to look over and bomb
the Pacific Fleet and its base. On this occasion, however, a heavy overcast
had produced disappointing results. The four bombs the flying boats aimed
at the enemy exploded harmlessly in the hills behind Honolulu. The
Japanese return on their effort was nonexistent, and an attempt to repeat
and improve upon the operation on 10 March only met with worse results.
The Mavis carrying out a repeat mission was intercepted and shot down by
U.S. Marine Corps fighters from Midway. The omens for yet another
operation, therefore, were hardly auspicious. But in support of Operation
MI, for which the most detailed and accurate information regarding enemy
movements was absolutely essential, the Japanese planned to revive Operation K in its original form. The two missions of March must have given the
Americans some idea of how Operation K was supposed to function, and a
third could hardly do anything except arouse American suspicions, so the
whole idea of reviving Operation K in May 1942 would seem questionable;
but the Japanese, perhaps because they had few options open to them,
reverted to the formula despite its earlier lack of success. Three units from
Captain Takaharu Miyazuki's Thirteenth Submarine Division were
ordered to be on station from 27 May onwards. The *I-121* and the *I-123*
were instructed to go to the Shoals while the *I-122* was directed to proceed
to Lisianski Island. The submarines each carried 40 tons of aviation fuel and
12 tons of oil for their charges.

Providing general and indirect support for Operation MI were the submarines put on station by the Combined Fleet for Operation MO. The five submarines from the Eighth Submarine Squadron were ordered to continue their operations, but further afield and, if need be, after returning to Truk for resupply. The *I-28* was lost on 17 May when upon returning to Truk she was torpedoed by the American submarine *Tautog*, but the other four conducted a series of reconnaissance and strike missions in the southwest Pacific from the middle of May onwards. The *I-21* looked in at Suva on 19–20 May and at Auckland four days later before moving on to the east coast of Australia, using her Glen seaplane to conduct a reconnaissance of Sydney on 30 May. Sydney had already been scouted by the *I-29* on 22–23 May before she moved on to examine Brisbane. Sydney was the focus of Japanese attention in the southwest Pacific because of its naval facilities and importance as a commercial harbor, and this interest culminated on 31 May in the so-called battle of Sydney, when the *I-22*, *I-24* and newly arrived *I-127* unleashed their midget submarines on the harbor. Thus far in the war the midget submarines had been notable failures, and the attack on Sydney did little to enhance their reputation. They certainly fell short of the performance of their sisters, who the previous night had carried out successful attacks on the battleship *Ramillies* and the tanker *British Loyalty* at Diego Suarez in Madagascar. The midget submarines of the battle of Sydney between them accounted for the accommodation ship *Kuttabul*, a solitary and unimpressive achievement. The torpedo that sank the ship with the loss of eighteen lives passed under a Dutch submarine that was tied up alongside, and it was probably aimed (by the midget from the *I-24*) at the American heavy cruiser *Chicago*. But with three cruisers, two armed merchant cruisers, a destroyer tender, one destroyer, three corvettes, one submarine and one accommodation ship in harbor on 31 May, it was somewhat ironic that the only ship the Japanese sunk was perhaps the least important one there. None of the midgets survived the incident (two were salvaged by the Australians in June). After the attack the mother boats dispersed. The *I-24* stayed in the general area of Sydney and bombarded the city (with her one 5.5-in gun) on 8 June, the same day the *I-21* carried out a similar attack on Newcastle in New South Wales. The *I-22* in the meantime made the long trip back to Truk via Wellington, Auckland and Suva. The Japanese made little effort to interfere with merchant shipping, but three merchantmen were sunk, and several others attacked unsuccessfully, by the Japanese submarines when they were off the Australian coast.

In close support of Operation MI, indeed as an integral part of it, the Combined Fleet planned to deploy nineteen submarines in three main groups, but the loss of the *I-164* to the American submarine *Triton* on 17

May some 250 miles off Kagoshima reduced this total to eighteen. To the north and Operation AL went the first group of six submarines: the *I-9* of the First Submarine Squadron; the *I-15*, *I-17* and *I-19* of the Second Submarine Division; and the *I-25* and *I-26* of the Fourth Submarine Division. Rear Admiral Shigeaki Yamazaki, in command of this detachment, set out in his Type A1 headquarters submarine, the *I-9*. The other five submarines were Type B1 reconnaissance units.

With five of his boats built for reconnaissance duties, Yamazaki was to scout the Aleutians and thereby raise the curtain for Operation AL. Yamazaki took the *I-9* to examine Kiska, while the *I-15* searched Adak, the *I-17* Attu and the *I-19* Dutch Harbor at the end of May.* His two remaining units were detailed to search the eastern Aleutians before running down the West Coast seeking opportunity targets and then settling down to keep watch on Seattle.† With the *I-25* and *I-26* thus employed, Yamazaki was to leave the *I-19* keeping watch on Dutch Harbor while he took the *I-15* and the *I-17* to form a patrol line, known as cordon line C or the *Tei*, along meridian 166°W between latitudes 49° and 51°N.

These three submarines were to form a "hard shoulder"—about 140 miles long—across two degrees of latitude, and behind them were to steam the forces for which they were to act as a picket line. In command of these forces was Hosogaya, his enthusiasm for the whole Midway-Aleutians venture having been recognized by his command of the Aleutians part of the grand design. His immediate tactical command consisted of the heavy cruiser *Nachi* and the destroyers *Inazuma* and *Ikazuchi*. Two oilers, the *Nissanmaru* and the *Fujisanmaru*, plus three supply ships, were with the Northern Force Main Body, the grandeur of the title no doubt being compensation for the small size of the formation.

Hosogaya was to supervise and control the operations that developed as his vanguard force deeply penetrated the sea area between the Aleutians and Yamazaki. This force consisted of Rear Admiral Kakuji Kakuta's Second Carrier Striking Force. This was made up of a support group of two heavy cruisers, the *Maya* and the *Takao*, from the Fourth Cruiser Division; a screen provided by the *Akebono*, *Ushio* and *Sazanami* from the Seventh Destroyer Division; and the oiler *Teiyomaru*. These units were gathered around the two members of the Fourth Carrier Division, the *Ryujo* and the *Junyo*.

---

*In fact there had been a preliminary reconnaissance of Attu and Kiska. On 6 May the seaplane tender *Kimikawamaru* left Atuseki and put scouts over the islands on the eleventh. She returned to Ominato on the eighteenth in time to take her place in Operation AL.

†Subsequently, on 20 June, the *I-25* was to bombard Fort Stevens, Oregon, while the *I-26* attacked the radio station and lighthouse at Estevan Point on Vancouver Island. This was the only time in the two world wars that Canadian soil was attacked by direct enemy action.

Kakuta, by crossing the international date line from west to east, was to gain a day in the course of his initial operations, and it was on the second 3 June that his force was to conduct offensive operations against Dutch Harbor. There was a twofold purpose to this attack. First, it was designed to pave the way for certainly two and possibly three landing operations in the western Aleutians. Second, it was intended to provoke the Pacific Fleet into giving battle in defense of American national territory.

The immediate objective was to secure the condition—the neutralization of Dutch Harbor—whereby the landing operations could be carried out. The Combined Fleet was concerned that in time the Aleutians might be developed by the Americans into a staging post for major operations. It was determined to secure what it saw as blocking positions on the line between Dutch Harbor and the Kuriles and Hokkaido. Fear of Dutch Harbor's being a major submarine base led the Combined Fleet to decide on securing an advance base from which to mount antisubmarine patrols. The base would be in the western Aleutians in the event that Unalaska itself was not secured. Unalaska was the desired goal, but for Operation AL the Combined Fleet, in the absence of the resources needed for an attack on Dutch Harbor, contented itself with the attempt to secure Kiska (Operation AOB) and Adak, scheduled for 5 June, and Attu (Operation AQ), set for the twelfth. The Japanese planned to land and occupy Adak only for the time it took them to destroy the enemy installations they wrongly believed were on the island, but this was not regarded as essential. Planning allowed for the landings on Adak to be dispensed with altogether.

The landing force destined for Adak or Attu or both consisted of 1,200 troops from the army's Attu Landing Force, alternatively known as the Army North Seas Detachment or by the name of its commander, Major Matsutoshi Hozumi. The formation was to be transported to its target(s) by the *Kinugasamaru*. She was to sail under the command of Rear Admiral Sentaro Omori in the light cruiser *Abukuma*, along with the *Hatsuharu*, *Hatsushimo*, *Nenohi* and *Wakaba* of the Twenty-first Destroyer Division, and the converted gunboat-minelayer *Maganemaru*. The *Kimikawamaru*, with eight Jakes embarked, completed this particular invasion force. She was to be under command from the time the force sailed to the time landing operations were completed. Thereafter she was to be detached and under the command of the Northern Force.

The 10,380-ton ex-liner *Hakusanmaru* and the 7,508-ton motor freighter *Kumagawamaru* were charged with the safe delivery to Kiska of the 550 men of the Third Special Naval Landing Force (direct from Port Moresby) of Lieutenant Commander Hikumi Mukai, along with 700 pioneers and equipment. Covering the troop ships were to be the *Kiso* and the *Tama* from the Twenty-first Cruiser Division; the three members of the Sixth Destroyer Division, the *Akatsuki*, *Hibiki* and *Hokaze*; and the armed merchant cruiser *Asakamaru*, complete with her four 5.9-in guns. In company were three auxiliaries from the Thirteenth Minesweeper Division, the *Hakuhomaru*, *Kaihomaru* and *Shunkotsumaru*. Command of operations was vested in Captain Takeji Ono in the light cruiser *Kiso*.

Important though the capture of a base in the Aleutians was deemed to be, the real objective of Operation AL was to act as bait. It was intended to lure out the Americans in defense of their islands. In the event of a direct but improvised American move from the central Pacific, the submarines on cordon line C and Kakuta's two carriers were expected to cope. In the event of a more deliberate American move, with major forces entering the waters north of latitude 40° N, the forces in the van would have the support of the so-called Guard Force or Aleutians Screening Force of Vice Admiral Shiro Gakasu. This force was built around the Second Battle Squadron. Gakasu flew his flag in the *Hyuga*. With his aging flagship was her sister ship *Ise* as well as the *Fuso* and the *Yamashiro*. The four battleships each carried two Dave seaplanes. Screening the battleships was a task entrusted to Rear Admiral Fukuki Kishi, who had for this purpose two light cruisers and twelve destroyers. With the battleships were two scouts from the Ninth Cruiser Division, the *Kitakami* and the *Oi*, and twelve destroyers. The latter came from three divisions, each with four units. The Twentieth consisted of the *Asagiri*, *Amagiri*, *Shirakumo* and *Yugiri*; the Twenty-fourth was represented by the *Kawakaze*, *Suzukaze*, *Umikaze* and *Yamakaze*; the *Ariake*, *Shigure*, *Shiratsuyu* and *Yugure*, released after Operation MO, made up the Twenty-seventh. The 7,335-ton *Kurementemaru* and the 10,050-ton *Toamaru* were on hand to refuel this force.

The chances of Hosogaya's combined forces encountering enemy main forces were remote, indeed as remote as Adak, Attu and Kiska themselves. But provision had to be made against the possibility, even though the Combined Fleet knew that battle in the central Pacific was more likely: the Americans, reacting to Operation AL, would probably move against Operation MI as that unfolded. The real Japanese hope was that any American reaction, either to Operation AL or to Operation MI, would be caught and overwhelmed by the forces committed to the second and far more substantial operation—of which the Americans would know nothing if they put to sea to meet Hosogaya.

As we have seen already, Japanese submarines were to lead the way to Midway. Just as Operation AL was to be scouted by Yamazaki, so the surface forces committed to Operation MI were to be warned of the possibility of a fleet engagement by the activities of the twelve submarines that were to form a dogleg bisecting the Hawaiian chain in the general area of French Frigate Shoals. On and after 1 June these submarines were to be in position on two lines. Cordon line A, or the *Ko*, was to be established to the south of the islands between latitudes 19° 30′ and 23° 30′ N along the meridian 167° W. Cordon line B, or the *Hei*, to the north, was to be formed between latitude 29° 30′ N, longitude 164° 30′ W, and latitude 26° 30′ N, longitude 167° W.

For the *Ko* the Japanese deployed the *I-169*, *I-171*, *I-174* and *I-175* from Rear Admiral Chimaki Kono's Third Submarine Squadron. These four units were from the Type KD6 class of attack submarine, amongst the best that the Imperial Navy ever built. This patrol line was to be reinforced by the three Type KRS units once their refueling duties with regard to Operation K were complete. What these were supposed to achieve is hard to discern: they did not carry torpedo tubes and their handling characteristics, especially when submerged, were not very impressive.

North of the islands were to be the seven survivors of Rear Admiral Tadashige Daigo's Fifth Submarine Squadron. All were members of the older Type KD classes. The Nineteenth Submarine Division provided the *I-156*, *I-157*, *I-158* and *I-159*, while the Thirtieth Submarine Division thickened up the *Hei* with the *I-162*, *I-165* and *I-166*. The Type KD6A submarine *I-168* was ordered to carry out a close reconnaissance of Midway itself. She would be on station on 1 June.

Both cordon lines came well clear of the sweep of the Hawaiian Islands. Line A stood across the direct route between Pearl Harbor and the Marianas, and line B reached out vaguely into the wastes of the northern Pacific. The lines were deployed away from the islands, since the Combined Fleet assumed that if the Pacific Fleet came out to give battle it would not hug the island line where shoals might hamper its freedom of maneuver. Accordingly, the Japanese extended their lines some 240 miles from the islands, the few submarines deployed having no overlapping fields of vision. They were not employed on mobile searches but deployed to fixed positions. There was no question of their using the tactic of advancing during the night on a possible contact and withdrawing during the day as German submarines did in the Atlantic. The Germans would never have considered use of such "hit-and-miss" methods, but to the Japanese such arrangements seemed perfectly in order, especially when the First Carrier Striking Force came up to a position some 300 miles clear of Midway on the open flank of line B on approximately 6 June.

For Operation MI the six fleet carriers that had raided Pearl Harbor would be deployed with the First Carrier Striking Force. These carriers were the *Akagi* and the *Kaga* from Vice Admiral Chuichi Nagumo's First Carrier Division; the *Hiryu* and the *Soryu* from Rear Admiral Tamon Yamaguchi's Second Carrier Division; and the *Shokaku* and the *Zuikaku*. Command of the force was vested in Nagumo, whose flagship was the *Akagi*. The major units of the support group similarly remained all but unchanged from those that had taken part in the Pearl Harbor raid, though there had been many changes in personnel in the meantime. Rear Admiral Hiroaki Abe now commanded the support group. His formation consisted of the seaplane cruisers *Tone* and *Chikuma* of the Eighth Cruiser Division, and the *Kirishima* and the *Haruna* from the Second Battle Division, Third Battle Squadron. The *Haruna* had displaced the *Hiei* from the force that had raided Pearl Harbor. Rear Admiral Satsuma Kimura's composite Tenth Destroyer Division, with the light cruiser *Nagara* and eleven destroyers, would screen the ten heavy ships. From the Fourth Division were the *Arashi*, *Hagikaze*, *Maikaze* and *Nowaki*. The *Hamakaze*, *Isokaze*, *Tanikaze* and *Urakaze* represented the Seventeenth Division. The *Kazegumo*, *Makikumo* and *Yugumo*, from the original Tenth Division, completed the screen. The task of escorting the six oilers supporting the force was given to the *Akigumo*, sister ship of the units from the old Tenth Destroyer Division. Of the oilers, five, the *Kyokutomaru*, *Kokuyomaru*, *Nipponmaru*, *Shinkokumaru* and *Tohomaru*, had taken part in the Pearl Harbor operation—the *Kyoeimaru No. 2* had not. Two other ships, the 6,534-ton ammunition ship *Nichiromaru* and the 1,521-ton refrigerated victualler *Hokkomaru*, were detailed to provide for the force should the need arise, but they did not sail with the formation.

The initial task of the First Carrier Striking Force was to begin its approach on Midway as the Aleutians operation opened on 3 June. By running down on the atoll from the northwest the carriers would steam into the prevailing wind and thus facilitate their flying operations. On the morning of the fourth the six carriers were to strike and neutralize Midway. This was to be achieved in one single attack, or so it was hoped; the probability of a second strike being needed to record decisive results was recognized.

With Midway neutralized, the initial landings would take place on 5 June, but not on Midway. Kure Island, some 60 miles to the west of Midway, was the first Japanese objective. This tiny inlet was the target of Rear Admiral Ruitaro Fujita's Seaplane Tender Group. Fujita had earlier been involved in securing various settlements along the northern coast of New Guinea with the *Chitose* and a small force of escorts. For this operation he again had the *Chitose*, but this time she was in the company of the *Kamikawamaru*, fresh from Operation MO. Originally the *Kamikawamaru* had not been earmarked for Operation MO but had been forced to join the order of battle after the loss of the *Mizuho*. With the two tenders were the destroyer *Hayashio* and patrol boat *No. 35*, both with troops embarked. This force was to secure Kure and establish on the island a base from which the seaplanes from the tenders could operate on the sixth in support of that day's landings on Midway. The *Chitose* was almost at full strength since she had seven Alf and sixteen Dave seaplanes; the *Kamikawamaru*, on the other hand, had only her operational quota of twelve seaplanes, four of which were Jakes, as opposed to her ferrying load of two dozen seaplanes.*

The landings on Midway were entrusted to 5,000 troops drawn from both the army and the navy. In command of the ground forces as a whole and the navy's Second Combined Special Naval Landing Force in particular was Captain (IJN) Minoru Ota. The naval unit was to secure Sand Island. Eastern Island, the other "half" of Midway, was to be secured by the military detachment that bore the name of its commander, Colonel Kiyonao Ichiki. True to form, the army wanted the Ichiki Detachment withdrawn from Midway at the earliest possible opportunity, since it was to be used in the course of subsequent operations in the southwest Pacific. Two construction battalions and various specialist support troops needed to maintain Midway as an air base were in company with the front-line units. The troops bound for Midway sailed from Yokosuka if they came from the army and from Kure if they belonged to the navy. Both were to leave on 24 May for a four-day passage to Saipan. There they had to rendezvous with their escort and with the force bound for Kure Island. At Saipan they came under the command of Rear Admiral Raizo Tanaka, later to receive widespread acclaim (and dismissal) for his handling of the transport forces during the Guadalcanal campaign. He commanded from the light cruiser *Jintsu*, and had with him the *Kuroshio* and the *Oyashio* from the Fifteenth Destroyer Division; the *Amatsukaze*, *Hatsukaze*, *Tokitsukaze* and *Yukikaze* from the Sixteenth Division; and the *Kagero*, *Shiranui*, *Arare* and *Kasumi* from the Eighteenth Division. The transports bound for Midway were the *Argentinamaru*, *Brazilmaru*, *Azumamaru*, *Hokurikumaru*, *Kanomaru*, *Kirishimamaru*, *Kiyozumimaru*, *Meiyomaru*, *Nankaimaru*, *Toamaru*, *Toamaru No. 2* and *Yamafukumaru*. With the transports were other troop carriers, the ex-destroyer patrol boats *No. 1*, *No. 2* and *No. 34*, and the oiler *Akebonomaru*. Four other oilers, the *Sata*, *Tsurumi*, *Genyomaru* and *Kenyomaru*, were detailed to succor the force, but they did not sail with it from Saipan.

In support of the Invasion Force were three more forces, two of which sailed from the Marianas. From Saipan a minesweeper group, under the command of Captain Sadatomo Miyamoto, sailed independently, putting in at Wake en route for Midway. This force consisted of three members of a new class of 438-ton submarine chasers, the *Ch. 16*, *Ch. 17* and *Ch. 18*, four steam whalers that had been converted for minesweeping duties, the *Tamamaru No. 3*, *Tamamaru No. 5*, *Shonanmaru No. 7* and *Shonanmaru No. 8*, and

---

*Some confusion surrounds the identification of the seaplanes carried by the *Kamikawamaru*. Certain records suggest that she carried four Alf and eight Dave seaplanes, but the serviceability returns for 15 and 23 June indicate that she deployed Daves, Jakes and Petes. (The fifteenth gives returns of two Daves, four Jakes and four Petes operational; the twenty-the 3,800-ton ammunition ship *Soya*. From Guam came the Close Support Group of Vice Admiral Takeo Kurita. This force contained the elite of the surface forces, the frighteningly formidable Seventh Cruiser Division. With their 35 knots and a collective strength of forty 8-in guns, the *Kumano*, *Suzuya*, *Mikuma* and *Mogami* were evidently considered capable of looking after themselves; they were given an escort of just two destroyers, the *Arashio* and the *Asashio*, from the Eighth Destroyer Division. The 10,020-ton oiler *Nicheimaru* completed this group.

The Invasion Force Main Body provided distant cover, with Kondo, despite his skepticism about the whole operation, in command of the overall invasion effort. Under his command were the heavy cruisers *Atago* and *Chokai* from the Fourth Cruiser Squadron, and the *Myoko* and the *Haguro* from Takagi's Fifth Squadron. All four heavy cruisers carried one Alf and two Dave seaplanes. Completing the heavy element of this main body were the fast battleships *Hiei* and *Kongo* from Rear Admiral Gunichi Mikawa's Third Battle Squadron. Rear Admiral Shoji Nishimura commanded the screen provided by the Fourth Destroyer Flotilla. This was made up of the light cruiser *Yura*; the *Harusame*, *Murasame*, *Samidare* and *Yudachi* from the Second Destroyer Division; and the *Asagumo*, *Minegumo* and *Natsugumo* from the Ninth Destroyer Division. Completing the Main Body was perhaps its most important single element, the light carrier *Zuiho*, and the plane guard, the destroyer *Mikuzuki*. For Operation MI the *Zuiho* carried twelve Claude fighters and an equal number of Jean torpedo bombers on her 13,950 tons.

In Operation AL the two invasion forces planned to sweep onto their objectives in the wake of the carriers and behind the cordon line established by the submarines; similarly, in Operation MI there was to be a synchronization of movement as Tanaka, Kurita and Kondo brought their forces to the objective and Nagumo's carriers, their neutralization of Midway accomplished, moved clear of the atoll to take up a position on the disengaged flank. Only in the last two days of the approach phase were the various forces earmarked for this part of the operation to be in close proximity as they closed on Midway from a little south of west. Tanaka's group was to be wedged between Kondo to the north and Kurita to the south. Kondo was to take up the van position during the crucial final stages of the approach, when the transports would come within range of what remained of enemy air power on Midway. During the actual assault phase Kondo was to stand to the north of Midway between Kurita and the First Carrier Striking Force.

---

third two Daves, one Jake and three Petes.) It would appear that the *Kamikawamaru* carried four Jakes rather than Alfs and a combination of Daves and Petes rather than just Daves. Japanese records, however, do not break down the number of Daves and Petes other than to state that there were eight of them overall. This text treats these eight as Daves.

But whereas Operation AL worked according to a relatively leisurely timetable, this was not the case with Operation MI. The schedule that had to be followed by the forces involved in this operation was frighteningly tight because the carriers, in anticipation of a general fleet action, had to be on station beyond Midway and on the flank of cordon line B after 6 June. By that date, the Combined Fleet estimated, any American reaction to events would have materialized, so Midway would have be secure and handling aircraft and seaplanes in support of the carrier force.

The Japanese therefore allowed themselves just three days between the opening of their offensive against Midway and the possible overture to main force battle, and only one day to secure Midway and get it into working order. Thereafter, the Combined Fleet would have a mere seven days to secure a victory in a fleet action before it had to turn back west. By any standard this self-imposed timetable was severe: it allowed very little time in which to overcome a reverse or delay. But with the Japanese convinced that only small ground and air forces were stationed on Midway, and with a submarine line in position between Pearl Harbor and the western Hawaiian Islands, there seemed little chance of mishap.

Certainly the forces available to meet an American sortie seemed adequate to the task. The submarines on cordon line B and Nagumo's six carriers were expected to deal in a preemptory manner with an American attempt to improvise an attack in response to Operation MI. But to guard against the possibility of a more deliberate enemy move made by the bulk of American forces, the Japanese planned to have various forces at sea in support of Nagumo's carriers. The most important of these forces was to be one under the command of the fleet commander himself.

Yamamoto planned to go to sea to take command of this operation. This was the first occasion since the war began for which he chose to lead his forces in battle, having previously exercised command from the fleet base at Hiroshima. He intended to sail in his new fleet flagship, the *Yamato*, in the company of her two colleagues of the First Battle Division, the *Nagato* and the *Mutsu*. With the battleships were to be two groups. The first, the Special Group, consisted of the tenders *Chiyoda* and *Nisshin*. The second, the Carrier Group, consisted of the old *Hosho* and the destroyer *Yukaze*. The *Hosho*, the world's first purpose-built carrier, was pulled off training duties to take part in this, her only operational mission of the war. She had embarked nine Claudes and six Jean torpedo bombers. Completing what was known as the First Fleet Main Body or, more simply, the Main Body, was Rear Admiral Shintaro Hashimoto's Screening Force. This consisted of the Third Destroyer Flotilla with the light cruiser *Sendai* and the Eleventh Division's *Fubuki*, *Hatsuyuki*, *Marakumo* and *Shirayuki*; and the Nineteenth Division's *Ayanami*, *Isonami*, *Shikinami* and *Uranami*. The fuel needs of this entire force, which initially included the battle force bound for the Aleutians, were to be met by three oilers that sailed independently but made a midocean rendezvous with the Main Body and stayed in company until battle was joined. These oilers were the *Naruto, Sacramentomaru* and *Toeimaru*.

The Main Body trailed the First Carrier Striking Force by about 600 miles. With the carriers destined to mark time to the northeast of Midway after the fourth, as they waited for that island to be secured and a possible fleet action to develop, this distance was to close to about 300 miles, the equivalent of one day's cruising. The Japanese anticipated that, if a major American counteroffensive showed signs of materializing—and once it did it would almost certainly be to the south of latitude 40° N—the warnings given by their submarines would allow time to halt Operation AL and bring Gakasu's Screening Force and Kakuta's Second Carrier Striking Force south to link up with their Operation MI counterparts. The four major formations involved in these two operations were to be in roughly rectangular form, both sets of battle forces some 300 miles behind their carriers with about 500 miles of sea between the forces in the north and those in the south. By concentrating their forces the Japanese could put eight carriers and two battleships in the van and have a battle force in support. This latter formation would consist of seven battleships and one light carrier. Even further south would be the various invasion forces, which would be free to go to the support of either the battle forces or the carrier forces once the occupation of Midway was completed. A total of one light fleet carrier, two fast battleships and eight heavy cruisers in the combined forces of Kondo and Kurita represented a massive reinforcement for the surface forces seeking battle with the enemy.

Detailed planning did not extend beyond Operations AL and MI, but as planning and preparations for these two operations and for Operations MO and RY pressed ahead in April and May, the two general staffs and the sections of Imperial General Headquarters concerned themselves with future operations. Discussion, planning and the issue of warning orders continued until 4 June, when preliminary arrangements were overtaken by events.

The discussions within the navy and between the two services in April and May were not easy, but in the end there was agreement untainted by the discord that had characterized earlier discussions. This was the result of two conditions. First, it was possible for the navy to come to an agreement with the army in April and May on the matter of the southwest Pacific, because the two general staffs had already agreed in principle on operations in this theater in March. The seemingly bottomless pit of Australia and the Indian Ocean having been avoided, the army was willing to accept the navy's case for the southwest Pacific. Second, the Combined Fleet did not reject the Naval General Staff's proposals for the southwest Pacific after

Operation MI. Its objection had been to this option being pursued before and at the expense of Operation MI. Indeed, a campaign that in effect would be designed to exploit the victory won at Midway was desirable. The way was clear for the factions within the navy to reconcile their differences and for the army and navy to renew their agreement, and on 28 April the army for a second time endorsed the navy's proposal for an offensive in the southwest Pacific theater.

Initial consideration of the theater led the planners to decide to mount simultaneous operations to secure New Caledonia, Fiji and Samoa. To achieve this Imperial General Headquarters ordered the raising of a new army on 2 May. This, the Seventeenth Army of Lieutenant General Haruyoshi Hyakutake, was theoretically the equivalent of a western corps, but in reality it was never more than a reinforced division. Planning, however, was to be complicated by Operation MI's miscarrying, and Inoue had to inform the Naval General Staff that unless he received substantial reinforcement in the shape of carriers and fast transports, a renewed attempt to secure Port Moresby could not be made before July. Initial Japanese planning had assumed that Operation MI would meet with considerable success. The Naval General Staff and the Combined Fleet were to agree in May that there could be no question of halting the arrangements for Operation MI in order to support a second attempt to secure Port Moresby. That had to be deferred to July, and the staffs had to recast their plans to schedule the repeat of Operation MO for the same time as the operations against New Caledonia, Fiji and Samoa.

For these four operations the navy planned to keep the South Seas Force where it was, in support of the proposed operation against Port Moresby, and to bring the bulk of the Combined Fleet to the south to support the more distant operations. After Operation MI Kondo and Nagumo were to bring their forces to Truk and there complete their arrangements to support the landings on New Caledonia, Samoa and Fiji. Yamamoto and Takasu were to take their battle forces back to Japan. Such arrangments—the withdrawal of the battleships and simultaneous landings across an immense area of operations—are explicable only in terms of the Japanese assumption that they would not encounter any substantial enemy resistance on land, in the air or at sea.

For the landings the First Bureau had to consider using four separate detachments, since there could be no question of any single force being able to secure more than one objective. The Seventeenth Army had one formation in position, Horii's South Seas Detachment. This, it will be recalled, was the three-battalion 144th Infantry Regiment detached from the Fifty-fifth Infantry Division. It had already been involved in securing various objectives in the west and southwest Pacific, and it had been tasked to secure Port Moresby. Under the redrafted plans it was to carry out the attack on New Caledonia; its previous mission was to be discharged by the Aoba Detachment. This was the three-battalion Fourth Infantry Regiment, part of the Second Infantry Division. As part of the Sixteenth Army it had already seen service in Java. Against the main target in the southwest Pacific the First Bureau planned to use high-quality troops that had been proved in battle. From Malaya was to come the command organization for the Fiji operation, the Thirty-fifth Infantry Brigade, with one of its two formations, the 124th Infantry Regiment. These, from the Eighteenth Infantry Division, were actually involved in securing Cebu and then Mindanao at the time when the Army General Staff was considering their commitment to the southwest Pacific. To stand alongside the three battalions of the 124th Infantry were to be two battalions from the Forty-first Infantry Regiment; its remaining unit was used to secure Samoa. Originally part of the Fifth Infantry Division, the Forty-first Infantry Regiment was then involved in bringing an end to enemy resistance on Panay. These provisional arrangements were sanctioned by Imperial General Headquarters on 4 June, but the venture was postponed two months on 11 June and finally abandoned on 11 July.

Had the Japanese been able to adhere to their original order of battle all might have gone well for them, though there is much to be said for the argument that even with their intended order of battle their plan of campaign was so fraught with inconsistencies that it was doomed to failure. But the Japanese were unable to abide by their initial intention to deploy ten carriers for Operations AL and MI. At the battle of the Coral Sea the Japanese lost the *Shoho*, and the *Zuikaku* and the *Shokaku* were both put out of the running for Operation MI. The *Shokaku* suffered severe structural damage, while the air group of the *Zuikaku* was badly mauled. Neither could be readied in time to sail in the last week of May with the other members of the First Carrier Striking Force.

These unexpected setbacks would probably have resulted in either a change of plan or a delay in mounting the offensive had any navy other than the Japanese found itself in such a situation. Indeed, the Naval General Staff sought delay. It wanted to postpone the operation until the *Zuikaku* could be put back into service. (Events were to show that she could have been ready to go to sea as early as 10 June.) At the very least there was much to be said for delay. To return to Kusaka's argument, the extra time could have been used for further training of the air groups, and there was no disputing the fact that delay would have yielded two worthwhile results: better-trained air groups and five rather than four carriers in the van. But any thought of postponement was anathema to the Combined Fleet. As far as Yamamoto was concerned, the date for Operation MI had to be fixed by meteorological considerations. The amphibious forces needed a full moon, and this meant that their operations would have to be carried out before the moon began to wane after 7 June. Any delay would result in Operation MI being put off a full month, to the detriment of operations in the Aleutians. The meteorological assessment was that operations in the Aleutians were only possible between March and May and in September and October. June, therefore, was at the very end of the "open season," and the Japanese could not contemplate a July operation in the north. In fact, there is something to be said for the idea that nothing could have been better calculated to serve Japanese interest than a delay to Operation MI that involved foregoing the Aleutians venture. There was nothing to be gained by persisting with Operation AL if, as a result, the all-important carriers of the vanguard force were left understrength at the point of contact. This, however, was not how Yamamoto saw matters. His unwillingness to suspend operations stemmed not from concern about moon phases or even the fogs, snow and icebergs of the Kuroshio and Oyashio currents of the Aleutians: it stemmed from the conviction that every day that passed with no attempt to bring the enemy to battle was another day lost, another day that enabled the Americans to add to their strength and make the Japanese task of destroying the Pacific Fleet that much more difficult. As far as Yamamoto was concerned, four carriers in June held out better hopes of success than five in July or six or seven in August.

There would seem to be a strong case for Yamamoto's refusal to recast or delay his operation in the central Pacific in the aftermath of setbacks suffered in the Coral Sea. But the case cannot stand up to real scrutiny. To proceed with an eight-carrier operation when only four carriers were with the First Carrier Striking Force could not be justified since the situation against which Miyo had warned the Combined Fleet in April still applied: the administrative arrangements for replacement aircraft and aircrew could not meet a June deadline.

The *Zuikaku* had to be left "on the beach" in spite of her undamaged condition, for when she arrived home, one week before Nagumo sailed, no fully trained air group awaited her. The factories and the training schools had not been able to keep pace with the extremely heavy losses incurred by the Naval Air Force even in its period of relatively easy and cheap conquests. Even when Japan went to war her carrier force was below establishment. Its First, Second and Fifth Carrier Divisions were at full strength, but only because the Third and Fourth Divisions were stripped and then starved of replacements. The Yokosuka Air Corps, the training unit for the navy, lost its best instructors at the very time they were needed as never before to cope with the influx of trainees. Between 7 December 1941 and 30 April 1942 the navy lost 315 aircraft in combat and a further 540 aircraft operationally. Losses of this order could not be covered. As we have seen, two of the carriers committed to Operation MI did not have time to convert from Claudes to Zekes, while the *Ryujo* and the *Junyo* were equipped with

Zekes only in the very last days before they sailed for the Aleutians. Moreover, only two of the eight carriers involved in Operations AL and MI sailed with a full operational establishment, and two, the *Hosho* and the *Zuiho*, were equipped not with front-line but with trainer aircraft. But the Japanese dilemma was not confined simply to aircraft and pilot numbers: pilot quality was also a serious problem, as we have already noted with regard to the *Zuikaku*, which did not receive an air group upon return to Japan. The Yamamoto notion of four carriers with the strike force, two more in the Aleutians and two more with the battle forces might have been valid had all his carriers been at full strength with crews of the quality of those with whom Japan had started the war. He needed the aircrew and aircraft of December 1941, but neither were available. He was determined to do what the carrier aircraft—through no fault of their own—had failed to do at Pearl Harbor in December: to destroy the carriers of the Pacific Fleet. Yamamoto planned to do this in June with less than half the number of aircraft the carrier force had deployed for the raid on Pearl Harbor. For this operation Nagumo was to have fewer carriers than he had deployed when he raided Ceylon in April and only the same number that the Japanese had used against Rabaul in January and Darwin in February, when both the prizes and risks had been infinitely smaller than they would be off Midway. Moreover, in June the Japanese planned to attack two targets, and to do so with an aircrew less proficient than the one at Pearl Harbor. But on this occasion the Japanese would not have the chance to strike at enemy ships taken by surprise at their moorings.

Clearly, things did not add up properly. Somewhere along the line the process whereby the Combined Fleet allocated forces proportional to the task in hand left something to be desired. The decision to press ahead with Operations AL and MI with an unaltered order of battle after the Fifth Carrier Division had been removed from the lists would seem to suggest a willingness to accept the principle of economy of effort far beyond the point where ordinary common sense—not to mention the prudence that should have been part of normal staff practice—should have prevailed. The Japanese knew that the Americans in the summer of 1942 had to have a minimum of four carriers: the latter had started the war with seven and the Japanese believed that their forces had accounted for three of them. As late as 15 May the Japanese knew that two American carriers were operating in the southwest Pacific and that neither had been present one week earlier in the battle that had deprived them of the services of the *Shokaku* and the *Zuikaku*. But with no contacts with enemy carriers after 15 May, and with no knowledge of overall American strength, the only point that the Combined Fleet could conclude with any degree of certainty was that the Fifth Carrier Division still retained its assured margin of superiority over the Pacific Fleet. To embark upon an operation with no margin against error or uncertainty when the enemy's presence and whereabouts were unknown was little short of criminal negligence. Moreover, under these circumstances it was bad policy to persist with an arrangement whereby half the carriers available for Operations AL and MI were consigned to secondary tasks while the First Carrier Striking Force was left without the means to meet its possible obligations. If Operation AL ever had any relevance at all—and that is doubtful—it was lost when the *Shokaku* and the *Zuikaku* were forced out of the running for Midway. What the *Hosho* and the *Zuiho* were supposed to achieve some 300 to 500 miles behind the point of contact is equally hard to discern. They could defend neither themselves nor their task group in the face of enemy air superiority, yet they were too far away to help the carrier force. But in support of the First Carrier Striking Force all four of any three of the *Hosho*, *Junyo*, *Ryujo* and *Zuiho* could well have proved effective beyond the sum of their individual strengths. Together these four carriers had an operational capacity equal to that of the Fifth Carrier Division, and on 2 June they embarked between them the equivalent of a strong air group. Any three of them collectively had more aircraft than the *Akagi*, *Hiryu* and *Soryu* had individually. Even if the *Junyo* were discounted from the lists because her top speed of 22.5 knots precluded her from a fully fledged fleet action, the other three carriers between them carried more aircraft than any single member of the First Carrier Striking Force.

These considerations naturally lead to one of the most vexing aspects of Midway—the air strength of the Japanese. Accounts of the battle differ drastically in their assessment of numbers. One gives two tables that cannot be reconciled—the first for original strength and the second for losses—and a narrative that contradicts both. In general most accounts place the original strength of the Japanese carrier force at Midway between 227 and 280 aircraft, with the 250–262 range being the one most favored by historians.

The recounting of the air order of battle that follows must be judged in light of the carrying capacity of the carriers of Nagumo's force. This was a total of 325 aircraft. The individual breakdown was the *Akagi* with 91 aircraft, the *Kaga* with 90, the *Hiryu* with 73, and the baby of the party, the *Soryu*, with 71. But the Japanese practice of reserving space for a considerable number of spare aircraft on their carriers kept the operational capacity of Nagumo's force at only 248: the *Akagi* had 66 operational and 25 reserve aircraft; the *Kaga* 72 and 18; the *Hiryu* 57 and 16; and the *Soryu* 53 and 18. What the absence of the *Shokaku* and the *Zuikaku* meant can be measured by the fact that as the most powerful single carriers in Japanese service, both had 72-strong air groups with another 12 aircraft in reserve.* As for the other carriers, the *Hosho* had a theoretical capacity of 21 aircraft with 15 operation and 6 spares, though in reality 15 was her optimum capacity; the

---

*This statement is based on the fact that the *Akagi* and the *Kaga*, despite their size and establishments, seldom had more than 60 or so aircraft in their groups. In theory the aircraft of the *Shokaku* and the *Zuikaku* were outnumbered, but in practice they were not.

Junyo had room for 48 operational and 5 reserve aircraft; the *Ryujo* had space for 48 aircraft of which 12 would be spares; and the *Zuiho* could handle 27 operational and 3 replacement aircraft.

Excluding from all calculations the aircraft carried by carriers for the intended Midway base and those seaplanes on board submarines, the total number of seaplanes and aircraft allocated to the forces involved in Operation AL was 79, of which 51 were aircraft and 28 were seaplanes: for the forces involved in the amphibious side of Operation MI (those commanded by Kondo, Kurita and Tanaka) the total was 85, of which 24 were aircraft and the remainder were seaplanes; for Yamamoto's Main Body the total was 23, of which 15 were aircraft and the remaining 8 were seaplanes; and the total for the First Carrier Striking Force was 246, of which 17 were seaplanes, 4 were reconnaissance aircraft and 225 were combat aircraft. The full breakdown of seaplanes and aircraft embarked for Operations AL and MI is given in table 3-1.

From the totals in table 3-1 it can be seen that the Imperial Navy deployed on Operations AL and MI a total of 315 combat aircraft, 4 reconnaissance aircraft and 114 seaplanes. Of this grand total of 433 aircraft and seaplanes, 354 were committed to the various forces involved in Operation MI. Not part of the order of battle but embarked on certain carriers were the 33 Zekes scheduled to form part of the Midway Expeditionary Force.

Before examining these figures in detail, it is appropriate to deal once and for all with the orders of battle for land-based air formations allotted to Operation MI and for the Midway Expeditionary Force. As part of the operation the Imperial Navy organized three task groups under the auspices of the Eleventh Air Fleet. Two of these, Task Groups 24 and 26, were established on a temporary basis; the other, the Midway Expeditionary Force, was to be permanent. Task Group 24, commanded by Rear Admiral Minoru Maeda, deployed bombers and flying boats in the Marshalls and on Wake. It had two Emily flying boats from the Twenty-first Squadron, Toko Air Group, and six Mavis flying boats from the Twenty-fourth Squadron, Fourteenth Air Group, under command. The latter, brought to Wake on 4 June, were detailed to form part of the Midway formation when the atoll began to function under new management two or three days later. Completing the order of battle of Task Group 24 were 12 Betty bombers from the Twenty-second Squadron, Mihoro Air Group, and 43 Nell bombers from the Chitose and First Air Groups. The second formation, Task Group 26, was made up of 49 Betty bombers from the Misawa and Kisarazu Air Groups. Parts of this task group were held back in the homeland at Kisarazu (near Tokyo) and Chitose (on Hokkaido), but 12 from the Misawa formation were on Marcus with orders to proceed to Midway after the atoll's fall.

Table 3-1. Orbat chart for Operations AL and MI

	Combat Aircraft					Seaplanes				Recce Aircraft		Total
	Type 96 A5M4 Claude	Type 00 A6M2 Zeke	Type 96 B4N1 Jean	Type 97 B5N2 Kate	Type 99 D3A1 Val	Type 94 E7K2 Alf	Type 95 E8N2 Dave	Type 00 E13A1 Jake	Type 00 F1M2 Pete	Type 97 B5N2 Kate	Type 2 D4Y1 Judy	
OPERATION AL												
Second Carrier Striking Force												
Ryujo		12		18								30
Junyo		6			15							21
Guard and Invasion Forces												
Maya						1	2					3
Takao						1	2					3
Hyuga							2					2
Ise							2					2
Fuso							2					2
Yamashiro							2					2
Kimikawamaru								8				8
Abukuma						1						1
Kiso						1						1
Tama						1						1
Main Body												
Nachi						1	2					3
Total for Operation AL		18		18	15	6	14	8				79

Table 3-1. *(continued)*

	Combat Aircraft					Seaplanes				Recce Aircraft		Total
	Type 96 A5M4 *Claude*	Type 00 A6M2 *Zeke*	Type 96 B4N1 *Jean*	Type 97 B5N2 *Kate*	Type 99 D3A1 *Val*	Type 94 E7K2 *Alf*	Type 95 E8N2 *Dave*	Type 00 E13A1 *Jake*	Type 00 F1M2 *Pete*	Type 97 B5N2 *Kate*	Type 2 D4Y1 *Judy*	
OPERATION MI												
Midway Invasion Forces												
Main Body												
Zuibo	12		12									24
Atago						1	2					3
Chokai						1	2					3
Myoko						1	2					3
Haguro						1	2					3
Yura						1						1
Close Support Group												
Kumano						1	2					3
Suzuya						1	2					3
Mikuma						1	2					3
Mogami						1	2					3
Transport and Occupation Force												
Chitose						7	16					23
Kamikawamaru							8	4				12
Jintsu						1						1
Subtotal	12		12			17	40	4				85

Main Force Main Body

										Total
Hosho	9	6								15
Yamato								3		3
Mutsu						2				2
Nagato						2				2
Sendai							1			1
Subtotal	9	6				4	1	3		23

First Carrier Striking Force

										Total
Akagi			18	18	18				1		55
Kaga			18	27	18				1		64
Hiryu			18	18	18						54
Soryu			18	18	18					2	56
Haruna								3			3
Kirishima								3			3
Tone						3		2			5
Chikuma						3		2			5
Nagara							1				1
Subtotal			72	81	72	6	1	10	2	2	246
Total for Operation MI	21	18	72	81	72	19	54	10	5	2	354
Total for Operations AL and MI	21	18	90	99	87	25	68	18	5	2	433

The Midway Expeditionary Force, with its commander-designate Captain Chisato Morita, was to have under command the three subgroups already mentioned: the 6 Mavis flying boats that were to come up to Midway via Wake from Jaluit; the 12 Betty bombers from Marcus; and the 33 Zekes of the Sixth Air Group, which were on their way to Midway by sea. Of the fighters the *Akagi* carried 6, the *Kaga* 9, the *Hiryu* and the *Soryu* 3 each and the *Junyo*, destined for the Aleutians, the remaining 12.

The first, and perhaps least important, observation to make about the order of battle of the air formations relates to the *Junyo*, her role and her passengers. Quite clearly she could take her extra aircraft with no difficulty, since even with them she was but three parts full. But there would seem to be an inconsistency here. The *Junyo* formed part of a force intended to operate in waters some 20 degrees of latitude to the north of Midway, waiting for a fleet action that was almost certain not to take place in these waters, yet she carried aircraft that supposedly had to be rushed to a base the capture of which was so important and urgent that no fewer than 44 major warships had been directed to its capture. There was another inconsistency about the *Junyo* and the formation of which she was a part. With a paltry total of 51 Kates, Vals and Zekes on its two carriers, it is rather difficult to see how the Second Carrier Striking Force justified the middle word of its title. If this formation was to neutralize Dutch Harbor and then possibly fight a naval action in northern waters, its allocation of 18 Kates, 15 Vals and 18 Zekes was derisory. Indeed, everything about the Aleutians operation and the Second Carrier Striking Force becomes more incredible the more it is examined. Between them the *Junyo* and the *Ryujo* had the capacity to operate one strong air group, but they were a hopelessly ill-matched pair that made a hopelessly unbalanced force. The *Junyo* was too slow to operate heavy torpedo bombers, and in fact she was fit only to handle fighters, while the *Ryujo* was just able to handle Kates. The *Junyo* and the *Ryujo* were not able either together or individually to operate properly constituted air groups. The fact that the *Junyo* was commissioned on the day that Imperial General Headquarters sanctioned Operations AL and MI was silent condemnation of Combined Fleet arrangements.

Second, the total of 354 aircraft and seaplanes committed to the forces involved in Operation MI was an impressively high one. (It does wilt a little in comparison with the 355 aircraft used in the two attack waves at Pearl Harbor and the 463 aircraft on the carriers in that operation.) The Midway figures, however, are misleading in the sense that seaplanes accounted for nearly one quarter of the total number of aircraft. They had little offensive value, though their usefulness in the antisubmarine and reconnaissance roles cannot be underestimated. Yet of the 86 seaplanes embarked for Operation MI, no fewer than 69 were unable to carry out effective reconnaissance. The forces with good reconnaissance capabilities were in the rear, and they lacked the offensive air power to support landing operations; Nagumo's carrier force, on the other hand, was in the exposed and vulnerable vanguard with virtually no reconnaissance capability.

Third, there was the most serious failing of the operation. As has been mentioned, the First Carrier Striking Force was understrength. In terms of strike power the Nagumo force was weaker than it had been at Pearl Harbor, when circumstances were more favorable. The 153 bombers available for Operation MI contrasted unfavorably with the 140 used in the first wave at Pearl Harbor and the 134 used in the second. It had just 4 aircraft and 17 seaplanes with which to conduct antisubmarine and reconnaissance duties. But these weaknesses, serious though they were, quail beside the realization that for Operation MI the Japanese had more seaplanes and ships with the First Carrier Striking Force than it had fighters for the combat air patrol.

Between them Nagumo's carriers had 225 combat aircraft, of which 72 were Zekes. The Japanese operational plan called for an opening assault against Midway with 108 aircraft, evenly divided between Kates, Vals and Zekes. A second wave of 96 aircraft was to be held for a follow-up attack if one was needed or was to deal with an enemy task force if one was encountered. This second formation was to be made up of 36 Kates, 36 Vals and 24 Zekes, which left just the 9 "extra" Kates in reserve, plus 12 Zekes. With each carrier having 18 Zekes and deploying 9 for the first wave and 6 for the second, all four carriers had 3 Zekes left, and these represented the combat air patrol's standing force. Readiness fighters would have to support the combat air patrol's standing force, but these could not double when the bombers were committed. There was, moreover, the danger of using them to supplement the combat air patrol before individual attack waves were committed against the enemy; the fighters could not defend the fleet and escort attacking bombers at one and the same time. And of course there could be no guarantee that once battle was joined the Japanese would have time to shuffle their meager total of fighters to carry out these divergent and irreconcilable tasks.*

If not earlier then certainly at this point in time the case in favor of Operation AL and the deployment of two carriers with battle forces breaks down entirely. For the main force to have a marginal strike ability, a small reconnaissance capacity and no aircraft for a permanent combat air patrol at a time when four other carriers were positioned in such a way that they were no more than impotent irrelevancies was worse than carelessness. If

*Nagumo has had to shoulder much of the blame for the subsequent debacle, but perhaps the full extent of his difficulty in juggling an inadequate number of aircraft has not been appreciated. Lest this be deemed a plea on behalf of Nagumo, it should be noted that Nagumo showed few signs of being aware of these potential difficulties and lacked the imagination and ability to come up with possible answers.

the *Hosho* and the *Zuiho* were retained with the main surface forces for reconnaissance and antisubmarine patrols—and that was all that could be expected of them—they could have gone forward to join Nagumo and these duties could have been taken over by seaplanes from the tenders *Chiyoda* and *Nisshin* of the Main Body's special group. Twelve seaplanes were, after all, the maximum capacity of the *Chiyoda* and the minimum capacity of the *Nisshin*. But such a neat rearrangement was out of the question for one reason, which in a sense comments on the whole plan of campaign: neither seaplane carrier had any seaplanes.

Of course it would have been too easy for the Japanese to have had seaplanes with their seaplane carriers for Operation MI. The *Chiyoda* had eight Type A midget submarines embarked, the *Nisshin* five motor boats, probably of the Type T1 class. Both carriers were bound for Midway, where their units were to provide local defense for the garrison after the atoll's capture. In some ways it is unfortunate that the *Chiyoda* had been so tasked; had she been ordered to operate with the fleet, she would have been the last piece of the jigsaw that showed Operation MI for what it was—a plan of campaign based on a prewar tactical doctrine that had been overtaken by events. The division of forces with submarines in the advanced reconnaissance and strike roles, carriers leading the battle force to incapacitate the enemy, battleships held back with carriers and midget submarines—this was the hallmark of prewar tactical thought. Operation MI was no more than the old plan for a decisive gunnery action taken from its pigeonhole, dusted down and given an offensive twist; it was not given the strength to ensure a reasonable degree of security and flexibility for the vanguard, nor was it given support from land-based aircraft in the battle phase.

A host of critical comments could be directed against this plan of campaign, but perhaps the most pertinent is the one that returns to the original theme, that Operations AL and MI constitute "the Schlieffen Plan of the Pacific War." In seeking to seize the initiative with a surprise move that concentrated overwhelming force on the disengaged flank of an enemy whose reactions were to follow an anticipated pattern, Operations AL and MI bear a striking resemblance to the German master plan of 1914. But the parallel does not end there. Both the German and Japanese plans were bound by frighteningly tight margins of time, and both depended on the initiative and qualitative superiority to blunt the impact of the enemy's counterattacks. Both plans depended on various forces achieving their individual objectives in a set pattern that would then enable the plan as a whole to move forward, the anticipation of "decisive battle" after skirmish and maneuver, the vast wheeling movement to roll up the enemy's forces and positions—in the case of the Schlieffen Plan, across northern and eastern France, in the case of the Japanese plan, across half the width of the

Pacific. Moreover, both plans assumed that difficulties would be dispelled by the very momentum of success. Events in 1914 showed that the Germans had far too much confidence in their initial strategic advantages and (assumed) qualitative superiority, and that they underestimated the strength and effectiveness of their enemies' countermoves. The same was to prove true of the Midway venture. At every stage it was based upon a casual, sanguine assumption that any difficulty could be overcome without too much trouble, that everything would run with the smoothness of a well-maintained watch.

This deliberate discounting of unpleasant prospects was most obvious in the way the problem that lay at the very heart of Operation MI was simply wished away. Every part of the plan supposed that the Japanese would be using their carrier force to reduce a land target before the enemy could come on the scene. Yamamoto would maneuver his carrier force into a position allowing him to strike at two targets in turn, and it was the Japanese calculation that there would be three days between dealing with the first and the second. But the attack on the first objective had to be made without knowing the strength or whereabouts of the enemy, and there was no genuine consideration of the possibility that three days of grace might not be available. By definition, the attempt to secure the central position in order to strike at a divided enemy ran the risk of being caught between the would-be victims, and this risk, as we have seen, could only be aggravated by the wretchedly inadequate number of aircraft with the carriers.

The war games played on the *Yamato* should have brought home to the various commanders and their staffs the extent of these risks; at the very least the games should have revealed to all concerned that the Japanese faced problems of a kind that they had not previously encountered and that threatened to be serious. The person who should have been most troubled by this was the commander of the First Carrier Striking Force, but Nagumo's reaction to the games was one of "bored indifference," which was passed on to his staff. What was notable about the games was that the players, with months of success behind them, were prepared to treat the results casually. Even allowing for a belief in the ability to rise to any crisis, there was no excuse for playing the games in such a way that a Japanese victory was always ensured. In one attack on the First Carrier Striking Force by aircraft from Midway, nine hits were recorded and the *Akagi* and the *Kaga* were lost as a result. Ugaki, disliking the outcome, unilaterally and arbitrarily reduced the number of hits to three and ruled that only the *Kaga* was lost; subsequently she reappeared to take part in another stage of the battle. At the very end of the games Yamamoto himself raised the one matter that should have attracted the attention of the First Carrier Striking Force from the outset, namely how the Japanese carriers were to deal with an enemy carrier attack that was delivered while the Japanese were engaged in operations against Midway. No answer to this question was forthcoming from any member of the First Carrier Striking Force. Miwa merely rose to his feet to pronounce that Japanese defensive power was "unbreakable." This was a grotesquely unreal answer—it simply did not address the problem—but it was an answer that apparently reassured everyone present. In the end the best suggestion for dealing with this potential situation was made by Yamamoto himself. At the end of the war games the fleet commander specifically instructed Nagumo to keep at least half of his Kates permanently armed with torpedoes. This was not an answer to the defensive needs of the force, but at least it had more to recommend it than banal hyperbole. Yamamoto was impatient with the staff of the First Carrier Striking Force for its inability to think through the implications of the situation, but in a sense he had no right to be: his own chief of staff fixed the games and discussions and had no idea of operational priorities. Kusaka, at the staff discussion held on 26 May, the very eve of the carriers' sailing, specifically tackled Ugaki on this very point. He wanted to be given an unequivocal answer to the crucial question of whether taking Midway or tackling an enemy fleet that might put in an appearance was the primary task of the carrier force. He was told the choice would not present itself. When Kusaka then demanded an answer he was told that the decision would have to be made on the spot by the Striking Force, and without any guidance from the fleet command because of the need to maintain radio silence.

The fact that as late as 26 May Combined Fleet policy with regard to Operation MI was still being questioned by subordinate commanders indicated that, despite the diktat of 5 April, opposition to Yamamoto's plan of campaign persisted until the last possible moment. No notice was taken of this opposition by the Combined Fleet, and in a sense this was understandable. Having fought for and secured the principle of the central Pacific offensive at the expense of the Naval General Staff, Yamamoto had little time for criticism from his own subordinates, even when they happened to include a fleet commander. This proved unfortunate for the Japanese cause, for little of the criticism was directed against the principle of the plan. Most of the criticism was directed against its various aspects, two of which were under particular fire.

The first line of criticism, many of whose aspects were covered earlier, amounted to a suggestion to postpone the operation until the *Zuikaku* could be put back into service. Among the most percipient arguments was the one made by Kusaka, who said that nothing should be attempted because the carriers needed three to four months away from operations to rest jaded crews, allow time for the ships to be overhauled, train aircrews and integrate them into existing air groups. It was beginning to dawn on many officers that the quality of the naval air force was in decline, as if the ruthless efficiency with which the *Cornwall* and the *Dorsetshire* had been sunk in April represented a pinnacle of achievement that ruined those who made it. Certainly, the results registered by the air groups in the exercises preceding Operation MI were so bad that the umpires, drawn from the elite Yokosuka Air Corps, were left wondering how past results had been obtained on the evidence of present showing.

The Japanese had begun the war with carrier pilots who had averaged more than 800 hours of flying time. Many had had 2,000 hours, plus combat experience over China. These elite aircrews sustained heavy losses in the opening months of the war and, as we have noted, the capacity of the Yokosuka Air Corps to train replacement aircrew had actually fallen before the start of the war. By the beginning of 1943 pilots with no more than 150 hours in their logbooks were joining combat formations. This was tantamount to a death sentence for the draftees. By May 1942 the situation had not yet reached this point, but the pattern of decline had begun, and the June deadline made no allowance for it. Yamamoto's timetable compressed training programs into thirty days. When the carriers returned from the Indian Ocean the air groups were dispersed, the *Akagi*'s to Kagoshima, the *Hiryu*'s to Tomitaka in Miyazaki Prefecture and the *Soryu*'s to Kasanohara air base in the Kagoshima Prefecture. Thus there was no chance for the groups to exercise together until just before the operation, and with these three carriers entering dockyards for all-too-rapid overhauls, only the *Kaga* was available for sea training. The *Kaga* could not carry out four months' worth of training for four carriers in four weeks. The old hands were allowed just one dusk landing in the time before Operation MI, and newcomers could only be given rudimentary training. With senior flying officers detailed to courses of instruction, even the individual squadrons and groups were not able to train together properly. The result was quite predictable. The carrier force was to sail with pilots whose capacity for night operations was minimal at best and whose capacity for daylight operations was weaker than it should have been. Thus, overall, the situation was stupifying: Operation MI was to be spearheaded by an understrength carrier force whose air groups were understrength and undertrained. Moreover, about 28 percent of all the combat aircraft involved in Operations AL and MI were anywhere but the place they were needed. And the whole plan of campaign depended for success on the carrier air groups of the First Carrier Striking Force first neutralizing Midway and then dealing with their counterparts if the enemy gave battle.

The second suggestion to improve Operation MI was for Yamamoto, if he was to go to sea, to take the *Yamato* force into the van and exercise command of the battle from there. This would have involved recasting the composition of the various task forces, with more heavy units being brought into the screens surrounding the carriers. The two separate considerations, easing command problems and bringing extra support to the carriers, tended to reinforce one another.

Hindsight leads one to the conclusion that the carriers could hardly have fared worse with a strengthened screen than they did without extra ships being moved into their tactical formation. The prima facie view would suggest that a more powerful screen, with heavy units either off the bows or astern of the carriers, would have been an improvement on the situation that actually prevailed. But matters were not quite so simple as this. Events were to show that in 1942 heavy ships were undergunned and that, far from being able to provide extra cover for the carriers, they did not have the means to fend for themselves. The *Yamato*, for example, carried a twelve 5-in, eight triple 25-mm and two twin 13-mm antiaircraft tertiary armament; the *Mutsu* and the *Nagato* were less well equipped to beat off air attack. The massed batteries and wall of fire put up by carrier screens belonged to a later period, not mid-1942. But, of course, at this time the Japanese did not know that their units were undergunned, and it is somewhat difficult to believe that the Japanese carriers would not have benefited by having units off the bows to break up torpedo bomber attacks and astern to counter dive-bombing attacks.

But the real problem that surrounded this question of strengthening the screen of the carrier force was that in 1942 no one in this or any other navy knew how to fight carriers defensively. By 1944 it was obvious that there was only one way to do so: by concentrating carriers together within a single task force and putting as much artillery into the screen in order to supplement the efforts of the combat air patrol. In 1942 navies were feeling their way into unknown territory. When Operation MI was put together the first carrier battle was yet to be fought, and no navy had come up with answers to the problems that had defied solution throughout the interwar period. Whether carriers should stay together or separate, whether screens should come in close or give searoom to the carriers, whether carriers should seek protection in evasion and maneuver or en masse—all these were questions for which no answers had been forthcoming. There was also the problem of marrying slow battleships with fast carriers when there were not enough destroyers to provide screens for both. It was not until the development in the late thirties of the fast battleship that part of the equation could be solved, but until the first battles between carrier aircraft took place there could be no answers to most of the problems of fighting carrier forces defensively. In 1942 each type of warship was regarded as capable of providing for itself, and carrier aircraft were considered the main means of defense against enemy air attack. Both the Japanese and the Americans tended to think in terms of carriers and assigned escorts dividing within a task force to fight separately. Neither side realized the extent to which all warships were interdependent and had to stay concentrated in what was in effect an "all-arms" battle group.

For these reasons, therefore, no criticism that centers upon the alleged failure of the Japanese to bring heavy forces to the defense of the carriers is automatically valid. It is probable that more heavy units with the carrier forces would have been beneficial; beyond this cautious statement nothing can be said with certainty except that the deployment of the *Yamato*, *Mutsu* and *Nagato* to the screen of the First Carrier Striking Force would not have been an effective substitute for the absence of the *Shokaku* and the *Zuikaku* or, alternatively, for the *Junyo*, *Ryujo* and *Zuiho*. Yet one further consideration should be noted. For a man with so formidable a reputation as a pioneer of naval aviation, Yamamoto's failure to come to grips with this problem of defensive measures and tactical organization and doctrine is surprising. It is not that Yamamoto did not provide an answer to the problems of defensive fighting; it is that he seems to have made no attempt to tackle the problems in the first place. Much of the praise that has been bestowed upon him for his advocacy of air power seems to have ignored this particular matter.

On the matter of Yamamoto taking the heavy units into the van to ease problems of command and control the situation is somewhat clearer. Like Nimitz, Yamamoto believed that the proper place for a fleet commander in a battle was ashore. There a commander could watch a battle develop and have access to information not necessarily available to a fleet or task force commander afloat. Ashore a commander would not be beset with the distractions that arise at sea. He was certain to have one facility that a commander at sea would lack: the ability to communicate with his forces. At sea any force had to observe radio silence until its position was known to the enemy. Yet for Operation MI, when close supervision and coordination of the actions of a large number of task forces was essential, Yamamoto chose to go to sea—and to take up a position, the only position, where he could not exercise command during the critically important advance to contact phase. On two occasions during this phase Yamamoto decided not to compromise his position by making signals to Nagumo's carrier force—with catastrophic results. He would have been able to communicate had he either stayed ashore or gone to sea with the carrier force.

Yamamoto's ostensible reason for staying back from the vanguard force was his desire not to break up the existing task forces and patterns of operations which had been built up over the previous months. An unwillingness to break up a winning team was a good reason not to alter existing arrangements, and as a fleet commander he obviously had no wish to add to his already considerable responsibilities the extra duties regarding the conduct of a carrier battle. Yet there was an obvious inconsistency on this score. Yamamoto had little confidence in Nagumo. A deep personal antipathy of many years' standing divided the two men, and Yamamoto blamed Nagumo for having bungled the attack on Pearl Harbor by not carrying out a follow-up attack on 7 December. Still, for the Midway operation he chose neither to replace Nagumo nor to go into the van himself. Clearly he regarded even Nagumo as capable of discharging the tasks that he had been set, and he believed that by staying behind the carriers his own Main Body would be in the right position to take advantage of Nagumo's assured success.

The reason Yamamoto refused to recast the composition of his task forces and take himself and his battle force into the vanguard with the carriers returns, once more, to the nature of the battle he expected to fight. As Yamamoto saw matters, he, Takasu and Kondo would be in position to pounce as the Americans rose to the bait of the Aleutians and/or Midway. The battle forces would lurk in the wings, out of sight, until the carrier exchange was over, when they would emerge and deliver the coup de grace. But against what? The enemy battle line, which had been destroyed at Pearl Harbor? According to Japanese intelligence estimates the Pacific Fleet might have two battleships and about one dozen cruisers with which to oppose the Japanese, and the *Yamato*, *Mutsu*, and *Nagato*, plus Takasu's *Hyuga*, *Ise*, *Fuso* and *Yamashiro*, hardly needed to be on hand to deal with such a meager force.

The various parts of the plan for Operation MI did not hang together. The cardinal error was to divide the objective into two parts, or three with Operation AL. Then there was the erroneous assumption that the battle line was to be the main instrument of destruction in a fleet engagement. It is surprising that "battleshipitis" still pervaded Combined Fleet planning for this operation after all that had happened over the previous six months. The lesson that should have been drawn from the opening encounters of the Pacific war was that surface units could only operate under conditions of assured air supremacy and that their separation from carrier forces could be nothing more than an insurmountable handicap, in this case self-imposed and unnecessary: surface forces had no capacity for an existence independent of the carrier orbit, except under certain specific circumstances which did not apply to Operation MI. It was understandable that the gunnery club disliked being tied to carriers, especially when an artillery duel might be in the offing; under those circumstances carriers were no more than a dangerous liability. But such circumstances were certain to be occasional and not the norm, and in most instances battle and heavy forces could be useful only if they were with the carriers.

Such matters passed unappreciated by a commander in chief and a staff convinced of their own infallibility in assessing the nature of the battle they intended to provoke. Yamamoto's plan of campaign was unreal. It was put into effect at the insistence of the fleet commander, despite the considerable body of opinion within the navy that was opposed to the plan either as a whole or in part. The leading members of the Naval General Staff—Nagano, Ito and Fukudome—seemingly had their reservations, though their collective attitude was so contemptibly supine that perhaps they deserve the greatest share of responsibility for such an inane operation. The two most important members of the Plans Division, Tomioka and Miyo, had done their best to oppose Operation MI, but without the support of their superiors they could do nothing. The most important officers in the carrier force, Nagumo, Kusaka and Yamaguchi, and Captain Tomeo Kaku of the *Hiryu*, were opposed to the air part of the plan. Kondo was resolutely opposed to the whole plan, as was Inoue.

In the face of this formidable assembly of skeptics it is surprising that the plan ever managed to get under way. That it did so was the result of several circumstances. First, many of those who doubted the wisdom of Operation MI had opposed the Pearl Harbor operation, and Yamamoto had been proved right on that occasion. The commander in chief of the Combined Fleet had shown infallible judgment to date, and this placed his opponents at a decided psychological disadvantage. Second, two of the main personnel in the Naval General Staff, Ito and Fukudome, had come to the staff after having served as Yamamoto's chief of staff. This must to some extent have prevented their formulating the type of opposition that Operation MI should have provoked amongst the upper echelons of the staff. Third, Nagumo did not speak out against the plan. He is generally regarded as having been indifferent to the proposed operation and of the opinion that his carrier force could carry out its mission with little difficulty. It would appear, however, that having been upbraided by Yamamoto for his mis-handling of the Pearl Harbor attack, Nagumo was reluctant to express his real feelings with regard to Operation MI. His silence on the matter of the operation helped prevent the opposition to it from taking coherent form, and herein was one main reason Yamamoto was able to overcome all criticism of his plans. There was no collective opposition. The objections crystallized at different times and focused on different details with the result that they were each dismissed in turn.

What wrecked any chance of these fitful objections injecting some note of realism into the planning of the Combined Fleet was two events: the Doolittle Raid of 18 April and the battle of the Coral Sea. While this is neither the time nor the place to consider the Coral Sea in any detail, its importance should not be underestimated. In the action the Japanese lost the *Shoho* and the Americans lost the *Lexington*, while the other three carriers engaged in the action, the *Shokaku*, the *Zuikaku* and the *Yorktown*, suffered varying degrees of damage. It has already been noted that in the aftermath of the battle the Japanese should have recast their plans for Operations AL and MI. For the Japanese the lesson that should have emerged was the same one that was drawn from the experience of 10 March, that they could only proceed with caution. But the Japanese navy read into the battle what it wanted, which was that the elite First and Second Carrier Divisions had little to fear if the somewhat despised Fifth Carrier Division (as was claimed) could put down a carrier of the *Lexington* class and either sink or incapacitate one of the *Yorktowns*. If the Coral Sea was the best that the Americans could do, the First Carrier Striking Force was not going to sweat over dealing with the enemy. Therefore while the Coral Sea should have had the effect of forcing the Japanese to tread more warily and of strengthening Miyo's arguments for delay, it did precisely the opposite. It confirmed Japan's low esteem of American fighting abilities, and it seemingly sanctioned the arrangements in hand for Operation MI.

It was the Doolittle Raid, however, that finally quashed the opposition to Yamamoto's plan of campaign. The outline of the raid can be recounted quickly, since it does not amount to much and will be told in full in a later chapter. What the Japanese tried to decry as the "Do Nothing Raid" was a strike by sixteen B-25B twin-engine Mitchell bombers from the U.S. Army Air Force's Seventeenth Bombardment and Eighty-ninth Reconnaissance Groups against Tokyo and other Japanese cities. The sum of the damage done in the raid was small, the only damage of military significance being that inflicted on the submarine tender *Taigei* in dry dock at Yokosuka. She was then undergoing a conversion that was to result in her being commissioned in November as the carrier *Ryuho*.

The significance of the raid was that it was mounted by a carrier task force consisting of the *Enterprise* and the *Hornet* and therefore pointed to the dangers that would face Japan until the time that the destruction of the American carriers was achieved. Another lesson that had to be learned from the raid was the permanent vulnerability of Japan and her conquests to attack from the east. With only Marcus and a line of converted trawlers in the vast wastes that separate Wake and Kamchatka, the whole of this Pacific area was Japan's Achilles' heel, and it was obvious to any thoughtful Japanese naval commander that nothing was to be gained by conquering and holding Southeast Asia and the Indies if Japan herself was left open to attack by an enemy who was certain to repeat his attacks in ever-growing strength.

Though Combined Fleet planning had suggested that the enemy might carry out a raid on the Japanese homeland, the reality of this attack still came as a shock and humiliation to a service that saw an assault on the sacred soil of Japan as a reflection of its competence and something that diminished its prestige and authority. In this way the raid played directly into Yamamoto's hands: it could not do anything but strengthen his argument that Midway should be taken as an outpost for Japan and as the means of bringing the enemy to battle. The Doolittle Raid did not support Yamamoto's arguments on any rational basis but transformed the operation that he planned into an article of faith. No one could argue with effect against Operation MI after 18 April; the raid belatedly forced the bulk of the Imperial Navy, hitherto intoxicated by its own success, to face up to the all-consuming need to move against the Americans. It was this almost frenzied determination to undertake an offensive into the central Pacific as a result of 18 April that stifled so much of the opposition to the dubious aspects of Operation MI.

Thus by the beginning of May the Imperial Navy found itself committed to a series of operations collectively designed to bring about an end to the war but all of which were flawed by inconsistencies and contradictions. Both Operation MO and Operations AL and MI combined a potentially dangerous division of forces with an overelaborate and mechanical naval ballet that largely relied on one element of war for success. The Japanese had to confuse the enemy and steal a march upon him, getting themselves into a position to decide the timing of events. To achieve surprise they had to have watertight security. On both matters the Japanese made fateful mistakes. They made the abstract and variable element of surprise central to their plans; they did not realize that surprise is an addition to adequate strength and not a substitute for it. Planning should always ensure sufficient means for success in case surprise is not achieved. In determining the arrangements for Operation MI the Japanese were confused about the nature and use of surprise. On the matter of security they made the mistake of thinking that their communications were secure. The Fourth Section of the Naval General Staff, which was in charge of codes, ciphers and security matters, believed that Japanese signals were not understood and that in any event the intricacies of the Japanese language were enough to baffle the enemy. To the Japanese there were no dangers in a practice that any Western armed service would have regarded as a serious breach of security. The raid on Ceylon in April was code named Operation C, and all three major operations on which the Japanese were to embark in May and June were given signatures that corresponded directly to the individual objectives: Operation MO involved Port Moresby, Operation AL the Aleutians, and Operation MI Midway. Though each objective had its own coded designator—that of Midway was AF—the choice of signatures for these operations was by any standard highly injudicious. In many other ways, moreover, security for the operation was lax. One squadron asked, in a low-grade cipher signal, for its mail to be directed to Midway from mid-June on. This is only one of many examples that can be cited of poor security procedures, which indicated an unusual carelessness—and confidence—about the forthcoming operation.

Thus the Japanese risked the element of surprise that was so crucial to success. The Americans knew that there was something in the making long before the Japanese task forces set sail for Operations AL and MI. Three matters convinced them that the Japanese planned to attack the Aleutians and Midway. First, in the course of the administrative preparations for Operations AL and MI the Combined Fleet was forced to use radio on an extensive basis. Over 1,500 high-priority signals dealing with a whole range of matters had been sent out by the Combined Fleet. Individual ships had been given their orders, their queries had been answered, the various force commanders had talked to other commanders and to their units. The sheer volume of radio traffic could only indicate one thing: that some major operation was being prepared. Second, through traffic analysis and reconnaissance the Americans found that the Japanese were concentrating their forces in the Marianas. This had to mean the Japanese were planning an operation in the central Pacific area. Third, and most critical of all, the Americans had broken the Imperial Navy's highest-grade codes and by May were reading an increasingly large part of Japanese signals. By cracking what to the Americans was known as the JN-25b code, they were able to piece together many aspects of Operations AL and MI. They had deduced the Japanese timetable and objectives, and even if they erred considerably in assessing the enemy's battleship and destroyer strengths the Americans had a very accurate idea of the number of carriers, cruisers and submarines that the Japanese intended to employ for their offensives. The Japanese believed that they had surprise and time on their side: the Americans knew that the former, at least, was denied the enemy. When he devised his plans for Midway Yamamoto knew that the odds were difficult to assess. What he could never have guessed was how the odds were being raised against his fleet by the breach of its security.

Yet for all these errors of commission and omission—perhaps because of them—there remains a paradox, the most perplexing of the many that litter the Midway story. The Japanese began Operations AL and MI with a bad plan that was compromised. They evolved an operational pattern and timetable that invited defeat. They committed themselves to a series of operations that broke every rule in the manual of staff procedures. Yet they should have won, both in the Coral Sea and off Midway. During both battles the Japanese stood on the brink of overwhelming success, and in each case they should have wrapped the enemy up with little difficulty—in spite of their plans. Instead they lost both battles, and their defeat at Midway was disastrous, so disastrous that never again did the Japanese carrier service give battle on the basis of real equality. Of all the paradoxes of the Pacific war in general and of Midway in particular, this is perhaps the most tantalizing and, for the Americans and their allies, the most satisfying.

PART II

The Allied Situation

CHAPTER 4

The Allies and the Southwest Pacific

By April 1942 the Japanese had all but secured every one of the objectives in Southeast Asia for which they went to war. When the *Lexington* and the *Yorktown* administered the first serious loss to any Japanese landing force off Lae and Salamaua, the British in Malaya and Singapore, Hong Kong and northern Borneo, and the Dutch in the Indies, had capitulated. The final defeat of the British in Burma and of the Americans in the Philippines was assured. When Inoue, the Combined Fleet and the Naval General Staff turned their collective attention to the question of Japanese policy in the southwest Pacific in light of the events of 10 March, they did so with a confidence that came from more than three months of solid achievement and success. The reverse of 10 March induced a degree of caution into Japanese deliberations, but their optimism and ambitions did not have to be modified. As long as sensible precautions were observed, as long as they took a little more care in future, there was no reason for the Japanese to suppose that they would not repeat their earlier successes.

In retrospect, however, it can be seen that the Japanese decision to expand the scope of their operations in the southwest Pacific, and to commit fleet carriers to the theater, came at least three or four months too late to be acted upon effectively. What in March and April seemed to be a "stabilizing of the front"—if it is realistic to refer in such terms to a theater of operations largely made up of sea and sky—along a line of mutual but temporary exhaustion was in fact something more than a passing phenomenon. In these months the Japanese prepared to carry the war forward into the Coral Sea, but events were to show that the "front" was to last longer than anyone on either side realized at the time.

This was strange, because in the first four or five months of the war the Allied "front" in the southwest Pacific theater was little more than a series of overlapping gaps. Yet by the time the Japanese undertook a major offensive in the theater their moment had passed. For a period the whole of the southwest Pacific had been all but undefended, and the small Allied forces in the theater could not have contested even a modest Japanese enterprise had such an effort been mounted immediately after the Rabaul and Kavieng operations on 23 January. If the Japanese had made an effort with their carrier forces in the southwest Pacific without waiting for the fall of Southeast Asia, they would have brushed aside the token opposition that was all the Allies could have mustered in the area at that time. After Rabaul, however, the carriers moved not to the south or to the east but to the west, where their efforts were largely superfluous. Theirs was a marginal contribution to the Japanese victories along the line of the Malay Barrier. Yet at the very time that carriers contributed so little to the speed and extent of Japanese success in Southeast Asia, the Allied position in the southwest Pacific was wide open to attack. At that stage of proceedings and with scarcely any effort on their part, the Japanese could then have registered the success that proved beyond them when they moved into the area in strength in May.

This was not how the Allies saw the situation at the time. The Japanese did not seem slow in developing offensive operations into the southwest Pacific; rather they appeared to be picking up the offensive option in the area far too quickly for the comfort of nations whose initial experiences in the Pacific war had been disastrous. None of the Allies—the Americans, Australians, British, Dutch or New Zealanders—were prepared for the ordeal they faced after 7 December. None had ever fought a major war in the Pacific, certainly not a war against a superior naval power that held the initiative and choice with regard to the timing and direction of operations. For the Dutch the experience was one from which there would be no recovery, and for Britain and her two dominions, Australia and New Zealand, the experience threatened to be the same.

In the opening weeks of the war the Japanese moved from victory to victory, seemingly impervious to the drag of miles on men and machinery. Their offensive seemed effortless, and it was conducted with a flair that rightly establishes it as one of the most impressive campaigns in the whole of military history. In these weeks the Japanese moved with a single-mindedness that was far beyond the reach of their enemies. By contrast, the Allied situation was one that resembled the chaos of an anthill after it has been disturbed. But the appearance was deceptive.

For the British, Dutch and Australasians the transformation of what had been until December 1941 essentially a European conflict into a global war could not be an orderly affair; for the Americans the change from neutrality to belligerency could not be a measured and regulated process. Confusion inevitably accompanied Allied efforts in the aftermath of the extension of the war to the Pacific, yet at the same time a certain order began to emerge

The Southwest Pacific

within their camp. This order was too little and too late to save the Dutch
and to deny the Japanese control of Southeast Asia, but it began to make
itself felt in time to frustrate Operation MO, and it proved crucial in
directing the course of the war into the hitherto neglected southwest Pacific
theater.

The Allied reaction to the outbreak of the Pacific war crystalized at three
distinct levels, and it took time for the efforts of the various powers to be
harmonized and take effect. First, there was the immediate reaction at the
local level as the British, Australians and New Zealanders attempted to
meet the emerging Japanese threat by sending reinforcements to their
various garrisons and possessions. Second, the two major Allied powers,
Britain and the United States, abrogated for themselves direction and
control of the Allied war effort. In the short term this was of small account,
since the immediate situation in Southeast Asia was beyond recall, but in

the long term they were successful in establishing a command system that stood the test of war—though it was not without its troubles and it was not to everyone's satisfaction. Third, the process of developing a joint Allied command was accompanied by structural, personnel and policy changes within the American high command. At the very time of their initial dealings with the British and the lesser Allies the Americans were forced to undertake a fundamental reappraisal of basic policy as the weakness of these newly acquired Allies became slowly apparent. This revelation gradually led to the inescapable conclusion, accepted by Washington during February and March, that there was no effective substitute for American power and that the United States would be called upon to help weaker associates who had earlier been regarded as potential sources of support.

This latter point was the significant one: it took time for both the Americans and their allies to appreciate the extent to which the power of decision rested with Washington after the start of the war. The habits of decades could not be discarded overnight. Before the war the Americans had dealt with the British more or less on the basis of equality, as they had done for generations. Minds that had been conditioned to think in terms of the reality of British power could not immediately grasp the implications of the eclipse of that power in the opening weeks of the Pacific war. During the Christmas season of 1941, for example, the Royal Navy had been reduced to the nadir of its fortunes, or so it seemed. In the forty days and forty nights between 14 November and 23 December the British had suffered losses that exceeded those incurred by the Americans at Pearl Harbor. The battleships *Prince of Wales*, *Barham*, *Queen Elizabeth* and *Valiant*; the battle cruiser *Repulse*; the fleet carrier *Ark Royal*; the light cruisers *Dunedin*, *Neptune*, *Sydney* and *Galatea*; and the fleet destroyers *Stanley* and *Kandahar* had all been lost to enemy action, and on Christmas Day 1941 the Royal Navy had but one modern battleship, the *King George V*, and two modern fleet carriers, the *Victorious* and *Indomitable*, in service.

The eclipse of British naval power in late 1941 lay at the root of American problems in these months. Prewar strategic thinking in the United States had been based on the assumption that in a two-ocean war the American priority would be the Atlantic and European theaters of operations. As far as the Americans were concerned, there was nothing the Japanese could do in the western Pacific and the Far East that could compare to the threat posed to American security by a Nazi-controlled Europe.[1] The Americans calculated that they would have to stand on the defensive in the Pacific while the German menace was eliminated. This calculation was made in the sure knowledge that the United States had the measure of Japan; there was never any doubt in the minds of American leaders that they would be able to crush Japan in the long run.[2]

The first weeks of the Pacific war brought home to the Americans the fact that two of the assumptions underpinning their basic strategic doctrine either were wrong or had been overtaken by events. First, their concept of a two-ocean conflict envisioned a war fought in the company of powerful allies. Even as late as the ABC-1 staff discussions of February 1941, American plans for conducting a defensive campaign in the Pacific while Germany was tackled included the active participation of the British in the defense of Southeast Asia and the southwest Pacific.[3] Accumulating evidence suggested that Britain was struggling for sheer survival in the Mediterranean and the Atlantic and that she could not possibly be an effective ally in the Pacific. Moreover, in the course of 1941 there were growing doubts in American circles about the British ability to hold on to Singapore. Yet up until December 1941 the Americans held fast to the ABC-1 arrangement dividing responsibility for the Pacific war between the two powers. The Americans were to assume responsibility for that part of the ocean in the western hemisphere, the British for the southwest Pacific between meridian 180° and meridian 155°E (i.e., the Australian east coast). The Americans, however, promised to help the British in their area of responsibility.[4] Second, before the war the American leadership reconciled itself to the fact that defeats and losses would be incurred if Japan struck the first blows, but it had not anticipated reverses of the magnitude that overwhelmed the Allies in the opening days and then weeks of the Pacific war. The assumption had been that the Japanese, by striking first and with their full strength, might rip a few holes in the Allied front. The first contact of war made it clear that by the time the last Japanese blows fell all that would remain of the Allied position would be debris.

In these circumstances all the Allies found themselves trapped between what they wanted to do, what they felt they had to do and what they could do as they tried to respond to events long past their control and influence. The outbreak of the Pacific war immediately increased the areas of responsibility and interest of each Allied nation without giving any of them the time to draw on the resources needed to meet widening commitments. None had the means to respond immediately and effectively to Japanese aggression. The American problem was that none of the Allies had the means of ensuring their own salvation. The friends who had earlier seemed capable of supporting the Americans in the common cause became liabilities that could only be sustained, if indeed they were capable of being sustained at all, by American power. America's new friends could not be relied upon to provide for their own defense, and they could not hold objectives that had to be held if American help to them was to be forthcoming. Washington was forced to the reluctant and alarming conclusion that Allied interests in the East could only be maintained if the Americans themselves provided the muscle, and herein lay three problems. First, the interests that had to be held lay in the southwest Pacific, across which American help had to be directed. Second, a widening commitment to the southwest Pacific would necessarily interfere with the American policy of "Germany first." Third, in the first six months of the Pacific war the Americans themselves did not have the proper means to secure this area.

War came to the United States when she was six months to a year from acquiring a minimum level of security and some three or more years from the point where her armed forces would be sufficient to guarantee victory over all aggressors. By December 1941 the United States was in the midst of a rearmament program whose scale was unparalleled in history. Already in hand were the provisions of successive annual construction programs that had culminated with the Two-Ocean Naval Expansion Act. By the end of the war the U.S. Navy was to have 5,718 major combat units in service. The U.S. Army Air Force was in the process of an expansion that was to enable it to take the lion's share of the 296,000 aircraft produced by American factories in the course of the war. The U.S. Army, similarly, was in transition, the two years before Pearl Harbor having witnessed an eightfold increase in its established strength. In December 1941 the army's officer corps alone was roughly half the size of the army's entire 1939 establishment, when 188,565 officers and men had been under arms. By 1940 this total had grown to 267,767; by December 1941 it had mushroomed to a total of 93,172 officers and 1,367,826 men, and the end of expansion was nowhere in sight. Under the terms of the 1940 mobilization program the army establishment in the spring of 1942 was to be 1,800,000 officers and men, and the terms of successive reviews conducted that spring ultimately envisaged the creation of an army of 334 divisions, plus antiaircraft units and formations. This total excluded the army air force.[5] But these goals seemed far away in December 1941. The navy at the outbreak of war found itself in possession of three fleets, with a two-ocean responsibility and a one-ocean capability, if that. The Pacific Fleet was unable to match the numbers—of any kind of ship—that the Imperial Navy commanded, even with the aid of transfers from the Atlantic Fleet. U.S. air losses at Pearl Harbor could be made good in less than a week in American factories, but new ships could not be improvised. The four units of the *South Dakota* class could be more than adequate replacements for the *Arizona, California, Nevada, Oklahoma* and *West Virginia*, lost at Pearl Harbor, but the first of the new battleships, the *South Dakota* herself, was not to be commissioned until 20 March, and the last, the *Alabama*, not until 16 August. The new *Essex*-class fleet carriers were not to appear in significant numbers until the second half of 1943. The army air force, in December 1941, was so weak in terms of offensive power that it was virtually insignificant. For example, there were only about 100 Flying Fortresses in the United States on which to draw for overseas service in December 1941. The army was no better placed. It was large but unready. The influx of manpower had not been matched by a commensurate growth of offensive power: supply, training and organization had failed to keep pace with the flow into the training schools. For all its numbers the army had but one infantry division and one antiaircraft regiment ready for combat in December 1941. It had already activated two cavalry, five armored and twenty-nine infantry divisions, but the first sixteen of these divisions were not to be ready until March 1942. In December 1941, besides the two formations ready for service, three divisions were almost ready for service and another five were to complete their training in the not-too-distant future.[6] The problem for the Americans, however, was that overwhelming numbers of warships, aircraft and military units in 1943 or 1944 were of no use in December 1941, when they had insufficient force to face up to the crises that confronted them and their allies, not just in the Pacific, but in the Atlantic, in the Mediterranean and, less immediately, in Russia. The real loss the Americans suffered at Pearl Harbor and the Philippines at the start of the war could be counted not so much in numbers of warships, aircraft and men but in terms of time.

At the very first opportunity the Americans assured their allies that they would not cut their losses in the Pacific after Pearl Harbor. At the first liaison conferences after the attack, in Chungking (17–23 December) and Singapore (18–20 December), U.S. representatives indicated their country's determination to pick up the Japanese challenge and to assume an increasingly active role in the prosecution of the Pacific war.[7] But, of course, this was easier said than done, and the declarations sat ill beside the initial intention of the chief of naval operations, Admiral Harold R. Stark, to renege on the original American promise to help the British in the task of securing the southwest Pacific. This promise had been given as part of the division of the Pacific into American and British spheres of responsibility at ABC-1, but in the aftermath of Pearl Harbor Stark was reluctant to contemplate any American involvement west of meridian 180°.[8] Given the nature of the losses sustained at Pearl Harbor, it was perhaps not surprising that Stark should attempt to limit America's immediate commitments in this way and confine her resources to those areas that had been defined in prewar American planning, which had ended at Eastern (or American) Samoa.

American strategic planning had concentrated upon securing Eastern Samoa, its line of communication with Pearl Harbor and various islands that acted as outposts for the latter.[9] Any American concentration on the latter islands hardly amounted to their becoming increasingly involved in the Pacific war, but as Washington was beginning to realize, there was a considerable difference between what was desirable and what was imperative. However much Stark might have wanted to limit American involvement to the defense of immediate national priorities, the logic of the situation pulled the Americans ever further to the west because the outbreak of war forced them to reconsider their Philippines policy.

Leaving aside the West Coast, there were three places the Americans had to hold to ensure their security and to conduct the war against Japan: Alaska, Oahu and the Panama Canal Zone. Retention of these latter two was essential if the Americans were to maintain a midocean capability. The Alaskan bases at Dutch Harbor and Kodiak were important, but they could probably have been lost without too serious an effect on the American war effort. The main base of the Pacific Fleet and the artery of the canal, however, were nonnegotiable. They had to be held and secured against attack at any price, since their loss or destruction would certainly cripple any American effort in the Pacific.

Distance conferred on the Canal Zone a large measure of immunity from attack (not that this deterred the Japanese from trying to devise the means to destroy the western locks and render the canal inoperable).[10] In the immediate aftermath of 7 December, however, the Americans naturally feared for the security of Pearl Harbor. Reinforcements were promised the garrison on a large scale, but as the extent of the Japanese commitment in Southeast Asia became obvious and the days passed with no follow-up operation against Oahu by the Japanese, the fears subsided. By the end of December Washington felt sufficiently confident about Pearl Harbor that it no longer considered the base's security its first priority in the Pacific.[11] Within another month the Americans were able to begin sailing merchantmen to and from Pearl Harbor independently, and between 16 January and 12 February a thorough review of Hawaii's needs resulted in the decision not to reinforce the garrison there beyond the level initially promised but yet to be achieved.[12] In retrospect it is all too easy to assert that this decision could have been made not on 12 February but on 12 January or even 12 December and, moreover, that the Americans need not have sent any reinforcements to Oahu at all, but such penetration of the situation was scarcely possible in the aftermath of the greatest defeat ever suffered by the U.S. Navy.

The initial concern for the security of Alaska, Oahu and the Canal Zone inevitably represented a loss of time, resources and effort that the Americans could not afford given the situation in the Pacific as a whole, especially when, as we have noted, events were dragging the Americans westwards and focusing their attention on the Philippines. These islands, which were the only American colonial possession in the Far East and which were scheduled to receive their independence in 1944, had a pernicious influence on American policymaking. Before the war the Americans had realized that the Philippines, like Wake and Guam, were indefensible. The U.S. Navy had based its war plans on the assumption that it would take two years to fight its way to the islands through the maze of Japanese-held islands between the Philippines and Hawaii.[13] U.S. Army plans had envisaged its garrison on Luzon being able to hold out for about six months.[14] In 1941, however, the Americans had decided to try to hold the Philippines as an air base, this idea of using concentrated air power on the islands being part of the deterrence policy they attempted to apply against Japan in 1941. In the second half of the year various reinforcements were directed across the Pacific to the Philippines as part of this effort. But there was an inconsistency in American policy that not even the outbreak of war dispelled. In the months before the start of the Pacific war the American high command was confused by the switch from a policy of abandoning islands that could not be defended to one of trying to defend islands as part of a deterrence effort—which many suspected was doomed to failure in any event. But even after the start of hostilities, when the twin policies of deterrence and the defense of the Philippines stood in ruins, confusion persisted because for political and emotional reasons the American leadership refused to face up to the loss of the Philippines and its garrison. The islands ceased to have any value to the American war effort unless left to their fate, unless the United States abandoned them to use to full effect the time their sacrifice bought the Allied cause. Japanese superiority on, above and around the islands was too great to allow any other course. But after the start of the war the Americans found it impossible to be as coldly clinical about the loss of the Philippines as they had been—in their own confused way—before. Despite the islands and their garrison being doomed from the first day of the war, Washington felt obliged to indulge in forlorn hopes and gestures to demonstrate that it had not abandoned them.

The only help that Washington could send to the Philippines after the start of the war took the form of bombers; fighters, with their restricted range, could not make their way to the islands. Yet scarcely had the decision been made to send heavy bombers to the Philippines than the logistical problems inherent in the action began to proliferate with bewildering complexity. All these problems narrowed down to the two that stemmed immediately from the decision. First, as we have seen, the U.S. Army Air Force lacked a strong strategic reserve and therefore had virtually no heavy bombers to spare for the Philippines. Second, there was no simple and effective way to get even the fewer bombers there were from the United States to the Philippines, and if there had been, problems of maintenance and supply would certainly have eroded any attempt to concentrate strength as rapidly and remorselessly as combat losses.

At the root of this second difficulty was the tide of enemy conquest, which had swept away the direct ferry route between Oahu and the Philippines as well as suitable bases in the Philippines. After the loss of Guam, Wake and the airfields of central Luzon, Midway was all that was left of the stations that had once made up America's central Pacific route to the Far East. Furthermore, the airfields of the southern Philippines that had not fallen to the Japanese could not be used by American heavy bombers, since they lacked the troops, antiaircraft guns and fighters that were needed to secure them against the attacks that their use was sure to provoke. Thus any American attempt to send bombers to the Philippines was made difficult by the lack not only of a direct route to the islands but of a secure base in the Philippines as well.

Not until it was too late had a serious attempt been made to pioneer other routes from the central Pacific to the Far East. The loss of Guam and Wake had been accepted before the war, but the full implications of this had been only belatedly appreciated. It was not until September 1941 that the army air force tested an alternative route to the Philippines by flying from Oahu through Midway, Wake, Port Moresby and Darwin to Luzon, but even this route was impractical because it staged through Wake.[15] The only option for the Americans was to bring a route farther back to the southeast and deeper across the southwest Pacific, rather than across the line of the central and western Pacific and Japanese possessions. The inescapable conclusion was that any attempt to stage aircraft to Luzon had to be carried out by using various islands in the southwest Pacific and northern Australia. Yet before October 1941 the Americans lacked the means even to explore the possibilities of such a route. Apart from Pago Pago on the island of Tutuila in Eastern Samoa, the Americans did not have any bases in the southwest Pacific and, what was worse, they had no other islands in the theater on which they could construct the 7,000-ft runways needed to handle heavy bombers.[16] Other countries owned suitable islands, but until October 1941, when its offending sections were repealed, the Neutrality Act prevented the Roosevelt administration from approaching such countries in order to seek facilities. In October, when the necessary authorizations were forthcoming, Washington approached various governments with a view to securing bases. Cooperation in meeting the needs of the U.S. Army Air Force was forthcoming, but these matters took time and, as we have seen, time was one of the many things denied the Americans in the last three months of peace and the first three months of war. Moreover, it was hardly surprising that while the various governments asked to provide bases proved willing to do so, the one authority that was unresponsive to the needs of the army air force was the U.S. Navy. It claimed that its own requirements on the islands where it had priority of construction would delay meeting the other service's needs until August 1942.[17]

As it happened, many of the airstrips that the army air force sought at such short notice were functioning in February 1942, and even in January a skeleton route, handling very small groups of Liberators and Flying Fortresses, stretched across the southwest Pacific.[18] But in the first desperate weeks of the war this route was not functioning, and the Americans had to resort to an even more hazardous expedient in order to get bombers from the United States to the Far East. Though the army air force feared it would incur prohibitively high losses in doing so, it sent its Flying Fortresses from the United States via the Caribbean, Africa and India in order to bring them to the Philippines garrison and to the British and Dutch on the line of the Malay Barrier. The rate of attrition turned out to be much less than what was feared: only nine of the fifty-three Flying Fortresses flown along this route failed to reach their intended destination.[19]

But the impact of the bombers sent along this route to the Indies and northern Australia proved negligible. They were too few and scattered for there to have been any real chance of checking or inflicting a significant loss on the enemy, and in the end the problems of maintenance and supply proved to be handicaps that could not be overcome. The Caribbean-Africa-India route was never anything more than a hazardous expedient to meet a hopeless situation; there was no effective substitute for a properly consti-tuted line of communication to Southeast Asia across the southwest Pacific. But this route could not be improvised any more than the eastbound route could be used once British and Dutch possessions in western Southeast Asia fell to the enemy. Handling small packets of bombers along the various hastily constructed airstrips on islands in the southwest Pacific was not the same thing as having a route with all the facilities needed to sustain a heavy traffic flow over an indefinite period. Yet from all the chaotic improvisation of the first days of the war, two things emerged on which the Americans had to act for want of anything better. First, given the situation throughout Southeast Asia, the only area from which heavy bomber forces could operate was northern Australia. Considerations of time, distance, aircraft ranges and security imposed a Hobson's choice on the Americans in this matter, though in reality their choice fit a pattern established at the begin-ning of the war. When hostilities began the Americans had a seven-ship convoy—carrying seventy aircraft, their crews, two field artillery regi-ments and supplies—en route to the Philippines. In the immediate after-math of the Pearl Harbor attack this convoy was ordered back to Oahu before proceeding to Brisbane, the revised American intention being to send forces northward to meet the advancing Japanese tide. The convoy reached Brisbane on 24 December, and after it arrived Washington in-formed General Douglas MacArthur, commander of the Philippines garri-son, that forces would be built up in Northern Australia, specifically around Darwin, to bring help to the beleaguered islands. In fact little came of this intention. On the twenty-eighth most of this particular convoy left Brisbane for Darwin, which it reached on 5 January. One of the units, the 1st/131st Field Artillery Battalion from the Texas National Guard, went forward to Java, where it was forced to surrender in the course of the general capitulation of the Indies in March. Five separate attempts were

made to fly fighters to Java from Darwin before the loss of Bali and Timor in
the third week of February brought that particular effort to a halt.[20] Second,
if the Americans were in earnest about the concentration of their strength in
northern Australia, they had to establish and develop lines of communication across the southwest Pacific to Australia, and they had to make them
safe from attack.

It was this matter of the lines of communication to Australia that began
to highlight the weakness of America's allies, to make inroads into the
"Germany-first" policy and to push the United States towards the conclusion that if the southwest Pacific was to be secured, it would have to be done
through American effort. The initial step in the process that was to lead to
the emergence of a binding American commitment to this area came at the
first Anglo-American "summit meeting" held after the American entry in
the war. This was the Arcadia Conference, held in Washington from 23
December 1941 to 14 January 1942.

In the course of the Arcadia Conference the Americans and British
accepted that if the former were to establish themselves in strength in
northern Australia, they would have to secure a line of communication
from Pearl Harbor through either American Palyra or British Christmas in
the Line Islands; Canton, an Anglo-American possession in the Phoenix
Islands ; Pago Pago and/or Tongabatu (in the British-owned Tongan Islands) and/or Suva on Viti Levu, the largest of the islands in Britain's Fiji
Islands. The passage from the Panama Canal, on the other hand, also had to
include a port of call, and Bora Bora in the Society Islands was naturally
recommended for selection. Its location in the center of the Pacific made it
geographically convenient, and it was in the possession of Frenchmen who
had rallied to the Free French cause. But Bora Bora had no facilities
whatsoever, and the same was true of most of the other islands penciled in
for consideration as bases on the routes to Australia. Even at Pago Pago,
which had been under the administration of the U.S. Navy since Eastern
Samoa had become an American possession in 1899, the airstrip was no
more than ten percent complete in January 1942.[21] Herein lay the seeds of
yet another American difficulty. Given the undefended and under-
equipped state of the islands needed as staging posts, it was inevitable that
any American troop movement to the southwest Pacific would be weighted
in favor of support and garrison troops at the expense of combat
formations.[22] Coastal and antiaircraft artillery, fighters and heavy engineering equipment had to take priority over combat units and this, combined
with the chronic shortage of Allied shipping at the time, had to mean that
the commitment of large combat forces to the southwest Pacific could not
take place until the second quarter of 1942 at the earliest. Moreover, by any
reasonable standard the Americans could not contemplate offensive operations in the southwest Pacific until 1943, because it would take about a year

to build up sufficient forces and material in the theater. This was a conclusion reached by the Japanese and many Americans alike, but events were to show that matters were not to work out the way the sliderules suggested.[23]

At the Arcadia Conference American and British leaders agreed to the demarcation of responsibilities in the Pacific. Because of their concern for the link with Australia, the Americans took responsibility for Palmyra, Christmas, Canton, Samoa and Bora Bora.[24] This represented no real change of prewar American policy. The area beyond Samoa, however, was turned over to the Australasians, whom both the Americans and British pledged to assist.[25] What this meant in effect was that external support for the dominions shifted from the British, whose remaining naval forces in the Far East were certain to be tied up escorting troop convoys to Singapore and in the Indian Ocean, to the Americans.

These arrangements did not really take the Allies beyond prewar terms of reference and would not have assumed any real significance but for three reasons. First, it quickly became apparent (as we will see later) that Australians and New Zealanders were totally unable to meet the commitment placed upon them at Arcadia.[26] Second, the definition of responsibilities was made within a much wider context of strategic policy at Arcadia that saw the Americans restate their commitment to the principle of "Germany first." At the conference the British and Americans confirmed their basic belief that the defeat of Germany had to be their first priority and that such a policy necessarily involved the deployment of "only a minimum of force necessary for the safeguarding of vital interests in other theaters."[27] Notwithstanding the disastrous turn of events in the Pacific, the American leadership still adhered to the view that Germany represented America's most dangerous enemy and had to be defeated first. The Arcadia Conference revealed persistence in thinking that if the defeat of Germany was accomplished, that of Japan would not long be delayed.[28] The very real American fear was that if Germany forced either Britain or the Soviets (or both) out of the war, her domination of Europe might become too strong to be overturned. Thus the European theater had to take whatever forces were immediately available to the Americans. This had obvious implications for the Pacific. The European priority meant that army air force resources would not be made available in any significant way to the Pacific, and the allied air position in the Pacific was precarious by any standard. In terms of ground forces the position was certain to be similarly dismal, though one indirect benefit would flow from an American buildup of ground forces in Europe. Since such a buildup could only take place in Britain, the arrival of American ground troops in the United Kingdom would free British forces for service elsewhere, particularly in the Indian Ocean and in the Mediterranean theater, from which the Australians wanted to withdraw.[29] On the other hand, this raised a distinctly unsettling possibility. By the

time such a shuffling of forces was complete, the British position in the Far
East might easily be beyond recall and the effort made could be rendered
worthless.[30]

The third reason surfaced towards the end of the Arcadia Conference
and then assumed increasingly serious proportions in the first seven months
of 1942. The meaning of such terms as "minimum of force" and "vital
interest" posed no problems to the British and American leaders at Arcadia,
perhaps because they remained undefined. There was no disagreement
about the overall balance of priorities. But notice had been served on this
unanimity as a result of changes within the American high command. The
twin architects of the "Germany-first" principle were Stark and his army
counterpart, General George C. Marshall, chief of the army staff. It was a
policy endorsed by Marshall's subordinate and commander of the U.S.
Army Air Force, Lieutenant General Henry H. Arnold. Much inferior in
caliber to Marshall, Arnold was essentially a lightweight but one whom
Marshall found useful on occasions. Agreement between Marshall and
Stark was critical in forging the "Germany-first" policy, but the position of
both men was uncertain in the aftermath of Pearl Harbor. Marshall's
priorities were challenged within the army high command by his most
senior commander in the Pacific, MacArthur, and by American public
opinion, which was not indisposed to a rapid settling of accounts with
Japan. MacArthur wanted to see the entire balance of American strategic
policy switched to his own command area in Southeast Asia. This challenge was not one that could be lightly ignored.[31] Stark's position was even
more precarious than that of Marshall because Pearl Harbor was regarded
as a naval rather than a military disaster. But even if Stark had proved able
to survive this debacle, his position had been fatally compromised by a
strange and unworkable decision made by Roosevelt in the aftermath of
Pearl Harbor. Roosevelt wanted changes, the most visible being the recall
of Admiral Husband E. Kimmel, commander in chief of the Pacific Fleet.
He was to be replaced by Admiral Chester W. Nimitz, then chief of the
Bureau of Navigation. At the same time Roosevelt decided to recreate the
post of commander in chief, U.S. Fleet, which he had allowed to slip into
abeyance when he appointed Kimmel commander of the Pacific Fleet in
January 1941. The pre-1941 navy had not had fleets but rather squadrons,
or in the case of the Atlantic, patrol forces. In such circumstances the post
of commander in chief, U.S. Fleet, had some meaning, but when in
January 1941 an administrative order created the Atlantic, Asiatic and
Pacific Fleets, the post was abolished or, more accurately, not filled.
Kimmel had been designated to the post in case his fleet and any other
operated together. In the wake of Pearl Harbor, however, Roosevelt determined to recreate the post and to appoint Admiral Ernest J. King, commander of the Atlantic Fleet, to it. This Roosevelt did on 18 December in

General George C. Marshall

the shape of his somewhat notorious Executive Order 8984. King was adamant about this post no longer being a seagoing one; it had to be exercised from Washington. This was Roosevelt's intention.[32] The inevitable side effect of this move was to pass a suspended sentence on Stark as chief of naval operations and on the unanimity that had established the "Germany-first" strategy.

Stark was not to be shunted from his post until 12 March, when he went to London to take command of American naval forces in Europe. Thereafter King wore two hats, those of chief of naval operations and commander in chief, U.S. Fleet.[33] But from the time that he took up his appointment as fleet commander in chief on 30 December, there was never any doubting with whom the power of decision lay within the U.S. Navy—and King was not altogether enthusiastic about the prospect of fighting a defensive war in the Pacific while Germany was tackled. A Pacific war was, after all, a naval war, the prerogative of the U.S. Navy, and in the opening months of hostilities King brought to American deliberations something that had been conspicuously absent from earlier proceedings: a fiercely partisan approach made obvious by an abrasive advocacy of the Pacific option. At the very least he wanted a redefinition of priorities to redress what he saw as an imbalance between the Atlantic and Pacific, and when he formulated this basic demand the way was opened for a major interdepartmental battle

Admiral Ernest J. King

within the American high command in the course of 1942. On the one side
was Marshall—with Arnold brought in to present a united army front—
who was determined to maintain the "Germany-first" option at all costs.
Marshall was totally committed to launching an invasion of German-
occupied western Europe, if not in 1942 then certainly in 1943, and such a
tight timetable certainly promised a poor diet for the Pacific. On the other
side was King, who was equally determined to reverse the balance of
priorities, and to do so by degrees. A conflict arose in regard to the
southwest Pacific. Marshall was determined to resist King's increasingly
vociferous demands that reinforcements be sent to this theater. What
stiffened Marshall's resolve on this matter was his certainty that much more
than local needs were at stake in any discussion of King's strategic priorities. Marshall correctly suspected that King was determined to use any
concession as the thin end of the wedge to make room for a much wider
commitment in the Pacific; he feared that King would try to make the
southwest Pacific an open-ended commitment that would spell an end to
the European priority and the 1943 venture. Marshall's distrust of King on
these matters was well founded, but King was not being unreasonable
when he argued that the seriousness of the situation in the southwest Pacific
was sufficient cause for a revision of priorities. The difference between
Marshall and King on this question of strategic priorities was best summa-

rized in an exchange in May, when Roosevelt was called upon to decide between them. King's view was that holding the Japanese had to be the United States' "basic strategic plan in the Pacific Theater." Marshall's retort was that American policy at that disastrous stage of the war had to be supporting the Soviets, not holding the Japanese.[34]

King's views about a widening American commitment to the southwest Pacific stemmed from the potentially disastrous situation confronting Australia and New Zealand. The outbreak of the Pacific war compressed the distances that had hitherto been the chief ingredient in the strategic stance of the two dominions. Neither nation had ever had any means to ensure its own defense other than the security granted by its distance from potential enemies. For example, Sydney is 4,970 miles from Yokohama, further from Japan than Singapore, Pearl Harbor and Vancouver. Though the Japanese had established themselves in the Marshalls, Carolines and Marianas as a result of the First World War, the nonfortification clauses of the Washington Naval Treaty meant that Japanese power remained effectively well to the north of the equator for most of the interwar period. Neither Australia nor New Zealand was immediately or directly threatened before the war, especially since the line of the Malay Barrier remained in friendly hands. Moreover, Australasian security had been underwritten by the British promise to send sufficient naval forces to the Far East in the event of a crisis to ensure the safety of Singapore and the two dominions.

The combination of the British guarantee and geographical remoteness gave Australia and New Zealand a degree of security they could not provide for themselves by military means. The Australasian commitment in the Pacific remained small even as the situation in the Far East deteriorated with alarming rapidity after May 1940. New Zealand had become the first dominion to provide a garrison for a British crown colony when on 1 November 1940 her Eighth Infantry Brigade Group took up residence on Viti Levu. This formation, commanded by Brigadier W. H. Cunningham, deployed the Twenty-ninth Infantry, Thirty-fourth Infantry and the locally raised First Fijian Battalions in and around Suva and Nandali, on the eastern part of the island. On the western part, at Lautoka and Namaka, were the Thirtieth Infantry and the Second Fijian Battalions. Supporting these five hopelessly ill-equipped units was an equally inadequate and unprepared amalgam of three artillery batteries, two of them coastal and fixed, an air group of twelve aircraft of unknown age and dubious value, and a "fleet" of five patrol launches. Elsewhere in the Pacific the New Zealanders provided company-sized garrisons for the cable station on faraway Fanning Island in the Line Group, Western Samoa, and by courtesy of native troops, for Tonga and Rarotonga. In addition, coast-watching detachments were in position in various island groups in the southwest Pacific. After July 1941 there were twenty-two volunteers in the Gilbert and Ellice Islands, while compatriots were employed on the same dreary duties in the less exposed Phoenix, Tokelau, Line, Cook, Tongan, Kermadac and Chatham islands.[35]

The Australians, similarly, had garrisons and coast watchers on their seaward approaches to the northeast. For part of the interwar period a considerable part of their naval effort had been geared to providing a reconnaissance capability in the area of and to the north of the Solomons, Bismarcks, Admiralties and northern New Guinea, thereby covering the eastern and forward part of a line held in the center by the Dutch and in the west by the British. For ten years, between 1928 and 1938, part of this effort had been discharged by the seaplane tender *Albatross*, operating between shore stations at Labaun, off northern Borneo, Kepi Bial in Dutch New Guinea and Rabaul in New Britain. To cover the rear of Rabaul a seaplane base was developed at Tulagi, the administrative capital of the Solomons. But by 1941 the *Albatross* had gone, and the Australians were dependent for coast watching on civil and service personnel who manned a line from Vila, in the New Hebrides, to Wuvulu Island (west of Manus in the Admiralties) via all the major islands in the Solomons and Bismarcks. This line was supported by a rear line along the northern coast of New Guinea, which extended down to Rossel and the Rennell Islands.[36] Further afield the Australians had provided garrisons of fifty men and single batteries for each of Nauru and Ocean. Both islands had been garrisoned in February 1941 following the disastrous raid of 8 December 1940 on Nauru, when the German raiders *Komet* and *Orion* sank 25,900 tons of shipping. On the twenty-seventh the *Komet* returned to inflict such destruction on the island's port facilities that even by December 1941 the vital phosphate trade had not properly recovered.[37] The main prewar Australian effort, however, was directed at Papua New Guinea and the mandated islands.

The Australians regarded Papua New Guinea and the Bismarcks in the same light as the Americans regarded the Philippines, only the Australian feeling was even stronger: the strategic location of their territories made them part of the homeland. On Papua (the Eighth Military District since this part of New Guinea actually belonged to Australia) about 1,000 troops were deployed, almost all of them reservists from Victoria. They constituted the Forty-ninth Infantry Battalion at Port Moresby. In the mandated territories the Australians deployed more than twice that number of men. Most were coast watchers or members of small garrisons and patrols who looked after the interior and the scattered settlements of the area. The only unit in the area, the Second/Twenty-second Infantry Battalion, was at Rabaul.[38]*

---

*This division of responsibilities between the two dominions had been settled at the tripartite Pacific Defense Conference of 1939. The Australian bases at Vila and Tulagi were established as a result of decisions taken at this conference, but the Australians had no

When war broke out in the Pacific both Australia and New Zealand set about strengthening their positions to the north. By stripping depots and training schools and diverting reinforcements already earmarked for service in the Middle East, New Zealand was able to send three more battalions to Viti Levu. The heavy cruiser *Australia* and her light cousins *Perth* and *Achilles* escorted two four-ship convoys to Fiji in January, the first arriving at Suva on the sixth, the second eight days later. These reinforcements all but doubled the garrison to a strength of about 7,600 men and allowed the island to be divided into two sectors. To the west the newly arrived Thirty-fifth and Thirty-seventh Infantry Battalions joined with the two resident units to form the Fourteenth Infantry Brigade. In the eastern sector the Thirty-sixth Infantry Battalion arrived to displace the Twenty-ninth Infantry Battalion as part of the Eighth Infantry Brigade Group. The latter battalion passed into the reserve of the island's new command, the Second New Zealand Expeditionary Force.[39]

The Australians looked to the state of their northern defenses at the same time, but their response to the new situation there was more complicated than that of the New Zealanders because of their country's great size—as large as British India or the mainland United States—and its relative proximity to the enemy. The outbreak of war and the Japanese advance on the south presented Australia with four separate areas of responsibility and interest. These were Singapore, to which the Australians had already committed their Eighth Infantry Division; the islands of the Lesser Sundas, since it was likely that if the enemy came to Australia he would cross the Banda Sea; Papua New Guinea; and the open Pacific flank to the northeast of New Guinea. In addition, of course, Australia had to look to the defense of her own soil, particularly the few but widely separated urban areas and the exposed areas of Queensland and Northern Territory.

Australian policy towards the Pacific flank was simple and quickly defined. On 12 December the Australian cabinet took the decision neither to abandon nor to reinforce Rabaul. Without the means to meet the enemy at sea or in the air, there was no point in sending reinforcements to New Britain. Those already on their way were to be held where they were at present, at Port Moresby. Subsequently, the decision was taken to evacuate Nauru and Ocean. Ocean was bombed on the first morning of the war, and garrisons put on the islands to deter German raiders were out of their depth when it came to a war with the Japanese. When, as part of their Rabaul

---

intention of trying to defend them or any of their other forward positions. The Australians intended to concentrate any defensive effort at Rabaul and Noumea, and since the garrisons at Vila and Tulagi in 1942 numbered thirty and nineteen respectively, this seems to be entirely reasonable. New Zealand protests that their intention to defend Fiji and Tonga demanded a similar Australian commitment to Tulagi and Vila went unheeded.[40]

operation, the Japanese attacked Tulagi and other positions in the Solomons, it became clear to Canberra that unless these garrisons were withdrawn quickly, they would never be withdrawn at all.[41] Accordingly, the Free French destroyer *Le Triomphant* withdrew the two garrisons in February.[42]

As for Singapore, the Australians made one reinforcement effort there. This was essentially an act of honor: the Australians after the start of the war had urged Britain to make every effort to reinforce Malaya and Singapore, and thus they had to do the same.[43] On 24 January 2,849 troops—the Second/Fourth Machine Gun Battalion plus 1,907 almost untrained and ill-disciplined "reinforcements" for the Eighth Infantry Division—reached Singapore, just three weeks before the capitulation. These troops had left Sydney on 10 January and been shipped in small transports off northwest Java for the run into Singapore.[44]

In the Lesser Sundas the Australian commitment was to Amboina and Timor, both of which had air bases that could handle aircraft flying between Darwin and Java. Retention of both islands, therefore, was vital to the defense of Java. For a time it was the Allied intention to concentrate air power on Amboina in order to contest any Japanese attempt to advance into the central Indies via the Molucca Passage.[45] Thus on 10 December 1,402 troops, members of the "Sparrow Force," which contained the Second/Fortieth Infantry Battalion, the Second/Second Independent Company and a coastal battery, left Darwin for Koepang, the capital of Dutch Timor. The transports *Zealandia* and *Westralia* arrived at the port on the twelfth.[46] Four days later the Second/Second Company, along with the 400 troops that made up the entire garrison of Dutch Timor, sailed for Dili, the capital of Portuguese Timor.[47] The city was occupied the next day in the face of strong Portuguese protests. The Allied move was designed to ensure that the Japanese, who had shown what was regarded as an unhealthy interest in Dili before the start of the war, would not be able to secure the city by a coup de main. The Portuguese correctly feared that the Allied presence was certain to provoke the very action it was designed to forestall, and that it would be too weak to counter any Japanese response. At the same time as these events on Timor were unfolding, the Australians took steps to ensure the security of Ambon. On 14 December 1,090 troops from the "Gull Force," which was built around the Second/Twenty-first Infantry Battalion, left Darwin in three Dutch freighters, the *Bold*, *Valentijn* and *Patras*, with the *Australia* and the minesweeper *Ballarat* providing escort. The convoy arrived at Ambon three days later. New supplies and miniscule reinforcement were subsequently delivered by a single escorted merchantman on 12 and 22 January.[48]

These reinforcement efforts had been decided upon early in 1941 in talks with the British and Dutch. The Australians had agreed to provide two battalions for Timor and one for the more distant Amboina. But in the opening weeks of 1942 the Australians were reluctant to send more than two of the battalions from the Twenty-third Infantry Brigade to these two islands, for they knew that the Indies were doomed and any reinforcements would be lost there. When the intention to concentrate air power on Amboina was abandoned as part of the new policy of surrendering the northern islands and investing everything in the defense of Java, the Allied garrison on the island, which included 2,600 KNIL (Netherlands Indies Army) troops, was not withdrawn. The Australians' worst fears were confirmed when 1,075 of their troops were amongst the number that surrendered on 2–3 February, after the Japanese had launched a four-battalion attack on Amboina on 31 January.[49] But in the middle of February, much against their better judgment, the Australians allowed themselves to be persuaded to support an American attempt to send a national guard field artillery battalion to Timor with an infantry battalion of their own. Fortunately for the Australians, the convoy carrying these two units was forced to return to Darwin after being subjected to fierce but ineffective air attack, and no subsequent attempt was made to bolster the island's defenses.[50] With this rather abject failure came confirmation of how sensible the Australian desire was to strengthen the defenses of northern Australia itself rather than attempt to hold isolated garrisons in the Indies.[51] Timor itself was forced to capitulate on 24 February, four days after it was invaded.[52] Some 1,137 Australian troops were forced to surrender, but others, plus some Dutch troops, managed to retreat into the hills, where they conducted a laudable guerrilla campaign until they were withdrawn to Australia between December 1942 and February 1943.[53]

In the remaining area of responsibility the Australians made two efforts. On 20 December the 333-strong Second/Third Independent Company was transported to New Caledonia from Brisbane. Escort was provided by *Le Triomphant*. The company arrived on 23 December.[54] The main effort, however, was directed towards Port Moresby. Three transports, including the giant liner *Aquitania*, sailed from Sydney on 28 December in the company of the *Australia*, *Canberra*, *Perth* and *Achilles*. They reached Port Moresby on 3 January, bringing with them 4,250 troops, including two infantry battalions, and 10,000 tons of supplies. The new arrivals brought the strength of the garrison up to one field artillery and three infantry battalions, plus a single antiaircraft battery. All the units were poorly equipped,[55] undertrained and, in the case of the Fifty-third Infantry Battalion, badly disciplined.[56]

It was small wonder that the British and Americans undertook to come to the help of the Australians and New Zealanders. Even without having to wait for these various movements to take place, the two senior Allied powers knew the basic facts of life in the southwest Pacific. Both dominions were desperately weak, as their attempts to reinforce their various garrisons and islands showed only too well. The nine battalions and the pitifully small number of cruisers of these orders of battle just about represented the sum of dominion strengths in December 1941, though substantial numbers of reservists remained in Australia. The reality of the situation was that in December 1941 Australia and New Zealand were forced to pay the price for their decision to stand by Britain. Neither had hesitated to join the mother country, and both had supported her subsequent effort in the Middle East, even while the Japanese threat to Southeast Asia began to assume ominous dimensions. The Australasian formations, the Sixth, Seventh and Ninth Australian and the Second New Zealand Infantry Divisions, fought in North Africa, Greece, Crete and Syria, where they established a reputation as perhaps the finest infantry in British service in the Second World War. It is probably fair to assert that only the original Fourth Indian Infantry Division was in their class. At sea, both nations had developed naval forces as supplements to the "Kipper Navy," as the Royal Navy was known to them. The British, with their battle fleet, were expected to defend the two dominions, while the Australasians were expected to provide no more than cruiser and light support. The Australians had the heavy cruisers *Australia* and *Canberra*, plus the light cruisers *Perth*, *Hobart*, *Adelaide* and (until November 1941) *Sydney*; the New Zealanders had just the light cruisers *Achilles* and *Leander*. Smaller escorts and minesweepers were in commission in some number in the Royal Australian Navy, but in December 1941 all such units were fully committed. In the air the two royal services were extremely weak: again their main effort had already been made in the Mediterranean and European theaters of operation. By December 1941 the two dominions had about one in twelve of their populations under arms, but they had virtually nothing to show for it as the tide of war approached them.

In these circumstances it was only proper that Australian thoughts should turn to the recall of the First Australian Corps from the Middle East and to the demand that the British honor their interwar promises to send naval and military forces for the defense of Southeast Asia and the two dominions. On the first count the Australians encountered sore disappointment when the return of their forces from the Middle East proved a long and difficult process. Between November 1941 and February 1942 the situation in North Africa was delicately poised, and Australian forces could not leave the theater unless and until the battles around Tobruk had been won. Australian forces could only leave the Middle East when replacement British troops arrived in Egypt, but the unfolding of events in the Far East forced the British to divert formations bound for North Africa across the Indian Ocean to Southeast Asia. The redeployment of Australian troops from the Middle East was certain to be a slow affair.

But the question of the redeployment of Australian forces, because it had ramifications far beyond Australia herself, had to form part of a global revision of commands forced on the Allies by the extension of the war into the Pacific. Such a revision was attempted at the Arcadia Conference, but it was not one that could be put into effect immediately. Moreover, the demarcation of responsibilities and the allocation of forces depended in large measure on factors beyond the immediate control of the Allies. Constant revision as priorities shifted to meet new crises gave rise to confusion, and in these circumstances it was remarkable not that the initial attempts to improvise failed but that so little dissension upset the ranks of the Allies during the process. The reason there was so little dissent was that the Americans and British deliberately chose to exclude the minor Allies from their discussions in the sure knowledge that their dependence would ensure their compliance with Anglo-American wishes.[57] But the First Australian Corps proved to be one of the controversial matters, since the Australian government made it the point of issue in its discussions with its senior partners, Britain and the United States. Australia refused to accept the role assigned her by more powerful associates.

To meet the Japanese onslaught, it was decided at the Arcadia Conference to create a supreme command for the American, British, Dutch and Australian forces in Southeast Asia. The ABDA Command was assigned to General Sir Archibald Wavell on 29 December 1941; the command was activated on 15 January. The process of creating this command, in the face of mounting defeats in the area that was to come under its authority, was difficult enough with just the British and Americans deciding policy. Aggravating the situation were the questions and complaints raised by Australia's prime minister, John Curtin, during the period of deliberation that resulted in the creation of the command and during the brief period of its functioning. Curtin's vociferous reaction to events reflected his growing concern for Australia's security and for the way his country was being treated by her seniors.

Curtin's concern and resentment were well founded. Australia had been rendered all but defenseless as a result of her past efforts and present British enfeeblement, and the Australian prime minister bitterly resented Australian exclusion from past British decision making. In the wake of the initial disasters that befell the British on and off Malaya in the opening days of the war, Curtin had little faith in British willingness and ability to defend Singapore, still less Australia. If Curtin justifiably resented the lack of consultation when the war had been concentrated in Europe, there was no doubting his right to be somewhat displeased by continued exclusion as war swept towards Australia. Churchill was to be embarrassed at the Arcadia Conference by the revelation of Curtin's downright skepticism and transparent lack of confidence in Britain.[58] Curtin sought a proper inter-governmental consultative body to decide strategy, and he would have favored (had he known about it) the type of authority that King himself unsuccessfully proposed in the course of the conference. He wanted an American general appointed to the post of supreme commander of the ABDA area, and he wanted that area to include Australia.[59] Curtin sought clarification of Allied command arrangements in the southwest Pacific because he feared, quite rightly, that with the British pinned back to the Indian Ocean and the Americans showing no immediate signs of moving beyond Samoa, Australia would be left to fall into the void. The process whereby the ABDA Command was presented as an Anglo-American diktat to the lesser Allies had nothing to commend itself to Curtin, and he was not impressed by Wavell's appointment and by the details of ABDA Command's strategic instructions. On all these matters Curtin had to settle for less than he believed Australia deserved, but his protests did produce one favorable concession of inestimable value to his country. His demands for clarification of the status of the southwest Pacific met with a response from Washington that was almost embarassing in its haste and enthusiasm. On 8 January Washington proposed the creation of a separate command in the southwest Pacific, and after much difficulty and delay at the Australian end, Curtin agreed to the creation of the ANZAC area on 27 January. This was a naval command, covering the southwest Pacific and the Australian approaches as far north as the equator and as far east as meridian 175° W. The sea area covered the whole of Australia's approaches beyond the Fiji and Solomon groups. The Australians were to provide the major part of the naval forces of the command—which was sufficient comment on the military value of the new organization—but that was not what mattered to Curtin or to his backer in Washington who, predictably, was King. Command of the area was to be vested in an American flag officer reporting directly to King himself.[60] A tacit understanding between Curtin and King brought about the realization of each of their aims: an entangling arrangement that saw the Americans committed as far as the Australian coast for Curtin, and the means of getting into the southwest Pacific for King.

But for Curtin the process of entangling the Americans was far from complete. He knew the Americans were the only people who could guarantee Australian security. By the terms of the ANZAC arrangement he had secured the commitment of American naval forces up to Australia's east coast. The Americans were already committed to using northern Australia as the base for their future air operations in Southeast Asia. There remained the question of an American commitment of ground forces to Australia, however, and this was not forthcoming. In fact on the same day the Americans set out their proposals for the ANZAC Command, the War Department decided not to commit ground forces to Australia.[61] This, of course, reflected Marshall's concern not to get involved in an open-ended commitment in the Pacific, but the march of events, set in train by the start of the Pacific war and the disasters that overwhelmed the Allies, was to include the revision of this decision in little less than five weeks of its being made.

The first move towards revision was made almost as soon as the decision itself. On 12 January, almost at the end of the Arcadia talks, the Americans committed themselves to sending ground troops beyond meridian 180° when they undertook to garrison New Caledonia. This, of course, conformed to the declared Anglo-American intention of going to the aid of the Australians and New Zealanders, but the move was significant in its own right as well. It marked a major departure even from the orders that King had issued to Admiral Chester W. Nimitz when the latter took up his appointment as commander in chief of the Pacific Fleet on 31 December. After being told that the difference in importance between Pearl Harbor's line of communication with the West Coast and eastern Australia was only marginal,[62] Nimitz was informed that his task was "maintaining communications between the West Coast and Australia, chiefly by covering, securing and holding the Hawaii-Samoa line which should be extended to include Fiji at the earliest possible date."[63] Thus the commitment of ground forces to New Caledonia represented a considerable advance beyond the earlier commitment of naval forces to Fiji, but the economic and strategic circumstances of New Caledonia undoubtedly called for special measures. The island seemed to consist of little more than metallic ores, particularly nickel and chrome, that the Japanese might be expected to covet. It also had an airfield being rushed to completion in accordance with American requirements. These considerations alone were enough to provoke unwelcome Japanese interest in the island, but the immediate Allied concern was that New Caledonia overlooked the lines of communication between Fiji and Tonga and the Australian east coast. The loss of New Caledonia would bring Japanese bomber forces to within striking range of Sydney and Brisbane and would divert shipping bound for these ports farther to the south. If merchantmen were forced to skirt round New Zealand and head for Melbourne and Adelaide because of the dangers facing Sydney, Newcastle and Brisbane, precious days would be lost for thousands of tons of shipping. The Allied problem, therefore, was that New Caledonia presented the enemy with minimal risks but maximum temptation. New Caledonia was all but undefended. The Australian presence on the island was minimal, and the regular garrison of 3,700 French troops who had declared for the Free French cause was perhaps the worst equipped and badly supplied of all the garrisons in the southwest Pacific.[64] With such considerations to shape policy for them, the Americans on 12 January detailed one reinforced brigade for immediate movement to the island.[65]

Ten days after the decision was made the as yet unnamed force left New York in convoy. By drawing on the Twenty-sixth and Thirty-third Infantry Divisions, the so-called Task Force 6184 consisted of the Fifty-first

Infantry Brigade with the 132nd and 184th Infantry Regiments under command, the 200th Field Artillery Regiment, the Ninetieth Coast Artillery (AA) Regiment, the 3rd/224th Coast Artillery Battalion and the light 754th Tank Battalion. With service troops and one air squadron, this force numbered about 12,000 men.[66] The troops had no more than their personal weapons, and before leaving their commander had been told not to expect reinforcement. The warning, which may have been an indicator that the War Department still intended to limit its commitment to the southwest Pacific, was wrong. Task Force 6184 reached Melbourne on 26 February, and there the convoy was reloaded before setting course for Noumea, where it arrived on 12 March. In the course of the passage across the Coral Sea the convoy, joined en route by two merchantmen, was given minimal close protection but powerful distant support by the *Lexington* and the *Yorktown*. They stood between the troop ships and the enemy in the course of their attack on Lae and Salamaua. Immediately after Task Force 6184 was safely established ashore it dispatched two reinforced infantry companies from the 184th Infantry and a company of engineers in the *Westralia* for Efate. The detachment left Noumea on 16 March and arrived two days later at its destination, where it set about the construction of an advanced air base, completed in the course of the following month.[67] Subsequently, on 14 May, Efate received a proper garrison of its own when 5,000 troops of the reinforced Twenty-fourth Infantry Regiment, supported by naval artillery and aircraft, arrived on the island.[68]

While the New Caledonia force was moving across the South Pacific, other American forces were moving to establish the line of communication to Australia. After the convoy carrying Task Force 6184 left New York it picked up the convoy bound for Bora Bora at Charleston. The 3,900 men from two battalions of the 102nd Infantry Regiment, plus the Nineteenth Coast Artillery (AA) Regiment, arrived in the Society Islands on 27 January. With the troops were 500 naval personnel who would be withdrawn when certain base facilities had been constructed. This proved not to be for some time. The island itself was inimical to the construction of a base, but most of the problems that plagued the Americans on Bora Bora were self-inflicted. Indeed, the Americans themselves came to regard this particular episode as a classic example of how not to conduct such an operation. The four ships in the convoy had been packed in the wrong order with the result that the machinery needed to unload the ships had been stowed under the equipment it was to move. The convoy had not been unloaded by the time the first resupply ship arrived, and it took a total of fifty-two days for all five ships to be turned round. The base was far from complete even in June.[69]

Farther north, the occupation of Canton and Christmas went ahead at the same time. Garrisons for the two islands left San Francisco on 31

January, the army having earmarked one infantry and two artillery battalions to Christmas Island, and two infantry companies and a couple of artillery battalions to Canton. Air squadrons were assigned to both islands. Canton, occupied on 13 February, was to deploy forty aircraft, the more distant Christmas a total of twenty-five.[70]

Elsewhere on the line between Pearl Harbor and the southwest Pacific certain other pieces of the great American jigsaw had already been put in place. The three outposts of Pearl Harbor—Midway, Johnson and Palmyra—were immediate priorities for the Pacific Fleet after the raid of 7 December, but these were small bases with relatively small needs that could be met with the local resources on Oahu. They were reinforced from Pearl Harbor in the course of December, though the main reinforcement effort for Johnson did not take place until January.[71] The reinforcement of Eastern Samoa, on the other hand, was a different story; the island was of manifest importance, but its distance from Pearl Harbor meant that it could only be strengthened through a very deliberate effort. For the reinforcement operation Nimitz chose to send a considerable part of the Pacific Fleet to the south on its first major operation since the abortive attempt to relieve Wake. On 6 January one defense and four marine battalions, comprising the 4,798-man Second Marine Brigade, sailed from San Diego in three transports in order to take over the defense of Tutuila, which had only a single battalion.[72] The convoy's passage was covered by Task Force 17, the *Yorktown* and her escorts, after the latter had passed through the Panama Canal. On 19 January, off Pago Pago, the *Enterprise* and her brood joined company, the two carrier task forces going on to raid Japanese positions in the Marshalls and Gilberts after the marines were safely established ashore.

The situation that confronted the Second Marine Brigade on Tutuila proved to be a microcosm of the one confronting Washington in January and February. As the marines set about making good the many shortcomings of the island's defenses—despite the heavy rainfall that wrecked much of their effort—the local command was appalled to find that the two islands that made up Western Samoa, at their nearest point some 40 miles from Tutuila, had a garrison of just 157 New Zealanders. It was almost as if the defenselessness of Western Samoa, and that of the French island of Wallis (with its radio station) further to the west, deliberately beckoned the Japanese to come east in order to undo the American attempt to secure Pago Pago. The New Zealanders, as part of the talks that took place when the ABDA Command limped to defeat, formally suggested that Wallis and Western Samoa (and Fanning) be turned over to the Americans on 19 February,[73] more than a month after they had brought the defenselessness of Wallis and Futuna to the attention of the British and Americans.[74] It was not until 20 March that American–New Zealand negotiations resulted in vesting responsibility for the whole of the Samoan group in the United

States. Eight days later the Seventh Defense Battalion arrived on Upolu and a detachment was sent forward to Savali. Later, as reinforcement in the shape of the Third Marine Brigade arrived at Pago Pago on 8 May, the Eighth Defense Battalion moved to secure Wallis. By June over 10,000 combat troops of the U.S. Marine Corps were stationed in Samoa, while two marine air squadrons and one naval reconnaissance unit were in support.[75]

Thus by the end of January the Americans were in the process of establishing themselves along the line of communication that led to the southwest Pacific and Australia. The army air force was building up its strength in northern Australia, though not on the scale and not with the speed that would enable it to have any real impact on events then in hand. The navy and the marines had secured Oahu, Oahu's outposts and Eastern Samoa, while the army, moving to secure the various islands between Pearl Harbor and Pago Pago, was on its way to New Caledonia. In no place, except on Oahu and possibly New Caledonia, were any of the assigned forces very strong, but the logic of the deployment was the same as the Japanese philosophy of establishing island bases. The islands and their garrisons were not expected to be able to resist invasion unaided: defense of the islands was vested primarily in the fleet.

What this added up to was a remarkable shift in American policy, even without a commitment of ground forces to Australia and despite Stark's initial attempt to limit commitments after the Pearl Harbor attack. In little more than one month of war, during which the U.S. Navy suffered the worst single defeat in its history and the U.S. Army did not fare well itself, the United States accepted and acted upon responsibilities that would have been unthinkable even three months earlier. The Americans had picked up the burden of commitment of air and land forces well beyond the 180th meridian, and the navy was doing the same with the creation of the ANZAC area. The implication of these developments was obvious and profound, but equally obvious at the end of January was that they could only be profound if they had time to be effective.

To the people in the combat zone it appeared that there would not be enough time for the Americans to arrive in sufficient strength to be effective, but events were to show that in the wider context time was available, despite appearances. Because the Japanese failed to develop an offensive anywhere in the southwest Pacific other than in the Bismarcks in the first four months of 1942, the Americans were to be given the time they needed to get reinforcements into the southwest Pacific before the Japanese plan of campaign in the area began to unfold. In fact the Americans almost had time to get one reinforced infantry regiment to Efate as an outpost defense for New Caledonia before Operation MO began against Tulagi and Port Moresby, and both of these Japanese objectives were hundreds of miles short of Efate. Even though the Americans had far to go before any reasonable margin against misfortune was secured, they had enough time to bring their strength in the southern Coral Sea and around the islands of the southern Pacific up to a level unsuspected by the Japanese, and well in advance of the timetable set down by the Japanese for their post-Midway operations. The Japanese drew up plans for their attacks on New Caledonia, Fiji and Samoa during May in the belief that there were but about 3,000 Free French and American troops as garrison, about 7,500 British and American troops in the Fiji Islands and about 750 soldiers on Eastern Samoa. Their plans were based on these estimates, which were accurate only for the period before the start of hostilities. The American buildup in the south and southwest Pacific went undetected, and the strength the Japanese allotted to the Seventeenth Army was totally inadequate to deal with the forces that had arrived on the Japanese objectives in the first half of 1942. By the time Imperial General Headquarters put the finishing touches on its plans for operations in the southwest Pacific, Task Force 6184 had been reconstituted as the Americal Division after the arrival in May of the reinforced 164th Infantry Regiment. Samoa, as we have seen, had two brigades, totaling 10,000 troops, for its garrison. Viti Levu was by this time held by about 9,000 New Zealanders and Americans, while 15,000 men from the Thirty-seventh Infantry Division sailed from the West Coast on 17 May in order to relieve the New Zealanders on the island. On Tongabatu, on the other hand, the relief of the New Zealanders by the Americans was already in hand. Some 8,200 troops, consisting of one antiaircraft, two infantry and three artillery battalions, arrived on the island on 14 May.[76] Thus in spite of the disastrous state of affairs that had beset the Allies at the start of the war, the failure of the Imperial Navy to move into the southwest Pacific in the first quarter of 1942, followed by the refusal of the Imperial Army to allocate major forces to the area, contributed to the American triumph in "the battle of the buildup" in this theater.

It was not in the central and southwest Pacific that time and troops were lacking but in Australia and the ABDA area. By the end of January 1942 the Americans had put in hand the various arrangements that would enable them to secure the south and southwest Pacific, but at the same time it was becoming clear that the Allied cause in Southeast Asia could not last much longer. The Japanese sliced into the Indies following their declaration of war on the Netherlands on 11 January, a fact more visible and immediate than the dispatch of American troops to certain islands in the Pacific. After less than three weeks the ABDA Command was foundering, with the Japanese on the point of breaking through its center and separating the British in the Indian Ocean from the Americans in the Pacific. It was the imminence of this danger and the troop shortages in both the ABDA area and Australia that explains the crisis the Allies faced in the second half of

February over the question of the deployment of the First Australian Corps.

In the course of a five-way consultation between Washington, London, Cairo, Delhi and Canberra, the Australian request for the return of their divisions from the Middle East met with the British concession to return two of the Australian divisions to the Far East. The return of the Sixth and Seventh Australian Divisions formed part of a reorientation that by mid-January envisaged the whole of the Middle East theater being downgraded temporarily to meet the crisis in the Far East. Six infantry divisions, one armored brigade, one light tank squadron, a considerable part of the antiaircraft strength of the Middle East Command and substantial air reinforcements were to be sent posthaste to the scene of the new conflict. Reinforcements bound for Iraq, which had become the scene of a pro-German coup, were redirected to the Far East. Overall the British chose to make available the Seventeenth Indian and the British Eighteenth, Fiftieth and later Seventieth Infantry Divisions, the two Australian divisions and the Seventh Armored Brigade for service in the Far East. Because of the strong objections of the Middle East Command, presented on 17 January, the Ninth Australian Division was to be kept in the Middle East until the arrival of a suitable replacement.[77] In the event this particular division stayed in the Middle East for the whole of 1942 and played a notable part in the victory at El Alamein before it sailed for home in February 1943.[78]

Initially both the Sixth and Seventh Australian Divisions were ear-marked to join the Eighth Australian Division in the defense of Malaya and Singapore, as were the Seventeenth Indian and Eighteenth British Divisions.[79] But this decision had to be revised for two reasons. First, during January the Japanese advance in Malaya was so rapid with the collapse of British resistance in central Malaya and northern Johore that there could be no question of getting the two Australian divisions into Singapore to do anything other than surrender—a fate that befell the Eighteenth British Division.[80] Second, a desperate shortage of shipping in the Middle East, in part the result of the extension of the war to the Pacific, meant that any faint hope of the Australians arriving in time to bolster Malaya's flagging defenses was dashed. In late January Canberra, Wavell and the Australian officers from the First Australian Corps who had gone ahead of their forces to the Indies learned that the first convoy from the Middle East, with a reinforced brigade from the Seventh Australian Division, would sail on or about 2 February. The rest of the division would leave on or about 19 February, and the Sixth Australian Division would follow between 19 and 29 March.[81] Accordingly, the decision was taken to send the two Australian divisions to southern Sumatra and central Java. The first part of the Seventh Australian Division was expected to arrive in the Indies on 1 March, the second part two weeks later.[82]

By the second week of February, however, it was becoming clear to all concerned that time and the enemy were not going to wait for the Australians. The Allied position throughout Southeast Asia was deteriorating with such rapidity and finality that there was no question of the Australians being able to arrive in Southeast Asia in time to do anything more than swell the ranks of the defeated. But in this calculation—that Allied resistance in the Lesser Sundas and southern Sumatra would not last beyond 2 March—was salvation for the First Australian Corps, because the 1–15 March schedule for the arrival in the Indies of the Seventh Australian Division proved overly optimistic. In a desperate attempt to get the division out of the Middle East as quickly as possible, it had been loaded piecemeal into whatever shipping was available. The result was that the division sailed not in two but in five convoys, none of which was tactically loaded. Units and formations were broken up and men separated from their equipment, a situation that could only be redeemed at the cost of time, which was not available to the Allies. Either the convoys would have to be reloaded and reconcentrated at a port of call en route to the Indies, or they would have to proceed to Java and the division reconcentrated and regrouped as it arrived on the island. Either way, by the second week of February the Australians and the rest of the Allies knew that the Seventh Division would not be ready for operations on Java until the fourth week of March.[83] By then the game would be up, and in any case it was doubtful whether the Australian formation would even reach the Indies in the first place. Thus the Australians came face to face with the reality that their desire to prop up the defense of the Malay Barrier was doomed to failure.

For all its predictability, the realization came as a shock. By the second week in February the Australians found themselves in the situation that they had suspected might arise but which in the interwar period the British had blandly assured them would never materialize. The British promise to send the fleet to Singapore in the event of a crisis had been proved an empty one. On 19 January Curtin was told for the first time of the full extent of recent British naval losses.[84] With most of the British fleet apparently littering the seabed, there would be no British naval support for Australia. And given the events at Pearl Harbor, there would be no American fleet to fill the gap. By this time, too, the battle of Singapore Island had begun with only one possible outcome. As if this was not bad enough, the Japanese forces in Malaya had only just entered Johore when compatriots struck at and secured Rabaul (3,000 miles from Singapore) and broke through the Makassar Strait and the Molucca Passage with contemptible ease. The Australians knew that very shortly the enemy would be on the far shores of the Coral, Arafura and Timor seas, and that there was every inducement for him to continue his advance. With nothing in the way of significant naval, air and military forces in northern Australia to contest a Japanese move, the Australians were confronted on every front by disasters that threatened to be overwhelming.

The shock to the Australians began to give way to desperate anger after 21 January, when Churchill, meeting his senior military advisers and the Australian representative in London after his return from the Arcadia Conference, set out for the first time the view that at this stage of the war the retention of Burma was more important than trying to reinforce Singapore.[85] In military terms Churchill was absolutely correct; British policy had to concentrate not on lost causes but on saving what might be saved. Nothing was to be gained by squandering the last available reserves that could be used to hold a theater that would otherwise be lost.

Churchill's newly acquired interest in Burma stemmed initially from a concern for the security and morale of India. India was the anchor of the British effort in both the Middle East and the Far East. She had to be held. Churchill realized the deplorable impression the loss of Singapore would have on India, and he was anxious not to add to it by losing Burma into the bargain. The state of the subcontinent was volatile, and British authority was so precarious that it could easily fail to survive a defeat on India's very doorstep. But there was a second factor in Churchill's interest in a country that before the war had been above only the Caribbean on the British list of priorities. At the Arcadia Conference Churchill became aware of the importance that Washington attached to the Chinese connection, and by extension Burma.[86] Throughout the war the Americans greatly exaggerated Chinese power and effectiveness. The British had many illusions of their own, but none at all about Chiang Kai-shek's regime. Nevertheless, the British could not be indifferent to American views about China, and indeed at the Arcadia Conference Burma was included within ABDA Command only on the insistence of the Americans. The latter sought a large measure of control over Burma, such was their interest in the Burma Road and the security of their only overland route into China.[87]

Churchill's suggested revision of priorities could only result in Burma emerging ahead of the Australasian dominions on Britain's list, and when Curtin was told of this by the Australian representative, the former prime minister Sir Earle Page, he telegraphed a stinging denunciation to London. Personal antagonism undoubtedly colored Curtin's observations, since he and Churchill had just indulged in a particularly unsavory exchange in the course of which the Australian remarked that Wavell, a good general for fighting Italians and blacks, inevitably needed Australians to get him out of the trouble he encountered when it came to fighting Germans. But there was certainly much more than slight justification for Curtin's comments of 24 January when he told Churchill that

> After all the assurances we have been given the evacuation of Singapore would be regarded here and elsewhere as an inexcusable betrayal. Singapore is a central

fortress in the system of Empire and local defense. . . . we understood that it was
to be made impregnable, and in any event it was to be capable of holding out for a
prolonged period until the arrival of the main fleet.

Even in an emergency diversion of reinforcements should be to the Netherlands East Indies and not to Burma. Anything else would be deeply resented. . . .
On the faith of the proposed flow of reinforcements [to Singapore] we have acted
and carried out our part of the bargain. We expect you not to frustrate the whole
purpose. . . . [88]

It was an intemperate and in many ways erroneous assessment, but in a
sense Curtin was right. For Britain to have done what was militarily correct
would have been morally and politically wrong. For the British to have
refused to reinforce Singapore while they still had the means and time to do
so would have been an "inexcusable betrayal," as Curtin suggested. On the
other hand, it would have been an inexcusable betrayal to other theaters
and to the troops sent to Singapore if such a deployment were made out of
some perverted sense of national honor rather than on the basis of common
sense. Churchill would have been right to accept the obloquy that would
have been directed his way from Canberra if he had cut losses at Singapore
and tried to salvage something from the wreck. Singapore had been lost
from the time the British failed to send a fleet that could defend it, but faced
with Australian intransigence Churchill decided to let events in train work
their way to the end that all foresaw. That was easier than taking the hard
option of changing policy, even though the policy in hand could only result
in humiliating failure. Curtin's strategic stupidity on this matter was
matched only by Churchill's moral cowardice.

But on 15 February, the very day Singapore surrendered, the leading
elements of the Seventh Australian Division arrived in the Indies, two
weeks earlier than expected. The fast transport *Orcades* went ahead of the
other ships to bring the vanguard of the division to the Indies. She carried
the Second/Second Pioneer Battalion (which had served as infantry in the
Middle East) and the Second/Third Machine Gun Battalion to Oosthaven
in southern Sumatra. Before the troops could be disembarked, however,
word was received that the Japanese had already landed on Sumatra and
that the all-important town of Palembang had been lost. Wavell gave orders
that the transport should not unload but should pick up the British light
armored squadron on Sumatra and then proceed to Java.[89]

For the Australians the evacuation of southern Sumatra without a serious fight had to imply acceptance of the loss of Java and hence the whole of
the Malay Barrier, for Java could only be defended if southern Sumatra was
held. For Curtin the lesson to be drawn was obvious. On that same day he
told London that in his view the Allied priority in the Far East from this
time had to be the defense of Australia herself. But two days earlier, on the
thirteenth, Wavell had suggested to his superiors in London and Washing-

ton that they consider whether or not to continue reinforcing Java, indicating that it might be better to use what forces were at hand to support Burma rather than a doomed effort in the Indies. On the sixteenth he repeated this view more forcefully:

> Burma and Australia are absolutely vital for war against Japan. Loss of Java, though severe blow from every point of view, would not be fatal. Efforts should not therefore be made to reinforce Java which might compromise defense of Burma or Australia. . . . In present instance I must recommend that I consider the risk [of sending the First Australia Corps to Java] unjustified from tactical and strategical [*sic*] point of view. . . . If Australian Corps is diverted I recommend that at least one division should go to Burma and both if they can be administratively received and maintained. . . . It is the only theater in which offensive operations against Japan possible in near future. . . .

The next day, 17 February, Curtin formally requested the return to Australia of all her forces in the Middle East. For good measure he also asked the British to send the Seventh Armoured Brigade, which had been en route to Egypt but which was now on its way to Rangoon.[90]

The following day Wavell returned to his theme, but this time he addressed himself directly to Curtin and for the first time he used Australian arguments in favor of the reinforcement of Burma. As commander in chief of Middle East Forces, Wavell had had under his command Lieutenant General John D. Lavarack and his Australian divisions. He now had Lavarack with him in Batavia. Lavarack, supported by his staff, had come to his own independent conclusion that the corps had to go anywhere but Java, and he inclined to Burma. On 18 February Wavell told Curtin, "I have been in close touch with Lavarack throughout and you may like to know that he agrees with my view that Australian Corps if diverted from the Indies should be used to reinforce Burma." Curtin did not like to know, and the tone of Wavell's signal must have reduced the Australian prime minister to a state bordering on apoplexy. Canberra, not a lieutenant general, made Australian policy, and the view in Canberra was that, with the line of the Malay Barrier broken, Australia, not Burma, had to be the priority. To Curtin this matter was non-negotiable. Lavarack's supporting signal to his prime minister was not quite so emphatic as Wavell's signal had suggested, as is evident from the following:

> . . . This opinion based on strategic considerations present situation and subject normal reservations in view of possible major deterioration Burma or elsewhere.
> . . . Believe future success dependent on retention of and action from main bases Australia and Burma. Future safety N.E.I. no longer possible by direct

defense and must depend on indirect influence operations from Australia and/or Burma. All Australian troops should be withdrawn from N.E.I. immediately for use in Australia or Burma. Best method imposing our initiative on Japan . . . to be direct threat against or attack on Japanese territory by air action. At present . . . most feasible by land and air from Burma into China and then against Japan from Chinese air bases. Believe establishment land and air forces Burma adequate repeat adequate strength will compel Japan conform to our initiative. This would tend to draw Japanese forces from Australian and N.E.I. regions [First Australian Corps]. Nearest available strong land and air forces. . . . Not personally in position judge Australia's home defense position owing considerable absence. If this reasonably satisfactory believe Australia's best interests served by course suggested. This despite natural desire . . . assist direct defense own homeland if considered necessary.[91]

By any standard this was a curious signal, setting out as it did the somewhat surprising idea of protecting the Indies by "indirect influence" when the enemy was all but on the shores of Java. Such an influence was to be exerted by unavailable bombers operating from nonexistent air bases in Burma and China at the end of an equally nonexistent line of communication from Burma to nowhere in particular—this must have served only to convince Curtin of the correctness of Australian defense priorities as seen by Canberra, not British and British-influenced generals.

Curtin met with his service advisers on 19 February, by which time the prime minister had before him the signals of Wavell and Lavarack from the previous day, plus Wavell's signal of the sixteenth, which had been forwarded by Page from London. But Page had other news for Curtin: it was clear that Wavell's suggestions had the backing of London and Washington. In order to placate the smaller powers that had been excluded from the Arcadia Conference, the so-called Pacific War Council had been established in London. This consisted of representatives from the Netherlands, Australia and New Zealand, who met with the British Chiefs of Staff under the chairmanship of Churchill. This was a cosmetic exercise as far as the British and Americans were concerned, the means of giving their Allies the impression that they were being consulted and kept informed about developments and policy. Any of the council's deliberations were certain to be weighted in favor of the British because of the disparity of strength between its members, Churchill's stewardship and Britain's relationship with the United States. Real power lay in Washington, with the American administration and with the Anglo-American policy and planning body, the Combined Chiefs of Staff, which had been established at the Arcadia Conference. To the British the Pacific War Council existed to support Churchill's strictures, and on 17 February it recommended to the Combined Chiefs of

Staff that no attempt be made to reinforce the Indies and that the Seventh
Australian Division be sent to Rangoon. The British were to send their
Seventieth Infantry Division there, though one of its brigades was to go to
Ceylon. The other two Australian divisions were to return to Australia.
The critical decision was the one concerning the destination of the Seventh
Australian Division. Its first convoy (after the *Orcades*) was then in the
Indian Ocean en route for Australia and nearing the point after which it
could not turn back for Burma. If, however, it was diverted to Rangoon it
could not be redirected back to Australia. Therefore a decision on the
deployment of the division had to be made quickly, and in his signal Page
told Curtin that the Australian government had twenty-four hours to
decide the destination of the convoy—that is, it had one day in which to
indicate its acceptance of Churchill's demand that the division proceed to
Rangoon.[92]

For Curtin there was no question of his compliance with Churchill's
demands. The view in Canberra was that Australian troops were coming
home, and on 19 February he spelled this out to the British prime minister.
In return he received two signals from London, one from the British
government and the other from Page. Both urged him to sanction the
change that Churchill wanted.

But if Page was seduced by Churchill's persuasiveness, Curtin, with
12,000 miles of shelter between him and London, was not. Indeed, events
served only to fortify his resolve. On February 19, war came to the
Australian mainland for the first time when Japanese land-based and carrier-borne aircraft all but flattened Darwin, and on the following day
Curtin signaled London, Washington, Wavell and, for good measure,
Lavarack, repeating that the Australian decision had been made and was
not going to be altered. That same day Page passed on to Curtin a message
from Churchill that the leading convoy of the Seventh Australian Division
was proceeding on course to Australia.[93] This was a lie. Churchill was
under terrible pressure at this desperate stage of the war. Months of defeat
had come to a shattering climax with Singapore, and with defeat in the
Indies inevitable, intransigence on the part of the Australians—of all people—must have been the final straw for such a person as Churchill. He
begged Roosevelt to press Curtin to comply with the demand that the
Seventh Australian Division go to Rangoon:

> The only troops who can reach Rangoon in time to stop the enemy and enable
> other reinforcements to arrive are the leading Australian division. These can
> begin to arrive there by the 26th or 27th. We have asked Australian Government
> to allow this diversion for the needs of battle, and promised to relieve them at
> earliest. All other Australian troops are going home at earliest. [This was at best a

half truth.] Australian Government have refused point-blank. I have appealed to them again in the interests of the vital importance of keeping open Burma Road and maintaining contact with Chiang. . . . I feel you have the right to press for this movement of Allied forces. Please therefore send me a message that I can add to the very strong cable I have just sent off. Our Chiefs of Staff here are most insistent, and I have no doubt our Combined Chiefs of Staff Committee in Washington feel the same way. There is no reason why you should not also talk with Casey [the Australian ambassador in Washington].⁹⁴

Roosevelt duly obliged Churchill, sending Curtin a signal whose moderation, sagacity and measured tones contrasted sharply with the signal Churchill himself sent Curtin—after he had first diverted the Australian convoy to Rangoon. The Australian reaction to Churchill's arrogant opening sentences is best left to the imagination. Suffice it to note that it could not have put the reader in a favorable frame of mind to accept the subsequent distortions and downright falsehoods.

I suppose you realise that your leading division, the head of which is sailing south of Colombo to the Netherlands East Indies at this very moment in our scanty British and American shipping, is the only force that can reach Rangoon in time to prevent its loss and the severance of communications with China. It can begin to disembark at Rangoon about the 26th or 27th.

2. We are entirely in favor of all Australian troops returning home to defend their native soil, and we shall help their transportation in every way. But a vital war emergency cannot be ignored, and troops en route to other destinations must be ready to turn aside and take part in a battle. Every effort would be made to relieve this division at the earliest possible moment and send them [sic] on to Australia. I do not endorse the United States' request that you should send your other two divisions to Burma. They will return home as fast as possible. But this one is needed now, and it is the only one that can possibly save the situation.

3. Pray read again your message of 23 January, in which you said that the evacuation of Singapore would be "an inexcusable betrayal." Agreeably with your point of view, we therefore put the Eighteenth Division and other important reinforcements into Singapore instead of diverting them to Burma, and ordered them to fight it out to the end. They were lost at Singapore and did not save it, whereas they could almost certainly have saved Rangoon. I take full responsibility with my colleagues on the Defence Committee for this decision; but you must also bear a heavy share on account of your telegram.

4. Your greatest support in this hour of peril must be drawn from the United States. They alone can bring into Australia the necessary troops and air forces, and they appear ready to do so. As you know, the President attaches supreme importance to keeping open the connection with China, without which his bombing offensive against Japan cannot be started, and also most grievous results may follow in Asia if China is cut off from all Allied help.

5. I am quite sure that if you refuse to allow your troops who are actually passing to stop this gap, and if, in consequence, the above ills, affecting the whole course of the war, follow, a very grave effect will be produced upon the President and the Washington circle, on whom you are so largely dependent. See especially the inclination of the United States to move major naval forces from Hawaii into the Anzac Area.

6. We must have an answer immediately, as the leading ships of the convoy will soon be steaming in the opposite direction from Rangoon, and every day is a day lost. I trust therefore that for the sake of all interests, and above all your own interests, you will give most careful consideration to the case I have set before you.[95]

Churchill needed and expected a prompt reply, but it did not come until 22 February. The time spent reviewing decisions, holding doubting colleagues and subordinates in line and then composing the reply to Churchill's bullying immoderation was well spent: Curtin's response was a model of restraint. Australian fury was all the more devastating for its being implicit.

I have received your rather strongly worded request at this stage, though our wishes in regard to the disposition of the [First Australian Corps] in the Pacific theater have long been known to you, and carried even further by your statement in the House of Commons. Furthermore, Page was furnished with lengthy statements of our viewpoint on February 15.

2. The proposal for additional military assistance for Burma comes from the Supreme Commander of the ABDA-Area. Malaya, Singapore and Timor have been lost, and the whole of the Netherlands East Indies will apparently be occupied shortly by the Japanese. The enemy, with superior sea- and air-power, has commenced raiding our territory in the north-west, and also in the north-east from Rabaul. The Government made the maximum contribution of which it was capable in reinforcement of the ABDA-Area. It originally sent a division less a brigade to Malaya, with certain ancillary troops. A machine-gun battalion and substantial reinforcements were later dispatched. It also dispatched forces to Ambon, Java and Dutch and Portuguese Timor. Six squadrons of the Air Force were also sent to this area, together with two cruisers from the Royal Australian Navy.

3. It was suggested by you that two Australian divisions should be transferred to the Pacific theater, and this suggestion was later publicly expanded by you in the statement that no obstacle would be placed in the way of [their] returning to defend [their] homeland. We agreed to the two divisions being located in Sumatra and Java, and it was pointed out to Page in the cablegram of 15 February that should fortune still favor the Japanese this disposition would give a line of withdrawal to Australia for our forces.

4. With the situation having deteriorated to such an extent in the theater of the ABDA-Area, with which we are closely associated, and the Japanese also

making a southward advance in the ANZAC-Area, the Government, in the light of the advice of its Chiefs of Staff as to the forces necessary to repel an attack on Australia, finds it most difficult to understand that it should be called upon to make a further contribution of forces to be located in the most distant part of the ABDA-Area. Notwithstanding your statement that you do not agree with the request to send the other two divisions . . . to Burma, our advisers are concerned with Wavell's request for the Corps, and Dill's statement that the destination of the Sixth and Ninth Australian Divisions should be left open, as more troops might be badly needed in Burma. Once one division became engaged it could not be left unsupported, and the indications are that the whole of the Corps might become committed to this region, or that there would be a recurrence of the experiences of the Greek and Malayan campaigns. Finally, in view of superior Japanese sea-power and air-power, it would appear to be a matter of some doubt as to whether this division can be landed in Burma, and a matter of greater doubt whether it can be brought out as promised. With the fall of Singapore, Penang and Martaban, the Bay of Bengal is now vulnerable to what must be considered the superior sea- and air-power of Japan in that area. The movement of our forces to this theater therefore is not considered a reasonable hazard of war, having regard to what has gone before, and its adverse results would have the gravest consequences on the morale of the Australian people. The Government therefore must adhere to its decision.

5. In regard to your statement that the 18th Division was diverted from Burma to Singapore because of our message, it is pointed out that the date of the latter was 23 January, whereas in your telegram of 14 January you informed me that one brigade of this division was due on 13 January and the remainder on 27 January.

6. We feel, therefore, in view of the foregoing and the services the [First Australian Corps has] rendered in the Middle East, that we have every right to expect [it] to be returned as soon as possible, with adequate support to ensure [its] safe arrival.

7. We assure you, and desire you to so inform the President, who knows fully what we have done to help the common cause, that if it were possible to divert our troops to Burma and India without imperilling our security in the judgement of our advisers we should be pleased to agree to the diversion.[96]

This telegram perhaps represented Australia's finest moment of the war, even though its contents were known to only a few. It was an assertion of Australian national rights and independence at the expense of the mother country, which had been tested and found wanting. It was a warning that Britain could not speak for Australia and could no longer treat Australia as an appendage. Perhaps 22 February rather than 26 January or 25 April was Australia's real national day.

The next day Curtin followed up his telegram of the twenty-second with another that was even more severe. By then he had been somewhat blithely informed by Churchill and an astonished Page of the unilateral diversion of the Seventh Australian Division to Rangoon.[97] Given Canberra's attitude Churchill, with a notable lack of good grace and contrition, had no option but to order the return of the dominion troops to Australia. He gave the necessary authorization on the twenty-third, but by then it was too late. The leading transport, the *Mount Vernon*, had to turn back to Ceylon to refuel, but she was able to resume her original course thereafter and bring her 4,668 troops to the safety of Freemantle on 10 March. The remainder of the division—less the troops who had gone to Java and been lost there—followed in the wake of the *Mount Vernon*. Twelve transports, totaling 97,741 tons between them, brought home 10,900 troops of the Seventh Australian Division. Their passage across the Indian Ocean was covered by the battleship *Royal Sovereign*, the heavy cruiser *Cornwall* and five escorts, three of them Australian.[98] Though the convoy reached Adelaide safely, it was somewhat fortunate to get across the Indian Ocean without mishap; its voyage coincided with the rampage by Japanese carrier and surface forces south of Java.[99] With an escort that would have been no match for any Japanese force that it encountered, the convoy escaped a contact with the enemy by what was a relatively small margin.

The emotions aroused in the course of this exchange over the fate of the First Australian Corps were natural, especially on the Australian side. The Australians were exasperated at being told to consider Chinese interests at the expense of their own; it was intolerable to have the newly discovered importance of China paraded as reason for not honoring the promises of two decades. But in a sense the bitterness, indeed the whole exchange itself, was largely unnecessary for two reasons. First, while the two heads of government fought their "battle of the wires," Burma was being lost. As London and Canberra bandied unpleasantries with a vehemence unequaled even at the time of the bodyline tour of 1933,[100] the backbone of the British defense of Burma, the Seventeenth Indian Division, was broken in a disastrous battle fought between the Bilin and Sittang rivers.[101] Thereafter the British could not hold Rangoon, a fact that the local commander appreciated well in advance of London and Wavell. (Not surprisingly, he was dismissed for his perceptiveness, though this was disguised amidst accusations of other failings.) Even though the Seventh Armoured Brigade arrived in Burma on 21 February in time to play a crucial role in covering the British withdrawal into central and northern Burma, the bulk of the First Australian Corps would not have been able to reach Burma before the fall of the colony's capital and main port.[102] Thus the real danger that the Australians dreaded, that of sending one formation to Burma and then more to support it with the result that all were lost to no effect, could not have come about: the British lost Burma too quickly to drag the Australians down with them.

The second matter, however, was the more important one. The exchange between the Australians and British was unnecessary because the Americans, on 14 February, made the decision to commit combat troops to Australia. This complete reversal of policy was proposed by the chief of the War Plans Division, Brigadier General Dwight D. Eisenhower, as part of a review of strategic policy ordered by Marshall on the eleventh. Eisenhower's proposal, prompted by the impending collapse of the ABDA Command and the need for increased American help to Australia, was endorsed by Marshall the same day it was made.[103]

The decision was made known to America's allies on the sixteenth, but it came too late to head off the Anglo-Australian clash of the following week.[104] No doubt the more immediate and dramatic events of the time, namely the fall of Singapore and southern Sumatra, overshadowed the full impact of the decision; moreover, it must be remembered that the American decision could not be translated into troops on the ground for some time. But on the day that America's allies were told of the new decision, Marshall allocated the Forty-first Infantry Division for the move to Australia, and three days later the shipping needed for the move was earmarked.[105] The division's first echelon sailed from New York on 3 March, and on the nineteenth the remainder of the division, less one infantry regiment, sailed from San Francisco. The initial movement of this understrength division was completed on 6 April, and the division was reconcentrated after its remaining regiment arrived at Melbourne on 14 May.

The Forty-first Infantry Division's errant infantry was not alone. It arrived in Australia with the Thirty-second Infantry Division. This formation had been dispatched by Washington in response to Churchill's request, made on 5 March, for the United States to send one division to Australia and one to New Zealand (on top of earlier commitments) and so allow those Australian divisions still in the Middle East to remain there.[106] The formation selected for New Zealand was the Thirty-seventh Infantry Division, whose 147th Infantry Regiment had already been assigned the task of securing Tongabatu.

It was the decision to send ground troops to Australia that enabled Roosevelt to adopt so conciliatory an approach when he signaled Curtin on 20 February about the diversion of Australian troops to Burma.

> I fully appreciate how grave are your responsibilities in reaching a decision in the present serious circumstances as to the disposition of the first Australian division returning from the Middle East. I assume you know now of our determination to send, in addition to all troops and forces now en route, another force of over 27,000 men to Australia. This force will be fully equipped in every respect. We must fight to the limit for our two flanks—one based on Australia and the other on Burma, India and China. Because of our geographical position

we Americans can better handle the reinforcement of Australia and the right flank.

I say this to you so that you may have every confidence that we are going to reinforce your position with all possible speed. Moreover, the operations which the United States Navy have begun and have in view will in a measure constitute a protection to the coast of Australia and New Zealand. On the other hand, the left flank simply must be held. If Burma goes it seems to me our whole position, including that of Australia, will be in extreme peril. Your Australian division is the only force that is available for immediate reinforcement. It could get into the fight at once, and would, I believe, have the strength to save what now seems to be a very dangerous situation. While I realize the Japs are moving rapidly, I cannot believe that, in view of your geographical position and the forces on their way to you or operating in your neighborhood, your vital centers are in immediate danger.

While I realize that your men have been fighting all over the world, and are still, and while I know full well of the great sacrifices which Australia has made, I nevertheless want to ask you in the interests of our whole war effort in the Far East if you will reconsider your decision and order the division now en route to Australia to move with all speed to support the British forces fighting in Burma. You may be sure we will fight by your side with all our forces until victory.[107]

Roosevelt's signal, if it did not succeed in moving Curtin, at least indicated the overall direction in which American strategic thinking was moving in mid-February. By then the Americans were reconsidering the wider implications of the fate that was certain to befall the Indies and the ABDA Command. The decision to send ground troops to Australia was the first part of a response to this situation, and the logic of defeat was to dictate an even wider revision of command arrangements made at Arcadia. As Roosevelt told Churchill on 18 February, the war in the Far East was producing a natural division of areas of responsibility, with the British confined to the Indian Ocean and the whole of the Pacific being turned over to the Americans. As the president noted, geography placed the Americans in the position to assume responsibility for Australasia.[108]

But however logical such a division of responsibilities would be, it still gave rise to problems. First, the immediate casualty of any decision to extend American commitments in the Pacific had to be the "Germany-first" principle. Marshall might still plan an emergency cross-channel invasion for 1942 and Roosevelt might still want the opening of a front in Europe in the course of the year, but these ideas, unrealistic even before the February decisions, died when the Americans accepted the burden of responsibility for the whole of the southwest Pacific. The decisions made by Marshall constituted a defeat for his own strategic policy and a victory, or at least a partial one, for King, but it was a situation that Marshall accepted with good grace at the time.

Second, settling command arrangements to take account of this change was no simple matter. For once the problem was not with the minor Allies or even with the British but within the American high command itself. In the final analysis the price that the minor powers had to pay for American protection was American hegemony, and the British were willing to go along with formal proposals made by Roosevelt on 7 and 9 March to divide the world's oceans into three areas of responsibility. The Pacific theater would be run by the Americans, the Indian Ocean (and the Middle East) by the British. The Atlantic was to be a joint Anglo-American responsibility. This arrangement—national control under the direction of the Combined Chiefs of Staff—was endorsed by Churchill on 18 March.[109] The command problems arose not because of interalliance trouble but because of departmental and personal differences within the American military establishment.

The root of these problems was that the U.S. Army and Navy had never agreed and could never agree on how a war in the Pacific should be conducted. Right up until 1945 the two services were at loggerheads on issues of strategic policy and the allocation of resources, and more often than not the service wrangling had to be resolved by either the president or the Joint Chiefs of Staff. After 1942 this potentially debilitating situation did not prove too serious; growing resources allowed the Americans to indulge in a series of compromises that more or less provided both services with what they wanted. In March 1942, however, the problem was more serious. By then the enemy held the initiative, and the Americans had to set up a structure to fight the Pacific war. Marshall, always an advocate of the principle of units of command, wanted to see a supreme commander appointed in the Pacific. King, on the other hand, was inclined to regard the principle as something of a panacea, a much overrated one, though he was never against the idea if an American admiral was in line for such a post.[110] The one thing King was never prepared to accept, however, was a general appointed to supreme command in the Pacific. The navy saw the Pacific as "its" war, the preparation for which had taken two decades, and it was not prepared to subordinate itself to the army. Thus King was opposed to Marshall's proposal on the grounds of principle, but to this was added an element of personal calculation. Marshall wanted MacArthur appointed to the post of supreme commander in the Pacific, and MacArthur was totally unacceptable to King and the navy.[111]

King had no confidence in MacArthur, and there was no doubt that the first months of the Pacific war confirmed his low regard of the general.[112] The first month of the war revealed how little had been accomplished in the years of MacArthur's stewardship of the Philippines Army, and the general's conduct of operations on Luzon, his misreading of the local situation and his manifest failure to grasp the strategic realities of his own and his country's situation should have led to his dismissal or retirement. Instead, MacArthur was awarded the Medal of Honor and went on to fill some of the highest military positions on the Allied side. Distance and defeat distorted the American view of MacArthur and his conduct of operations in early 1942. The American public needed an authentic hero, and it was given the photogenic MacArthur.[113] The failures in the Philippines were swept under the carpet, and in the circumstances of the time there was no good reason to lift it. If the well-connected general was in any way disgraced or retired, awkward questions were sure to be asked about the past and future conduct of the war. Some would reflect badly on MacArthur, but the general himself was in a position to make some damaging disclosures.[114] It might come to light that the loss of the Philippines had nothing to do with Pearl Harbor, that it had been foreseen before the war. An examination of Pearl Harbor could easily result in Marshall's share of responsibility being properly fixed for the first time. On that particular matter it was better to let the local commanders at Pearl Harbor take the rap, move Stark to London and keep MacArthur employed somewhere in the Pacific than to risk the scandal that was certain to accompany MacArthur if he returned to the United States. His penchant for Republican politics would obviously disconcert Roosevelt, and none of the service chiefs could be anything but apprehensive about the possibility of MacArthur arriving in Washington. He was senior to Marshall, having served as chief of staff for five years before his appointment as military adviser to the Philippines government. There was talk in congress of recalling MacArthur as head of a united military establishment, and Roosevelt (constitutionally commander in chief of the army and navy), Marshall, King and Arnold could hardly be enthusiastic about such a prospect. Moreover, MacArthur in Washington would be a liability to the president, Marshall and Arnold because he was certain to parade the "Pacific-first" option, a matter that inhibited even King's freedom of action. King wanted to upgrade the Pacific priority, yet he had to ensure that the beneficiary of any revision was the navy and not MacArthur. In all his attempts to realign strategic priorities King had to make sure that he did not play into the hands of the general.

MacArthur, therefore, had to be kept in uniform and abroad, and the scene of continued employment that recommended itself was the Pacific. But the navy was never prepared to subordinate itself to MacArthur, and it was impossible to place so senior a general under the command of an admiral. Thus in the end there had to be a compromise that broke the principle of unity of command. The Pacific was divided into two separate commands, one for the army and one for the navy. MacArthur was appointed supreme commander (a title he created for himself) in the southwest Pacific theater, while Nimitz was appointed commander in chief of the Pacific Ocean area with subordinate commands covering the northern, central and southern parts of the ocean. But demarcation of the boundary between the command areas proved difficult; while any command centered on Australia had to include its eastern approaches, it was the southwest Pacific, the Solomon and Bismarck Islands, that King on 2 March proposed as the scene of the United States' first offensive move.[115] Definition of responsibilities, liaison arrangements and matters of political control took time, and it was not until 31 March that Roosevelt finally approved the arrangements that had been made. The Southwest Pacific Command functioned with effect from 18 April, but the Pacific Ocean area did not become an operational command until 8 May.[116]

The settling of command arrangements did not produce troops on the ground or ships and aircraft in the southwest Pacific in the opening months of 1942, but it was significant to the story of the Coral Sea and Midway in two ways. First, conduct of the battle of the Coral Sea and Allied preparations for both this battle and the one off Midway were conducted by two separate commands. Second, the American commitment to Australia served to take the sting out of Anglo-Australian exchanges. With the Americans indicating that they would guarantee Australian security, Canberra became more receptive to British suggestions—not that this prevented all disputes. After the first Churchill-Curtin exchange over the destination of the Seventh Australian Division, another flared up when Churchill, with a notable lack of sympathy, suggested keeping Australian units in Ceylon when they arrived there for refueling. To Curtin it must have appeared that the British did not mind where Australian troops went as long as it was not to Australia, and he was not inclined to go over well-worn arguments yet again. When Page endorsed Churchill's suggestions, Curtin told him that he was in London to represent Australian interests, not to be Churchill's errand boy.[117] But the desperation had gone from the situation, and Curtin on 2 March suggested to Churchill that two brigades of the Sixth Australian Division stay on Ceylon when they arrived at the island. These two formations, the Sixteenth and Seventeenth Infantry Brigades, arrived in Ceylon on 23 March. There they joined a locally raised brigade, two brigades from the Thirty-fourth Indian Division, and two recently arrived formations, the Sixteenth British and Twenty-first East African Brigades. The two latter formations had arrived on Ceylon on 14 and 21 March respectively.[118]

Thus we conclude the examination of what the Allied powers did in response to the situation that confronted them in the Pacific in the first three months of the war. The process of replying to the demands of the war was a slow and painful one, in many ways bewildering in its manifestations and implications. Continual consultation between governments, constant revision of plans, the proliferation of troop and force movements over vast distances and in every direction combine to give the impression of disorder, unavailing improvization. Immediately after the start of the Pacific war, when the Japanese kicked over the Allied anthill, there was confusion and chaos. In those areas where the Japanese struck their heaviest blows the devastation was too great to lead to anything other than paralysis and defeat. But on the peripheries of Japanese conquest, where the ripples of sorrow could only lap gently around the Allies, Japan's enemies watched and reacted with increasing vigor.

Indeed the extent of the Allied reaction in general and the American response in particular was remarkable. At a time when the United States was committed to the "Germany-first" policy, she increased her troop strength in the Pacific from about 155,000 men at the start of the war to about 280,000 by 1 April, with another 38,000 en route. Of course this picture is distorted by the inclusion in the American order of battle of Alaska, the Canal Zone and the Philippines, but overall the facts speak for themselves. Between January and April 1942 more than 80,000 troops left the U.S. homeland for service in the Pacific. The effects of this increase on the order of battle are set out in table 4-1.

From the figures provided in table 4-1 and our earlier examination of the Japanese order of battle, one matter is clear. Even by April 1942 the Americans had ground forces roughly equal in strength to those of the Japanese in the combat zones of the Pacific. The Japanese had begun the war at the peak of their strength, but nonetheless they had encountered difficulty finding the eleven divisions needed for the Southeast Asia campaign. At the war's end the bulk of Japanese military power remained on the Asian mainland, and there was no slack that could be taken up to cover the needs of the new theaters of operation. The Americans, in four months, secured a rough numerical equality with an effort that had not even begun to assume serious proportions, and in doing so they marked out the battlefields of the Pacific war. With the central Pacific barred to them for the moment at least, and with no chance of a contact with enemy main forces as long as the latter were in the Indies and the Indian Ocean, the Americans marked out the southwest Pacific as the area where battle would be joined. They picked up the Japanese challenge, though there was no way of knowing the nature of the offensive that would be mounted in this theater. It would be determined by the outcome of fleet engagements, which would decide which side held the initiative in the area. The side that emerged victorious from any forthcoming fleet action was likely to choose the timing and location of any offensive in the southwest Pacific, and it was in this matter that the Americans had an advantage that was worth an army, an air force or a fleet. The American ability to read increasingly large parts of the most secret Japanese operational orders gave the Pacific Fleet the chance to meet the enemy in battle at a time and place of its own choosing or to decline

Table 4-1. Strength and Deployment of U.S. Army and Marine Corps Forces in the Pacific, October 1941–April 1942

	17 Oct 41	2 Apr 42		Projected		Divisions		Regiments		Aircraft	
	Total	Ground	Air	Ground	Air	Pre*	Pro†	Pre	Pro	Pre	Pro
The Philippines	54,000	60,000	8,000	......	......	......	......	......	......	......	......
Guam and Wake	676	......	......	......	......	......	......	......	......	......	......
Hawaii	42,000	62,700	8,900	100,000	15,000	2	3	8	9	275	358
Johnson	162	—	—	—	—	—	—	—	—	—	—
Palmyra	158	—	—	—	—	—	—	—	—	—	—
Midway	844	—	?	—	?	—	—	—	—	c 50	?
Alaska	22,000	26,500	4,300	33,200	9,000	1	1	4	5	56	81
Panama	31,000	35,800	14,400	51,000	20,000	—	—	4	6	412	626
Christmas	—	1,700	320	1,700	490	—	—	1	1	25	25
Canton	—	1,300	?	1,300	?	—	—	—	—	40	40
Bora Bora	—	3,850	—	3,850	—	—	—	1	1	—	—
Samoa	417	5,215	?	10,000+	?	?	?	1	?	?	?
Fiji	—	—	700	15,000	720	—	1	—	—	?	?
New Caledonia	—	16,000	2,000	23,000	2,500	—	1	3	1	?	?
Efate	—	450	—	4,900	?	—	—	—	—	?	?
Tongabatu	—	—	—	6,300	660	—	—	—	1	—	?
New Zealand	—	—	—	15,000	—	—	1	—	—	—	—
Australia	—	16,900	17,100	60,000	24,000	—	2	3	3	488	955

Note: In addition, there were 3,365 marines at various places in the Pacific.
*Present total.
†Projected total.

action if it so wished. The Japanese believed that they held the initiative and could continue to force their enemies to conform to their will, movements and timetable, but knowledge of enemy intentions gave the Americans a tactical advantage that was to prove devastating. The manner in which the Americans reacted to the onset of war was impressive; the speed with which they dispatched forces to the Pacific was an inspiration to their allies. But the process whereby they capitalized on their strengths and the enemy's weaknesses by breaking the enemy's communications security was nothing less than magical.

CHAPTER 5

Operation Magic and the Allied Deployment for the Battle of the Coral Sea

On 5 April, when the Naval General Staff sanctioned Operations AL and MI, the Imperial Navy had eleven carriers in service with another five nearing completion. Japan had gone to war with ten carriers: the fleet units *Akagi*, *Kaga*, *Hiryu*, *Soryu*, *Shokaku* and *Zuikaku*; the light fleet carriers *Hosho*, *Ryujo* and *Zuiho*; and the escort carrier *Taiyo*. Since the start of the war only the *Shoho*, sister ship of the *Zuiho*, had joined the fleet. She had been commissioned on 26 January but not activated in an operational capacity. Of the five carriers nearing completion two, the escort carrier *Unyo* and the fleet carrier *Junyo*, entered service during May, and the latter's sister ship, the *Hiyo*, was commissioned in July. Both the light carrier *Ryuho* and the escort carrier *Chuyo* were to enter service in November. Had the Japanese carriers enjoyed continued immunity from destruction after May, by 30 November 1942 the Imperial Navy would have boasted eight fleet, five light fleet and three escort carriers, with two more fleet carriers, the *Taiho* and the *Unryu*, under construction. For a nation of such limited industrial resources, Japan's carrier production program represented a prodigious effort.[1]

The American intention was to seek battle with Japan's carrier forces, but in the opening months of the war this had to be tempered by certain inescapable facts. First, at this time American carriers had to be employed on a number of defensive tasks, and they had relatively little offensive capability. As we have seen, in the first phase of the war the Americans had to be content with a number of small-scale offensive operations, little more than a series of short jabs against minor targets, while they tried to keep beyond the range of any possible counterattack. In military terms the American carrier operations against various Japanese islands and bases before April 1942 did not amount to much. Staged more for political and psychological reasons than for military purposes, they were no compensation for either battle or victory.[2] Second, the Americans were not able to initiate a fleet action because the enemy carrier forces did not present themselves as targets. In the first four months of the Pacific war Japanese carriers ventured but once into a position where they might have been contacted and brought to battle. On that occasion, the Pearl Harbor operation, the Japanese had evaded contact, and the chance to bring the enemy to battle did not recur before April. Third, a certain caution governed American actions because the American carrier position was inferior to that of Japan and was incapable of speedy improvement.

When war came to the United States she had eight carriers in commission. These were the fleet carriers *Lexington, Saratoga, Ranger, Yorktown, Enterprise, Wasp* and *Hornet*, plus the escort carrier *Long Island*, and of these three, the *Lexington, Saratoga* and *Enterprise* were in the Pacific when the Japanese struck. Another unit, the escort carrier *Charger*, had entered service, but at the outbreak of war she awaited assignment and in the event was confined to training duties for most of the war. By April the American situation, both overall and within the Pacific, had barely changed. Between 11 January and 22 May the Americans lost the services of the *Saratoga*, torpedoed by an enemy submarine off Johnson Island and then repaired at Puget Sound.[3] Her temporary absence was covered by the arrival in the Pacific of the *Yorktown*. She left the Atlantic in late December and became the flagship of Task Force 17 on New Year's Eve.[4] There were three other units in the Atlantic at the start of hostilities, but they were not ordered into the Pacific. The *Ranger*, considered unfit for combat duties in the Pacific, was assigned a number of tasks that included ferrying aircraft to west Africa, and she did not enter the Pacific until August 1944, when she became part of the Eleventh Carrier Division and the night-training program.[5] The *Wasp*, in the Atlantic at this time, was earmarked for two major operations designed to fly fighter reinforcements to Malta in April and May.[6] The *Long Island* was to enter the Pacific in the first half of 1942 and operate with the battleships of Task Force 1 on the West Coast at the time of Midway. Subsequently she took part in the Guadalcanal campaign.[7]

The *Lexington* (flagship of Task Force 11) and the *Enterprise* (flagship of Task Force 16) did not leave the Pacific in the first months of the war, and apart from the *Hornet* there was no means of reinforcing these two carriers (plus the *Yorktown*) after the turn of the year. Many new units had been ordered, but they were not coming off the slips quickly enough to influence the balance of power in American favor in the course of 1942. The *Copahee*, the first of no fewer than fifteen escort carriers launched or commissioned before September, entered service on 15 June; the first of the new light fleet carriers, the *Independence*, was launched on 22 August. But the first of the new fleet carriers, the *Essex*, was not commissioned until 31 December 1942, and the real expansion of American carrier power did not take place until the second half of 1943 and 1944. In the first half of 1942 the American high command was forced to try to get by with the few carriers that were available in the knowledge that replacement for losses or reinforcements were not available.

The *Hornet* was the exception to the general pattern. She was commissioned on 20 October 1941 and spent four months working up before bidding farewell to the Atlantic and the Caribbean in late February. After more exercises off the West Coast as she came northwards, the *Hornet* arrived at San Francisco on 1 April. There she embarked sixteen B-25B Mitchell bombers, an indication as far as the crew was concerned that months of hard work were to be rewarded with relegation to ferrying duties. The next day she sailed for the central Pacific as part of Task Group 16.2 in the company of the heavy cruisers *Northampton* and *Salt Lake City*; the destroyers *Balch*, *Benham*, *Ellet* and *Fanning*; and the oiler *Sabine*. This formation was not detailed to join Nimitz's command in the defense of either the central or the southwest Pacific. In fact the *Hornet* had been selected for something different from ferrying duties. Her flight deck was 5 feet wider than those of her two sister ships, and she was one of the few carriers that could operate a Mitchell. This had been proved in the course of trials conducted on 2 February. Thus when Task Group 16.2 left San Francisco on 2 April it was not for ferrying duties or to support the other carriers in defense of the central or southwest Pacific; it had been ordered to take part in the first raid of the war on the Japanese homeland.

The idea of using army medium bombers from the decks of a carrier for a raid on Japan was broached on 10 January by Captain Francis S. Low, King's operations officer. With King's enthusiastic support, Low and Captain Donald B. Duncan, the air operations officer,[8] worked out an attack plan over the next five days.[9] But the plan had to be shelved over the next two months, partly because of the need to train air crews to coax bombers into the air from a short takeoff, but also because the Pacific Fleet was so overcommitted that it had no chance of conducting such an operation.[10] But on 19 March, with the *Hornet* obviously on the point of becoming available for operations, Nimitz fell in with Washington's demands for a raid on Japan and made Task Group 16.1, formed around the *Enterprise*, available to support the *Hornet*.[11] Because the latter had to carry the Mitchells on her flight deck—they were too large to be stowed below—the *Enterprise* and

Task Group 16.1 had to accompany the *Hornet* and her group to provide combat air patrol. Task Group 16.1—consisting of the *Enterprise*; the heavy cruiser *Vincennes*; the light cruiser *Nashville*; the destroyers *Grayson, Gwin, Meredith* and *Monssen*; and the oiler *Cimarron*—sailed from Pearl Harbor on 8 April and made a rendezvous with Task Group 16.2 five days later in latitude 38° N and on the international date line. The American plan was for their combined task force to advance to a position 450 miles to the east of Tokyo before flying off the Mitchells during the afternoon of 19 April. The bombers were to attack various targets under the cover of darkness and then arrive at friendly airfields in China the following dawn. By launching late in the afternoon the carriers would have their own withdrawal covered by darkness, a vital consideration in view of the amount of time they would be within range of shore-based aircraft.[12]

Hardly had Task Group 16.1 sailed from Pearl Harbor than Nimitz had cause to regret having parted with it. The dictates of time and distance meant that half of the American carrier strength in the Pacific would be tied up until the end of the month with this single hit-and-run raid; Task Force 16 could not return to Pearl Harbor before 26 April. Thereafter it would need several days to get ready for sea again. But within a day of Vice Admiral William F. Halsey leading the *Enterprise* and her escorts out to sea, Nimitz and his staff became aware that trouble might be brewing, and Halsey might be needed, in the southwest Pacific.

Nimitz was alerted to this possibility by his intelligence services on 9 April. Prior to that there had been a few straws in the wind suggesting a possible enemy move south of Rabaul. Towards the end of March the Americans had detected signs that the Japanese intended to build up their air strength at Rabaul, which raised the question of whether the Japanese had designs on the southwest Pacific.[13] It was not until the second week of April, however, that accumulating evidence confirmed this alarming suspicion.

In the absence of prisoners, captured documents and reliable and extensive reconnaissance, the Americans had to depend upon one major source for uncovering enemy plans and intentions: signals intelligence. This particular effort was directed from Washington by an organization designated OP-20-G, the U.S. Navy's cryptologic outfit or, more correctly, the Communication Security Section of the Office of Naval Communications. OP-20-G was part of the Office of the Chief of Naval Operations. While it was dependent on the Office of Naval Intelligence (particularly OP-16-F2, its Far Eastern Section) for linguists and other branches of the Office of Naval Communications for signals personnel, OP-20-G was a largely autonomous organization. It contained a number of subsections whose various responsibilities covered the security of America's own communications and the navy's assaults on enemy signals. The specializations of OP-20-G relevant to this story were in the fields of traffic analysis, direction finding (OP-20-GX) and cryptanalysis, the prerogrative of OP-20-GY.[14]

Direction finding and traffic analysis were vital to gleaning information of enemy plans and movements. In the former the position of an enemy transmitter would be located by plotting a number of cross bearings from stations monitoring a signal. In this way the position, course and speed of a ship or submarine making frequent use of its radio could be calculated. But direction finding provided more than so mundane a return. Over a period of time, and in conjunction with traffic analysis, it could often trace individual ships and by their association with others identify task groups and forces.

Direction finding was carried out by the Mid-Pacific Direction-Finding Net, established in 1937. This was a series of listening stations established between Cavite and Pearl Harbor, between Dutch Harbor and Eastern Samoa. While some of the stations had been lost in the opening weeks of the war, enough remained to keep the coordinating body at Pearl Harbor fully occupied. Traffic analysis, similarly, was a full-time occupation; indeed it employed far more personnel than the highly specialized fields of direction finding and cryptanalysis. Traffic analysis sought to uncover the pattern of enemy signals. Given that Japanese possessions and forces were widely dispersed and in many cases lacked secure cable facilities, the Imperial Navy had no option but to use high-powered long-range radios on a large scale. This provided the basis of the activities of OP-20-GX, and in practice the Americans monitored about 60 percent of all the major signals made by the Imperial Navy.

Japanese operations usually originated with an operational directive that involved intercommand communications and the various commands "talking" with their subordinate formations and units. When preparations were complete and an operation began, the talking would stop because the forces at sea would observe radio silence. Commands ashore would continue to send signals to their forces, but the latter would not respond; one-way communications were hallmarks of an operation in progress.

The analysts of OP-20-G had learned to detect the pattern of Japanese signaling from the multitude of messages bouncing around the ether. In July 1941 they had given advanced warning of the Japanese descent on Indochina, and in November and December they had deduced that the Pacific war was about to begin after discovering the movement of Japanese forces towards Southeast Asia. They had not sniffed out the Japanese intention to strike at Pearl Harbor because the Japanese carrier force that carried out the attack was involved in a total two-way radio silence before the operation; it neither sent nor received signals. This, the Americans observed, had happened twice before in February and July 1941, and on both occasions the American assumption that the Japanese carriers were in home waters had been proved correct. Pearl Harbor was a case of third time wrong.[15]

Direction finding and traffic analysis could often detect operations by identifying active commands and areas of concentration. Obviously both had their limitations, but because the Japanese could not confound the Americans with a total blackout for any length of time, they were certain to have some usefulness even under the most unfavorable of circumstances. Although the Japanese did have recourse to a wide range of ploys designed to mislead the enemy, they could not ensure absolute security by making no signals at all: so drastic an action would have a debilitating effect on operational efficiency. The primary means of keeping the enemy ignorant of Japanese plans were the codes and ciphers devised by the Imperial Navy's Fourth Section, the equivalent of OP-20-G, and the section that dealt with signals security.

The basic principle of signals security is simple. To prevent an unauthorized body from reading a message, the latter is subjected to a two-part process, coding and ciphering. Initially a message is stripped of all superfluous words and punctuation to produce what is known as a plaintext, to which is added an authentication and the call signs of both sender and addressee. In coding, codegroups are substituted for words. The coded message is then enciphered—that is, processed against an electronically selected random numbers system. Sender and addressee possess common code and cipher books, the latter being known as one-time pads. With them, the sender can construct a message into plaintext, then into first a coded and then a ciphered signal; the addressee is able to reverse the process. As long as a signal is not garbled in either the sending or the receiving, the process is simple and theoretically secure.

The Japanese, like all the major combatants, operated a bewildering number of codes and ciphers. Different organizations used different systems, and even within one organization a variety of systems could be used depending on the source, the area of operations or the nature of the contents of any given system. In the course of the war the Imperial Navy is estimated to have employed several hundred codes; of these two were critically important. The first was the *KO*, reserved for flag officers. This was known to the Americans as *AD* and was extremely complicated. It proved invulnerable to American attempts to break it, but it induced so many errors in transmission and reception that it was virtually incomprehensible to its users, and it was abandoned in either 1942 or 1943.[16] The second was the *D*, or later the *RO*, which carried about half the Imperial Navy's operational traffic. This was the code known to the Americans as JN-25. In the opening months of the war the Americans were working on the second version of the code they had encountered, known simply as JN-25b. To ensure the code's security, D had been devised as a double-coded polyalphabetic superenciperment, which involved transposition of individual numbers in a prearranged pattern. The final defense of the Imperial Navy's signal lay in the complexity of Japanese, which had over 3,000 characters, and in the fact that signals were sent in Japanese morse.[17]

By a process that will always defy the understanding of anyone not involved in cryptanalysis, the JN-25b code had been compromised. The assault on the code had been led and directed by OP-20-GY, the head of the cryptanalysis units in the U.S. Navy. The Washington station, code named Negat, ran and directed the entire cryptanalysis effort, known as Operation Magic, but given the geographical separation of the stations— Hypo at Pearl Harbor and Belconnen at Melbourne—there was an element of autonomy in each unit's activities. Liaison between the units, and with a British station that was initially at Singapore and then at Colombo, was conducted on secure and reserved frequencies. This arrangement was known as Copek.[18]

Intelligence on Japan was made available to the United States from several sources and agencies. The British, for example, gave the United States the contents of many German signals they were reading which dealt with Japan and her intentions. The Americans themselves had an agent within the German Foreign Office who was able to supply them with certain information.[19] But these and other sources were secondary to the signals intelligence provided by Negat and its army counterpart, the Signal Intelligence Service. These two had cooperated in breaking the Japanese diplomatic code known as Purple. Hypo, on the other hand, had tried to chip away at KO without much success. It met with better results in its efforts against low-grade routine and administrative codes. The Americans were therefore placed in the odd position of being able to read some of the most and the least sensitive Japanese signals, but nothing in between and virtually nothing with regard to naval operations. Pearl Harbor acted as the spur to American cryptanalysis, and thereafter Hypo was directed to concentrate its efforts against JN-25b. Copek allowed stations to pool their activities, but it would appear that Belconnen (originally station Cast at Cavite on Luzon, before its evacuation) and the British between them made the first crucial entries into the code. Thereafter the main assault was spearheaded by Hypo and Negat together, the former having the most experienced cryptanalysts and intelligence operators of the four Allied stations. By April, after much trial and error and cross-checking, the various units were able to get an insight into about 40 percent of all the messages they received, and of these they could read from 10 to 15 percent of their contents.[20] This meant that about two percent of all the Japanese signals traffic could be read, but years of monitoring Japanese radio activity had provided the sixth sense that told the Americans what to ignore and where they should expend their efforts.

In the course of April the substantial break into JN-25b took place. The Americans were able to read as much as 85 percent of signals. Complete recovery, though, was rare, and the various stations were forced to work on a labyrinth of fragmented information. Still, through April the Allied operation recovered increasing evidence from enemy radio traffic that the Japanese were planning an operation in the southwest Pacific. In making this discovery the Americans were unwittingly helped by the carelessness of the Japanese, though they would have been able to build up the picture for Operation MO even without decryption. Traffic analysis in April alone gave the Americans enough warning of Japanese intentions.

Because operational messages must take a standard form, the constant use of a single code and cipher produces repetitions that will result in a loss of secrecy if the signal's pattern can be discerned by an enemy with time to build up and sift evidence. The counter to this—the standard operational procedure of signals security—is to change codes and ciphers at set intervals. In 1940 the Imperial Navy changed its JN-12 code because the British and Dutch were suspected of reading it.[21] Just before the outbreak of war the Japanese changed their codes twice in a month for extra security—a precaution that implied that war was about to begin.[22] A subsequent change of codes was scheduled for 1 April, and it had to be made in one move. There could be no question of using old and new codes alongside one another, for any compromise of the old code would be automatically transferred to the new one. But the Japanese failed to make their planned change. It seems that there was confusion in the libraries of the Fourth Section, and that the Japanese had considerable difficulty distributing new code and cipher books to their formations and units. Even so, there was certainly an unusual complacency in deferring the code changes first to 1 May and then to 1 June. This proved to be the Japanese undoing. Had they adhered to the April deadline, or even to their May schedule, there would have been no time for the stations monitoring Japanese signals to build up the repetitions needed to break the codes before Midway.[23]

As we have seen, the first signs of a buildup of Japanese air power in the southwest Pacific were noted by intelligence in late March, but it was not until 9 April that the Americans were able to glean information suggesting that the Japanese had designs on the area. Hitherto the Americans had noted that the enemy had the means and opportunity to move in this area—on 9 April a piece of the jigsaw suggested that they had the inclination as well. On that date the Pacific Fleet command was warned by intelligence that the *Kaga*, then believed to be in Sasebo, was expected in the New Britain area at the end of the month. After she received her orders of 5 April from the Combined Fleet to go south, the *Kaga* had communicated with the South Seas Force. For a member of the carrier force to talk to a local command was unusual, and did not go unnoticed by people intent on her destruction. The fact that she was talking to Inoue's command was an indication that she, and perhaps other members of her formation, might be bound for the southwest Pacific in the near future. The *Kaga*'s "conversation" with the South Seas Force was the first real indication that the Japanese might be planning some move beyond Rabaul.[24]

Confirmation of the suspicion came from two sources in the course of the next six days. First, on 10 April the Americans recorded their agreement with the Colombo assessment that the then-current Japanese rampage in the Indian Ocean was being conducted by six enemy carriers. (In fact the raid on Ceylon was over by the time this conclusion was drawn; the Japanese, by the tenth, were in the process of withdrawing from the Indian Ocean after having raided Trincomalee on the previous day.)[25] The assessment, which was correct, led the Americans to believe that the Japanese had two fleet carriers, the *Kaga* and the *Ryukaku*, available for operations elsewhere.* The Americans also concluded that the forces involved in the Indian Ocean raid could not be made available to support any offensive in the southwest Pacific before the end of the month.[26]

Second, on the fifteenth, Negat recovered the full text of a signal sent by Hara as the Carrier Striking Force passed through the Straits of Malacca. This was a situation report, sent by the Fifth Carrier Division to Inoue, made in response to an order for the division to proceed to the support of the South Seas Force. In the signal Hara reported that his force would be able to leave Formosa for Truk on 28 April. The Americans made two errors in their handling of this signal. First, departure and arrival dates were confused, the Americans taking the signal to mean that the *Shokaku* and the *Zuikaku* would arrive at Truk on the twenty-eighth. Second, because the Americans were reading so little of the overall traffic, they were not in a position to know that the Fifth Carrier Division had been ordered to the southwest Pacific in the place of the *Kaga*. The Americans believed that the two carriers had been ordered to join Inoue's flag in addition to the *Kaga*.[27]

Thus when Nimitz and his staff met on 17 April to discuss what to do about an enemy carrier operation in the southwest Pacific, they possessed erroneous and incomplete evidence of the enemy's intentions. The conclusion of this meeting was that the enemy was planning to develop an offensive into the southwest Pacific at the end of the month, his probable target being Port Moresby. As yet there was no evidence to confirm a

*Both before and during the battle of the Coral Sea, and for some time afterwards, the Americans confused the *Shoho* and the *Ryukaku*. The error arose through a mistransliteration of Japanese script.

Japanese plan to develop a double attack, one against Port Moresby and the other against the Solomons. The possibility of an enemy move into the Solomons had been suspected as early as 3 April, but to date there had been no evidence to confirm a Japanese plan to develop a double attack against both Port Moresby and the Solomons. Nor, for that matter, was there conclusive evidence that Port Moresby was the Japanese objective, but throughout the southwest Pacific only Port Moresby retained a significance that could justify the use of fleet carriers in an operation against it. After 17 April evidence began to confirm both suspicions, that the Japanese planned a double offensive and that their main objective was the seizure of Port Moresby. It was not until the end of April that the Americans secured confirmation of any enemy move in the Solomons, and it was only on the eve of battle, on 30 April and 1 May, that the cryptanalysts were able to identify Port Moresby as the enemy's target with any certainty. Then they were able to discern the enemy's intention to establish a seaplane base at Deboyne Islands on D-5 (five days before D-Day)[28] and thereafter to establish similar bases at Cape Rodney and Samarai Island.[29]

These discoveries left little room for doubt, but on the seventeenth Nimitz and his subordinates had to plan on the basis of less precise information, which suggested that four carriers would be in the Japanese order of battle: the *Kaga*, *Shoho*, *Shokaku* and *Zuikaku*. Before another week this estimate rose to five as suspicion hardened that the Japanese had committed the *Taiyo* to a venture that was now known to be code named Operation MO.[30] Actually the *Taiyo* and her two sister ships, unfit to take part in a fleet action, were confined to ferrying and training duties for the whole of the war, but the Americans were not to know that at this time.[31] The American problem in trying to frame a response to the impending Japanese move was obvious. At this time they had only the overworked *Yorktown* in the area. Three days earlier, on the fourteenth, Nimitz had taken the precaution of ordering her to put into Tongabatu for replenishment. She was to return to her station in the Coral Sea by the twenty-seventh. Her erstwhile companion, the *Lexington*, had arrived back at Pearl Harbor on 26 March and had been docked for a quick refit, which included the removal of some of her 8-in guns.[32] Her admiral, as we have seen, was put ashore. In his place Nimitz appointed Rear Admiral Aubrey W. Fitch. On 10 April Fitch received orders to take Task Force 11 to sea in five days and exercise to the south of Pearl Harbor with the battleships of Task Force 1 until 4 May.[33]

Nimitz's problems on 17 April were many, but the most serious was that the lone *Yorktown* could neither deter nor offer effective resistance to an enemy with four or more carriers. If Nimitz was to try to counter the enemy's move, the *Yorktown* would have to be supported. But with the *Enterprise* and the *Hornet* committed to the raid on Japan, the *Lexington* could

Admiral Chester W. Nimitz

not be sent to the southwest Pacific for the moment. Nimitz therefore had to await the outcome of the Doolittle Raid before he could think of sending Task Force 11 to join the *Yorktown*. But even if the *Yorktown* and the *Lexington* joined forces in time to meet the enemy as he came into the southwest Pacific, the Americans would have no more than two fleet carriers to meet the anticipated four of the enemy. At this point it was obvious that the Doolittle Raid had been an unwise move. Its effect was to tie up three-quarters, and then half, of available American carrier strength for what could easily prove to be a disastrous period of time, and there was no getting away from the conclusion, recorded in the fleet war diary, that "CINCPAC [Nimitz] will probably be unable to send enough force to the southwest Pacific to be *sure* of stopping the Jap[anese] offensive."[34]

It was ironic that Nimitz's problems arose because of the enthusiasm of King for the Doolittle Raid. All along King had wanted to direct the war into the southwest Pacific—he had been instrumental in pushing American carrier forces into the area in the first place—yet by mid-April he and Nimitz had to face the prospect of being caught on the wrong foot because of the Doolittle Raid.[35] But at least by 19 April Nimitz knew that one of his immediate worries had been laid to rest. Task Force 16 had completed its raid on Japan, and with the *Enterprise* and the *Hornet* safe and returning to

Pearl Harbor, Nimitz was free to order the *Lexington* to discontinue her exercises with the battle force and head for the southwest Pacific.

Moreover, Nimitz was advised on the nineteenth by King of Washington's estimate that the impending enemy operation would have to be delayed until the first week of May as a result of the Doolittle Raid. Such had been the overreaction of the Imperial Navy to the American operation—as many Japanese warships had given chase as possible—that reorganization of Japanese forces in time to meet a deadline of the last week in April was unlikely. On the other hand, Nimitz also received a report that the *Shoho* and the Fifth Carrier Division were expected to arrive at Truk on 25 April.

The Pacific Fleet staff meeting of 20 to 22 April saw Nimitz and his subordinates begin to settle their response to Operation MO. On the twentieth, when Nimitz sent a warning order to Task Force 11 to prepare for major operations, the Pacific Fleet began the process of examining in detail what was known of Japanese intentions and forces. Its first conclusion was that the enemy would begin operations in the general area of New Britain, New Guinea and the Solomons on or about 3 May with a force perhaps of five carriers, probably two battleships, about five heavy cruisers, light units and an army division. No doubt Inoue would have wished that this assessment was correct. The Americans assumed that the enemy's objective was to secure Port Moresby and the Solomons rather than just Port Moresby, and they rejected the possibility that the enemy would aim to cut right through the area in an effort to secure New Caledonia and/or Fuji. They believed that the Japanese were likely to adhere to a step-by-step process, and that they would not risk sending their forces beyond the range of land-based aircraft. This was in accordance with Japanese practice to date. The Pacific Fleet staff also thought it likely that the enemy would keep his main forces back in the opening moves, preferring to use them to exploit success or to reinforce in the event of trouble.

Nimitz's reaction to this scenario was to accept battle. His orders to the *Yorktown* and the *Lexington* had already served notice of his intention to fight for Port Moresby, and he was thus inclined for two reasons. First, the enemy's forthcoming operation would be a chance to meet his carrier forces in battle for the first time. Given the American determination to break these forces and with them the whole offensive power of the Imperial Navy, it was inconceivable that Nimitz would pass up the first chance he had of accepting battle. Second, and contrary to some accounts of events, at this stage of proceedings, when the Americans accepted the prospect of battle in the southwest Pacific, they had not picked up any signs that the Japanese contemplated a move into the central Pacific.

Nimitz in fact planned to make an all-out defense of Port Moresby. On the assumption that the central Pacific would remain quiet, he was prepared to deploy all his carriers to the southwest Pacific in an effort to secure a favorable decision in that area. The staff calculation was that a rendezvous of Task Forces 11 and 17 could be made on 1 May, and it was proposed that Task Force 16 be sent to the southwest Pacific in the wake of the *Lexington*. The linkup of all four carriers could be accomplished between 14 and 16 May, though as the subsequent plan of campaign showed, the arrival of the *Enterprise* and the *Hornet* was more likely to result in the rotation of American carriers in the southwest Pacific than in their concentration. The *Yorktown* was probably the most overworked of the American carriers in the Pacific, having been continuously at sea for all but a ten-day period at Pearl Harbor since the time she left San Diego on 6 January.[36] Depending on the situation, the arrival of Task Force 16 in the southwest Pacific would result in the departure of the *Yorktown* for Hawaii.

In arriving at any decision, however, Nimitz was confronted by two problems. First, the arrival of Task Force 16 in the southwest Pacific might be too late to be effective if the Japanese stuck to their assumed timetable. There was nothing that the Japanese could do on this score other than hope that the Japanese were late in getting under way. In view of the dispersal of Japanese forces in the aftermath of the Doolittle Raid, this was not an unrealistic hope. If, however, as seemed likely, Japanese forces in the homeland came south to support the South Seas Force when it became clear that Allied opposition was more substantial than had been anticipated, Task Force 16 would arrive in time to play its proper part in proceedings. Nimitz's second problem was that the American capacity for prolonged operations in the southwest Pacific was doubtful. A four-carrier force could be sustained until 1 June, but it could not be sustained if it went south with the battle force or if the latter proceeded independently, was held south of Hawaii or was kept at Pearl Harbor. Because of its heavy demands on oil, slow speed and lack of any independent role, Nimitz's inclination was to send Task Force 1 back to the West Coast. But even without the battleships, the Pacific Fleet could sustain its carrier forces in the southwest Pacific in June only if it requisitioned, and then only if its oilers were not lost. That operations could hang on so slender a thread as a single oiler had been revealed back in January when an operation against Wake had to be abandoned after the task group oiler was sunk.[37]

Once these considerations had been discussed the important decisions could be made and the basic plan of campaign could be framed by the fleet staff. Under its terms Nimitz proposed to rid himself of the battle force; it was to return to California. The *Lexington* was to make tracks for a rendezvous with Task Force 17; Halsey and Task Force 16 would be sped on their way to the southwest Pacific after their raid on Japan. In addition to the carrier deployment to the area, the Pacific Fleet planned to double the number of Catalina reconnaissance flying boats on New Caledonia to

twelve and to send submarines against Truk. To mask these various movements the Pacific Fleet planned to mount a diversionary raid on the Kamchatka fishing grounds with the light cruiser *Nashville*, in the course of
which she was to simulate carrier operations.[38]

Such were his intentions, but Nimitz had to secure approval from his
superiors to implement such a plan of campaign, because it contained two,
if not three, potentially contentious proposals. First, the plan envisaged
battle with inferior forces. Simply in terms of fleet carriers, picking up the
Japanese challenge in the southwest Pacific meant acceptance of odds of
three to two against. Second, the plan would empty the whole of the central
Pacific in order to meet the enemy in the Coral Sea. From the start of the
war American policy had been to keep the greater part of American carrier
strength in the central basin of the Pacific. At least one-third of the carrier
force had always been in the Hawaii area, and there had usually been more.
Having two carriers in the southwest Pacific on two separate occasions, first
in January and February and then in March, was exceptional, the result of
the peculiar circumstances of those times.[39] What Nimitz proposed, therefore, was different from anything the Americans had previously undertaken. Though the justification for his present proposal was that the Pacific
Fleet had no alternative but to react to a specific threat with its full force, the
fact remained that to meet Operation MO Nimitz proposed to put the
whole of the fleet's offensive power into the southwest Pacific, more than
3,000 miles from Pearl Harbor. This represented a considerable shift of
strategic policy, and to secure approval for it Nimitz left Pearl Harbor on
the afternoon of the twenty-fourth for a conference at San Francisco with
King.[40]

The King-Nimitz conference lasted from the twenty-fifth to the twenty-
seventh. The result was that King endorsed virtually everything Nimitz
proposed. Without countering the arrangements Nimitz wanted to put in
hand for the forthcoming operation, King instructed Nimitz to maintain in
the future a force in the southwest Pacific equivalent to that in the central
ocean. But in undertaking the move into the southwest Pacific, Nimitz was
instructed to heed the state of Midway's defenses. As far as King was
concerned, Midway had to be made as secure as possible if the Pacific Fleet
was to be committed to the south.[41]

Nimitz's proposals were far too in tune with King's own thinking for
there to be any question of his refusing to sanction them. It was unfortunate
that the enemy offensive seemed likely to get under way before the Americans had the chance to concentrate all their carriers in order to meet it, but
the prospect of doing battle even on the basis of numerical inferiority was
not one from which King recoiled. With the experience of battle yet to teach
him otherwise, King was supremely confident in the ability of the carrier
forces to deal with the enemy. He may not have agreed with the arithmetic

of the crew of his old command, the *Lexington*, which claimed their ship was the equal of any four Japanese carriers, but there was no doubting that King, a former chief of the Bureau of Aeronautics and vice admiral of the carrier division, shared the general American overconfidence in the power of the carrier force that he had helped to create.[42] King welcomed the prospect of battle. It presented a chance to hurt the enemy and get rid of the "defeatists and pessimists" who he believed continued to stalk Pearl Harbor.[43] More important, it would take place in the southwest Pacific, where King himself wanted to fight the war. He had already set out the Solomons as the area where the Americans should make their future effort, and he had done this when no one else in the American high command had the least idea of how to fight a war in the Pacific. In a roundabout way the soundness of King's thinking was being demonstrated by the enemy: Operation MO was seeming confirmation of King's strategic vision.

Operation MO and Nimitz's preparations to counter it played into King's hands as he began to prepare for the second round in the battle with two other enemies, Marshall and Arnold. Already in April the battle lines for this round were being drawn, and for King the Japanese offensive in the southwest Pacific could be used to strengthen his case for a revision of American strategic priorities. Thus far in the war nothing had really been settled. Marshall had agreed in the opening months of 1942 to deployments that had already seen more men committed to the Pacific than to the Atlantic and Europe, but within the army high command opinion was hardening against further commitments in the Pacific. To Marshall the policy of holding the lines of communication to Australia and to the islands of the southwest Pacific meant that the theater had to be defended and that forces, particularly aircraft, should be available to facilitate that objective. To King, on the other hand, "holding" meant making the area secure, and that involved having forces so they would be able to do something more than indulge in passive defense.[44]

As far as Marshall was concerned, in April and May the Pacific had drawn on more than its fair share of resources and would have to get by with what it had, not what King said it needed. His view was supported by Arnold. Operation MO (and, as it proved, its immediate aftermath) gave King the chance to throw open the whole question of strategic policy. But there was one catch. Any defense of Port Moresby, any meeting of the enemy south of Rabaul, required that Nimitz's carriers enter the Southwest Pacific Command area—once there they had to come under MacArthur's control. That arrangement was explicit under the terms whereby the Pacific had been divided into the Southwest Pacific Command and the Pacific Ocean Area Command. To Nimitz and King, meeting for the first time just one week after the Southwest Pacific Command had been activated, the answer to this difficulty was simple: MacArthur would be ignored.[45] There could be no question of the general having any say over carrier operations. This would not prevent the navy expecting MacArthur's prompt compliance in meeting any demand it might make of him.

The navy's treatment of MacArthur on this occasion was dishonest, and not surprisingly its rather cavalier attitude towards the Southwest Pacific Command was repaid in the same coin on later occasions. But for the navy much more was at stake in April 1942 than observing the niceties of operational boundaries and command responsibilities, and more was at stake than the immediate safety of the carrier forces and the outcome of an enemy offensive. The wider question was how the war would be fought. When the navy was putting together its plan of campaign for the southwest Pacific, Marshall was in London trying to sell his idea of a cross-channel invasion in 1942 to a somewhat incredulous British audience.[46] With Marshall was Arnold, who was committed to winning the war by strategic bombing, thereby establishing the right of the air force to an independent existence. It was natural that his attention should be directed towards the European theater of operations. In the eyes of the War Department the overriding American interest at this time was to keep the British and Soviets in the war and to deny the Middle East to the enemy. As part of this definition of priorities Eisenhower, the architect of the commitment to Australia in February, had reversed his opinions and was now of the view that preventing a Japanese invasion of Australia was "not immediately vital to the outcome of the war."[47] As far as King was concerned, such views were nonsense. In a world where American military leaders acted as if they were Chinese warlords in pursuit of power, King continued to play his lone hand with Australia essential to his cause. It had to be held as the base for future operations and "because of the repercussions amongst the non-white races" that its loss would certainly provoke.[48]

King's concern for Australia was seconded by MacArthur, but as we have noted, such support was two-edged; MacArthur's interest was to use Australia as the means of using Allied strategy to his own advantage. As early as 24 April he requested carrier forces and reinforcements for the Southwest Pacific Command, and on the twenty-eighth Curtin signaled such requests in his own name, adding the source acknowledgment.[49] On the following day MacArthur continued his attempt to usurp, or at least infringe upon, the preserve of policymaking by setting out the southwest Pacific as the one and only theater of operations that counted.[50] On 8 May he informed Marshall—after the latter had admonished him for his antics and for certain press releases from his headquarters that could easily have compromised security—that if the American aim was to get support to the Soviets so that they would not collapse under the weight of a German summer offensive, then the effort had to be made in the southwest Pacific. His assertion that "nowhere else can [a second front] be so successfully launched, and nowhere else will it so assist the Russians" was ludicrous.[51] Washington did nothing about either MacArthur or his strategic "vision," and it was left to Churchill to put matters in perspective when he told Roosevelt that the general had crossed the line between political authority and military responsibility.[52] At the time the course of action was clear enough to King and Nimitz: it was safer to abjure than to enlist the support of MacArthur, since the general threatened to be a greater danger to the navy than the Japanese.[53] The navy was determined to go it alone, and Nimitz's role as commander in chief of the Pacific Fleet enabled him to fight a naval war anywhere in the Pacific and thereby provide King with an ace or two for the battles that would ensue in Washington. It was scarcely surprising, therefore, that at San Francisco King backed Nimitz to the hilt. He gave Nimitz his full support, even though he retained certain reservations about some of Nimitz's subordinates and his fleet commander's support of them.[54] King sanctioned Nimitz's nomination of Vice Admiral Robert L. Ghormley as commander of the South Pacific Area—an unfortunate choice as things turned out—but ordered Nimitz to assume personal responsibility for this command until Ghormley arrived from London and took up his appointment.[55]

In San Francisco Nimitz received the support he needed for a deployment of American carrier strength into the southwest Pacific, and by the time he arrived back at Pearl Harbor on 28 April most of the arrangements had been made. On 24 April, even before he left for the West Coast, Nimitz had informed Rear Admiral Frank J. Fletcher, commander of Task Force 17, of what was going on and of the reinforcements he might expect to receive. The next day, as King and Nimitz began their discussions, Task Force 16 arrived at Pearl Harbor.[56] At the same time Fletcher was told that his formation might be able to return to Pearl Harbor after 15 May, but notification of Nimitz's intention to develop the base facilities at Pago Pago hinted that American carrier operations in the southwest Pacific might well be protracted.[57] The matter of the Samoan base was one of the few areas of disagreement between King and Nimitz in San Francisco. From the time that he had first expounded the virtues of the southwest Pacific as the theater where offensive operations should be mounted, King had singled out the less-exposed Tongabatu as the base for American logistical support; events after 2 March had given him no cause to revise this opinion.[58]

On 29 April Nimitz issued detailed instructions to his commanders in the form of Operational Plan 23-42. It was similar in content to the 20–22 April appreciation, though in the intervening week intelligence had been able to pad out a great deal of the information relating to enemy intentions. By the twenty-ninth it could be predicted with a fair degree of certainty that the enemy intended to move against both Port Moresby and the Solomons.[59] Intelligence had also uncovered Operation RY, the plan to

Rear Admiral Frank J. Fletcher

secure Ocean and Nauru, though the summaries that gave rise to this conclusion were met with some skepticism both ashore and at sea. Four major formations in the enemy's order of battle had been identified—a main force, a support force and two occupation forces, one destined for MO and the other for RZP. The correct intelligence guess was that *MO* stood for Moresby and *RZP* for Tulagi. Intelligence had also correctly connected the Fifth Carrier and Fifth Cruiser Divisions with the South Seas Force, thus coming to the conclusion that the enemy would have just three carriers in support of Operation MO.[60] The Pacific Fleet concurred with the Australian assessment that the enemy would have three carriers, five heavy cruisers, four light cruisers and twelve destroyers, plus lighter units, in their overall order of battle.[61] This assessment was not correct, and the Australians were wrong in presuming that Port Moresby was the sole enemy objective. The Pacific Fleet assessment was faulty in another sense as well. Still with no inkling of Operation MI, American intelligence continued to work on the assumption that the Japanese intended to make their main effort in the southwest Pacific and would probably move through the Coral Sea to strike at New Caledonia and Fiji if they were successful in Operation MO.[62] Even as late as 1 May Pacific Fleet intelligence continued to believe that the Japanese had no plans to develop an offensive into the central Pacific.[63]

Countering Operation MO involved more than just Operational Plan 23-42, the Pacific Fleet plan and disposition for the defense of Port Moresby and the southern and central Solomons. But leaving aside the contribution of air and naval forces from the Southwest Pacific Command, the American plan of campaign, as laid down by Nimitz, stated that "Rear Admiral Fletcher will operate in the Coral Sea from 1 May onwards and will be in command of all forces assigned to him. He will have discretion to take action to intercept the enemy and keep open vital lines of communication between the United States and Australia."[64] The forces that were to be assigned to him were his own Task Force 17, that of Fitch, Task Force 11, and that of Rear Admiral John G. Crace, RN, Task Force 44. On 1 May Task Force 17—consisting of the *Yorktown*; the heavy cruisers *Astoria*, *Chester* and *Portland*; the destroyers *Morris*, *Anderson*, *Hammann* and *Russell*; plus a replenishment group of two oilers and two destroyers—was to rendezvous with Fitch at Point Buttercup, latitude 16° S, longitude 161° 45' E, roughly equidistant from San Cristobal to the north, Espirito Santo to the east and the northern tip of New Caledonia to the south. Fitch's command consisted of the *Lexington*; the heavy cruisers *Minneapolis* and *New Orleans*; and the destroyers *Phelps*, *Dewey*, *Farragut*, *Aylwin* and *Monaghan*. Crace commanded the ANZAC Squadron, an American-Australian formation that was a leftover from the old ANZAC area. The heavy cruiser *Chicago* and the destroyer *Perkins* were at Noumea, while the cruisers *Australia*, *Canberra* and *Hobart* were at Sydney, all undergoing repairs. The two American units were ordered to join Fletcher at the same time as Fitch and to be in the company of the oiler *Tippecanoe*, which would have to refuel Task Force 11 at the end of its run from the north. The Australian ships, in the company of the American destroyers *Whipple* and *John D. Edwards*, were to join later, and did so on 4 May, though neither the *Canberra* nor the *John D. Edwards* were able to go to sea. The Australian heavy cruiser was refitting and could not be made ready for sea in time, and the American destroyer developed engine trouble that could not be corrected quickly enough to allow her to take her place in the Allied order of battle.[65]

The means by which Fletcher chose to oppose the Japanese was left to his discretion. He was to exercise overall command of all the Allied naval forces in the southwest Pacific until about 15 May, when he was to hand over command to Halsey, who would arrive with Task Force 16. Halsey's orders were to "check further advance of the enemy in the New Guinea–Solomons area by destroying enemy ships, shipping and aircraft."[66] Depending on the prevailing situation, the arrival of Task Force 16 in the theater would allow the departure for Pearl Harbor first of Task Force 17 and then of Task Force 11, 15 May and 1 June being fixed as the tentative dates of their respective farewells. With these arrangements Nimitz hoped to ensure a full concentration of his carrier forces should the situation

require it, or the division of the carrier forces between the southwest Pacific
and the central Pacific theaters, as King had demanded in San Francisco.
Nimitz had Task Force 16 take with it a fighter squadron for the marines at
Efate, and he ordered Halsey to scout Howland and Baker en route to the
south. Task Force 16 was instructed to tackle any Japanese force that might
be encountered heading for Ocean and Nauru. In addition, Nimitz instructed the *Pensacola* to make her way south as soon as she could. She was
to go with a solitary destroyer as escort. The new light antiaircraft cruiser
Atlanta, plus a destroyer and two oilers, was also to head for the southwest
Pacific in the course of May.[67]

Events were to conspire to prevent the integration of Fletcher's formations into a single task force until the morning of 7 May, three days after
battle was joined. When concentrated, the new formations took on the
Yorktown's designation, Task Force 17, which was then organized into three
tactical groups. Task Group 17.2 was to consist of the *Lexington*'s screen,
augmented by the *Yorktown*'s heavy cruisers. Task Group 17.3 was to be
the reconcentrated Task Force 44. Task Group 17.5 was to be made up of
the two carriers with a screen provided by the four destroyers that had been
with the *Yorktown*. Under command were two other groups. The first,
Task Group 17.6, was the detached oiler group. The second, Task Group
17.9, was theoretically part of Fletcher's task force but actually beyond his
control. It consisted of twelve Catalinas operating out of the tender *Tangier*
at Noumea in New Caledonia. Until 4 May this group had just one
squadron of six flying boats, but in the afternoon of that day the second
squadron, earlier promised by Nimitz, arrived on station.[68] Fletcher exercised overall command of Task Force 17, but tactical command of Task
Force 17.5 was assigned to Fitch in the *Lexington*.

Fletcher's plan, issued on 1 May, stated that the objective of his force was
to "destroy enemy ships, shipping and aircraft at favorable opportunities in
order to assist in checking further advances by [the] enemy in the New
Guinea–Solomons area." His orders were virtually the same as those given
to Halsey, but while Halsey's had to be left deliberately vague, because the
situation that might exist when Task Force 16 arrived in the southwest
Pacific was unknown, those issued by Fletcher had to be precise. Fletcher
was in possession of the enemy's assumed order of battle, timetable and
objectives. He stated that his forces would "operate generally about seven
hundred miles south of Rabaul. Upon receiving intelligence of enemy
surface forces advancing to the southward, [the Allied force] will move into
a favorable position for intercepting and destroying the enemy."[69] In this
manner Fletcher set out the main theme of his plan of campaign. His
intention was to keep the carrier force on the disengaged flank of any enemy
movement on Port Moresby. He planned to hold his formation in the
general area of the northeast Coral Sea, inside the sweep of the New

Hebrides and southern Solomons, to the west of Rossel and Tagula, and to the south of a line between these two islands and Rennell. The area in which Fletcher chose to operate was away from the direction of the enemy's main thrust, and Japanese reconnaissance there was expected to be at its least effective. From that area Fletcher intended to counterattack as the enemy showed his hand. In this way he stood a good chance of inflicting loss on the enemy while running the least possible risk to himself. This was the eventuality that the Japanese hoped to forestall by establishing a reconnaissance base at Tulagi as the final objective in preliminary phase operations, before the main effort to secure Port Moresby unfolded.

While the carrier force was to be in the east, the western sector of the Coral Sea, around southern New Guinea itself, was to be covered by naval and air units from the Southwest Pacific Command. The naval forces of the command were under the orders of Vice Admiral Herbert F. Leary. He had command of a single formation, nominally Task Force 42, but in reality this was no more than the solitary Task Group 42.1, made up of two submarine squadrons. These operated out of the tender *Griffith* at Moreton Bay, Brisbane. Task Group 42.1 numbered eleven submarines, all of them units of the old *S*-class that had not been intended for offensive operations in the Pacific. They had been designed for defensive duties, and they did not have the range, armament and communications to operate effectively in the vast Pacific, but in the emergency of early 1942 they were the only units on hand. Six of the eleven had come from the Atlantic in the company of the *Griffith*, arriving at Brisbane via Panama and Bora Bora on 15 April. The other five had come from the Asiatic Fleet after its futile defense of the Philippines and the Indies. They had been stationed at Freemantle following the withdrawal from Southeast Asia and then sailed round to Brisbane via Melbourne. Like their six other colleagues, they arrived in Brisbane in need of proper overhaul.[70] Such was the serviceability of these submarines that only four, the *S-38*, *S-42*, *S-44* and *S-47*, were able to go to sea before Operation MO began. The *S-38* was to sail on 28 April to scout the southern coast of Papua and the Jomard Passage, returning on 24 May. The *S-47*, *S-44* and *S-42* left Brisbane on 22, 24 and 25 April respectively. All operated in the New Britain and New Ireland area, and they returned to base between 20 and 23 May. In fact, between 13 and 20 May Task Group 42.1 had ten of its eleven boats at sea, going on or returning from patrol or on station. However, such a high rate of serviceability was exceptional, and in any event it came one week too late to have any effect on the outcome of the Coral Sea engagement. But, ironically, the only success to come the way of Task Group 42.1 was registered after Operation MO was over, as the Japanese prepared to put Operation RY into effect, and the little success that was achieved was recorded by members of the original four, not the subsequent six. On 11 May the *S-42* caught the *Okinoshima* with two torpedoes from a salvo of four, the minelayer being lost the following morning. That same day the *S-44* accounted for the *Shoeimaru* off Cape St. George. She was a 5,644-ton repair ship returning to Rabaul from Buka after a vain attempt to reach the *Okinoshima* before she foundered. Welcome though these two successes were, they represented a poor return for the efforts of Task Group 42.1.[71]

Main responsibility for covering the Solomons, eastern New Guinea and the sea approaches to Port Moresby had to be vested not in the submarines but in the air arm of the Southwest Pacific Command. This, activated as the Allied Air Forces on 20 April, was commanded by Lieutenant General George H. Brett, until recently Wavell's American deputy in the ABDA Command. Brett had under his orders what appeared on paper to be an impressively strong collection of American and Australian units and formations, but in reality the Allied Air Forces was much weaker than its paper strength suggested. For a variety of reasons, very few of which were of its own making, the Allied Air Forces failed to make much impact on forthcoming events.

Of the many problems that served to confound the efforts of the Allied Air Forces, five can be highlighted for consideration. First, its strength could not be concentrated to good effect. With the whole of Australia's east coast, particularly the vital ports of Brisbane and Sydney, open to attack, part of its strength had to be siphoned off to provide defense for areas not directly involved in the immediate combat theater. Moreover, the Australians had to provide routine maritime reconnaissance for the protection of coastal and oceanic shipping, and this commitment involved Australia in operations in two oceans, not one. Furthermore, though western Australia was threatened for the simple reason that Perth was no further from the Sunda Straits than Darwin, northern Australia faced an immediate and double threat: from Rabaul came the more obvious one, but from Kendari, Ambon and Timor came one that was no less severe. The basic problem that confronted the Allied Air Forces in trying to counter attacks on Port Moresby and eastern Australia was that substantial forces had to be held around Darwin.

Second, it was not possible for the Allied Air Forces to maintain striking power where it was needed—at Port Moresby itself. The airfields there were far too exposed for Brett to risk stationing his few, expensive and vulnerable heavy and medium bombers at a base that could be subjected to attacks from either Rabaul or Lae. Port Moresby was bombed for the first time on 3 February, and it suffered its first daylight raid three weeks later. On the twenty-eighth a single raid accounted for three Catalinas and one Hudson, nearly half of the reconnaissance strength there. With its dearth of antiaircraft guns, Port Moresby had virtually no capacity to protect its few aircraft, and heavy tropical rains made the ground little more than a swamp, preventing effective dispersal.[72]

Exacerbating this problem, Port Moresby was one of the few stations in northern Australia that could handle bombers such as the Flying Fortress and Marauder. Horn Island, in the Torres Strait, could operate them, but the appearance of Japanese bombers on 14 March over the airfield there put a momentary end to its use. The only other airfields that could handle bombers that needed long takeoffs were around Townsville. Prudently, Brett chose to keep his bombers in this area, out of the range of enemy attacks. Yet in doing so he had to accept the disadvantage of having his only worthwhile target, Rabaul, at the extreme range of his own strike aircraft. Rabaul was about 1,200 miles from Townsville and 525 miles from Port Moresby. The only way for American bombers to strike at Rabaul was by staging through the New Guinea base, about 450 miles from Horn Island and 750 miles from Townsville. The only way Rabaul could be attacked from Townsville was by a shuttle run, the bombers (seldom more than ten in any single raid) flying into Port Moresby in the late afternoon in order to arrive at or after sunset, spending the night refueling and arming, and then being sped on their way with the dawn. This was an altogether impossible arrangement, and it was one that boded ill for any Allied Air Forces effort to support the naval attempt to deny Port Moresby to the Japanese. The sea areas to be covered in the course of forthcoming operations pushed bomber and reconnaissance forces near the prudent limit of endurance. The Jomard Passage was 657 miles from Townsville, and beyond it lay the Solomon Sea. The simple calculation of distance against fuel consumption suggested only a limited role for Allied bombers in northern Australia.

The third problem for the Allied Air Forces was that service facilities in northern Australia and at Port Moresby were, by any standard, rudimentary. In the chaos of the retreat from Southeast Asia and the advance of the Americans into northern Australia, administration had fallen behind deployment. All forms of equipment were in desperately short supply and, in some cases, so were the ground crews. Basic human facilities were primitive, and in all too many cases morale was as low as serviceability rates. To get ten bombers into the air for a mission represented a major effort.

Four, the quality of Allied aircrews in northern Australia was questionable. The Australians were generally better than the Americans, because most of the few Australian formations had a nucleus of men with combat experience or a knowledge of local conditions. But by the end of April many Australian aircrew and aircraft had been in almost constant service since the threats to Australia had emerged in February. Eighty to ninety hours of flying a week, every week, was taking its toll of men and machines. Many of

the Australians were tired and jaded. The situation was not much improved
by the Americans, most of whom were too inexperienced to be operationally effective. The Forty-ninth Pursuit Group, for example, had arrived in
Australia in February with a commander and deputy commander who had
7,400 hours flying time between them. Five of their men had more than 600
hours, and another nine had 15 hours. The remaining eighty-nine pilots
had no experience in fighters.[73] At the other end of the spectrum the men of
the Thirty-fifth Pursuit Group were experienced, but theirs was the experience of defeat. In the fight for Southeast Asia they had seen action of the
kind that all too frequently shatters a formation rather than welds it into an
effective fighting force.

With regard to the bomber forces the lack of training and experience was
crippling. Bomber crews had undergone little if any training in ship recognition, still less bombing practice against moving targets. American navigation was generally poor. Furthermore, the lack of knowledge about local
conditions placed the Americans at a considerable disadvantage. Weather
could be far more dangerous than the enemy. Over the Owen Stanleys
powerful down draughts were always a hazard, and on the ocean there were
many perils other than those caused by error and the enemy. In late 1942,
for example, three Flying Fortresses were lost without trace when they
encountered a storm. In the course of its operations the Eleventh Bombardment Group lost twice as many aircraft to the weather as it did to enemy
action.[74] Indeed, American inexperience was enough of a problem that, at
the time of the Coral Sea battle, it was not unknown for Australian advisers
to fly with American bombers.

For the Allied Air Forces' defense of Port Moresby there was also a fifth
problem. The Southwest Pacific Command was a new one, and though it
had been organized for at least a month before it was activated on 18 April,
command and control arrangements proved troublesome. There were also
manifest problems with the liaison between naval and air forces, not just
within the command but with neighboring commands. Brett and Leary did
all they could, but the Allies did not have an adequate command infrastruc-
ture, and improvisation had its limits.[75]

In April 1942 Brett had six American air groups within the Allied Air
Forces. He had assessed his command's needs at fifteen—six fighter groups
and three light, three medium and three heavy bombardment groups—to
which he later added three more transport formations.[76] At this time Brett
had, in theory, eight groups under command, namely three fighter, one
light, two medium, and two heavy formations. In reality he was one
medium and one heavy group short of establishment, since neither the
Thirty-eighth (Medium) Group nor the Forty-third (Heavy) Group was
operational. Both had been assigned and had ground crews in Australia,
but neither had aircraft.

The Americans had within the Allied Air Forces the Eighth, Thirty-fifth and Forty-ninth Pursuit Groups, and the Third Light, Twenty-second Medium and Nineteenth Heavy Bombardment Groups. Of these, two of the fighter groups were effectively out of the fray. After a period of successful service on Horn Island, the Forty-ninth Pursuit Group had made its way to Darwin, its Ninth, Seventh and Eighth Squadrons arriving there on 17 March, 6 and 15 April respectively.[77] The Thirty-fifth Pursuit Group was in effect the reserve, stationed at Mascot Airfield, Sydney. It had been in the process of reorganizing before reentering the battle, and this it did in late May when it relieved what was by then the badly depleted Eighth Pursuit Group in the north.[78] At the time the Allied Air Forces was activated, the latter was at Archerfield, Brisbane; in the initial stages of the Coral Sea battle Brett was forced to deploy the Airacobras of its Thirty-fifth and Thirty-sixth Squadrons to Port Moresby in an effort to counter the attentions being paid the town by the enemy.[79]

Whereas the pursuit groups were more or less at full strength, the position of the bomber groups varied. The Third Light Group, formed by merging the original Third with the depleted Twenty-seventh Light Group (from the Philippines) after the fall of Java, had only three operational squadrons. The Eighth Light Squadron had the A-24 Dauntless dive-bombers from the old Twenty-seventh Light Group, and the Thirteenth and Ninetieth Light Squadrons had Mitchells that had been intended for the Dutch in the Indies. The Eighty-ninth Light Group was awaiting the arrival of its complement of A-20 Bostons, its ground crews filling in by working on Flying Fortresses at Townsville.[80] The Twenty-second Medium Group, on the other hand, had a uniform issue of forty-eight Marauders, delivered in March, and was at full strength. The Nineteenth Heavy Group, like the Third Light Group, was a composite formation, created by reforming the original Nineteenth Light Group with the Seventh Heavy Group after the fall of Southeast Asia; part of the Seventh, still keeping its number, went on to the China-Burma-India theater.[81] Its fourteen Fortresses joined up with another twelve that had been flown into eastern Australia to operate as a reconnaissance and photographic force. Beginning on 20 March two Fortresses a day were supposed to fly across the Pacific until the minimum strength of both the Nineteenth and Forty-third Heavy Bombardment Groups reached forty, with a similar number in reserve. This effort was abandoned after only nine Fortresses had set out. Without a flow of reinforcements the operational strength of the Nineteenth Group plummeted to just six aircraft at one point in April, and throughout May averaged only seventeen, the equivalent of just one and a half squadrons.[82]

The American commitment to northern Australia was due in part to the realization that the Australians were unable to defend the area. However

weak the American contingent within the Allied Air Forces, it was still
stronger than the Australian contingent. By April the Australians had
thirteen operational squadrons within the command, but their strength in
the northeast was negligible.

The war in the Pacific had begun with the Royal Australian Air Force
deploying a meagre 177 aircraft in Australia, New Guinea and the Indies.
Of these, nine were Seagull flying boats (better known as Walruses) used
for patrolling and air-sea rescue; twelve were Catalinas; fifty-three were
Hudson light reconnaissance bombers and the remainder were Wirraways,
used for training, liaison and observation duties.[83] Given the imbalance
between types of aircraft and flying boats, most of which were of extremely
dubious fighting value, and given the presence of some 101 observation
aircraft out of the total of 177 planes, one can only conclude that the
Australians must have believed they needed an extraordinary number of
reconnaissance and observation aircraft to report the massacre of the others
and the unimpeded advance of the enemy.

Needless to say, Australian efforts in the defense of Southeast Asia,
New Guinea and Australia itself resulted in the eclipse of their air force by
April. Far from being a means of useful support to the American groups, by
April the majority of its squadrons in northern Australia were no more than
tired cadres, and those formations that were available and fit for operations
were at Darwin, not in the northeast. In fact, only four squadrons were in
the threatened area. These were the Eleventh and Twentieth Squadrons,
both equipped with Catalinas and at half strength, the Thirty-second
General Reconnaissance Bomber Squadron, equipped with Hudsons, and
the Seventy-fifth Squadron. The latter, which had been equipped with
American Kittyhawks, in fact existed only in name by the time the battle of
the Coral Sea began. It had been deployed to Port Moresby on 21 March,
one of its number being lost on arrival to "friendly" antiaircraft fire. By 30
April the squadron had been wiped out twice over and was down to just
three serviceable aircraft; its plight was the reason the Eighth Pursuit
Group was deployed to Port Moresby at that time. It was not that the
Seventy-fifth Squadron had been unsuccessful. In the course of its operations it had exacted a steady toll on the enemy, and its finest moment had
been its first offensive operation, when it had the advantage of surprise.
Striking at Lae on 22 March, it had accounted for fourteen enemy aircraft
and lost only two of its own.[84] But the Seventy-fifth Squadron had been
beset by the same problem that had confounded the whole Allied air effort
in the Indies before March. It had never had an initial strength that would
enable it to operate effectively over a period of time, and as a result losses
were disproportionately heavy as the force diminished in size. Its lack of
numerical strength, combined with the inferiority of its pilots and aircraft,
made the Seventy-fifth Squadron a wasting asset, thus reflecting the gen-

eral state of the Royal Australian Air Force at this stage of the war. Losses could not be absorbed because Australian resources were so few, and in this respect the Australians and Americans differed considerably, at least with regard to their fighter positions. Between 23 December and 18 March no fewer than 527 American fighters arrived in Australia, yet by the latter date no fewer than 374 had been lost, put out of service or transferred to the Australians, and some had yet to be assembled.[85] By the end of April, though, the Americans had about 300 fighters in service with their three pursuit groups. Thus the Americans were able to sustain themselves at a reasonable (though dispersed) level of strength while the Australians declined in numbers and effectiveness. By the time that the preliminary moves in the battle for Port Moresby began, the four Australian squadrons at Port Moresby and Tulagi probably numbered no more than thirty aircraft in service between them.

The position of the Allies in the air, therefore, was a little precarious, but of all the Allied weaknesses in the theater of operations the most glaring concerned the ground forces at Port Moresby itself. Even allowing for the fact that a brigade group was about the limit of the base's administrative capacity in February and March, the failure to either reinforce or relieve the garrison was inexplicable.[86] In 1943 MacArthur claimed that he had intended to fight for Port Moresby from the time that he took up command, and that the Australians had not.[87] The glacial observation of the official Australian historian on this claim was that the garrison at Port Moresby at the outset of the battle of the Coral Sea was no stronger than it had been in January when, as we have seen, it was made up of reserve units low on morale, discipline and equipment.[88] Two months of frequent air attacks and a sense of having been written off had not improved the situation of these units. By April the Australians had four first-line regiments, and the Americans had delivered combat troops to Australia. The decision not to send any of these troops to Port Moresby had to imply that the base was considered expendable, and that the Australian government and the Southwest Pacific Command were determined to hold back high-quality forces for the defense of Australia itself. Certainly, formations were pushed into Port Moresby quickly enough on ce the battle of the Coral Sea had been won, though surprisingly the first to be sent, the Fourteenth Australian Infantry Brigade, was not a veteran formation.[89]

Such was the Allied plan of campaign and deployment designed to deny the Japanese control of Port Moresby. Had it not been that the plan devised by the Japanese was infinitely worse, history would have been more damning of Allied intentions. As it is, the Japanese failure to achieve their objectives in the course of Operation MO, and the quick overtaking of events in the southwest Pacific by Midway, has obscured the weakness of the Allied operational plan. Perhaps the naval part, devised by Nimitz, sanctioned by King and put into effect by Fletcher, was the worst single part of it.

In overall terms, the most striking feature of the Allied arrangements is the seeming contradiction between the willingness of Nimitz and King to send their irreplaceable carriers to the defense of Port Moresby and the southwest Pacific, and the unwillingness of MacArthur, close up to the front line at Melbourne, to commit forces to Port Moresby. Thus the whole of the Allied strategic stance presents a curiously lopsided picture: the Allies were weaker the closer they were to the Japanese objective. Port Moresby itself was barely secure: the whole of the left flank, where the enemy's main effort was to be made, was virtually exposed. On the right flank, where the enemy's secondary effort was to be made, the Allies were strong, at least at sea. As far as the naval plan of campaign was concerned, it was no less rigid then the Japanese plan in that it anticipated the battle developing along predictable lines. It stretched the principle of economy of effort to the danger point, if not beyond it, accepting the prospect of battle on the basis of inferiority of numbers. Thus the American plan proved that the Japanese did not have a patent on frugality. Moreover, the same racial confidence that colored all Japanese planning tainted Nimitz's thinking. His initial acceptance of battle, when the carrier odds were believed to be four to two against him, was based on an awareness that American carriers had more aircraft than their counterparts. But his acceptance of the odds was prompted by the belief that "our superior personnel in resourcefulness and initiative, and the undoubted superiority of much of our equipment," would balance them.[90] It was a dangerous and ill-founded assumption.

The Nimitz-Fletcher plan in many ways bears an uncanny similarity to that of the Japanese plan for Midway. Neither side possessed an assured superiority of carrier or aircraft numbers, yet both sought to secure a central position from which to strike at enemy formations in turn. Still, the censure applied to the Japanese on this matter cannot be leveled against the American plan of campaign for two critical reasons. First, the element of risk built into American planning was calculated on the basis of a detailed though not complete knowledge of the enemy's order of battle, his intentions and his timetable. It was not based on a combination of supposition and wishful thinking, as was the case with Operation MI. Second, the American plan of campaign, for all its faults and its miscalculations, gave the Americans at the start of the battle of the Coral Sea advantages that eluded the Japanese both here and later off Midway: the Americans had the benefit of good timing and, far more crucial, of basic equality in the air and more warships at the all-important point of contact.

American victory at both the Coral Sea and Midway is commonly considered to have been gained against odds. But a careful recounting of both sides' order of battle, first at the Coral Sea and then at Midway, reveals

something that to the author's knowledge has never been noted: in bot
engagements the Japanese possessed overall numerical superiority, which
at the point of battle degenerated into quantitive inferiority.[91] At Midway
the Japanese deployed seventy-two warships, the Americans twenty-four,
yet despite their three-to-one advantage, on 4 June they had to do battle
against the full strength of the enemy with but twenty of their own number.
At the Coral Sea the Japanese had twenty-three warships, the Americans
nineteen warships and two Australian units.* Given the American intention to fight with all their units in a single tactical formation, the overall
Allied strength consisted of two fleet carriers, one light and seven heavy
cruisers, and eleven destroyers; this is compared with the Japanese division
of one light and two fleet carriers, one light and six heavy cruisers, and
thirteen destroyers between three major task forces, none of which could
meet the enemy on the basis of equality. Their single most powerful force,
with two fleet carriers, two cruisers and six destroyers, was considerably
inferior to the Allied task force in terms of escorts and gun power, slightly
inferior in air power but equal in the number of carriers at sea.

The exact state of the air balance is impossible to establish. In terms of
carrier aircraft the Japanese possessed no more than parity with the Americans, or a very slight advantage if the detached *Shoho* were to be added
(wrongly) to the *Shokaku* and the *Zuikaku* for purposes of comparison.
Regarding land-based strengths, the relative positions are hard to calculate
because of the impossibility of defining the number of aircraft available at
any one time and the number of aircraft outside the immediate battle zone
that could be deployed to the battle. Compounding the difficulty of proper
calculation are the distance-range problems both sides encountered.
Moreover, it is impossible to prove that the Japanese enjoyed a qualitative
superiority of aircrew and a probable edge in aircraft. Nevertheless, it is
clear that the Allies held the upper hand south of the Owen Stanleys. Even
before battle was joined the Japanese knew that they had failed to subdue
Port Moresby, and that their final approach to the town would have to be
conducted under conditions of enemy air superiority.

But the decisive imbalance lay in the effectiveness of both sides' intelligence agencies. As we have seen, the Americans knew the enemy's plans
and schedule with a large degree of certainty. The Japanese, on the other
hand, had virtually no knowledge of the enemy's position, intentions and
strength. More critical, they made the understandable but disastrous error
of assuming that the Americans would be unable to respond, or able to
respond but weakly, to Operation MO on account of the Doolittle Raid. As
early as 10 April, before the *Enterprise* and the *Hornet* had made their

---

*These totals exclude transports, minor units, auxiliaries and submarines, and those major
units deployed on subordinate escort duties, such as destroyers with oilers.

rendezvous, Japanese traffic analysts had detected the American move and reasoned that a force of two or three carriers was heading towards their waters.[92] Subsequently, the *Nitto Maru No. 23* had been able to get off a sighting report of two enemy carriers on the morning of the eighteenth, before she was overwhelmed by the *Nashville*.[93] With the Americans lacking interior lines of communications, the Japanese calculated that the enemy would not be able to get their carriers back from the raid in time to arrive in the southwest Pacific and meet Operation MO. The Japanese were correct, but that was not the relevant point. The Japanese error was in the calculation of overall American strength. They failed to realize that the Americans, within two weeks, were able to deploy a force in the southwest Pacific equal to the force that had raided Tokyo. In the forthcoming operation this miscalculation, coming on top of the others, could well prove disastrous—the Japanese had no idea what to expect of the opposition, whereas the Americans labored under no such handicap.

As both sides shaped up for what was to be the first carrier battle in history, the odds favored the Americans, though they did not fully realize it. The odds were only marginal, however, and there was no guarantee that the advantage of surprise would be turned into the ability to launch the first and hopefully decisive blows. There were many loose ends, many matters that had to be left to chance. When Midway was over Fletcher remarked, "After a battle . . . people talk a lot about how the decisions were methodically reached, but actually there's always a hell of a lot of groping around."[94] It was an observation born of the experience at the Coral Sea and Midway, and it is a suitable comment with which to begin examining the first of these encounters, a battle that could easily be called the "Battle of Mistakes."

PART III

The Battle of the Coral Sea

CHAPTER 6

The Preliminaries to Battle

The Japanese determination to secure Port Moresby and the equally strong American determination to prevent their doing so produced the first major fleet action—the lamentable Oran affair excepted—for more than a quarter of a century. One month short of twenty-six years separate Jutland and the Coral Sea. The former is often considered the greatest and last of the classic artillery duels that decided naval warfare from the late sixteenth century on; the latter is regarded as the first battle of a new era of naval warfare in which the carrier, through its aircraft, dominated war at sea.

The change from fleets fighting within sight of one another to fleets exchanging blows over the horizon is arguably the single most important one in the history of war at sea. It is perhaps inevitable, then, that the differences between the Coral Sea and Jutland have been more obvious and more commented upon than their surprisingly large number of similarities. In both actions men fought with weapons that were generally untested in fleet actions, and they faced unknown dangers without any body of combat experience on which to draw for guidance. Each side had to contend with uncertain communications and the misunderstandings and confusions that followed, and they had to cope with poor reconnaissance. Intelligence varied from the scarce and the abundant, but regardless of the quantity it was almost invariably misapplied and its full value went unrealized. In both battles what may be termed for simplicity's sake "target identification" and "fire distribution" were more often wrong then right, and in both actions probably more bad decisions than good were made by commanders who, for a variety of reasons, had only a vague notion of what was happening around them and where the enemy might be. Neither new weapons nor advanced communications systems altered the impact of nature on events. The effects of light, wind, sun, clouds and, above all, nighttime proved as important at the Coral Sea as they had at Jutland. In both battles concern about such matters as logistics, range and endurance, and the safety of costly ships went some way to ensure relatively indecisive outcomes. A decisive success of Trafalgar or Tsu-shima proportions slipped through the fingers of the various commanders. Here, indeed, is the closest similarity between the action in the North Sea in 1916 and the battle in the southwest Pacific in 1942. In both the defender prevailed, despite the heavier losses he incurred. The defender was better placed to absorb his losses in the long term than the attacker, and in both cases the latter, despite his apparent "numbers victory," turned back from the scene of battle and never again made a serious or sustained effort in the area of his "triumph." In 1916 and May 1942 the defenders won victories the extent of which were not properly realized at the time, but which were of critical strategic significance.

The battle of the Coral Sea began in the same manner as Jutland—with the defender, forewarned by radio intelligence of the enemy's general intentions, moving into a position from which to strike the unsuspecting foe. Neither the Germans in 1916 nor the Japanese in 1942 expected to encounter anything like the opposition that confronted them. Neither the British in 1916 nor the Americans in 1942 knew the full details of the enemy's plan of battle, but they knew enough to be able to take up positions from which they could frustrate their enemies quite effectively, and they were moving to such positions long before the enemy's offensive began to get under way. On 27 April Fletcher left Noumea in New Caledonia with Task Force 17 and headed back to the Coral Sea in accordance with his orders,[1] to be joined by Fitch and Task Force 11 at latitude 16° 16′ S, longitude 162° 20′ E at 0615, on 1 May, a position some 250 miles to the west of Espirito Santo.[2] Making their rendezvous at Point Buttercup in the last minutes before sunrise, the two carriers of the task forces between them mustered a total of 141 aircraft. The *Yorktown* had a seventy-one-strong air group that was made up of twenty-two Wildcat fighters, eighteen Dauntless scouts, eighteen Dauntless bombers and thirteen Devastator torpedo bombers. The *Lexington* had one less aircraft than the *Yorktown* in each of her three attack squadrons, but two more fighters.[3]

Immediately on carrying out the rendezvous Fletcher began refueling his task force from the oiler *Neosho*, at the same time ordering Task Force 11 to take itself a few miles to the southwest and refuel from the *Tippecanoe*. As instructed, she had come north from Noumea in the company of the *Chicago* and *Perkins*. The American intention was that these three units would stay in the company of the carrier forces until they were joined by the other units of their parent formation, Task Force 44. Because of mechanical problems, there were only three other members of this task force. The Australian cruisers *Australia* and *Hobart* left Sydney on 1 May, met up with the American destroyer *Whipple* in Hervey Bay (north of Brisbane) and then steamed into the Coral Sea to join the other forces on the morning of 4 May—though in circumstances very different from those expected.[4]

From the time that he joined up with Fitch and Task Force 11, Fletcher encountered unexpected difficulties. The main problem was refueling. Refueling at every conceivable opportunity was standard operational procedure, and in this enormous theater of operations no commander could afford to overlook any chance to keep the oil tanks of his units full. The needs of the escorts in this respect were far more acute than those of carriers and cruisers. The *Yorktown*, for example, carried 7,500 tons of fuel oil, enough to keep her going at 20 knots for seventeen days.[5] A few hours of high-speed steaming would barely affect her steaming capacity. But high-speed action quickly brought a typical destroyer of the day to the limit of endurance. On a normal displacement of about 1,900 tons, such a unit would have about 500 tons of fuel. This would be enough to steam about 4,700 miles at an economical cruising speed of about 15 knots. But fuel enough to last thirteen days at such a speed would be used up at a rate of approximately sixteen tons an hour if the ship was forced to work up to 34 knots, at which speed a destroyer had an endurance of about 32 hours and a range of about 1,100 miles. Given the prospect of high-speed action in this theater of operations, and the size of the theater itself—Rabaul and Tulagi were separated by some 620 miles, Deboyne and Tulagi by about 560 miles—the need to keep all ships topped up with oil was urgent. But unlike Fletcher, Fitch did not begin to refuel until the following day, 2 May, and perhaps surprisingly the first units to refuel from the *Tippecanoe* were her erstwhile companions, the *Chicago* and the *Perkins*. Thus when Fletcher rejoined Fitch after refueling Task Force 17, he found that Task Force 11 had barely begun to take on fuel and that Fitch did not expect to complete replenishment until about noon on the fourth, a little less than forty-eight hours hence.[6] Yet by dusk on the second, Fletcher had two good reasons to consider moving from his present location. First, during the afternoon a Dauntless antisubmarine patrol from Task Force 17 found the *I-21* some thirty-two miles from the *Yorktown*. Fletcher suspected that the location of his force might well have been discovered—as it would have been had the *I-21* chosen that day to launch her Glen seaplane on reconnaissance. But she did not. Seemingly she shrugged off the Dauntless's attack with no difficulty and did not give the matter another thought.[7] Obviously the American nuisance had come from Noumea, and there was no need to report an unsuccessful enemy attack to command. Thus the American carrier forces managed to get behind the advanced reconnaissance line the Japanese were forming without being found, but Fletcher could not be certain that he remained undetected. What he did know was that there was a clear inducement to move away from the general area of the *I-21*. Second,

Fletcher received word from the Southwest Pacific Command that air reconnaissance had found the enemy coming south from Rabaul. Thus at 1800 Fletcher, joined by the *Chicago* and the *Perkins*, turned away from the southeast and headed westwards, into the central area of the northern Coral Sea.[8] By steering such a course Task Force 17 closed the enemy, but at the same time it drew very slowly away from Task Force 11, which was still steaming slowly into the southeast trade winds as it continued to take on fuel from the *Tippecanoe*. Before parting company Fletcher instructed Fitch to make for a new rendezvous at latitude 15° S, longitude 157° E, at 0800 on 4 May.[9] At this stage Fitch's delay in refueling was irksome and no more; with the enemy nowhere near the line of the Louisades there seemed to be plenty of time in which to reach the anticipated battle area.[10] Fletcher was probably more concerned by the arrival of a half-expected signal from Pearl Harbor warning him that Task Force 16 would not be joining him until 12 May.[11] Thus by the first hours of daylight on 3 May, Fletcher knew that there was no possibility of the *Yorktown* and the *Lexington* being joined by any force other than Crace's before the onset of battle, and he knew that battle could not be long delayed.

His counterpart, Inoue, was even then approaching Rabaul in his flagship, the light cruiser *Kashima*, having left Truk on 1 May.[12] When Inoue left the Carolines Operation MO was well under way and seemed to be progressing favorably. But by the time he arrived in the Simpson Roadstead on the fourth, Inoue was reminded that intention and performance are not necessarily the same thing.

On 28 April the *Nikkaimaru* arrived at Shortland, and by the end of the day the Japanese had improvised a seaplane base there and had five Mavis flying boats on station.[13] The following day Marumo led his Support Force and Shima his Tulagi Invasion Force out of Rabaul, while Goto cleared Truk with his Main Body Support Force. Two days later, on the same day that Inoue left Truk, Takagi left the Carolines with the Carrier Striking Force.[14] The immediate purpose of these various departures was the securing of Tulagi, due to be assaulted on the morning of 3 May. Shima's force, tasked to secure what had been up until this time the outpost of Australia in the Solomons, set course from Rabaul directly towards New Caledonia; Goto coming south from Truk made for the channel between Bougainville and Choiseul in order to pass through the line of the Solomons and take up a supporting position south of the New Georgia group. With both Shima and Goto evidently steering courses in large part designed to conceal the real destination of the Japanese moves for as long as possible, the Shima force turned for Tulagi only at dusk on the second. But other Japanese supporting operations that day served partly to defeat the object of deception. Throughout the hours of daylight, Tulagi was subjected to heavy and almost constant air attack from Rabaul, while the Support Force landed at

Thousand Ships Bay, Santa Isabel Island. The latter was reported to the Australian authorities by the local coastwatcher, Major D.G. Kennedy. With no illusions about what was on the way, the Tulagi garrison began the evacuation of its base on Tanambogo Island on the morning of the second, and demolished remaining installations before pulling out to Florida Island under the cover of darkness. From Florida the garrison embarked on the island trader *Balus* and sailed for Vila in the New Hebrides.[15]

The following morning the Japanese landed as planned, the Third Kure Special Naval Landing Force dividing its attentions between Tulagi and Gavutu islands.[16] These unopposed landings were supported by aircraft from Rabaul, by three seaplanes brought down to Santa Isabel the previous night and by aircraft from the *Shoho*. Goto had brought his Main Body Support Force to a position about 180 miles west of Tulagi by dawn on the third, and from there some of the *Shoho*'s ten Zekes, four Claudes and six Kates had supported Shima before Goto turned his force back towards southern Bougainville and a rendezvous with the *Iro*.[17] With little time in hand before his force had to move to support the transports heading for Port Moresby, Goto could not afford to loiter too long in the role of support for Shima. Similarly, the Marumo force, which stood some 60 miles to the west of Tulagi during the invasion, also turned back towards the central Solomon Sea in order to give itself time to be in position for the next phase of Operation MO.[18]

Thus by 1100 on the day of the attack on Tulagi, both supporting forces had turned back and Shima was left without any cover. This did not pose any danger because, as we have seen earlier, the Japanese did not expect any Allied reaction to their operation to materialize for several more days; for the enemy to be in a position to counterattack was something for which the Japanese made no allowance. In any case, by dawn on the fourth Takagi's task group, built around the *Zuikaku* and the *Shokaku*, would be in a position 120 miles to the north of Tulagi. From there it would be able to cover

The Aircraft Carrier *Shoho*

The Aircraft Carrier *Zuikaku*

Tulagi. Unfortunately for the Japanese, the Carrier Striking Force was not 120 but 340 miles north of Tulagi, and it was in no position to cover Shima.[19] Even if it had been in its correct position, it would not necessarily have been able to influence the course of events on the fourth.

The reason the Carrier Striking Force was so far north of its anticipated position had to do with a relatively minor task it had tried to carry out. When the two fleet carriers left Truk they had nine Zekes embarked in addition to their own air groups. These were to be flown into the Vunaka-nau airfield on 2 May, when the force was nearer Rabaul than at any other time in the course of its run to the south. The task did not appear to pose the least difficulty, but on 2 May the Zekes returned to the carriers when they encountered bad weather on their way to Rabaul. Takagi therefore had to decide between pressing on and not flying the fighters off or accepting the loss of time and flying the fighters off the next day. He chose the second course of action, and because the weather prevented refueling he decided to postpone replenishment until the next day, after the nine fighters had been sent on their way. On the third, however, the events of the second were repeated, only this time one of the fighters was lost. Takagi then decided to refuel and make a third attempt to fly off the eight remaining aircraft the next day, before his force resumed its course to the south.[20]

This episode was more significant than it would appear at first glance. What Takagi's loss of two days off Rabaul meant was that the synchronization on which Operation MO depended for success began to fall apart even before the amphibious forces bound for Port Moresby sailed from Rabaul. Takagi's decision to accept the loss of one and then two days was largely forced upon him by Rabaul's insistence that the fighters be delivered. At this time the whole of Operation MO stood in real danger of failure because of the inability of the Japanese to win air supremacy over Port Moresby and its approaches.

The Aircraft Carrier *Shokaku*

Operation MO would stand or fall on the outcome of this air battle—this the Japanese knew before they began the venture. Thus far in the war they had shown a marked reluctance to send slow, vulnerable and valuable transports into waters not already controlled by their air power, and in April, with the army nervous about air support for the amphibious forces, the Imperial Navy was not inclined to run risks that it had declined to face on earlier occasions. It intended to stick to its past practice of using its fighters to secure air supremacy and then to advance behind a secured front. Thus they had to fight and win a battle for supremacy over Port Moresby and its sea approaches before Operation MO proceeded.

In attempting to win such a battle the Japanese set themselves an impossible task. The difficulty was not so much the neutralization of Allied air power at Port Moresby but the fact that this power was only an extension of Allied air power in northern Australia. Even if the Japanese proved capable of curbing Port Moresby, they still had no answer to enemy air power in northern Australia. Allied planes would still be able to strike at any Japanese force in the western Coral Sea.

In fact the Japanese were in an unenviable position. They had to embark on a mission that could not be brought to success with the resources available to the South Seas Force. In the course of their attacks in April the Japanese air groups struck heavy blows at Port Moresby, but their own losses were severe as well. By 25 April the groups under command mustered between them just fourteen Mavis flying boats at Rabaul and seventy-eight aircraft, of which only thirty-eight were fighters. Over the next few days some of the flying boats of the Yokosuka Air Group made their way to Lae which, on 25 April, was home for twenty-four Zekes of the Fourth Air Group. This formation also had another eight Zekes and fourteen Betty bombers at Rabaul. Also at Rabaul were twenty-six Nells of the Motoyama Air Group and six Claudes of the Tainan Air Group.[21]

This was a hopelessly inadequate force with which to bring Port Moresby to heel, and in this sense Operation MO was a reflection at the local level of an overall failure of strategic policy. Too much was being attempted with too little over too great an area. To overcome their problems only one of two courses of action was open to the Japanese. Either they could build up a massive concentration of force at Rabaul and make one all-out attempt to smash Allied air resistance over Port Moresby, or they could make a sustained effort by massed carrier forces against not only Port Moresby but northern Australia and the feeder routes to the theater. The second alternative was out of the question. Even with their full strength the Japanese did not have enough carriers to consider it. (This was the type of operation mounted by the Allies in 1945 against Okinawa, and that involved twenty fleet carriers and eighteen escort carriers.[22]) Thus there could be no question of directing the carrier force against Australia, and as we have seen Yamamoto had specifically instructed Hara not to take the *Zuikaku* and the *Shokaku* against enemy airfields on the mainland. Not only did the two carriers lack the means to conduct such an operation—they did not even have full complements. Between them they had just 121 aircraft, excluding the Zekes earmarked for Rabaul. The flagship's air group consisted of twenty-two Vals, twenty-one Kates and twenty Zekes; the *Shokaku* had twenty-one Vals, nineteen Kates and eighteen Zekes. Of these, thirty-six Vals, a similar number of Kates and thirty-seven Zekes were operational when the Carrier Striking Force entered the Coral Sea.[23]

With just thirty-seven Zekes between them, it is easy to see why the carriers had to be kept well clear of Australia, and with so small a fighter element it is equally easy to see why Takagi and Hara were unenthusiastic about Goto's request, made on 2 and 3 May, that they part with three Zekes in order to beef up the *Shoho*. The request was vetoed by Inoue, but his decision was small comfort to the Carrier Striking Force: on 3 May it received orders from Rabaul to proceed by 7 or 8 May to a position where it could join in the battle for control of the skies over Port Moresby.[24]

The orders represented a dangerous widening of the responsibilities of the Carrier Striking Force. After flying off fighters to Rabaul and then covering Shima and Tulagi as it came around the Solomons, it would underwrite four different objectives simultaneously. It was to continue to provide cover for the Solomons, though this would be increasingly indirect; help provide cover for the amphibious forces during their approach to and assault on Port Moresby; take a major part in the air battle for the control of the skies over Port Moresby; and fight and win any naval battle that might result from an enemy task force arriving on the scene. There was no doubting the importance of any one of these objectives. The Solomons group was a two-way street that lured the Japanese towards Fiji and New Caledonia, the Americans in the direction of Truk.[25] Port Moresby could prove a crucial blocking position against any enemy attempt to move against Rabaul and Truk; it could serve as a vital springboard for further operations against eastern Australia. The security of the troop ships was an obvious concern, and so was the need for a naval victory over the enemy task force that was suspected to be in the area. Yet with thirty-seven fighters and seventy-two bombers the Fifth Carrier Division was hardly well stocked to meet any one of its responsibilities, much less all four. Even if they were allowed to keep the eight remaining fighters that seemed so unwilling to leave, by themselves the *Zuikaku* and the *Shokaku* were too weak to have a reasonable margin against failure in any single part of their endeavors.

Thus the Japanese found themselves with a problem entirely of their own making. Their difficulties stemmed directly from the deadlines imposed by Operations AL and MI, and from the belief that the weakest of the three front-line carrier divisions had the time and means to provide the backbone for one quick "limited" offensive before it returned to the homeland. This was the situation that the pioneers of massed carrier strikes should have avoided. It had been the Japanese who had shown that the only chance of obtaining decisive success with carriers was by concentration. For their efforts the Japanese had been unrewarded, but there was no doubting that their reasoning was correct. In December 1941 they had launched a six-carrier operation against a single target. It was not until October 1943 that the Americans were able to do the same, and the British took until January 1945 to mount their first four-carrier operation.[26] Yet in May 1942, after an operation with six carriers at Pearl Harbor, four carriers at Rabaul and five carriers off Ceylon, the Japanese were expecting two carriers, with 121 aircraft between them, to pick up a multiple strategic success. The notion was grotesque, as grotesque, indeed, as the notion that nine Zekes would determine the success of the air battle being conducted from Rabaul. Of course the planes were important—by 4 May the Japanese had been reduced to twelve Zekes at Rabaul and six at Lae, out of thirty-two that had been available eight days earlier—but nine fighters were irrelevant when set against Japan's real needs, which were more on the order of nine fighter squadrons.[27]

As it was, between 2 and 4 May the Japanese became caught in a trap of their own devising. First, the effort by their land-based air power had been undertaken without initially ensuring a concentration of strength sufficient for success. By starting with resources that were inferior to the task in hand and inferior to those of the enemy, the Japanese ensured that their losses would be relatively greater than those incurred by the enemy. The inevitable result of this situation was that aircraft sent as reinforcements arrived as replacements. Second, the Carrier Striking Force was overloaded with responsibilities and some twenty percent understrength. As events showed, there was little chance of discharging its various tasks, and here the Japanese did not really help themselves. Of all their carrier divisions, the

Fifth was the least capable of conjuring a victory out of nothing. Third, the operational timetable was so tight that there could be no delay in any single part of Operation MO. Thus while the Carrier Striking Force fell behind the clock as it came south from Rabaul, there was no attempt to postpone the operations in the Solomons and there was no recasting of the timetable for the operations against Port Moresby. Units tasked to help construct the seaplane base in the Deboyne Islands moved out from Rabaul on 3 May, and the transports and the Attack Force prepared to move out the following day. Their intention was to negotiate the Jomard Passage at midnight on 7 May.[28] With the fleet carriers two days late they would no longer be able to take station on the left flank of the amphibious forces as they came south from Rabaul. Hurrying across the Coral Sea the carriers were to leave these forces astern—with their left flank unsecured—and move to beat down the opposition at Port Moresby once and for all. Something was clearly wrong with such a plan of campaign and with a conduct of operations that allowed such a situation to develop. Thus far the air battle had been poorly conducted, and now the main part of the enterprise was in the process of being bungled. There was something to be said for holding back the various forces still at Rabaul or at sea so the carriers could make up for lost time. Delaying the forces in the general area of the western Solomon Sea was the least the Japanese could have done, but apparently this was never as much as considered at Rabaul.

These matters, however, relate to only one half of the Japanese problem. The other half was that the Japanese could not anticipate a repetition of the events at Lae and Salamaua on 10 March. The two carriers, the *Yorktown* and the *Lexington*, that had struck at these places in the immediate aftermath of the Japanese landings there were again present on 3 May and in a position to do something about the landings at Tulagi. They were as well placed on 3 May to interfere with the Tulagi operation as they had been on 8 March with regard to Lae and Salamaua, and the Americans were prepared to repeat and improve on their earlier effort. In fact, however, events conspired to frustrate them. Fletcher did not receive reports of the enemy's invasion and occupation of Tulagi from the Southwest Pacific Command until 1900,[29] and by then, in the words of one commentator, "most of the birds had flown."[30] Moreover, a strange sequence of events had taken place with regard to the refueling of Task Force 11.

Throughout the hours of daylight on 3 May, Fletcher and Task Force 17 continued to head slowly westwards into the central Coral Sea. The *Yorktown* flew combat air patrol and mounted reconnaissance missions. At dawn that day the force was some 500 miles to the south of Guadalcanal and about 750 miles to the southeast of Goto and the *Shoho*. Fletcher knew that he had to rely on the Southwest Pacific Command for the sighting reports that would enable him to move against enemy formations.[31] All day Task

The Aircraft Carrier *Yorktown*

Force 17 refueled from the *Neosho*. It did not know when it would next have the means to do so, and battle, if it came, could not be long delayed. Moreover, after the third Fletcher would have to share the *Neosho* with Fitch. Task Force 11 was certain to drain the *Tippecanoe*, and she had been ordered to replenish from the *E. J. Henry* at Noumea on or about 10 May. Since the *Platte* was not expected to enter the Coral Sea until 13 May, and the *Cuyama* and the *Kanawha* not until the seventeenth, Fletcher had to consider giving battle with just one oiler on hand to service two task forces.[32]

By dawn the *Yorktown* and the *Lexington* had drawn about 100 miles apart, and they continued to separate until just past noon,[33] when Fitch, the refueling of his task force completed one day earlier than expected, turned his ships back to the west on a course for next day's rendezvous.[34] Thus both American task forces were ready for action, and they could have joined up much earlier than expected had it not been for Fitch's failure to inform Fletcher of his situation. Precluded from using his radio, Fitch could easily have dispatched an aircraft with a weighted message for Fletcher. This was standard practice, but Fitch chose not to employ it. Fletcher, with no good reason to suspect the accuracy of Fitch's earlier estimate, did not know that his two carrier forces could join up well before dusk if they steered converging courses for three or four hours.

The Aircraft Carrier *Lexington*

The 1900 signal informing Fletcher of the situation at Tulagi thus found the Americans unnecessarily divided, but Fletcher had no hesitations in turning the *Yorktown* towards the enemy. As he himself noted in his battle report, such an opportunity had been awaited for some two months, and there was no possibility of his force passing up the chance when finally it arrived.[35] Fletcher detached the *Neosho* and the destroyer *Russell* to deliver fresh orders to Fitch to make for the preselected rendezvous position at latitude 15° S, longitude 160° E. This would leave Fitch with the whole of the fourth to steam about 200 miles back to the east, while Task Force 17 moved against the Japanese beachhead at Tulagi.[36] Since Fletcher expected Fitch to be nearing the end of his refueling by dawn the next day, it was perhaps surprising that he did not order Fitch to take Task Force 11 to the north to cover Task Force 17 in case the *Yorktown* had to retire quickly.

Fletcher turned to the north at 2030, working up first to 24 and then to 27 knots in order to reach a suitable flying-off position against Tulagi by dawn. In coming north Task Force 17 ran into weather conditions that were unfavorable to flying operations. As the *Yorktown* approached Guadalcanal she neared a cold front, which was to affect the course of operations not just on the following day but over the next four days.

The prevailing meteorological feature of the Coral Sea is its southeast trade winds. These blow for most of the year, but they are punctuated by cold fronts that move off the Australian continent towards the northeast. The normal characteristics of a cold front are massive cumulus clouds, heavy rain and high wind. These rapidly give way to clear weather as the front passes. In the southwest Pacific, however, cold fronts tend to slow down as they come to the indefinable area that marks the meeting place of the Coral and Solomon seas. As they slow their bands of bad weather widen. A widening front can spread over 150 miles, in which circumstances the winds at its back slacken. The front will then come under the influence of stronger winds from the north, which push the front back to the south.

Rear Admiral Aubrey W. Fitch

By this time the front is a warm one, exhibiting the altocumulus and altostratus clouds, falling visibility and heavy rainfall that are characteristic of warm fronts. When and if the fronts merge, the result is towering cumulus, strong winds and heavy showers.

As Fletcher led his task force north on the night of 3–4 May, he ran into a cold front that could not decide whether to go north or south. Its northern edge was just to the south of Guadalcanal, stretching back 100 miles into the Coral Sea. South of the front flying conditions were excellent. Fletcher hugged the front, keeping under heavy cloud cover to stay out of sight of enemy reconnaissance patrols. In such a position, moreover, he would still be able to recover aircraft. Because they knew the position of their carrier they, unlike enemy scouts, could come home at low altitude. The front, therefore, was ideal for the approach to contact that Fletcher intended to carry out. The problem was that attacking aircraft would have to fly through the front to reach the objective, and that the target itself might be obscured. On the latter point, however, the Southwest Pacific Command was able to advise Fletcher that the front was not expected to reach Tulagi on the fourth. This proved to be the case. The northern limit of the front on the morning of the fourth straddled the Sealark Channel, leaving Tulagi in clear weather but hiding the advance of American ships and aircraft alike. Circumstances could hardly have been better. But there was a catch. The attack on Tulagi was certain to betray the presence of an American carrier task force in the Coral Sea; the enemy could not but be alerted to the danger to his overall position even before the main part of Operation MO began to unfold. Still, the risks would be justified if in the course of its attacks Task Force 17 really hurt the enemy. Unfortunately for the Americans, however, this was hardly likely. Fletcher and Task Force 17 were one day too late on station to hurt the enemy in any significant way, and Fletcher was to betray his presence for no commensurate return.

By 0630 on the fourth, some ten minutes before sunrise, Task Force 17 began to turn towards the southeast, into the prevailing wind, to launch the first of what proved to be four strikes against Tulagi that day. The *Yorktown* was then about 50 miles northwest of Rennell, which she approached as she launched fifteen Dauntless bombers, thirteen Dauntless scouts and twelve Devastators. With only eighteen operational Wildcats available and no air opposition anticipated, no escort was provided for the bombers. The fighters were held for combat air patrol over the force, and were divided into three flights of six. The first combat air patrol was flown off at 0700, the cruisers with the *Yorktown* having flown off their seaplanes for antisubmarine patrols some time before.[37] After the bombers left, Task Force 17 settled down on a course that was to lead it in an irregular and jagged semicircle around Rennell Island. By following this course Fletcher was able to keep to within about 100 miles of Tulagi for most of the morning while maintaining a southeast course during the afternoon, when his force would have to retire from the scene of the crime. By coming around the north of Rennell Task Force 17 was able to keep circling around to the east, staying close to the prevailing wind.[38]

This first American attack suffered from two weaknesses. First, the Dauntlesses all used 1,000-lb bombs with impact fuses. None of the bombs had the quarter-second delay that would have allowed a direct hit to explode well within a ship or to produce a mining effect for a near miss. Most damage inflicted by the Americans therefore tended to be topside and superficial. Second, the commander of the *Yorktown*'s air group commanded the combat air patrol from his flagship. This meant that the bomber attacks were neither led nor directed, and the result was a lack of coordination in all the attacks and poor target selection. The various squadrons attacked without proper reconnaissance and with no attempt to spread their efforts over the few but worthwhile targets in the harbor. The result was a great deal of ordnance expended for a very small return, which Nimitz was to comment adversely on after the battle.[39]

The first attack on Tulagi began at about 0820. The three major units of Shima's force, the *Okinoshima* and the destroyer transports *Kikuzuki* and *Yuzuki*, were assigned as guard ships while the lesser units scurried about on a number of small tasks. Surprise was nonetheless complete. Results, however, were not so emphatic. The Dauntless scouts, attacking first, seemingly met with the greatest success, the best single result being achieved by a bomb that penetrated to the starboard engine room of the *Kikuzuki*, causing widespread damage and flooding. With the ship taking a list, she was towed to Gavutu and beached, but she fell back into the sea on the next tide.[40] The destruction of two minesweepers, the *Wa. 1* and the *Wa. 2*, is also attributed to the scouts during this attack, and the converted minesweeper *Tamamaru* is generally deemed to have been sunk by the Devastators. This is not impossible—the Devastators used Mark 13 torpedoes set at 10 feet for this attack—but it seems unlikely that so small a target as the *Tamamaru* would have been torpedoed. The Dauntless bombers, which apparently carried out the scouting function before making their attacks, are generally regarded as having drawn a blank.[41]

These forty attacking aircraft were all recovered safely by the *Yorktown* by 0931. Suspecting that results were not as impressive as those that were claimed, Fletcher ordered a second strike by the same aircraft. A minimum turnaround time of sixty minutes enabled fourteen bombers, thirteen scouts and eleven Devastators to be launched between 1036 and 1120, their attack on Tulagi beginning at 1210. What happened in the course of this attack is not entirely clear, and there is a possibility that one of the minesweepers and the *Tamamaru* succumbed in this rather than in the previous raid. It is certain, however, that two Mavis flying boats were destroyed and one of the attacking Devastators was shot down. Before the survivors landed at 1319, a third strike had been launched. This consisted of two sections, each with two Wildcats, flown off at 1310 to deal with three Mavis flying boats reportedly moored at Makambo Island. This they did, and they also attacked the *Yuzuki*, which they found steaming out of Tulagi as fast as she could when the attack materialized. With only 0.5-in machine guns they could only strafe her, and in doing so they killed ten men, including her captain, and wounded another twenty. Two of the Wildcats were forced down near Cape Henslow. Both pilots were to be rescued during the night by the destroyer *Hammann*. Once more Fletcher suspected that the claims made with regard to the second strike had been exaggerated and ordered the bombers out for a third time. On this occasion the torpedo bombers were left behind; only twelve scouts and nine bombers were available for the attack. These took off at 1400 and arrived over Tulagi one hour later, this time to be met by an almost empty harbor. The Japanese, tiring of being targets, had pulled out, and the Dauntlesses had to be content with their claim to have sunk four landing barges. The recovery of the twenty-one Dauntlesses was complete at 1632,[42] and by 1700 Task Force 17 had settled down on a course to the south and its appointment, next day, with Task Force 11.[43]

Fletcher's natural skepticism about the accuracy of his pilot's claims was well founded, but even his attempted objectivity proved to be wide of the mark. In his report to Nimitz he claimed the destruction of two destroyers, one freighter, four patrol boats and one light cruiser forced ashore. An additional destroyer, a freighter and a seaplane carrier were reported to have been damaged. These claims were roughly substantiated by the local coast watcher on Guadalcanal.[44] The real picture was rather different. The *Kikuzuki*, the two minesweepers, the *Tamamaru*, the four landing barges and five flying boats were destroyed, but nothing more. Shima's mine-laying flagship, the *Okinoshima*, the *Yuzuki* and the chaser *Tamamaru No. 8* were lightly damaged. The total Japanese casualties of the day were 87 killed and 124 wounded.[45] These results were "disappointingly meagre," particularly in view of the intensity of the American effort.[46]

Disappointment over the results was to set in later as a proper picture of the day's events emerged. For the moment, however, the Americans enjoyed a sense of exhilaration. That they believed they had done well was good for morale. Nimitz sent his congratulations to Task Force 17 after he received Fletcher's initial report.[47] Even if he was not prepared to accept all his pilots' claims, Fletcher himself believed that success had been substantial. He turned south and ordered his cruiser admiral to detach two units to Tulagi to "clean up the cripples." Rear Admiral William W. Smith chose to go with the *Astoria*, and he selected the *Chester* to accompany him.[48] Subsequently Fletcher thought better of his order and cancelled it, thus sparing the two cruisers from an almost certain encounter with an enemy force that most definitely was not in the class of the halt and the lame.[49]

The importance of the Tulagi affair was twofold. First, it boosted American morale on the eve of battle, and it gave Americans valuable combat experience, which was in short supply. Tulagi provided the *Yorktown* with a dry run with live ammunition, even if it was against an almost defenseless enemy.[50] This was no small matter. It was better for the *Yorktown*'s pilots to cut their teeth on an opponent such as Shima than on a more substantial enemy who had the ability to strike back. Second, by nightfall on 4 May both sides knew that the other was at sea. As we have seen, the Tulagi raid could do no other than betray the presence of an enemy task force to the Japanese. The problem the Japanese faced was that they had no idea from which side of the Solomons the Americans had operated, and to compound their problem there was no way of finding out. The means of doing so had been destroyed, and perhaps the single most significant aspect about the events at Tulagi was the destruction of those five Mavis flying boats in the harbor during the second and third American attacks. Japanese reconnaissance was hamstrung as a result of their loss. The Americans, on the other hand, knew that the Japanese were out, and not just with light forces. At 1135 an Australian-based Mitchell from the

Ninetieth Bombardment Squadron reported the presence of a force, supposedly with aircraft carriers, off Bougainville.[51] Intelligence in the Southwest Pacific Command entertained suspicions that either the *Shokaku* or the *Zuikaku* was with this force, but in the course of the afternoon Fletcher was warned that this force, which had been sighted, appeared to include a *Kaga*-class [*sic*] carrier and two warships, either battleships or heavy cruisers.[52] What the Mitchell had sighted, of course, was the *Shoho* and the *Sazanami*, detached from the remainder of the covering force. Fletcher suspected that the sighting was of a light rather than of a fleet carrier.[53] With no knowledge of the whereabouts of the fleet units, Fletcher felt no inclination to tangle with even a light carrier at this stage, despite the temptations. His cancellation of the earlier order to Smith and his cruisers was occasioned in part by his awareness of a carrier force off Bougainville, in part by the uncertainty of the location of the enemy's main strike force.

Fletcher's immediate concern was to get clear of the area. All the American raids thus far in the war had been notable for speed with which the carriers put distance between themselves and their targets, and Tulagi was no exception. Given the presence of enemy carriers, Fletcher had even more incentive to disappear from the target area than was usually the case. Throughout the night, therefore, Fletcher led his force south at a good speed, though not so quickly that the *Hammann* and the *Perkins*, detached during the night on air-sea rescue, were not able to rejoin Task Force 17 before it met up with Task Force 11 at 0816 on the following morning in latitude 15° S, longitude 160° E.[54] There Fletcher found that Crace was in company, the latter having carried out a rendezvous with Task Force 11 at 0900 on the previous day. Crace had stayed with Fitch in order that Task Force 44 might gather itself together again when the *Chicago* and the *Perkins* reappeared with Task Force 17. An hour before Crace had joined him, Fitch had carried out his prearranged rendezvous, not with Task Force 17 as expected, but with the *Neosho* and the *Russell*. Informed for the first time of Fletcher's actions and orders for the following day, Fitch decided against heading northwards in order to stand by Fletcher and cover his operation. Instead Task Force 11 mounted reconnaissance missions towards the northwest, almost to Rossel, in the belief that with Task Force 17 presumably searching on its own behalf to the northeast, this was the most practical help the *Lexington* could give the *Yorktown*. After launching the searches and linking up with Crace, Fitch led his ships around to the southeast, widening the distance between the two carrier forces. Late in the day Fitch came around on a course that would take him to next day's rendezvous with Fletcher.[55]

When the rendezvous of 5 May was carried out, the Allied task forces were some 320 miles to the south of Guadalcanal. Immediately on joining up, Fletcher settled his three forces into parallel formations and set course for the southeast as he refueled Task Force 17 from the *Neosho*. After the previous day's high-speed action this was a matter of urgency, and the Americans were fortunate enough to spend the hours of daylight refueling undisturbed. The Japanese, after the events of the previous day, were looking for the enemy, but the only scout to come anywhere near the task forces, a Mavis operating from Rabaul, was intercepted and destroyed by a Wildcat from the *Yorktown*'s combat air patrol at about 1100. It did not have a chance to send out any signal before it was shot down.[56] In the course of the day most of the combat air patrol and reconnaissance chores fell to the *Lexington*, and almost all her energies were directed to the west and to the north.[57]

Thus far the Americans had every reason to be pleased with their efforts. They had shocked the enemy and caught him flat-footed. The Japanese found themselves in a position they had never envisaged. They had assumed that the enemy would be forced to react to their moves and that by the time this happened, on or about 8 May, they would have secured positions from which they could deal with his countermoves. On 4 May the Japanese found that it was they, not the Americans, who had to respond to enemy moves, and long before their arrangements were complete. But the Tulagi affair did not see the initiative pass to the Americans. After the attack the latter were not able to dictate the pattern of events; they did not have the strength to do this, and in any case American policy was to deliver a counterpunch at this stage, not to go forward. For the Japanese Tulagi was an inconvenience, a small embarrassment that did not threaten to have too serious an effect. In fact, they were almost correct: the events of 5 May served to undo many of the slight advantages the Americans gained the previous day, and for two reasons.

First, Fletcher's refueling in the course of 5 May took him to the southeast, into the prevailing wind and therefore out from under the cover of the cold front that had shielded him the previous day. For the next two days the American carrier forces operated beyond the southern limit of this bad weather front, which from the fifth onwards tended to favor the Japanese. Second, American attentions were becoming increasingly fixed on the western Solomon Sea and the obvious buildup of enemy forces in the area south of Rabaul. Concern about the area to the north of the Jomard Passage was understandable, given the Allied anxiety over the security of Port Moresby and the clear intentions of the enemy. But it diverted the Americans from the real and immediate threat, which was going to emerge not in this area but further to the east, where American weakness after 2 May was critical. If the truth is told, of course, the Americans could be said to have been feeble across the whole theater of operations. But there was one region of considerable weakness: north of latitude 15° S and east of longitude 154° E. After 2 May Allied reconnaissance of this sea area was tenuous to say the least.

Before 2 May the Southwest Pacific Command had three bases from which to conduct reconnaissance missions. Lack of aircraft and flying boats prevented all but one of the allocated search areas from being scouted more than once a day. The search areas, moreover, barely overlapped and then only in two locations. But the Solomon Sea, the Solomons and the line of the Louisades were more or less covered from Townsville, Port Moresby and Tulagi. The weak spot was Tulagi. Tulagi anchored the Allied position in the east, but when it was abandoned the Allies were left with no reconnaissance capacity over the Solomons south of Bougainville and to the south in the sea area between Rossel and Rennell. The loss of Tulagi was not countered by any attempt to tie in the operational boundary of the Southwest Pacific and South Pacific Commands. The theater of operations where the whole of the battle of the Coral Sea was to be fought was in the Southwest Pacific Command area, but its operational boundary followed meridian 160° E until it reached latitude 17° S and then it sliced its way to the position latitude 10° S, longitude 165° E, before following the meridian line northwards to the equator, where three command areas converged.

Thus the sea area between the southern Solomons and the Santa Cruz Islands was divided between the South Pacific and the Southwest Pacific Commands. The touchy relations between the two, plus sheer lack of time, precluded the Americans from coordinating their efforts along the line of weakness that constituted their common border. The Allied Air Forces of the Southwest Pacific Command did not have the aircraft to watch this gap, and in any case its interest had to be directed to the sea areas south of Rabaul. The South Pacific Command did have the means to watch the gap, but it chose to keep its search forces—the Catalinas from the *Tangier*—at Noumea in New Caledonia. It was not prepared to make use of the improvised but quite adequate seaplane facilities at Efate. Had it done so, the Catalinas could have covered the gap between San Cristobal and Santa Cruz and scouted as far north as Tulagi and Malaita. From Noumea the Catalinas could not cover the whole of this gap, and they could not cover any of the Solomons channels from the Pacific into the Solomon Sea. They had only the capacity to reach just short of San Cristobal, and they had only a limited ability to cover even this relatively restricted search area. The Catalinas lacked the means to launch a two-phase reconnaissance. The practice of the force on Noumea was to mount a search with three Catalinas in a pattern 50 miles apart. With a visibility of 25 miles, this arrangement gave a search front of 150 miles, which was not enough to cover the area effectively. Thus, in effect, the seas around the southern Solomons were unwatched, or not watched effectively, and it was precisely in this sea area that the threat emerged. The Japanese plan was for the Carrier Striking

Force to come around south of the Solomons, between San Cristobal and Santa Cruz, and then enter the Coral Sea.[58] With Tulagi gone, the Americans lacked the base in the east that was essential to their defense.

When Inoue arrived at Rabaul on the morning of 4 May to gather together the threads of battle, difficulty confronted him. The Port Moresby side of Operation MO was under way, with the Attack Force leaving Rabaul at 0600 and Marumo moving on Deboyne to assist in the construction of the seaplane base on the islands.[59] In the light of events at Tulagi, however, Inoue had to decide whether or not to proceed with this side of the venture, and how to respond to the presence of the enemy somewhere in the vicinity of Tulagi. The trouble was that the dispersal of forces involved in Operation MO, plus the unforeseen turn of events involving the Carrier Striking Force, precluded rapid and effective redeployment. Thus the events of 4 May presaged events one month hence off Midway. Both of the Japanese forces with carriers were in the process of refueling when the enemy's blows fell. The *Shoho*, as we have seen, was with the *Iro* off Shortland, and she set out for an intercept position when word of events at Tulagi was received, but Takagi and Hara remained ignorant of events to the south until the afternoon. For the first but not for the last time in this battle, the vagaries of the Japanese radio net let them down. The *Zuikaku* and the *Shokaku* completed refueling from the *Tohomaru* about noon, but it was not until they received orders from Inoue that they set off at high speed to the south, along with the cruisers and whatever destroyers had finished refueling.[60] Since the latter had not all completed that task, Takagi had to divide his force, and he had to do something else that was inimical to his long-term interest. The long approach to the south, made at speed, could only involve another replenishment, and his progress eventually had to be geared to the speed of the slowest ship, his oiler. At some stage or another he would have to go into a box course to await her arrival and reconcentrate his forces, and his run to the south used up fuel for no useful purpose.

As the carrier force came south the *Zuikaku* and the *Shokaku* flew off reconnaissance missions. The two carriers searched the Pacific Ocean side of the Solomons as they came south.[61] In the course of the afternoon, however, it appeared that there was little prospect of Japanese forces contacting the enemy, and perhaps because of an awareness of the inadequacies of the *Shoho* Inoue recalled her. Hers was not a fleet role—indeed she hardly merited any role at all, being a strong contender for the unwanted title of worst-converted aircraft carrier to see service in any navy, her only possible rival being the *Zuiho*, her sister ship.[62] She could not be risked, unsupported, in an action with an enemy fleet carrier, and in any event Inoue needed her for close support, antisubmarine patrols and air defense for the forces bound for Port Moresby,[63] since he had decided to adhere to his original timetable and plan of campaign.[64] Thus Abe's transports left Rabaul at 1800 and Takagi, the chase called off, was ordered to proceed according to plan but still to fly off the Zekes to Rabaul when circumstances permitted.[65] These orders could not get around the Carrier Striking Force at some time having to regroup and refuel after its run to the south.

It was not until noon on 5 May that the Carrier Striking Force rounded the southern Solomons and entered the Coral Sea, and by the time it did so the overall position was developing along lines that were not unpromising for the Japanese, despite Tulagi. If the enemy was still in the area, then by entering the Coral Sea from the east the Japanese carriers placed themselves across or on the flank of any enemy withdrawal from the area.[66] Rabaul suspected that the missing Mavis had been shot down, but it had no idea where the loss might have occurred, and Inoue did not have another scout available for follow-up. Caught as he was between two objectives and with resources enough to deal with only one, on the fifth he chose to persist with Operation MO in unamended form and to send his air strength against Port Moresby rather than over the Coral Sea.[67] However serious the situation over Port Moresby might have been, it is hard to resist the notion that this was a confused decision. The destruction of an enemy carrier force that might be in a position to play havoc with Japanese forces in the Solomon Sea should surely have been Inoue's primary objective. Moreover, though there was much to be said for Takagi taking up a position across the enemy's line of retreat, there were also certain drawbacks, and to these Takagi and Hara remained curiously indifferent over the next two days. Taking up a position between an enemy and his base had attractions, and if the enemy did move against the Jomard Passage then it was in the Japanese interest to be on the disengaged enemy flank. From there the *Zuikaku* and the *Shokaku* might well be able to strike without being struck. Certainly the Japanese carrier force over the next few days showed a real concern, perhaps an inordinate one, lest the enemy manage to get into a position on its flank or rear,[68] and on the sixth the Carrier Striking Force continued to believe that it could afford to allow the enemy to get between it and those Japanese forces in the Solomon Sea.[69] But the weakness of this assumption is obvious. The Japanese might have thought in terms of catching the Americans between the hammer from the east and the anvil in the west, but the forces in the Solomon Sea were hardly an anvil of tempered steel. Protection of the transport and light forces had to be the primary Japanese objective. Success against an American carrier force was a high priority, but success at the expense of the various forces between Rabaul and the Jomard Passage could hardly be anything other than a Pyrrhic victory.

The way the Japanese shaped up to battle after Tulagi indicates a curious inability to readjust to a changing situation. Of course, this was not directly the fault of the local commanders, who had been given a task and inadequate means to see it through to a successful conclusion. But they reacted to events with a wooden orthodoxy, passing current orders down the chain of command without regard to the dictates of the existing situation. The Japanese were being forced to improvise, which was precisely what they were trying to avoid in their desire to make the original plan work. By the fourth their failure to recast plans when the presence of the enemy was revealed put them in danger of inducing a first-class disaster if the Americans were able to strike first at the forces in the Solomon Sea and then against the Carrier Striking Force. The odd thing is that the Japanese do not appear to have been unduly concerned at the prospect of the enemy holding a central position between their own dispersed forces, even though the Combined Fleet planning for Operation MI had selected a central position as the one from which a Japanese victory would be won.

CHAPTER 7

The Carrier Contacts

When the Carrier Striking Force rounded San Cristobal and entered the Coral Sea on 5 May, history's first carrier battle was in the making. The wonder of the events that followed was not that there was a battle between two fleet carrier formations but that this exchange did not take place until 8 May. Almost three days separated the Carrier Striking Force's entrance into the Coral Sea and its exchange of blows with Task Force 17. The exchange could easily have taken place on any of the three preceding days, and the fact that it did not occur until the eighth was perhaps a major factor in the Japanese inability to force a favorable decision. Their best chance of success fell between the fifth and the seventh, and by the time battle was joined on the eighth the odds had tilted slightly but significantly against them.

The events prior to 5 May and then on and after the eighth were relatively simple. Before the fifth there had been a series of preliminary moves on both sides that had culminated with the Tulagi episode. On the eighth both carrier striking forces found one another and tried to live up to their names. Both struck and were struck, and as they reeled away under the impact of their exchange both thought that the encounter had ended in their favor. Both believed that the other was the more grievously hurt, and neither knew the battle was over after just one attack by each of the main carrier forces. The latter, however, proved to be the case. Despite Japanese efforts to regain contact and resume the battle, and despite an initial American willingness to continue the fight, the battle ended on 8 May with the actual exchange between the two forces lasting less than an hour.

The three days from 5 May to 7 May, particularly the fifth and the sixth, form the most curious and complicated part of an engagement that was never straightforward. At that time five major task forces were at sea. Of these, four were north of the Rennell-Rossel line. Both the Coral Sea and the Solomon Sea were being crisscrossed by reconnaissance aircraft from both sides. In spite of all this activity, however, contact between the main forces proved impossible. With so much air and naval activity concentrated in a relatively restricted area, it would seem inconceivable that contact should elude both Fletcher and Takagi. But it did. Both choice and circumstance combined to all but snuff out any chance of contact between the two main forces, yet in the end contact materialized.

The chances of either or both sides obtaining contact were slimmer than might appear at first glance for three reasons. The first and probably most important was that both sides were determined to remain undiscovered. They sought to stay to the east, ready to move against the enemy when he was found. Both were playing a waiting game, a passive role that explains in part their failure to contact one another. Second, the two carrier striking forces were to the east, but almost all their air and naval activity was concentrated in the western and central sectors of the Solomon Sea and the northern Coral Sea. American and Japanese attention was fixed on the area south of Rabaul and north of the Jomard Passage. Each main carrier formation was at the edge of the other side's search area. This factor leads to the third reason for delayed contact: Japanese reconnaissance practice, or lack of it. The Japanese carriers did not conduct any reconnaissance on the fifth and sixth. The *Zuikaku* and the *Shokaku*'s reconnaissance of the fourth, when they came south in response to events at Tulagi, was exceptional. According to Japanese doctrine it was not a carrier's job to search for the enemy. The carrier was an offensive instrument, a strike weapon, and strength detached for reconnaissance was always wasted. The Japanese relied on flying boats and particularly the seaplanes from their escorts to provide reconnaissance for their carrier forces. Their two seaplane cruisers, the *Chikuma* and the *Tone*, had been built and had trained for this role. Yet on this occasion the two cruisers were not with the Carrier Strking Force because they had been assigned training duties in preparation for Operation MI. On 18 May, for example, they were to be the practice targets for Kate torpedo bombers, and it is somewhat hard to believe that in this role the *Chikuma* and the *Tone* were more important than they were acting as the eyes of the Fifth Carrier Division, that other units could not have been relegated to training duties.[1] With only standard heavy cruisers in the Carrier Striking Force, Takagi and Hara were ill provided in terms of reconnaissance capabilities, yet even this seems an inadequate explanation for the failure of the carrier force to mount reconnaissance of its own when it knew that an enemy carrier force was somewhere in the area. Given the Japanese tactical situation, there would have been little reason for the Japanese carriers to wait passively for reports from land-based aircraft. It cannot be stated for certain that, had Takagi and Hara conducted their own reconnaissance, contact with the enemy would have been made in circum-

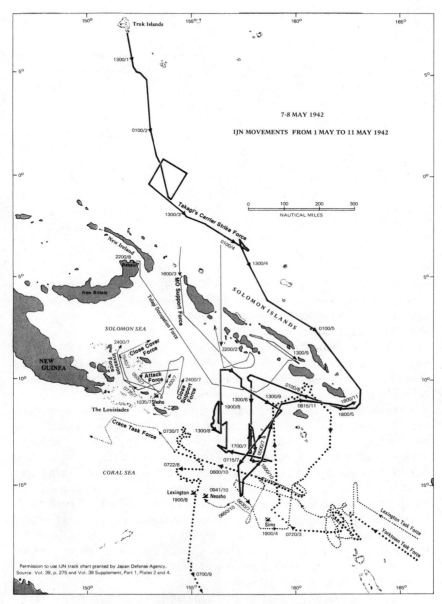

7-8 MAY 1942

IJN MOVEMENTS FROM 1 MAY TO 11 MAY 1942

Permission to use IJN track chart granted by Japan Defense Agency.
Source: Vol. 39, p. 275 and Vol. 39 Supplement, Part 1, Plates 2 and 4.

Battle of the Coral Sea, 7–8 May 1942, and IJN Movements,
1–11 May 1942

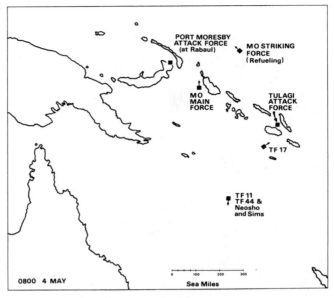

PORT MORESBY
ATTACK FORCE
(at Rabaul)

MO STRIKING
FORCE
(Refueling)

MO
MAIN
FORCE

TULAGI
ATTACK
FORCE

TF 17

TF 11
TF 44 &
Neosho
and Sims

0800 4 MAY

Sea Miles

The Situation at 0800, 4 May

stances more favorable than those of 8 May. But given these facts and errors of omission, what happened to the Fifth Carrier Division appears to have been a case of self-inflicted wounds.

Despite the circumstances, contact with the enemy could easily have come the way of both the Americans and the Japanese. In fact it almost did for the latter. Though the carrier formations of both sides sought to maneuver beyond the range of land-based enemy aircraft, a Mavis flying boat of the Yokohama Air Group actually found and shadowed Task Force 17 on the morning of the sixth. It accurately reported the location and composition of the task force to Rabaul; Rabaul received the report and retransmitted it; Pearl Harbor picked up the signal; the Carrier Striking Force missed it. It was coincidental that, at the same time, the *Lexington* launched a Dauntless that failed to obtain contact with the Carrier Striking Force by less than 20 miles. Such were the narrow margins by which contact for both sides was missed.

More serious for the Japanese than their badly overloaded and inconsistent radio net was their overall lack of system and policy. On the fifth and sixth the Japanese had to do two things: first, make a decision about whether Operation MO was to proceed and, second, contact the enemy carrier force known to be in the area. Though the two moves were interre-

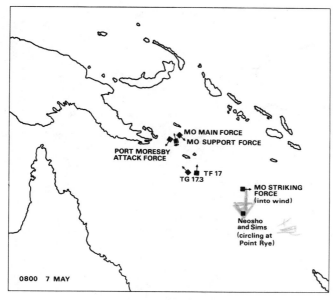

The Situation at 0800, 7 May

lated, the second was the crucial one: unless the enemy task force was eliminated Operation MO could not proceed. And yet the earlier decision to press ahead with Operation MO remained in force and was confirmed on the afternoon of the sixth—an extraordinary state of affairs given the fact that by then the Japanese had manifestly failed both to win air supremacy over Port Moresby and to bring the enemy task force to book.

When the Carrier Striking Force entered the Coral Sea it enjoyed an advantage that did much to offset any loss that might have been incurred off Tulagi. By making an indirect and undetected approach to contact, the force regained an element of surprise for the Japanese. In fact by the afternoon of 5 May they were in a position conducive to rolling up the enemy from the east. The problem that confronted Takagi and Hara seemed to be that they were four days in front of their operational schedule and that the enemy was at sea. The Carrier Striking Force had four days in which to sweep the enemy aside, but its attitude was that these were days that had to be lost in order to bring movements back into phase. Once the Carrier Striking Force entered the theater of combat on 5 May, it had to use these days either to bring the enemy to battle quickly or to go to the support of the forces in the western Solomon Sea. If the Carrier Striking Force could not deal with the enemy, its minimum obligation was to ensure that

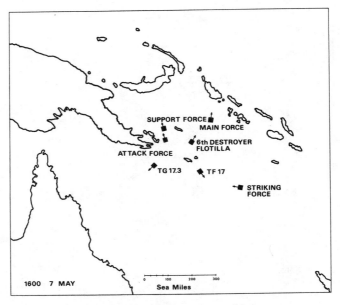

The Situation at 1600, 7 May

he not attack the transports and light forces. The force took neither action. It waited to the east, refueling and regrouping on the sixth, all the time concerned lest the enemy carrier force should fall upon its rear. From the time that Takagi and Hara rounded San Cristobal their overwhelming concern was to get across the enemy's line of withdrawal and into a position from which to attack his rear. The Japanese carrier formation showed more concern about the enemy on its tail than about the security of the amphibious forces. When time itself was against the Japanese, when they had to strike out firmly in order to dictate the operational pattern of forthcoming events, the Carrier Striking Force played the waiting game. This, as we have seen, was the prerogative of Fletcher and his task forces. Fletcher could wait because on the fifth he knew that the enemy amphibious forces were at sea and would have to try to force the line of the Louisades some time in the next three days. Thus Fletcher placed himself on an interception course and slowly steamed toward the enemy, knowing that he would have the time to close him at high speed should the need arise. The course he set would have taken him to a position about 120 miles due south of the Jomard Passage by midafternoon on the seventh, had he not turned his command away to the north to make contact with the enemy on the morning of the same day.

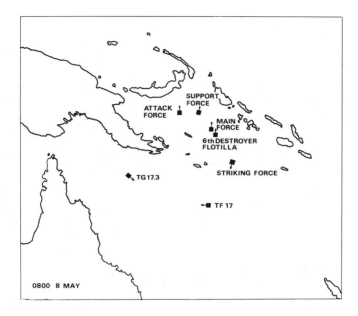

0800 8 MAY

The Situation at 0800, 8 May

Fletcher's task after Tulagi was to be patient while events to the north of the Louisades unfolded. He had to remain undetected and wait for MacArthur's command to pass him information on what was happening in the western Solomon Sea. This, however, did not mean that the role of the American carrier forces was a passive one. All the time they operated their own combat air patrol and carried out their own defensive reconnaissance. As we have noted, it was this reconnaissance on the morning of the sixth that so narrowly failed to obtain a contact with the enemy.[2] Moreover, in this period the Americans did three things to make final their order of battle. First, in the hour after dawn on the sixth Fletcher integrated his forces. The task had been outlined in his orders of 1 May, but he had delayed its execution until this time. Finally putting his order into effect, he reconstituted his three separate task forces into one task force, numbered on his extant formation. Henceforth the new Task Force 17 consisted of three combat formations at sea: Task Group 17.5, the carrier task group; Task Group 17.2, the attack group; and Task Group 17.3, the support group. Task Group 17.5 consisted of the flagships of the two American carrier formations, the *Yorktown* and the *Lexington*, plus the four carriers that previously had formed part of the former's screen, the *Morris*, *Anderson*, *Hammann* and *Russell*. Fletcher's intention was to hand over tactical command of Task Group 17.5 and control of its air groups to Fitch on the eve of battle, but for the moment he chose not to effect this change. Task Group 17.2 consisted of the heavy cruisers *Minneapolis* and *New Orleans* from the original Task Force 11; the destroyers *Phelps, Dewey, Farragut, Aylwin* and *Monaghan* from the same task force; and the heavy cruisers *Astoria, Chester* and *Portland* from the original Task Force 17. This task group was commanded by Rear Admiral Thomas C. Kinkaid, until this time commander of the *Lexington*'s screen and senior to Smith, his counterpart from the *Yorktown* force. Task Group 17.3, commanded by Crace, was the reconcentrated and redubbed Task Force 44, with the *Australia, Chicago, Hobart, Perkins* and *Walke* under the flag of the senior Allied admiral present in the Coral Sea.[3] Under special arrangement, the British and Americans had agreed that the senior American flag officer would take command of any task force that contained ships of the U.S. Navy and the Royal Navy, just as later in the war it became standard practice within the U.S. Navy for carrier admirals to assume tactical command even when they were junior to admirals with the screening forces.

The second arrangement made to solidify the order of battle related to Task Group 17.6. This was the Oiler Group, a title that was something of a misnomer. By 6 May it consisted of just the one oiler, the *Neosho*, and whichever destroyer had been detached as her chaperon. During the sixth the ever-thirsty Fletcher took one last chance to double back on the track that he had set at 1930 the previous night towards the northwest to top up his tanks before the tanker, in the company of the *Sims*, was detached at 1755.[4] Task Force 17 turned back on its original course some ninety minutes later, by which time Task Group 17.6 was en route to a patrol area where danger and convenience overlapped. The only available tanker, with what remained of her original load of 25,000 tons of oil, had to be ordered to an area where she ran as small a chance of being discovered by the enemy as possible, yet at the same time she had to be close enough to the carrier force to resupply it quickly. Risk and necessity had to be calculated meticulously, since the *Neosho* was the only tanker available to supply Task Force 17. Two other oilers were off the Australian coast, but neither was equipped to carry out replenishment at sea. Accordingly, the *Neosho* and the *Sims* were ordered to proceed to a patrol area south of a line between latitude 15° S, longitude 158° E, and latitude 16° S, longitude 160° E. These two points, code named Rye and Corn respectively, were just two of seven such preselected locations that had been assigned as possible refueling rendezvous positions. Both Point Rye and Point Corn were just within a 600-mile search radius from Shortland and just outside the range of shore-based attack aircraft. Fletcher ordered the group to be on Point Rye on odd days and on Point Corn on even days, passing through the positions within one hour of sunrise. At all other times they were to be south of these points.

The third matter relating to the order of battle had to do with Task Group 17.3. On the morning of 7 May, at 0645, Fletcher ordered Crace to proceed to the Jomard Passage while the remainder of Task Force 17 turned northwards towards Rossel. To strengthen Crace's force Fletcher detached the *Farragut* from Task Group 17.2, thereby leaving Crace with a command of three cruisers and an equivalent number of destroyers. Subsequently, Fletcher stated that this decision, described as "bold" by one commentator, was based on the calculation that even if something untoward happened to the carrier force when it came to fight its counterparts, the Allies would still have a force in position to contest any enemy attempt to force the line of the Louisades.[5] The Naval War College, in its tactical analysis of the battle, later pointed out the fallacy of this line of reasoning:[6] if the American carriers failed to stop the enemy, then cruisers and destroyers were not going to do any better.[7]

There was something wrong with Fletcher's decision. If the American carriers failed, Task Group 17.2 would be swept away with them; if they succeeded, they and not Crace's ships would either deter the enemy from trying to force the line of the Louisades or prove to be the agents of destruction should the Japanese persist with Operation MO. The only possible value of the deployment of a separated task group off the Jomard Passage would come if the two carrier formations cancelled one another out. Yet even in the event of mutual neutralization, the case for moving a force to the Louisades remained dubious. On 5 May the intelligence agencies at Pearl Harbor passed to Fletcher the text of the 3 May orders from Rabaul to Takagi directing him to take the carrier formation against Port Moresby. From that order Fletcher and his staff might well have inferred that the Japanese felt they could not persist with their operation against Port Moresby unless they won command of the air over the objective. This was precisely what the Japanese did believe, but it was not until 8 May that they faced up to the fact that this was one battle they could not win. Under the terms of Japanese arrangements it would be impossible for them to adhere to Operation MO unless a carrier battle was won decisively and in such a manner that Japanese units were free to close the enemy at Port Moresby. Any other result was of no use to the Japanese, and the Americans might have realized that Operation MO would have to be shelved (if only for the moment) in the event of the two carrier striking forces neutralizing one another. In that eventuality, Crace's being off the Louisades was quite superfluous to the situation. Hence by any definition the policy of separating Task Group 17.3 from the rest of the task force was an error, one that could and perhaps did prove costly by weakening a carrier screen that was already somewhat thin. With one other destroyer detached during the night of 7–8 May by Fletcher, Task Force 17 was left with twelve rather than nineteen escorts around its carriers on 8 May. Of course there is no way of knowing if the loss of the *Lexington* on the eighth would have been avoided had Task Force 17 been kept concentrated, but it is rather difficult to believe that Fletcher helped his cause by detaching more than one-third of his strength on the very morning of the battle. Quite unexpectedly, however, Task Group 17.3, as it approached the passage and then patrolled off its southern exit, attracted a disproportionate share of enemy air attention. An enemy reconnaissance mission stumbled across this force and grossly exaggerated its size and importance. Task Group 17.3 thus attracted numerous attacks by Japanese land-based aircraft that might otherwise have been directed against the carrier group. Crace inadvertently acted as bait that was swallowed whole by the Japanese, and with no ill effects for the six ships of his task group. Nevertheless, that happy state of affairs can hardly serve as retrospective vindication of Fletcher's decision.

On the fifth and sixth, however, the main events took place well to the north and northwest of Fletcher. Japanese forces were continuing their progress across the western Solomon Sea en route for the Louisades and Port Moresby. The Transport Group and Attack Force joined company on the fifth,[8] while Marumo's task force made for Deboyne Islands to give the *Kamikawamaru* time to put seaplane units on station before the amphibious forces approached the channel.[9] Marumo was then to take his force to patrol between New Guinea and Woodlark, ensuring the security of the relatively unthreatened right flank of the amphibious forces as they came south from Rabaul.[10] Likewise, at about 0830 on the sixth, the *Shoho*, after having completed the refueling that had been interrupted on the fourth, came south from Bougainville to provide the Transport and Attack Groups with close support as they approached the Jomard Passage.[11]

In the course of these two days aerial reconnaissance enabled the Americans to build up a picture of what was going on north of the Louisades. The process took time; even with the information provided by intelligence it was difficult to piece together conflicting and often erroneous sightings. The *Shoho*, for example, was demoted from a *Kaga*-class carrier on the fourth to a light cruiser on the sixth,[12] not that the lowliness of her latter status prevented four Flying Fortresses from the 435rd Squadron, Nineteenth Heavy Bombardment Group, from unsuccessfully attacking her at about 1030 when she was some 70 miles south of Bougainville.[13] In spite of such failings, by the afternoon of the sixth the Allied intelligence picture was beginning to fit together, except in one crucial area.[14] A partially recovered signal, sent by Inoue to Takagi after the Tulagi episode and forwarded to Fletcher by Pearl Harbor, seemed to suggest that the enemy carrier force would make for Bougainville before entering the Coral Sea. Given his knowledge that the Japanese carriers had been ordered against Port Moresby, Fletcher was inclined to believe that the Japanese would approach from the north rather than from the northeast or the east, and unfortunately for the Americans there was no way this deduction could be disproved.[15] The Carrier Striking Force came the long way around to enter the Coral Sea from the east, and thereafter it had taken up positions in the many sectors where the Allied Air Forces of the Southwest Pacific Command could not search for want of aircraft. After rounding San Cristobal Takagi kept his force close to the southern edge of the Solomons and spent much of the sixth in the same general area in which the *Shoho* had covered the Tulagi landings on the third. There the Carrier Striking Force spent most of the day refueling. Thus with the one Dauntless from the *Lexington* failing to find the Japanese on the morning of the sixth by some five or six minutes' flying time, Fletcher remained in ignorance of the danger in which his force was placed. Neither on the fifth nor the sixth did Fletcher have any inkling of the Japanese intention of rolling him up from the east. He had no idea that rather than being to the northwest for most of those two days, the *Zuikaku* and the *Shokaku* were generally to the northeast and north of Task Force 17.[16]

Quite clearly the ball was in the Japanese court on the sixth. Choice was theirs to make, and thus far they had made their critical decision not to amend their plan of campaign in any way. But this was not a final decision: the nature and timing of Operation MO meant that the Japanese constantly had to return to the question of whether or not to proceed with the operation. Two problems increasingly pressed on them. First, with the enemy carrier force unlocated and Port Moresby still resisting Japanese attempts to control its skies, the Japanese were running out of time. The fleet carriers were on loan, and Operation MO had to be completed as soon as possible. The Fifth Carrier Division had to return to Japanese waters in time for Operation MI. Second, Inoue could not keep his invasion forces indefinitely in the sea area south of Rabaul. The menace posed by Allied submarines and aircraft was too great to be ignored. With the Japanese nearing the Jomard Passage, decisions had to be made. The passage represented the point of no return for them: beyond it they would have to commit themselves to the stark alternatives of all-out victory or total defeat. But the Japanese forces in the western Solomon Sea could not wait on a decision from Rabaul indefinitely, and when on the afternoon of the sixth Inoue was called upon for the third time to decide whether or not to press ahead with Operation MO, it was perhaps predictable that for the third time he decided to proceed. He and his senior commanders realized full well that everything would depend on how well the Carrier Striking Force dealt with the enemy, but even this does not explain the basic lack of prudence in the Japanese conduct of operations.[17] To have persisted with the operation at this stage without making any change of timetable or force composition must have involved an act of faith rather than reasoned judgment.

At this stage of the battle in the southwest Pacific the Japanese plan of campaign was beginning to fall apart. The Japanese believed that the presence of their fleet carriers was unknown to the Americans and that surprise was on their side.[18] In this they were half right, but still there was little justification for the Carrier Striking Force dividing to refuel on the sixth, when it came within 70 miles of Task Force 17.[19] At that particular time the Americans were not flying reconnaissance missions, and even if they had been the chance of finding the Japanese was slim, since they were operating in bad weather that was worsening. Takagi, belatedly made aware of the presence of the enemy after one accurate signal reached him amidst a welter of inaccurate reports, decided against trying to force the issue on the afternoon of the sixth. The Carrier Striking Force believed that it still had a day or so in hand. It was therefore willing to hold off for the moment and make its main effort the following day, when the Japanese force would be reassembled after fueling. Though the general feeling in the force was that next morning the enemy was likely to be south of the Louisades preparing to counterattack forces coming through the Jomard Passage, Hara prevailed upon Takagi to search to the east as well as to the west of south. Initially the Japanese intention had been to search the area between south and west, but on Hara's insistence this was extended 20 degrees back towards the east.[20] Hara wanted to ensure that his carriers sat on the tail of the enemy, not vice versa, but the extension of the search area by a mere 20 degrees—a sector for one, perhaps two aircraft—was really neither here nor there. If the Carrier Striking Force really was concerned about this matter, it should have launched a full reconnaissance between east and west through south. As it turned out, the extension of the search area by even 20 degrees proved unfortunate for the Japanese.

Though battle was not joined on the sixth, the pace quickened as the day passed, with both sides preparing for a battle that had to come with the next day's dawn. Sunrise on the seventh found the various forces scattered at extreme range from one another. The American task force, which as we have seen divided shortly after dawn, was about 120 miles due south of Rossel, some eight or nine hours cruising distance from the southern exit of the Jomard Passage.[21] Beyond the Louisades, and hence nearest to Fletcher, were the transport and attack formations, under the overall command of Abe. Goto and the *Shoho* group were some 35 miles east of Woodlark and about 30 miles to the northwest of the convoy.[22] Marumo was almost in company with Goto, on the disengaged flank of the amphibious forces. Thus within a matter of two or three hours' steaming from the northern entrance of the Jomard Passage were more than thirty transports and warships. About 280 miles to the southeast of Fletcher's dawn position was Point Rye, where the *Neosho* and the *Sims* were obediently on station. About 200 miles to the north of the Oiler Group and about 280 miles southwest of Tulagi was the Carrier Striking Force. It was approximately 200 miles a compass point or two to the south of east of Fletcher and his carrier formation.[23] Fletcher, therefore, was in the central position between Takagi and the transports, the *Shoho* being on the far side of the latter force.

With dawn both sides mounted major reconnaissance efforts. After the poor results of earlier days neither side was taking any chance of relying on shore-based aircraft for reconnaissance. With success probably dependent on the relative effectiveness of their scouting forces, both carrier forces launched aircraft to supplement their other efforts. Allied aircraft from Australia, Port Moresby and New Caledonia took to the skies, but with battle about to be joined in the central area of the northern Coral Sea Fletcher had to rely primarily upon his own scouting squadrons. The dawn reconnaissance—still directed by Fletcher since he had yet to devolve tactical command of the task group and its aircraft to Fitch—was mounted from a position in latitude 13° 20′ S, longitude 154° 21′ E, by ten Dauntlesses. They began launching from the *Yorktown* at 0619 before Crace parted company, and were directed to cover the sector between 325 degrees and 085 degrees to a range of 250 miles. This would take them to and beyond the line of the Louisades.[24] The Japanese, on the other hand, committed aircraft, seaplanes and flying boats from Rabaul, Shortland, Tulagi and Deboyne to a blanket search south of the Louisades.[25] The Carrier Striking Force, well to the east, committed twelve Kates to the search of the sector between 160 degrees and 270 degrees to a range of 200 miles.[26]

Contact was inevitable. With so many ships in a shrinking area and with so many flying machines of all description in the air, there was never any question of the two sides missing one another. The operative question was which force would be sighted first. The balance between the two sides was delicate. The Americans, with 123 operational aircraft, were slightly closer to the forces beyond the Louisades than they were to the Carrier Striking Force, which had 108 aircraft available for missions.[27] This slight advantage of range and numbers was enhanced by the Americans' superior position; the enemy was in clear weather while Task Force 17 was just to the south of the trailing edge of the bad weather front. But these advantages were offset by Fletcher's ignorance of the whereabouts of the Carrier Striking Force, which had managed to maneuver itself into a position on the Americans' tail. It was on the rear of Task Force 17, where Takagi and Hara had wanted it, but just a little too far to the east to be ideally placed.

There were to be many sighting reports that morning, but the day's events were to be decided by just four, all made between 0810 and 0840. The first sighting was made by a seaplane from Deboyne, the second by a scout from Task Force 17. The third contact with the enemy was made by a scout from the Fifth Carrier Division, and the fourth by another seaplane from Deboyne. The two most important contact reports were those sent by the scouts from the carrier forces.

The American contact was made at 0815. It reported the presence of two carriers and four heavy cruisers in latitude 10° 03′ S, longitude 152° 57′ E.[28] This placed a major enemy task force beyond the Louisades at, or really just beyond, maximum attacking range from Task Force 17. The first contact, made some five to ten minutes earlier by the Japanese, established contact with Crace's force. This contact would not have proved significant had the strength of the task group not been greatly exaggerated. Mistaking cruisers for battleships, the seaplane reported that Crace's formation contained two battleships, one cruiser and four destroyers.[29] This erroneous report was to have a baleful influence on subsequent Japanese operations. The fourth report was also in error, signaling the presence of an enemy carrier force but giving the wrong coordinates. Rabaul, however, proved able to unscramble the mistake and informed Takagi that the enemy was some 200 miles to the south of Deboyne. This information, which came over the air to Rabaul at about 0840, was in the hands of the Carrier Striking Force at about 0900.[30] But arriving at that time it was too late to influence events. At 0830 the search by the Carrier Striking Force had discovered a carrier and light cruiser about 200 miles to the south.[31] Freakishly, its signal was picked up by Pearl Harbor, and in plotting the report the staff of the Pacific Fleet noted that this force had been seen at a position that corresponded with Point Rye.

In some way or another every one of these four reports was wrong, but the balance of error was to favor the Americans. This can be attributed primarily to the circumstances that surrounded the third report. Initially bewildered by a report that placed their carriers far from the Jomard Passage, the Americans at Pearl Harbor suspected that the report they had intercepted referred to none other than the *Neosho* and the *Sims*. Hara, on the other hand, never doubted the accuracy of the report. It would appear that in this instance the wish was father to the fact. The enemy force had been found in that part of the search sector that had been added to the original area on Hara's insistence and, half expecting to find an enemy force in that area, Hara convinced himself that the report was of the enemy task force the Carrier Striking Force was seeking. The Japanese questioned neither the reason an enemy task force should be out of range of the Jomard Passage at the time nor the composition of the reported force. A single carrier in the mighty company of a lone cruiser hardly constituted a sound tactical formation. After sending off a Kate on a second-phase reconnaissance, Hara committed the whole of his striking power against this meager target to the south without waiting for an amplifying report. Thus eighteen Zekes, twenty-four Kates and thirty-six Vals were well on their way to the south before the report from Rabaul, giving the true location of Task Force 17, was received by the Carrier Striking Force.[32]

One does not need much imagination to realize what impact this signal must have had on Takagi and Hara, particularly when the composition of the enemy force to the south was reported. The second Kate sent out to scout did not even give the *Neosho* and the *Sims* serious consideration—it was obvious they were not a carrier and cruiser.[33] Japanese problems really began when their attack formation arrived over the two American ships. It had to decide whether or not these were the reported carrier and cruiser or whether the search should be continued. The Japanese, not surprisingly, compromised. Limited range meant that not all the aircraft could scout, and the attack commander, Lieutenant Commander Kakuichi Takahashi, had to divide his force. Takahashi, leader of the dive bombers of the first attacking force at Pearl Harbor, was generally regarded as one of the steadiest and most dependable of senior aviators. He ordered his Vals to search while the Kates carried out a series of desultory high-level attacks. Returning to the position of the *Neosho* and the *Sims* after their fruitless searches, the Vals began their attacks at noon. Having come so far it was rather pointless not to attack, and they did so with a vengeance. In the best service tradition the *Sims* fought hard to save her charge, stationing herself about a mile off the *Neosho*'s port quarter. In this position the *Sims* stood between the *Neosho* and the sun, out of which the Vals dived as they attacked the tanker from over her stern. With all her guns firing and working up to full speed, the *Sims* was ripped apart by a mere four-aircraft attack. Three bombs hit her, two in the engine room. It was an impressive feat, one that contrasted with the results that had been obtained at Tulagi, but it hardly commended itself to the crew of the *Sims*, only fourteen of whom ultimately survived.[34] A massive internal explosion took place as the *Sims* settled by the stern, and her depth charges detonated as she sank.[35] With the destroyer sunk in a matter of minutes, the *Neosho* took the brunt of the Japanese attack. In the course of an eighteen-minute attack the Vals straddled the 75-ft wide target with fifteen 550-lb bombs, seven of which hit. One Val, hit by antiaircraft fire from the tanker, crashed into the *Neosho*, destroying one of her gun positions, but the surviving aircraft were able to head back to their carriers convinced that they had accounted for the ship.

So they had, but celebrations were premature. The natural bouyancy of the tanker was sufficient to keep her afloat until the eleventh. The Japanese attack had destroyed the ship's communications and machinery and split open her tanks. Flame spread across the whole of her upper deck. Yet despite her abandonment by almost half of the crew, the *Neosho* was saved by those who stayed with her. The fires were brought under control after considerable difficulty, and the ship was secured against sinking despite a 30 degree list to port. Without power, however, she drifted helplessly before the trade winds towards the northwest. She was eventually discovered on the eleventh by a patrolling Catalina. The *Henley* set out from New Caledonia to intercept and then scuttle the *Neosho*, after first having taken off her 109 survivors, plus those from the *Sims* who had taken refuge on her after their own ship sank. Those who had abandoned ship before the order to clear the *Neosho* was given were less fortunate. The sea claimed all but four men, who were saved by the destroyer *Helm* on the seventeenth. One of these men subsequently died.[36]

But much more than one Val and two American ships were to be lost in the course of this episode. The crippling of the *Neosho* left Task Force 17 without an oiler, thereby impairing its freedom of action. The loss of the *Neosho* forced Fletcher into the position of having to fight and win, if not on the seventh or the eighth, then certainly on the ninth. Thereafter the destroyers would be beset by increasing fuel problems, and without an oiler Task Force 17 would have little option but to leave the area.

The more obvious loss affected the Japanese. One dive bomber shot down was not important, but tying up twenty-four Kates and thirty-six Vals for this attack, when the enemy carrier formation was in the very position to be attacked in the manner that Takagi and Hara had intended, was an unacceptable loss. The Carrier Striking Force had worked itself into what it considered an ideal attacking position, and then it had revealed its position south of the Solomons and behind the enemy with an attack on an oiler and a destroyer just at the time when Takagi and Hara became aware of the enemy's true position and their own vulnerability. There was little they could do about this, especially when they decided against the dangerous practice of recalling or trying to divert their aircraft in response to the correct report of the enemy's position. But if the Japanese were quick they might redeem the situation. If they were able to recover their aircraft and launch a second strike before the Americans could do the same, the day might yet be won by the Carrier Striking Force. However, there seemed little chance that this might prove the case. The attack on the *Neosho* and the *Sims* tied up the offensive power of the Carrier Striking Force for most of the day; the last bomber did not get back to its carrier until 1515.[37] But on the seventh, fortune favored the Japanese in one vital respect. Their exact position remained unknown to Task Force 17, and the danger of their being beaten to the punch with the second strike failed to materialize. Fletcher's carriers were able to assemble a second strike force some two hours before the Japanese were able to do the same, and the Americans were able to concentrate a larger formation than that of the Japanese. But for a number of reasons Fletcher decided "to keep his powder dry." Thus the miscalculations of the Carrier Striking Force were in large part offset by those calculations that were correct. It believed that Japanese amphibious forces to the north of the Jomard Passage would act as a magnet and draw the enemy to them, thereby distracting his attention from the Carrier Striking Force. Nonetheless, Takagi and Hara were unable to take advantage of this distraction. Nor did they realize how punishing the result of an American effort beyond the Louisades might prove.

American actions on the morning of the seventh were determined by the report that placed two carriers and four heavy cruisers beyond the Louisades. This sighting had two immediate results. First, it brought Task Force 17 hurrying to the north at best speed to close the range. Second, it formed one part of the process that led Inoue to order his forces then approaching the Jomard Passage to turn back north. Just as the Japanese had ordered their transports to turn to the north when Allied forces gave battle in the course of the engagement in the Java Sea in February, so now Inoue tried to put distance between his forces and the enemy. The Japanese knew that their forces had been sighted by enemy air reconnaissance; they knew that Crace was to the south of the passage; they knew of the presence of Task Force 17 to the southeast. They had no illusions about what was going to happen, and at 0900 Inoue instructed his light forces to turn back, hopefully out of range of the anticipated enemy air attack.[38] At the same time Goto ordered the *Shoho* to provide cover for the various forces in the area and to prepare to attack the enemy with her bombers.[39] But the *Shoho* was fully stretched by her existing commitments without having more added to her load, and she was manifestly incapable of dealing with two enemy fleet carriers by herself. In the previous two hours she had flown off fighters for a combat air patrol over the all-important transports, and she had flown off reconnaissance missions.[40] About half of her few aircraft were already committed, and she simply did not have the means to put more than a couple of planes into a standing air patrol overhead at any one time.

Inoue's order to withdraw was right, but unfortunately for the Japanese it was too late for their forces in the western Solomon Sea to seek safety through dispersal and to put distance between them and the enemy. As if to ensure that Inoue's belated realization of his vulnerability would be properly punished, nature added the final touch. The area to the north of the Louisades was bathed in bright, clear sunlight. Visibility at 15,000 feet was up to 30 miles. In these circumstances the area covered by one degree of longitude and one degree of latitude (nearly 6,000 square miles in the tropics) could be searched in little more than a matter of minutes by a comparatively small number of aircraft. It was inevitable, then, that the Americans should find a target, and it was perhaps inevitable that the target would not be the one they were looking for. That target, of course, did not exist. What had been misidentified was Marumo's otherwise insignificant force, the smallest and by far the least important of the various task forces operating beyond the Louisades. The *Yorktown*'s pilot had misaligned the key and code in trying to make his sighting report, with the result that the enemy force was reported not as two cruisers and four destroyers but as two carriers and four cruisers.[41] By the time the *Yorktown* recovered this scout and the error was discovered, it was too late to rectify the outcome of the mistake. At 0926, with Task Force 17 then 210 miles from the enemy's reported 0815 position, the *Lexington* began launching the fifteen Dauntless bombers, thirteen Dauntless scouts, twelve Devastators and ten Wildcats that she had earmarked for the attack; at 1000 the *Yorktown* followed her colleague's example and started launching seventeen Dauntless scouts, eight Dauntless bombers, ten Devastators and eight fighters. Of the Dauntlesses committed to the attack, three belonged to the group led by the *Lexington*'s air group commander; once more his counterpart from the *Yorktown* did not accompany his squadrons. There was no overall commander of the attacking force. The three members of the attack group, in common with all the Dauntless bombers from the *Lexington*, carried a combination of 500-lb and 100-lb bombs; all the others carried 1,000-lb ordnance. Both carriers committed four of their Wildcats to the defense of their torpedo bombers and the others to the protection of their Dauntlesses. This inadequate scale of protection was recognized by American commanders but accepted as inevitable: without enough fighters to provide for both escort and combat air patrol, it was the former that had to suffer.[42] When the launchings were completed and before the reporting error was discovered, everything seemed to be in favor of the Americans. Though they knew that they had been sighted, the Americans believed that they had found the enemy's main force and had committed no fewer than ninety-three aircraft, seventy-five of them bombers, against it. Moreover, by the time the launchings were over not merely was the enemy north of the Louisades silhouetted against clear sunlight, but the American formation was on the point of getting back under the cold but comforting protection of the weather front.[43] This situation had been calculated during the previous night in the *Yorktown* and had worked out exactly when battle was joined.[44]

Thus by about 1015 the situation was that both carrier forces had simultaneously committed the bulk of their offensive power against misidentified targets. It was about this time that the American commanders, like their counterparts, realized something had gone wrong with their operations. Simultaneously the breaks began to work out in their favor. At 1022 Task Force 17 received a report from the Southwest Pacific Command that had been made some two hours earlier by a Flying Fortress. It reported the presence of a massive concentration of enemy shipping almost at the Jomard Passage, the enemy formation consisting of one carrier, ten transports and sixteen other units.[45]

This report presented Fletcher with something of a dilemma. It was possible that both it and the sighting report of the Dauntless were correct. Intelligence had warned that three enemy carriers might be at sea, and obviously the two reports between them accounted for just that number of carriers. But the report from the Southwest Pacific Command placed the enemy formation about 60 miles to the south of the Dauntless's "two carriers and four cruisers." It was unlikely that both reports were correct. The question that faced Fletcher was which of the reports to believe, and with no indication of the whereabouts of the enemy's fleet carriers over the last few days, a wrong decision would be dangerous. As it was, the contents of the 1022 signal were radioed to the strike mission, and within a short time the various American mistakes began to cancel each other out. First, the error of the Dauntless was realized after the scout was recovered by the *Yorktown*. During the debriefing the mistake that had been made by the aircrew surfaced, thereby revealing that Fletcher had committed the whole of his striking power against a secondary or even tertiary target. The deadly danger in which the Americans then stood was perfectly obvious. The *Yorktown* and the *Lexington*, with about seventeen fighters between them, a handful of Dauntlesses on antisubmarine patrol and the *Yorktown*'s scouts, had virtually nothing with which to oppose an enemy whose position remained unknown at this time. Second, hardly had this danger been recognized than it began to abate for the moment: when the *Neosho* and the *Sims* signaled that they were under attack Fletcher knew for the first time that the enemy was somewhere to the east, and that an attack clearly aimed at the *Yorktown* and the *Lexington* had fallen on the hapless Task Group 17.6. Third, the realization that for the moment Task Force 17 was immune to attack coincided with the realization that its own strike mission was certain to encounter a major enemy formation—even though the report from the Fortress placing a major enemy formation to the north of the Jomard Passage was in its own way as inaccurate as the earlier report from the *Yorktown*'s scout. The 1022 signal gave wrong coordinates for an enemy that had to be to the northeast of his reported position, and the report of a formation with a carrier was simply not accurate. The Fortress had not chanced upon Goto and the *Shoho* but rather upon the transports and their escorts, and one of the transports had been misidentified as a carrier. But with the *Shoho* actually in the area and the weather clear, the ultimate irony was about to be played out: the bombers from Task Force 17 were on their way to attack a carrier that was in the western Coral Sea, that had been reported to be in that area, but that had not actually been sighted by either of the reporting aircraft.[46] By any standard it was a remarkable situation. With cloud cover no guarantee against discovery and attack, Fletcher's command might easily have suffered a disaster for which two cruisers and four destroyers would have been but poor compensation; as it was, Task Force 17 seemed likely to fare better than the Japanese in what was certain to be an exchange less of blows than of mistakes.

In Japanese *shoho* means "luck-bringing phoenix." If the *Shoho* was ever expected to rise from her own ashes then she needed to bring more than luck to the scene of battle. She needed armor, plenty of aircraft and good protection from her escorts. Goto had deployed his four heavy cruisers at 8,000 yards from the carrier, ahead, astern and on either beam. Only the *Sazanami*, in her role as plane guard, was near the *Shoho*. It was almost as if the cruisers were trying to dissociate themselves from the carrier in the hope that they might escape attack themselves. They were certainly not in positions to provide the *Shoho* with flak support.

The attack on the *Shoho* was mounted in three distinct waves. The first, made at about 1100, was conducted by the Dauntlesses of the *Lexington*'s command group which, coming over Misima, sighted and ignored Marumo and concentrated on the *Shoho*. By that time the transports were then beyond the carrier and the horizon.[47] The lesser targets were ignored as the three Dauntlesses, led by the group commander, moved into the attack, though it was not part of the group commander's duties to be the first into the attack when his loss might mean destruction of the means of command. As it turned out none of the Dauntlesses were hit. Nor was the *Shoho*, though one of the bombs aimed at her was a near miss which swept overboard five of the aircraft parked aft.[48] The *Lexington*'s scouts, brought to the scene by the command group, moved into the attack at about 1110. The *Shoho* managed to evade all of the bombs aimed at her in this phase of the action except for one, a sign that desultory antiaircraft fire and passive evasion could not protect her forever. When the American attacks began she had just two fighters in her combat air patrol, having already provided the transports with cover and flown off reconnaissance.[49] Most of these aircraft had been recovered, and it was the Japanese intention to fly off the reserviced fighters in defense of the carrier. It was the attempt to put these fighters into the air that helped to pave the way to disaster. The two earlier attacks had been evaded by high-speed jinking, the slenderness and lightness of the *Shoho* being assets in this respect. But as she turned into the wind and held a steady course as she prepared to launch her fighters, the third and final American attack materialized.

This attack began with torpedo bombers from the *Lexington* and Dauntless scouts from the *Yorktown* joining in a simultaneous unplanned attack. Two 1,000-lb bombs hit the carrier just forward of her rear elevator, and one torpedo hit her on the starboard bow. With the *Shoho*'s having no armor and poor subdivision, the effect of these hits was lethal. She immediately began to lose power and headway. Other hits from these two squadrons were recorded before the coup de grâce was administered by the *Yorktown*'s bomber and torpedo squadrons. By the time these squadrons moved into the attack the *Shoho* was almost stationary, and in the course of about five minutes the carrier was literally ripped apart. American claims were far greater than Japanese estimates of the number of hits the *Shoho* received, but even according to the latter's figures as many as thirteen bombs, seven torpedoes and a crashing dive-bomber were said to have hit the carrier.[50] Probably no carrier could have survived such an attack, and at 1135, four minutes after the order to abandon ship was passed, the *Shoho* capsized and sank at latitude 10° 29' S, longitude 152° 55' E. She was the first of twenty Japanese carriers to be sunk in the course of the war and the first of twelve to be destroyed by enemy carrier aircraft. Goto's cruisers made no attempt to rescue survivors but withdrew at high speed towards the northeast, flying off their seaplanes to Deboyne as they did so.[51] By steering such a course Goto ensured that he stood between the transports and the Americans, though it is doubtful whether the former derived much comfort from Goto's position in view of his cruisers' manifest inability to protect the *Shoho*. The *Sazanami* was detached during the afternoon by Goto with orders to turn back and pick up survivors from the *Shoho*. She was to rescue 225 of a crew of more than 800 from the water. The Americans, on the other hand, lost three aircraft, but some of their aircrew were recovered. One of these aircraft, a Dauntless from the *Yorktown*, became lost after a skirmish with an enemy fighter, and with Task Group 17.5 refusing to provide directions home its pilot, Lieutenant J. W. Rowley, had the good fortune to encounter Task Group 17.3. This formation provided a bearing for Port Moresby, but without sufficient fuel to reach the town Rowley was forced to ditch off New Guinea. He and his gunner drifted ashore and were rescued by friendly natives.[52] Natives also rescued a pilot who crashed on Rossel.[53] All the other aircraft that survived this mission were recovered by the *Yorktown* and the *Lexington* between 1240 and 1338.[54]

Sinking a light carrier, however welcome, was not an effective substitute for the failure to deal with her big sisters; it did nothing to ease the position of Task Force 17 with respect to the Carrier Striking Force. What it did do was to blunt the Japanese thrust from the west, leaving Task Force 17 with little if anything to fear from that direction. More importantly, it confirmed to the Japanese the wisdom of turning their transports to the north—away from Port Moresby. In reality, this was the most significant outcome of the American raid. The destruction of the *Shoho* was a poor haul for an attack with so many bombers, especially when there were several other credible targets in the vicinity. The Americans claimed to have sunk two other ships in the course of this attack, but in reality no other ship was even damaged. There was good execution in the course of these attacks, much better than anything that had been achieved at Tulagi, but coordination was fortuitous, command was weak and the end product was the result of overconcentration. In fact, the attack on the *Shoho* was wasteful. The *Yorktown*'s bombers hit the *Shoho* when flames were already licking both sides of her flight deck, and the *Yorktown*'s Devastators hit a target that was obviously doomed.[55] The Americans could ill afford an attack that left the *Yorktown* with just fourteen torpedoes, the carrier having used up about three-quarters of her allocation in this mission and during the attacks at Tulagi. Additional hits on the *Shoho* and credits against light escorts did not make up for the fact that the *Yorktown* was left with just enough torpedoes for one more mission, and she had yet to face the enemy fleet carriers.

But with the *Yorktown*'s strike aircraft spotted at 1400 and Task Force 17 as a whole ready to launch a second strike by 1450,[56] Fletcher was left with the decision of what to do next.[57] He was in a strong position because he had now recovered all his aircraft without an enemy attack materializing. He had to decide between three possible courses of action. His first option was to try to press his advantage against the enemy forces known to be north of the Louisades and retiring in a state of some disarray. His second option was to turn east to search for and attack the Carrier Striking Force. In the event, however, Fletcher chose the third option—to do neither. His initial inclination was to resume the attack beyond the Louisades, but Fletcher decided that his best course was to break contact by steering towards the southeast before turning back west for a position south of the Jomard Passage.[58] From this position Task Force 17 would still be able to block any renewed enemy attempt to force the line of the Louisades (which made the earlier detachment of Crace even more meaningless) and at the same time stand beyond the range of the Japanese carriers. Task Force 17 still lacked precise knowledge of the whereabouts of the enemy carrier force, and Fletcher was not prepared to commit his aircraft to a search and an attack in worsening weather and rather indifferent light. Fletcher knew full well that any attack the task force might be able to make could hardly take place much before sunset, which meant that the *Yorktown* and the *Lexington* would have to run the hazards of night landings. These risks were unacceptable to Fletcher. The Americans had yet to carry out a major night operation, and with the situation so delicately poised he regarded the Coral Sea as being neither the place nor the occasion on which to break new ground. He was prepared to renew the battle on the following morning, hopefully with reconnaissance support provided by shore-based aircraft.[59]

Fletcher knew that he was able to decline further action during the afternoon of the seventh, for his formation had partially fulfilled its primary objective. It had barred the route to Port Moresby, and the enemy had had to turn back, if only for the moment. The Japanese forces in the western Solomon Sea were withdrawing, and Fletcher's prime concern was to ensure that their advance was not resumed. He was in the position to achieve this aim by opposing either the transports or the carriers. After the sinking of the *Shoho* Fletcher was in the fortunate but temporary position of being able to take as much or as little of the battle as he chose. The Japanese had no such freedom of choice: with time running out they had to force the issue to a conclusion. But their situation was difficult. The events of the day showed that their passage through the Jomard Passage was blocked not by one but by two enemy formations, and that any attempt to continue the offensive would have to wait on a reorganization of their task groups.

The immediate consequence of the loss of the *Shoho* was that Inoue delayed the date of the proposed landings at Port Moresby by two days. This, as we have seen, was a decision that was certainly one and perhaps as many as three days too late. At 1330 Inoue also ordered the warships in the Solomon Sea to concentrate off Rossel while the transports pulled well clear of the danger zone.[60] Goto's cruisers and most of the Attack Force were to congregate for a night attack, but Inoue did not specify whether this effort should be made against the enemy carrier force suspected to be to the southeast of Deboyne or against the force known to the south of the Jomard Passage. Neither was a realistic target, as Inoue subsequently recognized. He cancelled these orders and instructed Goto to keep half his cruiser force in the western Solomon Sea with the Attack Force. The other half of his force was to go to the support of the Carrier Striking Force.[61]

Most of the Japanese activity on the afternoon of the seventh was directed against Task Group 17.3, with the bombers that were to have attacked Port Moresby being diverted against Crace's force.[62] Normally such a switch of target would have been wise, a significant enemy task force being a more important target than an enemy force and position that could not run away. On this occasion, however, the switch was an error. This second enemy task force was not going to count for much if and when the Carrier Striking Force dealt with the enemy carriers, and the neutralization of Port Moresby remained the most important service that the air groups at Rabaul could contribute to Operation MO. But this error did not make the afternoon any less anxious for Crace. He and his force had no idea what was happening around them, and Crace was unable to drum up air support from Australia while operating within range of enemy aircraft from Rabaul. He had taken the precaution of avoiding the immediate vicinity of the exit of the Jomard Passage, steering instead for a position some 40 miles to the southwest of the channel. The only information that he received as he steamed to take up his blocking position came from interceptions of aircraft radio traffic. This strongly suggested that the enemy carrier reported to the north of the Louisades had been put out of the reckoning. Given his potentially vulnerable position, this information was welcome to Crace.[63]

There remained, however, the danger of attack by land-based aircraft, and not merely by the enemy. The *Perkins* had the misfortune to be attacked by three Mitchell bombers. After the battle Crace remarked that the accuracy of their attack was disgraceful compared with that of past Japanese performances, but the Southwest Pacific Command refused to discuss the incident and tried to pretend that it never happened.[64] Fortunately for Crace, the Japanese attack, though it may well have been more accurate than that of the Mitchells, was still not good enough to deal with Task Group 17.3. Crace had his formation in arrowhead, the flagship *Australia* having the other two cruisers on either quarter at a range of 1,600 yards and one destroyer 1,200 yards ahead of each cruiser.[65] This formation, combined with fierce antiaircraft fire and skillful shiphandling, allowed Task Group 17.3 to beat off two attacks by Japanese bombers between 1506 and 1516. The first attack was made by twelve Nell torpedo bombers, the second by nineteen Nells in the high-level role. Fortunately for the Americans and Australians, the torpedo bombers launched at too great a range— between 1,000 and 1,500 yards—to have a good chance of hitting such relatively small and fast-moving targets as the cruisers. All the same the flagship and the *Chicago* had to display some degree of gymnastic finesse in evading the torpedoes that were aimed at them. The *Australia* dodged two and the *Chicago* three of the more skillfully directed torpedoes. The high-level bombers attacked at 18,000 feet and came against Task Group 17.3 from the northwest, out of the sun. The attack, directed against the *Australia*, achieved a close grouping that straddled the flagship within a radius of about 250 yards, but none of the bombs actually hit the *Australia* and none caused anything more than slight damage topside.[66]

Not a single ship of Task Group 17.3 was hit by a bomb or torpedo, but the attackers claimed to have sunk one *California*-class battleship and one heavy cruiser of the *Augusta* class (of which the *Chicago* was a member). In addition, they claimed to have badly damaged one *Warspite*-class battleship, and to have possibly damaged a *Canberra*-class cruiser. Though the *Australia* and the *Canberra* were sister ships and members of the *Kent*-class heavy cruisers, the obvious discrepancy between, on the one hand, identification and claims, and on the other, those ships actually present and the results obtained, was in the words of one Japanese commentator "so great as to be ridiculous." Part of the reason for the divergence between claims and results may well have been, as this same source asserts, that the aircrews who made the attack were those who had arrived at Rabaul after the annihilation of the Fourth Air Group on 20 February.[67] These replacements are deemed to have been greatly inferior in quality to those who had been lost to the *Lexington*'s Wildcats nearly three months before. Be that as it may, the attack by the torpedo bombers was foolhardy. After launching their torpedoes the Nells did not break off but rather pressed home their attacks with machine gun and cannon, as if that was going to have an effect on battleships and heavy cruisers. Two men on the *Chicago* were killed, but the exchange rate was ruinous: four Nells were shot down, another was damaged beyond redemption and five more were holed. By contrast, only three of the high-level bombers suffered damage, and it was minor.[68]

The Japanese felt that they had done well in the course of their attacks on Task Group 17.3, but not well enough to ensure the safety of their transports. Even after the attacks by the Nells the Japanese command at Rabaul suspected the continued presence of a strong enemy force southwest of the Jomard Passage. A sighting report seemingly confirmed this at 1700, when a scout from Rabaul reported the presence of eight warships, including one carrier, south of the Louisades. Given the inaccuracy of their scouting and action reports, it is difficult not to have some sympathy for Japanese commanders, but this same sympathy cannot be extended to the Carrier Striking Force. Scouting errors were in part responsible for its misfortunes, but they were mostly brought about by command mistakes—and the already doleful list of such errors was to grow during the afteroon of the seventh.

The same lack of choice that had governed the Japanese decision to proceed with Operation MO as a whole characterized the Carrier Striking Force's dealings with the enemy carrier force, though not quite for the same reasons. Certainly all the calculations that molded Rabaul's decisions shaped the decisions of this formation, but other factors were also involved. The reputation of the navy had been tarnished by the morning's debacle, and in full view of the army. Responsibility for the loss of the *Shoho* was keenly felt, as it should have been. But equally keen was the sense of danger that belatedly overtook the Carrier Striking Force as a result of the sinking of the *Shoho*. During the American attack on the *Shoho* the carrier and her escorts sent out contact reports that suggested an onslaught by about ninety aircraft, and the Japanese did not need genius to realize that such numbers could not come from just a single carrier. Until this attack they had worked on the assumption that the Americans would be able to respond to Operation MO with only the *Saratoga* (in fact the *Lexington*) and that the carriers involved in the attack on Tokyo three weeks earlier would not have time to get to the Coral Sea in time to counter Operation MO. The sinking of the *Shoho* suddenly brought home to the Japanese the reality of their position— two enemy carriers were at sea and given the chance they could strike telling blows. The margin of superiority on which the Japanese had previously depended for success had disappeared.

Under these circumstances Takagi and Hara evidently believed that they could not afford to pass up any chance to strike against the Americans in the course of the afternoon. They had done so the previous day with results that were now only too obvious and unfortunate. But after the loss of the *Shoho* the Carrier Striking Force was prepared to accept risks that Fletcher had declined. In fact, the risks that the Japanese faced were worse than those Fletcher had refused, because the Carrier Striking Force was some ninety minutes behind the Americans. The Japanese did not know the enemy's location, and the weather was taking a turn for the worse. There was little chance of any mission that was launched being recovered in daylight. These were handicaps that Takagi and Hara were prepared to accept in exchange for an attack that might yet decide the battle in their favor.

The decision to launch a second strike to reverse the verdict of the first bordered on the line that separates bold determination and desperate stupidity, and for four reasons. First, such an attack could only be made with aircrew who had experience in night operations. The dangerous practice of milking forces of their elite is so well known as to need no further elaboration. Second, the aircrew that would be selected for this mission would already have spent up to seven hours in the air before setting out on this operation. The fiasco around Point Rye had taken up half the day, and simply on the grounds of pilot fatigue there was much to be said for letting the battle of 7 May die and striking at first light on the following day. Third, the trail of the enemy was already cold. The Carrier Striking Force had no idea where he might be. He had been sighted some two hours after dawn, but since that time a number of seaplanes and flying boats had been shot down by Task Force 17's combat air patrol, and the Japanese carriers had not been able to keep a plot on the enemy. The destruction of the *Shoho* meant that the American carriers had been to the west rather than to the south or southeast of the Carrier Striking Force, but beyond that there was little for the Japanese to work on. To redeem this situation Hara ordered a search that afternoon of the sector between southwest and northwest to a distance of 200 miles. Scouts were launched at 1530 but prematurely recalled because the approach of dusk brought with it no contact with the enemy and increased the chances of loss. It was something, perhaps, that Hara should have foreseen.[69] Fourth, an attacking force, in searching for the enemy, would have to fan out in a scouting line across a bad weather front. In these circumstances the chances of finding the enemy were not good, and the odds against a coordinated attack, still less a successful one, were high. Alternatively, the attackers could be concentrated into a single group until they reached a designated but relatively small search area, and there they could hunt for the enemy. This, however, was a poor alternative to the extended scouting line because it confined the attack force to a single-chance sighting on both its outward and inward flights and to finding the enemy in a search area the selection of which could be no more than guesswork.

For the attack Hara committed nine Kates and six Vals from the *Zuikaku* and six Kates and six Vals from the *Shokaku*.[70] No fighter escort was allocated to the attack.[71] The reason for this omission is normally deemed to be that the fighters were too prone to navigational error and attendant loss to be risked on so hazardous a venture, but this seems an inadequate explanation of the Japanese arrangements on two counts. First, the fighter pilots from the *Shokaku* and the *Zuikaku* were experienced. Second, the tactical pattern adopted for this mission was the alternative plan that should have minimized fighter pilot difficulties—the concentration of aircraft into a single group with orders to proceed to a given area, preselected as 280 miles to the west of the Carrier Striking Force at the time of launch.[72] It would appear, therefore, that considerations other than those of pilot difficulty influenced the decision to send out an unescorted strike force. When it made its arrangements for this mission the Carrier Striking Force did not know that an enemy attack was not in the offing. In putting their plan of attack together the Japanese in their own turn had to guard against the possibility of enemy attack. In view of this consideration, there was no getting around the fact that the *Zuikaku* and the *Shokaku* did not have enough fighters to provide for both a combat air patrol and an escort for their strike force. Moreover, the Japanese may well have calculated that since any attack they made was likely to take place in bad weather and at about 1800, conditions might well provide as effective a cover for bombers as fighters could provide.

What is certain is that the aircrew who made this attack were far superior to the quality of their operational plan. The plan may have deserved to fail, but the men who flew this mission deserved a better fate than the one that befell a third of their number. Far from being 280 miles to the west, the American carrier force was some 150 miles a little to the north of west of the Carrier Striking Force when the bombers began to launch at about 1615.[73] With just two hours available to them before sunset, the Kates and Vals had to claw their way westwards through frightful weather conditions. Towering cloud formations and lashing rain forced the bombers, which again flew under Takahashi's command, to make detours they could ill-afford in the fading light. With the day rapidly drawing to a close the Japanese bombers arrived at what they believed was their assigned search area, though the probability is that they were short of it. They had no time in which to mount a full and proper reconnaissance before turning back on an apparently empty ocean. To improve the chances of getting back to their carriers the bombers divided into three groups and jettisoned their weaponry, thereby lightening themselves and cutting down fuel consumption.[74]

In the course of their return flight, however, the Japanese bombers encountered the American combat air patrol. In the gathering gloom the first group of Japanese aircraft failed to find the enemy task force, but the *Yorktown*'s radar found them and the *Lexington* flew off Wildcats for an interception. The *Yorktown* was slower to launch, but her seven Wildcats arrived to join a fight that was developing favorably for the American fighters.[75] The Kates proved vulnerable, but the more agile Vals, surprisingly quick without their bombs, gave a good account of themselves. Two Wildcats, one from each of the carriers, were lost in the course of the air battle and another, a fighter from the *Yorktown*, was lost when it could not find the carrier after the battle, even after being in radio contact with the *Yorktown* for more than an hour.[76] Japanese losses in the course of this encounter are uncertain, but it would appear that seven bombers, including one Val, were lost. After dark, when Task Force 17 had recovered its combat air patrol, the other two groups of Japanese bombers separately approached the American carriers in the clear belief that they had found their own ships. The Americans held their fire and allowed the bombers to approach, trying to deceive them into thinking they were cleared to land by replying to their flashed signals. The tired Japanese pilots, no doubt confused by the signals from the ships, must still have been somewhat trusting until the flak started to burst about them. One was shot down but the others made good their escape under the cover of darkness.[77]

The Japanese carriers were about 100 miles to the east of Task Force 17 between 1900 and 1930 when these attempted landings took place, the two carrier forces having steered slightly converging courses over the previous three hours. Both sides were aware of the proximity of the other. The attempts to land on the *Yorktown* by not one but two groups of enemy aircraft were proof: the enemy's aircraft would not have tried to land had the carriers been widely separated. Moreover, the *Lexington*'s radar tracked enemy aircraft circling some 30 miles to the east between 1900 and 1930, the very time that the *Yorktown*'s hospitality was being sought by the enemy.[78] This information, suggesting the presence of an enemy not far beyond the horizon, was not received by Fletcher until 2200, seemingly because the *Lexington* tried to signal the information by low-frequency transmission to avoid betraying her position to land-based Japanese installations. Fletcher, however, disbelieved the report when he received it. The *Yorktown*'s radar had not picked up any similar contact, and if the contact were real, he reasoned, then it was with aircraft that were lost rather than with bombers circling their carriers. Nevertheless, it was clear that the Japanese carriers were not very far away. The Japanese themselves were soon to learn that the enemy was close at hand as their aircraft returned and they debriefed their pilots. Recovery was not completed until 2300, but only one aircraft, a Kate from the *Shokaku*, was forced to ditch from lack of fuel. Contrary to many accounts of the battle, the night recovery was successful. Despite the dangers, Hara ordered his carriers to turn on their searchlights. Eighteen bombers were recovered, none of them damaged. Overall, the mission cost the *Shokaku* three Kates, two of them shot down and the other ditched, while the *Zuikaku* lost one Val and five Kates.[79]*

---

*Figures from Japanese sources give a slightly different picture. Yoshida asserts that the *Zuikaku* recovered five Vals and four Kates while losing one Val and five Kates; the *Shokaku* recovered five Vals and two Kates and lost four Kates. These totals, however, do not agree

The pilots who returned to the *Zuikaku* and the *Shokaku* placed the enemy some 40 to 60 miles to the west. The *Lexington* was actually between 90 and 100 miles away. Given their proximity, it was inevitable that both sides should consider the possibility of conducting a night attack on the enemy with surface forces, but the Americans and the Japanese, for exactly the same reasons, rejected this course of action. They preferred to rely on their aircraft the next day rather than their guns that night to do the talking, and neither side was prepared to order a night attack against an enemy whose exact position was unknown. Both feared that a night attack would unduly weaken their screens during the night and the next morning if their detached units proved unable to rejoin before air operations began.[80] Given that more than 90 miles separated the task forces, both sides were wise not to launch a night attack. An encounter would have proved elusive, unless the two surface forces ran into one another while they looked for the other side's carriers.

Thus 7 May ended with the two carrier forces drawing away from one another with the issue between them unresolved. For both sides the day had been a disappointment, though the Americans had the compensation of doing something that had thus far in the war proved beyond the ability of any American or Allied task force—sinking an enemy carrier, albeit a light and vulnerable one, in open battle. That was an achievement that could not be gainsaid, but it was one that had to be balanced against the loss of the *Neosho*, the consequential loss of Task Force 17's freedom of action and the recognition that the real battle remained to be fought. For the Japanese, however, the situation was much worse. The day's operation had cost them an overall total of fourteen strike aircraft, of which all but two had been lost. The morning's reconnaissance had cost the *Shokaku* two Kates, which were forced down in the sea. The attack on the *Neosho* and the *Sims* cost the *Zuikaku* three Vals, one of which had been shot down by enemy gunfire, the two others damaged in trying to land back on the carrier. The afternoon's strike mission had cost the Japanese nine bombers. On 7 May the *Zuikaku* and the *Shokaku* lost one in seven of their bombers, and all they had to show for this was an oiler and a solitary destroyer. Pearl Harbor, in comparison, cost the Japanese five Kates, nine Zekes and fifteen Vals. But from a strategic standpoint a far more important loss than numbers and types of aircraft was the chance to hit the enemy while remaining immune themselves. On the seventh the Japanese managed to get themselves into the

---

with the total of twenty-seven bombers launched by the two carriers on this mission, the discrepancy being one Val from the *Shokaku*.

Since it is now more than forty years since the battle was fought it is unlikely that the "final" word can ever be written on this matter. One thing, however, is clear: the many accounts that tell of the Japanese losing eleven aircraft in the recovery phase are wildly wrong. Had the Japanese lost this number, they could not have launched the next day's strike in the strength they did.

position that they had wanted to assume—on the rear of a distracted enemy. Having secured it, the Japanese then squandered their chance and lost 14 percent of their striking power in the process. Given this situation, it is possible to argue that 7 May was the "turning point" of the battle, perhaps of the Pacific war itself.

Any interpretation of 7 May as a turning point has to explain how it marked a watershed in the conduct of this battle and of the entire Pacific war. For the Americans the previous day, 6 May, was their nadir: on that day their forces on Corregidor surrendered. Assessments that take this fact into account presuppose that the auspicious events of the seventh were somehow assured, that the Americans, in one day, moved from a position of disadvantage to one of advantage according to some preordained decree. This was definitely not the case. The sequence of events on 7 May was not inevitable. But on the eighth the Japanese suffered crippling losses amongst their air groups, and these rendered the *Zuikaku* and the *Shokaku* ineffective not merely for what might remain of Operation MO but, as it transpired, for Operation MI as well. On the eighth the Japanese had to give battle more or less on the basis of equality, whereas on the seventh they had secured, by a combination of calculation and good fortune, advantages on which they failed to capitalize. This failure and the resultant losses incurred on the eighth cost the Japanese not only their chance to bring Operation MO to a successful conclusion but their margin of superiority at Midway. Had the Japanese realized their intention to catch the Americans between two fires on the seventh, it is possible that Operation MO would have been pushed through to a successful conclusion and the Americans denied the instrument of their success at Midway. Loss of the *Shoho* would have been an acceptable price to pay for such a return. The Japanese difficulty at Midway is often thought to have arisen as a result of the events of 8 May, yet in reality the events of the seventh were more crucial. In the twenty-four-hour period that straddled the sixth and seventh the Japanese lost two good opportunities to force battle on the *Yorktown* and the *Lexington* when the odds were in their favor. On the first occasion, the afternoon of the sixth, the Japanese carriers, had they risked an attack, would have found Task Force 17 in the process of refueling. On the morning of the following day, had they found and attacked Task Force 17 and not the *Neosho* and the *Sims*, the Japanese fleet carriers would have caught Task Force 17 attacking the *Shoho*. By the time the Japanese finally managed to put their act together on the seventh—more by luck than by judgment—the aircraft that found the enemy had no ordnance. Perhaps this incident, around 1900 on the seventh, was the turning point of the war—but the turning point where events did not turn. Even if the Japanese bombers had had their weapons when they encountered the enemy, there was no guarantee that they would e registered success. The odds would have been against them, and to the

best of the author's knowledge there was not a single instance in the course
of World War Two of carrier aircraft registering nighttime success against
an enemy carrier force at sea. This encounter proved to be the last occasion
in the war (with the possible exception of the final stages of the battle of the
Eastern Solomons in August) when the Japanese were in a position to which
the Americans could not respond. It was ironic that on the seventh the
Japanese should have found the enemy after a fruitless day but at a time
when they had no means of attack. With the aborted mission of 1615 on 7
May, the last remaining hope of a cheap and substantial victory over the
Americans in the Coral Sea finally slipped away from the Japanese.

During the rest of the night both sides prepared to join battle as they
drew away from one another, the Americans heading towards the south
and then the west, the Japanese reversing course to the north. In steering
these courses their relative positions were changed in one important way.
The American run to the south took Task Force 17 clear of the front that
had proved so good a friend the previous day. By dawn the Americans were
well to the south of the front and in an area of good visibility. The Japanese,
on the other hand, stayed inside the front except for a brief period after
dawn, when they emerged beyond its northern edge before a reversal of
course brought them back under cover. Thus the Americans lost but the
Japanese retained their cloud cover.

Such a situation should have benefited the Japanese, but in fact the
Americans held three other assets that offset what might otherwise have
been a crucial advantage for their enemy. The first was the greater number
of aircraft the Americans had. At dawn on the eighth the *Yorktown* and the
Lexington deployed a total of 121 aircraft, of which 32 were Wildcat fighters,
33 were Dauntless scouts, 35 were Dauntless bombers and 21 were Devastators. The Japanese, on the other hand, had only 109 aircraft left to the
Shokaku and the *Zuikaku*. Of these no fewer than fourteen were nonoperational, an increase of two over the previous day's situation. For the forthcoming battle the Japanese had 37 Zekes, 33 Vals and 25 Kates.[81] These
figures speak for themselves. The Japanese had a better balance between
their fighters and bombers than the Americans, but only because of the
heavy losses amongst their bombers on the previous day. In fact both sides
were inadequately provisioned with regard to fighters. Both had an offensive capability that outstripped their defensive capacity, but American
striking power was considerably superior to that of the Japanese. Compared
with the 89 Devastators and Dauntlesses of the *Yorktown* and the *Lexington*,
the *Shokaku* and the *Zuikaku* could only muster 58 Kates and Vals.

The second major advantage the Americans held was in terms of defensive fire power. After the *Monaghan* was detached from Task Force 17 at
0055 to search for survivors from the *Neosho* and the *Sims* and to transmit
various messages on Fletcher's behalf, five heavy cruisers and seven de-

stroyers remained with the *Yorktown* and the *Lexington*.[82] The Japanese had their screen strengthened soon after dawn when the *Kinugasa* and the *Furutaka* joined company, but this still left them with one less heavy cruiser and one less destroyer in their screen than in that of the Americans.[83] With American carriers having about 60 percent more guns than their counterparts, the defensive fire power of Task Force 17 was roughly twice that of the Carrier Striking Force. In terms of fire power and numbers of escort under command, the *Yorktown* and the *Lexington* were better able to defend themselves than the *Shokaku* and the *Zuikaku*. Had Fletcher not detached one light cruiser, two heavy cruisers and four destroyers in the twenty-four hours before battle, the American defensive advantage would have been even more pronounced.

Thus the Americans had a marked gunnery advantage to go alongside their considerable superiority in aircraft numbers, but the third asset counted for much more than either of these two. Unlike the *Shokaku* and the *Zuikaku* the American carriers had radar and homing devices. These went a long way to canceling out the imbalance created by the position of the weather front relative to the two carrier formations. The location of Task Force 17 in clear weather left it exposed and without cover; but no Japanese air group that came against it would have friendly clouds in which to hide. There would be no refuge from the American combat air patrol, and American antiaircraft gunners would have the same chance to see and select their targets. There could be no question of a sudden attack coming against American ships out of low or broken cloud. The Japanese were not as fortunately placed. They were under cloud, but it was not so thick and protective as the overcast that had sheltered Fletcher's activities on the fourth and the previous day. The Japanese were under medium cloud and operating in frequent and sudden squalls and showers. The weather gave some cover, but it was erratic. The cloud that offered Japanese warships partial cover also sheltered American aircraft from the enemy's guns and combat air patrol, and in these circumstances lack of radar placed the Japanese at a considerable disadvantage.

Thus the Americans held several crucial advantages over the Japanese before sunrise on the eighth, when both carrier forces launched reconnaissance missions. Both had a fair idea of the enemy's probable location. The Japanese suspected, quite rightly, that the Americans had gone south during the night. With Japanese forces to the north and the east, and islands to the west, there was really no other course that the Americans could steam. Thus at 0600 the Japanese began a search of the sector between 145 and 235 degrees to a range of 200 miles.[84] For the mission the *Zuikaku* flew off three Kates, the *Shokaku* four.[85] Whether the search sector was small because there were few aircraft to scout or vice versa is unclear, but the commitment of seven Kates to reconnaissance duties reduced the number of torpedo bombers available for an attack mission to the bone. Just eighteen were left to the two carriers after the dawn reconnaissance was flown off.

The Americans were not so fortunate at guessing the location of the enemy. It was likely that the Japanese would try to place themselves between Task Force 17 and their forces in the Solomon Sea, but the American commanders felt obliged to take a double precaution in case this calculation was incorrect—as it would have been on the previous day. To guard against an unorthodox deployment, Fitch decided upon a full 360-degree search with eighteen Dauntlesses, fourteen of them scouts and the others bombers. Those ordered to search the sector from east to west via south were directed to a range of 150 miles; those in the northern sector were directed to a range of 200 miles. With the *Yorktown* not contributing any aircraft to the search, the *Lexington* began to fly off her aircraft at 0625.[86]

Japanese calculations and American suspicions were equally correct. The Japanese estimation that the enemy was to the south was accurate, as was the American guess that the Japanese would take up a position where they should have been one day earlier. In the course of the night Abe had specifically requested Hara to bring his carriers to the direct support of the transports, and Hara complied. Interrogated after the war on this matter, Hara stated that the reason for his decision was that he "had [a] basic mission to fulfill, which was to protect the transports."[87] It was by any standard a revealing comment on the nature of Japanese command arrangements. It seems strange that Abe should have had to alert Hara into attending to his "basic mission," and for the Japanese it was perhaps unfortunate that Hara was not reminded of priorities somewhat earlier than the night of 7–8 May. But with Abe seemingly initiating policy, Hara making decisions and Inoue and Takagi nowhere in sight, this tiny episode provided the answer to the question of who commanded Japanese forces at the Coral Sea—nobody. Control of the battle slipped from Inoue's hands when it was joined, and thereafter no Japanese commander was able to impose his authority over events because of the sheer complexity of Japanese arrangements. In the absence of command from the top, subordinate Japanese commanders succumbed to technique. That was all that was left to them. With the Fifth Carrier Division now inferior to the enemy, the test of that technique was at hand.

The two sides found one another within a matter of minutes. The advantage of relative position and the speed of the Dauntless being higher than that of the Kate served to cancel out the advantage gained by the Japanese in launching their scouting mission before the Americans. The first American contact with the Carrier Striking Force was at 0815. The initial sighting report was made by Lieutenant J. G. Smith five minutes later.[88] The Japanese Kate that found Task Force 17 was piloted by Flight Warrant Officer Kenzo Kanno. He made his sighting report at 0822. His approach was detected by the *Lexington*'s radar at 0806 and contact was held for ten minutes, but attempts to direct the combat air patrol against the intruder proved unsuccessful, seemingly because Kanno kept his Kate at very low altitude to evade the Wildcats.[89] The result of these contacts brought about the situation neither side wanted. Neither had been able to steal a march on the other, and there was now no chance of one side or the other being able to strike without itself being the target of a counterstrike. Neither the Japanese nor the Americans had been able to secure the all-important first contact while remaining unseen themselves. With both sides attacking more or less at the same time, it was uncertain which if either strike force would have flight decks awaiting its return.

Neither side, however, launched its strike force immediately upon receipt of the sighting reports. For the Americans there was no choice in the matter. Smith's initial signal was garbled, the *Lexington* was unable to gain a bearing on the scout, and when the Dauntless repeated her contact it was incomplete.[90] Smith's initial contact report merely stated the presence of the enemy—identified as having two carriers, four heavy cruisers and three destroyers—but failed to give the position, course and speed of the Japanese force. Smith dodged amongst the clouds until 0838,[91] when he amplified his first report with the much-needed information that the enemy, now said to have "many" destroyers, was in latitude 12°S, longitude 152° 16' E and set on a course of 120 degrees at a speed of 12 knots.[92] It was only when this information was forthcoming that Fitch, in charge of the air operations and after 0907 placed in full tactical command of Task Group 17.5, was able to order the *Yorktown* and the *Lexington* to begin launching their aircraft against an enemy estimated to be 175 miles east northeast. The Japanese, similarly, delayed sending off their aircraft, though the reason for their delay seems less clear. It was not unusual for them to fly off a strike mission within an hour of launching scouts, the course of the first bisecting those of the latter. Perhaps the Carrier Striking Force did not do this now because so few strike aircraft remained to the Japanese after the losses of the previous day and the commitment of seven Kates to the scouting mission. Certainly the example of the day before pointed to the danger of committing forces to battle prematurely and on the basis of unconfirmed reports, and this time there was no room for error. It was not until 0915 that the *Zuikaku* and the *Shokaku* began to launch their aircraft,[93] some fifteen minutes after the *Yorktown* began to fly off her strike.[94]

For the attack the Japanese committed virtually everything that they had left with the Fifth Carrier Division. A total of sixty-nine aircraft were to be sent against Task Force 17, of which eighteen were Zekes, eighteen were Kates and thirty-three were Vals. The two carriers contributed equally to the escort, but the *Shokaku* contributed most of the bombers. This, of course, was inevitable. The *Zuikaku*'s losses had been the heavier on the previous day. For this attack the *Shokaku* committed nineteen Vals and ten Kates, the *Zuikaku* fourteen Vals and eight Kates. Excluding those aircraft that were nonoperational, all that remained to the Carrier Striking Force after this allocation was just four Vals and nineteen Zekes.[95] These totals— all the totals that relate to the situation on the eighth—exclude the eight Zekes of the Tainan Air Group that still remained with the Carrier Striking Force.

The Fifth Carrier Division may have been the weakest of the three first-line divisions with the First Air Fleet, but in terms of technical proficiency it was to prove superior to Task Force 17 in at least one respect on 8 May. In the matter of flying off aircraft together, assembling them into formation and then flying en masse to the objective, the *Zuikaku* and the *Shokaku* immediately demonstrated their superiority over the *Yorktown* and the *Lexington*. From the outset the American intention to use their groups in one concentrated assault fell to pieces because the aircraft from the *Yorktown*, once more without an overall commander to lead the attack, moved out without waiting for their colleagues from the *Lexington* to join company. To compound this error, the various attacking squadrons within each air group were to become separated as they flew into and through the weather front that partially hid the Carrier Striking Force.[96]

The first contact was made by Dauntlesses from the *Yorktown*. Despite flying at 17,000 feet with an intermittent cloud cover at about 3,000 feet, the dive-bombers found the Japanese carriers at about 1032.[97] But instead of moving immediately and directly into the attack the Dauntlesses chose to seek the cover of the clouds, thereby moving into a good attacking position while giving the Devastators time to come onto the scene. Thus despite the absence of a strike commander the force from the *Yorktown* prepared to mount a coordinated attack from high and low levels.[98]

Moving into position ahead of two fast-moving Japanese carriers and waiting for the Devastators took time. The Dauntlesses, led by Lieutenant Commander William O. Burch, Junior, took just over fifteen minutes from the time of contact to get into position, and another ten minutes were to elapse before the torpedo bombers, escorted by four Wildcats, were able to move into the attack. These minutes gave the Japanese time to thicken their combat air patrol and gave the *Zuikaku* time to get under the protection of a rain squall. Visibility for both sides fluctuated wildly as the Carrier Striking Force moved in and out of the showers, and one of the reasons Burch decided he could not delay his attack for long was his fear of being left with no target and little fuel with which to regain contact.[99] This plus various other considerations therefore conspired to prevent the Americans from dividing their attention between both enemy carriers, though the enforced concentration against a single carrier might well have been a blessing in disguise. Had the American effort in fact been divided against two carriers, the results might well have been even more meager than proved to be the case.

There was certainly one advantage for the Americans in this developing situation. The *Zuikaku* was under cover by about 1100 and the *Shokaku* was not, because the two carriers had not rejoined after the *Shokaku* had turned away from base course to launch her combat air patrol. When sighted, the *Shokaku* was some eight miles off the *Zuikaku*'s port quarter, and as the Americans were to discover in the course of the battle of Midway, this distance was too great for units to give one another mutual support. The two Japanese carriers were separated by such a distance that they could not share a combat air patrol, and they had to divide the screen between them. With the arrival of reinforcements from Goto's command, each Japanese carrier was supported by three destroyers and two heavy cruisers. The *Zuikaku* had the *Myoko* and the *Haguro* in company, while the *Shokaku* was escorted by the *Kinugasa* and the *Furutaka*, fresh from their failure to protect the *Shoho*. The *Zuikaku* was to be spared attack, but her security was to be achieved at the cost of exposing the *Shokaku* to an attack against which she was inadequately protected.

The Japanese had flown off a combat air patrol of three Zekes soon after the reconnaissance mission had been sent on its way, leaving them with a reserve of sixteen fighters for the defense of the force.[100] It would appear that after the Americans arrived the *Shokaku* flew off most of her remaining fighters. None of the nine Devastators were shot down as they moved into the attack, and none of the Wildcats were destroyed. The latter claimed to have shot down two Zekes that tried to tackle the torpedo bombers,[101] and Japanese records do confirm that two Zekes from the *Shokaku*'s combat air patrol were shot down, one crashed trying to land back on the carrier and another three were forced to ditch.[102] The invulnerability of the Devastators was surprising, an indication that the Japanese fighter defense was nowhere near as effective as it should have been. But immunity did not go hand-in-hand with effectiveness, and the combat air patrol was successful, if not in shooting down the enemy, then in preventing his getting close enough to launch a telling attack. The Devastators launched their torpedoes at ranges between 1,000 and 2,000 yards, and this was too far out to cause the *Shokaku* much trouble. She had time enough to evade the torpedoes aimed at her, and her task in this respect was made easier when the *Yorktown*'s Devastators passed up the chance to mount an anvil attack with the torpedo bombers split into two groups and attacking across both bows. Because a long approach to attack from off the starboard bow would almost certainly have involved heavy losses, the Devastators contented themselves with the single attack from off the port bow. The *Shokaku* simply turned away from the aircraft and sidestepped their attack.[103]

The Dauntless attack could not be dodged with the same ease. But the claims of the Dauntless pilots to have recorded six hits and a number of near misses on a carrier that was left in a sinking condition proved to be wildly optimistic. Similarly, the report that they destroyed eight Zekes from the enemy's combat air patrol were in gross error.[104]

But in return for the loss of four of their number—two shot down by Japanese fighters, a third lost for an unknown reason and a fourth forced to ditch with damaged landing gear—the Dauntlesses did manage to hit the *Shokaku* twice with their powerful 1,000-lb bombs. The damage was not inflicted by Burch and his Dauntless scouts, which attacked first, but by the Dauntless bombers.[105] The second of these two hits did relatively little damage, though its detonation in the aircraft engine room in the ship's starboard quarter was a blow that could not but affect the carrier's long-term operational efficiency.[106] The fires in this workshop were quickly extinguished, as indeed were the fires set off by the first and most serious of the two hits sustained by the *Shokaku* at this stage. This hit, taken well forward in the anchor windlass room, had two immediate effects other than the destruction of the room itself. First, it set off a huge avgas fire that led to the erroneous American belief that the carrier was finished. In fact the *Shokaku* was able to bring this fire under control and then extinguish it with relative ease. Second, the force of the explosion was directed upwards through the flight deck, thereby rendering the carrier incapable of flying off her aircraft.[107] This hit on the *Shokaku* was registered by Lieutenant Joseph Powers, who held his stricken Dauntless in a dive from which he could not escape, an action that was recognized with the posthumous award of the Medal of Honor. Powers was one of only two pilots lost in the course of this attack.[108]

Either the bomb that hit the anchor windlass room or the third hit that was to be sustained in the course of the attack by Dauntlesses from the *Lexington* must in some way have done damage to the arrester system, for the *Shokaku* lost her ability not only to launch aircraft but to recover them as well. Two aircraft tried in vain to land on the *Shokaku* after she had been damaged.[109] Yet if there was a lesson to be drawn from this attack about the capacity of carriers to absorb punishment, it was that the *Shokaku* managed to withstand and control injuries that would have been far more serious had they been incurred by any member of the First and Second Carrier Divisions. All Japanese carriers had their fuel tanks built as integral parts of the hull, but whereas the armor protection over fuel in the *Akagi* and the *Kaga* was virtually nonexistent, and in the *Hiryu* and the *Soryu* provided only on a modest scale, in the *Shokaku* a full 170 millimeters of armor sheathed the fuel and other vital areas. This, with the help of voids filled with inert carbon dioxide, stood the *Shokaku* in good stead when she was hit at the Coral Sea. Her four older colleagues were not to be so fortunate at Midway. After these battles the voids in the *Zuikaku* and the *Shokaku* were filled with concrete,[110] which was used in Japanese carriers with increasing frequency as supplies of steel were exhausted.[111]

With the *Shokaku* damaged and in some immediate though not serious distress, a coordinated attack by two air groups might well have produced a favorable outcome as far as the Americans were concerned. Unfortunately for Task Force 17 the aircraft from the *Lexinton*'s air group (CVG-2) were not able to follow hard on the heels of the *Yorktown*'s aircraft. Some thirty minutes elapsed between attacks. This not only allowed the Japanese to escape from a potentially embarrassing position, it temporarily misled the Americans about the success of their missions as well.

The attack by CVG-2 was flawed from the outset. Whereas the *Yorktown* had flown off a total of two dozen Dauntlesses, nine Devastators and six Wildcats—two of which became lost en route and did not rejoin until the attack was over—CVG-2 committed fifteen Dauntlesses, twelve Devastators and nine Wildcats against the Japanese.[112] Had the Americans been able to coordinate the efforts of all seventy-five aircraft sent against the Carrier Striking Force their success might well have been considerable, but granted the relative failure of the *Yorktown*'s air group in its attack on the *Shokaku*, it was really too much to expect the twenty-one aircraft from CVG-2 that found the Japanese to better the results that had been achieved to date. Almost at the start of the flight one of the members of the torpedo squadron turned back with engine trouble, and the three Wildcats that had orders to escort the dive-bombers were forced to return to the *Lexington* because they became lost trying to find the Dauntlesses.[113] The aircraft that continued to press on towards the target failed to coordinate with one another as they flew into thickening cloud. The original plan of attack for CVG-2 had the Dauntlesses flying at 16,000 feet, the Devastators at 6,000 feet. The link between the two was to be provided by the four Dauntlesses that formed the flight of Commander Ault, the air group commander. Increasingly thick cloud, reaching from 3,000 to 15,000 feet, was encountered during the approach to contact. Ault remained in visual contact with the torpedo bombers but not the Dauntlesses. The latter, however, had more than just the problem of retaining contact with Ault. By an inexcusable oversight they had not been fueled properly. The Dauntlesses were up to 30 gallons light, which did not leave them any margin to overcome navigational error or to conduct a search if the enemy, for some reason, was not in the position the plot indicated.[114] Inevitably, the Carrier Striking Force was not where the Americans expected to find them. The *Yorktown*'s group had been extremely fortunate in finding the Japanese, because the report by Smith regarding the enemy's position had been in error. The Japanese had been well to the north of the location indicated by Smith, and though a correction was supplied by Lieutenant Commander Robert E. Dixon, who moved into his subordinate's sector after overhearing and disbelieving Smith's

The *Shokaku* After a Torpedo Hit

report, this amendment was not available to Ault's formation.[115] The Dauntlesses, short of fuel and with no capacity to linger in the general search area, had to turn back to the *Lexington*, jettisoning their bombs to save fuel as they did so. This left Ault, with his three escorting Dauntlesses and the eleven remaining Devastators, to carry on. They were still being escorted by six fighters. Two of these were with Ault, the others were with the more vulnerable torpedo bombers.

When he saw an empty ocean Ault ordered his aircraft to spread into line and conduct a box search. He was quickly rewarded, contacting one enemy carrier and two heavy cruisers. The Japanese were dodging between the squalls and were under a heavy overcast. Ault led his aircraft over the cloud to hide from the combat air patrol before the Dauntlesses and Devastators left their cover to attack the carrier.

The Devastators conducted a spiral glide out of the cloud and emerged just two miles ahead of the enemy carrier—in the company of the enemy combat air patrol. Three of the escorting Wildcats were shot down as they tried to keep the Japanese fighters away from the Devastators, and only one of the torpedo bombers was shot down. Two of the Dauntlesses were also shot down and a third, that of Ault, was to be lost after the action when he was unable to get back to the *Lexington*. The Devastators claimed five hits on the enemy carrier, the surviving Dauntless aircrew a further two. One bomb apparently hit the target, causing a major but short-lived fire forward, though the overall claim that the enemy carrier was left in a heavily damaged state was as erroneous as the previous assessment by the *Yorktown*'s aircraft about the state of the carrier after they had attacked it.

The carrier that the *Lexington*'s aircraft had attacked bore no outward signs of damage. This was a silent comment on the effectiveness of the attack by the *Yorktown*'s aircraft, because both attacks had been directed

against the *Shokaku*. Thus rather than leaving one enemy carrier sinking and
another badly damaged, the surviving American aircraft returned to their
own ships having damaged only one Japanese carrier. Though mauled, the
Shokaku was in no immediate danger. Her fires were easily dealt with, and
she retained full power and maneuverability. But without the means to
launch and recover aircraft there was no role for her in the Coral Sea, and
Hara ordered her to set course for Truk and home.

At about 1300 the *Shokaku* turned back for Truk, and thence for Kure.
She sailed for the Carolines in the company of the *Kinugasa* and the *Furutaka*
and the destroyers *Yugure* and *Ushio*.[116] She arrived home more crippled
than she was when she left the Coral Sea. The Americans, by courtesy of
Japanese neglect, ultimately did better than they knew. Some of the near
misses had lifted a number of the carrier's plates, and though she was not
holed below the waterline, gradual flooding affected her stability long
before she reached home waters.[117] By the time she reached Kure her
condition had become serious, though if renewed American malevolence
had been rewarded she would never have reached her home base at all. By
monitoring Japanese radio traffic the Americans found that the *Shokaku* was
not sunk but damaged and making her way back to Japan. They therefore
tried to put four submarines on station at Truk and another four on the
direct route between Truk and Kure. The *Shokaku* was fortunate to avoid
contact with all these submarines.[118] But if she nevertheless arrived back in
Japanese waters in a state of physical distress, it was minor compared to the
mental anguish to which she and the *Zuikaku* were subjected. The Fifth
Carrier Division was generally regarded to have given a less than satisfactory performance in the Coral Sea, and the fleet's disapproval was quickly
voiced.

There was some justification for criticism, but the failure of the division
and the Carrier Striking Force in general should have been properly examined by a careful staff analysis—for which there was no time. The
demands of Operation MI precluded detailed study of what had gone
wrong in the Coral Sea, although in the experience of the *Shokaku* were
technical and operational lessons that could have been heeded to good effect
by the forces bound for Midway. One of the best built of Japanese carriers
had been forced out of battle after having incurred only moderate damage.
Equally disturbing were the faulty defensive arrangements of the Carrier
Striking Force. As we have noted, on the eighth the *Shokaku* lost six Zekes
from the combat air patrol (though only two were shot down in combat) and
none of the attacks on the *Shokaku* had been broken up. With the exception
of the Dauntless bombers from the *Yorktown*, none of the attacking American formations encountered serious and sustained opposition from the
Japanese fighters. Nor did they encounter much opposition from flak.
When the *Shokaku* came under attack for the first time at least one of her

escorting destroyers maneuvered independently, and the antiaircraft fire put up in defense of the carrier by her five escorts was no better than what had been put up over the *Shoho*. The defensive fighting of the Carrier Striking Force was inadequate. It would appear that the Japanese escaped the worst consequences of their shortcomings only by virtue of serious misting problems the Dauntlesses had in the course of their attacks. At Tulagi on the fourth and again on the eighth in action with the *Shokaku*, misting and condensation spoiled the aim of American pilots diving from high level into moist air. On the seventh the *Shoho* had been in the clear and there had been no such problems for the Dauntlesses.[119]

But the various Japanese failures on 8 May did not alter the fact that the *Shokaku*, though she did not perform well in her own defense, managed to carry out her primary function. She had made a full and effective contribution to the offense. In the time between her being attacked first by the *Yorktown*'s aircraft and then by those from the *Lexington*, her own aircraft struck at the enemy. Naval opinion of the day decreed that the outcome of simultaneous carrier strikes would be mutual annihilation, but thus far examination of the record has shown that the Americans failed to record the success that was expected of them. The Japanese, on the other hand, did better—though not as well as they had hoped and not as well as they believed at the time.

To meet the sixty-nine Kates, Vals and Zekes committed to the attack, the Americans retained a combat air patrol that was no more adequate to the defense of Task Force 17 than the force retained by the *Zuikaku* and the *Shokaku* was to meeting the seventy-five Devastators, Dauntlesses and Wildcats sent against them. Task Force 17 had only twenty-five aircraft left after launching planes for reconnaissance and attack. Of these, eight were Dauntlesses from the *Yorktown*. These were tasked to fly antisubmarine patrol, but they were under orders to discard their two depth charges and to join the combat air patrol in the event of an enemy air attack.[120] The remainder were Wildcats, nine of which were with the *Lexington*, eight of which were with the *Yorktown*. The first combat air patrol of the day was flown off shortly after dawn, both carriers contributing four planes.[121]

The only possible compensation for the smallness of the combat air patrol was an effective use of radar, and the key to successful fleet defense lay in the ability of the air controller to get fighters at altitude and in the correct sectors immediately on receipt of warning of the enemy's advance. The objective was to get fighters into the enemy formation before the latter reached the fleet. Given the high speed of aircraft during an approach and the relatively slow rate of climb for a fighter—2,265 feet per minute in the case of the F4F-3 Wildcat—there was not much leeway for error. Moreover, the defense always had to ensure against a premature deployment that might leave its fighters short of fuel. At the Coral Sea the Americans lacked the two things needed to make effective use of radar. They had virtually no experience in handling the combat air patrol in the face of an enemy attack, and they did not have enough fighters to provide cover at both high and low levels. The large number of fighters available to the defense and the slick professionalism that characterized American fighter direction and control was not to come until the last two years of the Pacific war. In 1942 the techniques of effective defense were still being learned by trial and error.

Evaluation of various reports on the *Lexington* suggested that the Japanese would obtain contact with Task Force 17 around 1100, some thirty minutes after the carrier force had changed from its earlier course of 125 degrees to one of 028 degrees to close the distance from the enemy.[122] In altering their course the American carriers would cut down the flying time for their aircraft after the attack on the Carrier Striking Force. Closing with the enemy's strike mission had to be accepted as the consequence of this action. Radar contact was obtained with the Japanese aircraft around 1055 at a range of about 68 miles, the Japanese forming a pattern that filled up about one inch of the radarscope's five-inch face.[123] That meant that the enemy force was spread deep. The American warships and Japanese aircraft were then on almost reciprocal courses. But in spite of the earlier assessment of the enemy's time of arrival, the air command had not brought down the combat air patrol before contact. Thus the eight Wildcats flown off as combat air patrol soon after daybreak were still aloft but now so low on fuel that they no longer retained the capacity for a high-speed interception at a distance from the fleet. Moreover, they had no margin that would allow them to indulge in prolonged combat over the carriers. By the time radar contact was obtained, it was far too late to remedy the situation.

Thus even before visual contact with the enemy was obtained, neglect had robbed the Americans of half their fighter strength. To make this potentially disastrous situation even worse, it took the two American carriers up to ten more minutes to launch their nine relief Wildcats. The *Lexington* did not begin to launch until 1100, the *Yorktown* not before 1105. This was too late for the pathetically small number of fighters to have any chance of effectively defending the task force. Indeed, none of these fighters were able to engage in battle before the Japanese attack on the ships began.

Two of the Wildcats from the *Lexington* were directed against the Kates, but these were too well defended by the Zekes for the fighters to have any chance of breaking up their attacks. The other three Wildcats from the *Lexington*, directed to make a high-level interception, were still climbing and below the Vals when the latter reached their pushover point. The four Wildcats from the *Yorktown* were still moving to their interception position—some 20 miles from Task Force 17 and at an altitude of 6,000 feet—when they were informed that the Japanese attack had already started. The eight Wildcats from the original combat air patrol similarly failed to intercept the enemy before the onset of the attack.

Air defense for Task Force 17 would have been nonexistent had the Americans not been able to improvise. The Dauntlesses from the antisubmarine patrol were available to thicken up the combat air patrol. Moreover, by 1030, when Task Force 17 came back to its original course towards the northeast, all but two of the Dauntlesses committed to the dawn reconnaissance mission had been recovered. With both antisubmarine and reconnaissance Dauntlesses available to supplement the defense, American sources claimed a total of twenty-three were launched in support of the combat air patrol. This is a suspiciously high number, and it would appear that not all the Dauntlesses put into the air were effectively controlled and directed, but there is no doubting that theirs was a better contribution to the defense of Task Force 17 than that of the fighters. Eight Dauntlesses from the *Yorktown* tried to tackle incoming Kates, but with the advantage of height, speed and position, they passed over the Dauntlesses, leaving the latter to tackle the Zekes. The Dauntlesses claimed to have accounted for four enemy Zekes, though they lost four of their number in doing so. The report was exaggerated, and so too was that made by the eight Dauntlesses from the *Lexington*. They claimed to have shot down one Zeke, one Val and eight Kates, four of them before they had the chance to launch their torpedoes. As the battle analysis drawn up by the Naval War College after the war points out, the total number of Japanese aircraft claimed to have been destroyed on 8 May was seventy-three, of which twenty-seven were Zekes, thirty-one Kates and fifteen Vals. Of these totals no fewer than twenty-two of the fighters, eleven of the dive-bombers and all of the Kates were deemed to have been destroyed in the course of this single attack on Task Force 17.[124] The analysis is dry in its comments on the veracity of these claims, and rightly so. Japanese losses were less than a third of the reported number. During the attack the Japanese lost twenty-two aircraft, shot down or forced to ditch. Another aircraft, a Val, was badly damaged when it tried to land back on the *Shokaku*. Of the aircraft lost in action, one was a Zeke, eight were Kates and thirteen were Vals.[125] It is rather strange that while the claims grossly exaggerated overall Japanese losses, they were almost correct in their estimate of casualties amongst the Vals.

One other Japanese aircraft was lost in the course of the attack on the *Yorktown* and the *Lexington*. This was the Kate, manned by Kanno and Petty Officers Tsuguo Goto and Seijiro Kishida, that had made the initial contact with the Americans.[126] This was the only Kate committed to the dawn reconnaissance that was lost. Returning to the Carrier Striking Force, it encountered the strike wave moving out to attack the Americans. To ensure that contact was not missed Kanno turned back and led Takahashi and his force to the enemy. In this way Kanno condemned himself and his two colleagues to death. Even if they had escaped destruction at the ha of enemy pilots or antiaircraft gunners, their bomber lacked the range t back to their carrier after Kanno's turned back towards Task Force 17. .

turned out, theirs was one of the first, if not the first, of the Japanese aircraft to be shot down.

With their fighters flown off, the American ships looked to their own defense. At 1112, three minutes after the radar plot showed the Japanese dividing into groups for the attack, the carriers came round to a course of 125 degrees and within a minute had worked up to 25 knots. At 1118, when the Japanese attack began, American ships were slicing through the sea at 30 knots and throwing up an antiaircraft fire of daunting proportions. At this stage the two carriers were together, within a single screen made up of five heavy cruisers and seven destroyers. This arrangement did not survive the attack. The two carriers, forced to dodge the torpedoes that the Kates sent in their direction, had to maneuver independently of one another. The turning circles of the two carriers being different, there was no way in which they could maintain their relative positions. By 1127 they were more than three miles apart and the gap between them was widening, the *Yorktown* heading towards the southwest, the *Lexington* towards the east. An hour after the attack began, and some thirty-five minutes after it ended, the carriers were still six miles apart. By that time both had turned back on their original course of 028 degrees for the purpose of closing the enemy and recovering their aircraft. During the battle phase, when the formation divided, the *Yorktown* was screened by the *Astoria*, *Chester* and *Portland*, plus the *Hammann*, *Russell* and *Aylwin*. All of the escorts except the *Aylwin* had been part of the carrier's original screening force. The price she paid for gaining the *Aylwin* from the original Task Force 11 was the defection of the *Anderson* and *Morris*, which supported the *Minneapolis*, *New Orleans*, *Dewey* and *Phelps* in the defense of the *Lexington*.[127]

If all the American claims about this part of the battle were true, the *Lexington* should have escaped attack and being hit by enemy torpedoes. The Americans claimed to have shot down ten Kates before they had chance to launch their torpedoes, and the *Yorktown* claimed to have dodged the minimum of eight aimed at her. With only eighteen Kates in the sixty-nine-strong attack force, no more torpedo bombers remained to attack the *Lexington*. That the giant carrier was hit on her port side by two torpedoes indicates that American claims on these matters were as erroneous as their claims about Japanese air losses, and as mistaken as the results claimed by surviving Japanese pilots. The plethora of exaggerated and conflicting reports makes the task of unraveling the sequence of events an impossible one, but it seems that the air group from the *Zuikaku* pitted itself against the *Lexington*, while the bombers from the *Shokaku* tested themselves against the *Yorktown*.* It is likely that the Japanese attack began

---

*For example, the number of torpedo hits on the *Lexington* claimed by the Japanese exceeded the number of Kates provided by the *Zuikaku*, and it has been claimed that the *Lexington* was attacked by nineteen Vals, which was the number of dive bombers put into the fray by the *Shokaku*.

with Kates moving first against the *Lexington* and then the *Yorktown*, the difference of timing between these attacks being very small. After the Kates had finished their attacks the Vals began their dives. Thus it appears that the Japanese did not achieve an exact coordination of effort in their attacks. The probable sequence of events is as follows: the Kates from the *Zuikaku* attacked the *Lexington* just before their counterparts from the *Shokaku* attacked the *Yorktown*, these efforts being made between 1118 and 1121 or thereabouts; the *Yorktown* was then dive-bombed, probably by Vals from the *Shokaku*, between approximately 1124 and 1130, while the *Lexington* was given similar treatment between about 1126 and 1132. A solitary attack on the *Yorktown* by a maverick Kate at 1140 is generally regarded as having brought proceedings to an end.

The general direction of the Japanese advance to contact was on a bearing of 20 degrees from the American force, which gave the Japanese the advantage of coming out of the sun against their targets. In their approach, as we have seen, the Japanese also had an advantage of altitude over the Dauntlesses, which were some four miles to the north of the carriers.[128] It was this combination that allowed the Kates to fly over and then outrun the Dauntlesses in the course of their attacks on the *Yorktown* and the *Lexington*.[129] A successful approach did not prevent the Kates from duplicating certain errors made by the Devastators in the course of their attacks on the *Shokaku*. Most of the Japanese attacks were delivered at ranges between 1,000 and 1,500 yards, twice the range considered by the Japanese themselves to be the ideal distance from which to attack. The Kates, therefore, attacked at roughly the same range as the Devastators, and the Type 91 torpedo was not so superior to the Mark 13 that the Japanese automatically commanded a success in torpedo attacks that was denied the Americans. Runs of almost two minutes gave the Japanese torpedoes too much to do, because the American carriers had time to maneuver out of their reach. Nevertheless, the Japanese were able to record hits on the *Lexington* and they were perhaps unlucky not to achieve more impressive results than they did.

The Japanese failure to obtain better results in part stemmed from their failure to mount scissors attacks on both American carriers. The *Yorktown* had to negotiate an attack that came at her only from port, and it came from abeam and abaft rather than from the ideal attacking position forward. To meet the first attackers the *Yorktown* heeled under a full rudder as she circled to starboard. Steaming at more than 32 knots, with the destroyers struggling to keep pace, the *Yorktown* moved inside the path of the Japanese torpedoes. The latter passed ahead of the carrier. The same turn also took the *Yorktown* inside the tracks of more torpedoes from port which, had they been just slightly delayed, might have registered results. By turning, the *Yorktown* presented her starboard quarter to Kates that had approached her from her port quarter, and by straightening as she came out of the turn, the

Yorktown avoided these torpedoes as they sped by harmlessly to starboard. Expert shiphandling and the carrier's high speed and relatively small size allowed Fletcher's flagship to sidestep the attack by the Kates.

The *Lexington* was not so fortunate. Nearly 80 feet longer and almost twice the full-load displacement of the *Yorktown*, the *Lexington* lacked her agility. It took about half a minute just to put her rudder hard over, and she had a turning circle that was almost double that of the *Yorktown*.[130] But her relative slowness did not prevent her from evading first an attack from port by putting her rudder hard over to starboard and then an attack off the starboard bow by throwing the rudder hard over to port. The third and last attack made off the port bow, however, was one that she could not dodge. At about 1120 two torpedoes hit her within a minute of one another. The *Lexington* was fortunate not to receive more hits. Two of the torpedoes aimed at her ran deep and, according to her captain, passed under the carrier from port to starboard.[131] Two other torpedoes were seen to pass ahead, one more astern, the estimation being that all three passed within 200 feet of the carrier. About four seconds and 20 feet of ocean separated the *Lexington* from the devastation of up to five extra hits.

More than 47,000 tons of carrier seemed to absorb these blows with ease. The first hit was sustained well forward, around frame 50 or just ahead of the forward gun positions on the port side. The second hit, also to port, was sustained around frame 60, just forward of the island but on the opposite side of the ship. At the time neither hit appeared very serious. The inspection parties realized only too well that the full extent of structural damage was difficult to determine, but they saw nothing that gave immediate cause for alarm. Three of the carrier's sixteen boiler rooms had to be shut down because of flooding from ruptured feed lines. This reduced the speed of the carrier, but overall the damage caused by the two hits seemed minor and localized.[132] The whiplash effect of the blows did not appear to have caused much damage. The electrical system remained intact, though the elevators were jammed in the raised position. The U.S. Navy, unlike the British and Japanese navies, used hydraulic power for its elevators, and a loss of pressure within the system locked the elevators in their safety positions. One of the generator rooms for the ship's internal communications system had to be evacuated when the forced ventilation system in the room stopped working. Though the *Lexington* took on a list as a result of her injuries, the extent of the apparent damage did not seem to be anything she could not live with.

The *Lexington* also seemed capable of absorbing the damage that the Vals inflicted upon her. Exactly how many bombs hit the *Lexington* is a matter of some dispute, the generally accepted version being two, some sources giving totals of up to five.[133] Whatever the number, only three bombs—two that hit the *Lexington* and one that was a near miss—had any significant effect. The near miss exploded alongside frame 90 in the area of the gig boat and flak guns, and like the two bombs that hit to effect, it caused heavy casualties amongst personnel but little physical damage. One of the bombs hit in a ready store of 5-in antiaircraft ammunition and exploded under the flight deck, leaving it slightly splintered and buckled. The blast of the explosion was trapped by the shields of the port batteries in the vicinity. The crew of one gun and half the personnel of another were burnt beyond recognition. The force of the explosion also killed many people in the communications center, which was next to the scene of the blast. The other main hit was on the smoke stack. Heavy casualties were suffered amongst the light-flak gunners stationed on the overhanging platforms. The detonation started fires in the marines' quarters and apparently damaged the carrier's siren. Some men in the vicinity of the siren were apparently scalded by escaping steam, and all were deafened by the sound until the supply of steam was shut off by a member of the damage-control party.[134] Overall the hits and near misses put one 5-in and three 20-mm guns out of action, did minor damage to some berthing spaces and caused minor flooding to three compartments. The ship was left with a seven-degree list to port, but damage control began to correct this by shifting fuel oil. Since the ship retained power and the torpedo hits failed to inflict widespread damage on the feeder systems, damage control had the means to bring the fires in the ship under control. For those on the *Lexington* it appeared not merely that the ship was not in any danger but that her fighting efficiency had not been impaired. She had not been penetrated to her machinery, and neither her flight deck nor her hangar deck had sustained any real damage.

The *Yorktown* came through her dive-bombing ordeal with equal facility. She, too, sustained damage, but as in the case of the *Lexington* this seemed to be no threat to her effectiveness. She was hit by just one bomb which struck the carrier some 23 feet forward of her second elevator and 15 feet inside her island. The bomb exploded in an aviation store room after slicing its way through three decks, but a fire it started in that room and the immediate vicinity was quickly brought under control and then extinguished. The bomb's blast sheared the rivets that held the pedestal of the ship's radar antenna. It was not until the antenna fell to the deck just before the next day's dawn that the damage was discovered. The blast also damaged the intakes to three of the boiler rooms. These had to be closed down and temporarily evacuated while running repairs were made, but this inconvenience had no real impact on the ship's speed and performance. The only other damage that the carrier sustained was inflicted by near misses. One bomb, glancing off the carrier, exploded on impact with the water and lightly peppered the starboard bow above the waterline. It also ruptured a fuel duct, but since that had been drained before action no fire resulted. One other near miss caused more serious damage. This exploded under water with a mining effect. It buckled the lower edge of the armor belt by about 50 millimeters. A tank began to spill oil, and the *Yorktown* marked her trail with a slick that ultimately reached ten miles behind her. On American estimations perhaps as many as seven other near misses shook the ship, one reputedly lifting the screws clear of the water, but none did appreciable damage. Nevertheless, the carrier was perforated over a quarter of her length, which affected her watertight integrity. The *Yorktown* was shaken by her ordeal, but elation at having survived and beaten off the attack proved a speedy remedy for shock.

Just as the American pilots who attacked the Carrier Striking Force mistakenly reported major success, so the Japanese pilots who attacked the *Yorktown* and *Lexington* grossly distorted the results of their efforts. Indeed, their exaggeration exceeded that of the Americans—they reported that two carriers had been accounted for. One—identified as the *Saratoga*—was claimed to have been left in a sinking condition. Another, correctly identified as the *Yorktown*, was said to have been left, if not sinking, then in a heavily damaged state. According to the pilots, the *Lexington* had been hit by nine torpedoes and ten bombs, the *Yorktown* by three torpedoes and eight bombs.[135]

Thus at the end of the carrier exchange both sides believed that victory was within their grasp. Both the Japanese and the Americans believed that the enemy's two carriers had been badly damaged at the very least, and both regarded their own injuries as tolerable. Neither side was yet able to evaluate the extent of their air losses, but by noon both forces were sufficiently confident that they would be able to resume operations when they had recovered their aircraft. Indeed with the attack on the *Lexington* lasting but about nine minutes the battle seemed hardly to have started. An exchange of blows, spaced over a period of perhaps forty minutes, appeared to be the first part of an engagement both sides were anxious to continue. In fact, however, the battle was over.

CHAPTER 8

The Reckoning
and the Withdrawals

When the air attacks ended both sides believed that the exchange had gone in their favor. All four carriers had survived an action that all prewar thinking had declared could only result in mutual annihilation, and to both the Americans and Japanese survival spelled success—especially when it was coupled with exaggerated reports of the damage inflicted on the enemy carriers and air groups. In reality, however, the outcome of the morning's exchange favored the Americans. In the battle they had driven one enemy carrier from the Coral Sea and had inflicted such damage on both Japanese air groups that they were destroyed as effective fighting formations. The Japanese, for the second time in two days, had struck at the enemy with their full strength but had been no more able to force a favorable decision than they had twenty-four hours earlier. On this second occasion they sustained such losses amongst their air groups that they would be condemned to fight in the future, if they fought at all, on a scale of declining effectiveness. American losses had hardly been much lighter than those of the Japanese, but because American resources were slightly but significantly superior to those of the Japanese before battle was joined, the Americans were better placed to absorb losses than the Japanese. Neither side realized it immediately, but after the exchange of blows between 1100 and 1200 only the Americans remained in a position to continue the battle. The strength left to them was such that they could continue to operate on roughly the same scale as before the attack. This was now beyond the Japanese who, of course, still had to deal with two enemies, one at sea and one at Port Moresby.

Though the Japanese had no means of knowing it at the time, by noon on 8 May the offensive power of the Carrier Striking Force had been broken beyond repair. Nearly half its ships were soon to turn for Truk and home as the *Shokaku* retired from the fight, leaving just the *Zuikaku, Haguro, Myoko,*

Shigure, Ariake, Shiratsuyu and *Akebono* to continue the fight. Likewise, less than half the aircraft with which the Carrier Striking Force had entered the Coral Sea were left. As we have seen already, the Japanese began the battle on 7 May with 121 aircraft on the *Zuikaku* and the *Shokaku*, and of this total 109 were operational. That day's operations cost the Japanese 12 aircraft with another 2 rendered inoperative, thus reducing their strength to 95 operational aircraft out of a total of 109. On the eighth the Japanese lost one of the *Shokaku*'s Kates that had been sent out on the dawn reconnaissance; they lost five of the same carrier's fighters from the combat air patrol—two succumbed to enemy gunfire and three were forced to ditch. The attack on the American carrier formation cost the Japanese a total of 22 aircraft, all but one of which were bombers. Two other aircraft tried to land back on the *Shokaku* after she had been damaged. Both of these aircraft, one a fighter from the combat air patrol and the other a Val which participated in the attack on the Americans, were written off in the attempt.

Had the Japanese been able to hold their losses at this level then they might yet have retained a reasonably strong and balanced force with their one remaining carrier. Thus far the Japanese had lost a total of forty aircraft—twelve on the seventh and twenty-eight thus far on the eighth— and had another two effectively damaged beyond recall. The Carrier Striking Force had lost 37 percent of its operational strength in the course of three offensive missions in little more than a twenty-four-hour period. This was a crippling, almost prohibitive rate of attrition made worse by the losses being concentrated amongst strike aircraft. They had lost exactly half of their operational bomber strength in the course of these operations, but worse was to follow in the recovery phase. The *Zuikaku* proved incapable of recovering the survivors from the two air groups. Forty-seven aircraft remained from the attack mission, and theoretically she should have had the capacity to take aboard all that returned from the attack on the *Yorktown* and the *Lexington*. With nine sets of arrester wires and three sets of landing barriers she should have been able to recover those aircraft that returned to the Carrier Striking Force.[1] As it turned out, the *Zuikaku* could not handle aircraft quickly enough to prevent further losses—losses that were both unnecessary and could not be afforded. Because she did not have time to handle recovered aircraft properly while others, low on fuel and some damaged, remained in the air, the *Zuikaku* consigned three Zekes, four Vals and five Kates to the deep, thereby raising the total number of Japanese aircraft lost so far on the eighth to forty-two, including the Zekes and Val that had been extensively damaged trying to land on the *Shokaku*. Thus far the Carrier Striking Force had lost five of every eight bombers. Of the total of seventy-two that had been operational when the battle began on the seventh, no fewer than forty-five had been lost to a variety of causes.

Throwing nine bombers plus three fighters over the side was the point where the nature of Japanese losses changed. Losses that hitherto had been serious became prohibitive, indeed prodigal considering that the *Zuikaku* had space enough for refugees from the *Shokaku*. Even with Zekes of the Tainan Air Group embarked there was no lack of room on the hangar decks for all the aircraft that had returned from the strike against Task Force 17. Yet the *Zuikaku* wrote off 10 percent of the original establishment of the entire force at a time when she did not have a complete air group of her own. By the evening of the eighth the *Zuikaku* had six Kates, nine Vals and twenty-four Zekes ready for operations. A total of thirty-nine aircraft was just over half the carrier's operational capacity. In addition she had one Zeke, eight Vals and four Kates deemed capable of being restored to operational effectiveness.[2] By the following morning it would appear that four of the Vals and two of the Kates had been so restored, for by that time the *Zuikaku* had an air group of forty-five planes, eight of which were Kates, thirteen Vals and twenty-four Zekes.[3] Presumably, therefore, she still had seven aircraft that could be brought back into service. Moreover, she retained fighters from the Tainan Air Group, and she had a number of aircraft, no more than seven, that were considered more difficult to put back into operational service.

It is estimated that at one stage during the afternoon of the eighth just nine operational aircraft remained with the *Zuikaku*.[4] Such a figure, if it is accurate, is artificial in the sense that it must represent the low point between the completion of recovery and having a fresh attack force spotted. Nonetheless Hara and Takagi knew the Carrier Striking Force was in no fit state to continue the battle. This did not concern them overmuch, because the two Japanese commanders believed that the enemy task force had taken a beating and was incapable of further serious resistance. They thought that both enemy carriers had been sunk or ruined beyond recall. The continuation of battle, therefore, could only take the form of the pursuit and annihilation of surface ships that no longer posed a real threat; with the loss of their carriers Allied surface ships could not prove much of an obstacle or a danger. Hara and Takagi felt little inclination to capitalize on the success they were assured was theirs. They believed that their air power had won the main battle and that the Carrier Striking Force had been left free to take as much or as little of what remained of the battle.

Their decision not to follow up success was reminiscent of Takagi's failure to follow up his partial victories during the battle of the Java Sea in February. It also foreshadowed the Japanese decision not to reap the spoils of the small victories that came their way during the Guadalcanal campaign after August. The exploitation of success by fighting a battle of annihilation in the midst of amphibious operations had never formed part of Japanese strategic doctrine. But on 8 May far more immediate considerations shaped the Japanese course of action. In fact, the Carrier Striking Force had surprisingly little choice in the matter. The attack on the Americans had come late in the morning, and the *Zuikaku* felt obliged to warn Rabaul that it was unlikely that she would be unable to launch a second strike in the course of the afternoon. She also warned Inoue of the possibility that a second strike might be beyond her even on the following morning.[5] It was not just consideration of losses and the lateness of the hour that prompted this assessment. On the afternoon of the eighth the Carrier Striking Force had to face up to the consequences of its failure to fuel properly during the course of the run south from Truk the previous week. The attempt to redeem this omission on the sixth had been interrupted and then never completed. By the time the high-speed action of the eighth was over none of the Japanese escorts had tanks that were more than 40 percent full, and some were down to 20 percent.[6] Fletcher might have shown himself overly concerned with refueling, but his formation would never have been faced with the situation that now confronted the Japanese. Even if they wanted to exploit their "victory" or press on with Operation MO, they had little ability to attempt either. With a screen as frail as the one that surrounded the *Zuikaku*, and with the six escorts unable to contemplate high-speed action, Hara and Takagi had little option but to turn back to the north and the line of the Solomons in order to make a rendezvous with the *Tohomaru*. The only good that could possibly come of this enforced action was that the time spent refueling could also be used by the *Zuikaku* to get more of her damaged or presently unserviceable aircraft back into commission.

Overall this situation was disastrous for the Japanese. Operation MO could not now proceed. After the carrier exchange the Carrier Striking Force no longer had the means to counter Allied air power at Port Moresby and in northern Australia. A cynic could argue that the Japanese never had the means to proceed with Operation MO before 8 May, but after the carrier battle an understrength *Zuikaku* could definitely not move against Port Moresby. With Port Moresby holding its own despite two weeks of attack from Lae and Rabaul, a crippled Carrier Striking Force could not press on with the original plan of campaign. Moreover, for the Japanese there were other considerations. On the seventh there had been a "battle force" south of the Louisades, and on the eighth Japanese forces in the western Solomon Sea had been attacked by American heavy bombers.[7] Though the Japanese believed that they had struck the battle force heavy blows and knew that the American bombers had been unsuccessful in their attacks, there was good reason to call a halt to Operation MO. This was how Inoue regarded matters. As far as he was concerned, the state of the Carrier Striking Force spelled an end to the whole venture. This, however, was not a cause for despondency. Two enemy carriers sunk or crippled was adequate compensation for the failure to secure Port Moresby, and Inoue saw the reverse as only temporary. He was prepared to renew the offensive after Operation MO by using the discretionary powers granted him earlier that day by Yamamoto. Authorized to alter the date of the landings at Port Moresby if he wished, Inoue now proposed to exercise this option, though not in the way that the Combined Fleet had intended. The power of discretion was granted in the wake of 7 May, when it dawned on the Japanese that the landings could not proceed with two American carriers on the rampage in the Coral Sea. But the power of discretion was granted so that Operation MO could be postponed if necessary, not cancelled. The afternoon of the eighth Inoue chose to abandon the operation. After a holding order—timed at 1240 but not sent before 1500—which told the Carrier Striking Force to retire to the north and make good its damage, Inoue ordered Hara and Takagi to proceed to Truk. This order was received at 1800, and at 2300 fuller instructions were issued. The forces in the western Solomon Sea were recalled to Rabaul, and the Carrier Striking Force was ordered to cover Operation RY in the course of its passage to Japan.[8] Even if Port Moresby remained beyond his grasp for the moment, Inoue saw no objection to picking up Ocean and Nauru as prizes to be displayed alongside the scalps of the *Saratoga* and the *Yorktown*. Inoue was prepared to let Operation RY go ahead as planned. After the defeat of the Americans in the Coral Sea the opportunity to take these islands seemed too good to miss, and the operation itself seemed small and easy enough to bring to a successful end. Inoue would give up the base at Deboyne, since it could not be sustained in the face of enemy air superiority, but would hold on to Tulagi and take Ocean and Nauru.[9] These, with the losses inflicted on the enemy, would represent a fair return on Operation MO.

A violent reaction to Inoue's orders came from an unexpected quarter. The military principle of the level of realism existing in inverse proportion to the nearness of the enemy is well known. Inoue's instructions to postpone Operation MO until 3 July were countermanded immediately by Yamamoto. At midnight Yamamoto issued instructions that Inoue's forces, including the Carrier Striking Force, resume offensive operations with a view to bringing about the utter annihilation of the enemy.[10] These orders flew in the face of all that was realistic. The forces south of Rabaul were too weak to contemplate serious and sustained offensive operations, and in any case too many hours had been lost for there to be any chance of contact being regained with an enemy that was unlikely to stand and fight. With American ships able to withdraw to the southwest, the south or the southeast, the chances of the Japanese finding the enemy were not good. The Japanese would have had to maintain contact in the hours after the carrier battle in order to annihilate the enemy. By the time Inoue and his subordinates tried to pick up the threads of battle in compliance with Yamamoto's orders, it was far too late to regain contact.

Nearly eighteen hours after the air battle the Japanese forces in the Solomon and Coral Seas turned in pursuit of the Americans. It was not until the afternoon of the following day, the tenth, that Yamamoto conceded that his forces, despite more than thirty-six hours of fruitless endeavor, would not be able to achieve the battle of annihilation he demanded. Only then did Yamamoto issue fresh orders confirming those that Inoue had given during the evening of the eighth; most forces were recalled to Rabaul, Operation RY was confirmed and Operation MO was postponed until later in the year. Rather belatedly, Yamamoto put Operation MO where it should have been from the very start—after Operation MI. Yet an irony in the situation had developed. By the time that realism replaced optimistic determination in Hiroshima, an event occurred of which the Japanese remained unaware. Just as they had no inkling of the extent of their defeat on the morning of the eighth, so they did not know of a development that went some way to providing substance to their otherwise hollow claims to victory.

The end of the morning's fighting saw the Americans well placed but not without problems. Both the *Yorktown* and the *Lexington* had been damaged, but their operational efficiency was unimpaired and both were able to handle aircraft. Neither seemed in any danger as they moved under their own power. The *Lexington* had slowed to 17 knots at 1142, but by noon she had edged up to 20 knots and at 1223 she was recording 25.[11] By about 1230 damage control had managed to get the ship back on an even keel, and she began to turn into the wind to recover her aircraft. With both elevators jammed and permanently immobilized and the avgas system on the port side of the ship in disarray, the effectiveness of the *Lexington* was certain to be limited in the future. She could not lower her aircraft to the hangars, and two early casualties of her disability were heavily damaged Dauntlesses that had to be pushed overboard. In all probability others might have to follow them, yet the important point was that the state of the *Lexington* at this time did not give rise to real anxiety.

Thus far in the battle the Americans had been remarkably lucky. Fortune had smiled on them on the seventh, when they had accounted for the *Shoho* while escaping from the consequences of their own success. For their relative immunity on the morning of the eighth they had to thank the matter of yards that separated minor from major damage and the smallness of Japanese bombs. Had the bomb that hit the *Yorktown*'s flight deck struck her 15 yards and not 15 feet from her island then the verdict of history, with respect to both the Coral Sea and Midway, may well have been different. Had the Vals carried a bomb load that compared with that of the Dauntlesses the verdict would certainly have been different. The *Yorktown* was hit by a 250-kg (551-lb) semi-armor-piercing bomb, roughly the same type and size of bomb used by Dauntless scouts but only half the size of those used by Dauntless bombers. Accounts of the battle that unfavorably contrast Japanese inability to get the *Shokaku* back into commission until July with American ability to complete running repairs on the *Yorktown* within three days at Pearl Harbor fail to take into full consideration their relative damage, the location of that damage, the number of times they had been hit and by what size and type of ordnance. The *Yorktown* was more fortunate than the *Shokaku* in being hit by a solitary and relatively light bomb in the comparatively unused lee of her island.

The bomb damage sustained by both carriers was no more than inconvenience. The fires did not threaten the carriers, and the human losses, unfortunate though they were, were tolerable for ships with crews of more than 2,000 officers and men. The torpedo hits on the *Lexington* similarly seemed to pose no serious or immediate danger. With a 6-in armor that was proof of her battle cruiser pedigree, the longest and most powerfully engined warship in the world seemed able to take the punishment inflicted by the Kates in stride. Her damage control parties believed that she was not in any danger, but this was not the case.

It is believed that the torpedo that hit the *Lexington* forward rather than the one that hit amidships ruptured avgas compartments in the forward part of the ship. This was not discovered by the damage control parties in the course of their inspections, and vapor seeped into those parts of the ship that had been evacuated because of the failure of the ventilating system. Without a means by which it could be dispersed, the vapor became increasingly concentrated.

Theoretically what then happened should never have occurred. The seepage should have been prevented because the Americans, like the Japanese, used inert carbon dioxide to isolate their aviation fuel.* Moreover, the Americans, like the British but unlike the Japanese, relied for the most part on natural ventilation to disperse vapor. The concentration should thus have been avoided. It occurred, however, where there was no form of ventilation whatsoever. As their final precaution against induced explosions both the Americans and British made lavish use of heavy insulation and located switches and circuits above a height of 8 feet from deck level, above the level of any likely vapor concentration.[12] These measures were passive recognition that the carrier was a contradiction of every safety precaution that existed; it was no more than a lightly armored box of

---

*The British used seawater to guard against what was to happen to the *Lexington*. This was a superior safeguard, but it ran the perpetual risk of accidental contamination and severely restricted the amount of fuel that a carrier carried.

machinery, ammunition and fuel. In the case of the *Lexington* on 8 May these precautions were not enough. The buildup of vapor in the forward part of the ship escaped discovery until 1242, and the motor generators had been left running when their room had been evacuated.[13] The motors were known to be overheating owing to misalignment. The subsequent report on the loss of the ship, largely based on the battle report submitted by her executive officer, blamed a spark from one of these generators for setting off a massive explosion that marked the end of the carrier. Its force blew inboard the longitudinal bulkhead between the generator room and the interior communications room, and simultaneously destroyed the transverse bulkhead between the generator room and the aviation fuel control rooms and tanks. The force is believed to have been carried through the ducts into adjoining areas, into the machine shop spaces on the third deck and into the chief petty officer's quarters on the second.[14] This record of events has been disputed, since certain of the damage control personnel placed the location of the explosion some way forward of the generator room.[15]

The explosion took place at 1247, more than an hour after the last Japanese attacks. It hampered but did not bring an end to the *Lexington*'s flying operations, yet with her fires and elevators out of action it was not until 1414 that the last of the aircraft she was to recover were brought down.[16] But even when the *Lexington* was fully committed to fighting her fires and recovering (and flying off) her aircraft, there was every expectation that the carrier would ride out the damage. Certainly her damage seemed less pressing than the problems that bore down on Fletcher and Fitch as they tried to juggle with various imponderables in deciding the course of action to be pursued by Task Force 17.

Fletcher's immediate problem was how to continue the battle, if indeed it was to be continued. When the final counts were made it was found that nineteen aircraft had failed to return after the attack on the Carrier Striking Force.[17] It was a total that would easily have been much higher but for the clouds that had provided cover for American aircraft both before and after their attack. If the losses were relatively small in comparison to the number of aircraft still left to Task Force 17, the American position remained difficult on three counts. First, though the number of aircraft lost was not crippling, the number of aircraft damaged cut a swath in the number that would be made available for any second strike. The *Yorktown*, after recovering her own aircraft between 1231 and 1300, ultimately collected nineteen refugees from the *Lexington*, and of these no fewer than seventeen needed repairs.[18] Second, the time needed for a second strike was running out. It took time to recover aircraft, strike them below, refuel and rearm them, and prepare their aircrew for a second operation. With the sun due to set at 1820, Fletcher found himself in a situation that was almost the same as the

The Big Explosion Aboard the *Lexington*

one that he had faced one day earlier after the destruction of the *Shoho*: enemy targets were available but time to attack and recover aircraft before nightfall was not. Third, Task Force 17 had relatively few aircraft to send against the enemy in a second strike. By about 1430 the *Yorktown* had been able to ready a total of thirty-one aircraft, of which eight were Wildcats, eight Devastators and the remaining fifteen Dauntlesses.[19] This was a healthy total compared with the nine believed to be available to the *Zuikaku* at about this time, but still it remained too small a force to be sent against the enemy. Moreover, the *Yorktown* could no longer provide a Devastator contingent for any attack. Due to the overindulgence of the Devastators at Tulagi on the fourth and against the *Shoho* on the seventh, the effort against the Carrier Striking Force on the morning of the eighth had to be the last unit effort by the *Yorktown*'s torpedo squadron. The attack on the *Shokaku* all but exhausted her store of torpedoes.

Thus the chance of a second strike being flown off on the eighth was remote. Moreover, Fletcher had little inclination to seek a night engagement, for the same reasons that he had decided against such a course of action on the previous afternoon after the destruction of the *Shoho*. But after 1422 Fletcher had to contend with an unexpected development. Until that time the Americans believed that they had found, attacked and damaged two enemy carriers during the morning. There had never been any doubt that two carriers had been present. Smith's navigation might have been corrected by Dixon but not his identification of the enemy. The pilots' claims to have attacked two carriers had to be believed initially, but there was a quick repudiation of the assertion that both had been left in a rather precarious state. Radio analysts listening into the enemy net realized from Japanese signals traffic that one of the enemy carriers had taken over responsibility for landing aircraft from her stricken sister. Since these monitors had predicted the arrival of the enemy over Task Force 17 at about 1100 that morning by listening to Japanese radio traffic, they were believed. The state of the other carrier was to remain unknown until the following day, when Hypo found her on her way to Truk.[20]

The attack by Fletcher's air groups had lacked continuity, hence the commander's inability to realize that rather than dividing their efforts the groups had attacked one carrier on two separate occasions. In the course of the debriefing, aircrew from the *Lexington* reported the presence of an undamaged carrier near the scene of battle.[21] A number of inferences could be drawn from this information: that the Americans had attacked one carrier twice rather than two carriers once; that one enemy carrier had made good its damage almost immediately; that a third carrier had arrived on the scene. Prebattle intelligence reports had said that the enemy might feed in forces during the course of the battle.[22] It was not impossible for the battle to be starting in all seriousness only now. The truth of the situation was suspected, but suspicion was not enough when it came to making decisions that involved the fate of half the carrier strength of the Pacific Fleet. In the circumstances Fletcher felt that he had few options; like its adversary, Task Force 17 found that its course of action was already largely determined. Unwilling to contemplate a night action, unable to launch a second strike during the hours of daylight, and not exactly sure of the composition of the enemy force to the north, Fletcher chose to lead his force to the south and out of the battle zone. He signaled to Nimitz his intention to send the *Lexington* back to Pearl Harbor after her aircraft had been completely transferred to the *Yorktown*. With a full air group on his flagship, Fletcher planned to renew the battle with the *Yorktown* the next day.[23]

Fletcher's signal apparently broke the tension that had been building up at Pearl Harbor as the staff of the Pacific Fleet followed developments in the Coral Sea. Thus far Pearl Harbor had received various reports from

Fletcher regarding his own situation and the assumed situation of the enemy, but the information that the *Yorktown* was fully operational and that the *Lexington* was safe was a relief to Nimitz. The staff at Pearl Harbor obviously believed that the day belonged to the Americans, hence Nimitz's signal to Fletcher: "Congratulations on your glorious accomplishment of the last two days. Your aggressive actions have the admiration of the entire Pacific Fleet . . . You have filled our hearts with pride and have maintained the highest traditions of the Navy." As one noted historian observed, the congratulations sounded a little hollow when they were received late on the eighth—by that time the *Lexington* was not there to receive her share of the credits.[24]

Although it did not appear too serious at first, the explosion of 1247 doomed the *Lexington*. It killed or severely wounded many of the all-important damage control personnel stationed in the main control room. Among those lost was the head of damage control, Lieutenant Commander H. R. Healy. Thus the command organization of the damage control establishment was put out of action at the very time it was needed as never before. The explosion destroyed various telephone circuits as well as the engine telegraph, the rudder angle indicator, the Walker Log and the forward gyro compass. Communications with the main control room broke down completely, and the ship was forced to rely increasingly on secondary circuits or sound-powered telephones. Thus the explosion initiated the progressive breakdown of communications that was to play a large part in the ship's eventual loss.[25] The explosion also destroyed the water main in this particular part of the ship. This proved disastrous. The damage control parties, who did not have sufficient foamite fire-fighting equipment with which to tackle flames that were spreading throughout the ship, were forced to fight the fires with water, and with the main destroyed they had to play out hoses from aft.[26] But the general collapse of circuits inside the ship as explosions ripped through the *Lexington* and the loss of power meant that pumps did not have pressure. What exacerbated the situation was the loss of so many damage control personnel and the breakdown of internal communications; under these circumstances damage control had to be attempted locally, and local personnel, without the training and experience of highly specialized controllers, could not attempt to flood their own areas.[27]

The problem confronting the damage control personnel was that the explosion of 1247 set off an irreversible chain reaction. As the fires took hold of the ship, they were fed by fuel and vapor from the main storage tanks, which had been split and could not be flooded. The fires and explosions further weakened bulkheads, thereby allowing air and fuel vapor to circulate. The vapor, in its turn, was ignited by flame or heat, causing further explosions and making even more of the ship uninhabitable. The gradual loss of power meant that the *Lexington* fought with decreasing effectiveness against her fires until a second massive explosion at 1445 proved to be her death warrant. This explosion destroyed the ventilation system of the boiler and engine rooms. Without the forced draught for the furnaces, the final loss of power could not be avoided.[28] Within seven minutes of this explosion the carrier ran up the Not Under Control signal, and at 1456 she requested her escorts to stand by her to take off survivors, if necessary. By 1502 the condition of the *Lexington* had deteriorated to such an extent that Fletcher felt obliged to ask the Southwest Pacific Command to provide air cover. At 1510 he reassumed full tactical command of Task Group 17.5 from Fitch, and ordered the *Minneapolis, New Orleans, Anderson, Hammann* and *Morris* to stand by the *Lexington* and give her whatever assistance was necessary.[29]

These five ships could do nothing to save the *Lexington*. Final acceptance of the inevitable came at 1630, when orders were issued to shut down the engine room. By that time all other stations below deck and even the gunnery stations forward had been abandoned as fires took over the whole of the forward part of the ship's interior. Flames could be seen in the hangar well. The real danger that threatened the *Lexington* was that the remorseless rise of temperature would spontaneously set off the torpedo magazine. Because of the loss of hydraulic power and the jamming of the elevators the torpedoes could not be moved, and while 5-in ammunition could be thrown over the side the heavier armament could not be disposed of quite so easily. The danger was that the magazines would explode and blow the ship apart, taking the ship's company with it, and at this stage of proceedings the safety of the crew took precedence over the unavailing struggle to save the ship. The order to abandon ship was passed at 1707, though the first of the destroyers to come alongside to take off the wounded and other personnel had done so as early as 1615.[30] This destroyer, the *Morris*, subsequently suffered topside damage as she lay alongside the exploding carrier, but apart from this the process of abandoning ship was carried out in ideal circumstances. The carrier herself was more or less on an even keel—she had a list of about three degrees to starboard—and she was not under way. Moreover, the sea was both warm and placid. With the process of abandoning an orderly affair, the destroyers and cruisers were able to approach the carrier and pick up the hundreds of men left in the water. It is believed that every man that entered the water alive was picked up.

Fitch and his staff transferred to the *Minneapolis*, and after dusk all the escorts continued to pick up men from the water by the light from their own searchlights and the flames of the *Lexington*.[31] With their recovery of survivors completed at 1853, the five escorts went off to the southwest to rejoin Task Group 17.5, leaving behind the *Phelps* to administer the coup de grace with torpedoes.[32] However much the task force might have regretted aban-

The Crew of the *Lexington* Abandoning Ship

doning the carrier, after dark her fires threatened the safety of the rest of her colleagues. The *Phelps* fired five torpedoes at the carrier, three into her starboard quarter from windward, two into her port quarter. The *Lexington* sank at 1952 with one final and massive explosion that was felt by Smith on his flagship more than 20 miles away.[33] The *New Orleans*, at a range of 14 miles, was shaken as if she had been hit by a torpedo.[34]

With the loss of the *Lexington* one quarter of the carrier strength of the Pacific Fleet disappeared. It was small wonder that one of the first signals to leave Pearl Harbor after news of her loss had been received was directed to the naval dockyard at Puget Sound ordering that the repairs to the *Saratoga* be rushed to completion.[35] The loss of the *Lexington* had an immediate tactical impact on the situation in the Coral Sea and a wider impact with respect to the balance (or imbalance) in the Pacific. The loss of the *Lexington* meant the continued safety of the *Yorktown* became essential to the Americans. No success she might register on her own could possibly compensate the Americans for any further damage that she might suffer, still less her loss. The destruction of the *Lexington* removed the American margin against error, and there could be no question of trying to resume the battle on the following morning. Though there were second thoughts on this matter when it was realized that in a day or so Halsey would be in the area with the *Enterprise* and the *Hornet*, Nimitz's order to Fletcher to take Task Force 17 out of the Coral Sea was undoubtedly sound. But what had added a final note of urgency to the breaking off of the battle was the explosion of 1445, which brought with it an end to the *Lexington*'s flying operations. After the first explosion of 1247 her flying operations had not been seriously affected, but the second explosion took place before the carrier had time to complete the transfer of aircraft to the *Yorktown*. At 1515 the *Lexington* asked the

Yorktown to recover those of her aircraft that were airborne, and Fletcher's flagship was able to take on five Wildcats and fourteen Dauntlesses. A total of thirty-six aircraft remained on the *Lexington* and could not be flown off. These thirty-six, one of which was a Wildcat from the *Yorktown*, were fated to go down with the *Lexington*.[36]

Fletcher set course to the south throughout the night and the following day, thereby eluding the belated Japanese attempts to regain contact with his force. In doing so he brought about an end to the battle and left the field to the enemy, not that that meant much under the circumstances. The Japanese, with no advantage they could press home, were forced to retire and abandon an operation that had provoked the battle in the first place. For both sides it was a rather unsatisfactory closing act, and for the Allies there was an embarrassing epilogue. On the morning of the ninth aircraft from the *Yorktown* and bombers from Australia managed to pull off the only properly coordinated operation of the battle. The planes were called to the location of an enemy carrier sighted by one of the *Yorktown*'s scouts. Fourteen Flying Fortresses put in an appearance in an attempt to complement the *Yorktown*'s efforts in dealing with a carrier 175 miles to the northwest of Task Force 17. But the carrier turned out to be the Lihau Reef.[37] It was a rather sad comment on the conduct of operations by both sides. Overall there was no question that the problems confronting each side in history's first carrier battle had rather overwhelmed the commanders involved. The conduct of air operations, both offensive and defensive, had been awkward, and neither the Americans nor the Japanese had been able to hold their tactical formations together when attacked. Cooperation between land-based and carrier-borne aircraft was nil, and land-based aircraft had been singularly ineffective in damaging any of the targets that they attacked. Both sides had sustained losses that could and should have been avoided. Both sides claimed victory, the Americans not admitting the *Lexington*'s loss until after Midway. These conflicting claims implied that the battle had really ended in a draw. Certainly the material losses were closely balanced. The Americans lost one fleet carrier, one destroyer and one oiler; the Japanese lost one light fleet carrier plus one destroyer and various minor units and auxiliaries at Tulagi. Two fleet carriers, one on each side, were damaged. In the air the American carriers lost a total of sixty-six aircraft to the Japanese total of ninety-two, of which seventy-seven were from the Fifth Carrier Division and the balance was from the *Shoho*. The Americans lost a total of 543 men, the Japanese 1,074. Losses on the carriers broke down as follows: 66 were killed from the *Yorktown*, 216 from the *Lexington* and 108 from the *Shokaku*. At the end of the battle all the Japanese had to show for their efforts were the bases at Tulagi and Deboyne, and the Japanese themselves realized that the latter was untenable as a result of the wider failure of Operation MO. It was quickly bombed into oblivion by American aircraft based in northern Australia.

The first carrier battle in history is generally regarded to have resulted in a tactical Japanese success and an Allied strategic victory. As one Japanese source has noted, "If the Coral Sea battle can be said to have been a Japanese victory, it was a victory only by the narrowest numerical margin, even without taking into account the thwarting of the Port Moresby invasion."[38] There is an element of truth in this. The battle resulted in the Japanese being unable to realize their objective. The Allies were successful in denying Port Moresby to the Japanese, and this was the first time in the Pacific war, with the exception of the first assault on Wake, that a Japanese undertaking had failed. A Japanese advance was turned back, and though the long-term danger to the Allied position in the southwest Pacific remained acute, the Allied powers were justified in taking heart from their success. Had the battle been lost the effect on morale would have been potentially disastrous, coming as it would have on top of the American surrender in the Philippines. As it was, the Americans believed that the Coral Sea marked the beginning of the way back, and in the disastrous days of mid-1942, with Allied forces throughout the world in retreat, this was critical.

On the tactical side, however, the only way the balance can be judged is with reference to Midway. The real effect of the Coral Sea could not be seen until after that battle was fought. Far from being a tactical success, the battle of the Coral Sea was a tactical disaster for the Japanese for reasons that have never been appreciated properly because they did not become apparent until after the battle of Midway. The battles of the Coral Sea and Midway will be evaluated together in the final chapter of this history. Suffice it to note here that on 10 May neither the American nor the Japanese naval command could give much consideration to the future and the verdict of history. That could wait. What could not wait were arrangements for the next phase of operations.

PART IV

The Battle of Midway

CHAPTER 9

Operation Magic and the American Deployment for the Battle of Midway

It will be recalled that one of the major considerations behind Nimitz's decision to fight for Port Moresby and the southwest Pacific with the full carrier strength of the Pacific Fleet had been the calculation, supplied by intelligence, that the northern and central Pacific theaters would remain quiet.[1] With no inkling of Operations AL and MI, Nimitz was prepared to uncover the central Pacific in order to hold open the line of communication to Australia. Nimitz had enlisted and received the support of King for this policy on the condition that carrier strength be equally divided between the central and the southwest Pacific.[2]

In the first half of May, however, intelligence strongly suggested that the King-Nimitz accord of April had been based on an erroneous assessment of the enemy's intentions. King and Nimitz had assumed that Operation MO would prove the overture to a sustained enemy offensive in the southwest Pacific. Intelligence information on 1 May had noted that the Aleutians were a secondary enemy objective and would probably be subjected to attack at some time. The Pacific Fleet's summary of the same date noted that any point as far east as Pearl Harbor could be raided.[3] But the conventional wisdom was that the Aleutians and Hawaiian Islands were less attractive to the Japanese at this time than the islands of the southwest Pacific. Like the Aleutians, the islands between Australia and Oahu were considered secondary enemy objectives, but ones that seemed more likely to attract the enemy's immediate attention. Thus on the day that the *Yorktown* and the *Lexington* made their rendezvous in the Coral Sea, the American belief was still that the enemy's main effort would be made in this general area.[4]

By 4 May, however, the Americans had secured enough evidence to suggest that their earlier estimation of enemy intentions might have been based on a false premise. By the ninth, the day after the *Lexington* was scuttled, enough information had accumulated to back the conviction—at least in Pearl Harbor—that the importance of the southwest Pacific had been overestimated. Intelligence had discovered that a major enemy offensive was in the offing, but did not know when and where the Japanese would strike. What it did know was that the blow need not necessarily fall in the southwest Pacific. It was a conclusion that ushered in two weeks of confusion and uncertainty in American councils that was not finally resolved until 24 May. By that date the Americans had in their possession virtually the whole of the enemy plan of campaign and order of battle for Operations AL and MI.

The confusion of early May was the result of the American intelligence effort and its relationship to command arrangements and operational deployment. Japanese secrets were being uncovered piecemeal and over many days at a time when this latter commodity was at a premium. Right up until the end there were gaps in American knowledge of enemy intentions that could not be filled, and there were doubts that could not be laid to rest until the onset of battle revealed that intelligence had been able to put the enemy's jigsaw puzzle together despite the missing pieces. The fragmentary nature of accumulating information presented problems of evaluation, interpretation and dissemination, which were exacerbated by the American use of three intelligence agencies and command organizations—one in Washington, one in Pearl Harbor and one in Australia—to deduce the pattern of enemy intentions from source material that was common to all. In the initial stages little of the evidence fitted together, so it was perhaps inevitable that the various authorities involved in Operation Magic, with their dissimilar perspectives, should have clashing interpretations of Japanese intentions. The authorities seemed to work on the premise that the enemy was intent on realizing their worst fears—and different authorities had different fears, so there was no agreement over what Japanese plans were. It was not until the middle of May that sufficient evidence had been gathered together to convince both Pearl Harbor and Washington that the enemy's main effort was to be made in the central Pacific. Even then, however, there were doubts about where in the central Pacific the Japanese would make their effort, and it was not until the fourth week of May that these uncertainties were resolved. Thus for much of May the Americans were trying to formulate a response to an anticipated Japanese attack without knowing for certain where the enemy intended to mount his offensive, and at the same time they were trying to hold off a Japanese effort to secure Ocean and Nauru. In this attempt the Americans found themselves in an increasingly impossible situation: their carrier strength had been halved as a result of the battle of the Coral Sea, and what carrier strength remained to the Pacific Fleet was farther away from Pearl Harbor than the enemy was from Midway. On 18 May, for example, the *Enterprise* and the *Hornet* were at Noumea, 3,954 miles from Oahu, while the First Carrier Striking Force was about 2,600 miles from Midway with its four carriers, battle units and light forces. For most of May the Americans were in the potentially disastrous position of being the weaker side, on the defensive and forced to await an enemy attack; their command organization made plans that were overtaken by events, giving rise to fresh disputes within the American high command on the critical matter of when and where the enemy would make his move. Thus on 11 and 12 May King could inform his colleagues at the fourteenth meeting of the Joint Chiefs of Staff that in his view the enemy would try to repeat his effort against Port Moresby, or alternatively would move against New Caledonia or the Fiji Islands. By the time he made these predictions intelligence had largely discounted these possibilities.[5]

This inevitable delay between intelligence and command assessments began on 1 May, the day the intelligence services at Pearl Harbor claimed that the enemy's main effort would be made in the southwest Pacific. On that day doubt began to emerge about earlier predictions because it was realized that a call sign in the Marshalls, hitherto identified as belonging to one of the battleships normally with the carriers, may have been miscast. Rechecking past signals suggested that the call sign belonged either to a submarine or a submarine command; in fact by the third the identification of twenty-seven separate call signs in the Marshalls dated 28–29 April hinted at a submarine offensive in the offing, with all that that implied for the identification of a battleship in the island group.[6] This conclusion was subsequently strengthened by the discovery that one of the fast battleships, the *Kirishima*, was not in the southwest Pacific as the Americans had assumed but in a dockyard undergoing repairs. On the surface these matters might not have seemed significant, but they were. In large part the assessment that Japanese carrier forces were bound for the southwest Pacific had depended on the identification of a battle unit in the Marshalls. When this link was broken and the *Kirishima* was found to be in home waters, part of the case supporting the view that the Japanese would mount their offensive in the southwest Pacific began to crumble. Moreover, what did not happen in the course of the battle of the Coral Sea further reinforced the suspicion that the earlier conclusion was untenable.[7]

If the initial American assumption about future enemy intentions in the southwest Pacific had been correct, it would have been natural to find Japanese units from home waters and the Mandates heading south to support Inoue at the first sign of trouble as Operation MO was put into effect. This did not happen. American intelligence searched in vain for any sign of the enemy "heading towards the sound of the guns." The absence of support for the forces involved in Operation MO was not conclusive, but it suggested that perhaps the Japanese had ideas other than a phased offensive in the southwest Pacific. Moreover, on 8 May the Americans became aware that the enemy intended to develop an immediate offensive against Ocean and Nauru. Operation RY had been compromised in late April, but over the next few days the mounting evidence of a Japanese move between the Solomon and Ellice islands fueled the notion that at least for the moment the southwest Pacific might be dropping out of Japanese calculations. The lack of forces heading south and the switch away from Port Moresby and the lower Solomons had to suggest that the enemy had no immediate intention to undertake a major fleet offensive in the southwest Pacific.

It appeared that the enemy had no major units in the southwest Pacific on 4 May other than those known to have been committed to Operation MO. This realization forced the Americans to reconsider what was meant by the concentration of the Combined Fleet in home waters for the first time since the war began. One fact alone was clear: the concentration in home waters allowed the Japanese to strike not simply in the southwest Pacific but against any position across a full 85 degrees of latitude, from Australia in the south to the Aleutians in the north. On 6 May the Pacific Fleet staff noted that the enemy's concentration in his home ports enabled him to move in strength in both the northern and central Pacific.[8]

Under these circumstances it was natural that the Pacific Fleet's attention should begin to refocus on the security of Pearl Harbor, the maintenance of which was an absolute priority. This concern automatically involved two matters of crucial importance: first, the protection of Oahu's outposts, and second, the arrangements that had to be made with the army and the army air force.

The first matter was already in hand. Either as a result of his own intuition or of King's directive on the matter, on 2 May Nimitz flew to Midway to inspect the atoll's defenses. Consultation with the atoll's commander, Commander Cyril T. Simard, and the ground force commander, Lieutenant Colonel Harold D. Shannon, USMC, convinced Nimitz that for the moment Midway was reasonably provided for and that through reinforcement it could be made as secure as any such base.[9] The second matter, that of coordination with other services, was a more difficult one to straighten out.

At stake was the issue that had been slowly coming to the boiling point since March—the concept of defense to be applied in the southwest Pacific. The question was made urgent by the outcome of the battle of the Coral Sea. Roosevelt himself had inadvertently raised the matter at the Pacific War Council meeting on 29 April when he tried to reassure his lesser allies that revised and increased troop and aircraft strength would be allocated to the southwest Pacific.[10] On 4 May Marshall bluntly told Roosevelt that reinforcement of this theater beyond the limits already agreed could only be achieved at the expense of the buildup of forces in the European theater of operations. Roosevelt's grand gestures, casual benevolence and largesse ignored the weeks of planning and could only end any prospect of American ground forces being committed to action against Germany in 1942.[11] But this exchange provided King with the opening he wanted to reexamine the argument over the "Germany-first" strategy. King's view was that the Allied position in the Pacific was now so serious that priorities had to be switched for the moment.[12] What he wanted was a further commitment of forces to this theater of operations. Marshall's proposal of 4 May to hold the Thirty-seventh Infantry Division at Suva rather than send it on to New Zealand was welcome, but it was by no means enough.[13]* King wanted more aircraft in the southwest Pacific area; he retained a healthy skepticism about the army air force's claim that its formations at Hawaii and in Australia could be switched to the area in the event of an emergency. There was nothing quite so certain as formations in position, and King had good cause for concern on this score. When he made proposals for the further reinforcement of the theater at the thirteenth Joint Chiefs of Staff meeting, King and his colleagues were awaiting the outcome of the first carrier battle. King was aware of the possibility that any enemy follow-up operation in the southwest Pacific in May might well coincide with the arrival in the area of the forces earmarked for the theater. But without further reinforcement the whole of the American position in the New Caledonia–New Hebrides–Tongabatu–Samoa complex was precarious, for none of these American-held islands was capable of withstanding a serious and sustained attack. Despite the evident dangers of such a move, on 6 May Roosevelt ruled out further reinforcement of the southwest Pacific.[14] The Marshall strategy of concentration against Germany prevailed for the moment over the King alternative, and the navy would have to get by with what was on hand.[15] Marshall attempted to sweeten the pill by assuring King that Arnold and the army air force would meet their commitments, but this was a rather backhanded promise and in any event it was one that was given before the action in the Coral Sea forced further examination of the whole problem of the defense of this particular area.[16] At the meetings on the eleventh and twelfth King argued that the Americans had two carriers in the whole of the Pacific to the possible ten of the enemy, and since he was still at this time of the opinion that the Japanese would renew their attack on Port Moresby or would move against Fiji or New Caledonia, he wanted practical demonstration of the air force's claim of its "strategic mobility" through rapid deployment to the threatened area.

---

*Interestingly this proposal was resisted by Churchill, who on 9 May tried to insist that the Thirty-seventh Infantry Division should proceed to New Zealand as planned. It was only when he was told by his own Chiefs of Staff that New Zealand had already agreed to the change that he dropped his opposition.

The prospect of another bruising round of interdepartmental negotiations on the question of the defense of the southwest Pacific was overtaken by events. On 9 May, two days before King reviewed the results of the Coral Sea engagement and sought a further deployment of forces to the southwest Pacific, the Pacific Fleet staff recorded the view that the anticipated Japanese offensive need not necessarily come in this area. In the days that followed the Americans picked up indications that an offensive outside the southwest Pacific was under consideration in Tokyo and Hashirajima; on 11 May the Belconnen station had evidence suggesting that the Japanese were using Guam and Saipan as their concentration area.[17] In addition, there were four partially recovered signals that could not be made to fit together. First, in a signal from the *Kirishima* to Nagumo on 3 May there was a reference to a forthcoming "campaign."[18] Second, there was a reference to an operation that appeared to be scheduled between 15 and 21 May, when Japanese units sortied from home waters.[19] Third, there was a reference to an operational objective that could not be identified because its code letters had not been noted by intelligence before this time, but which the team at Pearl Harbor believed was not within the southwest Pacific. Fourth, there was a signal from Nagumo to Truk warning the local authorities that main force units would arrive there on or about 20 June and would remain for about two weeks. This signal requested Truk to assign berths for ships and to arrange for something that the cryptanalysts could not understand.[20]

The question the various intelligence units had to answer was how these various pieces fitted together. A major operation was certainly under consideration by the enemy, and an intercept of a message of 5 May from the Combined Fleet to the Naval General Staff requesting the delivery of fueling hoses had to imply a long-range operation involving replenishment at sea. These were the tentative conclusions drawn from the otherwise tantalizingly incomplete messages. What was irritatingly obscure was the crucial matter of timing. The deployment of carrier forces to Truk had to indicate a move into the southwest Pacific, but all the other clues pointed to a buildup of strength in the Marianas—and that suggested a move into the central Pacific. It was not clear if the anticipated arrival of the carriers at Truk would be before or after the campaign to which the *Kirishima* had referred, and there were indications that the enemy's offensive could be made between 1 and 5 June anywhere along the Aleutians-Hawaii-Australia line.

With the Japanese attempt to secure Ocean and Nauru then under way and with Halsey's Task Force 16 moving into position to frustrate the attempt, the American staffs had to sort out their information. The central Pacific option for the Japanese could be aimed either at Midway or Pearl Harbor, though on the fourteenth Nimitz raised the possibility that the

Japanese might attempt a "reverse Doolittle" with a raid on the West Coast. It was not an option that King ruled out, indeed he put more stock in it than Nimitz. It was also an option that the army and army air force took seriously, and in the last week of May Marshall himself went to the West Coast to supervise defensive arrangements there. (For good measure he took along Doolittle, now a brigadier general.) Army intelligence continued to assert that the West Coast option, or a move into the Aleutians, remained the most likely course of action open to the enemy.[21] But aside from this possibility, which quickly faded from naval calculations, the question of the form of a possible attack in the central Pacific remained. King favored the view that Pearl Harbor would be the enemy's objective, and for a time so, too, did Nimitz, but the latter subsequently became convinced that the Japanese would be forced to reduce Midway before moving down the Hawaiian chain towards Oahu. There was also the possibility that the Japanese might attack both Midway and Pearl Harbor, or that they might feint to assault Midway and move further east to descend on Oahu. King for some time clung to the notion that an attack on Midway might be made with only limited forces, the aim of the attack being to neutralize the atoll's installations and to draw out the Pacific Fleet in defense of the atoll while the bulk of the enemy's strength was directed elsewhere, probably in the southwest Pacific. To complicate matters still further, the scope of interpretation had to be extended as details of another enemy move—this time in the Aleutians—slowly became available. The immediate question was whether a northern or a central Pacific thrust would be the enemy's main effort, whether they might be complementary or whether one might be a diversion. For a time Nimitz even suspected that the enemy, with almost his entire strength, might attempt simultaneous operations in the Aleutians, the central Pacific and the southwest Pacific, in the latter instance using the forces left in position at the end of Operation MO. Compounding these difficulties were two other matters that had to be answered. As the details of the Japanese objectives grew, the Americans wondered whether the enemy was seriously contemplating use of the whole Combined Fleet to capture islands in the wildly desolate western Aleutians and an atoll almost at the western end of the Hawaiian chain. And there was always the question of whether or not the Japanese were mounting a deliberate and elaborate hoax by radio deception. The Americans could make no sense of the enemy's apparent intentions.

But the sheer volume of radio traffic that initially raised doubts about authenticity in the end answered them. Both Nimitz and King were convinced that their cryptanalysts knew their business and accepted that, while their estimates could and did vary greatly, they would not be hoodwinked by a plan of deception. Too many highly classified signals had been made by the middle of May for there to be any real question that the signals themselves were genuine, and Nimitz was convinced that the enemy's overextensive and unwise use of radio had been necessitated by a tight operational schedule. In this Nimitz was correct. Because of the difficulties presented by his impossible timetable, Yamamoto had no means of distributing his orders other than by radio.[22]

The question of authenticity was not resolved until after 20 May. Before that time the American priority was to find out the contents of Japanese signals. The most important part of this effort involved the positive identification of the objective referred to as *AF* by the Japanese. Before May intelligence at Pearl Harbor suspected that *AF* referred to Midway, and for two reasons. First, one of the Japanese aircraft shot down over Pearl Harbor on 7 December had yielded a partially destroyed coded map. The code used letters in the place of bearings, and was known to the Japanese as their *chi-he* system. It was intended as much to confuse the enemy as to ensure simplicity and the minimum of error in voice procedure.[23] From the map the Americans had deduced that *AH* referred to Pearl Harbor, and by reconstruction of the map Pacific Fleet intelligence had come to the conclusion that *AF* was in the general vicinity of Midway. Given the virtual absence of anything in the vicinity of Midway except the atoll itself, the conclusion was that *AF* signified Midway. Second, a single scouting mission by flying boats over Midway in March had referred to *AF*, and this was remembered in May. Even more to the point was that when the Americans began to burrow into the Japanese plan of campaign they found reference to an Operation K, which they deduced would take place between 15 and 20 May. This they found out to be a mission conducted by long-range flying boats in the central Pacific, subsequently discovered to be in support of a certain Operation MI. The implication of the main operation's designation was not lost upon men who knew that Operation MO had been directed against Port Moresby. When this *MI* designation was tied in with the Operation K directive warning against American aircraft at *AF* and ordering refueling to be carried out at *AG*, the American intelligence teams worked their way along the island chain until they came up with what they believed were the correct answers. Since Midway alone had aircraft of which the enemy would take note, *AF* had to refer to the atoll and *AG* had to mean the French Frigate Shoals. The Pacific Fleet staff, however, was hesitant to endorse this conclusion. The reasoning was logical, but with so much dependent on the outcome of the intelligence effort, the staff demanded confirmation.

This was provided in the form of one of the best-known intelligence coups of the war. On or about 10 May the two men in charge of the navy's intelligence effort at Pearl Harbor, the fleet intelligence officer, Lieutenant Commander Edwin T. Layton, and the head of cryptanalysis, Lieutenant Commander Joseph J. Rochefort, obtained Nimitz's permission to "plant" information on the Japanese. Rochefort dreamed up a scheme that would have Pearl Harbor send Midway instructions to broadcast a plain language signal reporting that the atoll's water distillation system had broken down. Oahu's orders were to be sent by cable. The hope was that Midway's signal would be monitored and that the eavesdropper would then report the signal in a code that the Americans had already broken. If the Japanese obliged, any use of *AF* as geographical locator would be the confirmation that the staff hoped for. To add to the deception and give credibility to Midway's signal, Pearl Harbor would signal back to Midway that a unit would be sent posthaste to repair the distillation system. (This is how such an emergency would be handled. Any malfunction in the distillation plant was a serious matter, for the highest point above sea level on the atoll was 39 feet and there was no fresh water on Midway.) The Japanese took the bait. The monitoring station on Wake overheard Midway's signal and made the report that Rochefort wanted it to make. When Wake's message was recovered Layton had his confirmation, and subsequently he had the satisfaction of knowing that the alleged shortage of fresh water on the atoll had come to the attention of the Combined Fleet, whose staff made arrangements for a water ship as part of the logistics support for the intended garrison.

By the middle of May Nimitz had been given sufficient material by his intelligence unit to know that the main enemy effort would almost certainly be made against Midway. On 15 May the intelligence summary predicted that the enemy would also make an effort against Dutch Harbor between 30 May and 10 June, but the cryptanalysts had been unable to deduce whether this would take the form of a raid or a deliberate attempt to seize the base. Their conclusion, however, was that this operation in the Aleutians probably represented a diversion in support of the main effort in the central Pacific.[24] American planning had already begun to take shape at this point, as indeed it was obliged to do if preparations were to be made to meet an enemy attack in late May or early June. Though the evidence was nowhere near complete, Nimitz was aware by 13–14 May that he and King needed to define their priorities and put in hand certain preliminary arrangements over the next few days if the intention to counter an enemy offensive was to be given any substance.

Nimitz's opportunity to initiate such a move came in the form of a signal sent to him by King on 13 May. In many ways it was a curious signal, untypical of King in being both overly cautious and ill-considered. In it he opined that Port Moresby was likely to be the enemy's next objective and that Halsey should exercise great restraint in the handling of his task force. Worried about the safety of his last remaining carriers, and perhaps concerned because of Halsey's well-known aggressiveness, King indicated that Halsey should be directed not to operate beyond the range of Allied shore-based air cover and not within range of enemy land-based aircraft.[25] Compliance with this order would certainly result in Halsey's being unable to threaten or meet any moves that the enemy might make; "hamstrung and hobbled" was Halsey's own comment on the effect that these orders would have had on his operations.[26] King suggested as well that the service units from the *Yorktown* and the *Lexington* be put ashore at New Caledonia and Fiji, where they would be able to handle shore-based carrier air groups. King's inclination towards such an eventual deployment of carrier aircraft, in precisely the form where they lost their great asset of mobility, was a reflection of his pessimism after the battle of the Coral Sea and his despair over not securing timely help for the defense of the southwest Pacific from the army air force.[27]

Nimitz replied to the signal the same day, attaching a liberal interpretation of King's thoughts regarding Halsey's freedom of action. Nimitz set aside the unnecessarily restrictive effect that obedience to King's instructions would have involved. But this was not too important a matter, for King's wishes were to be overtaken by events. Nimitz had in mind for Halsey certain other matters which concerned not the tactical but the strategic handling of Task Force 16. Nimitz shared King's concern about the safety of the southwest Pacific. Like King, he had no real confidence in the notion of army air force formations in Australia and at Hawaii being able to move from those theaters in sufficient time and strength to prove an effective defense in this theater. Again like King, Nimitz wanted to see the southwest Pacific reinforced in its own right and on a permanent basis and not subjected to a reshuffling of forces on an ad hoc basis to meet emergencies as and when they arose. He had no desire to see the defenses of Australia and Hawaii denuded; he needed the forces present in these theaters to stay where they were to meet the various threats that the Pacific Fleet anticipated would materialize in the very near future.

Nimitz's belief was that the enemy would mount offensives against Port Moresby, against Ocean and Nauru, between Samoa and the Line Islands, and against Oahu. Thus Nimitz had to raise with King the whole question of the deployment of American carrier forces. With only two carriers the Americans could not cover all eventualities. Nimitz knew that with little prospect of reinforcement, a deployment had to be made and the choice was between keeping Task Force 16 in the southwest Pacific or bringing it back to the Hawaiian Islands. If the enemy's intentions were what Nimitz now assumed them to be, then he and MacArthur needed to know in whose theater the carrier force was to operate.[28]

On 15 May King replied to Nimitz's message. In his signal King elaborated his earlier arguments but covered no new ground. Though he acknowledged the signs of an enemy move against the Aleutians and Midway, he remained convinced that the enemy would make his main effort in the southwest Pacific. Any Japanese attack on Midway, King asserted, was likely to be a feint. In support of this view he cited the move of various forces to Truk. These were to include thirteen heavy cruisers and twenty-four destroyers of the Second Fleet, and between five and seven carriers, four battleships and eleven destroyers of the carrier force.[29] King's analysis was perhaps the inevitable consequence of trying to interpret incomplete information. What Negat and Hypo had picked up were deatils not simply of Operations AL and MI but also of the operations in the southwest Pacific—against Port Moresby, New Caledonia, Fiji and Samoa—that were to follow the initial and main effort against the Aleutians and Midway. Given the fragmentary evidence and the great uncertainty surrounding the all-important question of timing, Negat and King had reversed the correct sequence of anticipated events. Hypo and Nimitz, perhaps because the immediacy of the situation helped direct their deliberations, were in the process of putting the sequence in proper order.[30] Later events were to show who was right and who was wrong. They also showed something else— that neither the Belconnen station in Australia nor the British in Ceylon were fully taken into the confidence of Washington and Pearl Harbor. The exchange of views on intelligence assessments and command decisions was the closed preserve of King and Nimitz, and the two passed information that was deliberately withheld from the British.[31] It was a small indicator of the way in which King tried to exclude the British from events that as late as 21 May he wrote to the First Sea Lord, Admiral of the Fleet Sir Dudley Pound, informing him that at the battle of the Coral Sea the Japanese had lost one carrier and had had another damaged. King also claimed that the Americans had suffered only "damage" to two of their own carriers.[32] It was a rather shabby response to a request for information on the battle.

Nimitz, in the restrained manner of a subordinate telling his superior he is wrong, repeated the Pearl Harbor assessment in another signal sent to King that same day. Armed as he then was with the latest intelligence appreciations, Nimitz set out the view that although the Japanese seemingly intended to mount a triple offensive in the southwest, central and northern Pacific between 25 May and 15 June, their main effort would be made in the central Pacific. It was a measure of the urgency of Nimitz's position that at this time he was replying to King's signals within a matter of hours of their arrival; King was taking one or two days to reply to Nimitz. And it was a measure of the urgency of the Pacific Fleet's position that Nimitz had already resorted to a strategem designed to force King's hand.[33]

When he passed King's instructions regarding the handling of Task Force 16 along with his own interpretation of these orders to Halsey, Nimitz also sent a message that neither he nor Halsey recorded in their signals logs. Far from warning Halsey not to become involved with enemy land-based aircraft, Nimitz told Halsey to make sure that he was sighted the next day by the enemy. At the time Halsey was to the east of the southern New Hebrides, awaiting the assembly of all his task groups and killing time before he moved north against the Japanese forces bound for Ocean and Nauru. The odds favored the American operation: Halsey, armed with information supplied by intelligence at Pearl Harbor, knew of the timing of Operation RY and the composition of the forces involved in it. Moreover, the Americans knew that the Japanese air units at Tulagi and Makin lacked the numbers to mount more than a single-phase reconnaissance of the sea area bound in the west by the Solomons and New Hebrides and in the east by the Gilbert and Ellice islands. Since the daily flights from Tulagi and Makin barely overlapped, Halsey should have had few problems in timing his run towards Ocean and Nauru so that the enemy patrols would be sidestepped and the invasion convoys annihilated. He did not know the exact position and course of the latter, but he knew when the enemy landing was scheduled to take place and was thus in a position to time his own advance so that he could overwhelm the enemy with ease.

The Nimitz calculation appears to have been that the premature revelation of a carrier force in the area would force the Japanese to abandon Operation RY, and deny them Ocean and Nauru just as effectively as a successful naval action would. Indeed with the discovery of Task Force 16 on the morning of 15 May (the afternoon of the fourteenth in Pearl Harbor), the Japanese called off their planned landings, and Operation RY was formally abandoned the following day. In this way the Americans ensured that the two islands had a three-month respite from the rigors of Japanese occupation. The Japanese took Nauru on 23 August and Ocean three days later under circumstances quite different from those the South Seas Force had envisaged in April.[34]

But the real reason for Nimitz's course of action was the belief that the planned Japanese efforts in the southwest Pacific would be paralyzed by the sudden appearance and then equally rapid disappearance of an American carrier task force in the area. Nimitz hoped that he could check any relatively small-scale enemy operation in the southwest Pacific by instilling an element of uncertainty into Japanese minds. Moreover, he wanted to lead the enemy into thinking that American carrier forces were in this theater, when in fact it was his intention to pull them back to the central Pacific as quickly and furtively as possible. The difficulty was obtaining King's permission for the American withdrawal, but of course once Task Force 16 was discovered in the southwest Pacific Nimitz had every excuse to recall it. The immediate consequence of this otherwise peculiar set of circumstances—with the Americans seemingly ruining a splendid chance of registering a small but significant success—was that Nimitz was able to recall Halsey as a result of his being discovered. When Nimitz signaled to King for permission to recall on the fifteenth, no reply was immediately made. Nimitz recalled Halsey on his own initiative the following day.[35] Thus Nimitz deliberately placed King in a position of having to agree with him. If King failed to reply to Nimitz's move he endorsed it, and it was virtually impossible for him to deliberately counter it.[36]

Much to Nimitz's annoyance King did not signal until the seventeenth, but when he did he accepted the whole Pearl Harbor thesis. Because of the vast and irreconcilable difference between the estimations of the intelligence staffs in Washington and Pearl Harbor, King ordered a rechecking of all data with the Pearl Harbor interpretation given due regard. The reevaluation of information by the Washington intelligence establishment, made known to the army and army air force commands at Washington on the sixteenth, indicated that the Japanese indeed planned to move in the Aleutians and against Midway, probably at the end of May rather than at the beginning of the following month, and against the southwest Pacific in the middle or latter part of June.[37] King accepted the conclusion that the Japanese planned to land on Midway but still thought that the enemy might first raid Pearl Harbor.

Now that King had finally come round to the Nimitz assessment of enemy intentions, there was no question of his refusing to agree to the demand for the concentration of the Pacific Fleet for the defense of the Hawaiian Islands. Moreover, there was no disagreement between the two men over the measure of the American effort; neither Nimitz nor King considered for a moment the possibility of voluntarily ceding Midway. Both believed that in attacking Midway the enemy sought two objectives: to secure the atoll itself and to goad the Pacific Fleet into battle. Both agreed that there was no question of their rolling with the punch and then counterattacking the overextended and untenable lines of communication the Japanese would be called upon to sustain if they were to take full advantage of their newly acquired "asset."[38] King and Nimitz were determined to fight for Midway, and if nothing else Yamamoto showed that he was correct in judging American psychology on this matter.

For King and Nimitz the problem was how to oppose the Japanese. With the balance of forces favoring the enemy, and with no prospect of the Americans matching Japanese numbers before the end of 1942, the Americans could not risk a head-on fleet engagement. Rather they had to employ what King called "strong attritional tactics," by which he meant opposing the enemy with a combination of submarines, land-based air power and carriers, the latter being handled in a tactically defensive manner that minimized the risks to themselves and their escorting cruisers.[39]

Thus by 17 May the Americans had the basis of a response to the Japanese plan of campaign, yet it could be said that American difficulties actually grew worse over the next twelve days before they began to ease at the end of the month. The American problems entailed questions of coordination between the commands of MacArthur and Nimitz; of proper cooperation with the army and the army air force; of the deployment of naval forces; and, critically, of recovering as much information about the enemy's plan of campaign as possible. Even as late as 17 May intelligence had more gaps than pieces of information, and it was to be another week before the Americans were reasonably confident that they had all there was to know about Japanese plans. In fact after 24 May there was little the Americans could further discover; on that day, in the course of the celebrated Nimitz-Rochefort interview, Nimitz was informed that the Japanese had changed their operational code and that nothing more would be gained from cryptanalysis for several weeks.[40]

By the twenty-fourth, however, the Americans had secured just about the whole of Operations AL and MI, provided by Yamamoto himself four days earlier. On the twentieth Yamamoto had issued a complete operational order to all units involved in Operations AL and MI, its monstrous length being the clue that seemingly alerted Belconnen station to its nature.[41] Seven days later the order had been 85 percent recovered. Still the question remained of when the Japanese attack would begin. To date all calculations had been pieced together either from partially recovered text or by sliderule calculations involving ship speeds against distance. The problem was that the operational date-time group in the 20 May signal was locked in a special cipher, only encountered by the Americans in three earlier signals. Since one of these, made at the Coral Sea, was a garble, the cipher had defied American attempts to break it. But on 27 May two members of Rochefort's team, Lieutenant Commanders Joseph Finnegan and Wesley Wright, broke a system that they found to be polyalphabetic with independent mixed cipher alphabets and with the exterior plain and key alphabets in two different scripts of Japanese writing, *kata kana* and *hira gana*.[42] At this stage in proceedings so monumental an effort was probably unnecessary, for the Americans had already decided that the enemy's attacks would probably begin on 3 June in the Aleutians and on the fourth against Midway. Wright and Finnegan provided the best confirmation of these estimations there could be.

Thus by 28 May Nimitz had virtually every detail of the Japanese plan, though in reality he had all he needed to know on the twenty-fourth. He had had to make his initial deployments before that time. As early as 14 May he had declared a state of "fleet-opposed invasion" for the Hawaiian Islands, a means whereby he secured command of all forces in the islands except for tactical control of the army's ground forces.[43] A week later, on the twenty-first, King and Marshall between them gave the Aleutians a similar status.[44] For a time the Americans considered making no move to defend the Aleutians other than with what was already there. Nimitz was thus inclined because it seemed that an enemy offensive in the area would lead the Japanese nowhere. In the event, however, perhaps prompted by King's instruction of the seventeenth to form a North Pacific Force,[45] he chose to send what was not much more than a token force to Alaska.[46] To command this force Nimitz appointed Rear Admiral Robert A. Theobald. The latter left Pearl Harbor in the destroyer *Reid* on 22 May, arriving at Kodiak on the twenty-seventh.[47]

Before the final details of the enemy's intentions were sorted out, Nimitz had to arrange various force deployments. For the moment the question of task force allocations had to wait. Until the carrier forces arrived at Pearl Harbor and the state of the *Yorktown* was ascertained, there was no question of Nimitz being able to decide upon the composition of his task forces. As it turned out Nimitz had little choice in the matter, but he was called upon to make early decisions with regard to the deployment of battleships and submarines. Once more, however, the situation regarding the former resolved itself without Nimitz having to make any hard decisions.

The factors that had led Nimitz to dispense with the services of the battle force when confronted by the crisis in the southwest Pacific in April still applied in mid-May. The intervening weeks had not changed this situation, and the fact remained that in an action where American carriers might well have to run hard for safety, the battle force was a slow and dangerous liability. The logistics margin of Pearl Harbor did not allow Nimitz the luxury of using such thirsty ships, the desperate shortage of escorts meant that there was virtually no screening force for a battle line. The seven battleships of Task Force 1—the *Maryland, Pennsylvania, Tennessee, Colorado, New Mexico, Mississippi* and *Idaho*—were to be kept at San Francisco and did not return to Pearl Harbor until August, when the danger had passed. This did not prevent their putting to sea at the time of the battle of Midway in response to various sightings and alarms about the security of the West Coast,[48] but there was as much validity to these sightings and reports as there had been in February at the time of the somewhat notorious "battle of Los Angeles."[49]

No doubt Nimitz would have welcomed two newly commissioned battleships, the *Washington* and the *North Carolina*, as additions to his carrier forces, but at this time both were in the Atlantic—the former with the British Home Fleet—having been sent to support Royal Navy operations by King in response to a British request for capital ship support.[50] Nimitz, therefore, had no battleships available to support his carriers, a major though unrealized weakness on the American part. The intelligence effort had not been able to unearth the fact that the Japanese battle force would be at sea. The Japanese battle force was at its base at Hashirajima, where it formed the major part of Yamamoto's own tactical command; the commander in chief was in immediate contact with it and had no need to signal it. As a result, American intelligence teams never knew that more than two or four battleships would be with the enemy formations.[51]

The submarine question was complicated and urgent. If the Pacific Fleet was to deploy submarines in support of Midway and the Aleutians, the units would have to sail from the middle of May onwards or be recalled to take up positions on the enemy's lines of advance. On 16 May the Americans had about seventy-nine submarines in the Pacific, but less than a score of these were available for deployment. Of this total fourteen were immediately put out of the reckoning. These included ten boats—the *S-11*, *S-12*, *S-13*, *S-14*, *S-15*, *S-16*, *S-17*, *Barracuda*, *Bass* and *Bonita*—that were either stationed on the Panama Canal or patrolling its Pacific approaches. One more submarine, the *S-33*, had been similarly employed on such patrols, but at the time it was en route to San Diego for an overhaul. The *S-30*, *S-31* and *S-32* were already at that base. They were being made ready for operations in the northern Pacific, but they were not to be overhauled and repaired in time to be in the Aleutians to oppose Operation AL. Thus the effective American submarine strength in the Pacific was not seventy-nine but sixty-five. This total does not take account of such units as the *Growler*, then on her way to Pearl Harbor but yet to make her first operational cruise of the war. She did not proceed to sea on her first mission in time for Midway; her departure for war was to be delayed until 20 June.

On the Aleutians station, or proceeding to the Aleutians, were another six of the old short-range S-class submarines: the *S-18*, *S-23*, *S-27*, *S-28*, *S-34* and *S-35*. Because of their characteristics and the nature of the situation, these would have to be deployed defensively. As we have already noted in the order of battle for the Coral Sea action, eleven sister ships were deployed at Brisbane. The 201st Submarine Division, consisting of the *S-37*, *S-38*, *S-39*, *S-40* and *S-41*, was a refugee from the Asiatic Fleet; the other six units that made up the Fifty-third Submarine Division—the *S-42*, *S-43*, *S-44*, *S-45*, *S-46* and *S-47*—had been sent out to Australia from America's East Coast. Though some of these boats were at sea in late May and early June, their moment had been at the time of the Coral Sea battle. Then they had not been able to play much of a part in the action; now they had no role to play as events unfolded in the central and northern Pacific.

On the other side of Australia, at Freemantle, were nineteen boats. Like the units of the 201st Submarine Division, they were survivors from the Asiatic Fleet, and the local submarine command, located at Perth, had been established on 3 March as part of the reorganization that took place with the collapse of the ABDA Command and the fall of Southeast Asia. The commander, Rear Admiral W. R. Purnell, USN, who had raised his flag on 3 April, had modern long-range boats built in the late thirties under command.

There were no major base facilities at Perth, and the boats had to be rotated with units from Pearl Harbor. Boats from the two stations patrolled Japanese-held islands in the central and western Pacific, and the arrangement was such that units could be exchanged while Freemantle remained able to mount a major effort in the South China Sea and in the general area of the Philippines.[52] Thus on 16 May eleven of the nineteen boats from the Freemantle station were at sea. These were the *Porpoise, Pike, Pickerel, Permit, Salmon, Seal, Snapper, Saury, Swordfish, Searaven* and *Seawolf*. Of these the *Porpoise* and the *Pike* were employed on patrols that were scheduled to end in Pearl Harbor. The remainder—the *Skipjack, Stingray, Sturgeon, Sargo, Spearfish, Sculpin, Sailfish* and *Seadragon*—were all in base between patrols except for two, the *Stingray* and the *Sculpin*, which were to proceed to sea before the end of May. Like the *Pike* and the *Porpoise*, the *Stingray* was to end her patrol at Pearl Harbor, which she reached on 23 July. In return, four of the submarines then operating out of Pearl Harbor were on patrols that were to end at Perth. These were the *Tautog, Gar, Grampus* and *Grayback*, and it was in the course of these patrols that the first three were sent to Truk in the unavailing attempt to catch the *Shokaku* after the battle of the Coral Sea. They arrived too late to contact the *Shokaku* and they missed the *Zuikaku*, but it was in the course of their prowling around Truk that one of their number, the *Tautog*, accounted for the *I-28* as that particular submarine returned to base after the Coral Sea action. The same day the *Triton*, similarly having missed the *Shokaku* as she returned to Kure, accounted for the *I-164* with her last remaining bow torpedo.[53]

Of the remaining twenty-five boats at Pearl Harbor eleven were on patrol. These were the *Dolphin, Cuttlefish, Pollack, Pompano, Triton, Tuna, Grenadier, Gato, Greenling, Drum* and *Silversides*. All were involved in profitable patrols at this time. The concentration of the Combined Fleet for Operations AL and MI had left the American submarines with the run of the Pacific, and they made full use of it. May 1942 proved to be one of their most successful months of the war. Amongst the various Japanese ships sunk, two were particularly noteworthy. One was the *Taiyomaru*, a 14,500-ton passenger ship sunk by the *Grenadier* while carrying engineers, scientists and technicians to the Indies for work in the oil fields of Java and Sumatra.[54] The other was the seaplane carrier *Mizuho*, sunk by the *Drum*. She was the largest Japanese combatant sunk thus far in the war.

The boats either at Pearl Harbor or operating from the base had to be the backbone of any submarine contribution to the defense of Midway and the Hawaiian Islands. The newly appointed submarine commander, Rear Admiral Robert E. English, wanted to use his units offensively in long-range search-and-destroy missions, but Nimitz, a submariner himself, overruled him. He was determined to leave that role to aircraft from Midway, which were better provided than the slower submarines to carry out this role. Nimitz was determined to deploy the submarines defensively in front of Midway. Because the Americans knew the basic form of the enemy's plan of campaign, they were able to tie their submarines to a defensive role in the hope that the enemy's advance to Midway would take him over the patrol lines that were to be placed in his path.

To support the forces that were to be at sea and on Midway, the submarines were formed into a single organization, Task Force 7. This had three subordinate formations, of which Task Group 7.1 was the largest and most important. It consisted of twelve boats. The *Nautilus, Tambor, Grayling, Trout* and *Gudgeon* formed the core of the task group. The *Grouper*, then on her first patrol, and the *Cachelot, Dolphin* and *Flying Fish*, were moving out for operations when they received orders to steer for defensive positions in support of Midway, while three other units, the *Cuttlefish, Grenadier* and *Gato*, were recalled as they returned to Pearl Harbor to thicken up the screen. The returning units, along with the *Dolphin*, were assigned patrol areas farthest from Midway. The *Cuttlefish* was directed to a station patrol 700 miles due west of Midway, to a position that intelligence believed was where certain enemy formations were to rendezvous before the battle. The other three, the *Dolphin, Grenadier* and *Gato*, were instructed to deploy on the arc 250 to 310 degrees at a range of 200 miles from Midway. The *Tambor, Trout, Grayling, Nautilus, Grouper* and *Gudgeon* were deployed on the arc 240 to 360 degrees at a range of 150 miles from Midway. The *Flying Fish* and the *Cachelot* were placed on station patrol on bearings of 310 and 350 degrees from Midway at a range of 50 miles. Except for those on station patrol, all the submarines were assigned sectors of 20 degrees and ordered to operate within 20 miles of the midpoint of their sector chords. Like their colleagues of Task Groups 7.2 and 7.3, they were to operate at periscope depth during daylight hours.

Task Group 7.2 was to consist of three submarines, the *Narwhal, Plunger* and *Trigger*, deployed as a support group at 30-mile intervals on the line between 45 and 225 degrees with its midpoint on a bearing of 75 degrees from Midway at a range of 425 miles. This deployment placed the submarines to the east of east northeast of Midway and in a position either to go forward to support Task Group 7.1 or to support the carriers if they were forced to run for cover. The American plan of campaign was to allow their carriers to withdraw over this patrol line if the need arose. In the event, however, the *Plunger* was able to move to her allotted station in time for the battle; she was unable to leave Pearl Harbor on her second war patrol until 9 June, when she set out for Shanghai. In her absence misfortune attended Task Group 7.2. When the *Narwhal* and the *Trigger* were ordered to move forward to support Midway, the latter had the ill luck of running herself onto a submerged coral wall within sight of the atoll.

Task Group 7.3 was to consist of four units, the *Tarpon, Pike, Finback* and

Growler, but the latter missed the battle. She proved unable to leave Pearl Harbor until 20 June, when she set out for Alaskan waters—via Midway. The others were deployed some 300 miles to the north of Oahu. Like the units of Task Group 7.2, they were to conduct station patrol. They were deployed to guard against the faint possibility that the enemy might launch a diversionary raid against Pearl Harbor. The submarines were ordered to be prepared to chase the enemy if so instructed.

The units from Task Group 7.1 that were at Pearl Harbor sailed between 18 and 24 May. The *Narwhal* sailed on 28 May, the *Trigger* the following day. The *Tarpon* and the *Pike* sailed on the thirtieth, the latter just five days after she arrived at Pearl Harbor from Freemantle. Thus of the sixty-five boats in the Pacific or on the western Australia station, just twenty-three were available to support fleet operations in defense of Midway and the Aleutians. In addition, six boats on distant patrol were diverted to search for and attack the enemy during his withdrawal after the battle. These submarines were the *Porpoise, Pollack, Pompano, Tuna, Drum* and *Greenling*, the first named being one of the units from Freemantle.[55] A couple of fleeting contacts were obtained, but none of the boats were able to make an attack on any enemy unit.[56]

At the time the Pacific Fleet worked out its submarine arrangements, Nimitz had to attend to the problem of reinforcing the air group at Midway and the naval forces in the Aleutians. Both matters involved naval cooperation with the army air force, though obviously only the situation with regard to Midway directly and immediately affected Nimitz. In addition, Nimitz had to take steps to picket the line of the Hawaiian Islands, in particular ensuring that the French Frigate Shoals were denied to the enemy, who would use them to refuel the flying boats involved in Operation K.

Midway was Nimitz's special problem. The atoll was strategically significant, but it had taken the famous Hepburn Report of December 1938 to spell out the obvious and to initiate the chain of events that was supposed to lead to the atoll's development as a base second only to Pearl Harbor in importance. In August 1941 and some twenty million dollars later, the air station on the atoll was commissioned, the first squadron of Catalinas arriving on station in November. In May 1942 the base had to be made as secure as possible against air, naval and amphibious attack, and it also had to be given a hard punch in terms of strike aircraft and a good reconnaissance capability if the "strong attritional tactics" of King were to have any chance of success. With Midway consisting of only two islets which between them covered less than two square miles, it was impossible to provide defense in depth for the ground forces or effective dispersal and passive defense for the aircraft and flying boats that were at or to be deployed to the atoll.

At the outbreak of war Midway was garrisoned by the 834 officers and men of the Sixth Defense Battalion. A single naval squadron of Catalina flying boats was on station.[57] It was withdrawn soon after the start of hostilities, but in the course of December the Marine Corps provided both land and air reinforcements for Midway. Artillery that had been promised back in September began to arrive when the seaplane tenders *Wright* and *Tangier* brought in three batteries detached from the Fourth Defense Battalion, plus a light flak group from the same unit.[58] In addition, on 26 December the *Tangier* brought in the ground elements for the fighter squadron that had been flown into Midway the previous day from the *Saratoga*.[59] This squadron, the 221st, consisted of fourteen F2A-3 Buffalo fighters. On Eastern Island it joined the 231st Squadron, made up of seventeen SB2U-3 Vindicator dive-bombers, which had arrived on station on 17 December. Apart from the latter squadron being redesignated as the 241st on 1 March as part of the process of establishing the Twenty-second Marine Air Group command on Midway, there was no change in the American order of battle on the atoll before May. What did happen on Midway between January and April, however, was the slow but steady expansion of facilities, the base gradually securing the means to maintain a larger garrison and air group.

After Nimitz's visit to Midway on 2 and 3 May reinforcements started to move along the Hawaiian chain to the atoll. Though they did not arrive until the last week of May, these reinforcements were substantial. The light cruiser *St. Louis*, in the company of the destroyer *Case*, was to put into the atoll on 25 May with a battery of eight 37-mm antiaircraft guns from the Third Defense Battalion and two rifle companies from the Second Marine Raider Battalion. The latter battalion, in some ways the forerunner of special forces, quickly demonstrated its skill in supplementing the atoll's defenses with a formidable array of improvised antipersonnel mines and traps. Captain Donald H. Hastie's C Company was deployed on Sand Island; Lieutenant John Apergis's D Company went to Eastern Island.[60] The following day the aircraft ferry *Kittyhawk* arrived with sixteen Dauntlesses, seven Wildcats, twelve 3-in and eighteen 20-mm antiaircraft guns (like the other artillery detached from the Third Defense Battalion), plus a platoon of light tanks.[61] Subsequently the destroyer *Gwin*, after having returned from the southwest Pacific before the remainder of Task Force 16 did, made a high-speed run to Midway with more reinforcements, leaving Oahu on 23 May and arriving back there on 1 June.[62] On 31 May the merchantman *Nira Luckenbach*, in the company of the destroyer *Mustin*, brought in the last equipment and supplies that were to reach Midway before battle was joined.[63] She brought with her ground equipment for the air group and 3,000 barrels of high-octane aviation fuel. The latter was needed by the base because on 22 May some 400,000 gallons of avgas had been destroyed by an accidental detonation of the emergency demolitions that were then being laid at the islands' installations.[64] For the *Mustin*, escorting the *Nira Luckenbach* was a task that had her turn round twice in Pearl Harbor in a short period. Having only just arrived there from Samoa, she was ordered out to Midway on 25 May, returning to Pearl Harbor on 5 June. She sailed again on 7 June, this time to help in the search for survivors of a battle she so narrowly missed.[65]

If the order of battle for the submarines was relatively straightforward, that for the aircraft was much more confused. In the days immediately before the battle the number of aircraft at Midway fluctuated as reinforcements were sent to the atoll and various aircraft already there were detached on a variety of duties. It would also appear that in the last days before battle was joined the overcrowding on the atoll was such that a policy of dispersal was applied to the Catalinas, a small number of them being deployed to the Pearl and Hermes Reef.[66] And of course the paper strength of Midway was different from its operational strength.

At 0001 on successive dates between 31 May and 4 June inclusive, the total number of aircraft stationed on Midway was 109, 111, 118, 110 and 121. At 0001 on 3 June the operational strength of Midway appears to have been exactly 100, and 111 one day later. On 4 June, when battle was joined, the grand total of 121 aircraft on Midway was made up of 21 bombers from the Seventh Air Force of the army air force, 6 torpedo bombers and 30 Catalinas from the navy, and 64 aircraft of various types from the marine corps.[67] While the units had their own commanders, operational command of all aircraft (regardless of service) was excercised by Commander Logan C. Ramsey. Especially selected for this post by Nimitz and his chief of staff, he did not arrive at the atoll until 29 May.[68]

The total of twenty-one bombers from the army air force consisted of four Marauders, flown into the atoll on 29 May, eight Flying Fortresses, which arrived on the thirtieth, and nine more Fortresses, which reached the base on the following day. The Marauders were from the Eighteenth Reconnaissance and Sixty-ninth (Medium) Bombardment Groups; the Fortresses were drawn from the Twenty-sixth, Thirty-first, Seventy-second and 431st (Heavy) Bombardment Squadrons.[69] The six torpedo bombers were TBF Avengers, the latest aircraft to enter service with the navy. These six were from the nineteen-strong torpedo squadron of the *Hornet*. The squadron had flown from the East to the West Coast, been shipped to Hawaii and missed their carrier by one day. Six of its number were then directed up the Hawaiian chain. They arrived at Midway on 1 June.[70] The other part of the navy's contribution consisted of fourteen Catalina flying boats and sixteen Catalina amphibians. Pearl Harbor had calculated that a total of twenty-three Catalinas were needed to allow Midway to function effectively as a base. This figure was reached by calculating that Midway needed to search a full 180-degree sector between south and north through west and that at this time of year Catalinas could be expected to search 8-degree sectors.[71] On 22 May, the day before this calculation was formally set down on paper, just four Catalinas were at Midway. The total rose to twenty-four on the last day of the month, to twenty-six or twenty-seven over the next three days and then to thirty on 4 June.[72] The Catalinas came from the Twenty-third, Twenty-fourth, Forty-fourth and Fifty-first Patrol Squadrons, and formed the Second Patrol Wing, itself an amalgam of two wings, the First Patrol Wing of Commander Massie Hughes and the Second Patrol Wing of Lieutenant Commander Robert Brixner.[73]

The aircraft from the army and navy (plus the flying boats and amphibians) appear to have enjoyed a high rate of serviceability. This was not the case with the aircraft from the marine corps. The marines had been on station for months and their aircraft had been in constant service. They had a total of sixty-four aircraft on Midway, but accidents and enforced cannibalization reduced this total to fifty-four by 4 June. Of the latter total, seventeen were Dauntlesses, twelve were Vindicators, eighteen were Buffaloes and seven were Wildcats. The established strength of these was, respectively, as follows: nineteen, seventeen, twenty-one and seven. Various accounts also refer to two other units at Midway. One is alleged to have been an old biplane, perhaps an old Curtis, which was retained for some indeterminate purpose and was fated to an equally indeterminate end. The other, a decoy, was a JFU, its locally applied designation standing for "Japanese fouler-upper." It was conspicuously placed on the apron of Eastern Island and performed its suicide role to perfection.[74]

Simply in terms of numbers Midway possessed the equivalent of a carrier air group. But numbers are deceptive. Aside from the Catalinas, the combat aircraft lacked homogeneity. Nimitz had to send to the atoll what was on hand rather than what was needed, and amongst the various types of aircraft at Midway were some that were so obsolescent that they were totally unfit to be considered first line aircraft. Certainly this applied to the Vindicators and Buffaloes of the marine corps, and the uncharitable would have alleged that the same could be said of the Wildcat, even though it was to remain the navy's first-line fighter for some time to come. Of all the naval and marine aircraft on Midway only the Avenger was modern, and the forthcoming battle was to mark its disastrous operational debut. The army aircraft, on the other hand, were modern and good. But the quality of pilots, whether army, navy or marine, was varied. None of the army pilots had been trained to operate against shipping, and the Marauder crews were amazed when they were later armed with torpedoes for use against the enemy. Amongst the marines all-too-frequent rotation of flying personnel meant that standards were constantly slipping. One marine general noted that the pilots who were lost at Midway in June were inferior to those they

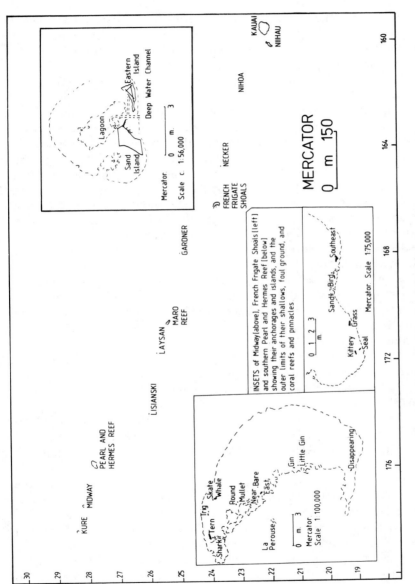

INSETS of Midway [above], French Frigate Shoals [left] and southern Pearl and Hermes Reef [below] showing their anchorages and islands, and the outer limits of their shallows, foul ground, and coral reefs and pinnacles

The Western Islands of the Hawaiian Group

had replaced and who fought at Guadalcanal after August.[75] Of the twenty-one pilots who arrived with the *Kittyhawk* were seventeen who had just graduated from the marines' flying school. Inevitably they were assigned the Vindicators, their low level of skill ensuring that they should be detailed the poorest quality aircraft available to the defense. Not surprisingly they wrote off two during their first familiarization flight. If the air group at Midway was to have any impact on the forthcoming battle, the aircrew would have to rise above the shortcomings of their own training and aircraft.

While the air group at Midway was augmented, Nimitz also had to attend to the problem of deploying various units along the Hawaiian chain. Patrol boats were allocated to Kure and Midway, and a single converted tuna boat was deployed to each of Necker, Gardner Pinnacles, Laysan and Lisanski. To the Pearl and Hermes Reef Nimitz was to deploy three ships, the minesweeper *Vireo*, the yacht *Crystal* and the gasoline tanker *Kaloli*. Likewise, three units were to be put on station at the sensitive French Frigate Shoals, not simply for the purpose of denying them to the flying boats of Operation K. The planning staff at Pearl Harbor had realized that the deployment of so many Catalinas to Midway in readiness for the battle had an unfortunate side effect: they would have to run for cover once contact was established and battle was joined. Because they could not run for Midway they would have to set course back down the chain. Their possible refueling needs and general welfare were major factors in the deployment of the *Ballard* and the *Thornton* to the Shoals. Both were old flush-deck destroyers that had been converted to serve as small seaplane tenders.[76] In company was the destroyer *Clark*, hitherto employed on convoy duties between San Francisco and Pearl Harbor. She was ordered not to put into Oahu at the end of her current mission but to proceed to the Shoals.

The settling of the defensive arrangements for the Aleutians was also a difficult problem, partly because it involved interservice cooperation and partly because the Alaska and Aleutians theater of operations with its severe climate and geography, was certain to all but defy any attempt to defend it. Moreover, the theater, being a low priority both before the outbreak of war and in the first few months of hostilities, had received few troops and aircraft. This may seem strange, in view of the fact that by May 1942 there had been an increase of almost fivefold in the number of troops in Alaska since the previous June. The number had risen from 9,946 officers and men to 45,417.[77] Nature, however, conspired to place formidable obstacles in the path of any attacker or defender of the area. These related to the distances within the theater; its almost total lack of roads and railways; and its climate and vegetation.

Of the whole unfederated Alaskan territory, only those areas washed by the Pacific were strategically important in 1942, yet they were isolated from one another by a harsh terrain and were as far-flung as places in better-known theaters of the Pacific war. Attu, the largest of the islands of the Near Group, was closer to Paramushiro in the Japanese Kurile Islands than it was to Dutch Harbor and Unalaska Island. Moreover, it was almost as far from Dutch Harbor to Juneau, the capital of Alaska, as it was from Midway to Pearl Harbor, and Juneau was not a fleet base that could sustain large-scale operations. The main base for the Aleutians was Seattle, more than ten degrees of latitude to the south of Juneau. Overland communications barely existed and airfields and port facilities were scarcely better provided. This situation was to have one immediate and important effect on military deployment. With so few troops to cover so large an area, and without roads and railways, there was no possibility of a concentrated reserve being moved to a threatened sector. In 1942 the local command had no option but to disperse its combat forces throughout the area. The policy of weakness everywhere through dispersal was one to which there was no alternative.[78] If distances were so great and communications so poor, the area's climate was worse. Fog, snow and rain, with the mercury hovering around zero, were normal. In such conditions navigation at sea and in the air was extremely hazardous. It was an indication of the severity of local weather conditions that of the twenty-five fighters and thirteen medium bombers directed to Alaska on 1 January 1942, no fewer than eleven were lost and six had still to arrive at their destination on the twenty-fifth.[79]

The difficulties experienced in this midwinter operation were so acute that in February the decision was made to build an overland route into Alaska, the Alcan Highway.[80] Such a project, however, was daunting. The mountainous terrain prevented rapid construction, and the tundra posed difficulties of its own. The spongy ground made wheeled movement all but impossible in many areas, and even tracked movement was difficult.[81] Building roads and runways on such ground presented problems of night-marish proportions.

Before the war Alaska had been a backwater, the Americans rightly discounting the possibility that the Japanese would undertake any serious effort to secure it. But the same consideration that had led to the Hepburn Report of 1938 recommending the development of naval air stations at Sitka, on Baranof Island, at Kodiak, on Kodiak Island, and for Dutch Harbor now forced the hand of Nimitz and his superiors: Alaska was national territory, and as such had to be defended.[82]

By May 1942 work on these three bases was so far advanced that they were operational and served as the major defense establishments in Alaska, far larger than the old bases that had been located there at the turn of the century. Sitka, along with Fort Ray, was the main joint operations base. Its weaknesses were remoteness from operational areas, overcrowding and lack of fueling facilities. Sitka had fuel enough for only two weeks.[83] Kodiak, in addition to its seaplane facilities, had an airfield, a submarine base and an excellent deep-water anchorage. Fort Greely was the location of the local military command in Alaska.[84] Dutch Harbor, protected by its garrison at Fort Mears, had also been developed as a submarine base. It did not have a colocated airfield, but Otter Point, alternatively known as Fort Glenn, on neighboring Umnak Island, had been developed as the local air base and as the main and most western American air base in the Aleutians. Its construction, authorized as late as November 1941, had been given top priority after the outbreak of war, and the laying of its steel-mesh airstrip was completed in April. The first operational mission from Otter Point was flown on 20 May. Speed of construction was not matched by quality of product, however.[85] The bounce of the matting on the soft tundra was the subject of much adverse comment by those unfortunate enough to have to fly from the base.[86]

In addition to these three bases, there was a fourth that came close in importance to Sitka, Kodiak and Dutch Harbor–Otter Point. This was the base at Cold Bay, the site of Fort Randall. It was overshadowed by Dutch Harbor to the west and Kodiak to the east, but herein lay its importance. It was vital as a staging post between two main bases and could be used to concentrate air power to support either place. After the outbreak of war the completion of its airfield was afforded the same priority as the airfield at Otter Point.[87] Moreover, the anchorage itself was reputedly the best of the many in the area. It was large enough to take the whole of the American fleet, and its approaches could be covered with relative ease. In May 1942 it had a garrison of about 2,500 troops, almost all of whom were with infantry, field and antiaircraft units. Sitka, by means of comparison, had a garrison of about 2,000; Kodiak an establishment of about 6,000; Dutch Harbor and Fort Mears a garrison of about 5,500 and Otter Point one of approximately 4,000 troops.[88]

A cursory glance at the map reveals that all the American bases were located too far to the east to have any real offensive role. American arrangements were overwhelmingly defensive, covering the eastern Aleutians, Alaska and the West Coast. With but twenty-three Catalinas shared between Kodiak and Dutch Harbor in late May, and these restricted to an operational range of only 400 miles, the theater of 1942 possessed only a minimal reconnaissance capability.[89] Even this role was eroded by the weather, and until the arrival of aircraft with radar, reconnaissance missions over the Aleutians and around Alaska were always difficult and dangerous. There was always the chance that a tired, inexperienced or unlucky crew would fly into a fog-shrouded mountain.[90]

In order to develop Sitka, Kodiak and Dutch Harbor the Americans had to build up a number of small but invaluable staging posts to the area. These

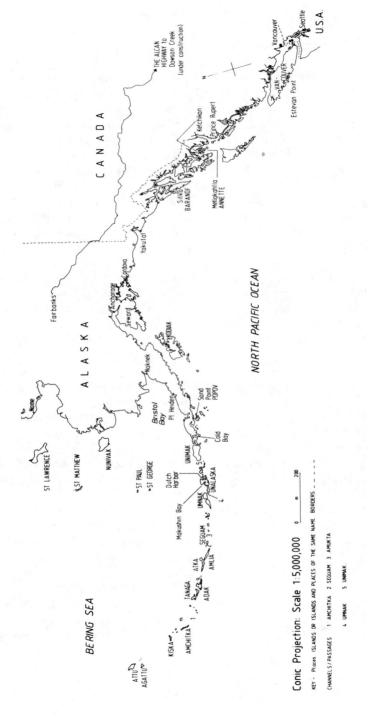

BERING SEA

ATTU
AGATTU

KISKA
AMCHITKA   1
                TANAGA
          ADAK   ATKA
                  AMLIA SEGUAM
                         3
Makushin Bay UMNAK
              2

ST LAWRENCE

ST MATTHEW

NUNIVAK

Nome

ST PAUL
ST GEORGE

Dutch
Harbor
UNALASKA
4
UNIMAK 5

ALASKA

Fairbanks

Naknek

Bristol
Bay
Pt Heiden

Cold
Bay

Sand
Point
POPOV

KODIAK

Seward

Anchorage

Cordova

Yakutat

CANADA

THE ALCAN
HIGHWAY to
Dawson Creek
(under construction)

Ketchikan
Prince Rupert

SITKA
BARANOF

Metlakahtla
ANNETTE

NORTH PACIFIC OCEAN

Vancouver
VAN-
COUVER
Estevan Point

Seattle

U.S.A.

Conic Projection: Scale 1:5,000,000

0   m   200

KEY - Places ISLANDS OR ISLANDS AND PLACES OF THE SAME NAME BORDERS – – – – –

CHANNELS/PASSAGES   1 AMCHITKA   2 SEGUAM   3 AMUKTA

                     4 UMNAK   5 UNIMAK

Aleutians, Southern Alaska and the West Coast Operational Areas, May–June 1942 bases had to be capable of serving seaplanes, flying boats or aircraft, though the base at Seward (Fort Richardson) was alone in having no capacity to service any form of flying machine. The bases that were developed as links on the air ferry route were at Metlakahtla on Annette Island, activated on 2 September 1940; Juneau, activated 1 March 1942; Yakutat, activated on 23 October 1940; Cordova, activated 15 March 1942; Anchorage, activated on 27 June 1940, which was the day after the army's Alaska Defense Command was itself established; Naknek, activated on 22 May 1942; Port Heiden on the Bristol Bay coast of the Alaska Peninsula; and, of course, Cold Bay. Of these air stations two were under Canadian control by the time that the Japanese attack on the Aleutians materialized. The Royal Canadian Air Force's 115th Fighter Squadron arrived at Metlakahtla on 5 May, and its Eighth Bomber-Reconnaissance Squadron occupied Yakutat on 3 June.[91] The major naval bases were at Seward, one day's overland travel from Anchorage, and at Sand Point on Popof Island. The latter had major seaplane facilities. The only other base of importance was at Ketchikan, headquarters of the U.S. Coast Guard in Alaska. As we have already noted, the only major naval base in the general area was at Puget Sound.[92]

Despite the plethora of construction between 1938 and 1941, at the outbreak of war the strategic center of gravity within the Alaskan theater was somewhere between Anchorage and the traditional heartland of Alaska around Fairbanks. This remained the case right up to May 1942 in one crucial respect. Until that time half of the army air force's strength in the theater was at Anchorage. In effect, until Otter Point became operational Dutch Harbor was in front of the forward air defense system, not that much of a system existed. Even as late as June 1942 there were only two radar sets in the theater, a supposedly mobile SCR-270 set at Anchorage and a sited SCR-271 set at Cape Chiniak, Kodiak.[93] This was a far cry from the minimum of twenty sets that had been deemed essential by the local command.[94]

What is clear from these facts is the matter referred to earlier, namely the paucity of overland communications in the area. Even if the Alcan Highway had been operational only half of American needs could have been met, for there was no adequate secondary road system in existence. There was no proper compensation for this sad state of affairs. Sea communication, while still superior to overland communication, was poor. Ice was often a danger, particularly around the turn of the year, and port-handling facilities were rudimentary in most bases. The construction of Otter Point, for example, took nearly four months; there was no port on Umnak, and men and supplies had to be transshipped to barges and moved to Umnak from Chernofski. Though the distance involved was only 11 miles, it was an extremely rough stretch. What is not evident on any map is that, excluding the Amchitka Passage between the Rat and Andreanof islands, there were only four good deep-water channels between the islands that divided the Bering Sea and the Pacific. These were the Unimak, Umnak, Amukta and Seguam Passages. If these channels were held, the way from the Pacific into the Bering Sea and Bristol Bay was effectively barred. One other matter is also not obvious from a map. Though Dutch Harbor was being developed as the major base in Alaska, Unalaska Island provided an alternative anchorage at Makushin Bay, around the coast from Dutch Harbor on the northern shore of the island.

Apart from Otter Point, Makushin Bay was the most western of the American bases in the Aleutians. With the exception of a ten-man weather station on Kiska, there were no other islands in the Aleutians with an American military presence. Before the war some thought had been given to the idea of developing heavy-bomber bases in the western Aleutians, but the notion had been dismissed for a variety of reasons.[95] Confirmation of the wisdom of that decision came on 20 May when the local army commander, Major General Simon B. Buckner, had to be rescued from Kiska by the seaplane tender *Williamson* after being trapped on the island by storm force 11 winds.[96]

Such, then, was the inhospitable area in which the Japanese were to mount Operation AL and which the Americans would try to defend. The various considerations of geographical remoteness, lack of local facilities and vile weather did as much to determine American policy and deployment as straightforward military considerations did.

Even before the declaration of a state of fleet-opposed invasion, the stance of the forces there was "strategically defensive" in accordance with the terms of the directive issued on the matter by Marshall on 18 March.[97] There had been talk in the winter months of developing the theater as a springboard for offensive operations against Japan if the Soviets participated in the war against Japan. In this case the Americans wanted to use as-yet-unbuilt airfields in Siberia for bombing missions against Japan. By the end of March such wild and unrealistic ideas had long since been consigned to oblivion.[98] Assigned a defensive role, the theater was almost up to its establishment in April. Buckner, responsible to Lieutenant General John L. DeWitt's Western Defense Command, had under command the equivalent of a single reinforced divison that was strong in flak support. The Eleventh Air Force, on the other hand, had only fifty-five aircraft in the theater in April, but this was a threefold improvement over the situation that had existed six months before, and even in April another fifty or so aircraft were en route to Alaska.[99] The naval forces, on the other hand, were negligible. Before the May crisis only the *Waters*, *Dent*, *Kane* and *Sands*, all old flush-deckers, had been assigned on a permanent basis to the sector command, and for the most part the local naval command had to try to get by with a motley collection of converted yachts, cutters from the coast guard and the pride of the theater, the gunboat *Charleston*. Armed with four 6-in guns, the *Charleston* contributed about half the weight of broadside available to the entire sector force. Had it not been for the small contribution of escorts that the Royal Canadian Navy in Pacific waters was able to make for the convoys to Alaska—convoys that were started back in 1940— it is probable that the American naval position in the sector would have been desperate.

The onset of the crisis in May brought about what had been recognized as necessary before—implementation of the principle of unity of command. Before May the ground forces comprised the Alaska Defense Command, activated on 26 June 1940. These were the forces commanded by Buckner. The Alaska Defense Command Air Force was established on 17 October 1941, reconstituted as the Eleventh Air Force on 5 February and in March placed under the command of Brigadier General William O. Butler.[100] After 11 December 1941 both were placed under the Western Defense Command, though the chain of command was confused because in certain matters the local theater commands were directly accountable to Washington. In December 1941 Buckner sought permission to assume command of all army and army air force elements in Alaska. The principle of unity of command was accepted by the army air force with the proviso that one of its generals be in charge.[101] With this deadlock it was perhaps inevitable that the issue would be put on ice and that, when an overall commander was appointed in May, he would come from the navy, until that time of only tertiary status amongst the services. Equally inevitable was that this commander would not be local. Before May the naval forces in the theater had formed the Alaska sector of the Pacific Northern Coastal Frontier, part of the Thirteenth Naval District.[102] The commander of the sector, a captain, was too junior to take command of the whole theater, hence the appointment of Theobald.

The strategic and tactical problems entailed in the defense of Alaska were exactly the same as those that had beset the theater command in the past. It had low priority in terms of men and equipment, and its subordination to the needs of the West Coast, the Hawaiian Islands and the southwest Pacific meant that it had to make do with leftover resources. The successful defense of Alaska could only be achieved by sea power, which in effect meant naval and air power, but neither the navy nor the army air force had sufficient force available or in reserve to have any realistic chance of meeting and defeating a sustained and large-scale enemy offensive. The ground forces, as we have seen, were too scattered and too small to have real chance of resisting heavy assault. The best that might be expected from the military in the event of any major seaborne landing by the Japanese was the imposition of undue loss or delay on the enemy. In every way it was fortunate for the Americans that Operation AL was intended as a small-scale landing and feint, not a main force operation.

With sea power the key to the defense of the Aleutians, Nimitz somehow had to juggle his forces to give Theobald the wherewithal to defend his command area. Thus far we have noted the situation that confronted Nimitz with regard to battleships and submarines: the former were not to be made available to the defense at all and the latter were deployed with six units in the north. Besides these, the Pacific Fleet had on its list three carriers, the *Yorktown*, *Enterprise* and *Hornet*; thirteen heavy and eleven light cruisers; fifty-three front-line modern destroyers; and thirty-two old flush-deckers, which were not up to the demands of fleet service. These totals exclude units either in dockyards or on their way to dockyards for overhaul, repair or reconstruction; they include such units as the *St. Louis*, *Clark* and *Mustin*, whose deployment was given earlier in this text.

Nimitz's problem was that the carrier forces had to be held to meet the main enemy threat in the central Pacific, and carrier forces, demanding the most modern and best ships in commission, ate into available strength at a prodigious rate. After the carrier forces had thus gorged themselves, existing deployments in various theaters accounted for most of what was left. Thus just as the Aleutians were able to secure a miserly 6 submarines from the 65 in the Pacific area, so the islands were doomed to secure a bare handful of ships, most of them elderly, from the 109 cruisers and destroyers in the Pacific.

When the question of the defense of the Aleutians was considered in the second half of May, seven heavy cruisers were either with the carriers or operating in their support. The neat symmetry of pre–Coral Sea deployment had disappeared with the loss of the *Lexington* and the damaging of the *Yorktown*. Committed to the south with the carriers were the *Minneapolis*, *New Orleans*, *Astoria*, *Portland*, *Vincennes*, *Northampton* and *Pensacola*. The latter, not part of the original screens, had joined company after she had completed the transfer of the Marine's 212th Pursuit Squadron to New Caledonia. She took the place of her sister ship, the *Salt Lake City*, which was detached at Noumea in order to strengthen the Southwest Pacific Command as the carriers returned to the central Pacific. Nimitz's policy was to leave the command with a cruiser force superior to that of the enemy in the area. With the *Chicago* and Australasian units already in the area, the *Salt Lake City* was deemed to provide the necessary margin of superiority and therefore transferred. She was the second ship detached to the Southwest Pacific Command by the carrier forces during their operations in the theater, the other ship being the *Farragut*. She had been transferred in the course of the battle of the Coral Sea.

The other original member of the carrier screens that had been detached was the *Chester*. Because of his need for an extra operational carrier as soon as possible, Nimitz instructed Fitch to make his way to the West Coast to expedite the recommissioning of the *Saratoga*. Fitch left the southwest Pacific for California in the *Chester* to take command of the new Task Force 11. At the same time the *San Francisco* was on the West Coast awaiting a move in the opposite direction as escort for the movement of the Thirty-seventh Infantry Division to Suva. Thus of his thirteen heavy cruisers Nimitz had only two, the *Indianapolis* and *Louisville*, which were not immediately committed and were therefore free to proceed to the Aleutians if so directed. The *Indianapolis* was at Pearl Harbor, the *Louisville* on the West Coast.

The light cruiser situation was no better. Of the eleven in service in the Pacific, one, the light antiaircraft cruiser *Atlanta*, had attached herself to the carrier forces in the southwest Pacific while a sister ship, the *San Diego*, was in her home port awaiting the recommissioning of the *Saratoga*. Three units, the elderly *Richmond*, *Concord* and *Trenton*, were in the backwater of the southeast Pacific, and one, the *Phoenix*, was detached to the Australian station where she spent part of her time on the Indian Ocean coast. The *Raleigh* and the *Honolulu* were engaged in escort duties in the south and southwest Pacific areas, while the *Detroit* was similarly employed in the central Pacific. The *Nashville* was earmarked for radio deception off Midway. The *St. Louis* was uncommitted and free to proceed to the north after her mission to Midway was completed. The *Honolulu*, returning to Pearl Harbor from the southwest Pacific, was to become available in time to be sent to join the North Pacific Force.

The destroyer situation largely revolved around the carrier position. A total of twenty-one destroyers had been involved in the Doolittle, Coral Sea and Nauru-Ocean episodes. Of these, two were no longer in service, the *Sims* having been lost at the Coral Sea and the *Fanning* having had to return to San Francisco after the Doolittle Raid for repairs. Of the remainder, no less than five had been detached by 19 May. The *Farragut* and the *Meredith* had been left in the southwest Pacific when the carriers returned to Pearl Harbor. The *Farragut* was assigned to general duties and the *Meredith* to the protection of the *Tangier* and the oilers at Noumea. The *Grayson* had had to go back to the West Coast for repairs while the *Morris*, slightly damaged in the course of rescuing survivors from the *Lexington*, returned early to Pearl Harbor for minor repairs. The *Gwin*, as we have seen, similarly made an early return to Oahu. The remainder—the *Dewey*, *Worden*, *Monaghan*, *Aylwin*, *Phelps*, *Balch*, *Benham*, *Ellet*, *Maury*, *Hughes*, *Russell*, *Anderson*, *Hammann* and *Monssen*—were still with the carrier forces or oilers in the southwest Pacific and could not be considered for deployment to the Aleutians.

Excluding the *Farragut* and the *Meredith*, the nineteen modern and nine flush-deck destroyers committed to the southern oceans represented the single largest drain on American destroyer resources in the Pacific. The areas involved were vast and American responsibilities were heavy—the term "southern oceans" referred to the southeast, south and southwest Pacific areas, the Australian station, and the lines of communication that ran from both Pearl Harbor and the West Coast to Australia and the south and southwest Pacific theaters. Given the enormity of this area, the total of twenty-eight destroyers was a desperately inadequate number with which to discharge a multitude of tasks.

Of the flush-deckers, five were detailed to proceed to Pearl Harbor from Australia. These Asiatic Fleet survivors were the *John D. Edwards*, *John D. Ford*, *Whipple*, *Alden* and *Bulmer*. The dates of their arrivals in June were, respectively, as follows: the first, second, sixth, seventh and sixteenth. Another Philippines veteran, the *Barker*, was also en route, but she was held at Tonga temporarily as a guard ship. Another erstwhile colleague, the *Paul Jones*, was making her way back to the West Coast. One of the two remaining flush-deckers, the *McFarland*, had been on the Pearl Harbor station since the start of the war. She was assigned to the South Pacific and cleared Oahu on 2 June.

In the southeast Pacific were the *Warrington* and the *Sampson*, with the last of the flush-deckers, the *Goldsborough*, in company. The *O'Brien* was at Samoa, pending the occupation of Wallis. On convoy duty between either the West Coast or the Canal and the south and southwest Pacific were the *MacDonough*, *Cummings*, *Conyngham*, *Mugford* and *Hutchings*. In addition, the *Gridley*, *Patterson* and *Jarvis* were involved in the Australia-Oahu run, the latter two leaving Pearl Harbor on 22 and 23 May respectively. The *Selfridge*, *Lamson*, *Flusser*, *Tucker*, *Perkins*, *Bagley*, *Helm* and *McCall* were engaged in coastal and escort duties within either the south or southwest Pacific areas. Of all the ships from these various areas only four were in Pearl Harbor at times that enabled Nimitz to redeploy them for the coming battles, and only three of them were available for such redeployment. The newly commissioned *Hutchins* arrived on 30 May for adjustments to her main armament and so could not be used. That left just the *Conyngham*, available to be earmarked for duty with the carriers, and the *Gridley* and the *McCall*, to be transferred to the Aleutians after their arrival at Pearl Harbor during the latter part of May.

Seven modern and seventeen flush-deck destroyers were operating either off the West Coast (in a variety of roles), as escorts between the Aleutians and the West Coast, or in the Aleutians. All the modern units— the *Porter*, *Drayton*, *Cushing*, *Smith*, *Preston*, *Craven* and *Henley*—were operating on the West Coast, as were eleven of their more venerable colleagues—the *Crane*, *Rathburne*, *Kilty*, *Kennison*, *Crosby*, *Gilmer*, *Brooks*, *Law-*

rence, Humphreys, Talbot and *King*. Either on the Alaska station or convoying from the West Coast to the north were the *Waters, Dent, Fox, Kane, Sands* and *Hatfield*.

Excluding the *Clark*, six destroyers were performing convoy duties between the West Coast and Pearl Harbor. These were the *Hull, Reid, Case, Dunlap, Blue* and *Ralph Talbot*, while on the Pearl Harbor station itself were the permanently assigned *Allen, Schley, Chew, Ward, Litchfield* and *Hulbert*.

The simple problem for Nimitz in trying to assign forces for the north was that he could not direct one or more carriers to the Aleutians in order to counter an enemy known to be taking such ships to the theater. Moreover, Nimitz might be able to pluck the occasional ship from the south or southwest Pacific areas that came into the central Pacific and direct it northwards, but for the most part he had no option but to redeploy units either from the West Coast or from convoy duties. In the latter case, of course, the most obvious candidate for attachment to the North Pacific Force were those units already plying northern waters. The vast majority of such ships were old and of little fighting value. The naval position in the Aleutians was thus one of serious weakness.

Serious weakness or not, however, knowledge of the enemy's intention to move against the Aleutians and the declaration of a state of fleet-opposed invasion forced the Americans to reinforce the northern theater and to revise their command arrangements there. Since there was little point in sending more ground troops to a command that was already almost at its authorized strength and administrative capacity, any reinforcement of the theater had to take the form of air and naval forces.

The command arrangements, the level of forces available both in the theater and as reinforcements, and the subsequent plan of campaign were intimately related. Under the terms of the declaration of 21 May a state of fleet-opposed invasion would exist unless and until there was a Japanese landing on either the eastern Aleutians or the Alaska Peninsula (that is, in the area bound by Otter Point to the west and Cold Bay to the east), or until it appeared that an enemy landing on either Kodiak or the Alaskan mainland was imminent.[103] In either instance, a state of land-opposed invasion would exist and the navy would conform to the orders of Buckner, the commander of the land forces. But in the present state of emergency the army was to coordinate its efforts in order to meet the navy's requirements. In addition, on the specific orders of King and Marshall air units from both the army and navy were to be placed under the single command of Butler, recently installed as commander of the Eleventh Air Force in Alaska. These aircraft in their turn were to be constituted as a single task group within Theobald's Task Force 8.[104] In this way the principle of unity of command, insisted upon by Washington, the Western Defense Command and the Pacific Fleet, was to be effected and maintained. The instructions Theobald received from Nimitz were quite specific on this matter. He was vested with the full powers of command. In the event things did not work out quite in the manner intended.

Of Theobald's manifold problems, two were critical. First, there was no real agreement over the deployment of available air power to meet a Japanese threat that was assumed to be directed against Dutch Harbor. Second, there was this very matter of the assumed threat. Theobald did not have anything like the detail of enemy forces, timetable and objectives that was available to Nimitz, Fletcher and Spruance. Indeed, it was not until 28 May that he was provided by Nimitz with the information that the enemy planned to descend on Attu, Kiska and Adak and then, because he was given neither the sources nor the reliability of this information, Theobald did not hesitate to discard it. [105] With every good reason he refused to believe that the enemy was embarked upon a madcap scheme to acquire such worthless real estate as the desolate islands of the western Aleutians, a view apparently shared by high-ranking army and air force commanders in Alaska. [106] It is hard to believe that Buckner, after his experience of 20 May, was not in sympathy with Theobald. The admiral believed that the information about the enemy's intentions did not make sense and that his superiors at Pearl Harbor had been sold a dummy. He thought that any move into the western Aleutians would prove to be a feint, designed to draw him to the west while the main assault would be delivered against Dutch Harbor or targets further to the east. Accordingly, Theobald chose to disregard his orders of 30 May to take his task force to a position 200 miles to the south of the western Aleutians. Fearing that if he did so the enemy would get between him and his base, Theobald was determined to take up a position some 400 miles to the south of Kodiak, where he would be handily placed on the flank of any enemy advance against the eastern Aleutians and Alaska. [107] Paralleling Theobald's decisions regarding his own naval deployment was a reluctance on the part of Butler and Buckner to consider a forward defense of the eastern Aleutians. Both wanted to concentrate the major part of their available air strength in the Anchorage area, beyond the range of any opening enemy attack but in a position from which it could be moved forward to counter Japanese moves. [108] These considerations were to have their effect on the American deployment for the battle.

It is something of a moot point how far these mistaken appreciations of the various commanders affected the forthcoming battle. While Theobald has been rightly criticized for the deployment of his task force in contradiction to his orders, when it came to his overall plan of campaign Theobald had little real choice but to concentrate most of his forces for the defense of the eastern Aleutians and Alaska. Considerations regarding the security of the bases, the distances involved within the theater and the range of ships and aircraft alike meant that there was not much the Americans could have done to defend the western Aleutians. But if Theobald's decisions on these matters were faulty and largely dictated by factors beyond his control, they did have the advantage of making a virtue of necessity: his deployment covered most of the major bases in Alaska.

As his last line of defense Theobald chose to use his submarines. Given the appalling weather and sea conditions in the area—one of his submarines was forced off station to land men injured by mountainous seas—the submarines were assigned to local patrols. There was little point in their undertaking long-range offensive patrols. Accordingly, the *S-27* and *S-28* were put on station just to the west of Cold Bay; the *S-18* and *S-35* were deployed to the southern entrance of the Umnak Passage; and the *S-23* and *S-24* were put on station at the northern exit of that same channel.*

Task Force 8.4 was to provide direct defense for Dutch Harbor and Cold Bay if the Japanese showed signs of making landings at either or both places. The group was to be deployed at Makushin Bay, and it was to consist of nine destroyers under the command of Commander Wyatt Craig in the destroyer *Case*. Two of the units, the *King* and the *Waters*, did not arrive on station until the fourth, and one of the others, the *Talbot*, did not arrive at Makushin Bay until the third. She had previously been involved in escorting three of the submarines bound for the theater, the *S-18*, *S-23* and *S-28*, to their patrol areas from Seattle. Excluding the *Talbot*, Craig had under command the *Reid*, *Kane*, *Brooks*, *Dent* and *Sands* in addition to the *Case* when Operation AL began to get under way with the preliminary air attack on Dutch Harbor.

To cover the approaches of the Aleutians, both on the Pacific Ocean and the Bering Sea sides of the chain, Theobald chose to deploy Task Group 8.2. This consisted of old sector ships, which were just about anything that could be scrapped together to meet the emergency. With the *Charleston* were fourteen converted yachts of the navy, the "gunboat-type" cutters *Haida* and *Onondaga* and the patrol boats *Bonham*, *Aurora* and *Cyane* from the coast guard. These twenty units were divided into three groups, two of the groups with a total of nine ships being on the Bering Sea side of the Aleutians. Four of the ships were deployed due east of St. Paul, and the other five between St. Paul and Atka. The other eleven were deployed on an arc between the southwest and southeast of Dutch Harbor at a range of 200 miles from the base. The units were supposedly spaced at 30-mile intervals and were to maintain stationary patrol.[109] Perhaps fortunately for all concerned, many of the units of this sorry and ill-assorted "armada" were late in arriving on stations that for the most part were not on the line of the enemy's approach, but the Japanese forces did cross the picket line on 3 June both during its approach and withdrawal from Dutch Harbor. None

*On 19 June the *S-27* ran aground at Amchitka and was lost.

of the American ships contacted the enemy and, more relevantly, none were contacted in their turn. The outcome of any such encounter would have been predictable.

It is hard to see what Task Group 8.2 might have been able to achieve other than putting its units into positions where they might well be sunk. But it was Theobald's intention that his forces, and not those of the enemy, should do the sinking. By using his picket boats and his Catalina reconnaissance flying boats, he would find and track the enemy and then, by means of the "strong attritional tactics" of his bombers, he would cripple him. While the fighter element was to stand in defense of its own airfields and bases, Theobald had to hope that the bomber forces that were to be on station in the theater would be in position and prove able to neutralize the enemy's carrier-borne air power. In the intelligence briefing of 21 May Theobald was warned that the enemy would lead with the *Ryujo* and one or two other carriers; between three and five heavy cruisers; one light cruiser; sixteen destroyers; and between eight and ten submarines in support.[110] This was an accurate overall assessment of the forces committed to Operation AL, and unless American land-based aircraft were able to counter the Japanese carrier threat, there was little prospect of American surface units being able to challenge the enemy's moves.

In order to have any chance of success the Americans would have needed to deploy their full strength to Otter Point and Cold Bay. This was Theobald's intention, but it did not meet with the approval of the local military command.[111] Buckner had been urged by DeWitt to move forces forward to Otter Point as early as 3 May.[112] That had barely been possible because of the unfinished airstrip there, and even by the time of the declaration of the state of emergency in the theater the prevailing belief was that Otter Point and Cold Bay could only handle one bomber squadron (twelve aircraft) and two fighter squadrons. Considerations of operational and administrative capacity therefore made the local commanders unwilling to engage in forward defense. This concern was backed by more solid considerations. The two airfields lacked dispersal and shelter facilities and had no early warning system in operation. Fear of being caught in the same way as their compatriots had been on various airfields at Oahu and Luzon on 7 December 1941 naturally made the local commands wary of a forward commitment. Moreover, the local feeling was that the best deployment was a concentration of forces around Anchorage and Kodiak, which would secure the Alaskan theater as a whole. This cut right across Theobald's inclination to establish a forward deployment of air power.

The difference in approach produced a compromise. Theobald subsequently admitted that he had been reluctant to use the powers granted him in light of the damage that might be caused to interservice relations if he insisted on policies that were both unsuccessful and contrary to the wishes and judgment of the other service commanders.[113] This was a lame reason at best, and in any case it did not prevent his being able to persuade Butler and Buckner on 27 May to sanction the deployment to the forward bases of at least a major part of their strike and fighter forces.[114]

But however many aircraft were available for offensive operations, Theobald would not have enough to entertain real hopes of countering the enemy. The success of Butler's groups in first finding and then striking at the enemy carrier force was essential to the defense of the Aleutians. Unless the enemy was hurt, the surface forces the Americans intended to deploy could not dare risk running the gauntlet of enemy air superiority. Moreover, Theobald was in the awkward position of knowing that he could not seek compensation for his weaknesses in the air by recourse to a night action; the hours of darkness in northern latitudes at this time of year were too short to hold out real hope of forcing a night action.

The main body that Theobald was to have at sea under his own command, Task Group 8.6, was to rendezvous some three hours after sunrise on 3 June in a position 400 miles south of Kodiak. It was to consist of two heavy and three light cruisers, four destroyers and the oiler *Sabine*. One other destroyer, the *Hulbert*, narrowly missed joining the force after she had been dispatched from Pearl Harbor. She proceeded to Kodiak and arrived there on 6 June.

The rendezvous of Task Group 8.6 was a complicated matter. Units converged on one point from three different directions. Theobald, who as we have seen arrived in northern waters in the *Reid* on 27 May, shifted his flag that same day to the *Nashville* immediately upon her arrival at Kodiak. She had left Pearl Harbor on 14 May and spent several days some 400 miles to the northwest of Midway transmitting false radio traffic to try to confuse the enemy. She set course for Kodiak on the twenty-second. The *St. Louis* and the *Case* arrived at Kodiak from Midway on 31 May, and within a matter of hours both had left. The *Case*, with Craig on board, set course for Makushin Bay via Dutch Harbor, and the *St. Louis*, in the company of the *Gilmer*, left for the rendezvous of Task Group 8.6. The following day, 1 June, the *Nashville*, *Humphreys* and *Sabine* cleared Kodiak to rendezvous with the *St. Louis* and *Gilmer* the next day. This nucleus of Task Group 8.6 then linked up on the morning of the third first with the heavy cruiser *Louisville* and then with the *Indianapolis*, *Honolulu*, *McCall* and *Gridley*. The *Louisville* had sailed independently from San Francisco on 31 May, the other four ships together from Pearl Harbor on the twenty-ninth.

Such, then, was the complete American order of battle in the Alaskan theater. By any standard, the American deployment and plan of campaign were tenuous, forced on the various commands by circumstances and not adopted by choice. None of the forces involved in the defense of Alaska were adequate to discharge the tasks they might be called upon to perform.

In the air the Americans had forces that could not carry out sustained or large-scale operations, be they defensive, offensive or in reconnaissance. On land the various American garrisons, even the one at Kodiak, were little more than hostages to fortune, unable to resist serious amphibious assault by an enemy certain to enjoy command of the sea and sky as the prerequisites for a landing attempt. At sea the Americans deployed numerically strong forces, including Task Group 8.6, the equivalent of a carrier formation—but without a carrier. With an improvised command structure and a commander who took himself to a position at sea from which he could not exercise command, American arrangements in this theater were extremely weak and vulnerable.

Defining policy and deployments for Midway and the Aleutians left one matter unsettled, though it had to be tackled at the same time as the other issues. This matter related to the situation of the south and southwest Pacific. While the demands of these two theaters lacked the overwhelming urgency that attended the problems of Midway and the Aleutians, their requirements were nonetheless real, for as the Americans knew, the enemy intended to switch the point of attack to these areas in the aftermath of Operation MI.

This problem resurrected the whole issue of army air force deployments, the Atlantic-versus-Pacific controversy and the complicated matter of interdepartmental and intertheater relations. After 16 May a new twist to the situation was provided by Nimitz's decision, communicated to Leary the same day, to bring Task Force 16 back to the central Pacific. In his signal Nimitz told of his intention to send air reinforcements to New Caledonia and Fiji. He also sought the cooperation of the Southwest Pacific Command in the defense of the southwest Pacific sea area. What Nimitz specifically wanted was for MacArthur to reach out to the right and help provide the islands of the area, which hosted the line of communication on which his command depended, with aircraft for defensive purposes. At this time MacArthur's command had more heavy bombers and fighters than any other single operational area in the Pacific, and the total number of American aircraft in Australia vastly exceeded the number in the southwest and south Pacific sea areas, on Hawaii, at sea or in Alaska. What Nimitz wanted was for MacArthur to thin out his air "front," now secure for the moment after the Coral Sea, to reach the least threatened areas, thereby extending his flank and helping secure the New Caledonia–Samoa complex. MacArthur would have to build up a reserve by taking risks elsewhere. Of course there was an element of dishonesty in Nimitz's request; he wanted MacArthur to put his faith in the concept of air force "strategic mobility," which he and King did not believe in at all. But such an act of magnanimity was far beyond MacArthur's capacity.[115]

In fact there was next to nothing that Nimitz and King could do for the south and southwest Pacific areas at this time. The navy had no forces that it could send and the army air force was dragging its feet on the whole question of reinforcement of the theater. As far as Arnold and the army air force were concerned, these theaters were not priorities. In March 206 heavy bombers had been agreed on by the Joint Chiefs of Staff as the quota for the Pacific, but the army air force had unilaterally reduced this to 160 (effectively lopping off a whole heavy bombardment group). In the South Pacific as a whole only 202 medium bombers and fighters had been allocated to the defense, and only 49 aircraft had been earmarked as reinforcements for 1943. Arnold's case was that the buildup of air power in Europe required paring the needs of the south and southwest Pacific to the bone. But the emergence of a threat to Hawaii forced his hand. Hawaii and the Seventh Air Force had not been reinforced since the start of the war. With the crisis in May reinforcements began to arrive and, moreover, aircraft began to filter down the island chain towards (but not to) Australia. By 1 June the equivalent of a bombardment group of B-17E Flying Fortresses was on Oahu, a threefold increase inside a month, in addition to a total of about 140 operational fighters. At the same time about 150 aircraft, 96 of them fighters, were deployed in the New Caledonia–Fiji–Tonga–Samoa complex.[116] The arrangements were far from ideal, not least because the South Pacific theater had virtually no offensive capability whatsoever, but given the refusal of Marshall and Arnold to consider further reinforcement of the area, the situation could not be improved. King's agitation on these matters was understandable but futile.[117]

The real problem, however, was not so much the divergence of views between King and his two colleagues but the fact that even after six months of war the Americans had not been able to make good lost time and increased responsibilities. The aircraft and aircrew that were needed in the southern theaters could not be sent because they were not available; even the forces sent to Hawaii were dispatched on an ad hoc basis. The seemingly endless supply of men and equipment that characterized the American war effort in 1943 and 1944 was simply not available in 1942. Moreover, it must be remembered that though the navy was resentful of the alleged shortcomings of the army and army air force in helping it fight the war in the Pacific, the Pacific theater as a whole had had more troops and aircraft deployed to it than had the Atlantic and European theaters of operation.[118] In May and June the Pacific had been allocated more than three times as many troops as the other theaters, and the number of troops either in the Pacific or on their way to the theater was already over the established limit.[119] In reality, despite the complaints of the navy, by June 1942 seven of the ten divisions and nearly all the air groups committed overseas had gone to the Pacific, mostly to the southwest Pacific theater.

Such matters were cold comfort to King and Nimitz. At this desperate juncture the idea of an Hawaiian Mobile Air Force of heavy bombers under the command of the Joint Chiefs of Staff, held as a reserve for immediate commitment anywhere in the Pacific, was an irrelevance. Such a force was to be established in June, after Midway, but what King and Nimitz needed were combat forces already in the area of operations. It was a measure of the weakness and desperation of the U.S. Navy at this time that King took a step that must have come close to the ultimate humiliation both for him personally and for the service that he headed. He felt obliged to ask the Admiralty for help with the crisis. His overture, developed as it was from one of MacArthur's olympian demands that masqueraded as suggestions, took two forms. First, it asked the British to deploy a carrier to the southwest Pacific and cover this area as the Americans drew back into the central Pacific. Second, it suggested a long-term buildup, beginning in July, of a concentrated Anglo-American carrier force in the Pacific that would be able to take the fight to the enemy. Perhaps because he had already committed the *Ranger* to ferrying duties to West Africa on behalf of the British and the *Wasp* to the support of British operations in the Mediterranean, King might have held hopes that the Admiralty would reciprocate. As King well knew, with the assault phase of the Madagascar invasion completed, the British had the *Formidable, Illustrious* and *Indomitable* in the Indian Ocean, and none of them were committed to operations, either then or in the immediate future.

The British were in a position to provide some form of reverse lend-lease on this occasion, and given the yawning disparity of strength and influence that was to emerge between the Americans and British over the next three years, it is easy to assert that the Admiralty should have seized the opportunity presented by King's plight to put the U.S. Navy deeply in its debt. But the British refused to accede to King's request and suggestion. The circumstances that surrounded their decision were somewhat strange, since the idea of a combined Anglo-American carrier force in the Pacific had already been favorably considered by the British Chiefs of Staff.[120] In the immediate aftermath of the Japanese raid on Ceylon the British chiefs had deliberated on the merits of building up a fleet in the Pacific from American and British resources. A fleet of nine fleet carriers and fifteen heavy cruisers was suggested as a total strength, battleships being discounted from consideration. Such a fleet was just about within the reach of the Americans and British. As the British planners and their superiors saw matters, a fleet this size would give the Allies a two-to-one advantage over the Japanese in carrier aircraft. This would enable the Allies to go on to the offensive. Moreover, it was recognized that so massive a concentration of power in the Pacific was the best possible guarantee of those possessions that remained to the British in the Indian Ocean. The British referred to this as "the indirect approach"; they calculated that the Japanese would never dare to move in the Indian Ocean if such an Allied fleet was concentrated in the Pacific.

The British had one other good reason to consider King's suggestion seriously and favorably. Before the Ceylon raid began the chief of the Imperial General Staff, General Sir Alan Brooke, sought to secure an American feint that would draw Japanese strength away from the Indian Ocean.[121] In a sense Brooke tried to do in April with regard to Ceylon what King was trying to do in May with regard to Midway. Both men failed to get any help from their ally, and for much the same reason. Neither the British nor the Americans could improvise feints and deceptions to help their ally; at this stage of the war coordination in two separate oceans of the efforts of two fleets, each inferior to the enemy, was meaningless. The lesson from this particular upshot in April for the British was precisely the point implicit in King's request for the second half of 1942: a concentrated Allied force in the Pacific protected India en passant.

But despite the incentive to pool resources, the British turned down King's suggestions for two reasons. First, they argued that sending a carrier to the southwest Pacific was irrelevant. The Japanese used theirs en masse, and a single British carrier in this theater would counter an enemy threat as long as there were none to counter; if the threat was real then a single carrier could do nothing but succumb quickly. Second, Pound told King that any British demonstration in the eastern Indian Ocean or against the Malay Barrier would have no effect whatsoever on Japanese strategic deployment.[122] He could have added for good measure that there was no point in even trying to make a demonstration during the monsoon. The British points were well taken, and the Americans had few grounds for dissent. But things were not quite so simple as that. If the British arguments were reasons, they were also rationalizations for more substantial calculations, and for the Americans the issue of the deployment of a carrier to the southwest Pacific or a diversion off Southeast Asia was not the real point. They stood in need of help, and if they could not get any help then at least they wanted a gesture of support. This was perhaps America's greatest crisis of the war, and to overcome it she turned to her only real ally, who refused to do anything. The situation of May 1942 and the issue of support was as much political and psychological as it was strategic, and the British decision not to render assistance could easily have become a cause of lasting bitterness had the battle off Midway gone against the Americans.

The root of the British refusal was that the clock told against their being able to make any timely or effective move to help their ally. Moreover, because Pound and his colleagues had no inkling of the desperate urgency of the American position in the Pacific, they could not understand why King should need such immediate help from them. When he turned down King's request on 19 May, Pound knew no reason for the American assumption that the enemy was soon to make his main effort in the central Pacific. Furthermore, he still had no idea of the extent of American losses at the Coral Sea. As we have seen, King had only himself to blame for this particular matter. As late as 21 May he wrote a personal letter to Pound claiming that only slight damage had been done to two American carriers at the Coral Sea; King, for reasons best known to himself, could not bring himself to reveal the loss of the *Lexington* to the only people who could help him. By the time the head of the Admiralty delegation in Washington, Admiral Sir Charles Little, was able to get to the bottom of King's request and inform Pound what was afoot, it was far too late.[123] Nothing the British could do after the twenty-second could have any effect on the Pacific situation, and the British Chiefs of Staff did not even discuss Little's signal until the twenty-fifth.[124] Pound had treated King's request as a naval matter and one on which no action could or should be taken.*

However, there is more than a fair chance that not even a timely and accurate recounting of King's position would have swayed the British from two overriding considerations. First, the situation in India was precarious. At the time of the Japanese rampage in the Indian Ocean British authorities sent from London were engaged in delicate negotiations with both Hindu and Moslem nationalists. The delegation reported to the War Cabinet in London that at that moment British prestige and authority in the subcontinent were at an all-time low. The thought was that the loss of Malaya and Singapore, and then of southern Burma, had severely damaged British standing throughout India, with two exceptions. These were in the Punjab and the North-West Frontier.[125] If British morale was going to hold anywhere it would be in these two areas. For India and the British this was the

---

*Sir Ian Jacob put these matters in some sort of perspective when he told the author that at no stage of the war was the U.S. Navy forthcoming about events in the Pacific. Sir Ian commented that planning for the European war had to take place without reference to the Pacific war because the British never knew what the U.S. Navy had in that ocean or what it planned to do. He indicated that the British were made to feel that the U.S. Navy regarded anything sent to the European theater of operations or the Atlantic as a waste, a distraction from the "real" war. In stating a case that suggested that King's behavior at this time was very characteristic of him, Sir Ian made three observations of special worth. First, he suggested that had King knuckled down to the "Germany-first" strategy, Italy could have been beaten more quickly than was the case, with incalculable repercussions with regard to the course of the European war. Second, he indicated that British ignorance of King's intentions but the awareness that the U.S. Navy was grabbing more than its share of American military resources made the British willing to go along with King's famous 30 percent-for-the-Pacific formula as the means of putting an upper limit on the American effort there. Third, he confirmed the basic unwillingness of Roosevelt to tackle King on any point of real policy or on the allocation of resources.

supreme crisis of the war.* One of the staff papers placed before the British Chiefs of Staff stated that "if the Eastern Fleet is defeated *and* we lose Ceylon, the threat to our sea communications is so serious as to likely to lead to a stoppage of military supplies to the Middle East and India."[126] In simple terms, the planners were telling the Chiefs of Staff that the war would be lost if the Japanese repeated their sortie into the Indian Ocean, this time with a force that overwhelmed an inferior British fleet and with a ground echelon that was able to take Ceylon, "the strategic keystone of the Indian Ocean."[127]

The second consideration stemmed directly from the first. The British were convinced that the Japanese intended to make their effort in the Indian Ocean in the course of 1942, and on 6 April, the day of the attack on Colombo, British confidence in their ability to withstand attack can be gauged by the fact that the British Chiefs of Staff ordered the preparation of an oil denial program throughout the Middle East.[128] The Naval Intelligence Division of that same day unhesitatingly set out the Indian Ocean as the theater where the Japanese would make their effort in 1942. This appreciation estimated that the Japanese priorities would be to try to consolidate their gains; to secure a settlement in China; to sever the Australian-American line of communication; and to sweep through the Indian Ocean.† These views were superimposed on another. They were set down in staff appreciations on 21 and 31 March claiming that Japanese diplomatic sources in Europe had been reported as saying that they, the Japanese,

> could not wait till the Allies had mobilized real strength in the Pacific. The intention was to conclude peace at an early date, which would be quite easy, as if the British and Americans suffered further territorial losses their Parliaments would raise a howl and would change their Governments or their policy. It is essential at any price to force a final decision as early as possible . . . and at the very latest before the spring of 1943.[129]

The British view was that in 1942 the Japanese would attempt an offensive specifically designed to force Britain or the United States out of the war. This was a view underpinned by the conviction that the Japanese had to win in 1942 or not at all. The idea that the Axis powers had to win in

---

*The Indian army recruited about half its numbers from the Punjab, while even in March 1942 the British had more troops in the North-West Frontier than they did in Burma and northeast India. With five incomplete divisions either facing the Japanese or training for front-line service, there were no fewer than fifty-four Indian infantry battalions on the border of the North-West Frontier, and another forty-one, plus seventeen British battalions, performing internal security duties.

†In view of the Japanese arguments on the matter, the British assessment was interesting: "Japan can probably accomplish her main objective . . . more easily and cheaply by placing herself astride the . . . approaches to Australia than by attempting to control the whole continent." No doubt the Japanese army and, to a lesser extent, Tomioka would have appreciated such an endorsement of their strategic thinking.

the current year or face certain defeat was neatly stated in the staff paper, *Allied Economic Warfare Strategy in 1942*, on 21 March: the Germans had the factories but not the raw materials and manpower to win a long war, while the Japanese had the manpower and resources but not the industrial base.[130] With these views in mind, it is easy to see the basis of British fears for the security of their Indian Ocean possessions in the second quarter of 1942. After the April raid on Ceylon the British expected the Japanese to renew their offensive, though they half expected the Japanese to attempt an overland drive into Assam in September or an amphibious operation in Bengal at this very time in May, when the Americans were asking for help in the Pacific.[131] Thus the British were unwilling to do anything that might undermine the fragile structure of their power in India, and in their caution they passed up the advantage they had foreseen in April on the subject of an Anglo-American concentration in the Pacific (see appendix B). Instead India and Ceylon would be strengthened to resist attack before the British redeployed their carriers to the Pacific in late 1942. Thereafter India would be defended at Truk.[132] The only problem for the British was that time did not wait for them: by late 1942 the Americans did not want the British in the Pacific in any strength.

Given all these considerations—the British fears and reading of Japanese intentions—it is more than likely that the British would have turned down any American appeal for help in May 1942. They refused to meet American requests on grounds that left the Americans with no real cause for complaint. The British reluctance to fall in with King's wishes was understandable, and unfortunate. One historian has asserted that this episode permanently embittered King towards the British and the Royal Navy.[133] This hardly seems to have been the case. Although King is widely regarded as having been an anglophobe, both during and after 1942 there were examples enough of his largesse towards the Royal Navy. At the various Anglo-American conferences, particularly those of 1943, he was involved in some singularly bruising exchanges with the British, but that was only to be expected. King was an American fighting an American cause, and because it was a cause that had to be argued with little help from his two service colleagues, he had to be in the forefront of any argument with the British high command. But whatever hostility he may have displayed towards the British was in any event secondary to his animosity towards the U.S. Army and the U.S. Army Air Force.* In May 1942 King's isolation within the

---

*To bring home this point, and perhaps to place the misinformation King fed Pound in its proper perspective, it is worth remembering that the army and air force members of the Joint Staff planners were not told of the nature and extent of the navy's losses off Savo Island for several weeks after the battle. Then the navy's losses were revealed accidentally by a newspaper correspondent who presumed that those responsible for the planning of future operations knew the outcome of the battle.

American and Allied high commands was as marked as the isolation of the U.S. Pacific Fleet; both were on their own with no prospect of support. Neither the British nor the other American services were in any position to help, and given the immutable constraints of time and distance, once King and Nimitz decided to fight in the central Pacific nothing could be done on behalf of the southwest Pacific theater. There might be a tinkering with minor units, a few bombers moved here and others put on readiness to move there, but for the most part the south and southwest Pacific theaters had to be left to their own devices. The best hope was that the defense of the two theaters would be secured by a victory at Midway, but not much reliance could be placed on this. By the last week of May there was little the Americans could do to help themselves. Arnold did order various squadrons to support the threatened areas, but the available numbers were far too small to have any real chance of turning back any substantial enemy offensive. American interests in the whole of the south and southwest Pacific theaters could only be secured by sea power, which in May 1942 was not sufficient to provide for the defense of those interests. If the enemy won off Midway there was little prospect of his being denied elsewhere, and an American victory might still not be enough to grant the Allies security in other areas. The only way a successful defense would be waged in any of the Pacific theaters was if something totally unforeseen happened at this time to redeem a potentially disastrous situation. Just how bad the situation was for the Americans at this stage can be judged from one of those "unofficial" comments-cum-orders that are never made and given. At a final briefing before Ramsey left to take command of Midway's air group, Nimitz told him to be certain "to get the heavies" out of Midway if the worst came to the worst.[134]

All these arrangements—involving the Southwest Pacific Command, Washington, Midway, Pearl Harbor, the Aleutians and the British—revolved around one matter. The various deployment of cruisers, destroyers, submarines and aircraft ultimately depended on the fleet being at sea to fight, and in the last week of May this was Nimitz's all-important consideration. Even before the carrier forces returned from the southwest Pacific the Pacific Fleet had to determine how it was to fight if it was to retain Midway. Until the state of the *Yorktown* was determined, however, deciding strategic deployment and tactics was problematic.

As it turned out, the basic form of American strategic and tactical policy was decided even before the condition of the *Yorktown* was ascertained. With the enemy possessing a clear superiority of numbers in all types of warships, the Americans knew that they could not risk a stand-up action. Because they could not trade blows with the enemy the Americans had to hit and run. At the final planning conference of 27 May, when the staffs of the two American carrier task forces that were to go into battle met with the fleet staff, it was determined that the American carrier force would stand to the northeast of Midway while the enemy approached from the northwest; the Americans would then advance to contact when the Japanese attacked the atoll. The enemy, it was assumed, would fly off strikes against Midway at dawn on 4 June, by which time the American carriers should have come to a position north of Midway and about 200 miles from where the enemy carriers should be. Relying on Midway's patrol aircraft to secure contact with the enemy, the American carriers would then be able to strike at an enemy distracted by Midway and minus a major part of his strength. At this planning conference the various staffs realized that there was a good chance of their being able to catch the Japanese in the process of recovering their aircraft after the strike on Midway.[135]

The problem for the Americans, however, was that they had to have three carriers to put into the battle. This was the absolute minimum if they were to have any reasonable chance of success. With only two carriers the Americans would have but about 150 aircraft, and this was not enough for the battle that was about to unfold. The Americans faced either four or five enemy carriers. To meet such a force they had to have the 220 or so aircraft that alone would provide a reasonable number of strike aircraft and sufficient strength for the combat air patrol. To have only two carriers against five would invite impossible odds—even two against four was not good. But three against four represented rough equality, and three against five was not too unreasonable either, since American carriers individually had larger groups than their Japanese counterparts. With knowledge of the enemy's plan of campaign and operational timetable, the Americans had a chance if they could put three carriers to sea. In marked contrast to the pre–Coral Sea days, this time there was no casual assumption that innate American characteristics would be enough to redress any numerical weakness. The Coral Sea had shown that the Japanese carriers were worthy opponents of the best that the Americans could put into battle. In these circumstances balancing the odds could only be brought about by careful preparation— and three carriers.

The *Enterprise* and the *Hornet* arrived safely at Pearl Harbor on 26 May, and with the *Saratoga* still on the West Coast the problem that confronted Nimitz was where to get the third carrier he needed for battle.[136] The *Yorktown* was the only possible stopgap, but in the immediate aftermath of the Coral Sea he had been told by Fitch that the carrier would need a ninety-day refit to make good her damage. Nimitz doubted the accuracy of his assessment for two reasons. First, on 8 May the *Yorktown* had recovered nineteen aircraft from the *Lexington*, and she had continued to operate her own air group after having been hit; this meant that her bomb damage had not affected her elevators and flight deck. Second, the carrier withdrew from the Coral Sea and then made her way back to Pearl Harbor under her

The Aircraft Carrier *Hornet*

own power. She had no need of assistance. The *Yorktown* might drag an oil slick ten miles long behind her, but with her power and flight deck she could continue to function as a carrier. The carrier could fight, and her captain informed Nimitz of this after she left Tongabatu.[137] The *Yorktown*'s difficulties centered around her structural strength and internal integrity.[138] These had been impaired, and the danger to the ship stemmed from the problem of what might happen if she incurred further damage without having corrected these initial weaknesses. As far as Nimitz was concerned, this was a risk that had to be accepted. He needed the *Yorktown* alongside her two sisters and he did not have ninety days in which to indulge her with a major refit. The forthcoming battle was not going to be postponed for the *Yorktown*, and Nimitz's intention was to allow the *Yorktown* time for nothing more than running repairs that would allow her to continue in action for two or three more weeks; thereafter she could have her full refit.

Nimitz was one of the first men to enter the dry dock at Pearl Harbor as it was drained, with the *Yorktown* inside it, on the afternoon of 27 May. His initial inspection confirmed Captain Elliott Buckmaster's assessment. Nimitz told the dockyard workers that they had three days in which to get the carrier back to sea.[139] The deadline meant that the *Yorktown* had time only for running repairs to be made to her hull and for her compartments either to be shorn up with wooden bracing or simply cut out and where possible rewelded. Unsatisfactory though these shortcuts were, they were acceptable given the circumstances. There were certain risks that had to be run with a deadline of just three days, but these were less than those that would be faced if the Americans had just two carriers off Midway.

The return of the carriers eased Nimitz's immediate problems, but also created two that related to command appointments. When the *Enterprise* returned to Pearl Harbor she brought with her an admiral suffering from eczema. It drove him to distraction and reduced him to about two hours of fitful sleep every night. As soon as he arrived Halsey reported to Nimitz that he was en route to the hospital. He recommended that command of his task force be turned over to his cruiser admiral, Rear Admiral Raymond A. Spruance.[140] Nimitz did not dispute Spruance's fitness for command of Task Force 16 even though Spruance—whom Nimitz had selected as his future chief of staff—was not an aviator and had never commanded as much as a carrier.[141] Nimitz's command problems centered not on Task Force 16 but on overall command of both task forces in the coming battle. With Halsey out of the running, command fell on Fletcher, but King had convinced himself that Fletcher's performance at the Coral Sea left much to be desired. Fletcher's signal of 17 May rebutting most of the criticism leveled at him had not placated King.[142]

Thus when Fletcher reported to Nimitz after the *Yorktown* reached Pearl Harbor he found himself in the embarrassing position of having to justify the handling of his forces in the Coral Sea. Though unconvincing in this interview, Fletcher the next day submitted verbal and written reports that convinced Nimitz that he should protect his otherwise hapless subordinate from King's impending wrath. In fact, Nimitz was pretty much stuck with Fletcher. With Wilson Brown long since on the beach and Fitch on the West Coast with the *Saratoga*, Nimitz really had no more than four officers from whom to choose for command—Fletcher, Spruance and the two cruiser admirals, Kinkaid and Smith. Nevertheless, Nimitz's decision to keep faith with Fletcher must have been made on grounds not of sentiment but of objectivity: Nimitz could not have placed the only carriers between the enemy and the West Coast under the command of a person whose competence was suspected. In some ways, however, events had unfolded in a convenient way for Nimitz. He is supposed to have said, more than twenty years later, that "it was a great day for the navy when Halsey had to enter the hospital."[143] The comment, although rather tasteless, was an indication that the impetuous and pugnacious Halsey, never widely acclaimed for his intellectual powers and surrounded by a hand-picked staff that left much to be desired, was perhaps not the best person to have commanded the fleet on this occasion.[144] The implication of Nimitz's comment was that the combination of Fletcher and Spruance was what was needed. Be that as it may, Fletcher retained command of Task Force 17 and, as senior admiral, was placed in overall command of the two carrier task forces. At the time of his appointment he agreed to grant Spruance full tactical command of his much larger task force.[145] With this question settled, both Fletcher and Spruance attended the staff conference held on the evening of 27 May, knowing that at that time all three carriers would be at sea to rendezvous in latitude 32° N, longitude 173° W, on 2 June. This juncture was designated Point Luck.[146]

The following morning Task Force 16 put to sea. The destroyers led the

The Aircraft Carrier *Enterprise*

way, followed by two tankers. The cruisers came next while the two carriers, the *Enterprise* leading the *Hornet*, brought up the rear. The task force went into box formation in order to allow the two carriers to fly on their eighty-strong air groups. In the event both had to be content with seventy-nine apiece because a Dauntless scout from the *Hornet* was unable to take off and a Devastator from the flagship had to ditch. As a result both carriers had twenty-seven-strong fighter squadrons and nineteen-strong squadrons of Dauntless bombers. The *Enterprise* had nineteen scouts to the eighteen of the *Hornet*, while the latter had fifteen torpedo bombers to the fourteen of the flagship.

In company was a formidable array of cruisers. A task force with two carriers needed no fewer than six cruisers under the command of Kinkaid. These were the heavy cruisers *New Orleans*, *Minneapolis*, *Vincennes*, *Northampton* and *Pensacola*, plus the *Atlanta*. The ships of the destroyer screen, like the cruisers, were almost all old companions of the carriers. The *Phelps*, *Worden*, *Monaghan* and *Aylwin* made up the First Destroyer Squadron; the *Balch*, *Benham*, *Ellet Maury*, plus a newcomer, the *Conyngham*, made up the Sixth. In company were the oilers *Cimarron* and *Platte*, from which the task force was to refuel for the last time before the battle on 31 May. The *Dewey* and the *Monssen* were assigned to the protection of the oilers. The *Gwin*, as we have seen, was to be ordered to join Task Force 16 after she returned to Pearl Harbor on 1 June after her dash to Midway, but she was never able to join company.

Shortly before noon the next day, 29 May, the repairs to the *Yorktown*'s hull had been completed and the dry dock was flooded preparatory to the carrier being towed into the roads. By that time most of the damaged compartments had been strengthened, but electricians and other specialists were still working on her twenty-four hours later when the carrier began to move down the channel under her own power.[147] In addition to the repairs that had been done she had been reprovisioned, itself a major task in view of the fact that the carrier's stocks had been all but exhausted after 101 days at sea. By any standard getting the *Yorktown* back to sea inside three days was an impressive achievement.

Task Force 17, like Task Force 16 before it, left Pearl Harbor and went into box formation to fly on the *Yorktown*'s air group. During the time at Oahu the group had been reconstituted. The original group (CVG-5), which had been with the carrier since the start of the war and had fought at the Coral Sea, was reorganized around squadrons provided by the *Saratoga*'s air group (CVG-3). The *Saratoga*'s Devastator torpedo and Dauntless bomber squadrons replaced those of the *Yorktown*, though the latter's bomber formation remained and was switched to the scouting role. The fighter squadron was reformed and at the same time reequipped with F4F-4 Wildcats in place of the Mark 3 versions with which the carrier had defended herself earlier in the month. This allowed the *Yorktown* to be equipped with a fighter squadron of twenty-seven aircraft, of which sixteen were piloted by original CVG-5 members. The remainder were drafted to the ship under the command of Lieutenant Commander John S. Thatch, formerly of the *Lexington* and already one of the Pacific Fleet's heroes. Some of the draftees had never been to sea with a carrier, and others were rusty after having been ashore for some months.[148] A lack of practice may have caused the accident that marred the *Yorktown*'s recovery of her aircraft. The carrier flew on her fourteen Devastators, eighteen bombers, twenty-seven Wildcats and nineteen scouts in that order, but one of the fighters missed the arrestor wires and bounced over the barriers, crashing into another Wildcat that was taxiing into position to be lowered to the hangar deck. The crash wrote off both fighters and killed the pilot of the fighter already on the deck. This pilot, the squadron's executive officer, Lieutenant Commander Donald Lovelace, was killed by the propeller of the other Wildcat.[149]

Protecting the *Yorktown* as she took on her air group was Smith's screening force. Smith had only two heavy cruisers, the *Astoria* and the *Portland*, after the *Chester* had been sent back to California with Fitch aboard for the *Saratoga* task force. In company with Smith were the five members of the Second Destroyer Squadron, the *Hammann*, *Hughes*, *Morris*, *Anderson* and *Russell*. No oilers accompanied the force; Task Force 17 would be refueled from the *Cimarron* and the *Platte* before the rendezvous with Task Force 16. Thereafter these two oilers, with their escorts, were to stay clear of the battle area yet sufficiently close to be on hand if needed, a repetition of the *Neosho-Sims* situation. As always, the concern about fuel was acute because of the needs of the destroyers. To safeguard against possible mishap a third oiler, the *Guadalupe*, was detailed to stand in support of the task forces. Escorted by the destroyers *Blue* and *Ralph Talbot*, which were taken off convoy duties between San Francisco and Pearl Harbor, the *Guadalupe* left Oahu on 3 June and arrived at Midway on the sixth.

The *Yorktown* and her consorts refueled from the *Cimarron* and the *Platte* on 1 June, when the *Hornet* flew reconnaissance missions to the west on behalf of Task Force 16. During its days at sea talk between ships had been banned by Spruance, and his pilots were under strict instructions not to use their radios. He refused to operate homing devices for his aircraft.[150] The next day, the second, Spruance's flagship provided the eyes of the force, which in the afternoon turned back eastwards to effect the juncture with Task Force 17 in latitude 30° 04′ N, longitude 172° 45′ W, just before 1600, some thirty minutes late.[151] The two task forces then settled down on courses ten miles apart, Fletcher ordering Spruance to stay within visual signaling distance of the *Yorktown*.[152] Like Spruance, Fletcher was concerned lest there be any signaling mistake that might alert the Japanese to the presence of the American carrier force off Midway. Fletcher's caution should have availed him nothing. His departure from Pearl Harbor on 30 May had been noted by traffic analysts not in Tokyo but in the *Yamato*. Tokyo had fallen for an elaborate deception being played out in the southwest Pacific by the *Tangier* and the *Salt Lake City*. These ships spent their time simulating a task force's flying operations, using the wavebands on which the Japanese were known to eavesdrop. The ploy fooled Tokyo but not the analysts with the fleet. The *Yamato* noted the telltale signs of increased air activity at Oahu on 30 May, which was the signature of the departure of a carrier force. Fortunately for the Americans, however, the *Yamato*, being at sea, could not send this vital information to Nagumo. Thus the carrier force was left in ignorance of the very real possibility that an enemy force might be awaiting it off Midway.[153]

On 3 June it was the *Yorktown*'s turn to provide reconnaissance for what was now a fleet, and Fletcher had decided that she would do the same the next day when, if intelligence was correct, battle would be joined. The latest intelligence calculation was that the Japanese would have four carriers, but Fletcher, no doubt a little more cautious as a result of the battle of the Coral Sea, wanted to ensure against being taken in the flank by an enemy whose presence was unknown.[154] He had no intention of playing the role of the biter being bit; he would not be caught by the selfsame tactic that he intended to use against the Japanese. To forestall this possibility Fletcher planned to use his flagship in the role of scout and reserve. The *Enterprise* and the *Hornet* would strike with their full force, leaving the *Yorktown* free to choose between joining a first strike, providing a second strike or operating defensively. In this way Fletcher hoped to keep the full power of decision in his own hands.

Such was the situation at nightfall on 3 June as the Americans settled down for the last time before battle was joined the following morning. The journey since 1 May had been a long and tortuous one, full of pitfalls, but by 3 June the Americans had arrived on time, in the right place and with a chance. That in itself was an impressive technical achievement, made more significant by the fact that the two carrier forces that were to clash the next day were very evenly matched. In the whole of the Pacific the Japanese possessed a clear numerical superiority over the Americans in every type of warship with the single exception of submarines. They had 11 battleships to America's 7; 10 carriers to 5; 18 heavy cruisers to 13; 20 light cruisers to 11; and 107 destroyers to 85. Of the Combined Fleet's 218 units no fewer than 113 warships and 16 submarines were deployed in Operations AL and MI. The Americans, on the other hand, had 47 warships and 26 submarines to defend the Aleutians and Midway. Yet, as we have noted earlier, where it mattered—off Midway on the morning of 4 June—the balance was in favor of the Americans. They had 3 carriers and 22 escorts at sea. With the carriers were 234 aircraft, with another 110 on Midway. For all their massive superiority of numbers spread across thousands of miles of ocean, the Japanese had an unsupported vanguard of 4 carriers, 17 escorts, 229 aircraft and 17 seaplanes. Because the Japanese forces were separated by distances that precluded mutual support, American hopes of victory were not ill-founded or fanciful. They might have seemed incredible at the time given past Japanese success and American ineffectiveness thus far in the war, but the fact was that the Americans had a chance and they knew it. Against the enemy's superior technique and aircraft the Americans had a slight advantage of numbers. They had a more simple objective than the Japanese. They had radar and homing devices, and they had a knowledge of the enemy's order of battle, timetable and plans.

History has not recorded how closely the odds were balanced in this battle. The hypercritical observer could argue that with all these factors in their favor, Midway was a battle that the Americans should have won. Perhaps some future revisionist will argue thus. Suffice it to say that the material balance was much closer than has been generally recognized. The forces were closely balanced owing to the combination of Japanese miscalculation and the careful calculations of the Americans. On the evening of 3 June both sides were at sea and moving to their stations. The Americans, at sea, at Midway and at Pearl Harbor, could do no more than wait and see if on the morrow fate would bring them victory because of their efforts or give victory to the Japanese in spite of themselves.

CHAPTER 10

Approach to Contact

Throughout April and early May there was a steady stream of ships of the Combined Fleet returning to their bases to take on the supplies they needed for forthcoming operations. From the middle of May onwards there was an equally steady trickle of sailings from these bases as the units that were to open proceedings sailed to take up their positions and the ships that were to stage from the Kuriles or the Marianas moved to their assembly points.

The first of the surface forces to leave the homeland were those earmarked to make the landings in the Hawaiian Islands. The transports carrying the landing forces left Japan on 20 May and arrived at Guam on the twenty-fourth. Two days later the carrier force bound for the Aleutians cleared Ominato harbor, negotiated the Taugaru Strait separating Honshu and Hokkaido, and set course for the northeast. Within a matter of hours after leaving Honshu, the Second Carrier Striking Force was enveloped in a damp fog that stayed with it for the whole of the nine days that it took the force to reach its flying-off position.

At 0800 on 27 May the order was given for the First Carrier Striking Force to sortie. Through the assembled ranks of almost the whole of the Combined Fleet gathered in the Hashirajima anchorage, the *Nagara* and her destroyers led the two seaplane-cruisers, then the two battleships and finally the four great carriers themselves towards the sea. The rest of the fleet, waiting to follow in the wake of the carrier force, cleared ship to cheer Nagumo's units on their way. Few who watched or took part in the departure of the carrier force from the Hiroshima base could have remained unmoved. Bright sunlight beat down on what was the greatest assembly of Japanese naval power in any one place since the start of the war. Morale was high on this special day. The twenty-seventh was not just the day that happened to be chosen for the sortie because the carriers had to be off Midway nine days later to allow the capture of the atoll. It was the day *The*

Japan Times and Advertiser, with unconscious honesty, called "the moment of fulfillment."[1] It was Navy Day, the thirty-seventh anniversary of the greatest triumph in Japanese naval history, the victory over the Russians at the battle of Tsu-shima in 1905. Small wonder, then, that the Japanese were so confident. With so much force brought together for this single operation there was no alternative to yet another Japanese victory. But this confidence obscured the fact that if all this might, all this enormous agglomeration of power that surrounded them on every side, could not break the Americans then the Americans would never be broken at all. Take away the forces bound for the north, the few ships still in the south or on the China station, the *Zuikaku* and the *Shokaku* and the other units licking their wounds, and what was in hand was not an operation by the Combined Fleet—it was a combined fleet operation. There was nothing left in reserve. Two fleet carriers, five heavy and ten light cruisers comprised the total number of major units of the navy not assigned to Operations AL and MI either because of their damaged condition or the need for their presence elsewhere. No one who watched the departure of the all-conquering carrier force could have guessed that none of the ships that rode at anchor would ever see the carriers again, that the stark alternative to the anticipated victory at Midway would be a defeat that was ultimately to engulf every single ship that sailed on Navy Day. Not one of Nagumo's ships was to see August 1945, and very few of the ships that cheered the First Carrier Striking Force on its way were to survive a war that in June 1942 was not drawing to a close but only just beginning.

The next day it was the invasion forces' turn to begin their slow and plodding march to the east. The forces destined to land on Attu and Kiska set sail from Ominato, while the forces bound for Kure and Midway set out from Saipan. To shake off and confuse any enemy submarine that might be in company, the forces bound for the Hawaiian Islands initially steamed westwards before turning back to the east, passing to the south of Tinian as they made for the central Pacific. From Guam Kurita led his cruiser force to a position just beyond the horizon north of Tanaka's transports.

On 29 May the main battle forces cleared Hashirajima on what was to be for most of the battleships their first operational mission of the war. Kondo's force led the way, his light units, like those of Nagumo two days earlier, leading the heavy units as they negotiated the narrow Bungo Strait where enemy submarines were almost certain to be on patrol. To safeguard the battle forces strong antisubmarine patrols were flown from shore; the ships themselves made 20 knots through the strait in order to throw off any enemy submarine that tried to establish and maintain contact. In the wake of Kondo were the two main battle forces, those of Yamamoto and Takasu, the old *Hosho* bringing up the rear. Kondo's Invasion Force separated itself from the other two forces almost immediately. Yamamoto and Takasu were to remain in company for six days before they divided in midocean on the morning of 3 June. Takasu thereafter set course to the northeast to take up a position where he could support the Second Carrier Striking Force; Yamamoto continued to set a course towards the east to support the First Carrier Striking Force.[2]

Once the various forces were at sea, what should have been for more than one month past standard operational procedure within the navy, strict radio silence, was at last imposed. The sources that had provided the Americans with so much invaluable information over the last weeks finally began to fall silent, a fact in itself significant to the watching, waiting Americans. Yet, paradoxically, this time the Japanese needed their communications far more urgently than when they had used their radios with such prodigal abandon, for as the great ships made their way to the open sea, the first part of Operation MI miscarried—indeed, Operation K miscarried in part even before Nagumo's carrier force left Hiroshima.

The submarine *I-121* reached the French Frigate Shoals on 26 May, four days before Operation K was to begin. Subsequently she was to be joined by the *I-123* while the *I-122* went on to Laysan. To their discomfort, however, the Japanese found that they were not alone. The shoals were not the same desolate and deserted wastes that they had been in March when last the Type KRS submarines and Mavis flying boats had visited them. Nimitz's arrangement ensured that there would be a seaplane tender on hand to meet the Japanese, and she showed a disconcerting disinclination to move on. Indeed, as the Japanese watched the shoals over the next few days it became clear to them that this unwelcome trespasser was not alone. Seemingly the Americans were active along the length of the Hawaiian chain as other warships, seaplanes and flying boats put in fleeting appearances. By the twenty-ninth two enemy units appeared to have taken up permanent residence, and Lieutenant Commander Toshitake Ueno of the *I-123* had no alternative but to signal Kwajalein that with the shoals being watched, it would be impossible to execute Operation K. There was no possibility of the replenishment submarines being able to refuel flying boats as long as the Americans were at the shoals, and there was nothing the Japanese boats could do to eliminate the enemy. The Type KRS submarines did not have tubes and torpedoes, it being no part of their role to fight, and even if they had had offensive armament there would have been no point in using it against the units at the shoals: any attack on American units there was certain to be counterproductive in the sense that it would have brought more enemy units to the area. Thus the best that the Japanese could do was to hope that the American units would move on of their own accord. Kwajalein responded to this development by postponing the attempt to reconnoiter Pearl Harbor for one day, but the following night Ueno reported that the situation was unchanged. This time he received orders directly from the Eleventh Air Fleet. He was to stay at the shoals in case the tiresome Americans moved on; the other two submarines were to move to their appointed places in cordon line A south of the Hawaiian Islands. Operation K itself was suspended for the moment. Given the tightness of the operational schedule, suspension was a euphemism for cancellation.[3] Thus there was to be no reconnaissance of the enemy's main base before the start of the battle.

Worse was to follow this unexpected and thoroughly unwelcome development. On 30 May, the day Operation K was supposed to be put into effect, and again on 1 June, Japanese reconnaissance flying boats from Wake clashed with their counterparts from Midway.[4] In the course of these exchanges the Americans emerged second best, particularly on the thirtieth. That day two of their Catalinas were badly shot up, not that they were unable to stagger back to Midway. For both sides the clashes were ominous; they meant that the other side was pushing out reconnaissance missions to unprecedented ranges. Ramsey was in fact determined to send his reconnaissance missions to a range of 700 miles on 3 June and if possible on preceding days as well. His reason for doing so was obvious. He expected the Japanese to attack Midway at dawn on 4 June from a range of about 200 miles. With the Japanese carriers able to steam 300 miles at full speed under cover of darkness, the First Carrier Striking Force would be 500 miles (or less) from Midway at dusk on 3 June. The 700-mile search pattern therefore ensured that the Japanese carrier force would be found the day before it reached flying-off position. In addition, the slower transports and other forces would have to come within this 700-mile search area either at the same time or even before the carriers.[5] Evidence that the Americans were patrolling to ranges of 600 to 700 miles should have warned the Japanese that something untoward was afoot, especially since radio intelligence picked up what appeared to be enemy submarine sighting reports and other indications of enemy submarine activity west of Midway.[6] By any reasoned standard these signs suggested the presence of an enemy patrol line. Moreover, on Midway itself, according to reports received on 2 June, there were unmistakable signs of large-scale enemy activity. Lieutenant Commander Yahachi Tanabe of the *I-168* spent three days watching the atoll and his report was comprehensive. He assessed that flights from Midway averaged between ninety and one hundred every day with reconnaissance aircraft spending the greater part of the hours of daylight in the air. This was confirmation of the air clashes of 30 May and 1 June. For reconnaissance aircraft to leave before or at dawn and not return to the atoll until late afternoon meant that the Americans were searching out to ranges of 600 or 700 miles. Moreover, the sheer scale of American air operations, which hardly tallied with Japanese intelligence estimates that enemy air strength on Midway was small, indicated that the Americans were attempt

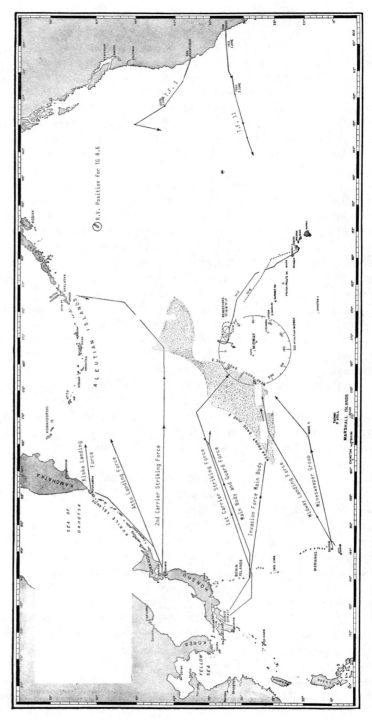

The Battle of Midway and the Aleutians Operations: Movement of Forces to 2400, 3 June 1942

ing to cover the whole of the western approaches to the atoll. At night the glare of work lights showed that construction work continued on both islands, again a clear sign of unusual and seemingly urgent enemy activity.[7] It was almost as if the Americans were expecting trouble.

Individually none of these matters amounted to much, but taken together they did. A pattern of activity should have been pieced together by any competent staff. At Midway, at the shoals, in the air and at sea there were indications of activity on the part of an enemy who was supposed to be in total ignorance of the fate that awaited him. All the signs suggested that the Americans were on their guard. Further information should have clinched matters and caused the Japanese to reconsider the plans that even then were getting under way.

The scale of signaling from Pearl Harbor, which the Japanese picked up, was itself a significant fact. After their success in working out the enemy's plan of campaign, timetable and most of the order of battle, it was ironic that the Americans in their turn almost compensated the enemy by duplicating his error. With their fleet at sea the Americans had to use their radio for communications, if not on the prodigal scale with which the Japanese had used theirs over the previous weeks then certainly with an intensity that ran the risk of compromise. By 30 May the Japanese had picked up so much radio traffic from Pearl Harbor that only one conclusion was possible: an American carrier force was at sea. Radio analysts in Japan suggested that 40 percent of all the signals were high priority. This was a suspiciously large proportion, one that could only confirm the conclusion that an enemy formation was at sea.[8] But as late as 31 May there was no clear indication of where this formation might be. Analysts in Japan placed American carriers in the southwest Pacific, though for the Americans to have deployed further carriers to that theater after their (alleged) losses in the Coral Sea and after the contact of mid-May scarcely seemed to make sense.[9] If the Americans had stripped their strength from the central Pacific to move into the southwest Pacific, the Japanese need have no fear of opposition at Midway, but there was a growing feeling that the Americans might conceivably have a task force at sea somewhere in the vicinity of Pearl Harbor.[10] In fact, Japanese attention had fixed upon the idea that the Americans had a maximum of three carriers available for battle but that there was little chance of their being able to deploy two to Midway. Their most liberal assessment was that the enemy might have a single carrier in the vicinity of the Hawaiian Islands.[11] Whether one, two or three, the presence of enemy carriers was certain to make things a little tighter than they need have been, but as far as the Japanese were concerned there was still no cause to worry. As long as they had surprise on their side and their submarines were between Nagumo's advancing carrier force and Pearl Harbor and therefore in a position to warn of an American sortie, there was every reason to presume that the First Carrier Striking Force was in no immediate danger and would be able to fulfill its objectives.

But submarine deployment and surprise were precisely the two areas of activity where Japanese preparations had miscarried. The presence of both the First Carrier Striking Force and the two major battle forces was compromised by breaches of radio discipline. The initial transgression was committed by the battle forces or, more accurately, by one of the oilers that was supposed to succor the battleships bound for Midway and the Aleutians. Refueling was scheduled for 31 May, but in thick fog the battleship forces did not find the *Naruto* and a search by aircraft from the *Hosho* failed to find the missing oiler. The oiler signaled its location in order that the refueling could be carried out, and from that time onwards the battle forces had to assume that their presence had been discovered.[12] The second breach of radio discipline came from the *Akagi* on 2 June. When it came time for Nagumo to turn his force so that it might start its run down on Midway from the northwest he could not see a single ship in his force. He had been able to tuck his formation behind a bad weather front that promised to keep him immune from detection in the critical approach to contact phase, but the fog played havoc with navigation and station keeping. In fact, Nagumo had been forced to deploy his ships single line ahead, each one trailing a marker buoy so that the ship astern could follow in the wake of an invisible leader. But such a drastic change of course in hazardous conditions was fraught with difficulty. It would be all too easy for a ship to miss the turn and become separated with little or no chance of rejoining. Nagumo had three options. He could reduce his speed and hope to get free of the worst of the fog before carrying out his maneuver; he could risk the turn; or he could break radio silence and order the change of course. The first option was out of the question. The operational schedule was too tight to give Nagumo any time to check his advance. Too much depended on Nagumo's carrying out his orders to the minute for even the slightest delay to be allowed; the synchronization of Operation MI robbed the Japanese of flexibility. The second course, equally, was out of the question. Nagumo therefore had to risk sending a low-powered signal to his units. Though it was the shortest possible signal—"Course 125"—the *Yamato*, then some 600 miles astern of the carriers, picked it up.[13] As in the case of the *Naruto* signal, common prudence had to assume that the signal had been heard by the enemy and that the presence of a force, though not necessarily its composition, would be known to the Americans.

These lapses of radio discipline, which would never have taken place during the more carefully prepared and executed operation against Pearl Harbor, might well have prompted any other navy in similar circumstances ⌐on the mission on which it was embarked. But not the Imperial .gumo's decision to resort to the radio had in large part been shaped by the calculation that the risk attached to using it was not very severe: since the enemy was probably in Pearl Harbor, he would be in no position to capitalize on any chance discovery. Even if the enemy acted promptly, the advantage of position would remain with Nagumo, who was presumably closer to Midway than the enemy. He would be able to deal with Midway and any American task force as it came upon the scene—exactly as the Japanese plan of campaign envisaged. In any event, the carriers could not be in any immediate danger because the submarines should be on their patrol lines and thus in position to report the advance of an American force that set out from Pearl Harbor in response to a radio interception. In fact Japanese luck held with regard to both signals. Neither was picked up by the Americans, though the Japanese still should have acted on the belief that the signals would be monitored by the enemy.

But the Japanese were out of luck on the matter of their submarines. They were supposed to have been on their patrol lines from 1 June onwards, but they were not. Their participation had been added as an afterthought to Operation MI when the war games played at the beginning of May showed that the carriers needed an advance guard. The initial failure to provide a submarine reconnaissance force for the carriers was rather strange—the submarines always led the fleet to sea and covered its withdrawal. The orders rectifying this situation were not issued until the second week of May.[14] This left the various units involved in the operation with about two weeks to complete arrangements, put to sea and take up station in front of the carrier force. With some units undergoing overhaul and others at sea when they received their orders, there was no possibility of all the boats being in their assigned positions by the appointed hour. The June timetable of Yamamoto was a killer; there was simply not enough time for the submarines to get on patrol in time. Some units did reach their operational sectors on 31 May, but the cordon lines across the arc of the Hawaiian Islands on which the Japanese depended for an early warning of an approaching enemy were not completed until 3 June—just twenty-four hours before the carriers arrived at their flying-off position.[15] By then, of course, it was too late for the submarines to discover the Americans; the enemy task forces had already crossed cordon line B on their way to Point Luck. Had the Japanese submarines been on time they would probably have found Task Force 17 but would still have missed Task Force 16. The *Yorktown* and her escorts crossed what should have been the Japanese patrol line shortly before midnight on 31 May, and they passed through the line a matter of hours in front of the submarines that were supposed to be in that particular sector. Overall, the crossing of the B line by the *Yorktown* was a close shave. Had she been sighted by the Japanese the consequences might have been highly unpleasant for both sides.[16] It seems probable that the Japanese would have been more profoundly shocked, even if the consequences for the Americans might have been more immediately detrimental. The discovery of an enemy task force could hardly have been dismissed as merely coincidental by the Japanese, despite their confidence; the sea area to which the Americans were heading was too remote for the Japanese to do anything other than draw the correct and alarming conclusion. But the submarines were late, and the result was that Nagumo's carrier force was all but in the van of the attack, with no reconnaissance being provided by either submarines or flying boats.* Nagumo, deprived of his eyes and ears, was left in the dark about most of the things that were happening, or not happening, about him.

Had the *Yamato* been with the carrier force many of Nagumo's problems would have disappeared. The presence of the new super-dreadnought in the vanguard would have solved many of the communications problems that plagued the First Carrier Striking Force. For a flagship the *Akagi* was poorly provided. She had had to reduce her aerials because they impeded flying operations, and her portside island, despite being redesigned to overcome previous shortcomings, remained inadequate for her needs.[17] If the *Yamato* had been with the carriers instead of 600 miles astern, the First Carrier Striking Force would not have been left unaware that an enemy force might be off Midway. It is clear from subsequent events that Nagumo was unaware of both the scale and range of American air reconnaissance from Midway.[18] Nor did he know that the submarines would fail to keep their operational schedule. It does appear, however, that he knew of the "suspension" of Operation K, though most of the accounts of the battle suggest that he was unaware of it. The discussions that surrounded the change of course, cited in what is generally regarded as the most authoritative of the Japanese accounts of the battle, indicate that the carrier force did know of the failure to reconnoiter Pearl Harbor.[19] This does not alter the fact that overall Nagumo was poorly served during his approach to contact, primarily because Yamamoto deliberately chose not to make information available to him.[20] It is hard to better the observation of the commentator who noted with regard to these arrangements that there is never a case for camouflage taking precedence over effectiveness,[21] yet this was precisely what was happening on the Japanese side. In an effort to ensure surprise and deception the Japanese deployed their forces in such a way that they could neither communicate nor support one another. This basic weakness of deployment led Nagumo to commit the first of a number of operational

*Perhaps the submarines were not even in the right place. It appears that the records on the Japanese side were tampered with. The account of the *Yorktown* crossing the B line is orthodox, drawn from standard accounts of the battle, yet as Toland has pointed out, one of the captains of the First Carrier Striking Force discovered after the battle that the submarines had gone to the wrong lines because the Combined Fleet had made errors in transmitting coordinates. This officer alleged that the Combined Fleet attempted to hush up its mistake.

The Aircraft Carrier *Akagi*

errors and miscalculations that were to result in the destruction of his force. That the First Carrier Striking Force sailed into deadly danger without its ever being aware of the peril in which it was placed was not the fault of Nagumo.

Contact between the Japanese and Americans was made on the morning of 3 June. Within a matter of an hour or so two events took place: American reconnaissance patrols from Midway at last discovered enemy forces bound for the atoll, and the Japanese bombed Dutch Harbor in the Aleutians. Though the two events were separated by more than 1000 miles of ocean, their coinciding marked the overture to the main battle, and both the Japanese and the Americans, for different reasons, could take comfort from the fact that things were unfolding more or less according to plan. For the Japanese the operation in the Aleutians, opening right on time with quietly acceptable results, seemed to augur well for the main effort, even if the discovery of their forces by the enemy had come much sooner than expected. The latter did not appear to be too serious. Japanese forces would surely be nearer to Midway than any American naval force, and the enemy's air strength on the atoll would pay for its presumptuousness when Nagumo's carriers entered the fray. For the Americans the same events showed that their intelligence surveys had been correct in assessing the enemy's intentions and timetable. In part this brought an end to mounting uncertainties within the American high command. During the previous day, 2 June, anxieties had multiplied as American air reconnaissance failed to establish any contact with an enemy that had to come within range of air patrols from Midway if he was to keep to his operational schedule. Even a Flying Fortress searching out as far as 800 miles due west of Midway failed to establish contact with a force or forces that the Americans knew must be in that area.[22] Even worse, there was no sign of the enemy to the northwest. The bad weather front coming down on Midway ruled out a search in that direction beyond a range of 400 miles.[23] Ramsey's intention had been frustrated, at least in part, by a combination of bad weather and fine

Japanese seamanship. Thus the contacts made on the morning of the third came as something of a relief to the Americans. The first contact, at 0843, was made by a Catalina that reported the presence of a suspicious but unidentified ship; at 0904 the Catalina reported the presence of two enemy ships believed to have been detached from the minesweeper group that was at that time moving towards Midway from Wake.[24] A further report, made at 0927, proved to be more important. What at first appeared to Ensign Jewell H. Reid and his crew to be dirt on the windscreen turned out to be slightly more substantial. His initial contact report left something to be desired, but for the moment it was the contact itself that was so important.[25] Coming hard on the heels of the bombing of Dutch Harbor, it seemed to indicate that the enemy's plan of campaign was unfolding as it was supposed to—and as it had to if the Americans were to spring their trap.

The affair in the north was to prove a frustrating and highly unsatisfactory one for both sides. For the Japanese Operation AL began well enough, and at its end they had been able to strike some hard blows against Dutch Harbor and secure Attu and Kiska before their carrier force returned to Japanese waters on 24 June. But even these results were below expectations and in any case were to be completely overshadowed by events in less intemperate climes. As for the Americans, their counter to Operation AL proved equally disappointing. The whole of the Aleutians venture turned out to be little more than a potentially lethal game of blindman's buff played out in fog and subzero temperatures without benefit to either side.

During the Second Carrier Striking Force's approach to contact, both sides' reconnaissance failed them. On the Japanese side the *I-19* successfully conducted a reconnaissance of Dutch Harbor on 30 May with her Glen seaplane, but the fragile machine broke up when it tried to land alongside the parent submarine. This meant that a second scouting mission, scheduled for 2 June, could not be conducted other than by periscope.[26] There was nothing the Japanese could do about this unsatisfactory situation, and Kakuta was therefore obliged to make his way towards Dutch Harbor without the help of any advanced reconnaissance and without the means to provide for it out of his own resources. He had no idea what might oppose him, and he had nothing more than the vaguest notions about the geography and meteorology of this theater of operations. One old photograph and maps thirty years old were the sum of Japanese information about their target.[27] Few operations can have been so underprepared as Operation AL, though it must be remembered that the forces earmarked for the landings on Midway were scarcely better provided. The officer who had been tasked to plan the actual amphibious phase of Operation MI did not know of the existence of gaps in the coral reef of the atoll,[28] and H-Hour remained unfixed when the operation began.[29]

The Japanese carrier force intended to strike against Dutch Harbor soon after dawn on 3 June. With the long hours of daylight in northern latitudes at this time of year sunrise was at about 0250, but the fog that had provided the Second Carrier Striking Force with much-needed cover during the approach now stubbornly persisted and did its best to hamper flying operations. It was only about five minutes before sunrise—by which time visibility should have been quite adequate—when the two Japanese carriers sighted one another, despite their separation by more than half a mile of ocean.[30] Even then the cloud ceiling was down to about 400 feet. This proved to be the most important factor in deciding the outcome of the Japanese attack. The low ceiling extended all the way to Dutch Harbor and prevented the air groups of the two carriers from joining in a single formation. They proceeded independently, and after the Zekes from the *Junyo* broke formation to deal with a Catalina that unwisely chose this moment to put in an appearance, the two flights lost contact and never rejoined.[31] The Vals and Zekes of the *Junyo* had to abandon their attempts to regain touch with the Kates and Zekes of the *Ryujo*, and they were forced to turn back when they failed to find Dutch Harbor. Their successful recovery, under the circumstances, was a minor miracle in its own right, though the precision and extra punch that twelve dive-bombers would have added to an attack were to be missed.

The *Ryujo*'s aircraft, on the other hand, did rather better, even though their mission began inauspiciously when one of the ten Kates committed to the attack stalled on takeoff and crashed into the sea. While the Japanese carrier force stayed behind the bad weather front that had shielded its advance from the Kuriles, the *Ryujo*'s aircraft flew into the eye of the storm. By good fortune Lieutenant Masayuki Yamaguchi's flight and clear weather arrived together over Dutch Harbor. It was the first time in three days that the base and anchorage had lost their overhead cover, and the Japanese made the most of their fleeting opportunity.[32] Because Dutch Harbor's rather tenuous communications with Otter Point broke down at this critical juncture—even though Anchorage, Kodiak and Theobald picked up the base's alert—the Japanese bombers were unopposed in the air as they accounted for oil dumps, the hospital and the barracks at Fort Mears. They also destroyed the Russian Orthodox Church on the island with one of their misdirected bombs. The Zekes destroyed one Catalina as it attempted to take off and damaged several others.[33] For so small an effort the Japanese secured a reasonable return, but what they had found at Dutch Harbor surprised them and showed that they would have to continue their efforts to register any significant success. Over Unalaska the Japanese encountered heavy but not particularly effective antiaircraft fire that accounted for just one aircraft, a Zeke, which was destroyed during its attacks on Catalinas in the anchorage. The Americans appeared to be ready to meet the Japanese attack, and in other respects they seemed to be making themselves ready for much greater efforts, for on the island the Japanese found all the installations and roads of a major naval base. Moreover, as the Japanese reformed for their return to *Ryujo*, one of their pilots had chanced upon the destroyer squadron in Makushin Bay.[34] This information was immediately transmitted to the flagship, Kakuta thus being made aware of the need for a second strike even without receiving Yamaguchi's assessment that a second raid on the base itself would be needed. This Kakuta ordered to be carried out at about 0900, before the *Ryujo*'s aircraft were recovered.[35]

This second attack fared much worse than the first. By the time the aircraft committed to the attack came upon Dutch Harbor, the clear weather had moved on and the American base was back under its impenetrable cover. But even if the weather had proved kinder it is doubtful whether any major success could have been recorded: the strike force that Kakuta was forced to send against Dutch Harbor consisted of only the aircraft that had returned to the *Junyo* after their initial failure to find Unalaska, plus four Dave seaplanes from the two heavy cruisers with the carrier force. The extent to which the Japanese were scraping the barrel to mount even so modest an attack can be gauged from the fact that just two Alf seaplanes were left as combat air patrol for the entire task force, and one of them, from the *Takao*, was lost on landing.[36] The weakness of these various arrangements, particularly that of the attacking forces and defensive air patrols left to the Second Carrier Striking Force, was a condemnation of the whole of Operation AL. With so little in terms of striking power—just eighteen Kates and fifteen Vals—there was small chance that the Second Carrier Striking Force could register significant results against any type of target. With the main carrier force off Midway, the carriers might well have played a far more important role than the one they were called upon to play in the Aleutians.

Only the four seaplanes found their objective in the course of this second attack, the other aircraft from the *Junyo* being forced to turn back without finding Dutch Harbor for a second time. Since the Daves were armed only with two 30-kg bombs, they could not do anything more than the most superficial of damage, and they were hopelessly miscast for the task in hand. Theirs was not to attack destroyers, even World War One destroyers, which were contemptuously said to be liable to sink after colliding with a barnacle.[37] The Daves achieved nothing and lost two of their number when they were intercepted by P-40 fighters from Otter Point.[38] The other two seaplanes that managed to escape immediate destruction were able to make their way back to their cruisers, but both were written off trying to land.[39] In return, the Americans did no better than the Japanese. Bad weather accounted for no fewer than four Catalinas that were directed to enemy, and the only two that did find the Japanese were shot down.[40] One was destroyed in the course of the first mission against Dutch Harbor, three of its crew being rescued by the *Takao*. The other ran into the Japanese combat air patrol but managed to escape immediate destruction by maneuvering in the clouds; it suffered such damage, however, that it was forced down long before it made a landfall. Fortunately for its crew, the Catalina came down close to the cutter *Nemaha*, which picked up her SOS signals and rescued the crew. Unfortunately for the American command, static frustrated the efforts of both the Catalina and the *Nemaha* to send an accurate contact report back to base.[41]

When the *Junyo* had recovered her aircraft in the wake of the second abortive mission, Kakuta reversed course to get back into the foul weather and away from American search patrols while he decided what to do the next day. In fact he had little option but to renew the attack as the essential prerequisite for the planned landings in the western Aleutians. There was a certain simplicity about Japanese decisions at this stage. The wild weather and unneutralized status of Dutch Harbor meant that Kakuta could not proceed with the landings on Adak planned for the following day.[42] Thus he ordered his landing forces to mark time before moving against their objectives. The Second Carrier Striking Force, having approached to within 150 miles of Dutch Harbor, hauled off to seaward for the remainder of 3 June and then turned back during the night to resume the attack on Dutch Harbor the next day.[43]

The Americans were not in so fortunate a position as the Japanese. Virtually everything that could have gone wrong on the third did. American difficulties in large part arose from a divided command and lack of communications. Buckner and Butler were at Anchorage while the tactical headquarters for both the army and navy remained at Kodiak. With Theobald at sea and observing radio silence, no real command and control was being exercised over the various American forces in Alaska and the Aleutians. Local commanders were forced to act independently, as best they could with the resources at hand. Herein lay the cause of further difficulties. If the Americans were to find the enemy they would need reconnaissance aircraft and seaplanes with radar. The harsh climate, the low ceilings and poor visibility with which aircraft had to contend meant that the success of reconnaissance patrols, unless made by planes with radar, was simply a matter of luck. The Americans needed airborne radar to find the enemy and act as pathfinder for bomber forces without radar sets. The collection of Fortresses, Bolos, Marauders and Liberators that made up the bomber element of the Eleventh Air Force could not find the enemy unless they were led to him, and the Americans did not have enough reconnaissance units with radar to ensure contact with the enemy. Neither was there a chance of American surface units finding the Japanese. The screen in front of Dutch Harbor failed to do its job. And Theobald, of course, had been too clever for his own good: with Task Group 8.6 to the south of Kodiak rather than to the south of the western Aleutians where it was supposed to be, his formation "proved about as useful as if it had been in the South Atlantic."[44] But by the same token it was as safe as if it had been in that ocean. Which force might have found the other first amid the shifting banks of fog had Theobald taken his formation to its proper position is open to speculation. Apart from one high-speed dash back to Kodiak to find out what was happening, Theobald, with two heavy and three light cruisers plus their four destroyers, faded from the story.

From the time that Kakuta turned the Second Carrier Striking Force away from Dutch Harbor on the third, Operation AL began to lose its significance. In part this was the natural consequence of the Japanese plan of campaign—after this day the operation had to take a back seat to the main action as it unfolded off Midway; and in part it was the consequence of Operation MI developing along lines totally unforeseen by the Japanese. The effort in the North Pacific was to be downgraded in a frantic move to redeploy forces when the battle off Midway went against the First Carrier Striking Force. The attempt to redeploy forces on the fourth came after Kakuta had renewed the attack on Dutch Harbor and only after the Americans had launched a number of unsuccessful and uncoordinated attacks on the Second Carrier Striking Force.

For the same reason neither the Americans nor the Japanese were able to register major success on the fourth: neither side had the strength to strike powerfully at the enemy. Operations on both sides were too fragmentary for a major tactical or even strategic success to be achieved by either side. But there was one incident that was to have significant results for each side. In the attack on Dutch Harbor, during which their bombers badly damaged the accommodation ship *Northwestern* and destroyed four storage tanks with 750,000 gallons of oil, the Japanese lost a Zeke piloted by Petty Officer Tadayoshi Koga from the *Ryujo*. It was hit by a single bullet from a Catalina that Koga had shot down. The bullet damaged the Zeke's oil-pressure gauge and not the engine, but the zero reading on the instrument panel convinced Koga that his engine would quickly die on him. He therefore chose to set his plane down on uninhabited Akutan Island. This had been designated by the Japanese as the emergency landing strip for their aircraft, since crews ditching in these cold waters would die of shock and exposure in a matter of minutes. The Japanese intention was to recover their men by submarine. Koga presumably tried to put his Zeke down on what he believed was firm ground. Touching down on a bog his aircraft somersaulted, breaking Koga's neck but leaving the aircraft itself remarkably intact. Some five weeks later Americans sighted the wreck of the aircraft—a silent comment on the value of islands that the Japanese sent more than fifty

Captured Zeke Undergoing Repairs in San Diego

warships, submarines and auxiliaries to secure. Recovered and shipped back to the mainland, Koga's Zeke was the first of its kind to be captured intact since the start of the war. It was subjected to rigorous combat evaluation, and the Americans were as much amazed by the Zeke's performance as by its lack of structural strength. Tests revealed the aircraft's many weaknesses in full, weaknesses that had been hidden only too effectively by the first-class pilots who had flown the fighter in the opening months of the war. The initial evaluation report was available in September and the full report on 31 October. These, combined with the lessons that were being learned the hard way in combat, were critical in helping the Americans devise defensive and offensive tactics that in part resulted in the neutralization of the Zeke as an effective fighter.[45]

At about 0415 on June 3, some thirty-five minutes before sunrise, twenty-two Catalinas on Midway began to take off to conduct what had become over the last few days their routine reconnaissance patrols to the west of the atoll. The Fortresses on Eastern Island were ordered into the air after the Catalinas departed, and the whole of the garrison was put on alert just in case the anticipated attack materialized sooner than expected. If it did the atoll would be prepared. It was not until well after 0700 that the order to stand down was given and the Fortresses were brought in to land. By that time the lack of sighting reports from the Catalinas indicated that the enemy could not be within striking distance of Midway.[46]

But if the patrols began as routine they did not stay that way for very long. By about 1100 four Catalinas had established contact with enemy forces to the west and southwest of the atoll. None of their reports were very clear or complete.[47] The first significant sighting report, made at 0904, indicated the presence of two enemy ships at a range of 470 miles on a bearing of 247 degrees from Midway.[48] This contact, however, was immediately overshadowed by perhaps the most confusing of the reports made that morning, the one by Reid at 0927. It consisted of two words, *main body*.[49] In fact the real main body, the two battleship forces, had separated at 0700 at a point some 800 miles northwest of Reid, who had stumbled across what was Tanaka's transport force, then some 700 miles almost due west of Midway.[50] Nimitz, picking up Reid's report at Pearl Harbor, had it relayed to the fleet just in case Fletcher's ships had failed to pick it up, adding that the force that had been sighted was quite obviously not the enemy's striking force.[51]

The problem that faced the Americans at this point was to determine exactly what Reid had found and then to decide which of the various contacts, if any, was to be attacked. Reid's sector covered the area where intelligence surveys expected enemy forces to carry out a rendezvous, and it was not until 1100 that the force Reid had discovered was understood to be a major one. It proved to be the most important find of the morning. Reid stayed in the clouds above the transports for more than ninety minutes, sending back reports that gave the bearing, distance, course and speed of the enemy force, but not a very accurate assessment of its numerical strength and composition. At one stage he mistook a transport for an aircraft carrier. But at 1100 Reid signaled the presence of eleven ships in the force. This, combined with an earlier report of six large ships in single column, convinced the command on Midway that here was a force large enough to justify the use of heavy bombers against it. By this time, moreover, it had become clear that there was no enemy force within striking range of Midway, and that there was no chance of searching through the fog beyond 400 miles to the northwest of the atoll. Thus an attack on the force that Reid had found made sense. Recalling Reid, who was already nearing the end of his range, Ramsey ordered the nine Fortresses of Lieutenant Colonel Walter C. Sweeney's 431st Bombardment Squadron against the force that was some 670 miles to the west of Midway.[52]

The nine Fortresses, each armed with four 600-lb percussion bombs, took to the air shortly after noon on a flight that was to last more than nine hours and end with the last bomber staggering back to the atoll in darkness with scarcely any fuel left in its tanks. That the squadron did not lose any of its aircraft on this mission does not alter the fact that on 3 June, for the second time in four days, the Midway air group came perilously close to seeing a major part of its heavy bomber strength destroyed for no purpose. On 31 May, in response to a certain nervousness on the part of Nimitz, fifteen B-17s conducted a deep reconnaissance mission to the west of Midway. The last of its aircraft returned four and a half hours overdue, and several of them did not get back until well after the time when by rights they should have been lost.[53] On 3 June the nine bombers, operating in exactly the same area as they had on 31 May, made contact with Tanaka's transports at 1623 with no trouble at all; the enemy force was just where the preflight briefing had told the pilots to find it. The transports had not deviated from a course that took them directly to Midway. After sighting the Catalina in the morning the Japanese had expected attack, but five hours of undisturbed plodding towards the objective seems to have lulled them into a sense of false security. The Fortresses were to spend eleven or twelve minutes above the transports, maneuvering to get into ideal attacking positions without being sighted by the Japanese. The Japanese seem only to have spotted the bombers at the very last moment, and some of the transports were unaware of the presence of the enemy until bombs began to explode about them.[54]

The bomber pilots later claimed hits on two battleships or heavy cruisers and two transports, but this was a case, common to all air forces, of pilots seeing what they wanted to see. Not one of the bombs, aimed from a minimum height of 8,000 feet, hit anything other than the the sea itself.

Thus ended a raid that was important first in the immediate tactical context. Though the forces on Midway were numerically strong, in terms of quality and organization they were weak, and they were not capable of meeting the enemy on anything like a basis of equality. The only hope that the forces on Midway might play an effective part in the forthcoming battle lay in their ability to find, attack and destroy enemy forces beyond the range of Japanese air power or, when the battle was joined with the enemy attacking the atoll, when there was the opportunity to launch simultaneous strikes and counterstrikes. The latter was the less desirable option. Obviously it would be better for Midway if its heavy and medium bombers could strike without being struck in return. Because Reid's contact had come so late only one strike mission was possible on 3 June, and it had to be made with only half the aircraft that should have been available for offensive operations. Thus on 3 June the best hope for the Americans passed without their being able to take advantage of the opportunity.

Second, the operation by the Fortresses was important in being the first test of the assertion by interwar advocates of air power that the heavy bomber could deal with invasion forces. One of the claims made by the proponents of the strategic bomber was that it would prove superior to the surface ship and that it represented the most secure investment against the possibility of amphibious attacks. This belief was shown to be without foundation on this occasion, though the accounts given by the bomber crews confused matters for the moment. Admittedly, there were special circumstances involved in this operation. The small number of bombers available for the attack prevented their inflicting loss on the enemy; nonetheless, the Fortresses had been brought up to the atoll to provide a defense in depth to the west of Midway and had failed. Apart from peppering one single merchantman with bomb splinters, the high-le bombers achieved nothing, and future events would show that such attacks were ineffective against shipping. It was only when bomb-release points were brought down to very low levels that results were achieved. On the other hand, even though the Fortress proved ineffective in the strike role on 3 June, she had a great deal to offer in the reconnaissance role. She had structural strength and an ability to absorb punishment in pressing a close reconnaissance that the flimsy Catalina could not match. One of the Fortresses that attacked the transport force did an impressive job of counting (if not ship identification) when it reported the presence of twenty-six ships in the enemy force when in fact there were twenty-seven.[55] It was small wonder that after the battle the navy considered the possibility of ordering Flying Fortresses as reconnaissance aircraft.[56]

Yet in an exchange of roles and relative effectiveness, it was a Catalina that drew first blood. The honor to have been the first to inflict damage and loss on the enemy fell to this aircraft, of those flown from Midway the most manifestly unsuitable for attacks on shipping. The events that surrounded the Catalina's success were implausible from the outset. Three Catalina amphibians, stationed at Ford Island in Pearl Harbor, were ordered up the Hawaiian chain to Midway on the morning of 3 June. After a ten-hour flight they arrived at the atoll at about 1800. There they found themselves in the company of a fourth amphibian with whom they shared two common characteristics. First, all four were equipped with radar and therefore did not suffer from the night-blindness that inflicted less fortunate colleagues. Second, all four Catalinas were attended by armorers who prepared to arm the amphibians with torpedoes. The new arrivals not surprisingly assumed that some kind of mistake had been made. At 2130, aware now of who had made the mistake, the Catalinas took off, each with a single torpedo nestling under its starboard wing. Contact with the enemy was made at about 0115 on 4 June. Once more the Japanese gave no indication that they were aware of the presence of the enemy as three of the four Catalinas—the fourth had become detached—maneuvered into a position to attack the port column. Their intention was to attack from the north, thereby keeping the Japanese ships silhouetted against bright moonlight.

Of the three Catalinas that launched their torpedoes against Tanaka's force only the first to do so, the one piloted by Lieutenant Charles Hibberd, managed to secure a hit. His torpedo struck the oiler *Akebonomaru* near the bow, killing and wounding twenty-four of the ship's company but doing remarkably little damage to the ship herself. She managed to maintain her position at the rear of the line as the force continued on its course for Midway. The two Catalinas that followed Hibberd into the attack failed to secure hits as the Japanese, recovering from what was not so much surprise as utter amazement at being attacked by such unwieldy aircraft, took evasive action and threw up a hail of antiaircraft fire. In the exchange the

Catalinas strafed the *Kiyozumimaru*, killing several of her crew members.[57] The aircraft themselves were repeatedly but not fatally holed.[58] The fourth Catalina, coming late upon the scene, found that with the Japanese now on their guard there was little chance of pressing home an attack, and it made no attempt to do so. But even after breaking off contact with the enemy the problems of the Catalinas were far from over. By the time they reached Midway they found that the atoll was awaiting an imminent attack, and they had to fly further east to get out of range of the enemy. Three of the Catalinas went on to Laysan, one was forced to ditch near Lisanski.[59]

Thus ended the initial contacts—the first clash in the north and the opening skirmishes off Midway. In these contacts no real gain was made by either side and some losses were incurred by both. The Americans were more seriously inconvenienced by their losses than the Japanese for two reasons. First, throughout 3 June their reconnaissance patrols did not penetrate the bad weather front to the northwest of Midway and thus failed to obtain any contact with the enemy carrier force. They would have to look for the enemy again the following day while the American carriers waited upon their searches for the all-important first contact. Second, as we have seen, the chance the Americans had on 3 June to attack the enemy without being subjected to counterattack was unique and fleeting, and the air group on Midway failed to make the most of its opportunities. On the Japanese side "loss" was more intangible, involving as it did the First Carrier Striking Force. During the night of 3–4 June it increased speed to 25 knots to advance to its flying-off position some 250 miles to the northwest of Midway by about 0430. But Nagumo was not aware of what was happening to Tanaka's transports. Yamamoto knew of these developments but saw no reason to ensure that his carrier admiral was kept up to date.[60] Nagumo had to assume that the next day his formation was likely to come under attack, but his failure to make certain that battle had been joined very early and before he had time to come within range of his objective seems quite inexplicable. Obviously radio silence on the part of the *Yamato* was considered more important than warning the carriers that one part of the battle had begun.

During the night the American and Japanese forces increased speeds on courses that, had they continued, would have converged 40 miles northwest of Midway. Both sides prepared for action at the next day's dawn. For the Americans this was slightly easier, since Fletcher and his two task forces knew roughly what to look for and where to find it. The Japanese, on the other hand, had three eventualities against which to guard. Whereas the American carriers, in preparing to conduct a limited reconnaissance and mount a major strike against the enemy, could depend on the forces at Midway to provide the reconnaissance role, the Japanese had to carry out a precautionary reconnaissance, strike at Midway and retain a guard against the possibility of an enemy task force being at sea. As Nagumo shed his oilers and increased speed to reach flying-off position at dawn, so he moved ever closer to the dilemma that lay at the heart of Operation MI—the prospect of having to deal with two enemies when he had the strength to deal with only one.

After spending the daylight hours of the third marking time some 300 miles northeast of Midway, just before dusk Fletcher settled his fleet on a course intended to take it to a position some 200 miles north of the atoll by sunrise. In that position it would be reasonably safe from detection yet ideally placed to strike at the enemy force as it rushed towards Midway. As noted, the main hope of establishing contact with the enemy was vested in the forces at Midway. Fletcher ordered his flagship to conduct a dawn reconnaissance on the part of all three American carriers. This was to be mounted by ten Dauntlesses operating out to a range of 100 miles to the north of the fleet. This was a defensive precaution, designed to give some measure of protection against being taken by surprise by an incoming enemy air attack.[61] It was not a mission that was to be launched in the expectation of finding the enemy.

On Midway the intention of Ramsey was to get the Catalinas and Fortresses into the air at dawn. The former had to be sent out as the reconnaissance force; the bombers had to be dispersed so that they at least were not caught on the ground. The latter point was Ramsey's main fear. Thus far in the war American air power had been twice caught on the ground by attacking Japanese aircraft, on both occasions with devastating results. Ramsey had no intention of allowing Midway to add to this unwanted record. Ramsey's plan of campaign was to get the Catalinas, Fortresses and Wildcats into the air before sunrise, the latter providing the atoll's combat air patrol. The remaining aircraft were to held in immediate readiness at dawn, the bombers ready to move against any enemy that the Catalinas might find and the fighters ready to defend the base. The fighters were divided into two formations to meet what was expected to be a two-wave Japanese attack on Midway. The first formation, under the fighter commander Major Floyd B. Parker, was to consist of three divisions, one with six Wildcats and two each with four Buffaloes. The second formation, commanded by Parker's executive, Captain Kirk Armistead, would have two divisions, both with five Wildcats.[62] The corollary of this arrangement was that the bombers would not be provided with an escort for their attacks on the enemy.

Nagumo chose to tackle his problems with a single-phase reconnaissance sweep of his disengaged port flank at the same time as he struck at Midway. This was the idea of his air officer, Commander Minoru Genda, who had been the architect of the Pearl Harbor strike. Unfortunately for the ʼnese his recommendations for Midway were accepted without comment and amendment. In outline Genda's proposals seemed logical and adequate. According to the reconnaissance plan, issued to the force two days before battle was joined, scouting would be conducted along seven lines of search, numbered 1 to 7. Lines 1 and 2, along bearings of 181 and 158 degrees, were to be searched by Kate reconnaissance aircraft from the *Akagi* and the *Kaga* respectively. Lines 3 to 6 were allotted to the *Tone* and the *Chikuma*. Abe ordered the *Tone*'s seaplanes to search lines 3 and 4 on bearings of 123 and 100 degrees, while seaplanes from the *Chikuma* searched lines 5 and 6 on bearings of 77 and 54 degrees respectively. Line 7, on a bearing of of 31 degrees, was assigned to the *Haruna*. She was to commit a Dave to the operation. This short-range seaplane would search in the least important sector to a range of 150 miles before turning to port for 40 miles. All the others were to search to a distance of 300 miles before turning to port for 60 miles.[63] According to instructions issued just after midday on the fourth (the third Midway time), this reconnaissance mission was to be flown off at the same time the force flew off its preliminary strike against Midway and its first antisubmarine patrol of the day. With regard to the latter, the First Carrier Striking Force was to provide five three-hour patrols, beginning at 0430. Each patrol was to consist of two seaplanes. The first and third patrols were to be mounted by the *Tone* and the *Chikuma*, both of which were to provide one seaplane. The second and fourth were to be provided by the two battleships. The fifth and last of the day was to be mounted by the *Chikuma* and the *Kirishima*.[64]

The strike plan that accompanied the reconnaissance and antisubmarine patrol plans involved two attack formations. The first was to strike Midway with 108 aircraft. This was a seemingly large number with which to strike at so small an atoll as Midway, but it was a total that was marginal considering the number of individual targets on the islands that had to be destroyed, and it was only equal to the American air group on the atoll. The plan of attack involved the use of thirty-six Zekes, drawn equally from all four carriers, thirty-six Vals and the *Akagi* and the *Kaga* and thirty-six Kates from the *Hiryu* and the *Soryu*. The Kates were to lead the attack, flying from east to west (out of the early-morning sun) in the high-level role. They were to be armed with 1,770-lb Type 80 general-purpose bombs. The Kates from the *Hiryu* were directed against Sand Island while those from the *Soryu* were to pound Eastern Island. The dive-bombers from the *Kaga* were then to join the attack on Sand Island and its seaplane facilities. The *Akagi*'s Vals were to devote their attention to the various facilities on Eastern Island. The dive-bombers were to be armed with 532-lb Type 25 general-purpose bombs. The Zekes were to provide cover for the bombers and to strafe if circumstances allowed. Command of the attack was vested in Lieutenant Joichi Tomonaga of the *Hiryu*. Tomonaga had been promoted to overall command after the commander-designate, Commander Mitsuo

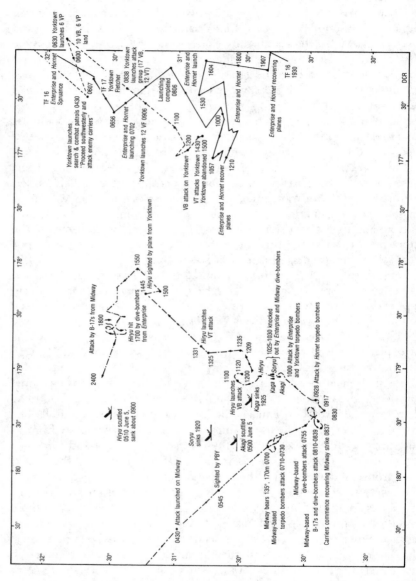

Battle of Midway Action on 4 June 1942

TF 16
Enterprise and *Hornet*
Spruance

Yorktown launches
search & combat patrols 0430
"Proceed southwesterly and
attack enemy carriers"

0600 *Yorktown*
0630 *Yorktown* launches 6 VP
10 VB, 6 VP
land

0607

0656

TF 17
Yorktown
Fletcher

0838 *Yorktown*
launches attack
group (17 VB
12 VT)

Enterprise and *Hornet*
launching 0702

Yorktown launches 12 VF 0906

Launching
completed
0806

Enterprise and
Hornet launch

1100

1530

1604

Enterprise and *Hornet*
1800

TF 16
1930

VB attack on *Yorktown* 1200

VT attacks *Yorktown* 1430

Yorktown abandoned 1500

1057

1000

1210

1907

Enterprise and *Hornet* recover
planes

Enterprise and *Hornet* recovering
planes

2400

Attack by B-17s from Midway

Hiryu hit
1700 by dive-bombers

Hiryu sighted by plane from *Yorktown*
1445

1550

1500

Hiryu hit
1700 by dive-bombers
from *Enterprise*

1331

1325

Hiryu launches
VT attack

1209

1235

Hiryu launches
VB attack

1100

1120

1200

Hiryu

Kaga & *Soryu*

Akagi

1025-1030 knocked
out by *Enterprise* and Midway dive-bombers

Kaga sinks
1925

1000 Attack by *Enterprise*
and *Yorktown* torpedo bombers

0928 Attack by *Hornet* torpedo bombers

0917

0830

Hiryu scuttled
0510 June 5,
sank about 0900

Soryu
sinks 1920

Akagi scuttled
0500 June 5

Sighted by PBY

0545

0430 Attack launched on Midway

Midway bears 135°, 170m 0700

Midway-based
torpedo bombers attack 0710-0730

Midway-based
dive-bombers attack 0755

B-17s and dive-bombers attack 0810-0839

Carriers commence recovering Midway strike 0837

DCR

Fuchida, underwent an emergency appendectomy. Tomonaga had overall command of the attack formation and direct tactical command of the bombers from the *Hiryu* and the *Soryu*. Command of the Vals was entrusted to Lieutenant Shoichi Ogawa of the *Kaga*. Command of the Zekes was vested in Lieutenant Masaharu Suganami of the *Soryu*.[65]

The four carriers provided six fighters each and reversed their bomber contribution for the second attack formation. This time the First Carrier Division provided the Kates and the Second the Vals. All bombers were armed with antiship ordnance, thereby ensuring that the carriers adhered to Yamamoto's instruction to hold half their Kates with torpedoes in case the enemy was encountered. The best of the aircrew were held back for this attack formation. Only if the reconnaissance patrols found no sign of the enemy and a second strike against Midway was judged necessary by Tomonaga would this force of thirty-six Kates, thirty-six Vals and twenty-four Zekes be rearmed and committed against the atoll.

The overall plan suffered from three inherent weaknesses. First, it assumed that the Japanese would be able to force events to conform to their operational timetable and would have the time to fight the battle as they had planned. Second, the plan assumed that the Japanese could find any enemy that might be at sea with a recconaissance force pared to the absolute minimum. Third, the plan envisaged the use of two attack forces, both of which were relatively weak, and a combat air patrol that numbered no more than a dozen Zekes unless it drew on readiness fighters. The test of all these arrangements was now at hand.

The matter of reconnaissance was crucial. The force earmarked for this operation was totally inadequate. The search sectors did not overlap. A predawn start should have resulted in a two-phase reconnaissance, with the seaplanes committed in the second phase being tasked to search the area covered by the earlier seaplanes in uncertain lights and the unscouted areas between the various sectors. In this way the Japanese carriers could have swept all the sea on their disengaged flank. It would have been prudent of them to do this before attacking Midway. Japanese reconnaissance arrangements, in the restrained comment of one observer, were "thin."[66] Genda had a reputation for cutting reconnaissance to a level that some regarded as rash or unwarranted.[67] Genda, however, subscribed to the carrier doctrine that units used on reconnaissance were always wasted. Off Ceylon in April the Japanese had been surprised on two occasions when their scouts found enemy warships at sea after the carriers had committed their striking force against land objectives. Both times the Japanese had been able to adjust to the situation and strike successfully against an enemy that lacked carrier air power of his own with which to strike back. The good fortune that came the Japanese way off Ceylon perhaps gave them confidence when it came to plan the attack on Midway. Midway, however, proved to be a case of third time unlucky. With their reconnaissance (and to a much lesser extent their strike) arrangements, the Japanese made the mistake of trying to repeat once too often a formula that in the past had worked despite its weaknesses. At some time or another these weaknesses were certain to be found out, and it was the Imperial Navy's misfortune that they were found out when the enemy had his first opportunity to take advantage of Japanese mistakes.

The weaknesses of the various Japanese arrangements became obvious in the last hour before sunrise on the fourth, as the carriers headed southeast at 19 knots to strike at Midway. With the first wave flown off, the second was brought from the hangar decks to be spotted on the flight decks. With the two attack formations allocated, just twenty-one combat aircraft remained in reserve, twelve of them fighters. Combat air patrol for the First Carrier Striking Force therefore had to be provided by these fighters and those from the attack formation detailed as readiness fighters. On first call were the six Zekes of the *Kaga*, with the six from the *Akagi* detailed as further reinforcement or replacement. This reliance on readiness aircraft for the combat air patrol, and the allocation of two dozen* fighters for the defense of the fleet, brought home the fact that the margin against error was nil. The Japanese were attempting to do too much with too little, the direct result of the loss of the *Shokaku* and the *Zuikaku* to an ill-considered diversion and the refusal of the Combined Fleet to recast the composition of its task forces or to delay the operation on account of their absence. Had the Fifth Carrier Division been present, Nagumo could have struck at Midway with 108 aircraft and had as many as 250 in reserve. Had the *Hosho, Junyo, Ryujo* and *Zuiho* been in company, collectively or in any triple combination, he could have held between 175 and 215 combat aircraft in reserve to meet any unforeseen development. As it was, he had committed his first major mistake of the battle. Unaware as he was of the enemy's presence and unwise enough not to delay his strike against Midway until after a precautionary reconnaissance was completed, Nagumo struck at Midway with a force about the size as that held on the atoll. At the same time he left himself at a two-to-one disadvantage with respect to the *Yorktown, Enterprise* and *Hornet*. After launching the first attack Nagumo's carriers would retain just 117 combat aircraft; the American carriers would have 223.

Thus at the very time that the Americans at sea were wondering which way next day's battle would go, the Japanese remained in utter ignorance of the danger in which they stood. The First Carrier Striking Force was in such an exposed position because of a bad and compromised plan, Yamamoto's refusal to use his radio to warn Nagumo of the hazards that could be ahead, and Nagumo's decision to commit half his strike force against

*A compromise between the one dozen that was allocated to the reserve, the two dozen that either committed or detailed to supplement the reserve and the three dozen that might be ble to the combat air patrol.

Midway before making certain that no enemy task force was in the vicinity. The danger to the Japanese carrier force was that it could be caught between two enemies. Much would depend on the outcome of the dawn reconnaissance. The Japanese were not without their chances, in spite of themselves, but the advantage lay with the Americans. That fortune had switched to the American side long before this day was unsuspected by the Japanese. It would become obvious with the rising of the sun on Thursday 4 June.

CHAPTER 11

Contact

Sunrise for the Japanese carriers and their escorts came at approximately 0156 on what was for them 5 June, since Tokyo time, and with it East Longitudinal Date, was used in his Imperial Majesty's ships regardless of location. For the American forces on Midway, ten minutes to the east of the Japanese, the sun hauled its way over the eastern horizon at about 0446, and for the American carriers the sun appeared a minute earlier—at 0645. The American carriers used zero + 10 time, which placed them two hours ahead of their Midway-based compatriots.* But while time was one of the elements separating the three parties to the coming battle—distance, nationality and race were amongst the others—sunrise found them all engaged in a common activity. Even before sunrise Midway and the carriers had flown off aircraft; when the sun arrived all were preparing to launch more aircraft in the event of a contact with the enemy.

Midway was the first to get aircraft aloft. At 0415 eleven Catalinas took off from the lagoon in search of the contact on which so much depended. After the previous day's failure to find the enemy, the search sector had

*Two points need to be made at this juncture. First, all timings hereafter relate to Midway local time and West Longitudinal Date, though the final dates when Japanese units reached home waters after Operations AL and MI will revert to Japanese practice. Second, there is a need to make certain definitions that will avoid the confusion that surrounds certain accounts of the battle of Midway because of imprecise use of the word *dawn*. According to the almanac office at Herstmonceux, the time for sunrise on 5 June 1942 for a position in latitude 31° N, longitude 179° W, was 0452, plus or minus two minutes. This position was roughly halfway between the two fleets at that time.

Civil twilight, when the horizon should have been clearly discerned, would have begun at or about 0425, but the first streaks of the new day would have appeared on the eastern horizon between 0315, the onset of astronomical twilight, and 0351, the start of nautical twilight.

Despite the error in so doing, this book uses 0452 as the time of sunrise for all four days of the battle of Midway, and accepts the timing with respect to all ships, American and Japanese, regardless of position.

been contacted. The Catalinas were ordered out to a range of 420 miles; if Midway was to be attacked this day there was no need to search beyond that limit.[1] The Catalinas took off at the same time that six Wildcats were flown off to provide the atoll's first combat air patrol of the day, and hard on their heels went sixteen Fortresses. On this occasion they took to the air not simply as a precaution against being caught on the ground but to regain contact with and attack the transport force that had been found the previous day. Behind them the Catalinas, Wildcats and Fortresses left an assembly of army, navy and marine bombers and fighters warming up so that they could go into action immediately in the event of either an attack or a contact.[2]

Some fifteen minutes after the first of the Catalinas left Midway both carrier forces began to launch aircraft. Some 200 miles to the north of the atoll the American carriers found that with the wind coming over their sterns they had to turn away from the assumed position of the enemy and set course towards the southeast as the *Yorktown* launched the ten scouting Dauntlesses that were to cover all three carriers against the possibility of being taken by surprise.[3] Simultaneously, air officers on the four Japanese carriers switched their signal lanterns to green, the order for the twenty-

The Aircraft Carrier *Soryu*

The Aircraft Carrier *Kaga*

seven aircraft lined up on each carrier's deck to begin the execution of
Operation MI.[4] At that moment the *Akagi*, *Kaga*, *Hiryu* and *Soryu* came into
their own, for then they were called upon to fulfil their raison d'être. Here,
for the last time, the carriers were moving to strike at a target beyond the
horizon. As the first of their aircraft climbed into the sky the four carriers
ceased to be intact and complete. None of the members of the First Carrier
Striking Force was ever to be complete again, and three of them were never
to be given another chance to strike at their enemies.

Within fifteen minutes all 108 aircraft committed to the attack on Midway had climbed safely into the air as their carriers held their course
towards the atoll at 19 knots.[5] An array of flashing red and blue navigation
lights circled over the carriers as the bombers and fighters drew themselves
up into their cruising formation and then set out at 125 knots for the
objective, less than two hours' flying time to the southeast. By the time they
arrived over the target, visibility would probably be good. Bad weather,
however, still shrouded the Japanese carriers. During the night Nagumo
had passed through the main weather front, but he remained in the company of the showers associated with an advancing cold front. Rather like the
situation that had prevailed at the Coral Sea, the Japanese carriers were
under low but light cumulus cloud, and whether this would protect the
Japanese formation from searching aircraft or offer protection for any
Catalina that stumbled across its path remained to be seen as Nagumo
brought his ships up to 24 knots.[6] In continuing to steer for Midway
Nagumo followed standard operational procedures. The concern of the
carriers was always to recover their aircraft, and by staying on a closing
course they cut down on the miles which damaged aircraft and which
wounded aircrew would have to cover on their return flight. The extra few
miles could easily prove the difference between aircraft being recovered or
lost, between life and death for the airmen, and on 4 June there was never
any question of the Japanese carriers doing anything other than following
their aircraft towards Midway. Immmediately after the launch of the first
attack mission was completed, the elevators brought the second attack
formation to the flight decks of the carriers.[7]

The reconnaissance missions that had been ordered were supposed to be
flown off at the same time Tomonaga's wave of attackers took to the air.
Two of the seaplanes, however, failed to get away on time. The *Haruna*
managed to launch her Dave as ordered, but both cruisers encountered
problems. The *Chikuma*'s second seaplane developed engine trouble on the
catapult, while the *Tone*, after a launching mechanism became jammed,
could not get her second seaplane away until 0500.[8] At the time the delay
seemed no more than irritating. The search that was being carried out was
merely intended to confirm the absence of the enemy, not to find out
whether his carrier forces were really alone. The delay to the *Tone*'s
seaplane did not appear any more serious than the early return of the late

Jake from the *Chikuma*. The seaplane, beset with continuing engine trouble throughout its outward journey and by bad weather in its search area, cut short its mission to return to its cruiser.[9]

The second of the Jakes from the *Tone* had only been airborne for a matter of minutes before the Japanese presence was discovered. The first of the *Tone*'s seaplanes had been tasked to search the sector immediately to the east of Midway, and its outward journey on a bearing of 123 degrees placed it on a course almost reciprocal to that of a Catalina piloted by Lieutenant Howard Ady, who was destined to find the First Carrier Striking Force.[10] Neither the Catalina nor the Jake made any attempt to interfere with the other's activities as they went their opposite ways, but both reported the contact to their respective commands.[11] The Catalina sent off two signals, the first a plain-language sighting and the second a proper amplifying signal, which could only mean one thing to the American commanders on Midway, at Pearl Harbor and at sea—the enemy had to be close at hand. At 0530, some twenty minutes after this contact, Ady encountered something a little more substantial. Coming out of cloud he found himself in the path of two oncoming carriers at a range of about 20 miles. Ady evidently was a man of few words when meeting strangers. His contact with the Jake had elicited a single-word signal, "Aircraft." Now he signaled "Enemy carriers" in clear before heading for the clouds and the protection they might provide from the enemy's combat air patrol. Ady's contact report with the enemy force was made at 0534.[12]

Six minutes later Lieutenant William Chase, in a second Catalina, almost found himself in the passing company of a swarm of Japanese aircraft heading in the opposite direction towards Midway. Chase, who left Midway some fifteen minutes behind Ady, had been tasked to conduct a reconnaissance of the sector to port of the one that Ady was to search.[13] Thus while Ady had set out on a bearing slightly north of northwest, Chase had steered to the west of northwest from Midway. Tomonaga's route to Midway, and that of Nagumo's carriers, therefore bisected the courses of the two amphibians, and it fell to Chase to obtain contact with the attack wave as it closed on Midway. The plain-language signal "Many planes heading Midway bearing 320 distance 150" was enough to provide the atoll with advance warning of an impending air attack.[14] It also indicated that enemy carriers were unlikely to be more than an hour's flying time from this point of contact.

The initial sighting and contact reports were enough to make Fletcher hesitate. It was not clear as the carriers listened in on the Catalina net that the sightings came from two separate patrols, and the first messages that were taken in did not give the number, position and course of the enemy carrier force. The initial reports that were received from Ady were fragmentary and, as events were to prove, erroneous. This was hardly surprising, since Ady prudently sought the cover of the clouds. The Japanese

DECISION

carriers, having been warned by the Jake of the approach of a Catalina, flew off Zekes within a minute of the intruder being sighted. But the lumbering flying boat, deftly using the clouds to compensate for its lack of speed and maneuverability, managed to elude the Japanese fighters and send back various reports.[15] Of course the cloud that provided Ady with protection also served to frustrate his scouting. It partially concealed Nagumo's force, and Ady reported the presence of only two carriers with the enemy force. Since Ady had veered to port on contact and had taken up a position on the enemy's starboard beam, it is likely that he encountered only the *Akagi* and the *Kaga* and failed to locate the more distant *Hiryu* and *Soryu* through the clouds.[16] Thus when Fletcher received Ady's signal of 0552, which gave the course and speed of "two carriers and main body of ships," and placed it alongside a report made at 0540 that gave the distance and bearing of the enemy from Midway, Fletcher was in a dilemma.[17] Armed as he was with the intelligence briefing that warned of the presence of four, perhaps five, carriers with the enemy strike force, Fletcher had to decide between striking quickly against what might prove to be only part of the enemy force or holding his hand until further reconnaissance was able to confirm or deny the presence of other carriers. His problem was that he did not know what had been found. With part of the enemy's strength committed against Midway he had a decided advantage. Eight complete bomber squadrons were with his three carriers. But the advantage the American carriers held was certain to disappear once their presence was revealed. Retribution was certain to be swift if the strike made by the Americans was bungled. If they attacked two enemy carriers and left two or three more unattended, the results were more than likely to be unpleasant.

Nonetheless, at 0607 Fletcher issued orders. Though the evidence was far from complete, Fletcher ordered Spruance to take the *Enterprise* and the *Hornet* to the southwest on an interception course while he held the *York-town* into the wind and recovered his scouts. Informing Spruance that he would follow as soon as his scouts were landed, Fletcher ordered Task Force 16 to attack the enemy as soon as the latter's position was known for certain.[18] Spruance led his ships away at 25 knots as the two task forces drew apart. From the plots that were being calculated on all three American carriers, it was clear that the *Enterprise* and the *Hornet* faced at least one and perhaps even two hours of high-speed steaming before they came within range of the enemy carriers. This calculation was based on the premise—a reasonable one—that the enemy would hold to his present course. It was figured that by 0700 the enemy would come within a range of about 155 miles. Spruance, however, was thinking in terms of closing to about 100 miles before launching. He had no wish to run the risk of his aircraft failing find the enemy for want of extra gallons of fuel.[19]

With the American carriers, as yet undiscovered, unable to get into action before 0700 at the earliest and their aircraft condemned to be incapable of contacting the enemy for at least ninety minutes after that time, the initial shock of battle had to be taken by the forces on and from Midway. In the clash between aircraft from the atoll and those from Japanese carriers, the latter struck the first blow, but neither it nor the American counterblow proved successful.

The reports of enemy aircraft sent by Ady and Chase should have given the Americans on Midway a little more time to prepare than they otherwise would have had with only the garrison's radar to warn them of the enemy's approach. About twenty minutes passed between Ady's sighting of the Jake and the radar station on Midway picking up the approach of the Japanese. Contact was obtained at a range of 93 miles.[20] Rather than helping the Americans, however, the extra time given by Ady's initial contact only added to the confusion that is a necessary part of any battle.

With the Ady signal things began to happen in the wrong order for the Americans on Midway. The contact came just after the garrison had been stood down from the dawn alert. Had it come a few minutes earlier, or had the stand-to been held for a few minutes more, all the aircraft at Midway would have remained in their state of readiness. As it was, contact was made just after the spot was broken. The basic simplicity of organization had been lost when contact with the enemy was obtained. Moreover, the combat air patrol was not properly recalled as Midway was stood down. Three of the Wildcats failed to receive the recall and only returned to the airstrip after the radar contact had been obtained. They had to be brought in to land just as the aircraft on the atoll were moved out to their takeoff positions. The three fighters, so important to the defense because they were (relatively) new, had to be refueled and put back into action immediately, with time running out as the enemy rapidly approached the atoll. To exacerbate the situation, one of the Wildcats slid off the runway when it landed and buried its wheels deep in the island's sand. It was hardly an auspicious start to the battle.

The problem that faced the American air command on Midway was twofold. First, all the aircraft had to scramble clear of the islands. Second, the fighters had to be arranged for the defense of the islands, and here Midway faced the same problem that had beaten the *Yorktown* and the *Lexington* at the Coral Sea some four weeks earlier. The fighters had to be ordered out to intercept at a good range from the atoll, and they had to be deployed early enough to climb the altitudes above those of the incoming enemy. These matters took time, and there was not much slack between the time that would be needed to get fighters in the correct position and their endurance time. With confusion engulfing the ground organization and command on Midway, the order to get aircraft airborne was not finally given until 0555. Various reports and radar contacts needed confirmation, but by then the Japanese were less than thirty-five minutes' flying time away and the Americans had some sixty-six aircraft on the strip waiting to get airborne. Error was inevitable amid the confusion on Eastern Island's runway when the order was finally given for the aircraft on the runway to get airborne. Some pilots had cut their engines, and many failed to hear the warning sirens above the roar of those engines that had been kept running. There was time only for flight commanders to be told of the enemy's likely position by officers who scurried over wings and fuselages to tell them of the developing situation. Even with this improvisation, at least one formation left Midway unaware that it was on its way to attack an enemy carrier force.[21]

American aircraft were so few in number, and their quality and that of their aircrew so uncertain, that their only hope of success and survival lay in the closest possible synchronization of effort on the part of the air group's various formations, which individually were vulnerable. The fighters, for example, were hopelessly outclassed. They could hardly be expected to fend for themselves in combat with Zekes, still less to provide either Midway or the bombers with effective cover. Such was the unfitness of most of the American fighters for combat duties that the bombers had to remain unescorted, and apart from the rugged Flying Fortresses and Marauders none of the bombers could hope to stand up to the depredations of the enemy combat air patrol. The Avengers and Vindicators, for different reasons, were particularly vulnerable, and the Dauntlesses scarcely less so. With the odds stacked so strongly against the bomber formations, they had to coordinate their efforts carefully if they were to avoid a series of individual and unsupported death rides against the First Carrier Striking Force. It was this coordination of effort that eluded the Americans in the confusion on Eastern Island when the enemy was contacted on the morning 4 June.

The fighters were the first to take off, getting airborne between 0600 and 0610. They were followed first by the torpedo bombers and then by the dive-bombers. Both fighter formations were ordered into the air as the American plan to divide their fighter strength into two groups fell apart. The first and larger formation was ordered out to a distance of 30 miles on a reciprocal course to the incoming Japanese. The second formation, joined by the last of the Wildcats from the earlier combat air patrol, was directed to a position slightly to the west of the other to guard against the possibility of a false reading on the radar plot or the arrival of more of the enemy on another bearing.[22] The first formation climbed to 12,000 feet to await the arrival of the enemy, its strength immediately cut back to a round dozen when one of its number was forced to turn back to Eastern Island with engine trouble.[23] Similarly, one of the Vindicators had to return home soon after takeoff when a cowling disintegrated.[24] The last of the strike aircraft did not get clear of Midway until 0616, by which time the Japanese were less than 30 miles away and almost within sight of the atoll's garrison.[25] After taking off the various torpedo bombers set course for an immediate contact with the enemy. The dive-bombers were directed to a standoff position some 20 miles to the east of the atoll, where they were to circle while awaiting fresh orders.[26] The only other strike force, the Flying Fortresses that had been sent out around dawn to find and attack the transports to the west of the atoll, similarly received new instructions. At 0555 they were ordered to abandon their search for the transports and to redirect their attentions against the Japanese carrier force.[27] Any synchronization of the American effort, both in attack and defense, was going to be as much a matter of luck as of good judgment.

The next phase, the air battle over Midway and the Japanese attack on the atoll's installation, is perhaps the most confused part of what was, by any standard, a confusing battle. While there has never been any dispute over the American air losses and the damage incurred by Midway's installations, Japanese air losses have been the subject of doubt. There has never been any way of reconciling the wildly different claims of the two sides. Nagumo's battle report admitted to the loss of just six aircraft: one Val, two Zekes and four Kates.[28] This source has been often used in English-language accounts of the battle, though other accounts, again using a Japanese source, give the total number of aircraft lost as eleven.[29] Japanese accounts claim that the American combat air patrol failed to account for a single Japanese aircraft. This is disputed by American sources. The official American sources, the histories of the navy and the marine corps, indicate that the minimum Japanese loss was at least one-third of their strength, while one of the most recent accounts of the Pacific war has assessed Japanese losses as thirty-eight aircraft lost and another twenty-nine rendered inoperable.[30] This gives the total Japanese loss as sixty-seven aircraft, nearly two-thirds of their strike force.[31]

The accounts that give eleven as the total number of aircraft lost by the Japanese in the course of this, their one and only air strike against Midway on 4 June, concur with the figures given in the official Japanese history of the battle. These, in turn culled from the battle reports of the carrier air groups, show that four Kates, one Val and two Zekes were lost in combat; another four Kates were lost when they were forced to ditch; one Kate and two Zekes were found to be unserviceable after returning to their carriers; and a total of sixteen Kates, six Vals and five Zekes incurred some form of damage. The *Akagi* and the *Kaga* each lost a fighter, the *Kaga* also losing the only Val that failed to return from the mission. The *Hiryu* lost three Kates in combat to the single loss of the *Soryu*, the light carriers each losing two of

The Val Dive-Bomber

the Kates that were forced down in the sea. The crews of three of these Kates were rescued, the unlucky exception being the crew from one of the *Hiryu*'s Kates. The Kate that returned only to be found to be unserviceable was from the *Soryu*, as was one of the fighters. The other came from the *Kaga*. Of the Zekes that were damaged three were from the *Akagi* and two from the *Hiryu*, while two of the *Akagi*'s Vals and four from the *Kaga* were also damaged to some degree. Of the damaged Kates one was from the *Hiryu* and the remainder were from the *Soryu*. This meant that every Kate from the *Soryu* was either lost or damaged, a fact borne out by Nagumo's battle report. The Japanese records indicate that all fifteen of the *Soryu*'s Kates that returned after the attack on Midway were damaged; thus it must be assumed that the unserviceable machine had been reduced to such a state because of its damage. The two Zekes similarly unfit to continue operations were presumably put out of the running by mechanical problems rather than battle damage; there is no indication that they were "injured" in any way. The Japanese statement of losses and damaged aircraft is as follows:

	Akagi		*Kaga*		*Hiryu*		*Soryu*	
	Zekes	Vals	Zekes	Vals	Zekes	Kates	Zekes	Kates
Lost in combat	1		1	1	3			1
Forced to ditch					2			2
Rendered unserviceable			1				1	1
Total lost	1		2	1		5	1	4
Total damaged	3	2		4	2	1		15
Available strength	?	?	?	?	7	9	?	10

Thus the overall situation as a result of the strike against Midway was that a total of eleven Japanese aircraft were lost, with a further three rendered incapable of further operations and another twenty-six damaged.[32]

A Torpedo-armed Kate

But even if these figures fail to dispel the lingering doubts about the extent of Japanese losses over Midway, there is little doubt about what their strike achieved.* First, in meeting the initial fighter formation between 0616 and 1630 and the second fighter formation during the actual bombing

*The author is obliged to point out that even though these figures represent the most complete returns available, they are not fully complete and they do not clear up certain elements of ambiguity about Japanese losses in this phase of the battle.

Official Japanese figures give the strength remaining to the Japanese after this attack only for the *Soryu*'s Kates and for the *Hiryu*'s Kates and Zekes. Thus there is no way of double checking five of the eight formations that were committed against Midway, and of the three where a check is possible, two of the figures may be in error. The only formation for which the various losses and damaged aircraft tally with those remaining is the fighter element from the *Hiryu*. A possible explanation of the discrepancies in the Kate strength remaining to the units of the Second Carrier Division is that the available number represented in the case of the *Soryu* the number that had been made ready for further operations when she was hit by enemy bombs, in the case of the *Hiryu* the number that had been made ready for further operations by the time she launched her second Kate operation of the day. Possible confirmation of this latter point may be the fact that in this operation the *Hiryu* launched six Zekes and ten Kates, one of which was unfit to take part in the attack. On the other hand the air officer of the *Hiryu*, in the course of his postwar interrogation by the Americans, stated that the carrier lost ten of her aircraft in the course of the attack on Midway; for the carrier to be left with sixteen aircraft from the Midway strike, plus three more damaged, might be an indication that the *Hiryu*'s losses have been understated.

But even allowing for the possibility that the flagship of the Second Carrier Division may have miscounted, there is still no way various contending claims can be reconciled. Moreover, phase, the Japanese destroyed the atoll's fighter defenses. Second, between 0635 and 1645 the Japanese raked over Eastern and Sand Islands and did more damage to their various installations than they realized at the time. But despite their success in destroying Midway's fighters and damaging its installations, the Japanese hit an empty base. As the apt simile drawn by one of the Japanese aircrew suggests, the atoll was like a snake that had crawled away, leaving its cast-off skin to be attacked.[33]

In the case of Midway's fighter defenses, annihilation was almost complete. At the end of the action Pearl Harbor was informed by Midway that only three combat aircraft remained to the defense; twenty-five fighters were lost in the air and on the ground to just one slashing Japanese attack. Of the aircraft that met the Japanese in the air just two, one a Buffalo and the other a Wildcat, remained undamaged at the end of the action, and another Wildcat suffered minor damage that prevented it from retracting its undercarriage. Ten aircraft survived to land on Eastern Island, four of them doing so while the Japanese attack was in progress. Of the ten, three came from the force that had been led by Parks and seven from the force led by Armistead. By definition, most of the ten that managed to get back to Midway were so extensively damaged that they never flew again.

Heavy American losses were not the result of a weak plan of campaign or the confusion that had arisen before takeoff. These factors had only a marginal impact on the situation. Losses were heavy because American pilots and aircraft were inferior to those of the enemy at this stage of the war. It did not really matter whether the Americans had Buffaloes or Wildcats—neither were good enough to stand up to Zekes in combat. This

---

certain odd features about Japanese losses over the Midway atoll on the morning of 4 June still remain. For example, the Kates bombed at 11,500 feet. This was well below the effective ceiling of flak, and according to Japanese official figures 25 percent of their level-altitude bombers were lost and another 41.6 percent of their number were damaged. In fact, two in three of the Kates sent against Midway were either lost or damaged. But certain American sources suggest that their antiaircraft gunners did not allow sufficient deflection, and it does seem rather odd that with so many Kates hit just one Val should have been lost, especially in view of the claims first by Fuchida that the Japanese dive-bombers attacked at a "perilously low altitude" and second by Nagumo in his official report that enemy antiaircraft fire was "vicious."

This relationship between losses, attack altitudes and heaviness of antiaircraft fire does not hang together easily, and it certainly sits strangely alongside the losses recorded by the strike forces at Pearl Harbor on 7 December 1941. On that occasion the Japanese lost five Kates, fifteen Vals and nine Zekes, and of these six Zekes and all but one of the Vals were lost from the second attacking wave. This second strike attacked in the face of a thickening barrage as the defense began to organize itself. Though the circumstances of the attacks on Pearl Harbor and Midway are different, it is curious that the balance of losses between attacking Japanese formations should have reversed itself from one attack to the other. It also seems strange to record the Japanese view that not one of their aircraft fell to the guns of enemy fighters. Even allowing for the fact that these were Buffaloes and Wildcats, this seems unlikely. The American fighters had an advantage of altitude over the Japanese, and the bombers were below and in front of the Zekes. American claims, by both surviving pilots and from the ground, are that the first enemy aircraft to be shot down fell from the skies well beyond the range of Midway's antiaircraft guns.

the surviving American pilots freely admitted. The Zekes ran rings around the Americans, and the number of instances the Japanese outperformed the Americans were too frequent to bear recounting. The reaction of the American pilots who survived this encounter was understandably bitter. One officer, Captain P. R. White, recorded the view that "any commander that [sic] orders pilots out for combat in a F2A-3 [Buffalo] should consider the pilot as lost before leaving the ground." Another, Second Lieutenant C. M. Kunz, said that the Buffalo "should be in Miami as a training plane."[34]

Though the damage inflicted on the atoll's islands was extensive, the attack was mounted in too small a strength to be properly effective. With only seventy-one bombers in the attack—one Kate had to turn back with engine trouble—the Japanese lacked the punch that was needed to inflict on Midway the kind of devastating treatment that had been handed out at Pearl Harbor, Rabaul, Darwin and Ceylon.

On Sand Island the Japanese accounted for the seaplane hangars and damaged the dispensary and parachute store. More seriously, the bombers hit the oil dumps and left them burning furiously. On Eastern Island the Japanese completely wrecked the power station and damaged the marines' galley and the mail exchange, though they did not destroy the hangars as they thought. The three runways received bomb hits, but these did not render them unserviceable. One of the underground command posts on Eastern Island took a direct hit, the sector commander, Major William W. Benson, USMC, being one of the small total of eleven men killed on Midway during the raid. Eighteen of the defenders were wounded.[35] Most of them, plus some of the wounded aircrew who managed to get back to Midway, were evacuated to Pearl Harbor after dark by a marine corps Dakota C-47 that flew up from Oahu.

Most of this damage could be shrugged off as inconvenience, but not the damage to the power plant and the fuel depot. The latter completed the destruction that had been caused on 22 May by the accidental triggering of demolition charges, which had resulted in the loss of half the atoll's fuel supplies. The raid on 4 June destroyed the distribution lines and pumps.[36] To overcome the problems this caused, the next night 3,000 barrels of avgas were transferred from Sand Island to Eastern Island so that the latter's aircraft could be serviced over the following days.[37] Before the attack Eastern Island had been using 65,000 gallons of avgas a day, a total that would have amazed the Japanese had they been aware of it.[38]* The events of 4 June reduced the needs of Midway, since so many of its aircraft were lost during the day. That night all remaining aircraft had to be fueled by hand—a slow, laborious and tiring process.†

---

*A carrier such as the *Yorktown* carried about 186,000 gallons.
†With a fuel capacity of 2,990 gallons, a B-17 needed 86 barrels for a mission.

The critical point about the raid was that "it hit air." The American attack units had gone, and this fact alone necessitated the second attack that Tomonaga, after reorganizing his formation once the attack was over, recommended to Nagumo at 0700.[39] The First Carrier Striking Force was under attack when this message was received; that the Americans were able to attack the carrier force from Midway was proof enough of the partial failure of the strike on the atoll. Thus Nagumo and his staff accepted Tomonaga's recommendation. It is possible to argue, however, that this second strike was not strictly necessary. Midway's fighter squadron was annihilated in the Japanese attack, and the losses inflicted on the American bomber units during their attacks on the Japanese carriers effectively destroyed Midway's offensive capacity. At least in terms of the atoll's air power, the Japanese had little to fear from Midway after the initial exchanges. On the other hand, Midway was not left totally bereft of its capacity to handle aircraft, and the atoll remained full of fight. With a garrison of 3,632 men Midway showed with her flak that she was far from neutralized, yet her resistance had to be broken if the atoll was to be successfully invaded on the sixth.

Tomonaga's recommendation had been more than half expected. Japanese planning had accounted for the likelihood of a second strike, and as early as 0520 Nagumo had taken the sensible precaution of issuing a warning order to his division to be prepared to switch ordnance if a second strike was considered necessary.[40] There was no overwhelming need to so instruct the Second Carrier Division—the *Hiryu* and the *Soryu* were to contribute dive-bombers to a second strike, and their bombs were equally adequate against land and ship targets. But Tomonaga's recommendation, though no surprise, was enough to make Nagumo and his staff hesitate. It represented the moment of truth. If Nagumo fell in with the suggestion and struck at Midway for a second time, the First Carrier Striking Force would be left for a period with no striking power whatsoever. There could be no going back if a second strike against Midway was ordered, because all that would remain to the carriers would be whatever returned from the first attack on Midway. With the elite of the naval air force in the second wave, Nagumo would be deprived of an offensive capability at least for a time. Much hung on the decision Nagumo was called upon to make.

Nagumo was in an impossible predicament. The Tomonaga signal forced him and his staff to address the insoluble problem that lay at the heart of Operation MI. The problem, dodged by Yamamoto and Ugaki, was how the carrier force, in the absence of a reserve, was to operate against one target while safeguarding against the possibility of encountering an enemy task force at sea. That Nagumo did not know of the presence of an enemy task force did not alter his problem. If Nagumo committed himself against Midway then he was certain to condemn his force to having no strike force for the time it took to recover, refuel and rearm the survivors of the first strike. In the phrase of its chief of staff, the First Carrier Striking Force was "like a hunter chasing two hares at once."[41] It was small wonder, therefore, that Nagumo hesitated before making a decision. It is hard not to sympathize with him, for although Nagumo cannot be absolved from some responsibility—the seeming casualness with which he had accepted his orders, despite any misgivings he may have felt, made Nagumo party to the fault—main responsibility rested with Yamamoto and the Combined Fleet staff. Between them they had insisted on four carriers doing the work of six. If the *Ryujo, Junyo* and *Zuiho*, or better still, the *Shokaku* and the *Zuikaku*, had been with the First Carrier Striking Force, Nagumo could have had the reserve to guard against the element of uncertainty that had been latent up to this point.

If Tomonaga's signal provoked some agitation on the *Akagi*'s flag bridge as Nagumo, Kusaka and Genda went into a huddle to decide on the best course of action, another disturbance was imminent. As Tomonaga's flight had approached Midway, it sighted and reported the American torpedo bombers flying in the opposite direction.[42] One of the Zekes made a single pass against the Avengers, but to no effect.[43] In response to the warning the Japanese thickened up the combat air patrol by drawing on the reserve from the *Akagi*.[44] The arrival of the six Avengers and four Marauders over the Japanese carrier force at 0705 forced Nagumo to postpone the decision about striking at Midway until after the enemy attack had been met.[45]

The original American plan had called for the Avengers and Marauders to synchronize their attacks, but with the Avengers setting off for the enemy without waiting for the army bombers this would be difficult to achieve. Nonetheless, the two forces arrived over the enemy at roughly the same time, the Avengers to starboard and the Marauders to port of the Japanese carriers.[46] The bombers actually managed to maneuver themselves into a near-ideal position from which to mount a scissors attack, but the Marauders chose to work their way around to what appeared to be the less well-guarded starboard side of the Japanese force.[47] In this way they condemned themselves to follow the Avengers into the attack and left the enemy fighters free to concentrate against the two sets of bombers in turn, with predictable results.

Though the American survivors from this attack claimed three hits on the enemy, none of the torpedoes aimed at the Japanese carriers found a mark.[48] Indeed, it would appear that few of the bombers actually managed to get within effective range of the enemy. The Zekes of the combat air patrol and the flak defenses began to pick off the Americans long before the latter came within range of the carriers, and by attacking in line-ahead formation the Americans made the Japanese task easier than it need have been. At the end of the attack only one Avenger and two Marauders

A Grumman Avenger Releases Its Torpedo During the Battle of Midway

survived to stagger back to Midway, and one of the Marauders (piloted by First Lieutenant James P. Muri) did so with three wounded gunners and fuel tanks full of bullets. The Avenger only survived because of Japanese misjudgment. The Zekes hacked it to pieces and believed it to be doomed, an opinion shared by the pilot, Ensign A. K. Earnest. But instead of an unscheduled meeting with the sea Earnest managed to coax his wrecked machine back to Midway after the Zekes turned their attentions from him to the incoming Marauders.[49]

The Japanese accounted for the first of the five Avengers they shot down as the torpedo bombers dived from their 4,000 feet cruising altitude, and they hacked away at the Americans all the way to the release points.[50] Most of the Avengers and Marauders that survived to attack selected the leading carriers as their targets, though Earnest may not have been alone in being forced to select the nearest ship as target—in his case the *Nagara*—as his aircraft began to disintegrate about him.[51] The *Akagi*, for all her 43,000 tons, proved nimble enough to dodge the torpedoes aimed at her. She initially made a complete 360-degree turn to starboard in order to comb the torpedoes from the Avengers, and then made another complete turn, this time to port, to evade the Marauders' attack.[52] The *Hiryu*, which had no such need for violent evasive action, apparently managed to detonate one torpedo that was aimed at her with gunfire.[53] The only damage sustained by the Japanese was on the *Akagi*. She was strafed by the Marauders as they came out of their attacks. The only real danger to the carrier was posed by the last of the medium bombers. This aircraft, a Marauder, made no attempt to pull out of its attack, and the *Akagi* found that it was on the receiving end of the form of attack for which the Japanese believed they had a patent. The suicide attack failed, though no one on the flagship's bridge was quite sure how the ship was missed. Though a collision had seemed inevitable, the Marauder cartwheeled into the sea off the carrier's port beam.[54]

This attack decided the Japanese course of action. The American effort had been uncoordinated, and no attempt had been made to attack from different directions to counter defensive maneuvering. Moreover, the torpedoes had been dropped at too great a range to be effective, and in any event the American Mark 13 torpedo was too slow and too unreliable in terms of depth-keeping to have much chance of recording hits on fast-moving targets. But if American equipment, technique and tactics were poor, there was no doubting that the attacks had been brave and determined and had come from Midway. The conclusion to be drawn from this attack, therefore, was that the carriers could not relax their effort against the atoll. Thus at 0715, as the American attack came to an end, Nagumo ordered the Kates on the *Akagi* and the *Kaga* to be lowered to the hangar decks and prepared for a strike against Midway.[55]

Nagumo had thus committed himself, and in doing so he had disobeyed Yamamoto's strict order to keep half his Kates armed with antiship ordnance. He had also left himself with little margin for error, not so much in terms of strength but in terms of time. The American torpedo bombers had not registered any significant material results—two men were killed, a signals aerial was cut and the *Akagi*'s flight deck pockmarked by machine-gun fire—but they had cost the First Carrier Striking Force ten minutes. It did not seem much then, but after 0700 the precious commodity of time began to run out for the Japanese. It would take about an hour for the Kates on the decks of the *Akagi* and the *Kaga* to be struck below and to have their torpedo armament changed to ordinary bombs.[56] Getting the bombers back to the flight deck and then the whole of the strike force into the air would take up to thirty more minutes. But on the basis of current calculations Tomonaga's flight would begin to circle its carriers as the first step to landing sometime between 0815 and 0830.[57]

Everything about the planning of Operation MI had been based on the assumption that the battle would unfold in a manner that would enable the Japanese to determine its timing and pattern. The delays incurred in making decisions about a second strike threatened this casual assumption. Nagumo had to decide between launching and recovering his aircraft—he could not do both at the same time. Nine sets of arrestor wires and at least two sets of crash barriers per carrier provided the theoretical capacity to launch Zekes and even Vals while landing aircraft, but this was not something that any carrier admiral lightly entertained.[58]

By delaying his initial decision for some ten or more minutes, Nagumo was left with the decision of whether to recover his aircraft from the first attack before or after flying off the second attack against Midway. At this time the problem did not seem insurmountable. There appeared to be no threat to the Japanese carriers other than the one posed by enemy forces on Midway. By the time Nagumo made his decision to commit a second strike against the atoll, the various scouts had been away for a minimum of two hours, some for nearly three. Since no sighting reports had been received in that time, Nagumo thought that the planners had been right all along, that he had only to deal with Midway at this time. With no sign of an enemy task force, it appeared safe for the First Carrier Striking Force to resume pounding Midway. Under the circumstances, resumption of the attack on the atoll was not only safe but essential. There was no way of Nagumo knowing that at 0702, almost the same time he received Tomonaga's signal recommending a second attack on Midway, the *Enterprise* and the *Hornet*, after having turned into the wind at 0656, began to launch aircraft against the First Carrier Striking Force.[59]

Some thirteen minutes after Nagumo committed himself to strike at Midway for a second time the radio intelligence unit at Pearl Harbor picked up a Japanese signal that Rochefort and his team of analysts took to be a message from a scout: "Sighted ten surface ships, apparently enemy. Bearing 10° 240 miles from Midway. Course 150° speed over 20 knots. 0728°."[60] Rochefort's reading of this signal was correct. What the Americans had intercepted was a sighting report of Spruance's Task Force 16 by one of Nagumo's reconnaissance seaplanes. Rochefort's immediate reaction was to take the signal to Nimitz, who may even have received the message before Nagumo himself. The Japanese commander had to wait for the message to be relayed to him by the *Tone*.[61] The reaction of Nagumo and Nimitz to the signal was the same: both noted that it made no reference to carriers.

It is always difficult for an historian, particularly one who deals with wars, campaigns and battles, to fit the elements of irrationality, uncertainty and luck into the rational mosaic of fact. To note that luck invariably has its say in any battle is almost trite, yet on some occasions events seem to have been organized in such a way as to mock the faltering efforts of the *dramatis personae*. Midway, at this point, seems to have been such an occasion; otherwise there would perhaps be no explanation for the fact that the signal read by Rochefort came from none other than Seaplane No. 4 from the *Tone*, the last of the scouts to leave the force after it had been delayed because of a jammed catapult. The seaplanes tasked to search sectors to either side of that allocated to the *Tone*'s second scout conducted their reconnaissance on time, but fate somehow arranged matters so that the Americans were found in the sector where the Japanese were operating thirty minutes behind schedule. One account of the battle has asserted that the sighting reports made by this seaplane both at 0728 and later were "not in time to affect the battle decisively." The comment seems to miss the point. It was the very lateness of these signals that was decisive, decisively disastrous for the Japanese.[62]

The sighting report of 0728 was one of the critical points of the whole battle. Why it had to be one of the two late seaplanes that made the all-important contact is inexplicable, but so were two other matters. First, a comparison of battle tracks suggests that one of the Jakes from the *Chikuma* (and not the one that was forced back prematurely) could and perhaps should have sighted the Americans some time before the seaplane from the *Tone* chanced upon the scene. Second, the *Tone*'s scout was unable to discern the distinctive silhouette of a carrier. By June 1942 Japanese scouts had become aware of the potentially lethal characteristics of American radar, and it may be that the seaplane deliberately stayed low on the horizon to evade the combat air patrol. This, in its turn, may account for the scout's inability to identify a carrier, but the fact was that throughout the day the American carrier forces were obliged to operate in front of the weather front that partially shrouded the Japanese. Indeed, with visibility up to 50 miles at 1,500 feet the Americans were uncomfortably aware of their potential vulnerability.[63] Yet in such ideal scouting conditions the Jake from the *Chikuma* failed to obtain a contact that it might have been expected to make, and the crew of the *Tone*'s Jake did not make out the shape of a carrier until 0820.[64]

The 0728 signal suddenly pinpointed Nagumo's problems. The force had to be American, and it was within striking range of Nagumo's aircraft—which in turn meant that the First Carrier Striking Force was within range of the enemy force if the latter contained a carrier. Nagumo had to know the composition of the enemy force immediately. The scout's information had been both alarming and unenlightening. According, at 0747 Nagumo instructed the *Tone*'s seaplane to ascertain the ship types in the enemy force.[65]

Two minutes before this signal Nagumo halted the rearming of the Kates on board the *Akagi* and the *Kaga*.[66] By that time, however, both carriers had completed the rearming of about half their bombers, while on the flagship only three Kates remained still with their original armament in place. Nagumo's caution was sensible, though perhaps it did not go far enough. He felt that it was far from clear which target would have to be attacked, and he was prepared to wait on amplifying reports before he made a final decision. In fact, however, between 0715 and 0745, between the time the Japanese broke the spot and the time the rearming of the Kates was halted, the First Carrier Striking Force lost a balance that it never really recovered.

Perhaps it would have been more sensible to order an immediate rearming of the Kates with their original weaponry. The uncertainty presented by the enemy naval force was more serious than any threat coming from Midway, at least on the showing of the Avengers and Marauders. Yet Nagumo's reasoning was sound enough as far as it went, which, unfortunately for the Japanese, was not quite far enough. If the Americans did not have carriers with them, it would be many hours before they could close the range and force an artillery duel, and the Japanese had plenty of time for a second strike against Midway before dealing with the enemy task force. If, on the other hand, the Americans had carriers, Nagumo would have to go after them immediately. By halting the process of rearming the Kates Nagumo allowed himself to stand between two options, ready to act on whatever reports he received. But Midway was never going to sail away, and the enemy force had been reported to be steering away from the Japanese force. Regardless of whether or not the sighted task force had a carrier, it should have been Nagumo's first and automatic concern. Had the Jake made its contact before Tomonaga made his recommendation there would have been no doubt about which course of action to pursue. Now, because the two signals had been received in the wrong order, Nagumo's ability to react had been impaired. The question of which target to attack should never have been raised, and it is perhaps surprising that no one picked up the significance of the course that the enemy task force was steering. A course of 150 degrees was suspiciously close to the one that the Japanese themselves were steering—one that led towards Midway, but more importantly into the prevailing wind.

These were the all-important points of which Nagumo and his staff lost sight over the next thirty minutes. Once the original order to rearm the Kates had been given, Nagumo had just the Vals of the *Hiryu* and the *Soryu* with which to strike at the enemy. Formidable as the Achi D3A1 was as a dive-bomber, it had to be escorted by fighters, and these were not fully available after all the Zekes from the *Akagi*'s and the *Kaga*'s combat air patrols were committed against the bombers from Midway. Nagumo therefore had to accept that if he chose to strike at the enemy task force without waiting for amplifying reports, he would be able to do so only with an unbalanced force of Kates, an understrength fighter escort and a full complement of Vals. On the other hand, if he chose to wait and rearm the Kates in response to the advice he received from his scouts, the whole question of whether to strike before or after recovering the Tomonaga force reasserted itself. Every minute that was lost making a decision about the armament for the Kates lessened the chances of the Japanese flying off a second strike before they recovered the first.

There was something else that should have been obvious about these various events but was lost on Nagumo and his staff. Less excusably, it was missed by Yamamoto and the staff of the Combined Fleet listening to developments some 600 miles astern. From the time the *Tone*'s statement was received Nagumo suspected the presence of an enemy carrier or carriers with the force that had been sighted. Japanese intelligence had suggested that the enemy could have three carriers, though the odds were that only one, perhaps two, might be encountered at some stage. Nagumo and his staff were not blind to the fact that the force that had been encountered was in an ideal position from which to counterattack if it had carrier aircraft. And there was no point in its being where it was unless it could attack with aircraft. This was the nub of the matter, yet it was a problem that Nagumo and Yamamoto neither considered at the time nor gave proper attention to after the battle.

The Japanese plan of campaign had assumed some two to three days between the attack on Dutch Harbor and a possible arrival of the Americans off Midway, but two to three hours after the start of the battle the Americans were found to be in the battle area. At the very least they were abreast of developments and not merely reacting to them. Such a situation should have alarmed any competent fleet commander and his staff, yet the reaction in the *Yamato* was casual by any standard. The appearance of the enemy at the outset of battle merely ensured his early destruction, and when the presence of his carriers was reported, the staff reaction was to envision an expansion of the size of the anticipated victory.[67] There was no consideration of what should have been evident—that the battle was developing along lines opposite to those that had been foreseen. In the face of such misplaced confidence on the part of Japan's allegedly best admiral and staff, Nagumo had little chance. For the First Carrier Striking Force, arrangements scheduled for three days became telescoped into thirty minutes, and it is scarcely surprising that under these circumstances Nagumo failed to come up with the correct answers to his difficulties.

The signal that Nagumo sent the Jake at 0747 telling Hiroshi Amari and the other two members of his crew to maintain contact with the enemy and report the types of ships in the task force inaugurated what was probably the most intensive phase of the battle. Between 0747 and 0830 the air was full of signals between the First Carrier Striking Force and its lonely scouts. The air was also full of attacking American bombers, a Japanese combat air patrol that was substantially increased during this phase of the battle and, at the end, Tomonaga's aircraft, which began to circle their carriers. In this period incoming messages from Amari and attacks on the Japanese ships by American aircraft followed one another in quick succession, overlapping in many instances. The period was one of considerable confusion.

Hardly had Nagumo's instructions been transmitted when the combat

SIDE MIDWAY

air patrol sighted a group of American aircraft approaching at about 9,000 feet from the southeast.[68] This was Major Loften R. Henderson's sixteen-strong force of Dauntlesses, which had left the eleven slower Vindicators from the 241st Scout-Bomber Squadron in its wake as it set course for the enemy. The Dauntlesses attacked between 0755 and 0812, using the glide-bombing technique. This unusual form of attack was settled upon by Henderson because it required less accuracy and skill than the demanding technique of dive-bombing, and he obviously believed that his hopelessly undertrained squadron could not be expected to do more than the bare minimum. Ten of its pilots, having arrived in the *Kittyhawk*, had been less than a week in the squadron, and only three of them had had previous time in Dauntlesses.[69] Henderson ordered his force to concentrate against the two carriers to port—the *Hiryu* and the *Soryu*—but neither of these were hit. The *Kaga*, attacked at the very end of the action, also escaped damage. The *Hiryu*, however, was shaken by five near misses, and units watching her under attack feared at one stage that she could not escape unscathed, such was the smoke that seemingly poured out of her. She emerged, however, with only four men killed by strafing. The American marines, on the other hand, lost half their number during the attack, and two more aircraft were found damaged beyond repair after they landed at Midway.[70] Undoubtedly American losses would have been heavier but for the many Zekes in the combat air patrol that had ammunition enough for only one pass. Among the pilots lost was Henderson who, instead of becoming one of the nameless thousands of Americans killed in the Pacific during this war, was to gain posthumous recognition of a kind. Just as the U.S. Navy named destroyers after its heroes, so airfields were named after its dead. Henderson had a captured Japanese airfield named after him. Henderson Field was later to prove the key to the battle that developed on, around and above the island of Guadalcanal.

DAUNTLESS

In the course of this attack Nagumo received two messages from Sea-plane No. 4. The first, signaled at 0758, reported the enemy's change of course to due south at 0755.[71] The report drew an immediate and exasper-ated reply at 0800: "Advise ship types."[72] Amari and his companions evidently caught the meaning and perhaps the menace of the signal. At 0809 the seaplane signaled the First Carrier Striking Force: "Enemy is composed of five cruisers and five destroyers."[73]

Even though the attack by the Dauntlesses was not over when this message was received, the signal of 0809 represented light at the end of the tunnel for the Japanese. Tension began to drain away with the realization that the enemy task force did not have the means to attack the First Carrier Striking Force. Inevitably the signal gave rise to some second-guessing on the flag bridge since, of course, there had never been any real chance that the enemy had a carrier with his task force.[74] But even Nagumo and Kusaka, who had suspected that the enemy force might have one or more carriers, could not but be reassured by this report. The First Carrier Striking Force would not have to fight a carrier battle at this stage, and it would not have to receive the first attack. Kusaka therefore recommended that the attack on Midway be resumed, though first the Japanese had to attend to one other matter. In the course of the American attack the Japanese cruising formation had loosened. It needed to be tightened. Moreover, the Japanese still had to see off the last of the American bombers. But no sooner had the Dauntlesses finished then another attack materialized, this time from high level.

This attack was different from the earlier ones. It was one that the Japanese had to sweat out because they could not counter it with the combat air patrol or with their antiaircraft guns. The attack was delivered by Sweeney's Flying Fortresses. They had decided that the 9,000 feet altitude from which they had attacked the transports on the previous day was too low for safety. Wisely, Sweeney kept his bombers at 20,000 feet, and at that height all but one of them proved immune to any kind of damage and mishap. But from that altitude the chances of the bombers hitting small elusive targets were slim. The rather ragged Fortress attack began at 0814 and lasted about five minutes. No hits were recorded. This, however, did not prevent a final claim being put forth of at least one carrier hit. Sweeney pared back the various claims in the belief that they had been grossly exaggerated, but like Fletcher at Tulagi he did not reduce the claims enough. Both the *Hiryu* and the *Soryu* were bracketed by bombs, but once more the Japanese carriers came through their ordeal unscathed.[75]

The attack by the Fortresses had not ended before the last of the forces from Midway, the eleven Vindicators of Major Benjamin W. Norris, came upon the scene. Approaching at a height of 13,000 feet Norris was immediately met by the combat air patrol. He led his aircraft into cloud in an effort to shake off the Zekes, and while he was there he gave orders for his men to attack Japanese carriers when they emerged from the safety of the clouds. When he led his formation into the attack, however, Norris, like Earnest before him, chose the first target available on the grounds that his aircraft were unlikely to survive long enough to reach the more distant carriers. Vindicators were known to the marines as either "Vibrators" or "Wind Indicators," and these derisive labels just about summarized the aircrafts' characteristics and chances of survival with Zekes at their heels. But only two of the Vindicators were shot down in the course of this attack. Another four were found to be damaged beyond repair when they arrived back at Midway. In part the relatively light casualties of the Vindicators can be attributed to the fact that they did not press their attack against the carriers and settled instead for the *Haruna*. She was attacked by Vindicators using a combination of techniques—glide-bombing, dive-bombing and some of indeterminate description—but to no effect.[76]

The Vindicators' attack lasted between about 0817 and 0830.[77] This coincided with the first great crisis of the battle for the Japanese. By 0830 the First Carrier Striking Force had beaten off successive attacks by Avengers, Marauders, Vindicators, Dauntlesses and Flying Fortresses with no more than a flight deck or two slightly grazed and a handful of sailors killed or wounded. But at 0820, during these last two attacks, the *Tone*'s Jake sent a report that wrecked the basis of Nagumo's earlier calculation: "The enemy is accompanied by what appears to be a carrier."[78] This destroyed the illusion of relative security that had settled upon Nagumo and his staff for the whole of the nine minutes since the message of 0809 was received.[79] Worse was to follow. Ten minutes later the Jake was back on the air to inform Nagumo that it had sighted "two additional enemy cruisers in position bearing 8° distance 250 miles from Midway. Course 150° speed 20 knots."[80]

Reaction to these two signals crystalized at three distinct levels. First, the contradictory reports provoked Abe, the commander of the Support Group and its two scouting cruisers, into sending out more scouts and issuing orders to the *Chikuma* to send out Jakes to relieve Amari.[81] Abe had lost confidence in Amari, and when the latter signaled that he intended to return to the carrier force, first at 0834 and then again at 0848 and 0850, Abe responded by ordering him to stay with the enemy task force until seaplanes from the *Chikuma* arrived on the scene.[82] He also ordered Amari to go on the air with his long-range transmitter so the carriers could take an exact bearing on the enemy.[83] If by ordering the latter Abe obliquely indicated that he had by this stage as little confidence in Amari's navigation as he did in his powers of observation, then the admiral's skepticism was well founded. When the newly dispatched scouts arrived in the position Amari had claimed to be operating in, they found an empty ocean.[84]

Second, also at about 0830, Yamaguchi, commander of the Second Carrier Division, made a signal by lamp—relayed by the *Nowaki*—to Nagumo. Yamaguchi had been no less alarmed than Nagumo by the turn of events, and he felt that it was ill-advised to delay a strike against a force that now seemed to be in two parts but collectively so large that a carrier had to be with it. His signal read, "Consider it advisable to launch attack force immediately."[85] In a service that could be so rigidly formal as the Imperial Japanese Navy, such a signal was tantamount to insubordination and certainly a reflection on Nagumo's conduct of operations. But Yamaguchi was not a person to be trifled with. In an organization not noted for high standards of personal behavior he was somewhat infamous. He had a reputation for unbridled aggression, but also ability, and Nagumo and

Kusaka could recognize the reasoning behind Yamaguchi's suggestion even though they disagreed with his diagnosis. Their solution was to be the third development that arose from the signals of 0820 and 0830.

In fact, Nagumo and Kusaka had no option but to discard Yamaguchi's prompting. Successive American attacks had forced the commander of the combat air patrol, Lieutenant Saburo Shindo of the *Akagi*, to use up increasing numbers of Zekes from the second attack formation. Even the *Hiryu* had been forced to commit some of her fighters to the defense of the task force before 0800.[86] This depletion of available fighter strength alone was enough to turn Nagumo and Kusaka against Yamaguchi's suggestion. As we have seen, at 0830 the carriers had a full complement of Vals, a hodgepodge of Kates and some Zekes available for operations. Nagumo and Kusaka had no intention of committing so unbalanced a force to the attack when the evidence of what would happen to it lay all around the First Carrier Striking Force. Four Japanese carriers were intact and at full fighting effectiveness despite having been attacked by successive waves of bombers for about ninety minutes. Enemy bomber losses had been prohibitive, a direct result of their lacking fighter cover. The American attacks had been a model of how not to conduct operations, and Nagumo and Kusaka were quite prepared to learn from American mistakes rather than from their own. To fall in with Yamaguchi's recommendation was to run the strong risk of writing off at least a quarter of the carriers' bomber strength with little prospect of their obtaining a commensurate return. If the bombers were to be launched against the enemy they had to be escorted, and this meant that the Zekes would have to be brought back to their carriers, refueled, rearmed and properly reorganized. Anything less would almost certainly result in the Japanese bombers being committed to a death ride. The problem with this course of action, however, was that the recall and the preparation of the Zekes would take time, and even as the last of the American attacks came to an end Tomonaga's aircraft appeared over their carriers.

Once the first attack formation returned from Midway time ran out for Nagumo and Kusaka. It would take some thirty minutes or more to get the second attack formation into the air, and the aircraft returning from Midway did not have thirty or more minutes in hand. All had been away for at least four hours. The endurance of the Vals and Zekes was about five hours; that of the Kates was about four and a half.[87] No one on the carriers knew the state of the returning aircraft, but some were certain to be damaged and some would have wounded crewmen. To keep these aircraft in the air while a strike was flown off was certain to condemn many of them to a watery grave. The whole of Tomonaga's attack formation would be put at risk by following Yamaguchi's recommendation, and as it transpired his division was the one most vulnerable to further losses because damage was largely concentrated amongst the bombers from his two carriers. Yamaguchi's recommendation was belligerent, simple and superficially attractive, but it made no more sense than the admiral's tactical solution to one of the problems that had plagued the attack on Pearl Harbor more than six months before. (When told that his division would not take part in the operation,[88] he had physically assaulted Nagumo and threatened to kill his superior if the attack miscarried.)[89] His solution to the problem posed by the fact that the *Hiryu* and the *Soryu* lacked the range for a round trip to Oahu had been to use the carriers' aircraft for the attack and then to abandon the two carriers off the Hawaiian Islands.[90] Yamaguchi's solutions had been discarded on that occasion, and Nagumo and his chief of staff did not hesitate to discard this particular recommendation. Writing off perhaps half their bomber strength was a luxury that the Japanese could not afford, and this was a view endorsed by Genda. Too much depended on these returning aircraft and aircrew, both immediately and over the coming months, for them to be consigned needlessly to the sea.

For the carrier force Midway was not the end of a campaign but the start of two months of intensive operations. Disposing of perhaps a hundred aircraft to launch possibly half that number at the start of the first battle was unthinkable. If Nagumo had had a couple more carriers, or just the *Zuikaku* with his formation, he might have been tempted, but with only four carriers he had no real margin against the unexpected that had now materialized. The inherent weaknesses of a plan that involved insufficient force to carry out a series of operations left the First Carrier Striking Force without the means to reorganize its strike formations quickly and effectively. Nagumo's decision, taken in consultation with Kusaka and Genda, was therefore logical and the only one possible under the circumstances: to clear the flight decks; to recover Tomonaga's aircraft and after them the combat air patrol; to rearm, refuel and regroup all available aircraft; and finally to strike with full force against whatever force might be to the east. At the most recovering the aircraft then in the air would delay an improvised strike for not much more than thirty minutes, while a full strike might be made ready in about ninety minutes, perhaps two hours. The Japanese situation was difficult, far more difficult than any situation they had encountered in the first six months of the war. But even if the carriers had never had to face such a crisis in the past, there was every confidence that they would rise to the occasion. It was not for nothing that they had registered success in the past and managed to break up the attacks that had been made over the previous two hours. In another two hours the account with the American task force, with or without its carrier, would be settled.

CHAPTER 12

Miscalculations

Once Nagumo decided to recover the aircraft returning from Midway before flying off a strike against the enemy task force, the landing signals were run up on the carriers and their flight decks were cleared. For the *Akagi* and the *Kaga* the latter posed no problems. Their flight decks had been clear, except for returning Zekes from the combat air patrol, for more than an hour, and when the *Akagi* flew off four fighters at 0832 she was quite free to recover her aircraft. She and her colleagues began to do so at 0837, though in the case of the flagship, flying operations had to be suspended at 0839 when two enemy aircraft were seen approaching off her port bow. Thereafter the Americans gave no more trouble, and in relative though temporary safety the *Akagi* and the *Kaga* set about recovering their aircraft and rearming their Kates. The initial rearming of the Kates was with 550-lb semi-armor piercing bombs,[1] but the subsequent reversal involved a change back to Mark 91 torpedoes.[2] This second rearming of the morning produced one unfortunate side effect. The emphasis of this change was on speed, and on this occasion the ordnance men did not have the time, inclination or discipline to ensure that discarded weaponry was stowed properly. Ordnance was left around the hangar decks instead of being returned to the magazines. Hangar decks were dangerous enough places under the best of circumstances since they combined the potentially disastrous brew of high explosive and avgas. After the Japanese carriers had refueled their aircraft and readied them for another strike mission, all eight hangar decks in the Japanese carriers were potential deathtraps. During rearming, the hangar decks were certain to be vulnerable, but the carelessness of Japanese arrangements increased the danger far beyond the point that was strictly necessary.[3]

The recovery of the first wave and the combat air patrol was completed without serious mishap. Tomonaga's flight was landed by 0900,[4] and the last of the Zekes to be recalled were recovered at about 0917.[5] At that point Nagumo ordered the execution of the next phase of operations. He had issued warning orders covering this phase at 0855, and these had told his force that after the carriers had completed the recovery of their aircraft, it was to turn north, away from Midway, to contact and destroy the enemy task force.[6] In this way Nagumo replied to Yamaguchi and gave notice of his intention to strike at the enemy with a concentrated and balanced force.

Nagumo issued his orders by lamp, but with his whereabouts known to the enemy there was no point in continuing to maintain radio silence. Nagumo recognized this and took the opportunity to send a sketchy situation report, full of factual errors, to Yamamoto at 0855.[7] The errors, however, were not particularly serious. What was important was that Nagumo kept the commander in chief informed of the course of events and his own intentions. At 0918 Nagumo turned his force away from Midway not to the north but on a bearing of 70 degrees. Such was their hurry, however, that the Japanese did not reverse order, and for the time that the First Carrier Striking Force had left to it, Nagumo's carriers steamed in a roughly rhombic form, the *Hiryu* leading, the *Soryu* and the *Akagi* roughly abreast of one another and the *Kaga* trailing in the wake of Yamaguchi's flagship.[8]

Responsibility for the disaster that overwhelmed the Japanese has largely been placed on Nagumo for his alleged mishandling of the First Carrier Striking Force during this critical phase of the battle. The criticism of Nagumo, though tempered by acknowledgment of the weakness of the Japanese operational plan and superior American intelligence work, has generally followed the line that when confronted with a series of difficult options, the admiral managed to make a series of poor decisions. The criticism made by Fuchida and Okumiya is typical of the general line of criticism. In their joint book, *Midway: The Battle That Doomed Japan*, Mitsuo Fuchida wrote the following:

> Unaware of these deliberations, I felt relieved that our second attack wave had not yet been committed to Midway, at the same time regretting the hasty rearming of our torpedo bombers for a land attack. At least, I thought, the dive-bomber group from the *Hiryu* and *Soryu* was ready to attack the enemy, and I expected that it would be ordered off the carriers momentarily. This expectation—and hope—waned as the recovery of the first wave got under way with no sign that the dive-bombers had yet taken off. It gave way to dismayed surprise when I learned of Admiral Nagumo's order issued at 0855, indicating that no attack would be launched until we had time to reorganize our forces while temporarily retiring northwards.
>
> Looking back at this critical moment, which ultimately was to decide the battle, I can easily realise what a difficult choice faced the Force Commander. Yet, even now, I find it hard to justify the decision he took. Should he not have

despatched the torpedo-bombers also, even though armed with bombs? He could have launched them to orbit until enough fighters could be recovered, refuelled and launched again to provide escorts. The plans back from Midway could have been kept in the air at least until the bombers had cleared. Damaged planes, if unable to remain aloft any longer, could have crash-landed in the sea, where destroyers would have rescued their crews.

'Wise after the event,' as the saying goes. Still there was no question that it would have been wiser to launch our dive-bombers immediately, even without fighter protection. In such all-or-nothing carrier warfare, no other choice was admissible. Even the risk of sending unprotected level-bombers should have been accepted as necessary in this emergency. Their fate would probably have been the same as that of the unescorted American planes which had attacked us a short while before, *but just possibly they might have saved us from the catastrophe we were about to suffer*. (Italics added)[9]

Coming from the person who led the attack on Pearl Harbor, this is powerful criticism. Fuchida's seeming willingness to write off a major part of the carriers' strength in carrying out "the only admissible course of action" cannot be disregarded lightly. Yet this criticism is not reasoned, and it fails on two counts. First, the statement is explicit about the view that aircraft and aircrew were expendable but the carriers were not. A carrier with no aircraft in the middle of a carrier battle was no use to the Japanese whatsoever. The value of a carrier lies with its aircraft, and Fuchida was willing to let Tomonaga's aircraft ditch and see prohibitive losses inflicted for the sake of saving an hour or two for launching the second attack. Even if such an attack was successful, what four carriers were supposed to do with virtually no aircraft and the invasion phase of Midway still to come is hard to discern. Second, Fuchida's final sentence is nothing more than irrelevant. Launching a second strike some time between 0830 and 0900 was never going to save the Japanese from catastrophe. By that time the American squadrons that were to crush the First Carrier Striking Force were already airborne and there was nothing the Japanese could do about it; at this late stage the best that an impromptu Japanese strike could achieve was success against carriers that had already flown off their own attack forces. That might in some way have compensated for the losses the Japanese were to suffer, but it would not have averted the losses. The incident regarding Seaplane No. 4's report of ten torpedo bombers heading for the First Carrier Striking Force has not been given the attention it merits.[10] This force (its size was underestimated) was one of six that were setting out to attack the Japanese carriers, and between them these six overpowered the Japanese. Following Yamaguchi's recommendation, said by Fuchida and Okumiya to be "in this critical situation . . . the only correct one," would not have affected this situation one way or another, except perhaps in denying flight decks to returning American aircraft.[11]

Walter Lord, in *Incredible Victory*, wrote about the Japanese at the time Nagumo ordered the rearming of the Kates to be suspended that

> despite their quandary, there was no reason to panic. They had plenty of strength: all they really needed was a little time. Time to switch back to torpedoes and armor-piercing bombs, if there were carriers around. Time to finish changing to land bombs, if they were to hit Midway again. Time to regroup the ships scattered by the enemy torpedo attacks. Time to replenish and tighten up the air patrol. Time to recover Tomonaga's planes. And, above all, time to think and plan intelligently, without too many twists and unexpected pressures.[12]

In the hour after Nagumo halted the rearming the situation did not change, and for that Nagumo must bear responsibility. Time had been wasted, but it had been wasted between 0728 and 0820, not after 0830. There is no ground for disputing Fuchida's comments on that particular score:

> Nagumo's reasoning was logical enough. His force was well balanced and appeared greatly superior in strength. Therefore, it would be easy to destroy the enemy if all his striking power were thrown into a single massive attack. Such strategy was orthodox, but it had one flaw—neglect of the time factor. Victory in battle does not always go to the stronger; it often goes to the side which is quicker to react boldly and decisively to unforeseen developments, and to grasp fleeting opportunities.[13]

This was precisely the point that is valid: Nagumo needed time, and the Americans, as much by luck as by judgment, did not give him enough.[14]

Yet by 0900 Nagumo had all but recovered his balance, and events were to show that when disaster struck he was but minutes away from the completion of his arrangements, arrangements that were superior in every way to those deemed correct by Fuchida. If any criticism is to be leveled at Nagumo, then it should be not for the decisions made between 0830 and 0855 regarding the priority of landing and launching but for the decision, which never seems to have been questioned, to set course towards the enemy. By setting course on a bearing of 70 degrees Nagumo deliberately shortened the distance between himself and the enemy. He steered into an attack that he knew from the signal of 0855 was then in the process of materializing, and he did this at the very time his four carriers were at their must vulnerable. The obvious justification for such a course of action was to maintain contact with the enemy and to take the First Carrier Striking Force to within striking range of the Americans. With one Jake, albeit an unreliable one, in contact with the enemy and others on their way to the presumed location of the enemy task force, the Japanese had little reason to shorten the distance between themselves and the Americans. The Americans were already within range and could not turn away because they

needed to recover their aircraft. The Japanese, with their scouts clinging to
the enemy task force and their direction finders helping to fix positions,
were reasonably placed for the moment. Nagumo needed to buy time, and
time was not to be bought by steaming towards the enemy at full speed.
Had Nagumo backtracked, turned north or steered for the west, he might
well have gained both time and cover. And he need not necessarily have lost
his contact with the Americans, because his scouts had an endurance
superior to that of their counterparts. Nagumo had much to gain and little
to loose by steering away from the Americans until he was ready to strike;
the course he adopted reversed these dangers and advantages. Perhaps this
was Nagumo's real error, not his vacillations of the previous hour.

The danger into which the First Carrier Striking Force sped after 0855
began to materialize from the time Fletcher and Spruance drew apart at
0607. After that Fletcher moved to recover his scouts, while Spruance took
Task Force 16 to a position from which to attack the enemy.[15] At this time
the Americans held a potentially decisive advantage: whereas the Japanese
believed that they had surprise on their side, the Americans knew better.
But the American advantage did not mean that Fletcher and Spruance had
clear courses of action or that their decisions were any easier to make. Both
admirals were aware of the restraining influence of Nimitz's "calculated
risk" admonishment, and they were equally aware of why such an order
was necessary: between them they had under command what amounted to
the only force that stood between the enemy and his complete domination
of the Pacific.

The basic problem that confronted Fletcher and Spruance during their
approach to contact was the size of the force to which they were opposed.
On this matter the two American admirals were no better served by their
reconnaissance forces than their Japanese counterparts. As we have seen
earlier, Fletcher's basic problem was that, during the initial phase, American contact reports referred only to two enemy carriers to the northwest of
Midway. But after the 0552 message that led Fletcher to embark on the
potentially dangerous policy of dividing his forces, the scent went dead for
the Americans. The carriers could not communicate with Midway because
they could not break radio silence unless they were compromised. All they
could work on was radio traffic from aircraft. Inevitably, this gave only
confusing fragments, and none of the American aircraft that attacked the
First Carrier Striking Force thought to report their position and composition before attacking. This was true even of the first of the carrier aircraft to
attack Nagumo's force after it had swung round on its new course. Between
0552 and 0838, when Fletcher committed the *Yorktown*'s aircraft to the
attack, the American carriers did not receive a single report giving the
strength, position and course of the enemy.[16]

The two American admirals were to react in very different ways to the situation in which they found themselves. When it came to making his decision, the junior admiral was to place his trust in the intelligence briefing that told him the enemy carrier force would be concentrated. Having seen intelligence proved correct thus far, Spruance assumed that it was probably correct on this matter. Fletcher, on the other hand, was more cautious and deliberate, and with good cause. At the Coral Sea he had learned the dangers of striking on the basis of a partial reconnaissance. On that occasion he had been both lucky and successful, but Midway was not the time and place to tempt fortune a second time. With but one carrier to the two of Spruance, when it came to the time for a decision Fletcher, unlike Spruance, chose to hold back a reserve.

But amid the uncertainties caused by the lack of reports, the Americans could draw one reasonable conclusion and entertain one hope. The enemy would have to recover the aircraft he had committed against Midway, and the initial contacts were secured at such a range from Midway that the Americans could calculate that the Japanese would be committed to recovery for some three to five hours after dawn. Thus the Americans could deduce that with the enemy showing no sign of turning away from Midway before the reports dried up, the Japanese would stay on a course towards Midway until the aircraft they had flown off against the atoll had returned. Thus the Americans had a reasonable idea of where the enemy might be until about 0900. With this calculation came the slow realization that the seemingly remote hope held at Pearl Harbor before the fleet sailed was becoming ever more realistic as Task Force 16 headed towards the enemy and remained as yet undetected. With luck the Americans might catch the enemy carriers recovering their aircraft after their attack on Midway or, better still, rearming and refueling their aircraft.[17] The reports that the Americans picked up before 0600 showed that it would be impossible to catch the Japanese carriers while their aircraft were still away attacking Midway. But as Spruance came southwest towards a flying-off point, the awareness that at 0630 the Japanese were over Midway raised hopes that Task Force 16 might yet strike at the Japanese carriers when they were recovering or servicing their aircraft.[18]

But the chance would evaporate if Spruance held to his original intention to close to within 100 miles of the enemy before launching. As Task Force 16 headed towards the enemy, its staff calculated that it would take until about 0900 for the force to close to such a range, and there was little if any chance of its continuing to remain undetected until that time. Spruance's intention, if adhered to, threatened the very advantage of surprise that the admiral had done so much to maintain over the previous week. As we have seen, on the voyage out from Pearl Harbor he had banned talk between ships, and he had ordered his aircraft to observe strict radio silence at all times except when in contact with the enemy. He refused to use homing devices to help his aircraft find their way home after search missions.[19]

On the morning of 4 June Spruance had every intention of striking at the enemy before the enemy could strike at him, and he was determined to strike with his full force. He was equally determined to strike at the Japanese before they had a chance to attack Midway a second time.[20] The initial Japanese attack could not have been prevented, but the retention of Midway was a major American priority, and Spruance was anxious to ensure that it remained in the fight. The problem was that these various intentions did not hang together. The best chance of hitting without being hit would come when the two opposing carrier forces came within range of one another, the Americans taking the first opportunity to strike at the Japanese. Maximum range for the Americans was 175 miles. That represented a dangerously small margin against mishap or navigational error.

In trying to strike a balance between these various intentions Spruance found himself involved in an increasingly acrimonious argument with Captain Miles R. Browning, the chief of staff he had inherited from Halsey. Browning had a reputation for being obnoxious that rivaled Theobald's, possibly even the infamous McMorris's. More to the point, Browning was damned as erratic and unreliable by King.[21] On this occasion, however, Browning had the right answers and Spruance, whom King regarded as the most intelligent officer in the navy, did not. Spruance was concerned that his aircraft would be sent out too soon and would either fail to find the enemy or be forced to return to their carriers for want of fuel. Hence his determination to close to a range of less than 100 miles. Browning, on the other hand, wanted to launch at about 0700, when the staff suggested that the distance between the two carrier forces would be about 155 miles, allowing for deflection (the distance covered by the enemy's ships in the time it took for aircraft to fly to them).[22] In support of his contention Browning could marshal two powerful arguments. First, the Americans could not hope to close to within 100 miles and remain undetected. Second, if Task Force 16 delayed flying off its strike mission beyond 0700, increasingly serious problems would be encountered with regard to aircraft handling. In fact, Task Force 16 would run into the same sort of problems that beset Nagumo and the First Carrier Striking Force in the shuffling of forces. If Task Force 16 was to launch an assault with virtually all its aircraft, it would need two flight decks from each carrier to handle the strike. American launching technique at this stage was not equal to that of the Japanese. Flying off so many aircraft was a time-consuming process. But at the same time Task Force 16 had to maintain its combat air patrol, and this would have to be relieved some time after 0700. But to bring down the combat air patrol and fly off more Wildcats would break the spot. The Americans would have to strike their aircraft, lower them to the hangar deck and return them to the flight deck once the combat air patrol was rearranged. A number of things could easily go wrong if the arrangement of lining up strike aircraft on the flight deck was broken. There was a difference between choosing not to attack until 0900 and adopting measures that precluded the possibility of attack before 0900. In Browning's estimation the dangers of an early strike were less weighty than a course of action that deprived the Americans of freedom of action during the first part of the morning. Spruance had far less choice about when and at what range he would attack than is immediately apparent, and Browning, not Spruance, had worked the situation out correctly. Browning prevailed upon Spruance to do as he suggested, but in return Spruance was adamant about one matter. He wanted to commit his full strength to the first attack, thereby breaking one of the cardinal rules of war, the maintenance of a reserve. Thus the policy of Task Force 16 was settled in favor of an all-out assault at or near extreme range, when the enemy was some 155 miles from the Americans at 0700.[23] It was the sort of decision of which Yamaguchi would have approved.

To launch such an attack Spruance could call on his two groups, CVG-6 from the *Enterprise* and CVG-8 from the *Hornet*. Lieutenant Commander Clarence W. McClusky and Commander Stanhope C. Ring were the respective commanders of the groups. CVG-6 deployed a fighter squadron (VF-6) of twenty-seven F4F-4 Wildcats under Lieutenant James S. Gray; a bomber squadron (VB-6) and a scout squadron (VS-6), both with nineteen Dauntlesses, under Lieutenants Richard H. Best and Wilmer E. Gallaher respectively; and a torpedo bomber squadron (VT-6) of fourteen Devastators under Lieutenant Commander Eugene E. Lindsey. The latter squadron was one of the most experienced in the navy; none of its pilots had less than 2,500 hours' flying time in their logbooks.[24] The *Hornet* carried exactly the same number of aircraft as the flagship. Lieutenant Commanders Samuel G. Mitchell and Robert R. Johnson were the commanders of VF-8 and VB-8 respectively, both units having the same strength as their counterparts from the *Enterprise*. Lieutenant Commander Walter F. Rodee's VS-8 had eighteen Dauntlesses, while VT-8, under Lieutenant Commander John C. Waldron, had fifteen Devastators. Thus Task Force 16 deployed a total of 158 aircraft: 54 Wildcat fighters, 75 Dauntlesses, of which 37 were with scout squadrons and 38 were from bomber units, and 29 Devastator torpedo bombers.[25]

At 0656, just four minutes before Tomonaga sent his signal recommending a second strike against Midway, Task Force 16 turned back to the southeast into what little wind there was and then divided in order to begin launching. The *Enterprise* took with her the lion's share of the screen with the *Vincennes, Northampton, Pensacola* and five destroyers; the *Hornet* was escorted by the *New Orleans, Minneapolis, Atlanta* and three destroyers.[26] This was standard operational procedure for the Americans at this stage of the war: carriers launched and recovered separately, even within a single task force. As we have seen in the course of the battle of the Coral Sea, the consequence of this practice was that the Americans did not combine their groups within a single tactical formation. The task force launched two separate attacks, one from each carrier and both supposedly with a balance of their own.

Another marked contrast to Japanese practice immediately became apparent when American flying operations began, at 0702 for the *Hornet* and at 0706 for the *Enterprise*. At this stage of the war the Americans were not as fast as the Japanese in the launch of attack formations, and it was to take Task Force 16 more than an hour to get all its aircraft into the air. But at the end of its effort Task Force 16 had a larger attack force in the sky than the Japanese had used against Midway, though this was achieved at a price. By the time the Americans completed flying off their aircraft their presence had been discovered by the enemy, and their two attack groups had both lost their cohesion.

Browning's view that Task Force 16 could not close to within 100 miles of the enemy without being compromised was well-founded. As we have seen, Amari's Jake, searching line 4, came across Task Force 16 at 0728. The *Enterprise*'s radar and gunnery rangefinder found the seaplane just above the southern horizon, fine on the starboard bow, at just about the time Amari sent his initial sighting report back to the First Carrier Striking Force.[27] The way the Japanese seaplane hovered on the southern horizon quickly dispelled any hope that somehow or another the task force might have escaped detection. Suddenly matters became more urgent for the Americans; they, like the Japanese, were suddenly made aware of their potential vulnerability. There was no way the Americans could know of the chain of events that was to give them another fifty minutes of relative security as a result of the shortcomings of Amari and his two companions.

By the time it was discovered, Task Force 16 had been able to fly off only the major part of its scouting and bombing squadrons. Thirty-three dive-bombers, led by the group commander, were either in the air or in the process of taking off from the *Enterprise*; the *Hornet* was in exactly the same position with respect to the thirty-five Dauntlesses she was committing to the attack. But even by 0745 neither the *Enterprise* nor the *Hornet* had been able to get its Devastators and Wildcats away. An obvious crisis was in the making. The Dauntlesses could not be kept circling the task force waiting for the others. The fifteen members of VB-6 were armed with 1,000-lb bombs, while their eighteen colleagues from VS-6 were armed with one 500-lb and two 100-lb bombs.[28] But whereas the scouts had a range of 775 miles, the bombers had a range of only 456 miles.[29] They did not have the endurance to be kept circling the carriers. By 0745 some of the Dauntlesses had been in the air for forty minutes, and a decision had to be made about what they were to do. The delay they were forced to endure was the direct result of Spruance's decision to launch an all-out strike against the enemy, for this required both carriers to undertake two flight deck operations. The Dauntless bombers, with their 1,000-lb bombs, needed the full length of the flight deck to get airborne, and this meant that the torpedo bombers and fighters had to be kept on the hangar decks when the Dauntlesses were launched. It took time to bring the Wildcats and Devastators up to the flight deck after the dive-bombers had gone, and it took even more time to fly the aircraft off. The American problem at this stage was exacerbated by last-minute breakdowns and reloadings that cost them time they could not afford. At 0745 Spruance felt that he had no option but to order McClusky to proceed with the attack without waiting for the others.[30] CVG-6, therefore, began its mission under the worst possible circumstances. The Dauntlesses, or at least some of them, had used up forty minutes' fuel even before they left Task Force 16, and they had to set out with no fighter escort. Moreover, by setting out before the Devastators they ended any possibility of there being a synchronized attack. Because the torpedo bombers were slower than the dive-bombers, the former could not catch up with the latter in the course of their approach to contact. Thus there was no way an assault could divide the enemy's attention between two different levels of attack.

CVG-6 thus found itself in a position that threatened to undo all the advantages conferred upon it by American intelligence work and by Spruance's initial decision to strike with full strength and at extreme range. As matters stood at 0745, there was more than a chance that the entire attack by the group could fall to pieces. The reaction of the *Hornet* and CVG-8 to this situation was rather different from that of the flagship. Her skipper, Captain Marc A. Mitscher, and her group commander were prepared to risk delaying back the Dauntlesses in order to ensure a coordinated attack. Mitscher and Ring would hold back the dive-bombers until Waldron led his fifteen Devastators well clear of the carrier, the calculation being that the higher cruising speed of the dive-bombers would enable them to catch up with the Devastators as they neared the enemy.[31] This attempted synchronization was sound enough in theory, but it failed to take proper account of the narrow margin against error that now beset the dive-bombers after their wasted time over Task Force 16, and it also underestimated the difficulties of station keeping that the various squadrons were to encounter. Waldron's squadron, organized into one division with four two-plane sections and a second division with two two-plane and one three-plane sections, would cruise at 1,500 feet; the others would make their way to the target at altitudes up to 19,000 feet.[32] Since CVG-8 had to advance towards the weather front in which the enemy still operated, the problems of command and coordination would be that much more difficult—even without speed differentials to complicate matters.

The weather front concerned Fletcher, but for a different reason. As a result of events at the battle of the Coral Sea, he was afraid of being attacked by an undetected enemy operating behind a weather front. He was wary of committing his single-carrier task force in an all-out attack when sighting reports failed to tally with intelligence appreciations. His position, with just one carrier, was more difficult than that of Spruance. Fletcher could not stretch his resources far. A single carrier could not provide fighters on a satisfactory scale for both the combat air patrol and the escort for the bombers.

Task Force 16 completed the launching of its aircraft at 0806 and then settled down on a course of 240 degrees for the rendezvous with and recovery of its aircraft.[33] By that time, however, the *Yorktown* was still not in a position to join the attack. The delays that Task Force 16 had encountered launching its aircraft were not enough to allow the *Yorktown* to make good the time she had lost recovering her scouts. It was not until after 0630 that the carrier was able to settle on a course towards the enemy, and then it was to take her another two hours of hard steaming to reach a launching position. She began to launch at 0838, first the twelve Devastators of Lieutenant Commander Lance E. Massey's VT-3 and then the seventeen Dauntlesses of Lieutenant Commander Maxwell F. Leslie's bomber squadron. Last to be launched were six Wildcats from the fighter squadron. These were led by the squadron's commander, Thatch.[34] The Devastators would fly in two six-strong divisions in the company of two of the six Wildcats. These would fly at low altitude, under the cloud base which was at 2,500 feet. The other four fighters, led by Thatch, were to fly at 5,000

Wildcat Fighters

THE BATTLE OF MIDWAY

feet. At that altitude they were to provide the link between the Dauntlesses and the Devastators; they would also be able to go to the aid of the vulnerable Devastators if and when the need arose.[35] Because of the commitment of the fighters to the torpedo bombers, the Dauntlesses flew at 20,000 feet in an attempt to keep above fighters from the enemy combat air patrol. This was recognized to be the best defense against enemy fighters, and the resultant discomfort caused by lack of oxygen in the dive-bombers was accepted.[36]

The *Yorktown* completed launching at 0906, one hour after the last of Task Force 16's aircraft managed to get away.[37] With only 35 of her aircraft committed to the attack, compared with the 57 of the *Enterprise* and the 60 of the *Hornet*, the *Yorktown*'s contribution was not merely the last but the smallest of three strike formations. This reflected Fletcher's determination to retain a reserve. The carrier's skipper, Buckmaster, elected to retain the scouting squadron—the only unit that remained from the ship's original air group—for this unpopular role.[38] This decision, and the retention of 19 Wildcats for the combat air patrol, kept the group commander, Commander Oscar Pederson, with the carrier. While there is little doubt that Fletcher's decision to maintain a reserve was solid, holding back a single squadron was really neither here nor there. Between them the *Yorktown*, *Enterprise* and *Hornet* committed a total of 41 torpedo bombers, 85 Dauntlesses and 26 fighters to the attack. One Dauntless squadron in reserve was unlikely to count for much if 152 aircraft were unable to force a favorable decision.

When the *Yorktown* finished launching her aircraft the situation was delicately balanced. Thus far things had gone wrong for both sides. The Japanese had found to their surprise that they were involved with an enemy task force long before Midway had been neutralized. On coming upon this enemy, the Japanese found that their aircraft, with all the blind obstinacy of inanimate objects, resolutely refused to arrange themselves in the "correct" order. Prompt and effective employment was an elusive goal. Thus for the first time in the war the Japanese carriers, caught without the means to strike first, were forced to fight defensively. For the moment the Japanese were vulnerable and unable to dictate the pattern of immediate events because the tactical advantage was in American hands. The latter was able to strike first, and to strike without being struck in return, but this was an advantage they had to take at the first time of asking; once the Americans made their move the balance of vulnerability would change sides. Thus far the American conduct of operations hardly suggested that success would crown their efforts. Between their three carriers the Americans had nine attack squadrons, and in theory they had committed themselves to three attacks, each of which was supposedly balanced. In reality they had committed eight squadrons in six separate attacks, and it remained to be seen whether the chances of success would be increased or diminished as a result of this fragmentation of effort. By prewar standards the lack of concentration and coordination would guarantee failure, but on the other hand the sheer number of attacks coming one on top of the other might bring success. There was no way of knowing which would prove the case, the Americans losing because of their failure to concentrate their efforts or winning in spite of it. One thing, however, was clear: the impending clash between the American bomber squadrons and the Japanese combat air patrol was likely to be decisive, one way or the other.

If the American deployment for the attack was not all it might have been, worse was to follow as soon as the major part of the attacking force set off for the enemy. It was one matter for the American carriers to launch their aircraft against an enemy whose position had been reported; it was quite another matter for these aircraft to find their target. To do so they had to rely on a course calculated for them by their operations staffs. This was plotted on the basis of the enemy's last-known position, course and speed, his probable intentions and thus the the position he was likely to be in when aircraft reached him on an interception course. On the American carriers the course plotted for the aircraft was one of 239 degrees, but this was based on information that was old. The operations staffs assumed that the Japanese carriers would continue to make 25 knots on their present bearing of 315 degrees from Midway. On this matter the staffs were correct. But the final calculation was wrong because they did not realize how much time the Japanese lost heading towards Midway as a result of their high-speed maneuvers in countering the various attacks from the atoll. The Japanese were much further from the atoll than the staffs of the *Enterprise* and the *Hornet* believed when they plotted the 239-degree course.[39] The failure of the various forces from Midway to report the location of the enemy when they established contact contributed to the error.

If all the aircraft from Task Force 16 had flown on a course of 239 degrees, none would have sighted the First Carrier Striking Force. This was the fate of the Dauntlesses and Wildcats from the *Hornet*. Ring led his aircraft along the prescribed course of 239 degrees until 0930, by which time he should have been directly over the enemy carrier formation. With visibility good in all directions Ring encountered an empty ocean. As a result he had to make an immediate decision about which was the more likely, that he was between the enemy and Midway or that the enemy had managed to get between him and the atoll. He chose to lead his formation around to port in order to sweep southwards towards Kure and Midway.[40] By the time the formation neared Kure and saw in the distance the black smoke from Midway's burning oil tanks, the pilots must have realized that their commander's guess had been less than inspired. To have been south of the calculated 0930 position the Japanese would have had to steam at something over 35 knots. It was apparent that the Japanese had been to the north, but by the time Kure was reached there was nothing that the formation could do about redeeming its error. Dauntlesses and Wildcats alike were too low on fuel to consider the possibility of backtracking. The mission had to be abandoned, and the various squadrons had to make for safety. For the bombers this meant Midway. The time they had spent in the air meant that there was no possibility of their getting back to the *Hornet*. Three of their number did not even manage to reach Eastern Island.[41] Two of these came down in the lagoon. Eleven managed to reach the airfield, where they landed and were refueled and rearmed by a garrison that had watched their approach with some apprehension. The Dauntless pilots themselves were not overenamored with the prospect of landing on a base that had been heavily attacked and whose garrison was likely to be trigger-happy. Fortunately for all concerned, the antiaircraft fire that greeted the Dauntlesses as they approached the atoll was quickly checked when the aircraft were identified. Three Dauntlesses received superficial damage.[42] Surprisingly, the fifteenth and last member of the bomber squadron, a Dauntless piloted by Ensign Clayton E. Fisher, made it back to the *Hornet*. Five of the scouts it flew with were forced to ditch.[43] All the Wildcats were also forced down in the sea. Their leader, Lieutenant Stanley E. Ruehlow, decided against landing on Midway. The atoll's fires convinced him that the situation there was dangerous. The Wildcats were better advised to try to get back to their carrier. With the *Hornet* out of range of the fighters, this was by any standard an unwise decision. The formation's search had indicated that there was no enemy in the immediate vicinity of Midway; the atoll's situation could not be so immediately precarious as to preclude landing there. In any event, the odds of landing on Midway could not have been as bad as putting down in the sea. The latter course automatically wrote off all the aircraft, and perhaps their pilots as well.[44]

Thus ended the first part of the American attack. It could hardly have begun more inauspiciously. The largest of the individual formations sent against the First Carrier Striking Force had divided into two, with its larger element, made up of fighters and dive-bombers, failing to secure as much as a single contact and losing 40 percent of their strength into the bargain. Eight Dauntlesses and ten Wildcats had been lost, and another eleven dive-bombers were out of the battle for the moment. This was a high price to pay for a conspicuous failure, and worse was to follow.[45]

The *Hornet*'s one remaining squadron did find the enemy. This was VT-8, whose fifteen Devastators were led to the enemy by Waldron. Waldron was convinced that the Japanese would haul round to the northeast after they had recovered their aircraft from the Midway strike and would thus be to the north of the position calculated by the staffs to be the place where the First Carrier Striking Force would make its inadvertent

rendezvous with CVG-6 and CVG-8.[46] As it turned out, the course followed by VT-8 led directly to the enemy, but not quite for the reasons that
Waldron had assumed. Nagumo did turn away from Midway after recovery was completed, but only a minute or so before the American squadron
made contact. The reason the Japanese carriers were where Waldron had
expected them to be was not their turn but the delays that they had incurred
in coming south.[47]

The price that Waldron and his squadron paid for finding the enemy was
threefold. First, the squadron's path and that of the other aircraft from the
Hornet diverged, so VT-8 came upon the enemy when it was alone and
unsupported. It was not in the company of Dauntlesses that might distract
the enemy and draw fire, and it was not with fighters that might offer it
protection from the Zekes of the enemy's combat air patrol. Second, VT-8
unintentionally deprived its companion squadron, VT-6, of cover. Lindsey's squadron from the *Enterprise* set off at roughly the same time for the
enemy, but on the prescribed course of 239 degrees. Before leaving, its
executive officer, Lieutenant Arthur V. Ely, made a personal arrangement
with Gray, leader of the Wildcats. Gray's intention was to cover the
Dauntlesses at 20,000 feet. The advantage for Gray was that, if he had to go
to the assistance of the Devastators, the speed his Wildcats would build up
in their power dives would stand them in good stead when it came to
tangling with the Zekes.[48] Ely would call Gray down in support of VT-6
should the need arise.[49] The problem was that when VF-6 was launched it
climbed in a spiral. Gray confused the two torpedo squadrons far below
him and attached himself to what he thought was VT-6 but was in fact
VT-8. Because the two groups (CVG-6 and CVG-8) were on different
frequencies neither Ely nor Gray realized what had happened. The result
was that neither of Task Force 16's torpedo squadrons had fighter support
when they moved in to attack the Japanese, and Gray led his fighters in
support of a torpedo squadron that did not know how to call upon him for
support.[50] The third price that Waldron and his squadron had to pay for
their success in finding the enemy was exacted when all these circumstances
began to converge.

The report in the official Japanese history of the action that followed was
brief and to the point: "0918. Enemy carrier planes begin torpedo attack.
Defense fighter planes. Shot down a large portion of the torpedo planes."[51]
Throughout the war the Japanese consistently exaggerated enemy losses,
but on this occasion they understated them. Every one of the fifteen
attacking Devastators was shot down, and all but one of their thirty aircrew
were lost.

It was the Waldron attack that made the most profound impression in the
United States after the battle. The attack, which became part of naval
folklore, had all the elements of Greek tragedy. Everybody was rushed, by

events beyond their control, to an end that all foresaw. Waldron's famous message to his squadron, attached to the plan of attack, had contained the following words: "My greatest hope is that we encounter a favorable tactical situation, but if we don't, and the worst comes to the worst, I want each of us to do his utmost to destroy our enemies. If there is only one plane left to make a final run in, I want that man to go in and get a hit."[52] The real tragedy of the squadron was that the last surviving Devastator did press home its attack in a desperate effort to get a hit that would justify the sacrifice of the whole squadron. But the Japanese carriers evaded this and all the other torpedoes that were aimed at them with the same ease with which all the earlier attacks from Midway had been turned aside.

Long before his squadron made contact with the Japanese, Waldron had formed it into an extended line to increase the chances of sighting the enemy. The scouting tactic was to be the attacking tactic: Waldron made no attempt to reform his squadron and lead his formation into a pell-mell attack. There was little point in attempted subtlety on the part of VT-8. It found, as had the Avengers and Marauders from Midway before it, that the Japanese knew how to deal with torpedo bombers. In the Coral Sea Japanese task groups had scattered under attack, but now, the third time they were faced with attacks by torpedo bombers, the Japanese ships kept station with their cruisers and destroyers well forward to give early warning of an enemy approach. Waldron and his squadron therefore had to run the gauntlet of an outer and an inner antiaircraft fire and a combat air patrol brought to the edge of the screen by the escorts. The *Chikuma* picked up VT-8 early in its approach, and despite the Devastators making their approach at full speed, the Zekes began to pick them out of the sky at a range of eight miles from the carriers.[53] Several accounts credit the Japanese with a combat air patrol of fifty Zekes at this stage of proceedings, but this seems to be an inflated figure considering that the Japanese carriers had only just completed recovery of the previous combat air patrol when this attack started.[54] It would probably have been impossible for the Japanese to put fifty fighters into the air by about 0920, though in the course of this and the subsequent Devastator attack some of the Zekes from the Midway Expeditionary Force were committed to the combat air patrol.[55] But whatever number of fighters were flown off by the carriers in their own defense, the Zekes knew their business.

The unescorted Devastators were hacked down with impunity even as Waldron called upon Ring and the fighters for help.[56] The Wildcats and Dauntlesses heard nothing, and only one of the torpedo bombers survived to break through the inner screen of destroyers to attack one of the carriers. Waldron had led his formation against the *Akagi* first and then had shifted to the right to attack the carrier next in line, the *Soryu*.[57] After he was shot down the remaining Devastators continued to bear down upon the *Soryu*.

When confronted by the last surviving bomber the carrier presented her bows and threw off the attack. In an attempt to defeat this ploy the last American aircraft, piloted by Ensign George H. Gay, aborted his run off the *Soryu*'s starboard bow and tried to back up to approach off the enemy's port bow.[58] But with Zekes cutting up his Devastator all the time there was little chance of Gay's plan working. The *Soryu* easily evaded his torpedo, and claimed to have dodged four in the course of the attack.[59] Gay was shot down by Zekes from the combat air patrol almost as soon as he launched his torpedo, the Japanese fighters on this and other occasions entering the antiaircraft fire from their own ships in order to tackle American aircraft. Gay proved to be only survivor of VT-8. He was picked up the following day by a Catalina from Midway after having had a "fish-eye" view of the events of 4 June.[60] With the destruction of VT-8, plus the losses that were to be incurred by the scouting, bombing and fighter squadrons over the next sixty minutes, the *Hornet* was reduced to half strength at the start of the carrier battle.

Hard on the heels of VT-8 came Lindsey and the Devastators from the *Enterprise*. They were brought to the scene of battle by the telltale vapor trails left by the Zekes as they cut into Waldron's squadron. Originally Lindsey had led his squadron too far to the south, but he had suspected that if he did not find the enemy at the designated location, the Japanese would be to the north. Thus he had turned northwards and was cruising at 1,500 feet, below the clouds, when he picked out the signs of battle at a range of 30 miles. At 0930 he sighted the enemy.[61]

By then VT-8 had been destroyed. Its attack had lasted perhaps ten minutes. VT-6 was destroyed as a fighting formation in about the same length of time. Its tactical situation was even more difficult than the one that had confronted Waldron and his squadron. The latter had found the enemy off his starboard bow and had simply led an attack that was little more than a head-on dash at full speed. Lindsey, coming from the south, engaged in what amounted to a stern chase to come around the flank of the enemy formation and launch an attack from ahead. He divided his squadron into two groups of seven to improve the chances of success and survival, but this availed him and his squadron nothing.[62] The time the Devastators spent warily working their way around the fast-moving enemy force, all the while being forced ever wider apart by Japanese antiaircraft fire, gave the Zekes the opportunity to get amongst the lumbering torpedo bombers.[63] Ten of the fourteen Devastators were shot down before the remaining four, evidently despairing of the situation, simply aimed themselves at the nearest carrier—the *Kaga*—and launched their torpedoes as best they could.[64] Under the circumstances there was little prospect of the Americans recording any hits, and none of the torpedoes found a mark on the *Kaga* or on any other Japanese warship. But the impromptu and disorganized attack

Devastator Torpedo Bomber

allowed the four remaining Devastators to make good their escape, and their pilots were able to coax them back to the *Enterprise*. In the case of Lieutenant Robert E. Laub this was not very difficult. His Devastator emerged almost unscathed from the attack, and he reached home with plenty of avgas to spare. The aircraft of Ensigns Edward Heck and Irving H. McPherson incurred greater damage, and Chief Machinist Stephen B. Smith's Devastator, with sixty-eight holes in it, was committed to the deep the following day after the armorers reluctantly decided not to try to repair it.[65] These four pilots, and the three aircraft, were the only survivors that remained available for further operations out of the total of twenty-nine Devastators from the two torpedo bomber squadrons from the *Enterprise* and the *Hornet*. The torpedo bombers from Task Force 16 failed to live up to their name through no fault of the men who flew them.

The attack by the *Enterprise*'s torpedo bombers took place between 0940 and about 1005, and scarcely had it ended when yet another one began. This time it was conducted by the *Yorktown*'s torpedo bombers. Like

Lindsey before him, Massey divided his formation to improve his hopes of making a successful attack.[66] His chances were marginally improved by the cover Thatch and his six fighters provided.

The value of the fighters, however, was countered by another factor. Lindsey had contrived to pull down the enemy's combat air patrol to low level, and it was therefore in an ideal position to attack VT-3 as it began its approach. Alerted to the enemy's approach first by the *Tone* and then by the *Chikuma*,[67] the combat air patrol tackled the Devastators at a range of 18 miles from the carriers.[68] The Wildcats fought to defend the torpedo bombers as best they could, but the odds were simply too great. The American fighters were able to look after themselves but not their charges. One Wildcat was destroyed in what proved to be the only fighter battle over the Japanese fleet on 4 June, and another was written off when it tried to land back on a carrier, in this case the *Hornet*.[69] In return the Wildcat pilots each claimed to have destroyed a Zeke, making a total of five between them. Ten of the Devastators were hacked down in return.[70] Massey divided his formation into equal parts with the intention of attacking off both bows, but the combat air patrol accounted for seven of the torpedo bombers before they were able to reach their launching positions, and another three were shot down almost as soon as they completed their attack. None of their torpedoes struck home.[71] The two Devastators that ran the gauntlet of the enemy's antiaircraft fire and combat air patrol and survived set course for the *Yorktown*, but both were forced to ditch. The pilot and gunner from one were rescued by the *Monaghan*, while the pilot of the other torpedo bomber, his gunner killed, was rescued by the *Hammann*.[72]

As these two surviving Devastators from VT-3 ran for safety, everything seemed all but ready for the First Carrier Striking Force to turn upon its tormentors. The tide of battle had run against the Japanese throughout the morning. The initial strike against Midway had been only partially successful, while the carrier force itself had been subjected to a series of attacks that had unexpectedly forced it back on the defensive. All these attacks had been broken up with heavy loss to the enemy, but the revelation of American determination in all the attacks, if not their technical skill and professionalism, had come as an unpleasant surprise to the Japanese. All their intelligence summaries and preoperations briefings had emphasized several recurring themes—the Americans' low resolve, poor fighting ability and inability to respond to Japanese moves quickly, in strength and to good effect. By 1020 it was quite clear that some of these conclusions needed rewriting. Moreover, those last two attacks had come as a surprise to the Japanese on two other counts. First, they had been pressed home with more skill than anything that had gone before. Indeed those led by Lindsey and Massey were superior to anything the Japanese had ever faced—hence, in part, the time it had taken for the First Carrier Striking Force to deal with them. Second, the Japanese now knew that they were opposed by a minimum of two enemy carriers.[73] The first attacks of the day had come from Midway, but the later ones could not possibly have come from the atoll. They had been mounted in such numbers and over so long a period that it was inconceivable that less than two American carriers were to the east of the First Carrier Striking Force. Too many American aircraft had been involved in these attacks for just the one carrier reported by the *Tone*'s Jake to be implicated. But the attacks had been met and frustrated. The tension that had mounted in the course of these attacks—only the most unimaginative could have failed to grasp the danger in which the carriers, little more than primed magazines surrounded by avgas, stood—turned into renewed confidence as the Zekes of the combat air patrol bought the time the carriers needed to recover their balance. When the two surviving Devastators from the *Yorktown* managed to break contact with the Japanese combat air patrol, Nagumo was but five to ten minutes away from that balance. This was the time the First Carrier Striking Force needed to start launching the all-out strike that would settle accounts with the enemy once and for all. There was no way the Japanese could have known that past success and future promise were mere illusion, that in fact the balance of fortune had decisively and irrevocably settled against them while they had beaten off the last two attacks by the enemy torpedo bombers.

Just when the Japanese believed they stood on the brink of their greatest victory, utter and irredeemable disaster was around the corner. In the time it had taken to repel the various Devastator attacks three things had conspired to present the Americans with victory: the gradual breakup of the Japanese battle formation; the arrival of the *Yorktown*'s Dauntlesses over the enemy carriers; and the belated appearance of the *Enterprise*'s Dauntlesses over Nagumo's force.

While it was beating off the attacks by the torpedo bombers from the *Enterprise* and the *Yorktown*, the First Carrier Striking Force had lost much of its cohesion. Its carriers had become increasingly separated from their screen. The force retained neither its cruising formation nor its proper battle order. When they launched and recovered aircraft all four carriers of the First Carrier Striking Force were supposed to operate together with the screen about them. When attacked the carriers were supposed to maneuver independently, each with a screen of escorts. The attacks that cost Waldron, Lindsey, Massey and most of their subordinates their lives also pried open the cruising formation without giving the Japanese time to tighten it up again. In fact the Japanese station keeping had never been quite right from the time—minutes before Waldron's formation attacked—the First Carrier Striking Force turned away from Midway. Thereafter the brunt of successive American attacks had fallen on the *Soryu*, *Kaga* and *Akagi*. All had had to put their wheels hard over at various times either to present their sterns to the enemy or to sidestep torpedoes that were aimed at them. With so much going on behind her, the *Hiryu*, having survived the various attacks directed against her from Midway's aircraft, steadily drew ahead of the other three carriers. The distances between the three trailing carriers began to open up disturbingly. By 1020 the *Hiryu* was out of sight of the *Akagi*. She was about six miles ahead of Nagumo's flagship and shrouded in a rain squall. Instead of the *Soryu* and the *Kaga* being about one mile from the *Akagi*, as they were supposed to be, they were some three and a half miles away. The screen had not broken and was not properly deployed around any of the individual carriers.[74] In some ways the situation was rather similar to the one in which the *Shoho* and the cruisers from Goto's command found themselves at the Coral Sea just four weeks and one day before.

As a formation, therefore, the First Carrier Striking Force had lost its cohesion, and individually the carriers were vulnerable on three separate counts, of which the first was by far the most important. Japanese carriers were not built with defensive requirements as a prime consideration. Of all the major navies, the Imperial Japanese Navy was least concerned with defense. The *Hiryu* and the *Soryu*, two ships usually described as fleet carriers, were really no more than light fleet carriers. The *Soryu*, for example, had virtually no horizontal armor. She had 25-mm armor over machinery and 55-mm armor over magazines and avgas tanks. The *Hiryu*, a large ship, had 90-mm armor over her tanks, but was only partially compartmentalized. The *Akagi* and the *Kaga* were twice the size of their two companions but scarcely better prepared to look after themselves. Moreover, all four Japanese carriers had three large elevators incorporated into flight decks that provided them with their longitudinal girder strength. In addition, none of the Japanese ships had enclosed hangar decks that were flash-tight and vapor-tight. Everything on Japanese carriers was geared to speed and ease of handling, and none of them were provided with sufficient damage control personnel and fire-fighting equipment. The extent of these weaknesses, largely unsuspected, was shortly to be revealed.[75]

There was a second factor contributing to the vulnerability of each individual carrier. To counter the last three American attacks the Japanese had had to recover many of their fighters from the combat air patrol, rearm them and then launch them again. The priority in this process was always rearming, since the Zekes had only sixty rounds for their cannon and thirty seconds of ammunition for their machine guns.[76] But regardless of the priority, to service the aircraft fuel lines had to be opened up and avgas bowsers brought to the flight deck.[77] There was simply not enough time for the Japanese carriers to lower their fighters to the hangar decks to service them there, not that these decks were any safer than the flight decks. As early as Waldron's attack the flight deck of the *Soryu* was alive with all the highly combustible impedimenta of flying operations. Gay, in the few seconds he had over the *Soryu* before the Zekes of the combat air patrol finally accounted for his Devastator, noted how vulnerable the carrier would be merely to machine gun fire.[78] Conditions in the hangars of all four carriers would have been as dangerous as they were on the flight decks as the service crews worked feverishly on the aircraft that had returned from the strike on Midway. All four Japanese carriers were like sticks of sweating gelignite: the slightest mishap could easily set off any one of them. Given the flammability of the carriers and their various structural weaknesses, any explosion, induced or otherwise, could hardly be less than lethal.

Third, as we have seen, the vulnerability of the Japanese carriers was exacerbated by the various Devastator attacks—particularly the last one carried out by Massey—which had the effect of either dragging down the combat air patrol to low level or keeping the Zekes already there on the deck. The rail bait for the Japanese fighters would seem to have been the Wildcats that flew with Massey; they apparently drew the Japanese fighters to them.[79] The effect was to leave the First Carrier Striking Force without overhead cover; as the Zekes tackled the Devastators and Wildcats none climbed to high altitude to protect the force. A Zeke needed about $7\frac{1}{2}$ minutes to climb to 20,000 feet from a standing start, and it is neither arithmetical nonsense nor pretention to suggest that sometime between 1000 and 1020 the Japanese ran out of $7\frac{1}{2}$-minute periods in which to rearrange their defenses. Without radar, the Japanese had no means of detecting approaching aircraft other than their eyes. Events were to show that Japanese lookouts had been distracted by the earlier American attacks. They had been guilty of watching the action rather than their stations, and because their attention had been brought down to low level by the Devastators they failed to spot American dive-bombers until the latter began their attacks on the Japanese carriers.

The attack by Massey's formation was the third and last of the efforts by carrier-launched torpedo bombers. The first attack, led by Waldron, took place between 0920 and 0930, while that led by Lindsey was carried out between 0930 and 1000. Massey's attack began at about 1000 and was over by 1020. The first two attacks were similar, being launched at the same time and made under like circumstances. Both Waldron and Lindsey led their squadrons into unsupported attacks on the enemy. They knew the risks and accepted the odds of attacking without support from fighters and dive-bombers. But the third attack by Devastators was different. The attack by the *Yorktown*'s torpedo bombers was deliberately intended to be one part of a coordinated attack by a balanced formation on the enemy.

Spruance had wanted his formations to mount such attacks, but in the end he had to divide his formations in order to pit something, anything, against the enemy. He gave up any hope of mounting coordinated attacks when he ordered his Dauntlesses to proceed without waiting for the

Devastators.[80] Task Force 17 put its attack formation together in a manner that was far superior to that of Task Force 16, though this did not prevent it from going wrong. As we have noted earlier, the *Yorktown* did not finish flying off her aircraft until 0906, an hour after the *Enterprise* and the *Hornet* completed their flying-off operations, but Massey was able to cut down at least thirty minutes on flight time as he followed Lindsey into the attack. The Devastators from the *Yorktown* almost caught up with those from the *Enterprise* because the operations staff of the *Yorktown*, unlike that of the *Enterprise* and Task Force 16, managed to get its plot correct. Pederson, retained in the *Yorktown* after his group was divided, made a calculation similar to Waldron's, though he started from the opposite end of the equation. Whereas Waldon did not believe that the enemy would continue on his course, Pederson allowed for the maximum possible advance by the enemy in the sure knowledge that a lack of contact meant that the Japanese would be to the north.[81] The course that Pederson calculated was one of 230 degrees, and it was a course that was to be flown in a precise order—the Devastators, the Wildcats and then the Dauntlesses.[82] Like Mitscher and Ring in the *Hornet*, Pederson and the *Yorktown* hoped to put things together in the correct order by relying on speed differentials to produce a concentration of force over the enemy formation. Initially it seemed as if the *Yorktown*'s aircraft would do better than the larger formations from Task Force 16, because her Wildcats caught up with the Devastators some twenty minutes after the latter set out and the Dauntlesses joined company after a further twenty minutes had elapsed.[83] Thereafter the American intention was to rely on the torpedo bombers for accurate navigation while Thatch and his fighters acted as liaison between the various attack forces.[84] Quite independently of Task Force 16, the *Yorktown* had picked out the good points from the other groups' plans of attack.

The organization and discipline within CVG-3 allowed the Devastators to obtain contact with the enemy while still in the company of the Wildcats and Dauntlesses, but thereafter the synchronization of effort fell to pieces. The dive-bombers lost sight of the torpedo bombers through cloud. The Devastators sighted smoke on the horizon at 1000, slightly to port. They came round to starboard, climbing as they did so. The Dauntlesses did not see the torpedo bombers change course, and they did not see the enemy until five minutes later, when the Japanese were spotted over the clouds at a range of thirty-five miles.[85] It was at this point that the effort of the *Yorktown*'s formation began to go wrong. According to the drill book, the Dauntlesses should have opened proceedings and the Devastators should have moved into the attack when the enemy was committed to dealing with the dive-bombers. The unfolding of events placed the Devastators in the vanguard of the attack, and they paid the inevitable price as the Japanese combat air patrol sliced into the Devastator formation at extreme range from the carriers.[86] Once caught by the Zekes, the American torpedo bombers could not hope to circle while waiting for the Dauntlesses to open the attack, since they would be shot down to no effect. As it was, Massey's formation drew the Zekes out of position and set up the conditions for the American victory that followed. Some accounts, the U.S. Navy official history included, have suggested that Waldron and Lindsey did so by drawing enemy fighters upon themselves.[87] This was not the case. The Zekes had plenty of time to get back into position after they had dealt with the Devastators of Task Force 16. Gallant though it was, the sacrifice of the torpedo bombers from the *Hornet* and the *Enterprise* was in vain; the torpedo bombers from the *Yorktown* were the ones that caught the Japanese out of position and denied them the time to regain their balance, leaving the Dauntlesses from both the *Yorktown* and the *Enterprise* free to move unopposed into positions from which to carry out their attacks.[88]

Leslie and VB-3 approached the First Carrier Striking Force from the southeast because the Japanese, as Pederson had predicted, had been detected to the north of the course of 230 degres that CVG-3 had flown. Leslie's formation approached the enemy force from off his starboard beam, the American intention being to pit the whole squadron against the nearest carrier. According to American tactical doctrine, one attack unit would grapple with a single enemy unit. Herein lay the element of calculated risk that bound American operations; the Americans did not really have enough formations to tackle four or perhaps five enemy carriers and therefore had to accept the possibility of being counterattacked by carriers not attacked in the American opening strike.[89] Leslie's decision to concentrate his Dauntlesses against a single target invited danger, but in fact he had no real option. He had led a formation of seventeen Dauntlesses off the *Yorktown*, and shortly after taking off he had given orders for his pilots to arm their 1,000-lb bombs. The Dauntlesses had been fitted recently with electrical arming and release devices, but the circuits had been crossed. In trying to arm his weapon Leslie had inadvertently released it, and three other pilots had done the same before the order was countermanded and arming was carried out manually.[90] Leslie had only thirteen effectives as he set course for the enemy, though he believed he had fifteen because he was aware of only one pilot other than himself who had lost his bomb.[91] With an understrength squadron Leslie could not divide his force and attack two enemy units. Adhering to orthodox doctrine, he therefore concentrated his squadron against the nearest enemy carrier. Fortunately for the Americans, Leslie's approach to contact coincided almost to the minute with the approach, from the opposite direction, of Dauntlesses from the *Enterprise*. These aircraft chose to attack the nearest enemy carriers, and the Dauntlesses' larger numbers allowed them to mark down two carriers for destruction. The target selection did not overlap. The distribution of targets, like the simultaneous arrival of the formations over the enemy, was entirely fortuitous and, indeed, neither formation was aware of the other's presence until after their attacks.

McClusky's flight from the *Enterprise* had been more than a little eventful. Like Lindsey, he set out on a course of 240 degrees only to find himself without fighter cover as Gray followed the wrong torpedo bombers. Radio failure and cloud prevented the Dauntlesses from obtaining the sighting that lured Lindsey to the enemy and death, and neither the Dauntlesses nor the *Enterprise* picked up Gray's signals indicating his position when he found the First Carrier Striking Force. Powerless to stop the massacre of Waldron's squadron, to find McClusky or to get an acknowledgment of his signals, Gray led his fighters back to the carrier while McClusky led the *Enterprise*'s two Dauntless squadrons ever further across the ocean.[92] At 0930 McClusky faced the same dilemma that had confronted Ring when the course that they both had followed led only to empty ocean. McClusky had to decide in which direction to look for the enemy, and like Ring he chose wrongly. When forced to pick between port and starboard Ring had opted for port. McClusky chose neither. He maintained his course for fifteen minutes before turning back to the northwest. Five and then ten minutes passed, along with the hopes that many Dauntless pilots had of getting back to the *Enterprise*. Three Dauntlesses had already turned back with engine trouble, and by 0955 it was clear that some of the Dauntlesses would never have enough fuel to make the return journey to the *Enterprise*.[93] McClusky had already decided to turn back east and head for the *Enterprise* at 1000 if nothing was sighted, but at 0955 contact was obtained. In the vast expanse of the Pacific Ocean, thirty Dauntlesses came across a lone Japanese destroyer.[94]

This ship was the *Arashi*, detached from the screen of the First Carrier Striking Force after an incident that had taken place some ninety minutes earlier. At about 0825 the Japanese carrier force had run across the line of sight of an American submarine deployed in front of Midway. On 4 June all but three of the American submarines were too far away to have any impact on the battle, and of the three that were in the enemy's vicinity only one, the *Nautilus*, made two contacts with the Japanese.[95] At about 0830 she found herself in the company of a large task force. Her skipper, Lieutenant Commander William H. Brockman, selected a battleship as his target and fired two torpedoes. One missed and the other resolutely refused to leave its tube. Brockman immediately took his boat down to 150 feet to sit out the inevitable counterattack. But at this stage one of the shortcomings of the First Carrier Striking Force asserted itself. Before the operation the screen had not had time to practice its antisubmarine drills as a group, and now it did not have the time, numbers or technique to conduct a systematic search for the enemy submarine. Nagumo's formation hurried on,[96] leaving the lone *Arashi* either to keep the enemy down or to administer the coup de grâce.[97]

When McClusky sighted the carrier she was on her way to rejoin. Her presence had been betrayed by her white wake, and her bow wave and trail suggested a high speed that could only be justified by urgent business. McClusky drew the conclusion that the direction indicated by the *Arashi*'s bows was the direction in which he should concentrate his future efforts, and ten minutes later, at 1005, "white slashes on a blue carpet" could be made out on the horizon, slightly to port.[98] McClusky and Leslie both sighted the enemy at just about the same time, in each case at maximum range. Without knowing it McClusky complemented Leslie's efforts by taking his formation round to port, thereby ensuring that the two American attack forces converged on different bearings. Unlike most pilots who attacked the Japanese that morning, McClusky saw all four enemy carriers, but as with Leslie, the orthodoxy of the drill book prevailed. With two squadrons under command McClusky decided to attack the two nearest carriers, one squadron for one carrier.

Below him McClusky could see the Japanese carriers maneuvering to escape the torpedo bombers from the *Yorktown*, and from 14,500 feet there was no opposition or any indication that the approaching Dauntlesses had been spotted. McClusky knew what was expected of his formation without any prompting, but if he had ever had any doubts they would have been dispelled by the *Enterprise*'s reply to one of his contact reports. The answer, in clear, was "Attack immediately." Made at 1008, this signal was picked up at Pearl Harbor and the voice was identified as Browning's.[99] Thus far in the battle Nimitz and his staff had been kept in the dark about what was happening some 1,300 miles to the west. Radio silence on the part of ships that did not want to reveal their presence meant that nothing was forthcoming from the American side, and very little could be gleaned from the enemy. But two messages, sent at about 1000 to an unknown addressee, gave Pearl Harbor an unexpected clue. There were the situation reports Nagumo sent to Yamamoto, and even though the cryptanalysts could not read them, they uncovered the call sign of Nagumo's flagship. One of the members of the Pearl Harbor intelligence team recognized the signals as having been sent by a chief warrant officer in the *Akagi*, his heavy hand having acquired some renown.[100] But other than these messages Nimitz and his staff heard nothing until Browning's voice cut across the ether—and then there was nothing. Just as things were clearly about to happen Pearl Habor suffered a communications blackout that lasted until 1100.

CHAPTER 13

Mortal Wounds

The message that Pearl Harbor intercepted at 1100 was a plain-language Japanese signal, "Inform position of enemy carriers." After fifty minutes of agonized waiting for some indication of which way the attack on the Japanese carriers had gone, the contents of this signal were not particularly encouraging as far as Nimitz and his staff were concerned. The message had been sent by either a carrier or a command ship to one of the scouting Japanese seaplanes. If there was some cause for quiet satisfaction in the indication that sometime during the morning the Japanese staff had lost the plot of the enemy's position, this paled beside the realization that the signal meant one or more of the enemy carriers was then ready to begin operations against an American force identified as having more than one carrier. This interpretation was correct. The signal that Pearl Harbor had picked up was sent by the *Chikuma* to Amari. The latter was ordered to stay on station to lead an attack formation to the enemy's location.[1] At this very time Japanese bombers were taking to the air to counterattack the American carrier force. Overall, the single sentence picked up at 1100 by Pearl Harbor did not seem to hold out much promise for Nimitz and the staff of the Pacific Fleet.

Some fifty minutes were to pass before the staff on Oahu took in another signal from the battle area, and ag. in it was one that had been made by the enemy. On this occasion it was encoded and hence unintelligible to the Americans, but a comparison with call signs from earlier signals revealed that once more Nagumo's flagship was sending a message to an unknown addressee. A member of Rochefort's team of analysts noticed that the signature of Nagumo's signaler was that of the senior member of the signals team of the light cruiser *Nagara*. For the first time Nimitz and his aides had some cause for cautious optimism. The fact that the *Nagara* had to handle Nagumo's signals suggested that the *Akagi* could no longer operate as a flagship; she must have been damaged in some way or another. Either

Nagumo had had to shift his flag or his signals had to be relayed via the cruiser.[2]

By about noon the staff at Pearl Harbor was coming to the tentative conclusion that perhaps something untoward had befallen, if not the First Carrier Striking Force, then certainly the *Akagi*. Some ninety minutes had elapsed since the flagship and two of her colleagues, the *Kaga* and the *Soryu*, had been transformed into fiercely burning torches by dive-bombers from the *Enterprise* and the *Yorktown*. It was not a case of the *Akagi* no longer being able to function as a flagship—she was totally incapable of any form of operations. She had less than a day to live, and the *Kaga* and the *Soryu* had been reduced to a similar condition. Only the natural bouyancy of the three carriers allowed them to survive for even the small length of time that was left to them. Perhaps it would have been better had they settled quickly; then the flames and heat that dealt out hideous forms of death and mutilation to hundreds of the ships' companies would have been rapidly quenched. In all three carriers fires induced explosions that seared men, tearing their limbs apart and turning them into flaming bundles of flesh and bone. Below decks, men suffocated in the smoke or found themselves trapped behind buckled and jammed doors through which they could not escape. Others must have been grilled alive as the decks above them became superheated with the fires that were working their way downward to do battle with the sea. On the flight and hangar decks the wounded were either engulfed in flames fed by fractured fuel lines or fried as the decks on which they lay began to glow beneath them. Perhaps a quick death in the cold impartial grip of an implacable sea would have been more merciful than the fate that overtook some 2,000 members of three carriers' companies on 4 June 1942.

What had happened, in the general sense, was relatively simple. The chance that American commanders had hoped for did indeed materialize. Inside the space of five minutes the Dauntlesses from the *Enterprise* and the *Yorktown* decided the outcome of the battle and, some would allege, the outcome of the Pacific War itself. In those five minutes, between 1024 and 1029, the dive-bombers caught the *Akagi*, *Kaga* and *Soryu* at their most vulnerable, their flight decks crammed with armed and fueled aircraft as the carriers turned into the wind to begin to launch. But even as the first Zekes attempted to get into the air, American bombs exploded on the flight decks and turned them into raging infernos. These explosions induced detonations that doomed ships which had ranged from Pearl Harbor to Colombo without receiving as much as a scratch.

Though a general picture of events is clear enough, a detailed account of what happened has never been satisfactorily completed. At the time of Midway and indeed throughout the war the claim of the army air force that its heavy bombers accounted for the enemy confused matters. Moreover, it is impossible to reconcile the conflicting claims of the American pilots involved in the attack on the First Carrier Striking Force. To complicate matters, the Japanese record is incomplete and cannot be used to settle disputes raised by such incompatible accounts. The nub of the problem was neatly summarized, with wry humor, by a noted historian of the battle:

> If the squadron action reports are taken at face value, everybody hit the *Akagi* or the *Kaga*. Nobody claims the *Soryu*—she presumably got back to Japan. Yet if the specific recollections of the three attack leaders are accepted, nobody got the *Akagi*. Each is convinced his target had its island on the starboard side—yet the *Akagi*'s island was to port.[3]

With nobody claiming to have sunk the *Soryu* or the *Akagi*—and as a consequence everyone claiming the destruction of the *Kaga*—the problem of unraveling the sequence of events between 1024 and 1029 is simple. The claims of the *Yorktown* pilots conflict with those of the pilots from the *Enterprise*, and the former have never accepted a formal division of the spoils that credited them with the destruction of the *Soryu* and the *Enterprise* pilots with the destruction of the *Akagi* and the *Kaga*.* To be credited with the *Soryu* instead of the *Akagi* or the *Kaga* was like being credited with the *Wasp* rather than the *Lexington* or the *Saratoga*, such were the relative sizes of the carriers involved in claim and counterclaim, and there was considerable resentment on the part of the *Yorktown*'s pilots about "being palmed off with a little one."

Leslie and the Dauntless bombers from the *Yorktown* were quite specific on one matter. They claimed to have approached the enemy with a choice between two targets, both carriers and one much larger than the other. The squadron insisted that they attacked the larger enemy carrier. Their report is difficult to dismiss. While claims based on silhouettes are often dubious, claims based on size are not so easy to dismiss. The pilots from the *Yorktown* said they were able to distinguish between two carriers, having seen them at the same time, and the *Soryu* was noticeably smaller than either the *Akagi* or the *Kaga*. This is one part of the "dissenting case" that the "official version" is not able to explain away. There is one other powerful argument that questions the generally accepted account of events. Such authorities as Professor Thaddeus V. Teluja and Vice Admiral William Ward Smith, supported by Pat Franks and Joseph D. Harrington in their account of the *Yorktown*'s career, have made great play of the idea that the *Yorktown*'s dive-bombers could never have attacked the *Soryu* unless the First Carrier Striking Force reversed its formation in the course of the morning. Their argument assumes that on the morning of 4 June the *Soryu* always had at least one member of the First Carrier Division to starboard.[4]

*This distribution of success, contained in the U.S. Navy's official history of September 1949, has been generally accepted since that time.

This premise, as it relates to the time the First Carrier Striking Force was closing on Midway from the northwest, has never been disputed. For the attack on Midway the carrier force had deployed into the square or rectangle, the standard formation adopted for attacks on land targets, with the *Hiryu* leading the *Soryu* in the port column, the *Akagi* leading the *Kaga* to starboard. The supporting heavy units were disposed around the four carriers. The *Chikuma* was deployed off the *Hiryu*'s port bow, while the *Kirishima* was off the *Soryu*'s port quarter. The *Tone* and the *Haruna* took up mirror images of these positions with regard to the *Akagi* and the *Kaga* respectively, while the *Nagara* took up a position between the *Chikuma* and the *Tone* ahead of the *Hiryu* and the *Akagi*. It was because of this deployment that the two heavy cruisers tended to be amongst the first of the escorts to contact the incoming American aircraft, and the position of the *Haruna* relative to the *Kaga* was explanation in itself of why she was attacked by Norris and his Vindicators when they abandoned their attempt to tackle the more distant carriers.

The *Soryu*, therefore, was the second ship in the port column during the approach to Midway, but after Nagumo turned his force away from the atoll and towards the enemy task force the First Carrier Striking Force did not resume its previous formation. The ships turned in their tracks together and did not maneuver to retain their relative positions. Thus the *Soryu* became the port marker of the four carriers, with the *Akagi* off her starboard beam and the *Kaga* trailing them both. The carriers were led by the *Hiryu*. But the turn loosened the tight discipline of the square, and this was loosened still further as individual ships fought off the attacks that were made on them. In the course of the attacks the *Akagi* presented her stern to Massey's squadron of Devastator torpedo bombers and turned to port, seemingly passing astern of the *Soryu*. It would appear that by this maneuver the *Soryu* and the *Akagi* did change their relative positions, and that the *Akagi* did come between the *Soryu* and the Dauntlesses of the *Enterprise* which approached from the southwest. But even if this is an accurate record of events, the whereabouts of the *Kaga* remain uncertain. It appears that when the *Akagi* tried to shake off *Yorktown*'s Devastators with her rather violent maneuver across the line of the *Kaga*'s advance, the *Kaga* turned to starboard, thereby keeping both the *Akagi* and the *Soryu* to port.

These maneuvers present a conundrum that cannot be solved unless one makes a certain assumption about the course of events and then attempts to marry that assumption with other material known to be more or less accurate. The other material relates to such matters as timing, details of claims of hits and near misses that can be substantiated by reference to the Japanese accounts, and target switches by the attacking American aircraft. For example, the Devastators from the *Yorktown* claimed to have shifted their attentions to a battleship and a cruiser when it was realized that the enemy carrier had been severely handled. In fact the cruiser turned out to be the destroyer *Isokaze*, one of the *Soryu*'s escorts then in the company of the carrier.[5] She suffered near misses but was not hit. It should be noted that in the critical matter of timing the Japanese and Americans concur in one vital respect. The *Enterprise*'s attack is supposed to have started at 1024, and the first of the Japanese carriers to be struck was hit then. The carrier was the *Kaga*.

Most of the evidence concerning the events of this time can be reconciled if it is assumed that the various maneuvers of the *Akagi*, *Kaga* and *Soryu* briefly brought them into a rather ragged single line at the very time they were struck. However implausible this might appear, the assumption is supported by members of the *Yorktown*'s Dauntless squadron who reported the enemy to be in a single line formation. Allowing for slight error in these reports, it would have been possible for the *Soryu* to be starboard of the *Akagi* yet still to port of the *Kaga*; it would also have been possible for the *Soryu* to be leading the two members of the First Carrier Division, whose order would have been maintained despite the violent changes of course they made to shake off attacking American aircraft. In this way all conflicting claims can be resolved except the *Yorktown* pilots' claim that they did not engage the *Soryu*. It is known that the Dauntlesses from the *Enterprise* and the *Yorktown* did not cross one another as they moved into the attack and that it was coincidental that they attacked different targets. Neither formation knew of the other's presence, and each attacked those enemy units that lay directly on their respective line of approach. With the *Yorktown*'s Dauntlesses coming in from the southeast and those from the *Enterprise* coming in from the southwest, a roughly linear deployment on the part of the Japanese carriers might accord with the usual version of events—the *Enterprise*'s Dauntlesses attacking first the *Kaga* and then the *Akagi*, the *Yorktown*'s dive-bombers testing their prowess against the *Soryu*. This division of the spoils, which accords with Walter Lord's detailed attempt to reconstruct events on the basis of timings and other criteria, is the one to be used here in recounting this phase of the battle.

McClusky divided his force of dive-bombers as it approached the Japanese from the southwest. He chose to lead the bomber squadron against the *Kaga*; the scouts were left to deal with the *Akagi*. It was a division of responsibilities that could easily have caused the attack to miscarry; it cut across standard operational procedures, and not all of the pilots took in McClusky's orders or those of his subordinate squadron commanders. With the bombers leading the scouts, the proper procedure would have been for each squadron to have attacked one enemy unit and for the leading squadron, the bombers, to attack the second target, the *Akagi*. This would have left the nearest target, the *Kaga*, to McClusky's trailing squadron. But in spite of the reversal of the proper sequence of attack and the communications failure that accompanied it, the last of the bombers, seeing that their target was already badly damaged, joined in the attack on the *Akagi*.[6] Regardless of the chaos above the clouds and an improvisation that robbed the attack of textbook symmetry, there was no disputing the outcome: the two members of the First Carrier Division were ruined beyond recall. The *Soryu*, the last of the three carriers to be attacked at this stage of proceedings, had a little more time than the others to greet the American divebombers with a ragged barrage, but this was ineffective. Neither she nor any of her escorts accounted for a single Dauntless.[7]

The *Kaga* was the first of the three carriers to be struck, though the first three 1,000-lb bombs aimed at her, including the one aimed at her by McClusky, missed. The fourth, and then three of the next five, struck the massive carrier before she could take evasive action.[8] The first of the hits landed on the starboard quarter amongst the Kates waiting to be launched. The next two hits were in the region of the bridge and second elevator, the fourth and last squarely in the center of the flight deck.[9] These four bombs were more than enough to doom the *Kaga*. Whether any more bombs smashed into the carrier after these four hits were registered is unknown and irrelevant; so many detonations took place within the confines of the ship that it was not possible to distinguish between explosions and their causes. The fact that some of the bombers switched away from the *Kaga* to the *Akagi* was proof of the effectiveness of the initial attackers.

The four bombs that hit the *Kaga* reduced the unprotected flight and hangar decks to a shambles, cutting down the damage control parties at their posts and destroying the equipment needed to bring the fires under control. The third bomb to hit the carrier exploded near the bridge, killing or maiming everyone there, including Captain Jisaku Okada. It also detonated a gasoline wagon that had been left on the flight deck, and this exploded over the island, ensuring that there would be no survivors from the ship's control centers. Commander Takahisa Amagai, the carrier's air officer, was left in command of a ship that had switched to emergency steering between the first and the third bombs. Such was the intensity of the fires on the upper decks that Amagai was forced to exercise his new and short-lived command from the starboard boat deck.

From the very start the position of the *Kaga* was hopeless. Japanese carriers, and particularly their early ones, were not built to absorb and survive damage. Between 1024 and 1700, when the order that the *Kaga* be abandoned was finally passed, fires slowly but remorselessly spread throughout her despite gallant but increasingly futile efforts on the part of the ship's company to contain them. The inevitable was recognized even as early as 1325, when with power failing and the ship beginning to acquire a list Amagai ordered that the ship's portrait of the emperor be transferred to the *Hagikaze*, the first part of a ritual of abandoning ship that was to become all too regular an occurrence over the next three years.[10]

The *Kaga* should not have long survived the transfer of the emperor's portrait. An attack at about 1400, which was claimed by the Americans to have been successful, should by rights have sunk her. This was made by the *Nautilus* which, after her shaking of the morning, had sighted large clouds beyond the horizon at about 1030. After she picked up signals indicating that an enemy carrier had been damaged, Brockman turned in pursuit of the enemy and at 1145 obtained visual contact with a burning carrier at a range of about eight miles. Approaching at half speed, Brockman ignored the temptation to attack one of the escorts and threaded his way into position to attack a carrier that he and certain other members of his crew identified as the *Soryu*, but which was actually the *Kaga*. Though the carrier was damaged, Brockman chose to attack her because of the high priority placed on sinking capital ships. He was fortunate in being able to evade the heavily committed escorts, two of which were virtually alongside, but fortune once more deserted him as he attacked. Four torpedoes were fired from a range of 2,700 yards against an almost stationary target. One failed to leave its tube. Two missed and the remaining torpedo struck the *Kaga* amidships. It failed to explode and broke in two under the impact of its collision with the carrier. The heavy warhead sank, but its air flask floated away to become a lifesaver to members of the *Kaga*'s crew who managed to cling on to it.[11] At this stage in the war many American torpedoes ran too deep—tests over the next two months revealed that they ran about 11 feet too deep on average—and many failed to detonate properly. But few submariners could have been so unfortunate as Brockman, who in the space of five hours maneuvered his boat into positions to attack two capital ships and failed to stake any claim through no fault of his own. He did not know of his second failure. He claimed to have sunk the *Soryu*, though he admitted that he did not see the carrier sink because he had to dodge the destroyers that came after him. At the time his report was accepted by the U. S. Navy, but postwar analysis of the Japanese record revealed the truth and the claim was denied.[12]

After 1700 the destroyers *Hagikaze* and *Maikaze* began to take off survivors from the *Kaga* while the four members of the Fourth Destroyer Division stood by the stricken carrier. Some two hours later, with the fires on the *Kaga* burning with seemingly less ferocity, Amagai attempted to reboard the carrier with fresh fire-fighting teams. They found the decks glowing red hot and had only enough time to get clear of the ship before two mighty explosions indicated that flames and heat had at last reached the aviation fuel tanks in the forward part of the carrier. The detonations all but blew the *Kaga* apart, and she rolled over and sank at about 1925. She took about 700 of her crew with her to a resting place in some 15,000 feet of the Pacific.[13]

The *Akagi* was attacked by Dauntlesses that took their dives down to 1,600 feet in an effort to record hits, but in spite of this only two of the bombs aimed at her found their mark.[14] The effect, however, was devastating, and her fate was sealed. The first struck the *Akagi* on the edge of her central elevator, penetrated the shaft and set off the torpedoes and bombs that had not been returned to their magazines. This explosion would have been enough to destroy the ship. The second bomb hit the ship's port quarter and exploded amongst the aircraft, fuel lines and ordnance lined up on the deck. The force of these explosions carried through the ship, jamming the rudder at 20 degrees to port, while a searing wall of flame swept the flight deck. The ship only narrowly escaped an early end. Her captain, Taijiro Aoki, ordered the magazines flooded to keep the ship from blowing herself to pieces immediately. While this was done with respect to the forward magazine, the explosions astern had so damaged the hoists that the after section of the magazine could not be flooded. It took until about noon for fire-fighting teams to make their way through the ship and bring the fires in the after section of the magazine under control, all the time losing members of the damage control parties as exploding ammunition exacted its toll.[15] By the time the most dangerous of the fires threatening the *Akagi* had been brought under control, the carrier was doomed in any case. Too many safety measures had been omitted for the carrier to have any chance of surviving her damage, and her captain and the force's staff drew the correct conclusions from the time that the flagship was hit.[16] Quite rightly, the chief of staff and his subordinates insisted that Nagumo shift his flag and leave the *Akagi* to her fate. Nagumo, no doubt partly as a result of shock and partly from a sense of fatalism, initially tried to resist Kusaka's increasingly astringent advice, but in the end he complied when the chief of staff more or less ordered him over the side.[17] It was a sign of the seriousness of the *Akagi*'s condition that the whole of the argument on the admiral's bridge lasted less than fifteen minutes, but even such a short delay was almost enough to doom the officers of the staff. By the time Nagumo's mind was changed for him all the exits from the bridge via the island had been sealed by fires, and the staff had to go out of a window and down a smoldering rope to safety. The small and wiry Nagumo managed this with no trouble. The rather less agile Kusaka did not do so well. He fell and sprained both ankles, but that was a small inconvenience compared with the sufferings of many of his compatriots. With the rest of the staff following and a boat coming alongside, Nagumo transferred to the *Nowaki* at 1046 and thence to the *Nagara* at 1130.[18] By the time he went over the side the *Akagi* had lost steering and all communications.

Efforts to save the ship lasted until 1925, about the time that the *Kaga* sank and the light finally faded. It was then that Aoki gave the order for the *Akagi* to be abandoned, but in all truth he could just as easily have given this order seven hours earlier. The efforts to save the carrier had become increasingly feeble in that time, and for two reasons. First, the explosions that had been set off when the two bombs hit the ship had carried right into the bowels of the ship. The explosions had not been contained by the hangar decks, with the result that damage was spread throughout the ship. This same damage also had the effect of decimating fire-fighting equipment and damage control parties. Had the *Akagi* been able to contain her damage topside she might have survived, but with so much lost in the initial explosions she had little chance of fighting her fires successfully. Second, the explosions caused fires and smoke that suffocated all those in the engine rooms, and from 1036 onwards the *Akagi* began to lose power. Once the boiler rooms were shut down, at 1042, the *Akagi* did not have the means to secure a stream from her pumps adequate enough to pour the ocean over her wounds.[19] Even though Aoki tried everything he could to confine the fires, he must have known that his efforts would be to no avail; at 1130, just after the second of two massive detonations rocked the ship, he gave orders for those members of the crew not involved in fire-fighting to transfer to the *Arashi* and the *Nowaki*.[20] Shortly after giving this order Aoki and his surviving officers were forced to move to the anchor deck, such was the intensity of the flames and heat on the flight deck and bridge.

From his new command post Aoki was faced with the increasing help-lessness of his ship. At 1350, some ten minutes after the emperor's portrait had been transferred, the carrier lost all power and began to drift. From 1400 onwards the crew was progressively withdrawn until the process was completed about 2000. Aoki, however, declined to save himself. After an argument that seems to have been as heated as the fires of the ship, Aoki was tied to the anchor deck to await the end. He ordered all his officers to leave the ship. But at 0300 on the following morning, with the ex-flagship resolutely refusing to sink, the *Akagi* was reboarded and Aoki was cut free and forcibly removed to safety.[21] At sunrise the *Nowaki* administered the coup de grâce to prevent the *Akagi* from being captured by the enemy. Thus the carrier had the unwanted distinction of becoming the first warship to be scuttled by the Imperial Navy. Official returns show the loss of 221 of her crew of 1,573 officers and men, but this total seems unreasonably low given the loss of the flight and hangar decks in the initial explosions and the casualties known to have been inflicted on damage-control personnel and the crews from the engine rooms.[22]

The *Soryu*, the smallest of Nagumo's carriers, was hit by three well-spaced bombs along the length of her flight deck. Both her forward and central elevators were destroyed, the forward one being blown out of its housing and against the island by the force of the explosions set off in the hangar deck. A series of massive explosions within the relatively small ship killed some men and catapulted others into the sea, where many were rescued by the *Hamakaze* and the *Isokaze*. Within ten minutes of being hit the *Soryu* lost steering and power, and at 1045 her skipper, Captain Ryusaku Yanagimoto, gave the order for his crew to abandon ship. Yanagimoto declined to save himself.

Like the other two carriers that had been struck, the *Soryu* took her time sinking. Nagumo, after a confused period of trying to regroup his formation and steer to the east in the hope that he might be able to force a surface action on the enemy with his remaining ships, returned to the stricken carrier in late afternoon to organize fresh fire-fighting teams as part of the renewed effort to save the *Soryu*. But before anything could come of this intention, the *Soryu* at 1912 began to settle by the stern. Within three minutes she was gone. At 1920 a massive underwater explosion erupted in her grave. At least 700 of her crew of 1,100 were lost with her, along with a large number of civilians, most of them pressmen who had sailed with the carrier on her final mission.[23] Thus the smallest of the seven carriers that fought at Midway was the first to succumb.

From the moment that they were struck, none of the three damaged Japanese carriers launched or recovered an airplane, and thereafter the *Akagi*, *Kaga* and *Soryu* ceased to play a positive part in the battle. But there remained the *Soryu*'s slightly larger sister, the *Hiryu*, unscathed and at almost full fighting effectiveness. On this single carrier now rested all remaining Japanese hopes of victory or, failing that, of recovering at least something from the wreckage of Operation MI.

CHAPTER 14

Three Against One

Operation MI was complicated, but the course of the battle on 4 June up until the time that the *Akagi*, *Kaga* and *Soryu* were damaged beyond redemption was relatively straightforward. The first six and a half hours of daylight spawned a superficially bewildering number of attacks, one by the Japanese and no fewer than eight by the Americans (excluding the one by the *Nautilus*). The Japanese had initiated the action with their partially successful strike on Midway itself, but thereafter they had been forced onto the defensive by a series of small-scale attacks, all of which were negotiated with relative ease until the final American assault, which reversed the pattern of events established throughout the morning. The margin between success and failure was improbably narrow. Some of the dive-bombers that attacked the Japanese carriers failed to get back to their own carriers as their fuel tanks spluttered dry, and one Dauntless actually ran out of fuel as it moved into the attack. Midway had been shorn of its never very great offensive capabilities, and only the scouts on the *Yorktown* remained in reserve for the Americans. The balance of carrier vulnerability was on the point of switching sides at 1030, after which time the Americans would be in the process of recovering aircraft while under enemy attack—the exact reversal of the situation over the previous three hours. In every respect, the American attack that crippled the *Akagi*, *Kaga* and *Soryu* was a last-gasp effort that against all the odds, against all that had gone before, succeeded.

Thereafter the basic simplicity of the battle disappeared for the Japanese as it divided, amoeba-like, into three separate struggles. First, there was the desperate but losing battle against the traditional enemies of sailors throughout the ages. The crews of the three stricken carriers fought flame and sea to save ships that were their homes and were to be, for many, their tombs as well. Second, the battle with the human enemy continued as the lone surviving carrier from the First Carrier Striking Force tried to redeem the situation, to do by herself, with less than her full strength, what Nagumo with half of his entire force had so singularly and disastrously failed to do between the first sighting of the enemy and the destruction of the overwhelming part of his force. Third, there was the desperate attempt by Yamamoto to regroup his forces in an effort to complement and support the efforts of the *Hiryu*. The Japanese had to strain every sinew to improvise if not success then a rough equalization of losses.

For the Americans the situation had been partially transformed. They had moved from a position of weakness, in which they were intent only on snapping at the heels of the most formidable carrier force yet seen on the world's ocean, to a position—if only for the moment—of distinct advantage. Uncertainties still abounded, the most important being the question of what force remained to the Japanese. Their original strength had still not been fully ascertained. But the destruction of the *Akagi*, *Kaga* and *Soryu*, and most of their aircraft, gave the Americans an advantage with regard to carrier aviation. Theoretically it conferred on them the right and ability to dictate the pattern of remaining events—if the *Hiryu*'s attempts to reverse the verdict of the morning were unsuccessful. There was every chance that they would be: the *Hiryu* by herself could hardly deal with three enemy carriers. Yet American tactics after the success against the *Akagi*, *Kaga* and *Soryu* were overwhelmingly defensive. Although the Americans had good reason for this, there was the seeming paradox of their carriers, when outnumbered by four to three, employing aggressive offensive tactics and then using more cautious and defensive tactics when they had a three-to-one advantage. This pattern of fighting defensively largely determined what was left of the battle, the American intention being to deny the Japanese the chance to gain compensation for their losses.

Had the battle ended at 1030, the Americans would have been able to make off with two substantial victories: first, blunting the cutting edge of Japanese naval power by the destruction of so many aircraft from the First Air Fleet; second, the destruction of three enemy fleet carriers. From this point onwards anything else that the Americans sank or destroyed was pure bonus. But, on the other hand, their three carriers still had to work to the terms of reference imposed by Nimitz's "calculated risk" formula. Thus far the Americans had made the enemy's eyes water, but even after the success of the morning the balance of naval power in the Pacific in general and off Midway in particular still favored the Japanese. The Americans had three carriers in the battle, but after their successful strike of the morning they had only about one carrier's worth of aircraft between them, and there were no more carriers immediately available in reserve. As we have seen, the *Saratoga* was four or five days away and could not come to the support of the fleet before the battle was almost certain to be over; the *Wasp* was not even in the Pacific. No new carriers could be expected to join the fleet before the end of the year. Thus Fletcher and Spruance knew that even with three scalps tucked under their belt they were not in a position to take risks in pursuit of an even greater victory than the one that had been achieved to date.

When the *Akagi* received the damage that for the moment rendered Nagumo incapable of exercising command of his force, responsibility for the conduct of operations temporarily devolved upon Rear Admiral Hiroaki Abe, commander of the Support Group, who flew his flag in the *Tone*.[1] Unless and until Nagumo could pick up the tatters of command again, Abe had to take control of the First Carrier Striking Force, and he clearly saw the way the battle should be prosecuted from the Japanese side. Three needs were immediate: first, to recover the stricken carriers and give them as much support as could be spared from the now all-important task of screening the one surviving carrier; second, to inform Yamamoto of the disastrous turn of events; third, to get the *Hiryu* into action immediately. At least on the last matter Abe had no problems: Kaku of the *Hiryu* knew exactly what was expected of him without any prompting. Recent events must have seemed like a bad nightmare coming true for Yamaguchi. Allegedly he had entertained no false hopes about Operation MI and had half expected not to return from it.[2] Now, having seen his 0830 signal urging speed and decisiveness on Nagumo set aside with such disastrous consequences, Yamaguchi had the *Hiryu* turn into the wind to launch eighteen Vals—twelve with 550-lb semi-armor piercing bombs and the remainder with 530-lb general-purpose ordnance—and six Zekes under the command of Lieutenant Michio Kobayashi. This was done at 1040, even before Nagumo and his staff went over the side of the *Akagi*.[3]

Matters would have been different had Nagumo not been denied those five to ten minutes he needed before 1030 to complete his arrangements for an attack with all his available strength. But small though this effort was, there seemed to be some reasonable hope of success. Now the enemy would have to labor under the same handicaps that he had so ruthlessly exploited in the fifteen minutes before the *Hiryu* began flying operations. With luck, the scenes even then being played out in the *Akagi*, *Kaga* and *Soryu* might be duplicated in their counterparts. This was the Japanese hope, but it was more fanciful than realistic. It took no account of the disparity that now existed between what force was available to the First Carrier Striking Force and what was needed to deal with the Americans. The aggressive, deter-mined but also desperate Yamaguchi, who at this point did not know that he faced three enemy carriers, set his flagship a task beyond her means. That the *Hiryu* could launch but eighteen Vals showed how narrow the thread was on which Japanese hopes were hung, and their disadvantage was made worse by the American's CXAM search radar. With their radar the Americans should be able to do to attacking Japanese aircraft what the

Zekes had earlier been able to do to every attacking wave of American aircraft but the one that really mattered. The scale of protection offered to the Vals by the Zekes of the *Hiryu* was derisory.

Though the *Hiryu* had lost the original plot of the enemy force,[4] Kobayashi's flight was helped to its target by Seaplane No. 5 from the *Chikuma*.[5] This seaplane was one of the scouts sent out by the First Carrier Striking Force with orders to clear up the confusion caused by Amari and the *Tone*'s Seaplane No. 4. The newcomer had come across Task Force 17 but like Amari failed to discover the presence of Task Force 16, even though the latter was but some 20 or so miles off the starboard bow of the *Yorktown* in the last hour of the morning. In ignorance of the whereabouts of Task Force 16, the seaplane guided Kobayashi to a single target. Thus his inadequate force was not offered the temptation of dividing to attack more than one enemy force. In this sense the reconnaissance failure helped the Kobayashi flight, but in the wider context the chain of events that kept Yamaguchi in ignorance of the enemy's order of battle had unfortunate consequences. One scout was in possession of the complete enemy order of battle. One of the two Judy reconnaissance aircraft from the *Soryu* had found the two enemy forces, but after the scout left the *Soryu* its radio ceased to function and it could not report the true situation until it returned to what remained of the First Carrier Striking Force. Finding the *Soryu* and two other carriers burning from end to end, the Judy located and landed on the *Hiryu* soon after 1200.[6] Thus when he ordered the attack Yamaguchi did not know the odds that he and his flagship faced, not that that would have affected his decision to commit his Vals against the enemy.

Kobayashi chose to fly at 13,000 feet,[7] and finding himself amongst American aircraft returning to their carriers he tried to conceal his advance to contact by joining the end of the stream of enemy aircraft heading towards the northeast.[8] The first of these aircraft to approach their carriers, Dauntlesses from the *Yorktown*, neared their task force at about 1115, the brevity of the return flight reflecting the converging courses of the carrier forces.[9] By this time the two fleets were about 135 miles apart, still not close enough to prevent a minor disaster in regard to aircraft from the *Enterprise*. Many of the command and control arrangements within the U.S. Navy in general and within Halsey's command in particular were casual at this stage in the war, and with no experience of major fleet actions between carrier forces this was particularly true of the procedure of recovering aircraft. The standard practice within Halsey's command was for pilots to assume that their carrier(s) would steam for the enemy at high speed in the time that they were away unless they were told to the contrary. The pilots of Task Force 16 had not been told to the contrary, and in accord with normal practice they assumed that their carriers would maintain a course of 240 degrees and a speed of 24 knots in the time they were away. No instructions

for the return and rendezvous of carriers and their aircraft were issued by
Task Force 16 before the Dauntlesses left the carriers. This was an arrangement that had worked well enough to date, but so far all the actions in which
the Americans had been involved were minor affairs. On the morning of 4
June such casualness began to claim victims. With the time the Dauntlesses
had wasted circling their carriers and then searching for the enemy, the one
thing they could not afford was to spend more time looking for their own
carriers at the end of the mission. Yet this was what the Dauntlesses from
the *Enterprise* had to do. Task Force 16 had not made 24 knots towards the
enemy in the time that its aircraft had been away. With turns into the wind
to launch or recover fighters, it had closed the enemy at perhaps 12 knots
and was therefore some 45 miles out of position by the time the Dauntlesses
from the *Enterprise* reached what should have been the rendezvous. No
correction had been issued by Task Force 16, and it was not until a lost
McClusky radioed the *Enterprise* that proper instructions were given to the
Dauntlesses. By that time it was too late to save many of the dive-bombers.
A total of eighteen failed to get back to the *Enterprise*,[10] though two were
recovered by the *Yorktown*.[11] The price of success thus far was little short of
disastrous: in effect Task Force 16 had lost four of the six squadrons it had
sent against the Japanese.

   The *Yorktown*, on the other hand, had managed things a little better. The
losses of the Coral Sea battle had not been pointless; the experience had
taught her to pay extra attention to detail, which had resulted in her finding
the enemy and then setting a course that enabled her surviving planes to
return to their carriers. The calculation of the plot by Task Force 17 was
superior to that of Task Force 16, but it had two unfortunate results. First,
Kobayashi tagged on the tail of aircraft returning to the *Yorktown*. The good
work that brought American aircraft back to the *Yorktown* also brought the
enemy. Second, it brought enemy at just the wrong moment for the
Yorktown. Nagumo had been unfortunate enough to have events occur in
the wrong order, and now Fletcher encountered a similar problem—as with
Nagumo, a problem partly of his own making, partly the result of factors
beyond his control.

   The first aircraft to return to the *Yorktown* were the Dauntlesses, but
apart from those from the *Enterprise* she refused to recover them immediately. The *Yorktown* had two other priorities. With her own Dauntlesses
having found the enemy and their own carrier with ease, there was no
urgency in landing them, and the *Yorktown* chose first to land her Wildcats.
These were low on fuel and the five surviving fighters had varying degrees
of damage. Two were extensively mauled as a result of their encounter with
the Zekes, and one made a bad landing that blocked the flight deck for a
time.[12] It was not cleared until 1150, when the *Yorktown*'s second priority
was revealed. This was to launch another search operation between 280 and

020 degrees, this time with ten Dauntlesses.[13] Fletcher was still concerned about the possibility of another enemy carrier being within range to do battle, and in any case he was now aware that one of the enemy's carriers had escaped attack. At 1150 the *Yorktown* began to launch her scouts, their orders being to search out to a range of 250 miles.[14]

Fletcher's decision proved to be amongst the more impressive ones made in the course of the battle. It was perhaps a little cautious, and it had one unforeseen and untoward result, but nevertheless it allowed the Americans to regain and hold contact with the *Hiryu*. This, in its turn, ensured a follow-up effort from any American carrier or carriers that the Japanese failed to put out of action. Because the enemy could mount nothing more than a broken-back strike after his losses of the morning, Fletcher's decision instigated a chain of events that led to the destruction of the *Hiryu*. Spruance and Task Force 16, having committed all their bombers to the opening strike and having lost heavily in that single effort, no longer had the means to conduct a reconnaissance. Browning in the *Enterprise* insisted that Task Force 16 carry out a further strike with the Dauntlesses that were recovered, but with no scouting capacity and only a vague idea of where the enemy might be, Spruance knew that resuming the attack would be futile. There was a catch in this situation: Spruance could not mount an attack without a prior reconnaissance, but neither could he scout without further compromising his already weakened strike force. Fletcher's decision had the fortunate effect of untangling Spruance's problems. Fletcher had sought to scout both for Task Force 17 and for the whole fleet, but events conspired to ensure that his reconnaissance was made on behalf of Task Force 16 alone.[15]

Recovering the *Enterprise*'s Dauntlesses and the Wildcats, clearing the obstructed flight deck and then flying off the scouts all took place with the *Yorktown*'s own Dauntlesses still in the air. The only other Dauntlesses remaining with the carrier were the seven scouts that had not been sent out. They were on the hangar deck being fueled and armed with 1,000-lb ordnance in readiness for any contact report.[16] The contact that was to occur, however, was with the *Yorktown*; at this point, shortly before noon, Kobayashi and his squadron of Vals came upon the scene. There seemed to be a chance that luck might have changed sides, since now it was the Japanese who were attacking and the Americans who were on the defensive. This, however, was not quite the case. The ploy of trailing an enemy to his base was one that airmen of all nations were always on guard against; in this case, moreover, Kobayashi was dealing with an enemy who had an unsuspected advantage. The Japanese were beginning to appreciate the importance of radar and the advantage it conferred upon the Americans, but they did not know that the CXAM radar then in service had an IFF capability.[17] Kobayashi actually managed to join the American stream of aircraft without being detected by it, but the radar found him and his squadron at a range of 65 miles.[18] The results were immediate and predictable. First, the *Yorktown* took the passive measures that had been so conspicuously neglected by the First Carrier Striking Force. The fuel lines were drained and the avgas was isolated under carbon dioxide at 20-lb pressure. A bowser, with 800 gallons of avgas, was simply and unceremoniously thrown over the side from its position on the flight deck.[19] Conscious of what had befallen her consort at the Coral Sea, the *Yorktown* tried to guard against the worst that induced explosions could do to her. Second, the *Yorktown* and her escorts worked up to full speed and assumed battle formation. Already at high speed because of her flying operations, the *Yorktown* worked up to 30 knots, a speed that was theoretically beyond her because of her unrepaired boilers. No doubt the proximity of the enemy coaxed the extra revolutions out of her turbines. Thus Task Force 17 was fully prepared for battle long before the enemy aircraft came in sight, though in deploying to meet the incoming attack the Americans had made one error. The *Yorktown* had two heavy cruisers and five destroyers to screen her, and her two cruisers, the *Astoria* and the *Portland*, were on her starboard side; she could have done with one of them to port.[20]

The third measure the *Yorktown* took was to wave away the Dauntlesses that were still in the air patiently awaiting recovery. The enemy attack materialized at about noon, just as her dive-bombers began to line up for their approach to the *Yorktown*. Not having discovered Kobayashi's approach, they had not realized that the task force was about to undergo attack. Certain of the Dauntlesses tried to join the combat air patrol in a repetition of the episode in the Coral Sea, but most made directly for Task Force 16 and the potential safety of an unattacked flight deck. As they made their way towards Task Force 16 they were attacked by Wildcats from the *Hornet* that were making their own way to Task Force 17, but the incident was inconsequential. Fifteen Dauntlesses were recovered, and the presence of fourteen of them with the *Enterprise* during the afternoon proved of vital significance in providing Spruance's flagship with a sizable Dauntless force for a second strike.[21] Quite fortuitously, the *Yorktown*'s Dauntless bombers were to replace those lost by the *Enterprise*, while the scouts of the *Yorktown* were to provide a refurbished *Enterprise* with the contact that Task Force 16 needed to mount an attack.[22] The two Dauntlesses that were not recovered belonged to Leslie and his wingman. They were trying to direct two destroyers from the screen, the *Monaghan* and the *Hammann*, to the locations of ditched aircraft.[23] In carrying out this duty the two Dauntlesses left themselves without enough fuel to complete the 20 or so miles to Task Force 16. Both put down in the sea alongside the *Astoria*.[24]

Fourth, the *Yorktown* deployed her combat air patrol into interception positions. Because she was by herself, the carrier could only provide twelve

Wildcats for her own defense, and these operated in two six-strong divisions.[25] They were directed out to a range of about 20 miles.[26] When it became clear to Task Force 16 that it was not going to be attacked, Spruance allowed its combat air patrol to move to the support of the *Yorktown*, but this decision came too late. Sixteen fighters from the *Enterprise* and the *Hornet* went to their sister ship's protection, twelve of them from the *Enterprise*, but they accounted for only one enemy aircraft (perhaps more) after its attack had been completed.[27] That Spruance initially hesitated in directing his fighters to the defense of the *Yorktown* was just as well for the Japanese. Naturally concerned with the security of his force, Spruance's decision to hold back his combat air patrol robbed the Americans of the chance to record an annihilating victory over the attacking Japanese force. Faced with only the *Yorktown*'s fighters (and the late arrivals from Task Force 16), the Vals became involved in "fierce engagements . . . between 1158 and 1240" while their fighters engaged in "a fight to the death."[28]

In retrospect it can be seen that the odds were stacked against Kobayashi and his Vals as they never had been with respect to the Dauntlesses that had attacked the First Carrier Striking Force. But no one on the Japanese side needed telling that this was one attack that had to succeed, regardless of the odds. Indeed, before the attack was launched Yamaguchi took the unusual step of personally briefing his pilots. He specifically warned his men against recklessness and foolhardiness; for Yamaguchi the desperateness of the situation called for dredging up the last reserves of skill, not bravado.[29] Unfortunately for Yamaguchi the commander of his fighters, Lieutenant Yasuhiro Shigematsu, could not have paid careful attention to the admiral's instructions. During the outward flight the Zekes encountered Dauntlesses returning to their carriers, and in the mistaken belief that the Dauntlesses were Devastators Shigematsu led his six fighters into an ill-considered attack. As both sides had shown at the Coral Sea, dive-bombers without their bombs were tough adversaries for fighters, and the overconfident Zekes came off second best in their affray with the Dauntlesses. Furthermore, the Zekes simply did not have the capacity to tackle empty American bombers, be they Devastators or Dauntlesses. The task of the Zekes was to clear a path through the combat air patrol to ensure that the Val dive-bombers could attack the enemy with the least possible interference from his fighters. Simply in terms of ammunition supply, the Zekes did not have the means to indulge themselves in an affair with Dauntlesses or Devastators when more serious business was at hand,[30] and Shigematsu certainly lacked the numbers to dispense with two damaged fighters that turned back for the *Hiryu*.[31] The four Zekes that rejoined the Vals after what must have been a rather chastening experience did not have long to dwell on the moral to be drawn from the encounter. If they could not pick off American bombers when undistracted by the defensive needs of the Vals, the prospect of their facing the American combat air patrol was not promising. In the event, only one of the Zekes survived to make its rather forlorn way back to the *Hiryu*, though it and the other Japanese survivors of the attack claimed between them seven "certain" kills.[32]

With the Zekes overwhelmed by the combat air patrol the Vals were hopelessly vulnerable, especially when they deployed into attack formation. Because the *Yorktown* had done rather better than she and the *Lexington* had done at the Coral Sea in managing the fighter control, the combat air patrol had considerable success in chopping down the advancing Japanese bombers well before they came within range of the antiaircraft guns of the surface ships. Just what happened in the course of the attack can never be stated with absolute certainty, but it appears beyond dispute that the Wildcats of the combat air patrol caught the Vals while they were still in their cruising formation and destroyed six of them in their first pass.[33] A running battle then ensued, and apparently only eight of the Vals survived to confront the fierce barrage of fire put up by the ships.[34] The *Astoria* fired 204 rounds of 5-in antiaircraft ammunition in ten minutes.[35] Two of the Vals that entered the flak were destroyed almost immediately,[36] before it had time to line itself up for the attack, the other as it released its bomb.[37] One more Val, shot down after its attack, perhaps by aircraft from Task Force 16, crashed into the sea near the *Astoria*'s stern.[38] It would appear that of the eighteen-strong squadron that flew from the *Hiryu*, only seven aircraft survived to attack the *Yorktown* and only five remained to escape back to their carrier at the end of their effort.[39]

Neither Kobayashi nor his deputy, Lieutenant Takenori Kondo, were amongst the survivors of the attack, and it was a reflection of the extent of Japanese losses that the situation report radioed to the carrier after the attack had to be sent by the third Val of the second bombing section.[40] The whole of the first section and the first two aircraft of the second were lost, and with them their pilots. These were amongst the best fliers in the Imperial Navy, and the seven Vals that broke through the fighter and flak defenses to attack the *Yorktown* put on a virtuoso performance that was begrudgingly acknowledged by the Americans.[41] The Japanese pilots held their dives down to under 1,000 feet in an effort to score hits. The fact that at Midway the Japanese were using the first team and not their reserves was never more clearly shown than in the results of this single attack.[42] While one of the bombs aimed at the *Yorktown* fell clear of the carrier, three were near misses that raised her stern out of the water and caused her to stagger and shake as her screws thrashed wildly in the air. Men on the fantail were cut down by shrapnel, and minor damage was caused to bulkheads, antisplinter mats and other impedimenta of the carrier.[43] But apart from the

losses amongst her crew, none of the bombs that so narrowly missed the
Yorktown caused her serious damage, either below the waterline or
topside.[44] This was not the case with respect to the three bombs that hit her.

Of these one—the second of the three hits and the third of the seven
intended for the carrier[45]—tumbled in its fall when the Val that aimed it was
caught by flak at release point.[46] The bomb exploded on impact with the
flight deck, just abaft the no. 2 elevator and inboard of the starboard
antiaircraft batteries and machine guns. The explosion on impact ripped a
hole some 10 feet square in the flight deck and set off a series of fires that
immediately enveloped the carrier in a thick black smoke seen easily on the
Enterprise, then hull down on the southern horizon. The devastation
wrought by this explosion was horrific, since the full impact was taken by
the third and fourth batteries of quadruple 1.1-in antiaircraft guns and by
the machine-gun positions improvised in the area. Of the battery guncrews
all but five men were killed, a number that had to be deduced by counting
the survivors, since there was no way of listing the dead amidst the mangled
and charred remains left in these positions. The gun shields, rather than
protecting the crews, concentrated the heat and force of the explosion. Men
were separated from their limbs, sliced in two or burnt beyond recognition.
Moreover, the force of this explosion carried through the screens into the
hangar deck and spent itself amongst the seven armed and fueled Dauntlesses that had been parked in this particular area. Three of these Dauntlesses ignited. Damage-control parties hacked the burning wing from one
aircraft to keep flames from reaching its fuel tanks in the fuselage. But what
saved the situation was the efficiency of the overhead spray system employed in the *Yorktown* and all American carriers. In the *Yorktown* this was
constructed in such a way as to bring down three vast cascades of water
across the width of the hangar, which was thus divided into four bays. The
officer in charge of the hangar deck, Lieutenant A. C. ("Ace") Emerson,
opened the spray system, thereby confining the fires to the last of the bays,
and fire-fighting teams were then able to extinguish the isolated blaze. In
this way Emerson forestalled the possibility of the sort of induced explosions that even then were rocking three enemy carriers many miles to the
west.[47] The fires were quickly extinguished, and it took only twenty
minutes for the ship's carpenters to make good the damage to the flight
deck.[48] It did not take any longer for the gun positions to be scraped clean of
human debris and manned with replacement crews.

The third and last of the bombs to hit the *Yorktown* sliced through both
the flight and hangar decks via the no. 1 elevator. It exploded on the fourth
deck, the same level on which the explosion had been sustained at the Coral
Sea. The bomb caused very little damage to the flight deck, and no one was
killed because it exploded in an area of the ship that was not heavily
manned. Though this forward part of the ship had many important com-

partments, the bomb searched out one of the least important in which to explode, a rag store, where it burned well and proved difficult to extinguish. Had the bomb landed a few feet in any direction, it could have had a disastrous effect for the forward part of the ship, comparable to what had befallen the *Shokaku* at the Coral Sea. The rag store was next to a magazine for 5-in ammunition and to an avgas compartment. Fortunately for the *Yorktown*, neither was affected by the force of the bomb's explosion, and the danger from heat caused by the fires in the rag store was set aside by two safety measures. First, Emerson's flooding of the hangar deck had simultaneously topped up the spaces around avgas compartments with carbon dioxide gas. Second, local damage control flooded the magazine with seawater. These measures proved sufficient to prevent the spread of damage.[49]

The remaining hit, which was in fact the first of the hits and the second of the bombs aimed at the *Yorktown*, was the one that did real damage. This bomb sliced into the ship from port—the two cruisers, it will be remembered, were to starboard—and penetrated the flight deck to the level of the second deck before detonating at the base of the uptakes from the ship's boiler rooms. The explosion wrecked many rooms of minor importance— the office of the ship's executive officer, various laboratories, the ship's laundry and various parts of the officers' accommodation.[50] But the serious damage inflicted by this particular hit was to the ventilation system of the boiler rooms. Without a forced draught the boilers could not provide steam for the turbines. The *Yorktown* went into battle with three of her boilers out of service, and the explosion of this bomb blew out the fires in five of the remaining six. Two were completely disabled, and the vents from three of them were wrecked, including the vent from the one functioning boiler. As that boiler continued operating it blew exhaust smoke back into the other boiler rooms.[51]

With the boiler rooms evacuated, no forced draught and one remaining boiler left to tick over at the minimum needed to keep certain auxiliary machinery in action, there could only be one result for the *Yorktown*. She quickly lost headway, and at 1220, just fifteen minutes after the Japanese attack had begun and four minutes after it ended, the *Yorktown* was dead in the water.[52] She was without speed, without power for her guns, without the ability to handle aircraft and, critically, without communications. The force of the explosion in the base of the funnel and the subsequent loss of power between them accounted for the radar and plotting rooms, and with the ship's communications system inoperative she could no longer function as a flagship in a fast-moving carrier battle. Though the *Yorktown* was in no immediate danger of sinking, Fletcher had no option but to shift his flag. He commanded both a fleet and an individual task force, and when it became clear that repairs to the *Yorktown* would take time, he decided to transfer to

Smith's flagship, the *Astoria*. She was ordered to come alongside, and by 1300 the heavy cruiser's no. 2 whaleboat was in position and Fletcher was lowered the 55 feet from the flight deck. Evacuation of the admiral and the most important members of his staff was completed by 1311, and at 1324 Fletcher boarded the *Astoria*.[53]

For seven Vals to score three hits on a carrier steaming at 30 knots was a formidably impressive performance, but it was incomplete and had to remain so because there were no Kates on hand to administer the coup de grâce with their torpedoes. When the *Akagi*, *Kaga* and *Soryu* were hit Yamaguchi opted for a quick rather than a balanced attack, and the price of that decision now had to be paid. The Japanese were caught in the worst of circumstances. The *Hiryu*'s Vals had been all but wiped out and were unfit for further operations, and the Japanese did not have the means to capitalize upon their achievement. They lost sixteen aircraft, almost a third of the total strength of the *Hiryu*, in recording a partial success that they could not exploit.

Even as Kobayashi's squadron was on its way to attack the enemy the *Hiryu* was preparing to launch a third strike, this time with Kates that had been recovered from the strike against Midway. For the moment the Japanese held the initiative, having recovered aircraft and not being under attack. The Japanese had a time advantage of some two or three hours, perhaps a little more, and they were determined to make use of it. On the other hand, when the *Hiryu* was preparing for her second effort against the enemy surface forces the Japanese became aware for the first time that they faced three enemy carriers. This information was provided initially by the *Soryu*'s Judy after it landed back on the *Hiryu* around midday. A rather nebulous confirmation was provided by Seaplane No. 5 from the *Chikuma*. The aircraft sent a signal at 1220 which was received at 1240.[54] Since this particular scout had been attacked and was to be subsequently shot down, its preoccupation with other matters was perhaps understandable.[55] In any event, its information was superseded after 1300 when Yamaguchi, along with Yamamoto, Kondo, Nagumo and Komatsu, came into possession of what they had needed one day earlier: the enemy order of battle.[56] It was provided by an ensign from the *Yorktown*'s Devastator squadron who had been picked up by the *Arashi* after the destroyer had inadvertently directed the dive-bombers from the *Enterprise* to their rendezvous with the *Akagi* and the *Kaga*. This unfortunate pilot was destined to be axed to death before the day was out, but not before he provided his captors with details of the American order of battle. In the course of a written interrogation the ensign identified the three American carriers at sea, stated that the *Yorktown* was operating alone and separately from the *Enterprise* and the *Hornet*, and gave the Americans an overall strength of six cruisers and about ten destroyers. He also told the Japanese that the American carriers had been on station off

Midway since 31 May. This information was not quite correct, but it was close enough to make no difference. In this manner the Japanese found out that they were opposed by one of the two carriers they thought they had sunk at the Coral Sea the previous month—while their own casualties from that battle were in home waters.[57]

Thus Yamaguchi found himself in dire straits, opposed by three carriers and with only what had returned from the strike against Midway available for operations against the enemy. But with time still in his favor, there was never any question of the Japanese admiral pulling back, and from the reports coming in from his returning Vals he had reason to believe that perhaps the battle was beginning to swing in his favor at last. The situation report informed him that the attacked enemy carrier had been brought to a halt and was burning fiercely. Yamaguchi correctly concluded that she had been hit by at least two bombs.[58] The carrier was not going to sink without a further nudge, but she was out of the battle for a long time to come. Thus the Japanese could afford to discount her and concentrate against the carrier they believed at that time was with her. When the Vals made their report on the state of the *Yorktown*, the general consensus on the *Hiryu* was still that the enemy had two carriers. Not surprisingly, the Japanese imagined still that they had a good chance against two enemy carriers, even with their depleted air group, when they found out that one of these carriers had been brought to a halt and that they had time on their side. The Japanese did not know of the effectiveness of the *Yorktown*'s damage-control arrangements; these brought the carrier back into service within an hour or so of Kobayashi's attack. The sudden revelation that the enemy had three carriers, two of which had not been attacked, suddenly made matters dangerously urgent for the Japanese; Yamaguchi and the *Hiryu* had no margin of safety—and no capacity to hit both of the enemy carriers that remained intact.

On the American side Fletcher and Spruance had to deal with equally difficult situations. When the *Yorktown* was seen burning, Spruance dropped the heavy cruisers *Pensacola* and *Vincennes* and the destroyers *Balch* and *Benham* from the screen of Task Force 16 at 1235 with orders for them to stand by and assist the *Yorktown*.[59] Beyond that there was little Task Force 16 could do to help the *Yorktown* other than recover any of her aircraft that still happened to be in the air. Even this seemingly small task was not without its dangers and tragedy. One aircraft, landing heavily on the *Hornet*, accidentally set off its machine guns, killing five and wounding twenty members of the *Hornet*'s crew. (Amongst those killed was the son of the commander in chief of the Atlantic Fleet.)[60] The American problem at this time was twofold. First, power had to be restored to the *Yorktown* as rapidly as possible. The Japanese hope was that either their submarines or their surface warships could complete the task begun so well by the Vals;

the *Yorktown*, therefore, had to get clear of the danger area. Second, the Americans had to try to account for their fourth and last enemy carrier, yet the means of doing so was small. The *Yorktown* had virtually no offensive power left to her. The same was true for the *Hornet*. In effect the *Enterprise* had two slightly understrength Dauntless squadrons available, one of them by courtesy of the *Yorktown*. A fleet that had begun an action six or so hours before with a couple hundred aircraft was now operating with a couple dozen, and so, too, were the Japanese. The two carrier fleets were like heavyweight boxers too tired and too weak to deliver a final telling blow. But even with their depleted forces both sides had just enough strength to make one final effort.

The odds favored the Americans, but the Japanese, having recovered their aircraft from the strike against Midway before the American carriers recovered their aircraft from the strike against the First Carrier Striking Force, still held an advantage of one to two hours over the Americans. The initial advantage of perhaps twice that length of time was shrinking rapidly, but there still remained enough for the Japanese to hope that one more effort could be made. After Kobayashi was sent on his way, however, the *Hiryu* found that all that she had available for a final strike was nine Kates, one of which had come in from the *Akagi*.[61] A tenth Kate, the one belonging to Tomonaga, had been hit over Midway by flak. The port wing, and with it its fuel tank, had been peppered and the *Hiryu*'s service crews could not ready the damage in time for this aircraft to take part in the pending strike. Fatalistically, Tomonaga ordered his aircraft to be armed and refueled, and turned down his subordinates' offers of intact aircraft.[62] With only two officers left to the squadron, Tomonaga was determined to lead his formation into the attack, knowing that he would never get back to the *Hiryu*.

This third strike by the *Hiryu*, therefore, was to consist of ten Kates, nine from the *Hiryu* herself and one from the *Akagi*, and six Zekes, two of which had come from the *Kaga*. Nothing more was available for the attack, and after having seen what had happened to successive American torpedo bomber attacks that morning, there must have been considerable misgivings on board the Japanese carrier as the time for launching approached. The odds were going to be very much against Tomonaga and his squadron, particularly because their orders were specific. With the *Hiryu* and Yamaguchi aware that Kobayashi and his men had been able to immobilize one carrier that had been operating alone—which had to be the *Yorktown*—the torpedo bombers were instructed to ignore any enemy carrier that was dead in the water and to concentrate against intact enemies, the *Enterprise* and the *Hornet*.[63] It went without saying that ten Kates and six Zekes pitting themselves against two carriers were not good odds, but they were odds Yamaguchi was prepared to accept.

Tomonaga divided his ten-strong formation into two divisions, each of five. One section he commanded directly while the other was under the command of his crewman, Lieutenant Tashio Hashimoto, who for this attack was flown in a separate aircraft. Hashimoto, a navigator, had been specifically warned that the stopped American carrier was somewhat to the south of her original estimated position. This information was passed to Hashimoto, but not to Tomonaga, in the last seconds before the formation took to the air at 1331. Unfortunately for the Japanese, takeoff time from the *Hiryu* was sandwiched between the time Fletcher boarded the *Astoria* and his former flagship regained most of her power. By 1340 four of the *Yorktown*'s boilers had been brought back into service as the vents were repaired. With two of her six boilers destroyed, four was the maximum she could get back into service,[64] and by 1350 the engine room was able to report that there was enough power for 20 knots, perhaps more.[65] At 1402 the square yellow flag with the blue diagonal cross of St. Andrew, which indicated that the ship that flew it had broken down, was lowered as the *Yorktown* worked up to 5 knots.[66] Within a quarter of an hour she managed to work up to 17 knots, and her escorts once more gathered around her in battle formation. This time, of course, they had four extra members in the screen.[67] There was no reason the carrier should not resume flying operations within a short time—aircraft were even then being prepared for operations—but with her radar and plotting facilities out of action she could no longer function either as a flagship or independently as a carrier.

Such was the situation when Hashimoto sighted a carrier task force at a range of 30 miles at about 1428.[68] Inevitably he and his colleagues assumed that the carrier could not be the one the Vals reported to have been burning furiously and dead in the water. There was no way the carrier so badly damaged by the Vals could have been brought back into service in so short a space of time. Unfortunately for the Japanese, they could not know of their error in this matter because the *Chikuma* had lost contact with her Seaplane No. 5, which had been shadowing and reporting the enemy force. The last contact between seaplane and cruiser was at 1345, when the former reported a change of course on the part of the enemy, presumably Task Force 16.[69] The *Yorktown*'s recuperation went unreported, seemingly because it was at about this time that a Wildcat from the combat air patrol of Task Force 16 accounted for Seaplane No. 5.[70] In fact the Japanese should have been in a position to protect themselves against loss of contact at this stage of the battle. The *Chikuma*, in response to a specific order from Abe, had brought her fourth seaplane, one of her two remaining Jakes, to the first degree of readiness just after noon, and had she launched it at this time the Japanese could have had a second seaplane in contact with the Americans until the arrival of the Kates from the *Hiryu*.[71] In those circumstances it would have been unlikely that the *Yorktown*'s recovery would have passed unnoticed by the Japanese. As it was, the First Carrier Striking Force was then doing what it should have done many hours earlier, in fact what it should have done even before it struck at Midway. The First Carrier Striking Force was putting together a second-phase reconnaissance mission. This was to be conducted by five seaplanes—a Dave from each of the battleships, a Jake from the *Chikuma* and two seaplanes from the *Tone*—to a range of 150 miles between 010 and 090 degrees.[72] Once more the Japanese managed to get their priorities in the wrong order. When they had needed comprehensive coverage they had opted for a less than adequate reconnaissance pattern; now, when they needed continuous contact, Abe sought to provide a general reconnaissance. Given the unsatisfactory performance of the scouts thus far in the battle, it is hard not to feel some sympathy for Abe on this matter, but the fact was that the Jake from the *Chikuma* sat on its catapult for eighty minutes before it took off. The Japanese lost contact with the enemy between the time this particular aircraft flew off and any of the five seaplanes sent out after 1340 came across the enemy. Thus the *Yorktown*'s change of situation was unknown to and unsuspected by the Japanese. Moreover the Jake from the *Chikuma* was the first of the seaplanes to take off on its reconnaissance mission, and under these circumstances it is rather difficult to see what she and her colleagues were supposed to achieve at this stage of the proceedings. The Jake was launched after the *Hiryu* began to launch her Kates, and the *Tone* was unable to get her seaplanes away for another twenty minutes. Thus the second-phase reconnaissance mission was launched after the Vals had been committed (and annihilated) and after the torpedo bombers had begun taking off. With the Dave, Kate and Jake being endowed with roughly equal top and cruising speeds, there was probably little point in launching a scouting mission after the attack missions began, especially after one scout had been available for operations for some time. Had that single scout from the *Chikuma* been committed early, much of the subsequent confusion might have been averted.

But these unsuspected failings counted for nothing when, about an hour after leaving the *Hiryu*, Hashimoto sighted a task force with a single carrier moving under its own power. The Kates had unwittingly come across the *Yorktown* and her escorts, but there was no doubt about the Japanese course of action. The formation of Kates divided into its two sections to take the enemy carrier in a scissors attack, the plan being for Tomonaga to lead his section into the attack from off the enemy's port bow while Hashimoto took his five Kates into the attack from the starboard bow.[73] Neither attack was going to be easy. The arrival of units from Task Force 16 had given Fletcher the chance to thicken up the *Yorktown*'s screen appreciably, and he had deployed the two cruisers that arrived astern of the carrier while the *Astoria* and the *Portland* took station off the carrier's bows. The Americans therefore had a single heavy cruiser covering each of the ideal lines of approach for both dive-bombers and torpedo bombers, and the augmented screen of destroyers was drawn into a distance of about a mile from the carrier, as if this was an indication of the escorts' extra determination to safeguard their injured carrier.[74] With the *Balch*'s radar finding the Japanese at a range of 50 miles, things promised to be difficult for the attacker. But against these considerations two crucial matters told against the *Yorktown*. First, she was not in company with the *Enterprise* and the *Hornet*, and she could not operate her aircraft. Since there was virtually no natural wind at this time and the *Yorktown* was only making 17 knots, a fully fueled fighter could not be launched. The job of refueling aircraft had been resumed on the *Yorktown* at 1350,[75] and by the time battle with the Japanese torpedo bombers was joined the carrier had ten Wildcats on her flight deck, none of them with more than twenty or so gallons of fuel in their tanks—which, in fact, proved rather fortunate.[76] The *Yorktown*'s real problem was that because she was not in company with her two sister ships, she did not have a properly balanced combat air patrol. She had to make do with a six-strong patrol provided for her at the last moment by the *Enterprise*. The first of these fighters had been launched at roughly the same time as the *Hiryu* launched her Kates, and of the six, three came from the *Enterprise* herself and the other three from amongst the *Yorktown*'s combat air patrol, which had been forced to land on the *Enterprise* when their own carrier was dead in the water.[77] With Task Force 16 unable to provide more aircraft for the *Yorktown* until it was sure it would not be attacked itself, and with the *Yorktown* unable to provide for herself, Fletcher's former flagship had problems. Second, and perhaps more important, the *Yorktown*'s slowed condition robbed her of an important element of protection. With five boilers out of action she was forced to operate at about half power and half speed. At the Coral Sea, and in meeting the attack by Kobayashi's dive-bombers, a combination of speed and an easy response to her helm had enabled the *Yorktown* to dodge most of the bombs and torpedoes that had been aimed at her. This time the situation was certain to be different. Two cruisers, two destroyers and fighters from Task Force 16 were welcome additions to the defenses of Task Force 17, but they were not to prove adequate compensation for the *Yorktown*'s loss of 10 knots between the attack led by Kobayashi and the one led by Tomonaga.

The attack by the Kates fared badly from the start. Ten miles from the *Yorktown* the combat air patrol claimed its first victim, a member of Tomonaga's section,[78] and as the two sections approached the carrier she put her wheel hard over to starboard.[79] This maneuver merely changed the direction of Hashimoto's attack, which moved in from port rather than from starboard. But the *Yorktown*'s change of course proved disastrous for Tomonaga's section, which was left astern of the carrier and was therefore committed to working its way around the flank again to attack across the bows. The time Tomonaga's section lost moving into the attack gave the combat air patrol the chance to get amongst the Kates, and between them the Wildcats and the antiaircraft gunners of Task Force 17 accounted for every member of Tomonaga's section. Two of the Kates were certainly shot down by flak, one by a shell that detonated the torpedo it was carrying.[80] The Americans claimed to have destroyed seven aircraft in the course of this attack.[81]

The *Yorktown*'s turn protected her from Tomonaga but left her open to Hashimoto. With difficulty the carrier began to fly off her fighters in an attempt to defend herself, but even though eight of her Wildcats were flown off none of Hashimoto's section was shot down.[82] Though the Zekes performed magnificently in defense of the torpedo bombers, it cost the fighters three of their number, and three of the Kates were damaged beyond repair.[83] Nevertheless, four of the Kates managed to drop their torpedoes, the fifth, the Kate from the *Akagi*, for some reason declining to drop its torpedo until it was clear of the enemy.[84] Two of Tomonaga's Kates may have managed to launch their torpedoes against the *Yorktown* before they were shot down, but the carrier was able to evade the torpedoes aimed at her from astern and even two of those aimed at her by Hashimoto's section. But with only 19 knots she was too slow to dodge the remaining two, and these struck home around frames 75 and 90, amidships and slightly abaft, on the port side of the ship.[85] Immediately after their attack the Kates fled for the safety of the *Hiryu*, Hashimoto signaling on ahead the good news that two hits had been recorded on an enemy carrier that was not the same carrier that had been disabled earlier in the day.[86]

Yamaguchi had good reason to be pleased with these results. With a full squadron of dive-bombers and a half squadron of torpedo bombers, the *Hiryu*'s attempts to avenge her three colleagues were impressive by any standard. At 1600 he passed on to Nagumo the information that two enemy carriers had been mauled, and from the first unevaluated report sent at 1445 by Hashimoto, the *Hiryu* believed that she was well on the way towards equalizing what were otherwise quite unacceptable odds.[87]

Thus in the immediate aftermath of this attack Yamaguchi believed that two enemy carriers had been hit, and hit hard, by his bombers. His various signals made this appreciation perfectly clear. Yet at the same time many of Yamaguchi's decisions made during this time simply do not make sense in retrospect. None of his senior commanders saw fit either to advise him or issue orders to him; he was left to fight his own battle without guidance from above. However, it would appear that Yamaguchi and the *Hiryu* learned only too late that one enemy carrier was out of action and that they still faced two enemy units. In the course of the afternoon the seaplanes that had been sent out in the second-phase reconnaissance provided a series of reports, but in the moments before disaster finally overwhelmed the *Hiryu* the suspicion arose that earlier assessments were wrong. At 1655 Abe, and at 1656 Yamaguchi, issued signals indicating their fear.[88] By then it was too late for the Japanese to redeem the situation. Acting on the initial reports after the Kates had attacked the enemy between about 1434 and 1452, Yamaguchi had told Nagumo in signals at 1531 and again at 1630 that the *Hiryu* intended to carry out an attack at dusk. In his 1630 signal he informed Nagumo that the attack would be launched at 1800 and asked the *Nagara* to provide her seaplane for night reconnaissance duties. The 1656 signal Yamaguchi issued told Nagumo that he had twelve bombers available for the forthcoming attack, six Kates and six Vals.

Though events were not kind to the Japanese at this stage of the battle, it is difficult to see what Yamaguchi was hoping to achieve. In his signals he was referring to attack formations of six Kates or six Vals and nine Zekes, but even with the refugees the *Hiryu* had recovered from the other carriers after they had been damaged, it is impossible to discern what such formations were supposed to achieve after a full-strength attack by eighteen Vals could not account for an enemy carrier. In fact, after the Tomonaga attack the *Hiryu* retained just four Kates, five Vals and six Zekes for offensive operations, and by 1700 the Japanese knew that the enemy had two operational carriers.[89] Yamaguchi did not know their state, but he did know that dive-bombers from American carriers had earlier accounted for the *Akagi*, *Kaga* and *Soryu*. The odds were disastrously against him because, as we have seen, the *Enterprise* recovered most of the Dauntlesses of the *Yorktown*, thus providing her with a strong second strike, and moreover, just after the Tomonaga attack drew to a close the *Hornet* received what would be the naval equivalent of a blood transfusion. Eleven of the missing Dauntless bombers that had made their way to Midway had been refueled at the atoll and even then were making their way back to their carrier. Yamaguchi in early afternoon thought that his bombers had equalized the odds; in fact in carrier numbers alone they had never been less than two to one, and in aircraft numbers, the only true measure of effectiveness, the odds were much greater against the Japanese.

Once the second strike against American surface forces was complete, Yamaguchi and the *Hiryu* had but one course of action—to get out of the danger area as rapidly as possible. By the time of the Kate attack the *Hiryu* had managed to get herself into the worst possible situation. She was little more than 110 miles from the enemy, and she was still little more than about 40 miles from the scene of the morning's devastation. The *Hiryu* was well within range of enemy aircraft, and the balance of vulnerability had changed once more. By the time Tomonaga led his formation into the attack, the Americans had had at least one hour to recover their aircraft and an hour or more in which to ready them for a second strike. The *Hiryu*, on the other hand, with virtually no strike force and a weakened fighter element, would again be reduced to the state that had prevailed throughout the First Carrier Striking Force before 1030. Even by his own logic Yamaguchi was at a disadvantage: one enemy carrier was certain to be ready or nearly ready to launch a strike against him while his own carrier was almost defenseless. The only possible course of action for Yamaguchi was to put as many miles between the *Hiryu* and the enemy as possible. With the balance of vulnerability changing sides, it was far more important for the Japanese to have the *Hiryu* available the next day, when the *Zuiho* and the *Hosho* would be on the scene and the *Junyo* and the *Ryujo* en route to add their support, than for the *Hiryu* to indulge in a course of action that smacked of self-immolation. There was no excuse for the *Hiryu* to loiter anywhere near the battle area. The Judy from the *Soryu* had found the *Hiryu* with ominous ease when she returned from her scouting mission, and far more seriously, at the very time Tomonaga and Hashimoto led their sections into the attack, the Japanese carrier force became aware that Fletcher's caution had paid off.

When Fletcher gave instructions for his flagship to fly off a scouting mission, his staff arranged for the ten Dauntlesses thus selected to fly in pairs. One of these pairs, which had flown for three hours and was en route back to the *Yorktown*, came across the First Carrier Striking Force.[90] At 1420 the *Chikuma* sighted the two American aircraft and began to lay a smokescreen, not that that was going to conceal the presence of the Japanese. Within a matter of minutes she and her sister ship started to use their main armament as well as their antiaircraft weapons against the intruders, and the *Hiryu* had flown off Zekes to shoot down the two enemy aircraft.[91] They failed, and in failing they should have given Yamaguchi and Kaku all the warning they needed. If the Americans could spare combat aircraft for reconnaissance at this stage of proceedings, it was hardly likely that they would follow them up with a social visit. Being discovered by the enemy should have been the signal for a high-speed dash to the west to get out of range, though even this might not have been successful. But at least the effort would have been more advisable than the course that was pursued. To stay in the general battle area, with a ruined strike force and virtually no fighter strength, was clearly a poor decision, perhaps the decision of a desperate admiral exhausted by the events of the previous twelve hours and sapped of sound judgment by the weeks of fatalism that had followed his being informed of the details of Operation MI. But even if Yamaguchi was unwise to keep the lone and weakened *Hiryu* in the danger area long after reasonable hope for further success had passed, blame was not his alone. At the least, responsibility had to be shared by Nagumo and Yamamoto, both of whom were in the process of redeploying the units and forces under their command in order to continue the battle.

The commander in chief of the Combined Fleet had received reports of the opening clashes with equanimity. He was not disturbed by the report of the need to strike a second time against Midway. This had been semi-expected, and arrangements had been made to cover it. He was equally unruffled by the reports of the presence of an enemy task force and the report that a carrier seemed to be with it. Whatever he might have thought about Nagumo and his fitness for command, Yamamoto judged that the carrier force was quite capable of looking after itself and fulfilling its mission. There was an initial alarm amongst the staff of the Combined Fleet when it was realized that the reported enemy strikes might fall after the second strike against Midway had been flown off but before the first had been recovered. For a brief period the staff believed that Nagumo might be facing the peril that had been so lightly discounted during the staff studies and war games that had preceded Operation MI. A quick check of the signals log showed that this fear was unfounded.[92] No one glimpsed at the tangle of events that led to the situation of 0837 onwards and the disasters that were to overwhelm Nagumo's command some two hours later. Once the immediate danger seemed to pass the old euphoria resurfaced amongst the fleet staff. It had a well-founded confidence that the Zekes could defend the First Carrier Striking Force and hold the enemy at arm's length, and as we have already seen the reaction of the staff of the Combined Fleet was so casual that one is forced to the reluctant conclusion that it lacked the imagination to realize the danger facing the fleet. Nagumo was expected to deal with the sighted enemy force with no difficulty, and when a carrier was tentatively identified it was the anticipation of victory rather than the fear of defeat that rose on board the *Yamato*. Yamamoto and his staff do not seem to have looked beyond the immediate situation. Any competent, alert and professional staff would have questioned a course of developments that invalidated the basic premise on which Operation MI was based. Nagumo did not have three days in which to subdue Midway and move into position to counter the Americans; the Japanese no longer had any chance of occupying Midway and getting the airstrip back into service to assist the operations of the Combined Fleet. The enemy was keeping pace with events and was not being forced to react to them. Yet no one on the *Yamato* questioned what an enemy task force was doing in the one position where it might be able to frustrate Nagumo's efforts, and no one questioned the process of events that had led to such a deployment. No one seems to have voiced the fear that because a maximum of three carriers remained to the enemy, it was inconceivable that the one carrier already identified should be alone.

With a battle clearly shaping up some 600 miles to the east, it was natural that there should be tension on the *Yamato*, but there was no basis for the "gratifying current of optimism" that went with it.[93] Certainly nothing could have prepared Yamamoto and his subordinates for the thunderbolt that arrived from Abe at 1050. The optimism that persisted despite the initial contact reports was killed when the next signal arrived: "Fires raging aboard *Kaga*, *Soryu* and *Akagi* resulting from attacks by enemy carrier and land-based planes. We plan to have *Hiryu* engage enemy carriers. We are temporarily withdrawing to the north to assemble our forces."[94] Yamamoto either said nothing or gave a grunt when he read the signal, depending on the source one reads. His face was said to have been "frozen" when he read the signal delivered by a silent Commander Yushiro Wada, chief signals officer of the fleet.[95]

Abe's signal, however, forced anything but a frozen response. Yamamoto had to make and then implement decisions. The personal command he was supposed to be exercising from his uncommunicative flagship could no longer remain the sham that it had been for the last week. For the first time in the war, in a sense for the first time in his life, Yamamoto had to take command of a situation, a situation that demanded inspired leadership and luck if the Japanese were to pull the situation round. Two things had to be done. First, the Main Body had to be taken immediately to the support of what remained of the First Carrier Striking Force. Second, all the Japanese formations had to be regrouped without delay. But it was unclear what general course of action to take, for the information Yamamoto had was incomplete. He was in the dark about the situation involving the *Akagi*, *Kaga* and *Soryu*. Yamamoto had no way of knowing if they had been able to fly off aircraft before they were hit or if any of the damaged carriers could be put back into service. Abe's initial report did not seem promising on either matter, and Nagumo certainly provided no reassurance when he came on the air from the *Nagara*. But even after the three fleet carriers were hit, the Japanese still had five carriers at sea, and excluding the aircraft with the *Hiryu*, some 120 or so fighters and bombers remained with the *Hosho*, *Zuiho*, *Ryujo* and *Junyo*. At 1050 it was far from clear that the First Carrier Striking Force had been overwhelmed by a disaster from which there was no recovery. Indeed, it was far from clear that the Japanese had decisively lost the air battle. For the eight or so hours of daylight that remained to Yamamoto after his receipt of Abe's signal, there was reason to believe that the verdict of the morning's encounter could be reversed. Inevitably, this was a belief raised falsely by the *Hiryu*'s erroneous reports of the afternoon, but even after the misfortunes that befell the *Akagi*, *Kaga* and *Soryu* the Japanese hoped that the loss of air superiority might only prove temporary. Yamamoto had no option but to try to continue the battle after he received news of the fate that had befallen Nagumo's command. The Japanese could not compensate for the disastrous turn of events unless they continued the battle, albeit in modified form. They could not break off the battle immediately after three carriers had been crippled. The battle had to be continued, and Yamamoto had to bring his force to the support of the First Carrier Striking Force and regroup his other formations. But in these matters he immediately encountered insurmountable problems of his own making. Any attempt to gather the threads of battle together again by bringing up forces in support of the *Hiryu* could only prove futile; the very dispersal of force previously deemed to be essential for the success of Operation MI now confounded all attempts to redeem the situation once the battle turned against the Combined Fleet. Yamamoto needed forces on hand immediately; this he did not have because regrouping would take time, and time was not available at this stage. Dispersal was all very well so long as the battle was won or at least developed favorably. Under any other circumstances it was a crippling liability. Command was forced upon Yamamoto as a result of the events of the morning, but despite the appearance to the contrary as a stream of orders flowed from the *Yamato* for the rest of the hours of daylight, command involved just one decision. The decision was to break off the battle, and it was not made until after midnight.

When the *Yamato* force received Abe's signal it was in the process of refueling amid the dense fog that earlier had concealed Nagumo during his approach to Midway. Getting the formation into action thus proved no easy matter, and it took more than an hour for Yamamoto to work his force up to 20 knots. Even at that speed he would need to steam for more than a day to reach the position of his three stricken carriers, and the Main Body was not making 20 knots due east because it had to zigzag as a routine precaution against enemy submarines. With the ships of the force all but out of sight of one another in the all-embracing fog, it was a reflection of the high standards of Japanese seamanship that no accidents occurred as fuel lines were jettisoned and the force worked up speed to come upon the scene of disaster with the least possible delay.[96]

During the time that the force was working up, the admiral and his staff conferred on the options open to the Combined Fleet. It appears that in common with the practice of many senior Japanese commanders, Yamamoto made no attempt to direct the proceedings but let his subordinates argue for an hour or more over the relative merits of various plans. But as discussion ran its course Yamamoto, unlike Nagumo and Nagano, made his own decisions, and he did not passively accept what seemed to be the general recommendation of his staff. The staff discussion was dominated by the topic of the First Carrier Striking Force and its misfortunes, but soon the deliberations were forced to focus on the one fact that became obvious after a signal from Nagumo was received on board the fleet flagship at 1130. From the *Nagara* Nagumo told Yamamoto that the *Akagi*, *Kaga* and *Soryu* had sustained "considerable damage" and would be unable to participate in any future operations.[97] It was what the Combined Fleet needed to know, though it was the last thing it wanted to hear. Except for the *Hiryu* the First

Carrier Striking Force was finished. Against this background the general trend of Yamamoto's thinking became clear in the series of orders that were transmitted to the various forces between 1220 and 1310. In his first order he issued the general instruction for all forces in the Midway area to engage the enemy. He gave the position of his own force, and he ordered Kakuta to bring the Second Carrier Striking Force southwards to join Nagumo at the earliest possible opportunity. He also ordered Kondo, with the Invasion Force Main Body, to detach part of his command to cover Tanaka and the transports, and he ordered the latter to set course to the northwest of Midway to await developments and further instructions. At the same time Yamamoto ordered the submarines off the Hawaiian Islands to move to a new patrol line along the meridian 168° W, between latitudes 26° and 36° N. In moving to their new patrol line the submarines would pass through the area where the enemy was operating.[98] Shortly afterwards Yamamoto elaborated his order to Tanaka with the more precise instruction to take the Transport Group to a position 500 miles to the west of Midway. There it would prove a safe distance from any force from the atoll, but it would still be sufficiently close to the objective to proceed with the planned invasion of the islands if things developed favorably.[99]

In an attempt to ensure that they did, at 1310 Yamamoto amplified his earlier instruction with a three-part order to all his forces. He temporarily suspended the planned invasions of Midway and Kiska and instructed all his forces to move to the scene of battle with the simple aim of contacting and engaging the enemy. He also instructed Kondo to detach another part of his force with orders to carry out a bombardment of Midway.[100] The general drift of Yamamoto's recast plans was becoming clear: Midway was to be neutralized and the battle area swamped by Japanese ships to secure the success that had eluded the hitherto successful First Carrier Striking Force.

These orders placed Kondo in a more than awkward situation. His immediate reaction to the turn of events had been to set course towards Nagumo without waiting for orders to do so. At 1227, just seven minutes after Yamamoto had issued the first of his orders, Kondo was able to tell the fleet commander that his Invasion Force Main Body was making for the First Carrier Striking Force at 28 knots.[101] But the order to detach a force to bombard Midway was not an easy one to comply with, for two reasons. First, in a fight between ships and a land target the odds invariably favored the latter; this fact had been well known to all navies for generations. Second, any force that he sent against Midway would have to use the cover of dark to guard it during its approach and would have to be well clear of the atoll by first light. There was the danger of being caught by aircraft from Midway, and scarcely less intimidating was the danger posed to any bombardment force by American submarines. The obvious candidates for a bombardment mission were the four heavy cruisers of Kurita's Close Support Group, but Kondo toyed with the idea of sending his battle squadron to support the night attack on Midway's installations. The effect of 14-in gunfire could well prove the difference between the success and the failure of a bombardment, but in the end Kondo rather reluctantly abandoned the idea. The battleships were over 400 miles from Midway, and even if they made a beeline for the atoll at top speed it was unlikely that they would get into action during the night. Any attempt to rush to the islands was likely to leave the battle force exposed to any air attack that might materialize the following day, and for no useful purpose. Kurita's cruisers were about 100 miles nearer the atoll than the battleships, but both Kurita and Kondo knew that even with the cruisers' shorter distance and higher speed, they were being set a task that had a perilously narrow margin against error. Kurita, in fact, was reluctant to attack Midway at all unless he had the support of Kondo's main force, complete with whatever air cover the *Zuiho* might provide. Neither was forthcoming, and Kurita had to accept the fact that his proposed bombardment would have to be unsupported. In any event, he had no alternative but to comply with Kondo's direct order, especially when it was in accord with Yamamoto's instructions. Accordingly, at about 1500 Kurita began his approach to Midway at 32 knots, his four cruisers unsupported but for their two escorting destroyers.[102]

Two different matters arise from these assorted developments. The first is a question: Why were there no warning orders either drafted or sent after 0728, when the initial enemy contact report was received? In the event, the five hours between contact with the enemy and Yamamoto's first orders did not make the difference between defeat and victory, and even if the orders of 1220 had been sent out some hours before it seems unlikely, but not impossible, that the course of events might have been changed. But even allowing for the fact that the staff of the Combined Fleet expected success to follow in the wake of contact with the enemy, it does seem a little strange that no steps were taken in the *Yamato* to consider redeployment. After the contact of 0728 the Japanese were going to be involved in a naval battle, perhaps not the battle that they wanted and expected, but some sort of battle that someone would have to command. With Nagumo committed to battle off Midway Yamamoto could no longer continue to play the role of casual, taciturn or uncommunicative spectator, especially when he had a better knowledge of what was happening than the commander of his vanguard. That no warning orders were discussed or prepared after 0728 is surprising.

The second matter, however, is different because it did not affect command. Put at its simplest, the problem was what Japanese formations were supposed to achieve and how they were to survive without air cover.

As we have seen, Kondo and Kurita hesitated to send heavy units into action in waters controlled by the enemy's air power. They realized this would be asking for trouble. Yamamoto might order the Second Carrier Striking Force down from the north; he might order the bombardment of Midway; he might hope that the *Hiryu* could turn the tables—but there was no blinking one fact. The *Ryujo* and the *Junyo* could not get their aircraft into action in the Midway area before other forces closed up on what remained of the First Carrier Striking Force. In the face of enemy air superiority these forces could not be expected to operate in the general area of the atoll without the protection afforded by carriers.

But it was not Yamamoto, Kondo and Kurita who had to deal with this problem immediately. It was Nagumo. Even before his flag replaced that of Kimura over the *Nagara*, the light cruiser had received word from her larger cousin, the *Chikuma*, that the enemy carrier force was now but 90 miles to the east of the badly scattered First Carrier Striking Force. [103] For Nagumo this information was both alarming and promising. It posed the danger of annihilation. Nagumo's formation was then divided into three separate parts: the *Nagara* with five destroyers; the three stricken carriers, each with their escorting destroyers; and the *Hiryu* and her consorts. If the enemy advanced further disaster might easily befall the Japanese. But an enemy advance was unlikely, as Nagumo and his staff knew. With the battle going well there was little reason for the Americans to close the range and present the Japanese with a chance to redeem their fortunes. On the other hand, if the enemy was only 90 miles away, the Japanese might yet be able to force a surface engagement. This course was urged upon Nagumo by members of his staff. Not surprisingly the admiral, torn between various options and no doubt conscious of the likely outcome of a chase towards the east, hesitated until 1150, when he signaled Yamamoto that he intended to regroup his force to the north after attacking the enemy. At 1153 he gave the order, repeated at 1156 and 1159, for his units to form into a battle line, with the destroyers in the van, in an effort to join battle with the enemy. [104]

For more than an hour Nagumo's ships converged from various directions to comply with his instructions, but without any advantage of speed over the enemy the Japanese could not close the range. In fact, it is difficult to see the point of this particular deployment: Nagumo's order of 1159 gave his ships a bearing of 170 degrees on which to steer and instructed them to make 12 knots, at which speed they would not be able to contact the enemy. But at about 1300 a seaplane from the *Tone* that had been sent out to trail the American task forces reported that the enemy had reversed course to the east, and admiral and staff realized that the Americans had no intention of giving the Japanese the chance that they, under similar circumstances, would never have offered a beaten foe; the Americans had no inclination to become involved in a hazardous brawl when they could keep their distance and pound the enemy with complete inpunity.[105] Shortly afterwards, there fore, Nagumo decided to retire westwards for the moment, though he hoped that after dark he might be able to resume the chase. Any hope that Nagumo entertained of closing the enemy in the hours after his own force had been shattered was no more than a chimera. Between about 1000 and 1100 the Americans had been steering towards the southwest, but after 1100 they had turned back to catch the wind and were then steering a little to the south of east. The first report that Nagumo had received from the *Chikuma* had been erroneous; the report from the *Tone* had been accurate but related. At this stage of the battle Nagumo had no chance whatsoever of engaging in a surface battle, though events were to show that in the final analysis the Japanese failure to force such an action at this time left them unable to force it at any time. Perhaps the only notable matter to come out of this rather strange set of events was that Nagumo's emasculated task force was the first Japanese formation to withdraw voluntarily in the face of enemy air superiority.

Nagumo rejoined the *Hiryu* at about 1445 and formed his ships into a tight protective ring around the last of the carriers, the cruisers and destroyers now but about 1,600 yards from their last hope.[106] Ten minutes before he joined company with Yamaguchi's flagship, however, Nagumo sent a signal to Kakuta which was taken in by the *Yamato* at 1430. The signal gave Nagumo's present position and set out his intention to head north after destroying the enemy task force to the east. Presumably the latter was to be achieved by the *Hiryu*, but if there was an element of ambiguity on this matter the instruction to Kakuta was clear enough: he was to bring the Second Carrier Striking Force south to rendezvous with what remained of the senior formation without delay.[107] Kakuta's reply, received by Yamamoto and Nagumo at 1530, marked the beginning of the end of the battle as far as the Japanese were concerned.

When Yamamoto's initial orders had been received by Kakuta, the Second Carrier Striking Force had been involved in the second-phase operations that the admiral had deemed necessary if he was to neutralize American power in the eastern Aleutians and allow the landings in the western islands to proceed as planned. It took time—time Yamamoto and Nagumo no longer had available to waste—for Kakuta to recover all his aircraft, regroup his force and turn towards the south. Even by 1500 Kakuta and his two now-vital carriers were still only about 120 miles to the southwest of Dutch Harbor. Kakuta's response to Nagumo's signal was to come south at top speed, but that was decided by the speed of his slowest unit, the 22½-knot *Junyo*. Moreover, his intention to comply with orders was qualified by the need to refuel the Second Carrier Striking Force the following morning. Thereafter Kakuta would be able to steer for an interception course.[108]

se disallowed the possibility of the Second Carrier Strik-
to the support of what was left of the First Carrier
il the afternoon of 7 June at the earliest. This the staff of
et should have known from the plan of campaign, and in
ould have been able to work it out for themselves. The
ne was too late for Kakuta to have any influence on the
he trail would be cold. Yamamoto needed the Second
Carrier Striking Force in the battle off Midway immediately, and he could
have had it were it not for his preoperational determination not to have the
force in this location. The regrouping that was essential was out of reach.
Thus any Japanese attempt to regroup on what remained of the fourth and
over the next two days had to be made with just the *Hosho*, the *Zuiho* and the
Hiryu. Given this situation only two conclusions were possible. First, both
individually and collectively the *Hosho* and the *Zuiho* were inadequate for
the task they were now called upon to discharge. The *Hosho* had just six
Jeans and nine Claudes; the *Zuiho* had only two dozen aircraft evenly
divided between Claudes and Jeans. Second, the *Hosho* and the *Zuiho*, and to
a lesser extent the *Ryujo* and the *Junyo*, could only have value if they came up
to support the *Hiryu*. One of the essential conditions for the Combined
Fleet's regrouping was the continued survival of the *Hiryu* and of as many
aircraft as possible. Yet here was the root of the problem. These light
carriers were incapable of forcing a favorable decision when the main
strength of the First Air Fleet had been broken. Theirs was a supplementary rather than a shock role, and they could not turn defeat into
victory—especially after more bad news began to come over the air during
the early evening. At 1755, with just one hour to go before sunset, Yamamoto learned that the fate that had befallen the *Akagi*, *Kaga* and *Soryu* had at
last overwhelmed Yamaguchi's flagship.[109] With the *Hiryu* gone the way of
the others, the end of the battle was in sight; it might linger for some time to
come, but the issue had been decided once and for all.

During the course of the day fortune slowly settled upon the Americans.
Throughout the morning the two sides had fought for the initiative, the
balance tilting one way and then the other before the Americans had won a
stunning victory with what was in effect their last effort. Thereafter the
Hiryu had had the misfortune to strike one and not two enemy carriers, and
in failing to hit two she left the initiative firmly in American hands. The
Enterprise and the *Hornet* had escaped attention throughout the morning and
early afternoon, though in the last hours before dusk only the former was
really in a position to launch a further strike against the enemy. Even as the
Yorktown was undergoing her second attack the *Enterprise* was preparing
Dauntlesses for what proved to be the last strike mission of the day. If this
mission was successful, the American victory would be complete.

As we have seen, when Tomonaga's torpedo bombers were moving into the attack against the *Yorktown*, the *Enterprise* was moving appreciably closer to total victory without any effort on her own behalf. At the very time the Japanese carried out their second attack on the *Yorktown*, the *Hiryu* was contacted by one of the scouts that Fletcher had sent out around midday. The scout patrol that found the *Hiryu* was the one detailed to the most westerly of the five search areas selected by the staff of Task Force 17, and the lead pilot, Lieutenant Samuel Adams, made a textbook report that was described by the U.S. Navy's official historian as "the best, clearest and most accurate carrier plane contact of the entire war."[110] Sent first by voice and then in code at 1445,[111] Adams's report read: "One carrier, two battleships, three heavy cruisers, four destroyers. 31° 15′ North 179° 05′ West. Course 000° Speed 15."[112]

Adams and his wingman made their contact just before 1430, and it was this contact, as we have noted, that should have convinced the Japanese of the need to get the *Hiryu* out of the area as quickly as possible, especially when the combat air patrol failed to account for the two snoopers. At this stage the *Nagara* claimed to have been attacked by a Dauntless, improbable though this appears.[113] She did not order the *Hiryu* (by semaphore) to set a course to the west until 1630.[114] By then, of course, it was too late for the *Hiryu* to seek safety in flight.

But before the *Enterprise* could launch a strike against the *Hiryu* in response to Adams's report, the problems of the *Yorktown* assumed alarming dimensions that threatened the American freedom of action and the extent of the victory then in the making. The *Yorktown* had survived her ordeal by dive-bombing with something akin to aplomb, but the torpedo attack by the Kates proved quite another matter.

The two torpedoes that hit the *Yorktown* struck within half a minute of one another, at about 1441. The first ripped into the fuel compartments outboard two of the boiler rooms that were divided by a bulkhead. The compartments and rooms were all destroyed by the explosion of this single torpedo. The watch that had kept the single boiler in action after the *Yorktown* had been crippled by the Vals were all killed in the explosion. They had come off duty after their exertions and were resting in the area where the first torpedo hit the ship. The second torpedo struck the *Yorktown* just forward of this scene of devastation. It exploded in a generator room, killing every one in it.[115]

The effect of these two torpedoes exploding within the *Yorktown* was disastrous. The immediate result was that she was torn open along some 65 feet of her length. The *Yorktown* had been trying to comb the tracks of the torpedoes from Hashimoto's formation when she was struck, and she did not have time to bring her rudder back before the torpedoes hit. The

The *Yorktown* After a Torpedo Hit

explosions jammed her rudder at 15 degrees to port, but her loss of steering was unimportant compared with her loss of power and her list.[116] Immediately on being struck she took on a 6-degree list to port and the sea rushed into fuel compartments whose contents were vaporized. A yellow haze engulfed the carrier's wounded port side, and the torpedo that did this damage also opened the way for the ocean to tumble unchecked into the *Yorktown*.[117] With tons of water rushing into the ship and the carrier rolling uncontrollably under the impact of the torpedo blows, the clinometer briefly recorded a 30-degree list. The carrier eased back to 17 degrees, then slowly settled until the clinometer showed a list of 26 degrees at 1455. There the list stabilized for the moment.[118]

The seawater that produced the list to port put out the fires in the two boiler rooms that took the full extent of the torpedo's detonation. This blast also extinguished the fires in the starboard boiler rooms, and both they and the engine rooms began to flood. The sick bay stood in danger of being flooded and the wounded had to be evacuated quickly. The force of the explosions wrecked and warped many of the watertight doors up to the level of the third deck, and with water reaching the first platform level in the

The *Yorktown* Listing Heavily to Port After Being Attacked

forward and aft engine rooms within a matter of minutes after the ship was
hit, the *Yorktown* stood in grave danger of slow but progressive flooding that
could not be checked.[119] With boiler and engine rooms flooded or flooding
and the forward generator room destroyed, the *Yorktown* lacked power;
without power she could not move, repair her damage or shift her oil to get
back on an even keel. The only power she retained was provided by the
emergency diesel generator that cut in when power failed, but this could
barely provide the ship with lighting and in any event its functioning had
distinct disadvantages. The generator's exhausts were next to the bridge,
and the noise they made deafened her men so that they could not function
properly. Moreover, the generator could not be switched off because its
controls were underwater. As Buckmaster noted, the only thing that
drowned out the sound of the generator was the sound of air being forced up
through the ship by the sea.[120] With damage to the carrier so extensive,
Buckmaster reluctantly ordered the carrier abandoned at 1458.

In the light of what was to happen over the next two days this order was premature. The *Yorktown*'s wounds were not serious and the carrier could have been saved. But these were the early days of the war, and the Americans had yet to learn how effective their damage control arrangements were. This class of aircraft carrier was exceptionally well compartmentalized. Subdivision below the waterline was both extensive and elaborate, and in this respect the Americans probably led all other navies. With only a 4-in armor belt and 3-in-thick horizontal armor, divided between the hangar deck and main armor deck, the whole emphasis of passive defense in the *Yorktown* class was upon containing the extent of damage.* These powers of resistance were unproven in mid-1942. When Buckmaster gave orders to abandon ship he did not know how effective construction and damage control would be, and he had no means of knowing if the damage incurred in this action would open up the old wounds sustained in the Coral Sea. All he knew was that the *Yorktown* was in danger of capsizing, and that if she did she could take more than 2,000 men with her to the bottom. The safety of his crew was Buckmaster's proper concern, and his decision to leave the *Yorktown* to her fate was one that was endorsed by Fletcher, though it seems to have blighted his subsequent career.[121]†

The process of abandoning ship was orderly. For the second time inside a month an American fleet carrier was abandoned under ideal conditions—a calm sea that endangered neither the men in the water nor the stability of the rescuing destroyers, and no enemy attack to threaten the escorts when their screws were surrounded by men in the water. Rescue operations were directed by Captain Edward P. Sauer. He had become senior officer in the destroyers when the *Balch*, having been detached by Spruance, joined Task Force 17.[122] Under his direction all the destroyers stopped and lowered their boats, then resumed their screening duties while two or three of their number moved in close to pick up the men in the water. About 2,300 officers and men were rescued, nearly 1,800 of them by the *Benham*, *Balch* and *Russell*.[123] With so many men aboard, these destroyers had stability problems. The *Russell*, for example, had to keep her rescued men below deck and ballast her empty oil tanks with seawater to avoid becoming top heavy.[124] Even though there were certain untoward events during this phase of operations—some of the *Yorktown*'s wounded were left behind in the darkness and confusion, and certain routine security procedures were similarly overlooked—the overall process of quitting the ship and recovering the carrier's crew was carried out with remarkable smoothness.

---

*The main armor deck met the top of the belt, thereby enclosing the ship's vitals.
†Buckmaster rose to the rank of vice admiral but never again went to sea after the loss of the *Yorktown*. This reflected a certain ambivalence on the part of his superiors, a compromise between approval of a decision that was correct and a reticence that suggested that Buckmaster had not done the right thing.

The *Yorktown*'s Crew Abandoning Ship

The ordeal of the *Yorktown* coincided with receipt of Adams's report of the whereabouts of the *Hiryu*. While the crew of the *Yorktown* set about trying to save first their ship and then themselves, Task Force 16 prepared to act on the contact report. In the event, it managed its planned attack badly. Spruance instructed Browning to put wheels in motion for an attack at about 1445, and by this time the *Enterprise* should have had the time to set up an attack with relative ease. Thirty minutes later the *Hornet* still had to be issued orders. It was then that she was informed that the location of the last remaining enemy carrier was unknown. That the *Hornet* could have contributed little to an attack at this stage does not excuse the mismanagement of a strike mission by the staff of Task Force 16 for the second time that day. The *Enterprise* turned into wind and began to fly off bombers even before the *Hornet* received orders to join the attack, but at least for this afternoon attack the dangers presented by a divided effort were not so great as they had been during the morning operations. By the afternoon the enemy had been gravely weakened and no longer possessed the offensive power that might have made the Americans pay for their mistakes, and his defensive power had similarly been sapped. Moreover, the same vulnerability that had plagued the Japanese during the morning returned after the attack on the *Yorktown*. At this point the *Hiryu* was exhausted. She had been involved in more than nine hours of constant action, in the course of which she had flown off three strike missions and battled with an estimated hundred enemy aircraft.[125] The carrier's weakened state concealed the shortcomings of staff organization and procedures within Task Force 16, which were to resurface on later occasions with graver consequences.[126] As it was, the lack of coordination between the *Enterprise* and the *Hornet* did not prove serious because the flagship's bombers were capable of dealing with the *Hiryu* by themselves.

Spruance's second and final attack of the day began when the *Enterprise* turned back into the wind and at 1530 started to launch her Dauntlesses.[127] She flew off twenty-five, but one was forced to turn back after it had taken off, leaving a round two dozen, ten of which were from the *Enterprise* itself.

The flagship provided six scouts and four bombers for this attack, and all were armed with 1,000-lb bombs. The other fourteen were refugees from the *Yorktown*, all armed with 500-lb bombs.[128] The plan of attack gave the lion's share of the intended spoils to the *Enterprise*'s aircraft. They were detailed to go for the enemy carrier, the others for the escorts.[129]

No escort flew with the Dauntlesses. Task Force 16 was so depleted, given the loss of half of the *Hornet*'s fighter squadron, that it was decided to keep all the available Wildcats for the combat air patrol rather than provide an escort for the fighters.[130] But even as the *Enterprise* launched her dive-bombers, extra help was arriving from an entirely unexpected source. To the considerable alarm of the fleet, aircraft were detected approaching from the south soon after 1500; fortunately these proved to be those Dauntlesses from the *Hornet* that had sought refuge and succor on Midway. Now, refueled and briefed, the eleven aircraft began landing on the *Hornet* at 1527, just before the *Enterprise* began to launch.[131] There was to be no repeat of the morning's fiasco with Dauntlesses circling while they waited for aircraft that never took off. The *Enterprise*'s aircraft went ahead with their mission, leaving the *Hornet*'s aircraft to catch up as best they could. When all the returning aircraft were refueled and prepared, the *Hornet* was able to spot a total of sixteen Dauntlesses for the attack. These began launching at 1603, but by the time they found the *Hiryu* it was clear that any effort they made against her would be superfluous.[132]

The caution that led to withholding the Wildcats for the defense of Task Force 16 was wise, for the Japanese had intended to strike again at the Americans with whatever force they had available at the end of the day. As we have seen, Yamaguchi wanted to make one final effort in late afternoon, and had he held to his initial plan the Wildcats of the *Enterprise* and the *Hornet* would have had to justify their existence. But Yamaguchi postponed his launch from 1630 to 1800.[133] This decision cost the *Hiryu* her last opportunity to strike at her tormentors before she herself was crippled by the attack from the *Enterprise*. Just as earlier in the day Dauntlesses from the *Enterprise* and the *Yorktown* conspired to deny Nagumo the minutes he needed to launch a full assault against the American task force(s), so at about 1703 the same Dauntlesses, this time flown from just the *Enterprise*, managed to deny Yamaguchi his last faint hope of success when they struck and devastated the *Hiryu*.

Two factors convinced Yamaguchi to defer his final strike of the day. His pilots were his initial concern. They, like the rest of the crew of the *Hiryu*, had been in action since before sunrise, and had not eaten for more than twelve hours. Yamaguchi put back his proposed strike until after they had eaten. This alone, however, was not sufficient cause for postponement. The real reason for delay was the pitifully small force that he had left for his fourth and final effort of the day. Though the *Hiryu* claimed only to have lost four Zekes in the battles over the First Carrier Striking Force and relatively few when they had accompanied the various strike missions, she had only six left at this stage; these could not be spared to escort the nine remaining Kates and Vals for their final attack on the enemy. To send nine unescorted bombers against the enemy could only have one ending, and in desperation Yamaguchi resorted to the same tactic that Hara had employed at the Coral Sea—a night attack on the enemy carrier force. The reason for this decision was simple. Japanese bombers would never be able to get through the enemy combat air patrol in broad daylight, but in the gloom of twilight they might have a chance. The Italians at Matapan and the *Bismarck* in the Atlantic had been caught by carrier attacks at sunset—perhaps the Japanese would enjoy similar good fortune. On this basis Yamaguchi made the decision to launch a strike at 1800 after his aircrew had eaten a hurried meal and the Judy that had come from the *Soryu* had taken off to find the enemy and lead the Kates and Vals to their targets.[134] In one vital respect this attack was certain to be different from the one that Hara had improvised in the Coral Sea four weeks before. On that occasion he had not hesitated to switch on his lights to recover his aircraft; with enemy aircraft and submarines known to be off Midway, Yamaguchi would not be able to do the same.

The Dauntlesses from the *Enterprise* never gave the *Hiryu* the chance to put the recast plan into effect. Led by Gallaher, the Dauntlesses came upon the *Akagi*, *Kaga* and *Soryu* at about 1445. They had no trouble detecting the wakes of ships steaming at high speed some 40 miles to the north. Belatedly, the Japanese were making 30 knots towards the setting sun in an effort to outrun the enemy before launching their own strike. With their advantage of range over the Americans this was what the Japanese should have done from the start, but now it was too late. Gallaher led his force around to the southwest, climbing as he did so until he reached 19,000 feet. It was his intention to come out of the afternoon sun against the *Hiryu*, but this plan miscarried.[135] The Dauntlesses were sighted by the *Chikuma*, and the *Hiryu* was alerted just as the dive-bombers reached their push-over point.[136] The Japanese carrier began to throw up flak in her defense and the Zekes from her combat air patrol belatedly turned to deal with the Dauntlesses. The *Hiryu* threw her rudder hard over, executing a full 90-degree turn to starboard.[137] At 30 knots the *Hiryu* made a small and elusive target, and in this first phase of the battle Kaku outguessed and outfought the attackers. All the bombs aimed at the *Hiryu* were dodged. But unfortunately for the Japanese the dive-bombers from the *Yorktown*'s squadron did not carry out their part of the attack as they should have done. With the two most senior officers in the squadron in the *Astoria*, the acting commander of the squadron, Lieutenant David Shumway, did not lead his bombers against the escorts. Rather he held back to see the result of the Gallaher's strike, and when that failed he led his bombers into an attack on the carrier that to date had twice crippled their own ship.[138]

Shumway and the Dauntlesses from the *Yorktown* had to contend with one problem that had barely begun to materialize when Gallaher attacked. Though complete surprise had not been achieved and one of their number was shot down before it was able to carry out its attack, the Dauntlesses from the *Enterprise*'s two squadrons faced a rather disorganized opposition. The matter of seconds that encompassed the attack by Gallaher and his men provided the Japanese with the chance to put together a much more serious opposition to Shumway's formation. The flak was more intense, and this time the Zekes pulled out everything in defense of their last surviving flight deck. Some of the Zeke pilots are supposed to have performed acrobatic prodigies in defense of the *Hiryu*, looping to attack more than one Dauntless in the course of a single dive, but these efforts were not good enough. The Japanese simply did not have enough Zekes to deal with any attack, and the *Hiryu*, a sister ship of the *Soryu*, was hopelessly vulnerable to damage. Two of the Dauntlesses were shot down, and three more were so badly damaged that they were written off after being recovered by the *Enterprise*, but between them the *Yorktown*'s dive-bombers avenged their ship with four direct hits on the *Hiryu* and a shower of near misses.[139] In fact, such was the immediate success of the first of the *Yorktown*'s Dauntlesses that the last two switched their attentions to the *Haruna*, but to no effect.[140] The American attack lasted no more than four or five minutes, and recovery of the twenty-one surviving Dauntlesses was completed by the *Enterprise* at 1834, just before sunset.[141]

This was not the last American attack of the day, but it was the last that registered success. The Dauntlesses from the *Hornet* were still to arrive on the scene as Gallaher and Shumway led their formations back to the *Enterprise*, and even more aircraft were coming, both from Midway and direct from Pearl Harbor.* It was as if everyone wanted to claim the honor of having delivered the last attack of 4 June.

The aircraft that attacked the escort ships of the First Carrier Striking Force after the *Hiryu* was devastated were the sixteen Dauntlesses from the *Hornet*; six B-17 Flying Fortresses flown from Pearl Harbor to Midway as

*The latter were numbered amongst the sixty B-17Es that the army air force deployed to Oahu between 18 May and 10 June as part of its defensive effort both before and during the battle for Midway. These were intended to replace the twenty-seven B-17Cs and seven B-17Ds then on station, these earlier marks being no longer considered fit for front-line operations; the E version carried a much heavier defensive armament and was a much more stable platform than the earlier marks. Most of these heavy bombers were kept at Oahu and not allowed to proceed to Midway. The price that the Fortresses had to pay for going into battle direct from Oahu was carrying only half their normal bomb loads; otherwise they would not have the range to get into action.[142]

reinforcements for the air group but diverted en route to attack the enemy; six Fortresses from Midway itself; and eleven Dauntlesses and Vindicators from the marine corps' Midway-based squadron which had survived the exchanges of the morning. The first three forces attacked over a single one-hour period, between about 1730 and 1832, and their attacks over-lapped. Each force bombed the enemy when it was in the company of at least one of the other forces. The exception was the marine formation. Six Dauntlesses and five Vindicators took off from Midway at 1900, after nightfall, to attack the carriers reported to be burning to the northwest of the atoll. No trace of the enemy was found, and the aircraft were forced to turn back. Ten managed to find Midway again, being helped back to the atoll by the reflection of the fires burning in the storage tanks on Sand Island, the illumination provided by searchlights, and homing beacons. One Dauntless, flown by Norris, the squadron commander, was lost in a down draft. Thus the 241st Marine Scout Bomber Squadron lost two commanding officers on 4 June.[143]

For all their efforts, no hits were recorded by any of the aircraft that went into action against the Japanese after the *Hiryu* was caught. The *Hornet*'s dive-bombers and the Fortresses between them launched their bombs against the *Haruna*, *Chikuma*, *Tone* and *Hiryu*, but apart from a strafing run by one of the Fortresses from Pearl Harbor, the Japanese ships escaped with nothing more serious than minor damage and shakings from near misses.[144] The *Haruna* had a few stern plates bent and loosened by a near miss, while the rangefinder for her main battery was jammed by another bomb which exploded in the water alongside. Running repairs were quickly made, and whatever slight damage was inflicted on any of the escorts at this time was shrugged off with indifference.[145]

But the *Hiryu* could not do the same. She had been caught in exactly the same state as the *Akagi*, *Kaga* and *Soryu* before her, with fueled and armed aircraft on her decks, fuel lines open and ordnance not properly stored away. In all probability her crew were so exhausted after seventeen hours of servicing and fighting the air group that the neglect of safety precautions was inevitable. Be that as it may, the price that the Japanese had to pay for their habitual carelessness was a heavy one. Of the four bombs that hit the carrier, two struck forward, two amidships. If any others hit, their effect was lost amid the series of explosions that immediately tore through the ship. One bomb bodily lifted the whole of the forward elevator out of its well and left it propped up against the island.[146] Though much bigger and better built than the *Soryu*, the *Hiryu* shared her sister ship's weakness: the flight and upper hangar decks provided part of the ship's longitudinal main strength. With three massive elevators to weaken the decks, the points of stress and weakness were the wells (hence the way Japanese carriers, when struck, had self-induced explosions that ripped upwards and outwards

The *Hiryu* Smoldering on the Morning of 5 June

rather than into the ship). The bombs that ripped the *Hiryu* open destroyed most of her fire-fighting equipment, but the *Hiryu* had with her four destroyers which came alongside to pour the ocean over her wounds. Moreover, the *Hiryu*'s machinery was undamaged, and with power she had some means of fighting the fires. Even after being struck the carrier could still make 28 knots, and at 2100 one of her escorting destroyers, the *Makikumo*, noted that this speed was still being maintained.[147] Kaku hoped that by maintaining this speed he could get clear of the battle area and bring the fires under control, but there was never any real hope for this. The 21,900-ton carrier was no better able to absorb punishment of this kind than any of the other members of the First Carrier Striking Force, and the decision to keep the carrier at full speed and to use her own power to fight the fires had one inevitable result. Power could only be provided if the crews of the boiler and engine rooms stayed at their posts as the fires worked their way downwards through the ship. They continued at their battle stations even as the paint on the ceilings over them melted to reveal decks that were glowing red hot. Most of the men were grilled alive in these rooms, and it is worth noting that Nagumo in his official report stated that the conduct of the *Hiryu*'s black gang "can only be described as heroic." For a service that regarded death as the minimum obligation, this comment must come close to being a supreme accolade.[148]

After 2123 the *Hiryu* lost power as the members of her boiler and engine room crews were overcome. After that time the *Hiryu* began to drift and slowly settle to port. Still the fight to save the ship continued, even after a mighty explosion ripped through her shortly before midnight. It was not until 0230 that the crew was mustered before abandoning ship. By then the *Hiryu* had acquired a list of 15 degrees to port and Kaku was in the same position Buckmaster had found himself in twelve hours earlier. At 0315 the transfer of some 800 survivors to the destroyer *Kazegumo* began, the first man to leave the *Hiryu* being the ensign charged with the safety of the ship's portrait of the emperor. In the face of overwhelming disaster discipline, ceremony and ritual were observed until the end. The national flag and Yamaguchi's flag were lowered to the strains of the national anthem, while the exchange of momentos and courtesies during the final scenes ensured that none of the staff and ship's officers stayed behind to share the fate that Yamaguchi and Kaku accepted.[149] Yamaguchi's last order was for the *Makikumo* to complete with her torpedoes what the Americans had begun with their bombs; then he and Kaku went their separate ways to join 414 of their companions in death.[150]

CHAPTER 15

Dusk and Dust

Sunset over the battlefield found all the major formations in the Midway area, Japanese and American alike, steering towards the east, though for different reasons. The Japanese were steaming at high speed ever further from their homeland in the hope that during the hours of darkness they might yet be able to reverse the disasters of the day. The Americans steered a similar course towards the east precisely to deny the Japanese this chance. Throughout the hours of daylight the Americans withheld from the enemy the victory that he had so casually and confidently expected. With sunset Spruance had absolutely no intention of presenting the Japanese with a chance to redress the present balance of losses.

Spruance had no doubt about his priorities, and he was prepared to act decisively on them despite criticism. Like Nimitz at Pearl Harbor, by sunset he knew that a great victory was in the making, notwithstanding the misfortunes of the *Yorktown*. By that time three enemy carriers had been burning for more than eight hours, and if the Japanese had been unable to bring these fires under control in that time they would hardly be able to do so during the night. The three carriers were obviously doomed, and now, in the last hour or so of daylight, a fourth enemy carrier had been reduced to a similar state. Thus far strong attritional tactics had worked with an effectiveness far beyond anything that could have been reasonably anticipated. But an hour or so after the fourth and last enemy carrier had been crippled and set on fire by dive-bombers from the *Enterprise*, Flying Fortresses coming upon the scene from Midway were attacked by Zekes flying combat air patrol.[1]

Contact with Zekes at this stage of proceedings could mean one of two things. Either the fighters could be now-homeless refugees from that fourth and last carrier, using up their remaining fuel before they ditched, or they could be from a fifth and thus far undetected carrier. Intelligence summaries had warned that a fifth carrier might be present in the enemy's order of battle. The possibility declined in the course of the day as combat sightings revealed that there were no more than four enemy carriers off Midway, but at sunset the Americans were not in a position to take chances. They had no idea of what might be to the west, and they had no good reason to try to find out during the night. Intelligence had credited the enemy with two to four battleships and eight or nine heavy cruisers.[2] If this kind of strength was indeed to the west of Midway and coming east at sunset, there was powerful inducement for the Americans to steer to the east to keep the Japanese at arm's length. They could handle trouble better in the light of the following morning.

At dusk on 4 June Spruance had one overriding priority—to ensure the safety of his own task force. The defense of Midway was clearly his second priority. Inflicting further loss on the Japanese was his third priority, but it was much inferior to the other two for the moment. With the approach of night, when carriers lost their value, Spruance had no option but to set course to the east to keep his task force beyond the reach of the enemy yet still close enough to Midway to support the atoll if the Japanese tried to go through with the invasion attempt despite their losses. Thus at 1915, some three minutes after the *Enterprise* and the *Hornet* joined company after having recovered their aircraft, Spruance settled Task Force 16 on a course due east at a speed of 15 knots. Five minutes later he was rejoined by the *Vincennes* and the *Pensacola*, directed to rejoin Spruance by Fletcher some 35 minutes earlier. Fletcher himself brought the major part of his truncated task force to a station some ten miles to the southwest of Task Force 16 after 2000, and he remained in company with Spruance until midnight.[3]

Spruance was prepared to leave the night to his submarines and the enemy, and as we have seen only the one rather ill-judged mission by the marines from Midway departed from the policy of passive defense adopted by the Americans for the hours of darkness. This particular mission had one unanticipated result. Because the Dauntlesses and Vindicators spent so much time looking first for the enemy and then for Midway before the air station switched on its searchlights and homing beacons, the recovery of the bomber formation was not completed before 0145.[4] The late hour meant in effect that these aircraft and their pilots would not be able to take part in any operations before and around dawn.

By steaming at 15 knots on a course of due east Spruance covered some 82 miles by midnight, Task Force 16 then being some 250 miles northeast of Midway.[5] He planned to kill time in that general position until the arrival of daylight, since there he would be well placed to move to support Midway if the Japanese showed any sign of seeing their operation through to the bitter end. If the Japanese main forces continued to come eastwards during the night, the American carriers would be ideally placed to strike at them in the morning without much possibility of being struck in return. On the other hand, if the Japanese turned back the Americans would have all the hours of daylight to go after them at high speed and force a decision. The course of the next day's events would depend on the decisions made by the Japanese; Spruance was willing to accept that his course of action would be decided by a combination of Japanese decisions and the effectiveness of his scouting forces. On the morning of the fifth Spruance was prepared to react to events, but to do so effectively he needed good reconnaissance—and in this matter his hopes were misplaced.

Once the decision was made by Spruance to turn Task Force 16 away to the east, his problems ended for the moment. The Americans had to wait upon events. The same was not true for the Japanese, who were in the position of having to initiate action. Their problems had begun from the time that Operation MI departed from the script and they had to make decisions. By nightfall the battle had entered a new phase in which certain critical steps would have to be taken.

After issuing his orders at 1220 Yamamoto had some four hours of relatively untroubled steaming to the east with his battle force while his formations began to react to their new instructions. There was nothing else that Yamamoto could do at this stage other than hope that the *Hiryu*'s attacks would help salvage the disasters of the day. After the situation report of 1150 (sent when Nagumo resumed command of his force from the *Nagara*), Yamamoto received no direct word of what was happening in front of him until 1615. It was then that Yamaguchi came onto the air with a situation report that for the first time told Yamamoto that he faced an enemy with three carriers, five heavy cruisers and fifteen destroyers. Yamaguchi added to this report of the enemy's strength that the *Hiryu*'s attacks had "accounted for" two of the enemy's carriers.[6]

At 1655 Yamamoto asked Nagumo for a situation report.[7] At this stage the situation seemed if not exactly promising then certainly full of possibility. With Kondo and the *Zuiho* rushing up to support Nagumo from the southwest and Kurita en route for Midway, something might yet come of Yamamoto's attempts to regroup and continue the battle. But Japanese success depended heavily on the screening units from the First Carrier Striking Force. Since they were closer to the enemy than any other Japanese units, an effective night action would in large part be determined by the fortunes of these ships.

When Yamamoto sent his signal to Nagumo the carrier admiral still intended to take his units eastwards during the night in pursuit of the enemy. Nagumo had come into prominence during the thirties not simply because of his unbridled belligerence and his threats to those colleagues who did not share his extreme nationalism, but because he had been a cruiser captain of note when the Imperial Navy had been developing its ideas of massed torpedo attacks at night as part of its battle doctrine. Quite clearly, with the *Akagi, Kaga* and *Soryu* damaged, Nagumo was reverting to such tactics as the only hope of overturning the verdict of the morning's exchanges. He must have suspected, however, that his chances of success were slim. Only one of the seaplanes with the *Nagara* had a night reconnaissance capability, and a single scout would most likely not obtain a contact on which the surface units might act.[8]

Yamamoto did not receive a reply to his request until 2130. The *Nagara* must have received Yamamoto's signal just as the *Hiryu* came under attack, and the series of American strikes that followed in the wake of the Dauntlesses from the *Enterprise* kept the First Carrier Striking Force fully occupied until 1832. Nagumo had too much to deal with during these attacks to give serious and immediate consideration to Yamamoto's signal. However, at 1730 he did send the one signal that Yamamoto did not want to receive. It told him that the last of the carriers had been hit by bombs and was on fire.[9]

It would seem that the 1730 report stunned Yamamoto and that at least for a few minutes he sat slumped in a chair on the bridge without saying a word.[10] At this stage he must have considered abandoning a pursuit that now seemed ever less likely to be successful and ever more hazardous. The attack on the *Hiryu*, so late in the day and after such high hopes of belated success, was in many ways the end of the line for the Japanese, particularly when it was added to the fact that the Second Carrier Striking Force could not come into action quickly enough to redeem the situation. The loss of the *Hiryu* showed that the Americans still retained a formidable offensive capability, in spite of the successes that Yamaguchi had claimed. As the day faded so did Japanese hopes—but not Yamamoto's determination. He gave no indication that he intended to do anything other than continue the battle. In this, of course, he was in some ways the prisoner of the logic that had led to the signals of and after 1220; if a surface night action was sought as the means of obtaining redress for Japan's initial losses, then further losses only reinforced the determination to continue the battle.

Only as the hours passed did the unattractiveness of persistence become more evident. Yamamoto had to face the full implications of the decision to continue steaming to the east. If the Americans were withdrawing beyond the reach of Japanese warships, the latter ran the distinct risk of being found the next morning by an enemy with air superiority and a full day in which to play havoc with the Combined Fleet. Because the Japanese had no speed advantage over the enemy and had only the *Hosho* and the *Zuiho* in company, Yamamoto at some time or another had to face the reality that an attempt to continue the battle would result not in a night action with the odds favoring the Japanese but in a "decisive battle" fought the next day between beleaguered Japanese surface warships and enemy aircraft. There were no prizes for guessing the probable result of such an encounter. Every mile the Japanese steamed eastwards lessened their chances of disengaging without problems. At some time after sunset on 4 June Yamamoto had to make a choice. He had to decide whether to continue in pursuit of the enemy or turn back, accepting that this particular battle had been lost and was best abandoned. At some time or another Yamamoto had to decide between taking further risks with his still powerful surface forces and ensuring that no further unnecessary losses were incurred. It was a decision that no one but Yamamoto could take. The staff in Tokyo had watched the day's developments with mounting anguish and with no sense of satisfaction in seeing its worst fears confirmed by events. The disasters were so great as to transcend any divisions within the naval high command, but in spite of what had happened Nagano made no move to take control of the battle or to advise Yamamoto. Just as Yamamoto had not seen fit to interfere with Nagumo's conduct of the carrier battle, so Nagano saw no reason to take control of a battle that his self-willed subordinate had forced upon the staff and had gone to sea to command. The battle was Yamamoto's, and Nagano would not tell him how to fight it.[11]

At 1915, just as darkness was beginning to obscure the ships of his force from view, Yamamoto issued a new set of orders to his formations. The first part of these orders, which became both controversial and notorious, began with the observation, "The enemy fleet has been practically destroyed and is retiring eastwards." The accounts that view this statement as nothing more than an attempt to stiffen morale for the dangerous hours ahead are correct; there were certainly no grounds for thinking that the enemy had been practically destroyed. Certainly morale needed to be strengthened, for with these orders Yamamoto made it clear that he wanted to go ahead with the operations to secure Midway and to force a night action. Kurita's force of heavy cruisers was ordered to proceed with its attack on Midway, while Kondo's Invasion Force Main Body and the surviving units of the First Carrier Striking Force were ordered to press forward to contact and engage the enemy.[12] Yamamoto's own battle force was both too slow and too far to the west to come into the action, but he was determined to bring it eastwards to provide the other forces with support. A little more than an hour later, at 2030, the *Yamato* issued a separate order to the submarine *I-168*, still off Midway. She was ordered to carry out a bombardment of the atoll until 0200.[13] Yamamoto's anticipation was that thereafter Kurita's heavy cruisers, with a combined broadside of about five tons, would take up the attack and complete the destruction of the atoll's installations.

Thus at 2030 Yamamoto's determination to continue the battle had not wavered, but success depended on all three of his senior subordinate commanders—Kondo, Nagumo and Kurita—achieving their individual objectives. Kurita had to neutralize Midway; the Japanese dare not venture within range of the atoll the next day without having broken its offensive power. Kondo and Nagumo needed to contact the enemy carrier force for exactly the same reason. Failure of any one part would all but certainly lead to failure overall. In the three hours after sending orders to the *I-168*, Yamamoto received three signals that told him that none of the three parts of his plan could work. Only then did the commander in chief of the Combined Fleet admit defeat.

The first two signals came from Nagumo, the initial signal being timed at 2130, the second at 2250. Both gave a situation report for the First Carrier Striking Force. Their combined effect was to produce Nagumo's dismissal by an irate Yamamoto, who even after the receipt of the second signal still seemed intent on continuing the battle.

Nagumo's resolve to pursue the enemy through the night was destroyed in the hour before sunset. This was the result of several factors, the most important of which was not the physical destruction so much in evidence around him but two sighting reports from the scouting seaplanes. The first, delivered by a seaplane from the *Tone*, was timed at 1733; the second, delivered by Seaplane No. 2 from the *Chikuma*, was timed at 1713 but was not submitted to Nagumo until 1830. The attacks on the *Chikuma* by dive-bombers from the *Hornet* and the general confusion of the First Carrier Striking Force as it dealt with the various attacks by carrier- and shore-based aircraft between 1701 and 1832 apparently accounted for the delay.

The signal from the *Tone* was discouraging. It told Nagumo that the enemy was heading eastwards, drawing away from what remained of the First Carrier Striking Force.[14] Nagumo needed the inadvertent cooperation of the Americans if he was to obtain a contact, but from what he was told by this signal it appeared that the Americans were moving ever further out of reach even before he was in a position to give chase.

As the escorts of the First Carrier Striking Force were fully occupied beating off the attacks made upon them by enemy aircraft, this signal from the *Tone* placed Nagumo on the horns of a dilemma. If the Americans were already withdrawing from the battle area, their pursuit could not be delayed. But Nagumo could not consider a chase with so much of his force standing by the *Akagi*, *Kaga* and *Soryu* and trying to ensure the recovery of the *Hiryu*. Well over half his destroyers were committed to this task, but every one of them would be needed for a pursuit. It was no comfort to know that soon more destroyers would become available as the first of the carriers sank; by 1800 the battle to save the *Kaga* and the *Soryu* had been decidedly lost. Both were slowly settling, and less than two hours after the *Tone*'s report was received both had gone. But even without the *Kaga* and the *Soryu* there still remained the *Akagi* and the *Hiryu* and, equally important, there still remained the crews of the carriers that had not been moved to safety. If, as seemed likely, the carriers were lost during the night while Nagumo took all his ships east in pursuit of the enemy, he would not be able to rescue the carriers' companies. The Imperial Navy could no more afford to lose its seamen than it could afford to lose its carriers; rescued seamen would form the nucleus of reformed Japanese carrier forces. Nagumo was naturally concerned not to take a course of action that would involve unnecessary loss of life amongst his sailors, but even the desire to save as many crewmen as possible had its drawbacks. Burning carriers could not help but act as beacons to enemy submarines, and the battleship *Kirishima* was not slow in pointing out to the *Nagara* that she for one felt uncomfortable as she stood by the *Hiryu*. Enemy submarines were known to be in the area after three contacts had been made in the course of the day.[15] This Nagumo acknowledged at 1837 when the battleship was ordered to leave the *Hiryu* and rejoin the *Nagara*.[16] Nagumo was being pulled in different directions by the various demands on his depleted resources.

But if the report of the *Tone* was discouraging, that of the *Chikuma* was positively alarming. The report spoke of the Americans coming westwards—towards the Japanese—with no less than four carriers, six cruisers and fifteen destroyers. The force was reported to be still some 30 miles to the east of the abandoned *Yorktown*.[17] The sheer implausibility of this report was not considered for a moment by the *Nagara*. Its contents were totally at variance with all the information that had been gathered slowly, and at immense cost, during the day. What had in fact happened was that the crew of the *Chikuma*'s Seaplane No. 2 had reversed a bearing through 180 degrees, and the air staff of the *Chikuma* had compounded this error by telescoping two reports instead of treating the second as an amplification of the first. A competent staff would have noted the various inconsistencies in the two reports and on that basis ordered a recheck of the reports on which the signals were based. In all likelihood the confusion of the *Chikuma* would have been realized. But competence was beyond Nagumo's coterie at this stage of proceedings.* The events of the day had sapped the staff's collective judgment and nerve, and at this point it was perhaps easier for the staff to accept the contents of this signal than to question them. It was, after all, impossible to accept defeat, and if any consolation was to be had it was in the notion that defeat had been suffered at the hands of five carriers rather than three. But more likely tiredness, shock and confusion (rather than a willingness to believe what they would have liked to believe) led Nagumo and his subordinates to accept a manifestly incorrect report at face value. The Americans, pushing ever more carriers into the battle with the dexterity of a magician pulling rabbits from a top hat, appeared to be heading westwards and growing in inverse proportion to the Japanese as the day progressed: first none and then one American carrier to oppose the four of the Japanese; then three against one; now, finally, four and one that had

---

*In fact, the *Chikuma* did correct her report. At 1942 she informed Nagumo that two carriers and six large cruisers constituted the enemy force.

been abandoned against none. If previous Japanese claims were correct and both the *Lexington* and the *Saratoga* had been sunk, the whole of the carrier strength of the U.S. Navy just so happened to be off Midway on 4 June, and four of the enemy carriers were bearing down on Nagumo's shattered force in the last two hours of daylight. It was small wonder, therefore, that Nagumo's reaction was to seek safety in flight—though if the report was true the Americans were actually providing him with the chance he needed to bring them to battle. Nagumo's force steamed away from the enemy when it believed that the distance between them was closing in the very manner that the Japanese wanted.

Initially however, Nagumo had to make a decision about his stricken carriers. If the enemy was advancing in such overwhelming strength that his advance could not be resisted, then the six destroyers with the three drifting shambles that had been the *Akagi*, *Kaga* and *Soryu* had to get clear of the area. Yet with the inconsistency that bedevils so much of Midway, Nagumo made no decision about these carriers and destroyers. In fact he had no decision to make about the *Kaga* and the *Soryu*: the decision was made by the two ships themselves. Coming up to the *Soryu* at about 1900, Nagumo belatedly tried to reinforce the attempts to contain her fires, but she was settling by the stern and the sea itself put out her fires long before his puny efforts could have any effect. The *Soryu* went down at 1913 in latitude 30° 38' N, longitude 179° 13' W, and seven minutes later the *Kaga* was gone in latitude 30° 20' N, longitude 179° 17' W. In the time between the loss of the two, the *Akagi* asked permission to scuttle. Nagumo never made any reply to this request.[18] The two destroyers with the ex-flagship, the *Nowaki* and the *Arashi*, therefore stayed with her and were joined by the two other members of the Fourth Destroyer Division, the *Hagikaze* and the *Maikaze*, after their responsibility, the *Kaga*, went down. The *Hamakaze* and the *Isokaze*, with the survivors from the *Soryu*, joined Nagumo in setting course towards the northwest.

Two more hours elapsed after this episode before Nagumo signaled his intentions to Yamamoto: "Total enemy strength is five carriers, six heavy cruisers and fifteen destroyers. They are steaming westwards. . . . We are retiring to the northwest, escorting *Hiryu*. Speed 18 knots. . . ."[19] Surprisingly, this signal did not provoke a response from the *Yamato*, or more accurately, it did not provoke a response that took the form of a signal from Yamamoto to the *Nagara*. The signal from the *Nagara*, however, meant that Yamamoto's best and perhaps only chance of a night contact was fast disappearing if Nagumo was steering towards the northwest and away from the enemy. Moreover, Nagumo was not operating as Yamamoto had instructed him to when orders had been issued at 1915.

Nagumo referred to this signal when he sent a second situation report at 2250: "There still exist four enemy carriers (may include auxiliary carriers), six cruisers and sixteen destroyers. These are steaming westwards. None of our carriers are operational. We plan to contact the enemy with reconnaissance seaplanes tomorrow morning."[20] Evidently this signal was the final straw as far as Yamamoto was concerned. Perhaps there was justification for doing nothing if Nagumo was trying to ensure the safe recovery of the *Hiryu*, but the notion of a contact with the enemy the next morning with the paltry assembly of Daves and Jakes available to the First Carrier Striking Force was neither here nor there. A seaplane contact with the enemy on the following morning was no use to the Japanese when what was needed was a contact that night. Under the original terms of Operation MI Yamamoto had allowed seven days for the Japanese to secure and win an action against the Americans after the fall of Midway. After the disasters of 4 June Yamamoto was left with about nine hours to achieve the same result. By the time he received Nagumo's second signal, four of those hours had slipped by without anything to show for their passing. Indeed, the relative position of the Japanese had worsened considerably.

It would appear that after Nagumo's first signal was received by the *Yamato*, doubts were expressed amongst the staff of the fleet about his willingness or capacity to carry through a night action. Five minutes after his second signal, one from the *Yamato* relieved him of command of all the ships of the First Carrier Striking Force except for the *Akagi*, the *Hiryu* and the destroyers standing by the two burning hulks. The other units were placed under the command of Kondo, then coming up from the southwest with Tanaka and his destroyers in furious pursuit.[21] Tanaka had left the transports he was charged to protect. They were to reverse course while he led his force to what he hoped would be "the sound of the guns."

A certain irony about the situation was developing at this point, but it is hardly likely that any of the participants would have seen and still less appreciated it. Whatever hopes Yamamoto held at this stage rested on Kondo, the commander who had never had much confidence in Operation MI. When Yamamoto had told Kondo and Nagumo of Operation MI, it was Kondo who had objected and Nagumo who had made no protest. Now, during the last hour of 4 June, the Japanese had to depend on the one commander who had had virtually no confidence whatsoever in the outcome of the operation, while the commander who had too easily assumed that his force could play a victorious role had failed during the conduct of the carrier battle and then during the first part of the night. Whereas Nagumo's response to his change of fortune had been, at best, somewhat irresolute, that of Kondo had been positive and immediate. He had pushed forward at 28 knots after disaster struck without waiting for orders, and from Yamamoto's signal of 2255 it was clear that Kondo was expected to rekindle the confidence and aggressiveness of the First Carrier Striking

Force. He seemed to be the admiral needed to restore an element of much-needed decisiveness to Japanese operations at this time. Yet in the end it was Kondo's inability to get his units into action during the night that made Yamamoto decide enough was enough.

The bad news broke for Yamamoto at 2340 when Kondo, responding to his new command, issued his first orders.[22] He set out his anticipated position at 0300 as well as his general intentions, and he ordered all the units from the First Carrier Striking Force (less the *Akagi*, the *Hiryu* and their escorts) to "immediately turn about and participate in the night engagement." The order was elaborated by a second signal, sent twenty minutes later. With this midnight signal Kondo instructed his various formations to organize themselves into an extended line for searching, their intended course to be 65 degrees and their speed to be 24 knots. Tanaka's destroyer formation was to take up position on the right flank of the sweep, while Kondo's destroyer force was to take up station on the left. Kondo's two cruiser divisions were to occupy the center. The destroyers and cruisers were to space themselves at intervals of four miles, and the *Kongo* and the *Hiei* were to tuck themselves in behind Kondo himself in the right center, some six miles astern of the *Atago*. With Kondo intent on flogging his forces eastwards, the remnants of Nagumo's old command—if two battleships, two seaplane cruisers and a number of destroyers can be regarded as remnants—were to sweep downwards from the north.[23]

In issuing these orders Kondo inadvertently ended any hope of bringing Operation MI to a successful conclusion. He stated in the course of his first order at 2340 that his main force would reach a position in latitude 30° 28′ N, longitude 178° 35′ W at 0300 and then search to the east "in an effort to engage the enemy at night." That would leave him slightly to the south of the *Akagi*, which was even then slowly dying. The staff of the Combined Fleet was thus made aware that Kondo had no chance of making contact with the enemy during the night. He might refer to a night action, but sunrise would be at 0452 and civil twilight would be at 0425. By then it would have been growing light for at least an hour. Kondo was not as far to the east as the Combined Fleet believed him to be, and at the very best Kondo was unlikely to have much more than an hour of "dark" in which to find and locate the enemy before the first predawn reconnaissance missions were flown from Midway and from the two, three or four carriers the enemy was supposed to have to the east. The result of such a situation would be entirely predictable. From the time that Nagumo's 2340 signal was taken in by the *Yamato* and its information transferred to the plot, Yamamoto knew that any attempt to continue the battle could only increase the potentially fatal vulnerability of Japanese forces to no useful purpose. It was a time, at last, for realism.

Throughout the evening, staff discussions and planning continued in the *Yamato* as the situation became ever more urgent, but in the end all the options except the night action were discarded as impractical. No alternative to the planned action emerged, and by midnight even that ploy looked empty. Various schemes, of dubious value and realism, were bandied about by the staff even as the bad news from Kondo was received, but these were scotched by Ugaki. There was talk about an attack next day with every aircraft and seaplane in the various forces in the hope that if enough damage was inflicted on the enemy, Japanese guns might yet record a victory or at least a draw. There was even a proposal, made by the hitherto infallible Kuroshima, for all the battleships and cruisers to proceed to Midway for an all-out bombardment of the atoll. It was incredible that the fleet's operations officer could come up with such a suggestion, and Ugaki reacted sharply against it. With a rationalism that would have been all the more welcome had it been displayed in May when war games were fixed in Japanese favor, Ugaki contemptuously dismissed such proposals, pointing out that enemy aircraft and submarines were likely to account for Japanese warships long before they came within range of Midway. As far as Ugaki was concerned, a battle and not a war had been lost, and it was time for the present mission to be abandoned to prepare for the next fight.[24] The navy might well have a special attack hymn called "The Song of the Self-Sacrificing Warrior," but the time to sing it had not yet come.[25] Yamamoto did not disagree. He had remained silent during the various staff discussions, but one comment was enough to end debate. When one of the staff officers, trying not to admit defeat, asked Ugaki how they were to apologize to the emperor for failure, Yamamoto cut in with the comment that he alone was responsible.[26] Whatever his personal or professional weaknesses, moral cowardice was not one of them; Yamamoto was prepared to admit failure while his subordinates were still clinging to illusions.

At 0015 he issued the first of a series of instructions that brought Operation MI to an end. The signal did not spell out that the operation was being brought to a close, but this was obvious; Kondo's formation and the survivors from the First Carrier Striking Force—less the *Akagi* and the *Hiryu* and their escorts—were ordered to join Yamamoto's task force. He gave his calculated position for 0900 as latitude 32° 08′ N, longitude 179° 01′ E, and he stated that his force would steer on a course due east at a speed of 20 knots.[27] This was a position over two degrees of longitude further to the east than the position Yamamoto had earlier given as the one he would reach by 0300. Therefore, he intended to bring his own force to the east even as the other forces were ordered to reverse course to join his flag. Perhaps Yamamoto did this because he felt he and his force had to run the same risks that the other formations had run, but be that as it may he was unnecessarily condemning his battle force to hazards that could have been avoided. Yamamoto had brought about the worst of eventualities. First by insisting on a night action and then by not canceling it until 0015, he had left his two major battle forces plus other substantial light formations in positions where they were likely to spend all the fifteen hours of daylight on 5 June within range of anything that the enemy might have on Midway—not to mention what might be on the flight decks of rampant American carriers. The daylight hours of the next day were going to be full of danger for the Combined Fleet.

What the Americans retained on Midway was going to have a major bearing on the events of the following day. The initial orders to Kurita to neutralize the atoll with gunfire thus still seemed relevant, but the calculations of the Combined Fleet staff showing Yamamato that Kondo had no chance of forcing a night action also indicated that Kurita could not reach Midway to begin the bombardment of the atoll's installations at 0200. Kondo's signals had revealed that he was farther to the west than the Combined Fleet had anticipated, and if it was impossible for Kondo to bring his force to the longitude of the *Akagi* before 0300, it was highly unlikely that the Close Support Group would be able to reach Midway much before sunrise. Far from being the vanguard of a massive invasion effort, the *Kumano*, *Suzuya*, *Mikuma* and *Mogami*, along with the *Arashio* and the *Asashio*, had become the most hopelessly exposed of all Japanese ships. In his general order of 0015 Yamamoto instructed Kurita to abandon his mission and join him. At 0200 Yamamoto specifically repeated this order. In fact there was no need for the second order; Kurita heard him the first time, and at 0045 he turned the Support Group back to the east and a *WEST* rendezvous with the fleet commander.[28]

After the orders of 0015 and 0020, only two more orders needed to be issued to bring Operation MI to a close—if the enemy permitted. First, the fate of the *Akagi* had to be settled. Second, the final orders putting an end to the mission and giving out new instructions had to be issued. Once the 0015 signal had been made there was no reason to delay either of the subsequent signals, but Yamamoto did not act until 0255. It was then that he issued a four-part order. The first part stated simply, "The Midway operation is cancelled." The other parts instructed the transports to proceed westwards beyond the range of aircraft on Midway, and told all forces to concentrate in order to refuel in latitude 33° N, longitude 170° E during the morning of the sixth.[29] The *Akagi* order was delayed for almost another hour, and seemingly for no reason. What support could be given to a burning and ravaged carrier that was certain to be slowly filling with seawater is hard to see, but Yamamoto prevented her being scuttled in the early evening of the fourth, perhaps because of his old connection with the ship. He had been her skipper in 1928 and 1929. Nevertheless, at 0350 he finally gave the order for her escorts to hasten her end, and at 0455, after her four destroyers had fired torpedoes into her, the *Akagi* went down in latitude 30° 30′ N, longitude 179° 08′ W, the first ship in the history of the Imperial Japanese Navy to be scuttled.[30]

It was one thing to order an end to the operation, quite another to make a clean break with the enemy. The *I-168* encountered problems because she did not receive any orders canceling her earlier instructions to bombard Midway. Her skipper, Tanabe, took in the signals relating to Kurita's recall, but without any further orders to the contrary he had to carry out a bombardment that was now utterly pointless. Originally his solitary 3.9-in gun was intended to provide the overture to the arrival of the Seventh Cruiser Division; when the cruisers turned back this gun was all there was for the bombardment. At 0125 Tanabe began his attack. He had time for only eight rounds, all of which landed harmlessly in the lagoon, before counterfire from three shore batteries convinced him that submarines, with their delicate and vulnerable pressure hulls, should never be given so ill-becoming a task as shore bombardment. At 0128 the *I-168* submerged and resumed a cautious patrol, though she was almost caught by searching enemy aircraft soon after dawn.[31]

If the *I-168* managed to extricate herself without much trouble, the same was not true of Kurita and his cruisers. Kurita turned his force back to the west at 0045 and maintained a course of 300 degrees until about 0215, when his ships were some 89 miles from Midway. Thus it would appear that the force was much farther to the east than Yamamoto and the staff of the Combined Fleet had appreciated and that it had been within range of Midway and a predawn bombardment when it was recalled. But at 0215 Kurita and his force were sighted by the American submarine *Tambor*, then coming south at top speed.[32] She, along with other submarines, had been redeployed to cover the atoll's western approaches. Kurita had evaded the submarines on his way to attack Midway, but during his withdrawal he encountered the *Tambor*.

The *Tambor*, with the advantage of position and first sight, found the Japanese at maximum range, but could not make a positive identification. In the dark the submarine settled down for a dangerous game of hide-and-seek with an enemy who did not suspect her presence, but even after maneuvering his boat to catch the surface ships silhouetted against the moonlight, Lieutenant Commander John W. Murphy was unable to distinguish whether the ships were friend or foe. All American submarines had been warned that friendly forces might cross their patrol lines during the night, and with six ships coming out of the east the problem of the *Tambor* was obvious. Murphy made a single contact report, stating the presence of "many unidentified ships" in a position 89 miles from Midway. He then settled down to maintain contact with the force and try to discover its identity.[33] By the time there was enough light for the *Tambor* to make out the distinctive silhouette of the *Mogami* class, the Japanese realized they were not alone. The *Kumano* put her wheel over 45 degrees to port and flashed a warning down the line. The *Suzuya* and the *Mikuma* conformed to the flagship's turn, but the *Mogami*, last in line, corrected her turnaway too quickly. She tried to resume her place in a line-ahead formation before the others corrected their turns and in attempting to take station on the *Mikuma* her navigating officer, Lieutenant Commander Masaki Yamauchi, failed to see the real *Mikuma* in the gloom and lined up on the next in line, the *Suzuya*. The *Mogami* ploughed into the stern of the *Mikuma* at 28 knots.[34]

In the light of subsequent events it is somewhat ironic that the *Mikuma* escaped this accidental ramming with remarkably little damage, while the *Mogami* lost 40 feet of her forecastle up to A turret. The bows of the *Mogami* were bent to port at a right angle, and only with difficulty did her crew shore up and secure her bulkheads as she gingerly worked her way up to 12 knots. The damage to the *Mikuma* was confined to a few loosened plates and a damaged fuel tank, but this proved more significant than the damage that the *Mogami* inflicted upon herself. From her wound the *Mikuma* left a trail of oil that was to lead the enemy to her.[35]

Kurita turned back when he became aware of the fracas at the end of his line. When he discovered that the *Mogami* could make 12 knots, he ordered the *Mikuma* and the force's two destroyers to stand by her while he took the *Kumano* and the *Suzuya* towards the northwest and the linkup with the main forces.[36] The two damaged cruisers, with their destroyer escort, then set course towards the west in the hope and belief that their safety would best be ensured if they got within range of air cover from Wake at the earliest possible opportunity. The more immediate danger of submarine attack did not materialize. The *Tambor* was unable to benefit from the accident that her presence had induced. When she dived she was about two miles from the Japanese cruisers but this distance more than doubled in the course of the enemy turnaway. Though heavily damaged, the *Mogami*'s ability to make 12 knots enabled her to get clear of the submerged American submarine. For about two hours Murphy tried to maneuver his boat into an attack position, but his slow submerged speed prevented this. The *Tambor* therefore broke off contact and set course for Midway after sending another contact report, this time correctly identifying the enemy ships and giving their course.[37]

If Murphy considered himself unfortunate in being unable to make a single attack on an enemy cruiser force in spite of being in contact with it for some four hours, Spruance and Pearl Harbor proved unsympathetic. From the first contact the *Tambor* failed to observe standard operational procedures and gave no indication of the course and speed of the "many unidentified ships" that she had encountered. The submarine command at Pearl Harbor, moreover, made no attempt to elicit this information. The result was that the one formation that could identify this force as enemy and perhaps move to deal with it, Task Force 16, did not know whether the contact was with a force advancing towards or withdrawing from the area of Midway. It was not until after 0600 that Murphy made a proper contact report, and by then there was no means by which it could be acted upon effectively. By that time the dawn reconnaissance from Midway had found by its failure to contact an incoming enemy that the Japanese were not persisting with their planned invasion, that they were in retreat. Had Murphy made a full report at the time of contact, or had he subsequently dispatched amplifying reports, this information could have been available to the American command up to three hours before the Catalinas were able to report the absence of the enemy. In that case Spruance would have been provided with information giving him the option to bring his task force westwards immediately, but in the absence of any definite indication of what was happening to the west he held back to the northeast of Midway until 0420. Task Force 16 did not begin its run towards the atoll until thirty minutes before sunrise, and by then it had lost the chance to catch a retreating enemy in the course of the morning.[38] The failure of the *Tambor* to report properly thus had major repercussions, not least for Murphy. After the battle Spruance, then serving as Nimitz's chief of staff, ordered Murphy's transfer from command, a decision with which Murphy himself said he could not find fault.[39] But that particular episode would not take place until later, and at sunrise on 5 June, despite the failings of the *Tambor* and the inability of the Catalinas to detect an incoming enemy, the Americans had good reason to suppose that battle would be resumed. If the *Tambor* had been unlucky in not being able to use her torpedoes against the enemy, it seemed unlikely that all American forces would be thus disappointed.

CHAPTER 16

The Final Exchanges

In the predawn hours of 5 June both the Japanese and Americans prepared to resume battle with the reappearance of the sun. On the American side there was confident anticipation born of the previous day's success; on the Japanese side there was only a nervous, despondent apprehension. The latter knew that they had been beaten, and they were only too painfully aware of their vulnerability, shorn as they were of the protection of Nagumo's carriers. The danger of being subjected to sustained air attack became all the more real when the day dawned fair. After ten days of fog, cloud and rain, the weather and visibility on the fifth were reasonable. Thus just when the Japanese would have welcomed the cold clammy embrace of foul weather in which to hide their nakedness, they steamed into weather if not ideal for easy and accurate air reconnaissance, then not such as to present serious handicaps to searching aircraft. With but about a hundred aircraft and seaplanes of all types with their various formations near Midway, the Japanese were in the dangerous position of simultaneously having lost the strategic initiative and exhausted themselves. For the moment they were the weaker side, and having spent themselves they had no option but to brace themselves to meet the inevitable American counterattack. All the advantages seemingly lay with the Americans.

But 5 June unfolded in a way different from what was anticipated by most of the people involved. The day was to pass with the Americans unable to bring enemy main forces to battle, and American carrier forces would barely manage to obtain contact with the enemy at all. On the following day, the sixth, the Americans enjoyed slightly better fortune, but contact with enemy main forces continued to elude them. Thereafter the battle was broken off by the Americans, who in this follow-up stage of the action failed to register the kind of success that seemed to be theirs for the taking after the destruction of the Japanese carriers on the fourth. The

Japanese, at the time of their maximum vulnerability, managed to extricate themselves from a potentially disastrous situation without further undue loss, though this was as much the result of luck as sound judgment. In many ways the Japanese were fortunate on the fifth and sixth, and even after the sixth they were somewhat lucky, for Yamamoto's attempt to continue the battle beyond this day could easily have resulted in further major losses.

The fact that success eluded the Americans after 4 June provoked much criticism in the United States, both at the time and later. Spruance was the target of most of it, the extent of his turnaway during the night being alleged to have been the cause of the American failure to press home an advantage during the last phase of the battle. There is some truth in this criticism, because his move did leave the Americans trailing the Japanese by a distance that was too great to close. But by any definition this criticism of Spruance can at best be only partially valid, and there can be no serious quarrel with the accuracy of one biographer's observation that the turn-away during the night of 4–5 June was "an eminently correct action."[1] It was an action dictated by a defensiveness that was subsequently endorsed by Nimitz and King, both hard taskmasters who were not disposed to support poor decisions. It denied Yamamoto the chance to fight the only type of battle that could have redeemed the Japanese cause at the eleventh hour, and it exposed the Americans to the least possible danger while leaving Task Force 16 with the chance to pick up the threads of battle on the morning of the fifth. That it proved unable to do so was not the result of the turnaway by Spruance during the night, except in the sense that the turnaway was combined with a similar maneuver on the part of the enemy. Moreover, this mutual standing off has to be considered in conjunction with three other factors that denied the Americans a major follow-up victory on and after 5 June.

Collectively, the three factors were the absence of those conditions that had produced the victory of 4 June. The success of 4 June was made possible by the Americans' knowledge of Japanese plans, intentions and order of battle; by Midway's ability to provide contact with the enemy at the very outset of the battle; and by the presence of three fully prepared American carriers on the disengaged flank of the enemy's advance. These had been the basic ingredients of American success, though even with these factors working in their favor victory had still almost slithered through American fingers. Leaving aside all other considerations, the Americans' success on 4 June was the result of concentrating all their forces at full strength and effectiveness in a position to frustrate an enemy who was ignorant of their presence and deployment.

None of these conditions existed on the morning of 5 June. Only two and not three American carriers remained operational, and neither was at full strength. The American carriers were not in a position to move against an enemy whose position, course and speed were unknown. Moreover, the carriers were not able to rely on Midway to provide the all-important contact as it had on the previous day. The atoll had neither the strength nor the exact knowledge of enemy plans that on previous days had enabled it to mount effective reconnaissance missions. The success of Midway's air group in finding the enemy on both the third and fourth can be attributed to the strong reconnaissance and bomber forces in position and able to work to an accurate intelligence brief. On the fifth, however, the situation was different. Once battle had been joined Midway proved no more able to maintain contact with the enemy than the Japanese had been able to maintain contact with the Americans. Just as the *Hiryu* had lost the plot on the morning of the fourth and during the late afternoon the Japanese command had been confused by a series of muddled sighting reports, so on the fifth the Americans suffered from Midway's inability to maintain contact with the enemy during the previous day and night and by the various incomplete and jumbled reports in the morning. On the fourth the losses of contact by both sides had not amounted to much. Surface forces could not outrun aircraft, and because of the relative positions of the two carrier forces, lost contacts were reestablished with little difficulty. On the fifth, however, the long hours of darkness could do nothing other than conceal Japanese intentions, giving the Combined Fleet thousands of square miles in which to operate and, if need be, to hide. On this day the Americans had to start from scratch since they lacked hard signals intelligence on which to draw up plans. They had to operate from Midway and from their carriers with smaller groups than had been available on the previous day. Moreover, the American problem was worse than that of merely having little information on which to work; what little information they had was also contradictory. The last-known position of the enemy had been to the northwest of Midway, yet the night mission from Midway against the enemy carriers had failed to locate him. At the same time the erroneous contact report from the *Tambor* placed the enemy to the west of the atoll.

On the fifth the initiative rested with the Americans, and the situation seemed to be overwhelmingly in their favor. Yet there were obstacles capitalizing on their success of the previous day. The intelligence picture was sketchy. The Midway air group was badly depleted. Between them, the *Enterprise* and the *Hornet* retained about sixty Dauntlesses and Devastators for reconnaissance and strike missions. The carriers themselves were not in a position from which they could intercept the enemy with relative ease. The Americans did not have the strength to be confident of making contact with the enemy and then of being able to follow up with sufficient power to secure a favorable result. What the Americans needed was for the *Saratoga* to put in a providential appearance on the battlefield, but on the fifth she was still one day's steaming east of Pearl Harbor.

Spruance turned his task force back towards Midway before it was known that the enemy was withdrawing to the west. At this stage, about 0420, Spruance was ideally placed to achieve his main objectives: to deny Midway to the Japanese, and to ensure the safety of his task force. Criticism of Spruance largely ignores this point, crucial though it is to Spruance's conduct of operations. He was in the right position to strike in defense of Midway while running the least possible chance of being struck in return, a neat reversal of Nagumo's situation on the previous day. It was not until 0600, however, that Spruance and Task Force 16 knew that Midway had been secured without a fight. By that time so much negative evidence had built up there was no room to doubt that the enemy had turned back in the course of the night. No attack on Midway had taken place, other than the bombardment by the *I-168*, and the absence of contact reports by submarines and Catalinas in the first hour or so after sunrise had to suggest that the enemy was not in the immediate vicinity of Midway and was unlikely to be heading eastwards. But beyond that there was no indication of where the enemy might be or what he was doing. As Spruance came westwards he was determined not to commit himself to any given course of action until a clear picture of what was happening in front of him began to emerge. It was the American misfortune that the picture Spruance wanted did not materialize. The reports he received on the morning of 5 June were confused and slow in arriving.

On the morning of 5 June Midway committed just ten Catalinas to search the sector between 250 degrees and 020 degrees to a range of 250 miles.[2] This was a much smaller and more restricted search area than the ones that had been covered on any of the six previous days. The size of the sector and the relatively few patrol planes committed to the search reflected the disorganization brought about by the previous day's raid and the dispersal of the flying boats. Equally, the restricted range of the reconnaissance suggested the defensive nature of the day's effort but left little chance of finding an enemy not coming out of the west and directly threatening the atoll itself. Moreover, this chance was not improved by the refusal of Task Force 16 to scout on its own behalf.

The Catalinas began to leave Midway at about 0415, and thereafter two sets of contacts were made.[3] The first was with the units to the west. The initial report, made at 0630, referred to two damaged battleships some 125 miles to the west of Midway. Sighted at 0617, these were reported to be making 15 knots to the west.[4] A second report, made thirty minutes later, indicated the presence of two cruisers on a bearing of 274 degrees at a range of 174 miles from Midway. They were reported to be on a course to the northwest at a speed of 20 knots.[5] The first report obviously referred to the *Mogami* and the *Mikuma*, and roughly confirmed the sighting report of the *Tambor*; the second report referred to the *Kumano* and the *Suzuya*. The second set of contacts, made by two Catalinas at 0719, 0735 and 0800, placed a concentration of Japanese warships roughly 240 miles to the northwest of Midway, but these reports could not specify what enemy task force might have been encountered.[6] The second and third contact reports, however, concurred in the assessment that two battleships, with heavy cruisers and destroyers, were in the company of a burning carrier.[7]

This combination of contacts to the northwest of Midway proved unfortunate for the Americans. The burning carrier had to be the *Hiryu*, though it is unclear what ships were supposed to be in company with her because by this time she was alone. The American misfortune was that contact was established before and at 0800. It was around this time that the *Hiryu* began to settle. A matter of a few minutes later and there would have been no burning carrier for any Catalina to report, and that would have saved the Americans a great deal of trouble. Moreover, the reported presence of a carrier to the northwest of Midway was to prove misleading; in the process of transmission to Task Force 16 the various signals made it appear that not one but two enemy carriers were in this area.[8] Midway and the two Catalinas involved in these sightings between them duplicated the error made by the *Chikuma* on the previous evening by running together more than one sighting report, thus producing a substantial overestimation of the size of whatever force had been encountered. Given these circumstances, what happened was entirely predictable. With Midway secure and not in any danger of coming under attack, Spruance's priority was to account for enemy main forces.[9] On the strength of the reports that were received, Spruance made the decision to go after the larger and evidently more important enemy force to the northwest of Midway rather than the cruiser force reported to be west of the atoll.[10] In making this decision he condemned himself and his force to an exercise in futility. There was no second carrier to the northwest of Midway on the morning of 5 June, and there never had been. Unfortunately for Task Force 16, there was no first carrier either: the *Hiryu* sank more than one hour before Task Force 16 came to the longitude of Midway.[11]

Spruance had come westwards at 25 knots after 0430, but it was not until 1115 that he set his task force down on a course for a contact with the carrier(s) supposedly to the northwest of Midway.[12] This did not mean that the *Mogami* and the *Mikuma* did not receive unsolicited attention on the fifth. The American carriers made no contact with the two heavy cruisers and their escorts during the day, but the forces on Midway attempted to follow up their initial sightings with two attacks. The first of these attacks should have been made by eight Flying Fortresses. These left Midway at

0430, fifteen minutes after the Catalinas, just in case all expectations were wrong and the enemy was moving in to attack Midway.[13] With four of their colleagues already sent back to Oahu because they were deemed unfit for further operations and the remainder out of service for the moment, the Fortresses represented the total heavy and medium bomber strength of Midway. They were ordered out after the force reported by the *Tambor*, but they encountered bad weather that cloaked the Japanese ships. Having missed the enemy the Fortresses made for Kure, where they circled whilst awaiting further orders. The first report by the Catalinas provided the contact that the Fortresses needed, but before they were able to find and attack the Japanese ships the second strike force, sent out by Midway at 0700, had found the *Mogami* and the *Mikuma* and completed an attack on the two cruisers. This force consisted of six Dauntlesses and six Vindicators.[14] Unlike the heavy bombers of the army air force, the marine aircraft flew at low altitude and thus had no difficulty picking up the trail of the enemy, finding the oil slick that the *Mikuma* dragged behind her at 0745. Twenty minutes later the marines contacted the Japanese ships, and three minutes after that the twelve bombers began their attacks against an enemy that fought back hard.[15] Such was the volume of fire that the Japanese ships threw up in their own defense that none of the bombs aimed at them by the dive-bombing Dauntlesses and the glide-bombing Vindicators found their mark. The *Mogami*, attacked out of the sun by the Dauntlesses, escaped with nothing worse than near misses that did minor damage to her superstructure but had no mining effect because the Americans used 500-lb bombs with impact fuses.[16] Similarly, none of the Vindicators that attacked the *Mikuma* managed to put their bombs within 200 yards of her, yet she was to pay a high price for this immunity.[17] When her antiaircraft fire accounted for the leading Vindicator at its release point, the pilot, Captain Richard E. Fleming, deliberately crashed his aircraft into the cruiser's X turret in the kind of attack American sailors were to become grimly familiar with in the course of the last year of the war. The resultant explosion spread flames across the whole of the cruiser's stern and these were then sucked down the starboard ventilation shaft. The fires set off an explosion in the engine room that killed the entire watch.[18] Fortunately for the Japanese the Fortresses coming on to the scene just as the marines' attack was drawing to a close were unable to add to the destruction.[19] No further attacks were made on this particular force during the remainder of the day, the Japanese being left undisturbed to lick their wounds. They were not subjected to any further attack, which could easily have proved overwhelming. Nevertheless, after these attacks the *Arashio* and the *Asashio* were left trying to tend to not one but two cripples, since Fleming's revenge left the *Mikuma* in no better a state than the prowless *Mogami*.

As we have seen, at 1115 Spruance set Task Force 16 down on a stern chase, the Americans steering a course for the enemy's last known position. In the course of the morning and early afternoon the American carriers flew only combat air patrol. The first of the day was made by twelve Wildcats from the *Enterprise*; all the other patrols, mounted at two-hour intervals, were made by six fighters. The reason for the extra strength in the first patrol was not fear of the enemy but the desire to equalize strength between the *Enterprise* and the *Hornet*. Six of the fighters flown off by the *Enterprise* on the first patrol of the day had come from the *Yorktown*, and these were recovered by the *Hornet* while the flagship provided the second patrol.[20] By early afternoon, however, Spruance and his staff had to reconsider the policy of flying nothing other than defensive patrols. As the hours slipped by with Task Force 16 holding on towards the assumed position of the enemy, no contact or amplifying reports were received. With the carriers dependent on shore-based reconnaissance patrols, this lack of reports was serious. The carriers could not afford to lose contact with the enemy; they were not to know that there was no contact to be had. Under the circumstances Spruance decided to conduct a reconnaissance in force in midafternoon. For the mission he decided to commit virtually every one of his strike aircraft. Apart from a handful of Devastators on the *Enterprise* Spruance put all his bombers into one single attempt to find and strike at the enemy.[21] At 1500 he turned his carriers back towards the east and into the wind to fly off his aircraft.

Between 1512 and 1528 the *Enterprise* flew off a total of thirty-two Dauntlesses, thirteen of which were her own. Seven were from her scouting squadron, six from her bombing unit. They were in the company of nine scouts and ten bombers from the *Yorktown*, which had been recovered by the *Enterprise*. The thirty-two Dauntlesses were ordered to fly out to a range of 265 miles on a course of 324 degrees with the scouts formed into an extended picket line and the two bomber elements tucked in behind at slight lower altitude.[22] The *Hornet* flew off a total of twenty-six Dauntlesses. These were detailed to scout to a range of 315 miles on the same course followed by the Dauntlesses from the *Enterprise*, which was to have one immediate effect on deployment. As soon as the first group of Dauntlesses from the *Hornet*—the attack leader plus eleven bombers—was airborne it was waved on by the air group commander, a fiery and seemingly irascible little man who rejoiced in the name of Commander Apollo Soucek. (His brother, who was also an officer in the navy, was named Zeus.) With his bombers committed to a scouting mission out to 315 miles, Soucek had no intention of keeping his Dauntlesses circling to form up. As a result the *Hornet* flew off two waves, the second being of nine scouts and five bombers that left the carrier at about 1545.[23]

All the Dauntlesses, whether from the *Enterprise* or the *Hornet* and regardless of their bomber or scout designation, were supposed to be armed with 500-lb bombs. When the briefing for the mission began McClusky was appalled to find that Browning and the staff had ordered the Dauntlesses to be armed with 1,000-lb bombs. McClusky, having been shot and wounded in the previous day's attack, was not involved in this mission, but on hearing Browning's orders he forced his way on to the admiral's bridge to confront the chief of staff in what was to become a somewhat notorious and unpleasant exchange. Browning had an infamous temper and an overweening confidence in his own judgment, but in the course of this argument McClusky, backed by the captain of the *Enterprise* and the officer who was to lead the mission, forced Browning to admit that he had never flown a Dauntless with a 1,000-lb bomb. His confession strengthened McClusky's assertion that the Dauntlesses could not be expected to scout to extreme range and carry a full payload. Forced to arbitrate between his quarrelsome airmen, Spruance decided in favor of McClusky on this matter, thereby overruling his own chief of staff and chief adviser on air operations. Thus humiliated, Browning had what can only be described as a hysterical screaming and sobbing fit, after which he took himself off the bridge and away from his duties to sulk.[24] The remainder of the staff seemingly made little attempt to placate him.

The concentration of Dauntlesses into a single search sector gave the Americans no more than a slim chance of finding the enemy they believed to be in the northwest, but this was only one of the difficulties that beset American operations at this juncture. First, the two carriers had to turn away from the enemy and run at high speed into a gentle wind to launch their aircraft, thereby opening the distance between themselves and the enemy at the very time they should have closed it. Second, fighters did not have the endurance to escort Dauntlesses expected to search for the enemy to the limit of their range. Third, Browning was right to insist on 1,000-lb bombs for the Dauntlesses. Only bombs of this size had any chance of inflicting substantial damage on the type of ships the Americans were expected to contact. On the other hand, McClusky was correct in maintaining that the Dauntlesses, with their restricted range, had little chance of finding the enemy if they carried 1,000-lb weapons. As a result of Spruance's ruling on the matter, the Dauntlesses of Task Force 16 flew off with bombs that were too small to register significant success against heavily armored targets. Fourth, the Dauntlesses were to fly at 18,000 feet for this mission, but with the cloud base at 13,000 feet and a distinct haze above 2,000 feet, the Americans were certain to have only fleeting opportunities to find the enemy through the thickening cover.

On that afternoon the Americans were to fly three strike missions, one by their carriers, one by a flight of seven Flying Fortresses that left Midway at 1320, and the last by a flight of five Fortresses that set out from Midway at

1545.[25] By rights, only the Fortresses should have had any chance of obtaining a contact with the enemy; only four-engine heavy bombers had the range to catch an enemy believed to be in flight. The inability of the carriers to get into action until midafternoon should have forced their Dauntlesses to turn back long before they came within range of the enemy. Nevertheless, all three American missions could have established contact on the afternoon of 5 June, since the Japanese were not withdrawing from the scene of their defeat. Had they been, they would almost certainly have been betrayed by their smoke and white wakes, which had drawn McClusky to the First Carrier Striking Force the previous day. But on the fifth, after the various formations had gathered around Yamamoto's flag, the Japanese hove to in order to transfer the wounded of the First Carrier Striking Force from the various destroyers to the more spacious and better-equipped sick bays of the *Haruna, Kirishima, Mutsu* and *Nagato*.[26] Perhaps significantly, the *Yamato* did not take her share of cot cases.

However important it was to render medical assistance to the wounded, it is somewhat hard to believe that such solicitude extended to halting the fleet in midocean while it was still within range of medium and heavy bombers from Midway and with enemy carrier forces at sea and in pursuit. The decision to complete the transfer of wounded before seeking safety in flight ran the greatest possible risk for the least possible return. Yet this course of action may well have been the only one that ensured that the Americans did not obtain the contact they sought. In late afternoon the *Nagara* sighted heavy bombers heading westwards, but with no funnel smoke or streaming wakes to attract the enemy's attention the Japanese warships remained unsighted under the clouds.[27]

The Americans did obtain one contact with the retiring Japanese, however, and this was with the destroyer *Tanikaze*. She, along with the Alf from the *Nagara*, had been detached at 0700 by Nagumo in response to a report from one of the *Hosho*'s scouts that the *Hiryu* remained afloat with men on her flight deck.* The *Tanikaze* was ordered back to destroy the carrier and rescue the men who had been left behind.[28] By the time she came across the area where the *Hiryu* was reported to be, the carrier had long since sunk and the destroyer could find no trace of ship or survivors. As she searched, the *Tanikaze* was all that stood between the Combined Fleet's battle forces and the rampant carriers of the enemy, and the perils of such a

*Many accounts of the battle claim that the *Hiryu* was found by a Japanese aircraft on 5 June, but most are deliberately vague about the incident because the survivors from the *Hiryu*, rescued by the seaplane tender *Ballard* on 19 June, said the carrier had been overflown by an aircraft with a fixed undercarriage. The problem with this statement is that the usual and inaccurate air orders of battle for the Combined Fleet have not included any aircraft that could fill the role. As we have seen, both the *Hosho* and the *Zuiho* deployed fighters and torpedo bombers with fixed undercarriages, so considerations of range and function would suggest that the aircraft in question on 5 June was a Jean from the *Hosho*.

position became evident in the course of that afternoon. After she abandoned her search and turned back to the west, she was attacked by successive waves of aircraft. First, she was found and attacked by the first of the Fortress formations from Midway. These bombers were on their way back to Midway after having abandoned their search for enemy main forces when they came across the *Tanikaze*. They began their attacks on the destroyer at 1635 from 16,000 feet, initially attacking with four of their number and then with the remaining three. The latter had to make two passes over the *Tanikaze*, the second drawing fire. Neither side suffered any damage in this exchange, the *Tanikaze* being missed by all fifty-six 500-lb bombs aimed at her.

The carrier force eavesdropped on the Fortresses' radio net when the heavy bombers made their attack, so the presence of the *Tanikaze* was known to it long before contact was made with the Japanese destroyer by its aircraft. The destroyer was found by Dauntlesses of the *Hornet*'s first wave on their outward journey, but the dive-bombers, intent on finding a more substantial enemy, did not engage at this time. On this day, however, there was to be no repetition of the previous day's success, when a chance encounter with an enemy destroyer led American aircraft to a contact with enemy main forces. The Dauntlesses moved on to search for the Japanese but without success, and they had to be content with just the contact with the *Tanikaze* when they came across the destroyer for a second time on their return flight. They attacked the *Tanikaze* at about 1810, some twenty minutes after the Japanese destroyer had been attacked by dive-bombers from the *Enterprise*. The Dauntless performance of 5 June was well below that of the previous day, and neither the flagship's nor the *Hornet*'s dive-bombers were able to improve upon the earlier efforts of the Fortresses. Commander Katsumi Motoi worked his ship up to full speed and twisted and turned her beyond the reach of all but one of the bombs aimed at her. That bomb, a near miss, gouged out Y turret and killed six of its crew, but other than that the *Tanikaze* emerged unscathed from her ordeal.[29] In return she managed to shoot down one of her tormentors from the *Enterprise*, though she claimed to have shot down four and to have seen two more crash into the sea at the end of their attacks. As if the gods were now intent on exacting their price for past success, the Dauntless shot down by the *Tanikaze* was the one piloted by the same Lieutenant Samuel Adams, who had made the all-important contact with the *Hiryu* on the previous afternoon.[30] Having survived these various attacks, the last one of the day, made by the five Fortresses that set out from Midway at 1545, posed no problems to the *Tanikaze*. She easily evaded this attack, made around 1845 in poor light and at the relatively low altitude of 11,000 feet, and it is possible that the Japanese destroyer was responsible for the destruction of one of the heavy bombers. This aircraft, The City of San Francisco, was lost without trace and no Mayday signal. It may be that flak from the *Tanikaze* inflicted damage on the Fortress that proved fatal, though one of the other bombers reported that the lost aircraft was seen jettisoning her bomb bay fuel tanks in the course of its attack.[31] Another of the Fortresses was lost when it was forced to ditch just short of Midway. All but one of its crew were rescued the following day.[32] These two Fortresses were the only heavy bombers lost in the course of the battle.

The remaining fourteen Dauntlesses from the *Hornet* did not find the enemy main force, nor did they find the *Tanikaze*. But they, like the other forty-three surviving dive-bombers, did encounter one enemy, the approach of night. The attack mission had been launched in midafternoon to extreme range, and after the Dauntlesses had searched and in most cases attacked the enemy, they had to find their carriers in failing light and with little fuel. Nevertheless, their recovery by the *Enterprise* and the *Hornet* proved as successful as the recoveries carried out by the Imperial Navy one month earlier at the Coral Sea. Spruance is alleged to have accepted the possibility of night landings before the launch and to have accepted the need to take all measures necessary to recover his aircraft. His belief that if the tactical situation was such that the commander was not prepared to take all possible steps to recover the aircraft with which he fought, then he had no right to send out the aircraft in the first place.[33] Accordingly, Task Force 16 had its carriers switch on their search and deck lights to guide home the Dauntlesses. Just one dive-bomber—from the *Hornet*—was lost as it ran out of fuel while attempting to land on the *Enterprise*, but the aircrew were rescued by the plane guard, the *Aylwin*.[34] All the other aircraft were recovered safely. When the final count was made it was found that five of the *Hornet*'s aircraft had sought refuge on the *Enterprise* and one from the latter had transferred its loyalties to the *Hornet*.[35] The Americans had been lucky in their recovery, and in a sense it was their only compensation for their failure to find the enemy. The recovery could not disguise the fact that the day had passed without Task Force 16 being able to improve upon its success of the previous day; failure to account for a single Japanese destroyer was a poor postscript to the destruction of Nagumo's carriers. Moreover, it was a second day of failure for the *Hornet* and her skipper, Mitscher. On the fourth the *Hornet* had no impact on the battle, and on the fifth she did no better. The same day Mitscher, who had already been selected for promotion to flag rank, incurred Spruance's displeasure when his Dauntlesses straggled badly and the first of them to get back to Task Force 16 returned with unused ordnance. These early returnees had been armed with 1,000-lb ordnance, the *Hornet* having varied the weaponry of her Dauntlesses despite Spruance's specific instructions to use 500-lb

weapons after the Browning-McClusky confrontation. That the performance of Mitscher and the *Hornet* at Midway was less than satisfactory seems
to have caused Spruance considerable irritation.

The Americans' lack of success in contacting the enemy main forces
meant that the daylight hours of 5 June passed with the Japanese main
forces escaping from their vulnerable position in far better shape than they
could have dared to hope when dawn broke. By nightfall the Combined
Fleet had been reconcentrated. Kondo and Yamamoto had effected their
rendezvous at 0700, their two forces having sighted one another soon after
dawn.[36] Kurita, with just two cruisers, joined company at 1155. Nagumo
did not join up until 1300. When he failed to put in an appearance immediately after dawn Yamamoto had ordered the *Hosho* to fly off an aircraft to
find him. A Jean found what remained of the First Carrier Striking Force
some 40 miles to the northeast of Yamamoto at 0800, and after the latter
reversed course the two formations settled down on gradually converging
courses until their juncture was completed. That Nagumo had with him
and the *Nagara* but two battleships, two seaplane cruisers and five destroyers from the seemingly invincible force that just one day before had
been on the brink of its greatest victory brought home the full enormity of
defeat.[37]

Nevertheless, Yamamoto had other matters on his mind as he gathered
his formations about him during the course of the day. He had to decide
what to do about Kakuta and the Second Carrier Striking Force now that
the operation they had been told to support had been canceled. At 1259
Kakuta was told to rejoin the Northern Force, but the final decisions with
regard to operations in the Aleutians were not made until later in the day.[38]
Yamamoto also had to attend to the problem of refueling, and he had to
consider how to extricate the *Mogami* and the *Mikuma* from their present
difficulties—or how to turn their discomfort to advantage. The balance of
losses still had to be redressed, and at least on that matter there was one
thing Yamamoto could do immediately and with little effort. At dawn
Nagumo had ordered the *Chikuma* to launch two of her seaplanes to conduct
a general reconnaissance towards the southeast. At 0630 Seaplane No. 4
sighted the abandoned and drifting *Yorktown*, and at 0652 she began to tap
out her contact report.[39] The destroyer *Hughes*, standing by the carrier,
detected the intruder on her radar, but without air cover she could do no
more than track the scout on her screen until the contact faded as the
seaplane turned for home.[40] On the strength of what turned out to be an
accurate fix of the *Yorktown*'s location, Yamamoto ordered his nearest
submarine, the *I-168*, to set course for the carrier and ensure her
destruction.[41]

For most of the day Japanese main forces played a passive role, either
joining up with Yamamoto's formation or taking part in the transfer of the

wounded. The general movement of the main forces through the day was to the northwest, and any thought of offensive action was clearly subordinate to considerations of immediate safety. It was not until nearly midnight that orders began to flow from the *Yamato* as Yamamoto tried to redeploy his forces with a view to continuing offensive operations. By this stage in the battle it was far too late for the outcome to be affected in a way that would be favorable to the Japanese unless the Americans blundered. Yamamoto might make plans and set traps, but the power of decision lay with Spruance. After Task Force 16 had recovered its aircraft, Spruance had to decide on his course of action for the coming night, but unlike the previous evening, when he chose to steer eastwards and away from the enemy, on this evening he chose to head towards the west. His decision was shaped by the knowledge that the enemy was unlikely to be less than 300 miles away and that the enemy formations were probably heading for the bad weather front that the Catalinas from Midway and the Dauntlesses had reported was to the northwest of the atoll. Thus, Spruance decided that his own course should be towards the west, and he chose to steam at 15 knots in that direction through the hours of darkness. On such a course Task Force 16 would have a chance of contacting any enemy force to the northwest or the surface formation to the west of Midway, but at the same time the relatively low speed of advance would keep it safe if the enemy tried to double back at night and force a night action. Moreover, the speed of 15 knots was one that took into consideration the needs of the destroyers. The American escorts were beginning to get low on fuel, and 15 knots was their most economical cruising speed. With these decisions went one to conduct a full 180-degree search between south and north through west to a range of 200 miles at dawn the next day.[42] This departure from Spruance's normal practice of not carrying out reconnaissance on his own behalf was in large part determined by the admiral's exasperation with the relative ineffectiveness of Midway's Catalinas on the two previous days.[43] Midway, on the other hand, planned to undertake a much deeper reconnaissance on the sixth than it had on the fifth, and at dawn on the sixth the atoll's air group flew off fourteen Catalinas to search the sector between 220 degrees and 330 degrees to a range of 600 miles. [44]

With Task Force 16 some 340 miles from Midway at 0500 on the sixth, the search from Midway was to extend just about 50 miles beyond the search area of the carrier force. This was not enough to find the Japanese main forces, which were by that time just out of range and in the friendly weather front. But by backing from northwest to west in the course of the night, Task Force 16 emerged at dawn in a position from which it could contact the *Mogami* and the *Mikuma*, plus their destroyers, as the Japanese formation tried to get under the cover that Wake and its air group would be able to provide. Unfortunately for the Japanese, the front that covered

Yamamoto did not extend to this particular formation, and the latter was not within 700 miles of Wake. Spruance had determined not to go within that range of the island. The Americans were aware that it had been reinforced before the start of Operation MI, and the conventional wisdom was that Japanese shore-based bombers could operate to a range of 600 miles—hence Spruance's determination not to approach within 700 miles of the island.[45] The Japanese ships needed to be within 500 miles of Wake to escape from the *Enterprise* and the *Hornet*, and dawn found them beyond that range. Thus the course of the day's events was predictable. Denied a contact with the enemy's main forces, the Americans were able to take their time to account for the cruiser force. Indeed, there was no reason to suppose that the day would see anything other than the total annihilation of this little Japanese force. The Americans had everything in their favor. There was no air opposition. Weather conditions were almost perfect. The wind had veered around to the southwest, blowing from the Japanese ships to the American carriers. During the last attacks the Americans were less than 90 miles from Japanese ships, and American pilots were able to see both formations at the same time soon after they had become airborne.[46]

But if the fifth had seen the Japanese emerge surprisingly intact from what should have been a one-sided encounter between the *Tanikaze* and fifty-six bombers, the sixth produced an equally surprising result: only the *Mikuma* was lost to the fearful pounding that all four Japanese warships endured as Task Force 16 launched three separate attacks on them. The other three ships managed to make good their escape, the *Mogami* first to Truk and then to Kure naval yard, whence she emerged in May 1943 as a seaplane cruiser, similar to the *Tone* and the *Chikuma*. In this role she displayed such formidable powers of resistance on the occasion of her loss in October 1944 that it was perhaps not surprising that on 6 June she evaded the end in store for the *Mikuma*.* The latter's fate was sealed when one of the eighteen Dauntlesses launched by the *Enterprise* on the dawn recon-naissance—fourteen of her own and four wanderers from the *Hornet*—sighted her and her companions at 0502.[47]

Despite the almost ideal weather conditions, this and subsequent con-tacts resulted in a number of erroneous and conflicting sighting reports. The first indicated the presence of a carrier, later amended to a battleship. The arrival of other Dauntlesses on the scene only added to the confusion.

---

*The dockyard cut away the *Mogami*'s X and Y turrets, both damaged beyond repair on 6 June, and provided the cruiser with a supported level deck from which she could operate up to eleven seaplanes, a considerable improvement over the *Tone* class's capability of operating five. The *Mogami* was to survive another seventeen months of war before being lost in the action in the Surigao Strait during the battle of Leyte Gulf. She succumbed to the devastation of battleship gunfire, bombing and, ironically, an accidental ramming. Even then she had to be scuttled by torpedoes.[48]

Seaplanes flown from the cruisers at 0749 were dispatched to clarify the situation. The second contact report was accurate with regard to the composition of the Japanese formation, but it placed the enemy more than 50 miles from the location recorded in the 0502 report.[49] Throughout the morning Spruance and his staff were not sure what was in front of them. It was not until the *Enterprise* launched a strike that the situation began to resolve itself. The strike commander deliberately flew beyond the *Mogami*, *Mikuma* and the destroyers to contact the phantom force. His failure to locate a second force did much to settle the matter; by then the American command finally realized that the *Mikuma*, *Mogami*, *Arashio* and *Asashio* were quite alone.[50]

This particular strike mission was the only one the *Enterprise* made that day, and it was the second of three made by Task Force 16 against the four enemy ships. With the flagship having carried out the dawn reconnaissance, it was all but inevitable that the *Hornet* should have been the first to strike at the enemy, particularly when the ferocious Soucek was there to urge speed on all and sundry. The first strike flown by the *Hornet* consisted of twelve Dauntless bombers, fourteen Dauntless scouts and eight Wildcats. This wave, flown off at 0800, delivered their attack at 0946. One of the scouts was lost to flak, probably from the *Mikuma*.[51] The second attack, made by the *Enterprise*'s mixed bag of thirty-one Dauntlesses, three Devastators and twelve Wildcats, was launched at 1045. After the disastrous losses among the torpedo bombers on the previous day, Spruance personally briefed the Devastator pilots and specifically instructed them not to attack in the face of flak. This strike was delivered at 1215, and after it was over three of the aircraft landed back on the *Hornet* by mistake. The third and final attack of the day was launched at 1330, the twenty-three Dauntlesses and eight Wildcats of the *Hornet* engaging the enemy at 1445.[52] Originally there had been twenty-four dive-bombers involved in this, but one had to turn back with engine trouble. All the other aircraft on the mission were recovered by the *Hornet* by 1528.[53]

These three attacks between them left both Japanese cruisers a shambles, barely afloat and with dead and wounded strewn throughout them. In large measure the American failure to sink both cruisers outright, and the high losses sustained by the crews of the two ships, can be explained by the impact fuses on the 1,000-lb bombs, which were used by all the Dauntlesses except the scouts of the first attack. They, like the scouts of the reconnaissance mission, had been equipped with 500-lb bombs. At the time the different sizes of bombs and fuse settings seemed irrelevant, since there was little to suggest that anything other than the rapid destruction of the Japanese formation was at hand. In the event, however, the instant fuses on the American bombs meant that the main effect of the bombs that struck the Japanese ships was to pound rather than to pierce their victims.[54]

Initially the *Mogami* seemed the stronger candidate for the unwanted distinction of being the first to be lost. In the initial attack she was hit by one of the few bombs that penetrated either cruiser's armor before exploding. This bomb exploded within Y turret and killed the entire crew. Another bomb exploded amidships, destroying the torpedo tubes and causing raging fires between decks. But it was the second attack, made by the aircraft from the *Enterprise*, that doomed the *Mikuma*. Five bombs hit her in the course of this attack. A series of fires raged throughout the ship and set off a massive internal explosion at 1358 that caused her to lose all power. The flames were so fierce that the destroyers could not come alongside to take off survivors.[55] The *Mikuma* began to settle, and there was really no need for the final attack from the *Hornet* to complete her destruction. It was this one, however, that caused heavy loss of life amongst the survivors gathered topside. The attack set off a series of explosions amongst the ship's torpedoes that prompted the *Arashio* and the *Asashio*—after having rescued 240 men from a ship's company of 890—to pull clear and leave the cruiser and the men in the water to their fate.[56] Among those rescued was the *Mikuma*'s captain; he died six days later in the *Suzuya*. The two destroyers, however, did not make their escape unscathed. Both were hit by a single bomb each, the *Arashio* losing thirty-seven men, her sister ship another twenty-two.[57] But the efficiency of neither destroyer was impaired by their damage, and both continued to shield the *Mogami* as best they could. The cruiser sustained a total of six hits in the course of the various attacks that were made upon her, but despite seemingly crippling damage and the 300 or so deaths that these hits caused, she was able to limit the extent of her damage and remain afloat. By 1515 she had worked up to 20 knots and slowly pulled her way to safety. The *Mikuma* capsized and sank during the night.[58] The next day the *Arashio* returned to the scene of her loss and picked up one man. He and two men picked up by the American submarine *Trout* on the ninth were the only people rescued of the hundreds that had been left in the water on the sixth.[59]

Hundreds of miles both to the east and to the west of the *Mikuma*'s last battle, other events were in train that marked the end of the Midway exchange. To the west Yamamoto followed the events of the morning and decided to try one last time to bring the enemy to battle. At 1230 he ordered Kondo to take his force south, along with the *Tone* and the *Chikuma*, to stand by the *Mogami* and the *Mikuma* and escort them to safety.[60] At 1500 he brought the remainder of his forces, including the battle force from the north that had joined up during the night, on a course to the south. At the same time Yamamoto ordered Kakuta and the Second Carrier Striking Force to rejoin Hosogaya, and he gave orders for the Aleutians operation to go ahead as planned.[61]

Yamamoto's decision in favor of the Aleutians operation was prompted by three considerations. First, the occupation of islands in the western

Aleutians would fulfill the strategic objective of Operation AL, namely securing points of defense on the northeast approaches to Japan. The alleged value of the western Aleutians was not affected by what had happened at Midway. Second, Yamamoto was not opposed to picking up a consolation prize when the main one eluded him. In the Japanese view occupation of the western Aleutians represented a gain in its own right, and occupation of American national territory would be some small political and psychological compensation for the defeat off Midway. Third and most important of all, by pursuing the Aleutians operation the Americans might be tempted to come north; in that case they could present the Japanese with the chance to reverse the verdict of Midway. This last consideration, however, was pure moonshine. If the Japanese could not secure victory with the *Akagi*, *Kaga*, *Hiryu* and *Soryu* in the vanguard and most of the Combined Fleet piled up behind them, there was little prospect of the *Ryujo* and the *Junyo* securing a favorable decision in the latest version of the "decisive battle." Admittedly, the Japanese took steps to augment their forces in the northern Pacific. The *Zuikaku* was ordered to join Hosogaya's forces, but the order was canceled on 12 June when it became clear that the Americans would not fall into their enemy's trap. [62] At one stage they did come north, but amid a welter of false sightings and growing skepticism about the value of fighting for the lesser islands of the Aleutians after the victory that had been secured at Midway, they turned back. The Japanese main forces that traveled to northern waters returned to Japan on 24 June, having failed to reverse the Midway verdict. [63]

Yamamoto's flirtation with Operation AL on and after 6 June was perhaps as ill-considered as the American decision not to force a battle in the north was unfortunate. It is difficult to see how any resumption of the battle after 6 June in the north could have ended in anything other than further Japanese losses—and this was something that applied to the Japanese forces in the central Pacific, not just those in the north. After they turned away on 5 June the Japanese should have had just one priority: to get back under the cover provided by shore-based aircraft at the first opportunity and reconstitute the carrier forces. To continue the battle in light of the losses suffered by the carrier force made no sense whatsoever, and could do no more than endanger those carriers that had survived and whose value and importance had been drastically increased as a result of the loss of the four fleet carriers.

On the sixth, with two options for continuing the battle open to him, Yamamoto relied more on the Aleutians than on the central Pacific to produce the compensation for the losses of 4 June. Proof of this lay in his signal of 2320 when, with no contact with the Americans during the first part of the night as his forces steamed to the south, Yamamoto issued warning orders for the *Hiei*, *Kongo*, *Zuiho*, *Tone* and *Chikuma*, along with the

Kamikawamaru and the submarines that had been involved in Operation MI, to prepare to join Hosogaya. Subsequently the warning order was confirmed, and after 8 June the various units detailed to form the Aleutians Late Support Group began to assemble. By 14 June its single carrier, two battleships, two cruisers, eight destroyers and two seaplane tenders were on station off Kiska and under the command of the Northern Force.[64]

By this time, however, the Japanese had been reduced to grasping at straws. Yamamoto at this stage of the battle depended on Spruance to provide him with a chance that he would never have given the Americans had the roles been reversed, and it was inconceivable that the Americans would fall for anything so obvious as the trap he was trying to set. Spruance had not made the mistake of venturing too far either to the west or the south of Midway. He had kept clear of enemy air power on Wake, and he had ensured that the enemy's battle forces were held out of range. Now, on the sixth, his well-justified caution was reasserting itself, just when Yamamoto needed rashness on the part of the Americans to spring his trap. Spruance had no intention of being drawn further to the west, and he had no inclination to go after the *Mogami* when it was known that the cruiser had somehow survived and was dragging herself within range of air cover from Wake. Spruance was prepared to let her go. Like Nimitz, he suspected that the *Mogami*'s transmissions were at least in part a bait to draw him within range of a counterattack, and he declined to be so drawn.[65] Yamamoto was to maintain his south-bound course for the night action that there was still a chance would materialize. He stayed on course until 0700 the following morning (the seventh), when he finally accepted that the battle was over. At that time he turned his forces away to refuel before they set course for their various home bases. Even then he ordered the *Chitose*, in the company of the *Haguro*, *Myoko* and three destroyers, to proceed to Wake and continue transmitting false reports in the hope that the enemy might yet be lured within range of the bombers on the island.[66]

But Spruance at that time was well to the east, heading for a rendezvous with his oilers which were still on station in latitude 32° N, longitude 178° W, where they had been since before the battle began. Task Force 16 was turned back to the east at 1907 on the sixth, partly because of Spruance's natural caution and partly because of hard practical fact.[67] Given Spruance's disposition as revealed both at Midway and at the Philippine Sea, it is doubtful whether he would have accepted the risks involved in venturing further than 400 miles to the west of Midway—his rough position when he turned back—even under the most favorable of circumstances. On the sixth these were far from favorable. His air groups were depleted and his aircrews, after three days of hard fighting, were tired. Concern for the well-being and effectiveness of the air groups seems to have weighed heavily with him at this point.[68] But equally serious and more urgent was that after midday on the sixth the *Enterprise* and the *Hornet* only had four destroyers in company. At noon the *Maury* and the *Worden* had been forced to turn back to refuel, and Spruance knew after 1240 that he had in the *Phelps, Aylwin, Conyngham* and *Ellet* the absolute minimum for a screen. All four, moreover, were low on fuel and had little capacity for high-speed maneuvering in the event of a night action.[69]

After turning back to the east Task Force 16 steamed for more than a day before making a rendezvous with the *Cimarron* at sunrise on the eighth. The *Atlanta* was detached to find the *Guadalupe* and bring her to the rendezvous position to speed the process of refueling. The task force was also joined by units from Task Force 17, and by 2000 a reinforced Task Force 16 had been refueled. With two carriers, one light and five heavy cruisers, twelve destroyers and two oilers, it headed for a new rendezvous position in latitude 34° 45′ N, longitude 167° 30′ W. Refueling continued throughout the next day as the force moved to its new position. Then the two oilers, with three destroyers, took their leave of the force and set course for home.[70]

The rendezvous for Task Force 16 was to be with a reconstituted Task Force 17. Before it could be carried out Spruance received orders from Nimitz indicating that this juncture would be the first of two that would end with the commitment of the fleet carriers to the North Pacific. On the eighth Spruance received instructions to effect a second rendezvous, this time with Theobald's Task Force 8 at 1600 on the twelfth. The position designated for this second gathering of forces, Point Blow, was some 280 miles due south of Seguam in latitude 48° N, longitude 172° W.

The initial rendezvous involved formations committed to very different duties since the time they parted company at midnight on 4 June. At that time Spruance had turned Task Force 16 to the north to prepare to resume battle with the dawn while Fletcher kept Task Force 17 on course to the east, clear of the battle area. Thereafter, while Task Force 16 carried out its attacks on first the *Tanikaze* and then the *Mikuma*, the *Mogami* and their escorts, Task Force 17 engaged in the slow and laborious tasks of refueling, regrouping and transferring the survivors of the *Yorktown* to the submarine tender *Fulton*. The latter task was ordered by a Nimitz determined to keep Task Force 17 in the battle but aware that it could not fight if its ships were jammed with the *Yorktown*'s survivors. He therefore ordered the *Fulton*, one of the largest tenders of any description in the Pacific, to make her way from the French Frigate Shoals on a course and to a position calculated by the intelligence staff to be clear of enemy submarines. At her assigned position she carried out her rendezvous with Task Force 17 and took on board 2,025 members of the *Yorktown*'s crew from the *Astoria, Portland, Morris, Russell* and *Anderson*. By the time this task was completed and the *Fulton* had set course for home, most of Task Force 17 had turned back to the west.[71] The remaining two cruisers and three destroyers settled down for a rendezvous with Task Group 11.1, which consisted of the *Saratoga, San Diego, Mahan, Mustin, Smith, Preston, Laffey* and the oiler *Kaskaskia*. This formation had sailed from Pearl Harbor at 0630 on the eighth after just one day in port. Embarked in the *Saratoga* were no fewer than eighty-four aircraft, of which forty-six were new F4F-4 versions of the Wildcat. Of the remainder twenty were Dauntlesses, ten were Avengers and eight were Devastators.[72] Task Force 17 and Task Group 11.1 made their rendezvous at 0843 on the eighth, with Fletcher transferring his flag from the *Astoria* to the *Saratoga* at 1034. Thus reconstituted, Task Force 17 set course for its meeting with Task Force 16, which was carried out at 0934 on the tenth. The *Kaskaskia* was immediately detached to join Task Force 16, but bad weather prevented Spruance's ships from refueling and forestalled the main business of the day. This was the transfer of aircraft from the *Saratoga* to the *Enterprise* and the *Hornet*, a task that could not be carried out until dawn the following day when the *Saratoga*, for four days the most powerful carrier in the world, flew off ten Dauntlesses and five torpedo bombers to the *Enterprise* and nine Dauntlesses and ten torpedo bombers to the *Hornet*. Shorn of her offensive power, the *Saratoga* and Task Force 17 turned back for Pearl Harbor.

Some three hours after dawn, however, Nimitz recalled Task Force 16.[73] The previous day the American command had become aware that the enemy had landed on Kiska, and Nimitz suspected that the Japanese had prepared a trap for his carrier force in the north.[74] With his task forces already having won the main battle off Midway, Nimitz was in a position to decline action in the Aleutians if that was his wish. The Pacific Fleet did not have to fight for the western Aleutians, not for the moment at least.*

---

*The situation for the local Alaskan command, however, was different, and in briefly setting out the immediate American reaction to Japanese landings in the Aleutians, it is convenient to summarize certain features of the final stages of Operation AL.

The orders and counterorders of 4 and 5 June referring to the Second Carrier Striking Force, the invasion forces and Operation AL in general left the various Japanese forces in the north in no position to carry out the original plan of campaign when Yamamoto finally decided to let operations in the Aleutians proceed. Accordingly, on 6 June the Northern Force abandoned the proposed landing on Adak in favor of landings on Attu and Kiska the following day. At the same time the *Kimikawamaru* was detached from Omori's force with orders to proceed to Kiska to provide Ono's force with some measure of air support. She arrived on station on 8 June, by which time both Attu and Kiska had been secured at the cost of one fatality—an American civilian on Attu.

The American command suspected that the Japanese had landed on Attu and Kiska because radio contact with the islands was lost on the seventh, but it was not until the tenth, when Japanese warships and auxiliaries were found in Kiska Harbor, that the Americans were certain that the enemy had landed in the western Aleutians. Thereafter the American reaction was as rapid as it was ill-considered, and not even a delay caused by bad weather led them to rethink a policy that saw Catalinas, based on the tender *Gillis* at Atka, used in a bombing role. Between 11 and 13 June the U.S. Navy, with some support from heavy bombers on the eleventh, carried out the "Kiska Blitz," a round-the-clock bombing of Kiska by Catalinas. By

But Yamamoto, recasting his plans as he set his forces on a course to the south in his vain attempt to ensnare the Americans did have one crumb of comfort. During the fifth and sixth, when he struggled to swing the battle in his favor, another battle had been fought hundreds of miles to the east. On the morning of the fifth the *Hughes*, directed to stand by the *Yorktown* during the previous night with orders to sink the carrier if her fires spread or she seemed in danger of being captured, signaled Pearl Harbor that because her list and fire had not grown worse during the night, the carrier might yet be saved. This had led to a major salvage attempt on the part of the Americans, but during the afternoon of the sixth Yamamoto learned that the enemy effort had almost certainly been in vain.

When the signal from the *Hughes* was received, neither of the two officers most directly concerned, Nimitz at Pearl Harbor and his own skipper on the *Astoria*, needed any second prompting. But in trying to bring the stricken carrier to port the Americans faced four problems, and in the end their combination proved insuperable. First, at this stage of the war the Americans had no standard operational procedure for salvage, and there were no permanently assigned personnel for such parties. The crew of the *Yorktown* on 5 June was scattered between eight ships, two cruisers and six destroyers, and many hours were to pass as Buckmaster and his staff assessed needs, selected and then traced key personnel and supervised the various transfers. During this process one of the *Yorktown*'s officers, Lieutenant Elgin Hulbert, is supposed to have changed ship one dozen times

---

the thirteenth the stocks of the *Gillis* had been exhausted, half the Catalinas committed to the attack had been lost, and Japanese antiaircraft fire at Kiska had much improved.

It was at this stage that forces from Operation MI arrived on station as part of the effort to draw the American carriers into battle. As we have seen, the Americans declined to be so drawn and the major Japanese units were quickly withdrawn from the area, arriving back in home waters on 24 June. They left on station the Seaplane Unit that consisted of the *Kamikawamaru* and the *Kimikawamaru*, plus escorts. This was on the Kiska station until 18 June, when it sailed to Attu to conduct search and antisubmarine patrols, and it left for Japanese waters on 4 July after an air raid the previous day had slightly damaged three of the *Kimikawamaru*'s seaplanes. On the fifth the seaplane carrier *Chiyoda* arrived at Kiska with six Type 2 A6M2-N Rufe seaplane fighters.

By this time both sides were in the process of being dragged into a widening commitment in the Aleutians. For the Americans the commitment was obvious and unavoidable, but this was not the case for the Japanese. Their commitment widened in part because their initial "victory" in the islands was used as a propaganda device to deceive the Japanese population on the matter of the Midway disaster. Having told themselves that taking the Aleutians was worthwhile, the Japanese found that they could not abandon islands that, contrary to Yamamoto's assertion, did not represent "an important gain." In fact, the islands were a liability, just as the army alleged they would be. On 18 June the oiler *Nissanmaru* was sunk by bombing in Kiska, and on 4 July the *Triton* sank the *Nenohi* off Agattu. The next day the *Growler* sank the *Arare* and heavily damaged the *Kasumi* and the *Shiranui* outside Kiska harbor, and ten days later the *Grunion* sank the chasers *Ch. 25* and *27* off the same island. Losses were not all one way, but the trend was clear from the start of a campaign that was to last until August 1943.

during the night of 4–5 June, and that even before the signal from the *Hughes* was received.[75] Second, the various warships were some 150 miles east of the *Yorktown* by the time the signal from the *Hughes* arrived. Though the organization of the salvage party took place during the return to the *Yorktown*, the Americans were losing time that they could not afford. Third, there was no fleet tug with the fleet. There were only two on hand, the *Seminole* and the *Navajo*, and only the latter, off the French Frigate Shoals, was available.[76] But she could not reach the *Yorktown* until the morning of the seventh at the earliest. Shortly before noon on the fifth the minesweeper *Vireo*, called to the scene from her patrol off Midway, arrived and put a line aboard. She began to two at 1436, but with the *Yorktown*'s rudder jammed and the carrier twenty-four times the size of her wouldbe tug, the *Vireo* had an extremely difficult task.[77] There was no way the *Yorktown* could be towed clear of the danger area until the *Navajo* arrived. But the *Navajo* was not the only unit making her way towards the stricken carrier. The *Gwin* had been on her way to join Task Force 16 when she was directed by Pearl Harbor to stand by the *Yorktown*, and the *Monaghan* also came up in support.[78] She had been detached from Task Force 16 when she turned back to recover a bomb sight from a ditched aircraft.[79] In addition, units from Task Force 17 were making their way back to their carrier. And finally, heading for the *Yorktown* was another unit, one beyond the control of the Americans, which was to prove the crucial factor in determining whether or not they saved their carrier.

Buckmaster selected 28 officers and 133 men of his crew to go back to the *Yorktown*, the *Hammann* being chosen as the destroyer that would make the journey and lie alongside to provide the carrier with power. In the early part of the evening she completed the transfer of personnel and in the meantime took the chance to refuel from the *Portland*. Then she set course for the *Yorktown* and arrived in company at about 0200 on the sixth. The *Hammann* stood off in order to wait for the dawn.[80]

Buckmaster and his staff had decided to lighten the carrier topside before using power from the destroyer to shift oil from port to starboard and bring the carrier back on an even keel. This had been anticipated by the *Hughes*, but until the *Vireo*, *Gwin* and *Monaghan* arrived she could do nothing for the *Yorktown* other than rescue two wounded men who had been left for dead when the carrier was abandoned. In the late afternoon certain salvage work was begun. Secret papers, codes and ciphers that had not been secured before the carrier was abandoned were recovered. Aircraft were thrown over the side and the anchor chains let go.[81] But little had been done before the various parties were recalled for the night at 1930. Morning saw the salvage effort begin in earnest, and by noon, the same time that the *Enterprise*'s aircraft were moving in to attack enemy ships hundreds of miles to the west, one of the *Yorktown*'s 5-in turrets had been cut away and unceremoniously committed to the deep. A second turret was just about to be pushed overboard. Power from the *Hammann* was being used to help fight the fire in the *Yorktown*'s ragstore, to pump out the after engine room and to shift oil. The ship's list had been reduced from 25 degrees to 23 degrees—a small but significant sign that at least for the moment the sea was not gaining on the carrier.[82]

With the *Hammann* providing power and five other destroyers circling the *Yorktown* and the *Hammann* protectively, the Americans had high hopes of saving the ex-flagship. The situation of the *Yorktown* was not good. She had been sliced open over one-sixth of her length, and with the structural weaknesses caused by the damage suffered at the Coral Sea beginning to show through at this stage, she was leaking over one-third of her length. Her two engine rooms had been flooded, as had her main generator room and two of her boiler rooms. Salvage was going to be difficult, yet there was no cause for despair: at least by noon on the sixth the team appeared to be making headway. But some six and a half hours earlier the *Yorktown* had been sighted by the *I-168*. Until that time it had been a long and in some ways frustrating search for Tanabe and his submarine. He had wanted to find the carrier early and come out of the west against her either before or at dawn. Had Tanabe been lucky, the *Yorktown* would have been set against a light horizon, the *I-168* hidden in the blackness of the sea. But the *Yorktown* was too far to the north for Tanabe to have his wish. By the time the *I-168* came across the carrier, at 0530, it was broad daylight.[83]

The *Yorktown* had been sighted at a range of 11 miles, and Tanabe began his approach from the west on the surface, diving when he decided that he was too close to the enemy destroyers for comfort. Thereafter he stalked the *Yorktown* slowly and deliberately, coming to periscope depth every ten minutes or so until he was close to the screen. The American destroyers were gathered around the *Hammann* and the *Yorktown* at a range of about 2,000 yards, and it was Tanabe's intention to bring his boat to a range of 1,500 yards to be certain of scoring a hit on the carrier. The *I-168* was equipped not with the Type 95 torpedoes but with the older nonoxygen version, which had a warhead of 446 pounds. Tanabe intended to fire two torpedoes together at a single spot to produce the smashing power of a single Type 95, or more accurately, he planned to fire four torpedoes on a two-degree spread. It was normal practice to fire on a six-degree spread, but with the *Yorktown* making only three knots under tow there was no need to aim off. Tanabe, determined to put as heavy a punch as possible into the center of the ship, did not want to waste torpedoes forward or aft. More-over, he intended to set his torpedoes to run at 19 feet so they would strike below the carrier's armor belt. Since he also planned to fire at a periscope depth of 60 feet, Tanabe needed 1,500 yards to run true. In fact he condemned himself to strike below the 19-ft mark. By approaching the

Yorktown from off her starboard quarter, the *I-168* was brought against the carrier's starboard side, which was being raised out of the water by the ship's list to port. A torpedo set to run at 19 feet would hit the *Yorktown* on the normal 25-ft mark.

In the final stages of the approach Tanabe came to periscope depth every thirty minutes. The submarine was able to slip through the screen without being detected. The listening posts in the boat noted a sudden silence on the part of American search gear as the *I-168* passed through the screen. Perhaps a thermal layer, oil or debris, or a combination of all three, shielded the submarine from American sonar as it made its approach. But in making its final run into the attack without visual contact, the *I-168* came in too close, to a range of about 700 yards. When Tanabe checked his position he found that in addition to being too close to the *Yorktown* he was off the carrier's quarter, not amidships where he wanted to be. He began to circle outwards to take up an ideal attacking position.[84] Afterwards Nimitz acidly commented that there was something wrong with American antisubmarine tactics if five or six destroyers were not enough to protect the *Yorktown*. That may well have been true, but nonetheless Tanabe, a submariner since graduation in 1928 and one of the few Japanese "aces" to survive the war, made a thoroughly professional attack, even if only two of the four torpedoes he fired actually hit the *Yorktown*.[85] One rogue torpedo ran wide and narrowly missed the *Benham* on the far side of the screen, while another ran shallow and sliced through the *Hammann*. The other two hit home at 1336, striking the *Yorktown* more or less opposite the two previous torpedo hits.[86] The effect of these later hits was to complete the destruction of six of the carrier's nine boiler rooms and to tear out her bottom.[87]

The impact of the hits on the *Yorktown* pushed the carrier and the *Hammann* apart. The destroyer, struck in her boiler room, had had her back broken and she sank within three minutes. Eighty-one members of her crew were killed outright, and the casualty list was swelled by two massive underwater explosions that smashed bodies in the water and added to the damage of the *Yorktown*. The *Benham* picked up 166 men from the water, but 26 of them subsequently died from appalling diaphragm wounds. In the aftermath of the attack quartered bodies floated around the *Yorktown* and her escorts. The explosions were the result of either the *Hammann*'s boilers bursting as the ship sank or the detonation of a torpedo that was set running in its tube by the concussion from the hit.[88]

The *Yorktown* seemed to absorb the two torpedo hits well. Since they found their mark to starboard the carrier's list corrected itself, but only at the price of the ship's settling ever lower in the water. In fact she was doomed; she could not take blows of this kind. Her after elevator was jolted from its housing. Virtually all of the vital machinery areas were flooded, and with her watertight integrity compromised, her flooding could not be confined. There was no means of checking the advance of the sea, a fact that the *Vireo* appreciated quickly. At 1410 she slipped the tow, tacit endorsement of Buckmaster's earlier order, his second in two days, for the carrier to be abandoned.[89]

While two destroyers picked up survivors and corpses from the water, the *Gwin, Hughes* and *Monaghan* reacted to the attack by combing the tracks of the torpedoes. This was not difficult because they were not Type 95 weapons. To escape from the attack that he knew would follow his action, Tanabe tried to take the *I-168* down to 200 feet (nearly her maximum depth) and underneath the *Yorktown*. Things did not work out quite as Tanabe had hoped; the American destroyers were too fast for him. They quickly obtained the contact that had earlier eluded them and pounded the *I-168* for more than two hours until lured away on a false contact. In those two hours the American destroyers brought the submarine to within an ace of destruction. Paint fell off the inside of the bulkhead as a result of the depth-charge attack to which she was subjected, and at one stage she was leaking when both the inside and outside doors of her no. 1 tube were damaged. She was also threatened by a leakage of chlorine gas from her forward batteries, but somehow or another she managed to ride out the storm and repair her damage. The one thing that Tanabe could not do, however, was come to the surface quickly. As the American destroyers moved away he took the chance to creep slowly away in the opposite direction, and he surfaced at about 1645. By that time he had put more than five miles between himself and the Americans, and the light was beginning to fade. The first sighting of the *I-168* on one of the American destroyers was confused; what had been seen was thought to be another destroyer coming up to join the hunt. When the error was realized the three destroyers gave chase, the *I-168* deliberately making as much smoke as possible to confuse their gunnery. Tanabe stayed on the surface long enough to recharge his batteries and freshen the air of his boat. Then he dived as American shells began to land around him. Once submerged, the *I-168* reversed course and passed directly under the onrushing American destroyers. Tanabe's hope was that the enemy's sonar would be blotted out by the high speed of the destroyers' approach, and so it proved. The destroyers did not withdraw from the scene until 2245, but they believed that the submarine's dive had been involuntary and that she had succumbed to artillery after having been previously mauled by depth charges. Tanabe was able to resurface and head for home in safety.[90]

The *Gwin, Hughes* and *Monaghan* returned to the *Yorktown*, but there was nothing that they could do at this stage to assist the carrier. She had needed assistance on the fifth when none had been available, and she had needed protection on the sixth when none had been given. By the time the three destroyers returned to her all they could do was await the end and be prepared to pay their final respects. During the night the *Yorktown* gave a violent lurch to port, and first light revealed that the meeting of the sea and the port side of the flight deck would not be delayed for long. A constant roar of breaking metal could be heard as the sea broke into the ship and prepared to claim its own. By 0443 the carrier lay on her port side, bearing the wounds that had been made the previous day by the *I-168*. Then, with her battle ensign at her mast, she turned on her beam ends and began to settle by the stern. She sank at 0501[91]—noisily but with none of the massive underwater explosions that had marked the end of the *Lexington* and of the Japanese carriers—and joined the mighty eternity of a 12,000-ft deep as her escorts turned for home.[92]

PART V

Final Perspectives

CHAPTER 17

Final Perspectives

There is nothing new in the observation that wars are invariably fought long after their outcome can be discerned by the parties to the conflict. Wars reach a point where further bloodshed, suffering and destruction could be avoided if the belligerents gathered to discuss the general situation, decided their respective fates on the basis of the prevailing circumstances and moved without further conflict to a peace settlement. Unfortunately states lack the means to act in so rational a manner once they are involved in war, and if they did perhaps war might be prevented in the first place. In the Pacific war such a sane and humanitarian arrangement might have been applied to good effect. The war's outcome could be predicted with absolute certainty at least fifteen months before Japan's defeat was an accomplished fact. It must be noted, however, that even after three years of constant defeat and the devastation of Hiroshima and Nagasaki by atomic weapons, there were still many senior Japanese commanders who tried to evade the reality and responsibilities of failure.

It is this rationalism which views the Pacific war in terms of its outcome being foreseen that lies at the heart of the problem of assessing the significance of the events between February and June 1942. A somewhat superficial assessment may be sketched quickly by setting out the overall pattern of the Pacific war. The war began with five months of almost unchecked Japanese success. Then the tide turned and the Japanese suffered creeping paralysis and enfeeblement as their enemies fought through various island groups in the central and southwest Pacific to bring the war to Japan itself. The months from April to June 1942 represent the period when the imbalance of power that had previously favored the Japanese shifted. But this statement of the obvious does little to explain how the events of these months fit the larger pattern of the war and how the battles of the Coral Sea and Midway shaped subsequent events.

In fact both questions effectively revolve around Midway, since this was both the larger and the more momentous of the two battles. Midway rightly ranks amongst the greatest naval battles of all times and was the most costly of all the engagements of the Pacific war in terms of losses incurred by Japanese carrier forces. But it is a battle that cannot stand apart from the Coral Sea or the series of battles fought on, above and around Guadalcanal between August 1942 and February 1943. Despite its overshadowing every other engagement between May and December 1942, Midway formed but a part, admittedly the single most important part, of a whole series of actions that collectively marked the watershed of the war. The battle broke the effectiveness of Japanese naval air power. It was not until the final stages of the struggle for Guadalcanal that the Japanese high command realized control of events had slipped from its grasp—hence its decision to abandon the fight for the island—but the Americans could never have undertaken an offensive in the Solomons had it not been for their triumph at Midway. Japanese losses at Midway compromised Japan's ability to meet the American challenge in the southwest Pacific. Between May and December 1942 the two sides fought for the strategic initiative, and in this period the Japanese incurred losses that were so prohibitive they were forced to abandon the struggle for the central Solomons. Between June 1942 and March 1943 no fewer than 1,590 naval fighters were lost, and in the eight months before 31 December 1942 (the day Imperial General Headquarters made the decision to break off the battle for Guadalcanal), the Imperial Navy lost the battleships *Hiei* and *Kirishima*, the fleet carriers *Soryu*, *Kaga*, *Akagi* and *Hiryu*, the light fleet carriers *Shoho* and *Ryujo*, the heavy cruisers *Mikuma*, *Kako*, *Furutaka* and *Kinugasa*, the light cruisers *Yura* and *Tenryu*, the seaplane tender *Mizuho*, seventeen destroyers and fourteen submarines, plus other auxiliaries and lesser units, including the *Okinoshima*. Of these losses, the two battleships, one light and one heavy cruiser, six destroyers and five submarines were lost in the last two months of the year, and it was these losses, coming on top of the others, that finally convinced the Imperial Navy and thence Imperial General Headquarters that the struggle for Guadalcanal could not be sustained. Given this situation, the losses suffered by the Japanese at the battles of the Coral Sea and Midway begin to come into perspective.

Both battles were strange affairs. Certainly the Coral Sea and perhaps even Midway should never have been fought, while the latter gives rise to a whole series of paradoxes of which one is crucial to any assessment of the battle and its conduct. Reference has already been made to this paradox: before battle was joined there was no way the Japanese could have lost it, but once it began there was no way they could have won it. In the course of the exchanges the Japanese secured a position of advantage that should have ensured their overwhelming success—and then the battle was irretrievably lost. For reasons that will always defy rational analysis Yamamoto insisted upon a tactical deployment that incorporated every possible risk and weakness and left his forces inferior to the enemy at the point of contact, despite their having what should have been an irresistible numerical and qualitative superiority in every type of ship and aircraft except for submarines, heavy bombers and reconnaissance patrol aircraft. The latter were of marginal value. Only in one field, intelligence gathering, did the Americans possess a definite advantage over the Japanese, but this, combined with Japan's muddled aims and errors of tactical deployment, produced a stunning American success.

Japanese confusion at Midway was but a symptom of a more general confusion of strategic direction, and in some ways this is better examined in the context of the Coral Sea than it is with regard to Midway. In general, history had treated the Coral Sea as significant because it was the first naval battle to be fought without the rival fleets sighting one another. As the curtain-raiser for Midway, it has been totally overshadowed by the second battle. The result of the battle of the Coral Sea is generally agreed to have been a tactical Japanese success but a strategic Japanese defeat; the balance of losses favored the Japanese, but they were denied their objective, which was Port Moresby. With regard to this latter point, the check of Japanese expansion has been seen by various commentators to be of considerable importance.

Undoubtedly Japan's enemies were heartened by news of the Coral Sea, though part of this feeling was misguided because the American public (and as we have seen the British high command) was not told of the extent of American losses until after the battle of Midway had been fought and won. The edited version of the Coral Sea made available to the American people went some way to offset their reaction to the surrender of Corregidor and the Philippines. Japanese morale was dented, but not appreciably; the reverse was considered no more than temporary. In terms of the local situation, the position of the Allies in the southwest Pacific was eased as a result of the battle of the Coral Sea, though in truth Japanese pressure in the theater was certain to ease in any event. Midway, not the Coral Sea, ensured that Japanese pressure was not reapplied in the manner the Japanese had intended. This cannot be disputed any more than the significance of the Coral Sea as the first carrier battle in history can be disputed, but it hardly agrees with the general assessment made of the Coral Sea action. A case can be made for the battle's constituting a Japanese tactical success, though this is extremely doubtful. On the other hand, if the battle was an Allied strategic victory it was not for any reason that related to Port Moresby and the local theater of operations.

It was irrelevant to the future conduct of operations and the outcome of the war whether or not the Japanese took Port Moresby in May 1942. A

Japanese victory in the Coral Sea enabling them to secure Port Moresby would have led nowhere, and certainly not to any significant strategic gain without a victory at Midway to confirm it. Taking Port Moresby would merely have added the demands of yet another air base to Japan's already chronic overcommitment to a growing number of similar such bases in the southwest Pacific. Port Moresby could never have provided Japan and her defensive perimeter with any measure of security compatible with the effort needed to secure and maintain it. Japanese conquests and continuing operations in the southwest Pacific had neither deterred nor impeded the Americans from carrying out the Doolittle Raid, and persisting with operations in and around southeast New Guinea was never going to reduce or end this vulnerability. The value of a Port Moresby in Japanese hands can be gauged by reference to the career of wartime Rabaul. Initially by choice and then by force of circumstances the cornerstone of the defenses Japan created in the southwest Pacific, Rabaul proved useless. The Japanese took Rabaul on 23 January 1942 and held it throughout the war—its garrison capitulated on 6 September 1945 and that of Bougainville two days later— but the possession of Rabaul did not prevent Japanese defeat either in the immediate theater of operations or in the Pacific as a whole. Possession of Port Moresby would not have changed this situation. If the Japanese could not hold on to the central Pacific by virtue of their bases at Truk and Rabaul and the presence of their fleet, their ownership of Port Moresby was not going to redress this situation. On the other side of the coin, however, the alleged Allied victory in denying the Japanese Port Moresby can hardly be deemed to have opened up glittering strategic and tactical opportunities that had been out of reach before the battle of the Coral Sea was fought.

If the Coral Sea was an Allied strategic victory—and it was—then the view that it was a Japanese tactical success must be questioned. In this particular battle the strategic and tactical aspects of success were blurred by the confrontation between two quite different philosophies of war. This returns us to the major Japanese error. To repeat the observation that began this book, the Japanese, in their concept of operations in the southwest Pacific and indeed throughout the Pacific, made the fundamental mistake of misunderstanding the nature of the war they unleashed. They were attempting to make it into something that it was not and could not be.

Despite all appearances to the contrary, the Japanese operation to secure Port Moresby was precautionary and defensive. As such it was irrelevant to Japan's real needs and served no useful purpose at this stage of proceedings. The philosophy to which the Japanese were committed and sought to further enact by taking Port Moresby was one of static warfare conducted from various bases on islands strewn across the length and breadth of the Pacific. It was, in effect, the naval equivalent of a Maginot Line strategy, yet no island and base in the Pacific, with the exception of Oahu and the

Japanese home islands, had a self-defense capability. At best, a base in the Pacific could defend itself only as long as it remained unthreatened, since any enemy that moved to attack it by definition had to be stronger than the force that was defensively deployed. No island base could be secure for longer than the time it took for enemy air and naval power to control the skies over and the seas around them—and that was from the very outset of a campaign.

Victory did not depend on holding any particular island or base. It depended on fighting fleets bringing sufficient power to push through to a successful conclusion either the offensive move (be it a raid or an invasion attempt) or the spoiling counterattack. The key to victory lay not in possession of a base or bases that lacked the fire power needed to counter an enemy move but in the availability of mobile concentrated fire power. As Churchill explained to Curtin, "Land and air forces holding bases in the Pacific [Australia, New Zealand, New Caledonia, Fiji, Hawaii] are built up to minimum defensive strength required to enable them to stand without *immediate* support from fleet."[1] The operative word, as Churchill noted, was *immediate*; carrier forces, not island airstrips with a handful of aircraft, were the key to success. Victory was not going to be won by the side that spread its resources in an effort to be protected and secure at every point, but by the side that was able to concentrate massed fire power to destroy the enemy's similar capability. The war was about the projection of mobile fire power into waters that in orthodox terms would otherwise have been controlled by enemy surface forces. Islands in the Pacific were as relevant as a Jutland-type battle line would have been. Mobile resources were superior to static assets. Herein lay the root of the Japanese defeat at the Coral Sea—a defeat that was both strategic and tactical.

On a superficial level the Japanese secured a tactical victory at the battle of the Coral Sea because the balance of losses apparently favored them. The fate of the *Shoho*, even when combined with the casualties incurred at Tulagi, appeared to represent sheer gain when set against the destruction of the *Lexington*, *Sims* and *Neosho*. A 47,700-ton fleet carrier, plus extras, for a 14,200-ton light carrier, plus minor additions, was a good rate of exchange in anybody's book, but it was not the relevant rate of exchange in May 1942. The outcome of the Coral Sea cannot be measured by comparing tonnages and numbers lost or by reference to possession of a tiny port on New Guinea's southern coastline. It cannot even be measured in the terms outlined by Curtin in a brutally honest appraisal of the battle:

> We knew the strength of the enemy . . . . We knew his intentions and we knew the prospective date of his attack, yet we were unable to marshal the superior strength to deal him a heavy blow and the whole of his convoy . . . fell back on Rabaul unscathed. Fortune will not continue to favor us with these opportunities if we do not grasp them.[2]

In regard to any other battle such an observation would have been fair and perceptive, but in regard to the Coral Sea it was neither. The important point was not so much that the enemy convoy had been able to fall back unscathed but that it was forced to return to Rabaul because of what had happened to Japanese main formations. The balance sheet for the Coral Sea has to be compiled in terms of the demands made on resources by time and distance. The ability to concentrate mobile forces to dictate the direction and tempo of future operations was the all-important factor in the conduct of the Pacific war. The true cost of the battle was not to be found in calculations of ship losses but rather in contrasting the effect of the battle on the carrier forces. The effort the Japanese expended at the Coral Sea could have been better spent preparing for the main endeavor, Operation MI, for that alone held out some hope of decisive strategic success if the Americans accepted battle. By rights, the chance to do battle with the Americans should not have arisen at the Coral Sea, and when it did the Japanese failed to make the most of it. The whole of their effort in the Coral Sea became no more than a prodigal waste when the enemy carrier force that was encountered was not annihilated. The margin by which such a success eluded the Japanese was narrow, but so too was the margin by which they escaped disaster. The relevant point, however, is that given the paucity of Japanese resources, the extent of their commitments and their assured long-term inferiority to the Americans, they had to assert their initial superiority early in the war to achieve a definite strategic result. The Coral Sea was the type of battle the Japanese had to win quickly, decisively and at small cost to themselves if they were to avoid ultimate defeat. Given their commitment to Operation MI, they could not afford the luxury of forgoing the services of three carriers for even the shortest period of time unless the losses were suffered in return for losses that compromised the enemy's *strategic* capabilities. The very reverse was the case with regard to the outcome of the battle of the Coral Sea: while the loss of the *Lexington* did not impair American strategic capabilities, the loss of the *Shoho* and seventy-seven aircraft, plus the damage that put the *Shokaku* and the *Zuikaku* out of service for between one and three months, cut into Japanese strategic potential. Though at first sight the proposition seems preposterous, and though it was certainly not apparent at the time, the balance of losses at the Coral Sea favored the Americans: they were better placed to absorb the permanent loss of the *Lexington* than the Japanese were to do without the services of the Fifth Carrier Division for ten weeks *at this stage of the war*.

Virtually everything that applies to the Coral Sea applies to Midway, only more emphatically. The confusion of objectives and the diminution and division of force that denied the Japanese a possible victory in the Coral Sea brought them to disaster off Midway. But confusion was not confined to the Japanese in their planning of the campaign; it has plagued the many accounts of the battle as well. Even one of the more recent and serious if somewhat controversial accounts of the Pacific war contains an ambiguous and contradictory analysis:

> Midway *was* the "decisive" battle of the war in the Pacific. If it had been won by the Japanese, it is unlikely that it alone would have brought about the defeat of America, but it surely would have prolonged the war. However, Japan's loss of the decisive battle doomed the Japanese Navy and insured the ultimate defeat of Japan, for she could never match the industrial capacity of the United States in the production of weapons and hardware. Even with the resources of the South Seas, her supply lines would later become vulnerable to air and submarine interdiction.[3]

It is hard to see how a battle's conclusion could possibly prove "decisive" if a different result could only have prolonged the war and not changed its outcome. For all its seeming plausibility, this analysis explains nothing. There could be no question of the Japanese ever matching the Americans ship for ship, gun for gun, aircraft for aircraft. Both sides knew that, before and during the war. Indeed, it was one of the major factors in Japan's decision to go to war in the first place. But a Japanese victory at Midway would not have changed this situation. The use of the word *decisive* about Midway's outcome implies one of two things: either that the American victory at Midway was one from which the Japanese could not recover or that it reversed a situation which could never have been turned around without such a battle and victory. At best, both are doubtful propositions. It is possible to argue that the Japanese never really recovered from Midway, that they were never again able to give battle with realistic hopes of success. This certainly was true of 1943 and 1944, but such a situation most likely would have arisen, if not exactly in the shape and form it did, with or without Midway. Even if the first proposition is true, it fails to explain certain events of the second half of 1942. When the Japanese fought the Americans at the second battle of the Solomon Sea in August and at Santa Cruz in October, they did so on the basis of general equality; Midway did not automatically condemn the Japanese to a position of numerical inferiority and declining effectiveness. But Midway was fought between one navy at the peak of its strength and another if not at its nadir then close to it. If the final defeat of the Japanese was assured because of the disparity of national resources, Midway was at best only a milestone on the road that led to defeat; it was not a signpost that marked a parting of the ways, one track leading to American victory and the other in precisely the opposite direction. The American victory in the Pacific war might have been inevitable. The American victory at the battle of Midway might have been decisive. But these statements cannot both be true. In short, the notion of an inevitable victory is irreconcilable with that of a decisive battle.

It is all too easy to focus attention on the alleged inconsistencies in the writings of others or to indulge in an exercise in semantics. Any summary of Midway is certain to encounter formidable problems of interpretation, if only for one reason. Japan's defeat in the Pacific war was total in every respect. It encompassed her political, diplomatic, financial, industrial and military efforts. She was beaten on land, at sea and in the air. With regard to her defeat at sea it is possible to argue, without any hint of facetiousness, that if Japanese lines of communication were to be destroyed by Allied air and submarine action, all the major surface actions of the Pacific war were unnecessary. Six-sevenths of Japan's merchant navy was destroyed in the course of the war, and even before 1945 she no longer had the shipping to sustain her civilian needs. Over half of Japan's merchant shipping losses were inflicted by submarines, and they would have recorded even greater success but for the aircraft that in the last months of the war both complemented and rivaled their efforts as the war moved into Japanese home waters. Prior to that, every major American amphibious operation had resulted in soaring Japanese merchant losses as the Imperial Navy was forced to undertake resupply and reinforcement efforts in the face of enemy air supremacy. But in 1945 Japanese failure was not in some confined or distant part of the empire; it visited coastal waters and home ports. This time, however, Japanese losses could not soar, for there was virtually nothing left to lose.

Long before atomic weapons devastated Hiroshima and Nagasaki, Japan's capacity to wage war and avoid defeat had been destroyed by her inability to continue to function as an industrialized manufacturing power. This was achieved in large part by American submarines, and trying to make sense of Midway is therefore a many-faceted problem. If Japan was in effect broken because of the Allied campaign against her shipping, the part that a defeat in a single fleet action played in the wider context of national failure is not easily defined. The victory over Japan was total. It involved an overall effort that could not be compartmentalized. Japan was pounded into defeat on land, in the air and at sea, and the naval defeat was divided between efforts above, on and under the surface of the sea. Japan in effect hanged herself with a rope of many strands, none of which was more important than any of the others but one of which was often uppermost at any given time. In mid-1942 the carriers were the dominant strand; for much of 1943 perhaps the light forces were most important; and by 1945 the heavy bombers were possibly the key element in the war effort. The nature of their campaign prevented the submarines from emerging from their anonymity, though this did not detract from their overall performance.

Midway was fought at the time when the fortunes of the two sides were determined in the main by the few units that made up the carrier forces, and the battle was emphatically lost by the Japanese. Allied successes to date

THE FINAL PERSPECTIVES521

had been fleeting, partial or quickly reversed. In June 1942 the Americans recorded the first irreversible Allied victory of the Second World War. This simple fact was one of the most important aspects of the battle of Midway. For Japan it was the first significant defeat since 1931, perhaps even since 1894. Yet however grievous the defeat at Midway might have been, in the period that embraces the Coral Sea and the struggle for Guadalcanal American losses were as heavy as those of the Japanese, and the balance of damaged ships probably favored the Japanese. Given that on 1 May 1942 American strength in the Pacific was less than that of the Japanese, the American losses were relatively greater. Any examination of the actions between July and December 1942 suggests that the losses incurred by the Japanese at Midway did not prevent them from more or less balancing the books by the end of the year.

If one elects to use comparative losses as the yardstick to measure the significance of Midway, the Japanese losses at the battle, and in the whole of the May-December period, pale beside their subsequent losses. In 1944, for example, they lost four battleships, no fewer than six fleet and four light fleet carriers, two escort carriers, a staggering total of eight heavy and sixteen light cruisers, and no fewer than fifty-eight destroyers and sixty submarines. Losses in 1945 showed a decline only because by that time little remained to be sunk. As the Imperial Navy ran out of places in which to hide its last survivors, it lost two battleships, two hybrid battleship carriers (the *Hyuga* and the *Ise*), one fleet carrier, one escort carrier, four heavy and four light cruisers, thirteen destroyers and twenty-two submarines. But circumstances in the last twenty months of the war were very different from those that prevailed between May and December 1942. The losses of 1944 and 1945 were incurred under a condition that Yamamoto declined to face on 5 June—assured enemy superiority in the air. At Midway and in the last seven months of 1942, the initiative was disputed and the balance of power, though gradually tipping away from the Japanese, still remained in their favor. The losses of 1944 and 1945 were those of a defeated navy that fought for two reasons: first, to stem the tide of defeat and disaster, and second, to die so that it could atone for failure. The losses of 1942 were those of a navy with hopes of victory; those of 1944–45 were incurred by a navy without hope. However unrealistic Japanese aspirations were, in 1942 the Imperial Navy had chances that never reappeared.

Perhaps the most appropriate terms of reference for Midway were provided before the war by Stark in talks with the Japanese ambassador, Admiral Kichisaburo Nomura:

> If you attack us we will break your empire before we are through with you. While you may have initial success . . . the time will come when you too will

have your losses, but there will be this great difference. You will not only be unable to make up your losses but will grow weaker as time goes on: while on the other hand we will not only make up our losses but will grow stronger as time goes on. It is inevitable that we shall crush you before we are through with you.[4]

It was hardly a diplomatic observation, but it left virtually nothing unsaid and was one that both admirals understood. The battle of Midway, indeed the whole of the Pacific war before 1943, was fought by two prewar navies, one at the peak of its strength and effectiveness, the other only slowly beginning to recover from its traumatic plunge into war and yet growing to a strength that even Stark could hardly have contemplated. When Japan went to war she possessed 10 battleships; 1 escort, 3 light and 6 fleet carriers; 18 heavy and 20 light cruisers; 111 destroyers; and 64 submarines. In the course of the war she completed 2 battleships; 14 carriers of all types; 7 light cruisers; 63 destroyers and destroyer escorts; and 116 submarines. Submarines excluded, in 1940 alone the U.S. Navy ordered a force equivalent to the entire Japanese navy built and being built, and in 1942, 1943 and 1944 the annual output of American yards at least equaled the sum of Japanese wartime production of main force units. In 1944 alone the Americans launched a force that rivaled in strength the Combined Fleet of December 1941.* Such was the scale of American industrial power that if during the Pearl Harbor attack the Imperial Navy had been able to sink every major unit of the entire U.S. Navy and then complete its own construction programs without losing a single unit, by mid-1944 it would still not have been able to put to sea a fleet equal to the one the Americans could have assembled in the intervening thirty months.

Herein lies the proper context of Midway. The massive eruption of American power during the Second World War came in 1943 and 1944, but it was in 1942 that the Americans secured the strategic initiative in the Pacific with their victories in the central, southern and southwest theaters. Success in 1942 was not the result of an existing supremacy. By 1944 victory and supremacy were synonymous, but the U.S. Navy mastered the enemy long before the unprecedented expansion of its power became a reality. Midway was a step, the first and extremely important step, towards

---

*In 1940 the United States authorized the construction of 9 battleships, 11 fleet carriers, 6 battle cruisers, 8 heavy and 37 light crusiers, 195 destroyers and 72 submarines. In 1944 the Americans launched 1 battleship, 9 fleet and 35 escort carriers, 8 heavy and 11 light cruisers, 68 destroyers, 103 destroyer escorts and 78 submarines. The following is a table of wartime commissionings:

	BB	CV	CVL	CVE	CA	CL	DD	DE	SS
Japan 1941–45	2	7	4	3	0	7	32	31	116
United States Dec 1941–42	5	1	0	11	0	9	85	0	36
1943	2	6	9	24	4	7	129	221	56
1944	6	7	0	33	2	11	77	192	82

this expansion. It was a battle that ended the enemy's dreams of further conquest and forced him back on the defensive. It was a battle that resulted in the destruction of more fleet carriers than were lost in any other engagement of the Pacific war, and because most of the losses were Japanese it robbed the Combined Fleet of a balance that was not properly recovered for two years, perhaps not at all. Midway shattered the offensive capacity of the Imperial Navy and gave the Americans the chance to turn their attention from defensive duties to the task of breaking down the protective barrier with which Japan intended to surround herself. Yet Midway was only the beginning. In December 1941 the United States was a power in the Pacific and the dominant influence in the Americas, but elsewhere she had only interests and newly acquired responsibilities. Midway initiated the process whereby the United States was transformed from a power in the Pacific to the power of the Pacific, and to a nation, the only nation, with the means to back her worldwide interests. It was the success at Midway and the mighty assembly of fighting strength then taking shape in the dockyards, on the production lines and in the training schools that provided the ingredients that transformed the United States into the first global power.

Nominal Orders of Battle of the Imperial Japanese and U.S. Navies Between 7 December 1941 and 2 September 1945

	Fleet Carriers						Light Fleet Carriers						Escort Carriers						Battleships						Heavy Cruisers					
	Japanese			*American*			*Japanese*			*American*			*Japanese*			*American*			*Japanese*			*American*			*Japanese*			*American*		
	1st*	cmd	ttl	1st	cmd	ttl	1st	cmd	ttl	1st	cmd	ttl	1st	cmd	ttl	1st	cmd	ttl	1st	cmd	ttl	1st	cmd	ttl	1st	cmd	ttl	1st	cmd	ttl
8 Dec 41	—	—	6	—	—	7	—	—	3	—	—	—	—	—	1	—	—	—	—	—	10	—	—	—	—	—	18	—	—	18
31 Dec 41	—	—	6	—	—	7	—	—	3	—	—	—	—	—	1	—	—	—	—	1	11	—	—	12	—	—	18	—	—	18
31 Jan 42	—	—	6	—	—	7	—	1	4	—	—	—	—	—	1	—	—	1	—	—	11	—	—	12	—	—	18	—	—	18
28 Feb 42	—	—	6	—	—	7	—	—	4	—	—	—	—	—	1	—	—	1	—	—	11	—	—	12	—	—	18	—	—	18
31 Mar 42	—	—	6	—	—	7	—	—	4	—	—	—	—	—	1	—	—	1	—	—	11	—	—	13	—	—	18	1	—	17
30 Apr 42	—	—	6	—	—	7	—	—	4	—	—	—	—	1	2	—	—	1	—	—	11	—	—	14	—	—	18	—	—	17
31 May 42	—	1	7	1	—	6	1	—	3	—	—	—	—	—	2	—	—	2	—	—	11	—	—	15	—	—	18	—	—	17
30 Jun 42	4	—	3	1	—	5	—	—	3	—	—	—	—	—	2	—	—	2	—	—	11	—	2	15	1	—	17	—	—	17
31 Jul 42	—	1	4	—	—	5	—	—	3	—	—	—	—	—	2	—	—	3	—	—	11	—	—	15	—	—	17	—	—	17
31 Aug 42	—	—	4	—	—	4	1	—	2	—	—	—	—	—	2	3	—	6	—	1	12	—	—	16	1	—	16	3	—	14
30 Sep 42	—	—	4	1	—	3	—	—	2	—	—	—	—	—	2	4	—	10	—	—	12	—	—	16	—	—	16	—	—	14
31 Oct 42	—	—	4	1	—	3	—	—	2	—	—	—	—	1	3	—	—	10	—	—	12	—	—	16	1	—	15	—	—	14
30 Nov 42	—	—	4	—	—	3	—	1	3	—	—	—	—	—	3	—	—	11	—	—	10	—	—	16	1	—	14	—	—	14
31 Dec 42	—	—	4	—	1	4	—	—	3	—	—	—	—	—	3	1	—	12	—	—	10	—	1	17	—	—	14	1	—	13
31 Jan 43	—	—	4	—	—	4	—	—	3	1	—	1	—	—	3	—	—	12	—	—	10	—	—	17	—	—	14	1	—	12
28 Feb 43	—	—	4	—	—	4	—	—	3	1	—	2	—	—	3	3	—	13	—	—	10	—	1	18	—	—	14	—	—	12
31 Mar 43	—	—	4	—	1	5	—	—	3	1	—	3	—	—	3	1	—	14	—	—	10	—	—	18	—	—	14	—	—	12
30 Apr 43	—	—	4	—	—	5	—	—	3	—	—	3	—	—	3	3	—	17	—	—	10	—	—	18	—	—	14	1	—	13

*See notes on p. 530.

	31 May 43	30 Jun 43	31 Jul 43	31 Aug 43	30 Sep 43	31 Oct 43	30 Nov 43	31 Dec 43	31 Jan 44	29 Feb 44	31 Mar 44	30 Apr 44	31 May 44	30 Jun 44	31 Jul 44	31 Aug 44	30 Sep 44	31 Oct 44	30 Nov 44	31 Dec 44	31 Jan 45	28 Feb 45	31 Mar 45	30 Apr 45	31 May 45	30 Jun 45	2 Sep 45	Total
	13	14	14	14	14	15	15	16	16	16	16	16	17	17	17	18	18	18	19	20	20	21	21	21	23	—	—	—
	—	1	—	—	—	1	—	1	—	—	—	—	—	1	—	—	1	—	—	—	1	—	1	—	3	—	—	12
	—	—	—	—	—	—	—	—	—	—	—	—	—	—	—	—	—	—	—	—	—	—	—	1	—	—	—	7
	14	14	14	14	14	14	14	14	14	14	14	14	14	14	14	14	8	8	6	6	6	6	6	6	5	4	2	—
	—	—	—	—	—	—	—	—	—	—	—	—	—	—	—	—	6	2	—	—	—	—	—	—	1	1	2	16
	19	19	19	19	19	19	19	19	19	19	19	20	21	23	23	23	25	25	25	25	25	25	25	25	25	25	—	—
	1	—	—	—	—	—	—	—	—	—	—	—	2	—	—	2	—	—	—	—	—	—	—	—	—	—	—	13
	—	—	—	—	—	—	—	—	—	—	—	—	—	—	—	—	—	—	—	—	—	—	—	—	—	—	—	—
	10	9	9	9	9	9	9	9	9	9	9	9	9	9	9	9	6	5	5	5	5	5	5	4	4	1	—	—
	—	—	—	—	—	—	—	—	—	—	—	—	—	—	—	—	—	—	—	—	—	—	—	—	—	—	—	2
	—	1	—	—	—	—	—	—	—	—	—	—	—	—	—	—	3	—	1	—	—	—	—	—	3	—	—	11
	17	17	18	21	23	27	30	35	39	43	48	53	57	63	65	65	63	64	65	64	64	65	66	69	70	71	—	—
	—	—	1	3	2	4	4	5	4	4	5	5	5	6	2	—	—	—	1	—	—	—	—	3	1	—	—	76
	—	—	—	—	—	—	1	—	—	—	—	—	1	—	—	—	—	2	—	—	—	—	—	1	—	—	—	6
	3	3	3	3	3	3	4	3	3	3	3	3	3	3	3	2	1	1	1	1	1	1	1	1	—	—	—	—
	—	—	—	—	—	—	1	—	—	—	—	—	—	—	—	—	—	—	—	—	—	—	—	—	—	—	—	3
	—	—	—	—	—	—	1	—	—	—	—	—	—	—	—	1	—	1	—	—	—	—	—	—	1	—	—	4
	4	5	6	7	8	8	8	9	9	9	9	9	9	9	9	9	9	8	8	8	8	8	8	8	8	8	—	—
	1	1	1	—	1	—	—	—	—	—	—	—	—	—	—	—	—	—	—	—	—	—	—	—	—	—	—	9
	—	—	—	—	—	—	—	—	—	—	—	—	—	—	—	—	—	1	—	—	—	—	—	—	—	—	—	1
	3	3	3	3	3	4	4	5	6	6	6	6	6	6	6	6	6	3	2	2	2	2	2	2	2	2	—	—
	—	—	—	—	—	1	—	1	—	—	—	—	—	—	—	—	—	—	—	—	—	—	—	—	—	—	—	4
	—	—	—	—	—	—	—	—	—	—	—	—	—	—	—	—	—	3	1	—	—	—	—	—	—	—	—	6
	7	7	7	8	8	8	10	10	11	11	11	12	13	13	13	14	15	16	17	17	18	18	18	19	19	20	20	—
	2	—	—	1	—	—	2	—	—	—	—	—	—	—	—	—	1	1	—	1	—	—	1	—	—	1	—	17
	4	4	4	4	4	4	4	4	4	4	5	5	5	2	2	4	4	4	4	3	3	3	3	3	3	3	2	—
	—	—	—	—	—	—	—	—	—	—	1	—	—	—	—	2	—	1	1	—	—	—	—	—	—	—	1	7
	—	—	—	—	—	—	—	—	3	2	—	—	—	—	—	—	—	—	—	—	—	—	—	—	—	1	—	11

Appendix A (*continued*)

Date	Light Cruisers						Destroyers						Destroyer Escorts						Submarines					
	Japanese			American			Japanese			American			Japanese			American			Japanese			American		
	lst	cmd	ttl	lst	cmd	ttl	lst	cmd	ttl	lst	cmd	ttl	lst	cmd	ttl	lst	cmd	ttl	lst	cmd	ttl	lst	cmd	ttl
8 Dec 41	—	—	20	—	—	19	—	—	111	—	—	168	—	—	—	—	—	—	—	—	64	—	—	112
31 Dec 41	—	—	20	—	1	20	4	—	107	—	2	170	—	—	—	—	—	—	3	—	61	1	3	114
31 Jan 42	—	—	20	—	1	21	—	—	107	3	4	174	—	—	—	—	—	—	3	—	58	2	3	115
28 Feb 42	—	—	20	—	2	23	1	—	106	—	2	173	—	—	—	—	—	—	1	4	61	1	1	115
31 Mar 42	—	—	20	—	—	23	—	2	108	4	3	172	—	—	—	—	—	—	—	—	61	1	2	116
30 Apr 42	—	—	20	—	—	23	—	—	108	1	6	177	—	—	—	—	—	—	—	1	62	—	2	118
31 May 42	—	—	20	—	1	23	1	—	107	1	4	180	—	—	—	—	—	—	2	2	62	—	4	122
30 Jun 42	—	—	20	—	—	24	1	2	108	1	9	188	—	—	—	—	—	—	—	1	63	—	4	125
31 Jul 42	—	—	20	—	1	25	2	—	106	—	7	195	—	—	—	—	—	—	1	—	62	—	4	128
31 Aug 42	—	—	20	—	1	25	2	3	107	4	10	201	—	—	—	—	—	—	3	3	62	1	2	129
30 Sep 42	—	—	20	—	1	26	1	—	106	—	9	210	—	—	—	—	—	—	1	2	63	—	3	132
31 Oct 42	1	—	20	—	1	27	4	—	102	3	9	210	—	—	—	—	—	—	2	2	63	—	4	136
30 Nov 42	—	—	20	2	—	26	4	—	98	7	9	212	—	—	—	—	—	—	3	1	61	—	1	137
31 Dec 42	1	—	19	—	—	26	2	3	99	—	11	222	—	—	—	—	—	—	2	4	63	—	3	140
31 Jan 43	—	—	19	—	1	27	—	1	100	1	8	225	—	—	—	—	1	1	1	2	64	1	4	143
28 Feb 43	1	—	20	—	—	27	2	—	98	1	10	234	—	—	—	—	2	3	1	1	64	1	3	145
31 Mar 43	—	—	20	—	1	28	6	2	94	—	9	243	—	—	—	—	2	5	—	3	67	2	4	147
30 Apr 43	—	—	20	—	—	28	1	1	94	1	13	255	—	—	—	—	10	15	1	3	69	2	4	149
31 May 43	—	—	20	—	—	28	3	1	92	—	12	267	—	—	—	—	15	30	3	3	69	—	5	154
30 Jun 43	1	—	21	—	—	28	—	—	92	—	8	275	—	—	—	—	18	48	2	2	69	2	4	156

31 Jul 43	1	—	1	—	20	—	28	7	3	88	14	—	—	19	67	5	5	—	6	162
31 Aug 43	—	—	—	1	20	—	29	3	—	85	11	—	—	28	95	2	1	—	4	165
30 Sep 43	—	—	—	—	20	—	29	—	—	85	13	—	—	28	123	3	6	2	5	168
31 Oct 43	—	—	—	—	20	2	29	2	1	84	7	—	—	31	154	—	3	3	7	172
30 Nov 43	1	—	—	—	19	6	29	6	—	79	12	—	—	35	189	7	5	2	5	175
31 Dec 43	—	3	—	3	20	2	32	2	2	79	12	—	—	32	221	—	3	—	5	179
31 Jan 44	1	—	—	1	19	2	33	2	—	77	6	—	—	19	240	3	5	3	5	184
29 Feb 44	3	—	3	—	16	6	33	6	1	72	9	—	—	28	268	7	4	7	5	186
31 Mar 44	—	—	1	2	15	2	33	2	—	72	10	—	—	20	287	2	2	—	8	193
30 Apr 44	1	—	—	—	14	3	33	3	—	69	6	—	1	22	308	6	6	1	8	200
31 May 44	—	—	—	2	14	3	34	3	—	68	8	—	1	27	334	9	3	—	7	207
30 Jun 44	—	—	3	—	15	7	36	7	3	61	8	—	3	18	351	11	2	2	8	213
31 Jul 44	2	—	2	—	14	3	37	3	—	58	7	—	1	20	371	6	3	2	7	218
31 Aug 44	—	—	1	—	14	3	38	3	—	55	3	1	3	16	386	—	4	2	7	223
30 Sep 44	—	—	—	2	12	2	40	2	1	53	4	—	4	9	395	2	4	—	5	228
31 Oct 44	4	—	—	—	8	11	40	11	2	42	2	3	11	8	400	6	2	5	7	230
30 Nov 44	2	1	—	—	7	11	40	11	1	31	8	—	12	4	404	4	2	3	6	233
31 Dec 44	—	—	3	—	7	5	43	5	5	28	6	2	15	1	405	4	2	—	9	242
31 Jan 45	1	—	2	—	6	3	45	3	—	26	3	3	14	2	407	7	2	—	3	244
28 Feb 45	—	—	1	—	6	3	46	3	—	23	8	—	15	1	408	2	2	1	6	249
31 Mar 45	—	—	—	6	6	—	46	—	—	23	12	6	21	—	408	7	1	2	5	252
30 Apr 45	2	—	—	—	4	5	46	5	4	19	5	—	22	—	407	—	1	1	5	256
31 May 45	—	—	—	—	4	—	47	—	5	19	8	3	25	—	406	2	9	1	2	257
30 Jun 45	—	—	2	2	4	1	49	1	2	19	7	1	24	1	407	3	2	1	5	261
2 Sep 45	1	—	—	—	3	1	49	1	1	18	13	3	21	—	406	1	7	—	5	265
	24	7	33	32	—	125	—	32	70	—	347	10	31	11	417	129	116	52	205	—

NOTES:

lst—the number of units lost in that month
cmd—the number of units completed (if Japanese) or commissioned (if American) in that
      month
ttl—the total number of units in service on that date

The figures given for 2 September 1945 refer to the number of units completed/
commissioned and lost by both sides between 1 July and 2 September and the number that
were in service on the day that the war ended.

No allowance has been made for ships out of service or time spent in dockyards for repair,
refit or conversion.

The Japanese submarine lists do not include the *Ha*-class transports, but do include as lost
one unit that was scrapped, and the figures have been adjusted to take account of the fact that
one boat was lost on two separate occasions.

The American destroyer lists have been adjusted to take account of the fact that after August
1942 a total of sixty-six units were taken from service for conversion and recommissioning in
other roles.

The American lists do not include units built directly for other Allied navies or which were
transferred after service, however minimal, with the U.S. Navy.

The three battleships and three destroyers lost by the Americans at Pearl Harbor and
subsequently returned to service have not been included in the lists for 8 December 1941 but
have been entered as they recommissioned, the *Shaw* being deemed to have returned to service
in August 1942.

The terms *completed* and *commissioned* give rise to certain problems of interpretation. American units are commissioned before completion and often some time before they are ready for
service. The *Essex*, for example, was commissioned six months before she was ready for
service. Japanese units, on the other hand, might not be commissioned until after completion
or prior service at sea. The *Shoho*, for example, has been variously considered to have been in
service before the start of the war, to have been completed in January 1942 and to have been
commissioned—activated in a fleet role—in April. Thus there must be a certain latitude about
these figures, though they do provide a general basis of comparison.

The Fate
of the Anglo-American
Combined Fleet

The British unwillingness to undermine the fragile structure of power in India ended a rather curious episode in which both the British and Americans proposed the creation of an Anglo-American fleet and rejected the idea when the other party showed any interest in it. Before the outbreak of the Pacific war the British had tried to persuade the Americans to deploy at least a part of their fleet at Singapore in order to defend southeast Asia. Apparently the first time the idea of a joint Anglo-American fleet—perhaps confusingly referred to as the Combined Fleet—was put forward after the outbreak of war was on 10 December 1941, when British joint planners shelved the idea.[1] One can only surmise that the loss of the *Repulse* and the *Prince of Wales* ended any further thought of a combined fleet for the obvious reason that there were no fleets left to combine after the tenth. It would seem that the idea remained on the shelf until 19 March, when John Curtin tried to make it his own. Conscious that Allied forces were weak because they were dispersed and deployed defensively against an enemy holding the strategic initiative, Curtin argued that offensive action alone could disguise Allied weakness. Thus he proposed a combined fleet, and in his signal to Churchill on this day he set out the strength that such a fleet should have. His suggestion was for nine carriers, fifteen heavy cruisers, two dozen destroyers and nine fast oilers. There does not seem to have been so detailed a proposal made before this time, and Curtin's suggestion was that this fleet should consist of three task forces, two American and one British. Such a force would be able to deploy between 400 and 500 aircraft but no capital ships. In Curtin's view "these valuable ships should be kept well away" from combat until the carriers had won air supremacy.[2] This particular proposal was made at the time of the various arguments over new command arrangements in the Pacific following the collapse of the ABDA area, and the idea was under British consideration at the time of the Japanese attack on Ceylon.

At this time the British rejected the idea of a combined fleet, and their main calculation, or at least the main calculation that was committed to paper, was that such a fleet could not operate from one single base and cover both the Pacific and Indian oceans.[3] Be that as it may, the British appear to have been influenced by the calculation that from mid-April onwards the U.S. Pacific Fleet would be roughly the same size as the Japanese Combined Fleet.[4] The implications of such a situation were obvious, and there seems to have been an ambivalence in British thinking on this matter after the Ceylon raid.

On the basis of very incomplete evidence, a tentative conclusion can be drawn that the only time the Americans and British considered the suggestion of a combined fleet was when they thought it would be to their own immediate advantage. Both were intent on preserving their freedom of action on the matter of strategic deployment, and it is clear that neither really had any confidence in their ally being able or willing to risk his own position in order to protect interests that the other deemed essential to its survival. King's suggestions in May have all the signs of a deathbed conversion, while the British reaction smacks of the agreement in principle that, according to Bismarck, indicates a complete refusal to do anything in practice. Probably the real views of both the British and the Americans read between the lines of the British minutes of the Anglo-American discussions in Washington on 21 June—after Midway had ended the sense of urgency on the part of the Allies. These minutes read, quite simply, "It was agreed that Admiral King should inform the British High Command of the action which he would like the British Eastern Fleet to undertake in support of his own operations in the Pacific."[5] It was a rather illuminating comment on the realities of Anglo-American relations, at least where the Pacific was concerned.

Source Notes

CHAPTER 1

1. Clausewitz, 121.
2. Rosinski, 103.
3. Dull, 18–19.
4. Storry, 208.
5. Jentschura, 38–40; Pelz, 33; Watts, 69–70.
6. Chihaya 1973, 137.
7. Hagan, 264. *See also* pp. 237, 240–41, 243, 247–48 and Pelz, 202–8 for details of previous American construction programs.
8. Pelz, 224.
9. Sadao, 151–56.
10. Rosinski, 106.
11. See, for example, the following articles in *Time* magazine:
    "Japan." Vol. 38, no. 15 (1941): 27.
    "Safety Razor." Vol. 38. no. 18 (1941): 23–25.
    "War Footing." Vol. 38, no. 24 (1941): 87–90.
12. Pelz, 196.
13. Dull, 28.
14. Marder, 328–29.
15. Bauer, 394.
16. Rosinski, 106.
17. Willmott 1981, 14–15; Prange, 21.
18. Rosinski, 103.
19. Lundstrom, 8–9.
20. Rosinski, 53–101.
21. Peattie, 65–69.
22. Reynolds, 1.
23. Reynolds, 485–86.
24. Kiralfy, 459.
25. Peattie, 65.

26. Rosinski, 112–13.
27. Hagan, 230, 257; Morton 1962, 61–64.
28. Sadao, 148.
29. Wilds, 402.
30. Morison 1968, 42–43; Reynolds, 510.
31. Agawa, 31.
32. Toland 1970, 94.
33. Slim, 537–38.
34. Spurr, 295.
35. Pelz, 33–34; Jentschura, 39.
36. Chihaya 1973, 130; Spurr, 24.
37. Watts, 288; Jentschura, 151.
38. Watts, 268.
39. Willmott, *Zero A6M*, 32–59.
40. Pelz, 32; Chihaya and Abe 1971, 265.
41. Kiralfy, 468.
42. Spurr, 25.
43. Jentschura, 40; Pelz, 34; Watts, 73–74.
44. Watts, 152–55.
45. Jentschura, 28; Watts, 41, 56.
46. Kiralfy, 469.
47. Pelz, 31.
48. Peattie, 67–68.
49. Jentschura, 163.
50. Pelz, 35.
51. Francillon 1970, 453.
52. Yoshida, 1.
53. Preston, 164, 170, 173.
54. Pelz, 29–32.
55. Kiralfy, 471–74.
56. Kiralfy, 468; Peattie, 65; Warner, 506.
57. Peattie, 66; Warner, 500–501.
58. Willmott 1982, 87.
59. Francillon 1970, 379.
60. Pelz, 31, 35.
61. Marder, 315.
62. Sadao, 148.
63. Agawa, 200.
64. Gill 1968, 27.
65. Pelz, 35; Willmott, *Zero A6M*, 7.
66. Chihaya and Abe 1971, 275.
67. Pelz, 36.
68. Pelz, 39.
69. Ito, 12.
70. Toyama, 209–10.
71. Toland 1970, 86.
72. Ito, 54.

73. Okumiya, 120.
74. Dull, 340; Fuchida, 240–43.

CHAPTER 2

1. This was a description used by Hugh Byas in his book of that name, *Government by Assassination*. London: Allen and Unwin (1944).
2. Browne, 76.
3. Lundstrom, 6.
4. Lundstrom, 5; Hayashi, 10.
5. Hayashi, 2; Pelz. 172–74; Sadao, 146, 159.
6. Hayashi, 33, 41.
7. Wenzel, 5.
8. Fuchida, 71.
9. Wenzel, 2.
10. Barker, 19.
11. Barde, 29.
12. Fuchida, 72; Lundstrom, 40.
13. Wenzel, 7.
14. Browne, 148.
15. Fuchida, 67–70.
16. Barde, 23–25.
17. Barker, 29.
18. Lundstrom, 41.
19. Adm 223/51; NID 24/T48/45.
20. Dull, 116; Hayashi, 43.
21. Toland 1970, 302–3.
22. Montgomery, 165.
23. Rosinski, 106.
24. Barker, 19–21; Fuchida, 67–70; Hayashi, 42–43.
25. Adm 223/51; NID 24/T47/45.
26. Kirby 1958, 116.
27. Adm 199/454.
28. Agawa, 294.
29. Wenzel, 12–13.
30. Kirby 1958, 146.
31. Willmott 1982, 423.
32. Kirby 1958, 109.
33. Wenzel, 11.
34. Toland 1970, 303–4.
35. Dull, 100.
36. Lundstrom, 23.
37. Lundstrom, 25.
38. Lundstrom, 27.
39. Lundstrom, 25.
40. Lundstrom, 27.
41. Lundstrom, 3, 23.
42. Forrestal, 3, 25.

43. Willmott 1982, 286.
44. Lundstrom, 24.
45. Brown 1974, 33.
46. Marder, 315–16.
47. Lundstrom, 33.
48. Lundstrom, 35.
49. Milner, 10; *Japanese Monograph* no. 37, 3.
50. Dull, 101; Gill 1968, 6–7.
51. Yoshida 1.
52. Miller, 5.
53. Gill 1968, 6.
54. Dull, 101.
55. Lundstrom, 37; Potter, 43.
56. Lundstrom, 38.
57. Brown 1974, 36.
58. Yoshida 1.
59. Lundstrom, 38.
60. Potter, 44.
61. Buell 1980, 174, 178.
62. Prem 3/470/388.
63. Yoshida 1.
64. McCarthy, 65.
65. Agawa, 129.
66. Lundstrom, 42.
67. Fuchida, 73.
68. Lundstrom, 46.
69. Barde, 99; Morison 1967, 72.
70. Yoshida 6.
71. Fuchida, 76.
72. Barde, 32–33.
73. Fuchida, 73–76.
74. Lundstrom, 45.
75. Barde, 30.
76. Fuchida, 75.
77. Barde, 31.
78. Fuchida, 74–76.
79. Prange, 234.
80. Agawa, 294.
81. Fuchida, 77.
82. Prange, 297–99.
83. Fuchida, 77.
84. Toland 1970, 304.
85. Barde, 27.
86. Barde, 34.
87. Barde, 40.
88. Lundstrom, 46.
89. Lundstrom, 39, 67, 70.

90. Jentschura, 47.
91. Dull, 111; Lundstrom, 60.
92. Prange, 375.
93. Lundstrom, 66.
94. Wenzel, 13.

CHAPTER 3

1. Sources

Given the nature of this chapter it proved impossible to credit sources for the Japanese order of battle within the text. The major sources consulted were Blair, Dull, Fuchida and Okumiya, Morison, Rohwer and Hummelchen, with Brown, 1974 and 1977, Billot, Francillon, 1970, and Jentschura, Jung and Mickel used as references in their specific fields. Lundstrom was relied upon in relating the intended order of battle and plan of campaign devised by the Japanese army for the southwest Pacific. The American operations that related to Operation K were drawn from Hough.

Because the various accounts of proceedings could not be reconciled, the author consulted, on the advice of Colonel D. O. Caton of the British Embassy in Tokyo, Commander Akihiko Yoshida, then of the Military History Department at the National Defense Academy. Commander Yoshida checked a series of questions and finally the completed text against official Japanese records, and where appropriate the text has been written to accord with these sources. Commander Yoshida's comments and corrections have been taken as authoritative except in the area of seaplane carrier development for the Aleutians and Midway, for which Professor Kanji Akagi was consulted.

2. Japanese air strength at Midway

The statement of the Japanese air order of battle given in this chapter is different from that given in any previous account of the battle. It has been drawn up on the basis of material provided by Commander Yoshida and Professor Akagi, and while inconsistencies and possible errors may still remain, it is the author's belief and hope that this order of battle is as accurate as the record permits and clears up several of the small—and not so small—inconsistencies that beset previous accounts of this battle.

It will suffice to provide but two minor examples of the clarification of inconsistencies by this order of battle. First, many accounts of the battle of Midway credit the *Akagi* and the *Kaga* flying off one Kate reconnaissance aircraft each in the course of the approach to Midway on 4 June, but no such Kate would have been available from the *Akagi* if the carrier deployed nine of her Kates for the first-wave attack and the remainder for the second. Second, the circumstances surrounding the sinking of the *Hiryu* on 5 June cannot be reconciled against most orders of battle. Shortly before she sank she was overflown by an aircraft from the *Hosho*, and survivors from the *Hiryu* noted that this aircraft had wheels—i.e., a fixed undercarriage. This is a point glossed over because normal orders of battle credit the *Hosho* and the *Zuiho*, the only carriers that could have put an aircraft over the *Hiryu*, with Kates and Zekes, both of which had retractable undercarriages. The author's suspicion was that the aircraft concerned was a Claude fighter, though how a short-range interceptor could have reached the *Hiryu* remains an obvious inconsistency. It was not until Commander Yoshida's letter of 1 March 1983 that matters fell into place with the realization that both the *Hosho* and the *Zuiho* were equipped with Claudes and Jeans.

I do not wish in any way to detract from other accounts of the battle, but the total of 433 aircraft and seaplanes embarked by Japanese forces for Operations AL and MI—246 of them with the First Carrier Striking Force—contrasts with the totals provided by other primary and secondary sources as follows:

Macintyre's *The Battle for the Pacific* and D'Albas's *Death of a Navy* give no figures at all, either for the Japanese forces before the battle or for their losses. Bruce's *Sea Battles of the Twentieth Century* (pp. 101–15) states that "Yamamoto's total force" (whatever that might mean) deployed 280 aircraft but gives no losses. Hezlett's *The Aircraft and Sea Power* places Japanese strength at 500 aircraft and seaplanes, and states that 250 were lost. Winton's *The War in the Pacific* (p. 52) gives a figure of 400 aircraft with the eight carriers involved in Operations AL and MI but gives neither breakdown nor losses.

Steeh's *Decisive Battles of the Pacific War* (pp. 46–59) does not give an original order of battle but states that the Japanese lost 332 aircraft. This is obtained from what is generally regarded as the most authoritative Japanese source, Fuchida and Okumiya's *Midway: The Battle That Doomed Japan*. Of this total 322 appear to have been from the carriers. But these two totals (on p. 246) contrast with the order of battle given three pages later, which credits the First Carrier Striking Force with 261 aircraft. On p. 161, however, reference is made to aircraft that would *appear* not to be within the order of battle on p. 249, though this matter is not without ambiguity. Barker's *Midway: The Turning Point* reproduces the figures of Fuchida and Okumiya with 261 as the original Japanese strength and 332 as their losses. Adding up individual totals, however, produces a total of 262 for the initial carrier strength. The total of 261 is also given by Ito in *The End of the Imperial Japanese Navy*. Ito does not provide an individual ship breakdown but does provide one by divisions, and this accords with Fuchida and Okumiya. Okumiya, when collaborating with Horikashi and Caiden in *Zero! The Story of the Japanese Navy Air Force, 1937–1945*, gives the total Japanese air strength for Operations AL and MI as about 1,000 aircraft. Teluja's *Climax at Midway* credits the Japanese with 685 land-based and shipborne aircraft and seaplanes, and states that the First Carrier Striking Force had 260 aircraft. He gives no figures for losses.

Morison, in *History of U.S. Naval Operations in World War Two*, volume 4, credits Nagumo's carriers with 272 aircraft on p. 88, but later states that the Japanese lost their "entire complement of planes, about 250 in number." Rohwer and Hummelchen, in *Chronology of the War at Sea, 1939–1942*, volume 1, state that Japanese losses totaled 253. Costello's *The Pacific War* states on p. 277 that the three American carriers, with a total of 230 aircraft, had parity with the Japanese, though on p. 286 it reads as if the Japanese had 270. It is a little ambiguous, and the cause of clarity is not helped by a misprint of totals on that page. On p. 308 Costello gives Japanese losses as 234, a total that is given by Dull in *A Battle History of the Imperial Japanese Navy, 1941–1945*. Apart from Fuchida and Okumiya, Dull is the only account to give a breakdown of Japanese strength by both ship and type of aircraft, but surprisingly his total does not include two Judy reconnaissance aircraft known to have been in the *Soryu*.

Brown, in *Carrier Operations of World War Two*, volume 2, gives a total of 254 (on p. 63), but in *Aircraft Carriers* he gives no indication of Japanese strength at Midway, which is not surprising given the different slant of that book. He does, however, give the operational capacity of the four carriers of the First Carrier Striking Force as 265, which is about the total given by Watts and Gordon in *The Imperial Japanese Navy* and by Jentschura, Jung and Mickel in *Warships of the Imperial Japanese Navy, 1869–1945*. Both sources agree that the total capacity for the carriers was 325, with 248 as their combined operational capacity.

The final source is one that in two separate accounts gives widely different figures, one of which is extremely accurate. Francillon, in *Japanese Carrier Air Groups*, gives the Japanese a total of 227 aircraft with another 21 as the air group bound for Midway. The breakdown of the 227 is correct, the only error being the exclusion of the two modified Kates. That particular book was published in 1979, and in the previous year *U.S. Navy Carrier Air Groups* gave the four carriers a strength of 297, less the 36-strong air group bound for Midway. This brought the total back to 261, which was the total given three paragraphs ago . . .

To recapitulate the actual order of battle, Japanese air strength excluding the group bound for Midway and those ashore was:

	Combat Aircraft	Recce Aircraft	Seaplanes
Forces in the Aleutians	51		28
Forces bound for Midway			
Main Body	24		61
Main Force	15		8
Carrier Force	225	4	17
	315	4	114

Subtotals: For the Aleutians   79 aircraft and seaplanes
             For Midway   354 aircraft and seaplanes
Total: 433 aircraft and seaplanes

3. The Madagascar Campaign

A lack of space precludes any serious examination of the Madagascar campaign, but because the subject has been touched upon in the course of chapter 3, this note has been included to provide a bare outline of Allied and Japanese operations on the island and in the western Indian Ocean in the time span set out by *The Barrier and The Javelin*.

The Allied—or to be more accurate, the British—interest in Madagascar dated from the time of the fall of France in June 1940, it being in Britain's interest to coax French colonial authorities into the Allied fold under the auspices of de Gaulle's Free French movement. It was not until Christmas 1941, however, that the British interest in the island sharpened, and then it was as a result of the Japanese successes in the first two weeks of the war and the evident danger of the Japanese bursting through the line of the Malay Barrier into the Indian Ocean. With virtually no Allied naval forces in the Indian Ocean at that particular time, the British for some time entertained certain alarmist and wildly exaggerated fears, including the one that the Japanese might either invade or mount raids on Madagascar or the Falklands or both. Incredible though it may seem, at that time the British approached the Canadians with a view to their providing the Falklands with a garrison, but in mid-1942 the British sent one of their own infantry battalions as the garrison for the islands.

At Christmas 1941 the idea of an Allied operation to secure Madagascar was not followed up, but in the first week of March—with the fall of Rangoon coming on top of the end of the campaign in Malaya and Singapore, the collapse of the Indies and British options in the Far East largely having resolved themselves—British interest in Madagascar revived. The British concern was to ensure the security of their lines of communication in the western Indian Ocean to and from Egypt and the Gulf and to ensure that the Japanese did not secure the port of Diego Suarez, either by a coup de main or as a result of some connivance with a Vichy regime pressured into concessions by Germany. Accordingly, between 12 and 14 March Operation Ironclad was sanctioned, the Allied intention being to use British naval forces from Gibraltar for the assault. The British Eastern Fleet provided reinforcement and distant cover while the Americans moved forces (including the *Wasp*) to cover the gap left at the western end of the Mediterranean.

The various invasion convoys involved in this assault assembled in Durban by 22 April and left between 25 and 28 April. Covering forces, consisting of the battleship *Ramillies*, the fleet carrier *Illustrious*, the heavy cruiser *Devonshire*, the light cruiser *Hermione*, nine destroyers, various corvettes, minesweepers and auxiliaries, were joined at sea by the *Indomitable* and two destroyers from the Eastern Fleet on 3 May. The *Formidable* was retained with Somerville's fleet and did not take part in this particular operation.

Landings were made before dawn on 5 May on the western beaches of Cape Amber, and Diego Suarez was taken from the rear by early afternoon. French resistance in the area of Diego Suarez Bay, however, was not quelled until the seventh, and thereafter things went wrong as the French in the other parts of the island refused to surrender. After a well planned and executed landing operation, the British found themselves caught with a commitment to clear the island, and from September onwards they undertook a series of operations designed to bring about the surrender of the Vichy authorities. Landings at Majunga, Tamatave and Tulear were successful in that they led to the taking of Tananarive (23 September) and Fort Dauphin (5 November), the surrender of the latter bringing the campaign to an end. In December 1942 control of the island was handed over to the Free French.

The Japanese submarines involved in the operation of 30 May that resulted in the loss of the *British Loyalty* and the damaging of the *Ramillies* were the *I-10*, which used her Glen reconnaissance seaplane to search Diego Suarez harbor on 29 May, and the *I-16* and *I-20*, which launched the midgets that carried out the attack. The *I-18* was to have joined the attack but was forced to withdraw with engine trouble. The *I-30* was also in the western Indian Ocean at this time, but she did not take part in this operation because she was en route to France.

The Japanese attack, deemed by the official British naval historian as "daring and successful," caused such heavy damage to the *British Loyalty* that she subsequently sank. During the attack a single compartment of the *Ramillies* was also damaged. Running repairs allowed her to leave on 3 June for Durban, where she was given repairs sufficient to allow her to return to Britain and a proper refit. She did not return to the Indian Ocean and the Eastern Fleet until September 1943. The two-man crew of one of the midget submarines involved in this attack managed to get ashore, but being surrounded by enemy forces they shot themselves (or one another) rather than give in to the ignominy of surrender.

(For further information, see Turner, 116, 131–41.)

CHAPTER 4

1. Morton 1962, 85–88.
2. Hagan, 261; Morton 1962, 125.
3. Kirby 1957, 58.
4. Morton 1962, 205.
5. Greenfield, 198.
6. Leighton, 144–45.
7. Matloff, 86.
8. Morton 1962, 205.
9. Hough, 64.
10. Watts, 352.
11. Leighton, 148.
12. Morton 1962, 217.
13. Cook Sep 1978, 66.
14. Morton 1951, 63–64.
15. Morton 1951, 41–42.
16. Gillespie, 41.
17. Craven, 180.
18. Gillespie, 41.
19. Willmott, *B-17 Flying Fortress*, 39.
20. Willmott 1982, 189.
21. Hough, 89.
22. Matloff, 118.
23. Agawa, 294.
24. Leighton, 151.
25. Willmott 1982, 279.
26. Hough, 64.
27. Conn 1960, 171; Morton 1962, 159.
28. Cline, 144, Morton 1962, 158.
29. Chandler, 20.
30. Williams, 19.
31. Willmott 1982, 183.
32. Buell 1980, 152–54.
33. Buell 1980, 178–79.
34. Harrison, 23–24.

35. Gillespie, 23–26, 30, 36, 38, 43.
36. Gill 1957, 422–23; Wigmore, 396; Gillespie, 43.
37. Gill 1957, 441–42; Muggenthaler, 81–86.
38. McCarthy, 12.
39. Gillespie, 42–48.
40. Cab 94/4/17.
41. Gill 1957, 486, 495, 634.
42. McCarthy, 38.
43. McCarthy, 182, 209.
44. Gill 1957, 524; Wigmore 258.
45. Connell, 93; Craven, 384.
46. Wigmore, 467.
47. Hoogenband, 158.
48. Gill 1957, 473, 487, 551.
49. Wigmore, 59, 69, 511.
50. Gill 1957, 555.
51. Kirby 1957, 348, 350.
52. Dull, 61.
53. Hoogenband, 159–60.
54. McCarthy, 38.
55. Gill 1957, 512.
56. McCarthy, 44–45; Paull, 11–13.
57. Buell 1980, 169.
58. Wigmore, 183.
59. Buell 1980, 168.
60. Gill 1957, 513–17, 519.
61. Williams, 13.
62. Morton 1962, 205.
63. Hough, 84.
64. Coakley, 150.
65. Matloff, 116.
66. Morton 1962, 209.
67. Gill 1968, 6, 10.
68. Morton 1962, 219.
69. Coakley, 179.
70. Morton 1962, 213.
71. Hough, 83.
72. Frank, 50.
73. Cab 84/42/184.
74. Cab 84/40/44.
75. Hough, 89–90.
76. Lundstrom, 125.
77. Craven, 434–35.
78. Morton 1962, 219.
79. Playfair 1960, 123–26.
80. Gill 1968, 187.
81. Wigmore, 272.

82. Willmott 1982, 310–35.
83. Wigmore, 272, 443.
84. Wigmore, 443.
85. Wigmore, 448.
87. Butler 1964, 416–17.
88. Willmott 1982, 399–400.
89. Wigmore, 225.
90. Wigmore, 286, 446, 454–56.
91. Churchill, 126–27; Connell, 171–73.
92. Wigmore, 446.
93. Connell, 175.
94. PREM 3/63/4, 40–41.
95. Wigmore, 449–50.
96. PREM 3/63/4, 33–34; PREM 3/470, 458–59.
97. PREM 3/63/4, 13, 16, 24–25, 35–36.
98. Gill 1957, 626, 632.
99. Willmott 1982, 352–53.
100. Blythe, 142–56.
101. Kirby 1958, 59–77.
102. Wigmore, 460.
103. Matloff, 129.
104. Morton 1962, 203.
105. Matloff, 129–30.
106. PREM 3/470, 426–30.
107. PREM 3/63/4, 27–28.
108. Matloff, 165.
109. PREM 3/470, 402–4, 414–17; Matloff, 166; PREM 3/165, 63–73.
110. Buell 1980, 182.
111. Pogue, 255; Manchester, 283.
112. Hagan, 275.
113. Cook Sep 1978, 58.
114. Cook Aug 1978, 72–73.
115. Buell 1980, 188–89.
116. Cook Sep 1978, 56; Gill 1968, 32–34. The Southwest Pacific Command came into effect on 18 April. The ANZAC area was abolished four days later. The Pacific Ocean areas were officially constituted on 8 May but were effectively in existence from mid-April.
117. Wigmore, 459.
118. PREM 3/154/2, 57; Kirby 1958, 109. Because of time differences this was sent on 3 March and received on the second.

CHAPTER 5

1. Ship classification as used by Dull, 343–50; information drawn from Brown 1977, 12–33; Jentschura, 40–59; Watts, 169–203.
2. Buell 1980, 172–73.
3. *Dictionary of American Fighting Ships*, vol. 6, 341.
4. Frank, 49.

5. Macintyre 1964, 145–46.
6. Polmar, 417.
7. NWCA-M70.
8. Cracknell, 59; Glines, 14–17, 24.
9. Polmar, 189.
10. Lundstrom, 79.
11. Potter, 65.
12. Potter, 67–68.
13. Costello, 247.
14. Kahn, 1–2, 9–10.
15. Kahn, 39.
16. Blair, 74; Kahn, 7, 512.
17. Kahn, 12.
18. Kahn, 25, 564; Lundstrom, 76.
19. Deacon, 220–21.
20. Kahn, 567–68.
21. Kahn, 27.
22. Kahn, 39; Farago, 268.
23. Kahn, 564–65, 567, 571.
24. Lundstrom, 75–76.
25. Tomlinson, 133–37, 139.
26. Lundstrom, 78.
27. Lundstrom, 79.
28. Costello, 248.
29. Lundstrom, 90.
30. Lundstrom, 80.
31. Jentschura, 58–59.
32. Hoehling, 32.
33. Lundstrom, 79.
34. Potter, 67.
35. Buell 1980, 196–97.
36. Frank, 50.
37. Morison 1968, 260.
38. Lundstrom, 82–85.
39. Lundstrom, 85.
40. Potter, 68.
41. Lundstrom, 88.
42. Hoehling, 36–37.
43. Costello, 250.
44. Matloff, 219.
45. Buell 1980, 197.
46. Pogue, 302–20.
47. Matloff, 181–82.
48. Buell 1980, 190; Costello, 222.
49. Lundstrom, 93–94; PREM 3/151/1, 21–22.
50. Matloff, 213.

51. Willmott 1982, 183.
52. Lundstrom, 94; PREM 3/470, 329–31.
53. Manchester, 284.
54. Buell 1980, 197–98.
55. Lundstrom, 87.
56. Cracknell, 67; Potter, 69.
57. Lundstrom, 87.
58. King, 383–85.
59. NWCA-CS, 21.
60. Lundstrom, 86, 90.
61. Gill 1968, 41.
62. Lundstrom, 88–89.
63. Millot, 35; Lundstrom, 90–91.
64. Millot, 35.
65. Gill 1968, 41; Morison 1967, 15.
66. Lundstrom, 89.
67. Lundstrom, 89.
68. NWCA-CS, 23. The complement was increased to eighteen in the course of the battle of the Coral Sea.
69. Lundstrom, 100–101.
70. Blair, 217-18.
71. *Dictionary of American Fighting Ships*, vol. 6, 199–210; Lundstrom, 148.
72. Gillison, 239, 453.
73. Craven, 412.
74. Willmott, *B-17 Flying Fortress*, 40.
75. Lundstrom, 95.
76. Craven, 411.
77. Gillison, 469.
78. Gillison, 547.
79. Craven, 425.
80. Craven, 414; Gillison, 471, 542.
81. Willmott, *B-17 Flying Fortress*, 39.
82. Craven, 412; Gillison, 471, 539.
83. Gillison, 238.
84. Gillison, 459–61.
85. Craven, 411.
86. Gillison, 446.
87. Lundstrom, 93.
88. McCarthy, 82, 112.
89. Gill 1968, 63; McCarthy, 111.
90. Lundstrom, 86.
91. Toyama, 175, makes the point with regard to the Coral Sea. This is the only such comment made about either battle known to the author.
92. Cracknell, 66.
93. Agawa, 299.
94. Lord, 87.

CHAPTER 6

1. *Dictonary of American Fighting Ships*, vol. 8, 535.
2. Morison 1967, 21.
3. Francillon 1970, 40.
4. Gill 1968, 41.
5. Brown 1977, 57.
6. Lundstrom, 101.
7. Morison 1967, 22.
8. Gill 1968, 43.
9. Dull, 120.
10. Millot, 43.
11. Lundstrom, 101.
12. Lundstrom, 103.
13. Lundstrom, 97.
14. Dull, 120; Gill 1968, 42.
15. Gill 1968, 42; McCarthy, 80.
16. Hough, 237–38.
17. Yoshida 3.
18. Lundstrom, 97–98.
19. Lundstrom, 103.
20. Dull, 120.
21. NWCA-CS, 8.
22. Polmar, 432–54.
23. Lundstrom 1.
24. Lundstrom, 99.
25. Dull, 116; Okumiya, 103.
26. Polmar, 318, 447–48.
27. NWCA-CS, 9.
28. Dull, 122.
29. Morison 1967, 24.
30. Gill 1968, 44.
31. Brown 1974, 49.
32. Lundstrom, 101.
33. Morison 1967, 24.
34. Gill 1968, 43.
35. Adm 199/1305, 57.
36. Dull, 120–21.
37. Morison 1967, 25–26; NWCA-CS, 36.
38. NWCA-CS, 34.
39. NWCA-CS, 35, 37.
40. Dull, 121.
41. Brown 1974, 49–50; Morison 1967, 26.
42. Morison 1967, 27.
43. Gill 1968, 45.
44. Gill 1968, 44 and 44fn; Feldt, 108–9.
45. Yoshida 1.

46. McCarthy, 80.
47. Potter, 70.
48. Smith, 28.
49. Morison 1967, 27.
50. Brown 1974, 50.
51. Millot, 51.
52. Gill 1968, 45–46.
53. Lundstrom, 102.
54. Gill 1968, 45; Morison 1967, 28.
55. Dull, 121.
56. Dull, 122.
57. Brown 1974, 50.
58. Dull, 122.
59. Gill 1968, 45.
60. Brown 1974, 50.
61. Lundstrom, 103.
62. Brown 1977, 21–22, 26.
63. Brown 1974, 48.
64. Lundstrom, 103.
65. Millot, 45.
66. Brown 1974, 50.
67. Dull, 122.
68. Dull, 124.
69. Lundstrom, 105; Millot, 55.

CHAPTER 7

1. Opnav-1947, 5.
2. Brown 1974, 51.
3. Morison 1967, 18–19, 29.
4. Morison 1967, 29.
5. Millot, 62.
6. Frank, 94.
7. NWCA-CS, 54.
8. Dull, 124.
9. Gill 1968, 45.
10. Dull, 124.
11. Brown 1974, 48, 51; Morison 1967, 29.
12. Brown 1974, 51.
13. Millott, 55.
14. Gill 1968, 116.
15. Lundstrom, 103–4.
16. Morison 1967, 20.
17. Dull, 124.
18. Dull, 124; Lundstrom, 106.
19. Gill 1968, 46.
20. Lundstrom, 106.
21. Morison 1967, 37.

22. Dull, 125.

23. Lundstrom, 106–7.

24. Adm 199/1305, 122.

25. Okumiya, 107.

26. Lundstrom 1.

27. Lundstrom, 106–7.

28. Dull, 124; Morison 1967, 40.

29. Gill 1968, 47; Okumiya, 110.

30. Millot, 59; Okumiya, 107.

31. Brown 1974, 53.

32. Millot, 55; Lundstrom, 107.

33. Millot, 60; Morison 1967, 34.

34. Polmar, 197.

35. Morison 1967, 34.

36. Morison 1967, 35–36.

37. Lundstrom, 107.

38. Brown 1974, 52.

39. Dull, 125.

40. Morison 1967, 40.

41. Frank, 98; Millot, 68.

42. NWCA-CS, 55.

43. Dull, 125; Morison 1967, 40fn.

44. Frank, 93.

45. Frank, 98; Morison 1967, 41fn.

46. Adm 199/1305, 128–29.

47. Gill 1968, 47.

48. Brown 1974, 52.

49. Dull, 124; Okumiya, 108.

50. NWCA-CS, 58.

51. Dull, 125.

52. Frank, 101.

53. Hoehling, 43.

54. NWCA-CS, 59.

55. Frank, 99–100.

56. Frank, 102.

57. Morison 1967; 42.

58. Dull, 126.

59. NWCA-CS, 59–60.

60. Lundstrom, 108, 110.

61. Yoshida 4.

62. NWCA-CS, 79.

63. Gill 1968, 49.

64. Costello, 256.

65. Gill 1968, 48.

66. Gill 1968, 50.

67. Okumiya, 110–11.

68. NWCA-CS, 79–80.

69. NWCA-CS, 68.
70. Yoshida 4.
71. Fuchida, 115.
72. Lundstrom, 109.
73. Brown 1974, 53.
74. Lundstrum, 109.
75. Frank, 103.
76. Frank, 105; Morison 1967, 43.
77. NWCA-CS, 60–61.
78. NWCA-CS, 61.
79. Lundstrom 1.
80. Millot, 79.
81. Lundstrom 1.
82. NWCA-CS, 83.
83. Yoshida 4.
84. NWCA-CS, 105.
85. Yoshida 4.
86. NWCA-CS, 83.
87. Morison 1967, 45.
88. Morison 1967, 48–49.
89. NWCA-CS, 83–84.
90. Hoehling, 52.
91. Frank, 109.
92. NWCA-CS, 84.
93. NWCA-CS, 105.
94. NWCA-CS, 87.
95. Lundstrom 1.
96. Belote, 78.
97. NWCA-CS, 85.
98. Morison 1967, 49.
99. Frank, 112.
100. Yoshida 4.
101. Frank, 114.
102. Lundstrom, 1982, 1.
103. NWCA-CS, 89.
104. NCWA-CS, 86.
105. Frank, 112–13.
106. Polmar, 203.
107. NWCA-CS, 88–89.
108. Frank, 113.
109. Yoshida 4.
110. Brown 1974, 6, 23.
111. Fukaya, 1035.
112. NWCA-CS, 85, 87.
113. Frank, 115.
114. NWCA-CS, 87.
115. NWCA-CS, 84–85.

116. Yoshida 4.
117. Brown 1977, 24.
118. Blair, 230–33.
119. Adm 199/1305, 5.
120. Adm 199/1305, 136, 240.
121. NWCA-CS, 90.
122. Morison 1967, 52.
123. Frank, 115.
124. NWCA-CS, 99.
125. Lundstrom 1.
126. Yoshida 4.
127. NWCA-CS, 97–98.
128. NWCA-CS, 92.
129. Belote, 80.
130. Morison 1967, 54.
131. Hoehling, 69.
132. Hoehling, 97–98.
133. Frank, 132; Hoehling, 90.
134. Hoehling, 82.
135. Belote, 82.

CHAPTER 8

1. Brown 1977, 23.
2. Lundstrom 1.
3. Yoshida 4.
4. NWCA-CS, 107.
5. Lundstrom, 112.
6. Lundstrom, 112.
7. NWCA-CS, 103.
8. Lundstrom, 112; NWCA-CS, 107–8.
9. Lundstrom, 113.
10. Dull, 128; Lundstrom, 113.
11. Hoehling, 104, 111, 113.
12. Brown 1977, 6.
13. Hoehling, 117.
14. BS/ND/WD-16, 10–11.
15. Hoehling, 124.
16. NWCA-CS, 100.
17. Lundstrom, 111.
18. Frank, 133.
19. NWCA-CS, 101.
20. Potter, 76.
21. NWCA-CS, 101.
22. Lundstrom, 111.
23. Potter, 75.
24. Lundstrom, 113.
25. Hoehling, 122–23.

26. Belote, 83.
27. Hoehling, 131.
28. Morison 1967, 58.
29. NWCA-CS, 102.
30. Belote, 103.
31. Morison 1967, 59.
32. NWCA-CS, 103.
33. Smith, 47.
34. Hoehling, 196.
35. Potter, 77.
36. NWCA-CS, 102–3.
37. Frank, 133.
38. Fuchida, 116–17.

CHAPTER 9

1. See pp. 182, 188.
2. See pp. 184–87.
3. Lundstrom, 90–91.
4. Lundstrom, 91.
5. Lundstrom, 165; Matloff, 223.
6. Adm 223/22/OIC/SI/J7.
7. Lundstrom, 137–38.
8. Lundstrom, 138–39.
9. Potter, 78.
10. Matloff, 217.
11. Matloff, 219.
12. Costello, 271–73.
13. Matloff, 222.
14. Matloff, 219.
15. Pogue, 324.
16. Matloff, 221.
17. Costello, 271.
18. Lundstrom, 138.
19. Lundstrom, 139.
20. Costello, 271; Lundstrom, 138.
21. Matloff, 225.
22. Potter, 85.
23. Kahn, 569.
24. Kahn, 567.
25. Buell 1980, 200.
26. Halsey, 106.
27. Lundstrom, 152.
28. Lundstrom, 152–54.
29. Gill 1968, 56–57.
30. Lundstrom, 159–60.
31. Lundstrom 2.
32. Adm 205/18.

33. Lundstrom, 160.
34. Gill 1968, 165.
35. Lundstrom, 160.
36. Buell 1980, 201.
37. Matloff, 224.
38. Kagan, 274.
39. Lundstrom, 162.
40. Potter, 82.
41. Kahn, 568.
42. Kahn, 570.
43. Morison 1967, 80.
44. Conn 1964, 260.
45. Lundstrom, 162.
46. Potter, 80–81.
47. NWCA-M, 64.
48. Rohwer, 221–22.
49. Craven, 283–86; Stacey, 170.
50. Dulin, 41; Morison 1948, 167–68; Roskill 1956, 134, 136, 186.
51. NWCA-M, 41.
52. Blair, 223-24; Harkness, 3.
53. Blair, 233.
54. Blair, 226.
55. Blair, 236.
56. Barde, 98–99.
57. Hough, 216.
58. Hough, 216.
59. Barde, 105.
60. Hough, 216.
61. Barde, 108.
62. Hough, 219.
63. *Dictionary of American Fighting Ships*, vol. 3, 193.
64. Barde, 104.
65. Lord, 54.
66. Hough, 220.
67. Barde, 111–12.
68. NWCA-M, 48–49.
69. Barde, 115–16; Lord, 53.
70. Craven, 456–58.
71. Lord, 55–56.
72. NWCA-M, 49.
73. Morison 1967, 92–93.
74. Hough, 220.
75. Barde, 107–8.
76. Adm 199/1302, 141–42.
77. SOTA, CSCSO-31, 42.
78. Conn 1964, 227–28; Rosien.
79. Craven, 304.

80. Conn 1960, 389, 394.
81. Craven, 306–7.
82. Conn 1964, 224; Morison 1967, 163.
83. Rosien.
84. Rosien.
85. Craven, 304, 306–7.
86. Craven, 464; Morison 1967, 164.
87. Craven, 304.
88. Conn 1964, 258.
89. Rosien.
90. Craven, 309.
91. Dziuban, 252–53.
92. NWCA-M, 46–47; Rosien.
93. Conn 1964, 257.
94. Craven, 308.
95. Conn 1964, 240–41.
96. *Dictionary of American Fighting Ships*, vol. 8, 374–75.
97. Morton 1962, 420.
98. Conn 1964, 253–54.
99. Conn 1964, 261; Craven 166, 303–9.
100. Craven, 307.
101. Conn 1964, 255.
102. Rosien.
103. NWCA-M, 57.
104. Conn 1964, 260.
105. Morison 1967, 167.
106. Rosien.
107. Potter, 88.
108. NWCA-M, 58.
109. NWCA-M, 61.
110. NWCA-M, 43.
111. NWCA-M, 58.
112. Conn 1964, 260.
113. NWCA-M, 59.
114. NWCA-M, 58.
115. Lundstrom, 163.
116. Lundstrom, 169–70.
117. Costello, 272.
118. Matloff, 355.
119. Matloff, 353.
120. Matloff, 358–59.
121. Morton 1962, 258.
122. Cab 79/20/119.
123. Cab 79/20/102.
124. Adm 205/18.
125. Roskill 1957, 37–38.
126. Cab 79/21/160.

127. Cab 79/21/160.
128. Cab 79/20/125.
129. Cab 79/20/107.
130. Cab 66/23/175.
131. Cab 66/23/113.
132. Cab 66/23/23.
133. Cab 79/20/102.
134. Cab 79/21/167.
135. Costello, 274.
136. Barde, 116.
137. Potter, 87.
138. Cracknell, 67.
139. Potter, 87.
140. Potter, 85.
141. Halsey, 107; Merrill, 44.
142. Buell 1974, 120.
143. Potter, 84.
144. Lundstrom, 177–78.
145. Barde, 87.
146. Potter, 84.
147. Potter, 85–86.
148. Morison 1967, 97.
149. Potter, 87–88.
150. Lord, 38.
151. Frank, 147–48.
152. Forrestal, 39.
153. Lord, 61; Morison 1967, 97.
154. Buell 1974, 129.

CHAPTER 10

1. Barde, 15.
2. Fuchida, 122–26.
3. Dull, 135–36; Lord, 39–40.
4. Lord, 53.
5. Barde, 123–24.
6. Fuchida, 137–38.
7. Fuchida, 132–33; Lord, 45.
8. Lord, 44.
9. Fuchida, 138–39.
10. Lundstrom, 138–40.
11. Barde, 49.
12. Agawa, 313.
13. Fuchida, 136–37; Lord, 56–57.
14. Lord, 9.
15. Fuchida, 132.
16. Lundstrum, 135.
17. Fuchida, 133.

18. Fuchida, 151fn.
19. Fuchida, 136.
20. Fuchida, 137–39; Lord, 44.
21. Bauer, 247.
22. NWCA-M, 54–55.
23. Lord, 65.
24. Barde, 126–27.
25. Belote, 89.
26. Brown 1974, 61; Garfield, 9.
27. Fuchida, 147.
28. Lord, 9.
29. Barde, 37. Documents in British possession state that H-Hour was believed by Allied intelligence services to be 1900 (Adm 223/22). This would have been in accord with Japanese practice at this stage of the war, which was generally to land before dawn rather than soon after dusk. But in the case of Midway—with the objective obvious because of the lack of any other target in the area—there was no point in approaching under the cover of dark in order to prevent a premature disclosure of intention (Monograph 156, 34).
30. Fuchida, 147.
31. Belote, 91.
32. Rosien.
33. Dull, 171; Garfield, 29.
34. Fuchida, 148.
35. Dull, 171; Fuchida, 148; Morison 1967, 176.
36. Brown 1974, 64.
37. Garfield, 13.
38. Conn 1964, 262; Garfield, 39.
39. Fuchida, 149.
40. Rosien.
41. Garfield, 34–36.
42. Conn 1964, 262.
43. Belote, 90; Dull, 171.
44. Potter, 88.
45. Willmott, *Zero A6M*, 32.
46. Lord, 65–66.
47. Lord, 68.
48. Forrestal, 41.
49. Lord, 67.
50. Fuchida, 144.
51. Potter, 92.
52. Craven, 457.
53. Lord, 67–68.
54. Barde, 126.
55. Lord, 68.
56. Adm. 199/1302, 40; Barde, 99; Craven, 461–62.
57. Fuchida, 144–45; Lord, 71–73.
58. Dull, 136.

59. Lord, 74–75.
60. Brown 1974, 66; Morison 1967, 100fn.
61. Belote, 89.
62. Brown 1974, 65–66; Morison 1967, 102–8.
63. Barde, 135.
64. Fuchida, 154; *Midway Kaisen*, 286.
65. ONI-1947, 12–13.
66. Lord, 91, 102–3; ONI-1947, 42–45.
67. Ito, 64.

CHAPTER 11

1. Hough, 221.
2. Brown 1974, 67; Teluja, 95.
3. Lord, 87; Morison 1967, 102; Teluja, 84, 88.
4. Lord, 90; Teluja, 84.
5. Fuchida, 158.
6. Morison 1967, 103; Teluja, 80–81.
7. Fuchida, 159–60.
8. Brown 1974, 66; Lord, 92; Teluja, 93–94.
9. Fuchida, 156.
10. Fuchida, 172; Lord, 79, 315.
11. Fuchida, 165.
12. Belote, 91; Lord, 94–95; Teluja, 89.
13. Hough, 221. Lord, 94.
14. Belote, 91; Lord, 95; Morison 1967, 103; Teluja, 93.
15. Fuchida, 165.
16. Fuchida, 165; Lord, 95.
17. Brown 1974, 67; Lord, 95; Potter, 93; Teluja, 90.
18. Teluja, 91.
19. Morison 1967, 113; Teluja, 92.
20. Lord, 96; Teluja, 96.
21. Lord, 96–97.
22. Adm 199/1302, 51.
23. Morison 1967, 104.
24. Hough, 223; Lord, 97; Teluja, 98.
25. Lord, 98, 100; Morison 1967, 106.
26. Hough, 223.
27. Lord, 96–98, 125.
28. ONI-1947, 43.
29. Belote, 93; Fuchida, 162–63.
30. Heinl, 28–32; Hough, 223; Morison 1967, 105.
31. Dull, 146.
32. *Midway Kaisen*, 302.
33. Lord, 107.
34. Lord, 108.
35. Hough, 219.
36. Belote, 93; Fuchida, 163.

37. Dull, 147.
38. Lord, 111.
39. Brown 1974, 68.
40. Lord, 112.
41. Brown 1974, 68; Morison 1967, 106.
42. Belote, 93; Dull, 148.
43. Dull, 146; Lord, 114.
44. Lord, 114.
45. Morison 1967, 106.
46. Lord, 113–14.
47. Lord, 113; Morison 1967, 110.
48. Lord, 113.
49. Belote, 93; Lord, 117.
50. Morison 1967, 106.
51. Fuchida, 167; Lord, 117–18.
52. Dull, 148; Teluja, 105–6.
53. Belote, 94; Morison 1967, 107.
54. Fuchida, 169; Teluja, 105.
55. Brown 1977, 14–16, 18–21, 56.
56. Brown, 1974, 68; Dull, 149; Morison 1967, 108–9, 113.
57. Potter, 94.
58. Fuchida, 170.
59. Belote, 91.
60. Morison 1967, 102; Teluja, 91.
61. Dull, 148.
62. Belote, 94.
63. Fuchida, 173.
64. Lord, 185–86.
65. Lord, 120.
66. Hough, 220.
67. Hough, 225.
68. Teluja, 109.
69. Lord, 124.
70. Teluja, 112.
71. Fuchida, 173.
72. Belote, 94; Lord, 125–27; Morison 1967, 110.
73. Brown 1974, 69; Hough, 225; Teluja, 114.
74. According to the *Haruna*, two of the ten (?) Vindicators attacked not her but the *Akagi*, unsuccessfully, at 0839. This assertion is unsupported by any other source. Quoted in Morison 1967, 111.
75. Belote, 95; Teluja, 113.
76. ONI-1947, 16.
77. Lord, 130–31; Teluja, 115.
78. Dull, 148.
79. Belote, 95.
80. Teluja, 118.
81. Dull, 151.

82. Fuchida, 174.
83. Toland 1970, 162.
84. Prange, 286.
85. Prange, 280.
86. Belote, 95.
87. Fuchida, 174–75; Lord, 131–32.
88. ONI-1947, 15.
89. Francillon 1970, 276, 377, 416.
90. ONI-1947, 43.

CHAPTER 12

1. ONI-1947, 16.
2. Fuchida, 175.
3. Agawa, 315.
4. Lord, 134.
5. Fuchida, 176.
6. Teluja, 118.
7. Fuchida, 176; ONI-1947, 17; Teluja, 118.
8. Lord, 134.
9. Fuchida, 176–77.
10. Lord, 134, 142.
11. Fuchida, 234.
12. Lord, 119.
13. Fuchida, 175.
14. Dull, 149.
15. Lord, 136.
16. Morison 1967, 114.
17. Potter, 87.
18. Potter, 94–95.
19. Forrestal, 39.
20. Forrestal, 43–45.
21. Buell 1974, 126.
22. Morison 1967, 113.
23. Lord, 137; Morison 1967, 114.
24. Barde, 178.
25. Dull, 142; Francillon 1978, 40; Morison 1967, 90.
26. Morison 1967; 113fn.
27. Lord, 140; Morison 1967, 113–14.
28. Smith, 80, 103.
29. Gunston, 66.
30. Teluja, 128.
31. Lord, 141.
32. Barde, 171.
33. Smith, 94.
34. Smith, 103.
35. Barde, 189.
36. Smith, 104.

37. Frank, 168.
38. Smith, 96–97.
39. Lord, 141, 151–52; Teluja, 125.
40. Lord, 151; Teluja, 130.
41. Lord, 177.
42. Teluja, 131.
43. Lord, 192; Smith, 100.
44. Frank, 165; Teluja, 131.
45. Lord, 151; Morison 1967, 116; Teluja, 130–31.
46. Teluja, 127.
47. Lord, 143.
48. Barde, 172.
49. Lord, 141–42.
50. Teluja, 128, 131–32.
51. Dull, 150.
52. Teluja, 124.
53. Belote, 98.
54. Fuchida, 179.
55. Lundstrom 1982, 1.
56. Lord, 144.
57. Lord, 143.
58. Lord, 145.
59. Lord, 147.
60. Lord, 281; Smith, 99.
61. Morison 1967, 120.
62. Lord, 148; Barde, 178.
63. Teluja, 136.
64. Teluja, 137.
65. Barde, 180–83.
66. Barde, 193.
67. ONI-1947, 18–19.
68. Frank, 171.
69. Barde, 193.
70. Smith, 101, 104.
71. Teluja, 140.
72. Barde, 195, 197.
73. Fuchida, 178.
74. Lord, 160.
75. Brown 1977, 5, 14–16, 18–21.
76. Francillon 1970, 377.
77. Fuchida, 180; Teluja, 139.
78. Lord, 145.
79. Lord, 218; Teluja, 162.
80. Buell 1974, 133.
81. Frank, 167.
82. Teluja, 142.
83. Lord, 157.

84. Frank, 166.
85. Lord, 157.
86. Smith, 104.
87. Morison 1967, 121.
88. Frank, 170.
89. Buell 1974, 131.
90. Frank, 169.
91. Teluja, 144.
92. Frank, 168; Smith, 99.
93. Belote, 100.
94. Morison 1967, 122; Teluja, 145.
95. Blair, 239–45.
96. ONI-1947, 6.
97. Lord, 160, 162.
98. Lord, 163.
99. Potter, 95.
100. Lord, 150.

CHAPTER 13

1. Opnav-1947, 44.
2. Potter, 97.
3. Lord, 290.
4. *See*, for example, Teluja, 215–23.
5. Belote, 101; Lord, 173.
6. Belote, 100; Lord, 164–67.
7. Lord, 169.
8. Brown 1974, 71.
9. Dull, 155; Lord, 171.
10. Dull, 156.
11. Fuchida, 187–88; Lord, 213.
12. Blair, 244–45.
13. Belote, 104; Dull, 156.
14. Brown 1974, 71; Dull, 153.
15. Dull, 154.
16. Brown 1977, 14.
17. Lord, 183.
18. Fuchida, 184; Lord, 184.
19. Lord, 182–83.
20. Dull, 154.
21. Dull, 155.
22. Belote, 104.
23. Dull, 152–53.

CHAPTER 14

1. Dull, 160; Fuchida, 192.
2. Agawa, 317.
3. Dull, 160–61; Fuchida, 193; Teluja, 153.

4. Dull, 151.
5. Dull, 161.
6. Fuchida, 194.
7. Teluja, 153.
8. Fuchida, 193; Lord, 195; Teluja, 153.
9. Frank, 180.
10. Buell 1974, 134–35.
11. Frank, 181.
12. Smith, 114.
13. Smith, 114.
14. Belote, 105; Frank, 181; Teluja, 153.
15. Buell 1974, 137.
16. Teluja, 153.
17. Belote, 105.
18. Smith, 114.
19. Frank, 182.
20. Frank, 188; Lord, 193.
21. Polmar, 222–23.
22. Smith, 125.
23. Barde, 197, 277–78; Lord, 206.
24. Smith, 117.
25. Frank, 183.
26. Lord, 194; Teluja, 155.
27. Lord, 200–201.
28. Opnav-1947, 44.
29. Lord, 188.
30. Willmott, *Zero A6M*, 30.
31. Fuchida, 193; LORD, 194–95.
32. Opnav-1947, 44; Teluja, 157.
33. Frank, 183–85; Smith, 115.
34. Fuchida, 193.
35. Lord, 199–200.
36. Belote, 105.
37. Lord, 197; Morison 1967, 133; Polmar, 224.
38. Lord, 200.
39. Opnav-1947, 44.
40. Lord, 202.
41. Prange, 530.
42. Belote, 105; Lord, 198.
43. Frank, 190–91.
44. Opnav-1947, 41, 44.
45. Smith, 115.
46. Frank, 192–94.
47. Lord, 197–98; Morison 1967, 133; Teluja, 156–57.
48. Lord, 192.
49. Dull, 161; Frank, 196–97; Teluja, 157.
50. Lord, 198.

51. Frank, 196; Lord, 203–4.
52. Polmar, 224.
53. Lord, 205.
54. Opnav-1947, 23.
55. Smith, 121.
56. Opnav-1947, 24.
57. Barde, 198–99, 426–33.
58. Fuchida, 193.
59. Lord, 216; Teluja, 159.
60. Frank, 200; Smith, 117.
61. Opnav-1947, 44.
62. Fuchida, 194.
63. Lord, 213–15.
64. Morison 1967, 134.
65. Frank, 199.
66. Lord, 216; Smith, 118.
67. Frank, 201.
68. Lord, 217.
69. Opnav-1947, 25, 29.
70. Smith, 121.
71. Opnav-1947, 23.
72. Opnav-1947, 24–25.
73. Fuchida, 195; Lord, 218.
74. Lord, 217; Smith, 118.
75. Lord, 216.
76. Morison 1967, 134; Smith, 118.
77. Frank, 202.
78. Brown 1974, 74.
79. Lord, 218; Teluja, 162.
80. Lord, 218.
81. Frank, 205.
82. Smith, 120.
83. Opnav-1947, 45–46.
84. Lord, 222; Opnav-1947, 45.
85. Belote, 108.
86. Lord, 222–23.
87. Opnav-1947, 26.
88. Opnav-1947, 27.
89. Fuchida, 196; Polmar, 224.
90. Smith, 125.
91. Opnav-1947, 26.
92. Fuchida, 205–6.
93. Agawa, 316.
94. Fuchida, 207.
95. Agawa, 316; Fuchida, 207; Lord, 187.
96. Fuchida, 207.
97. Opnav-1947, 22.

98. Fuchida, 207–8.
99. Fuchida, 208.
100. Fuchida, 209; Opnav-1947, 24.
101. Opnav-1947, 23.
102. Fuchida, 217–18.
103. Fuchida, 200.
104. Opnav-1947, 22.
105. Fuchida, 201.
106. Dull, 150; Fuchida, 202.
107. Opnav-1947, 25.
108. Fuchida, 209.
109. Fuchida, 211.
110. Morison 1967, 136.
111. Lord, 230.
112. Teluja, 167.
113. Fuchida, 189.
114. Fuchida, 202; Opnav-1947, 28.
115. Frank, 207–8.
116. Morison 1967, 135.
117. Lord, 219, 223.
118. Frank, 209.
119. Teluja, 163.
120. Smith, 119.
121. Frank, 211.
122. Smith, 122.
123. Frank, 214; Morison 1967, 153.
124. Smith, 124.
125. Opnav-1947, 46.
126. Buell 1974, 138–39.
127. Morison 1967, 136.
128. Teluja, 168.
129. Frank, 216.
130. Smith, 127.
131. Belote, 106.
132. Brown 1974, 75; Lord, 231.
133. Dull, 157.
134. Agawa, 318; Fuchida, 196–97; Lord, 233.
135. Smith, 127.
136. Opnav-1947, 29.
137. Frank, 217.
138. Smith, 127.
139. Smith, 128.
140. Lord, 236.
141. Lord, 242.
142. Adm 199/1302/140–43, 149–55.
143. Hough, 225.
144. Morison 1967, 137.

145. Lord, 239.
146. Teluja, 172.
147. Opnav-1947, 35.
148. Opnav-1947, 9.
149. Dull, 158–60.
150. Opnav-1947, 67.

CHAPTER 15

1. Morison 1967, 142; NWCA-M, 119.
2. NWCA-M, 41.
3. NWCA-M, 142–43.
4. NWCA-M, 120.
5. Morison 1967, 142, 146–47.
6. Fuchida, 210.
7. Lord, 243.
8. Fuchida, 202.
9. Fuchida, 211.
10. Lord, 244.
11. Fuchida, 212–13.
12. Fuchida, 211.
13. Fuchida, 219.
14. Teluja, 179.
15. Blair, 241–44.
16. Lord, 240.
17. Lord, 244.
18. Lord, 246.
19. Fuchida, 211; Opnav-1947, 36.
20. Teluja, 181; Opnav-1947, 36.
21. Fuchida, 212; Lord, 251.
22. Fuchida, 212.
23. Opnav-1947, 36.
24. Fuchida, 213–14.
25. Prange, 338.
26. Agawa, 320.
27. Fuchida, 214–16.
28. Yoshida 2.
29. Fuchida, 215.
30. Fuchida, 186.
31. Fuchida, 219–20; Lord, 258; Teluja, 189–90.
32. Morison 1967, 144.
33. Lord, 259.
34. Teluja, 185–87.
35. Lord, 259.
36. Fuchida, 219.
37. Blair, 246–47.
38. Brown 1974, 77; Lord, 242.
39. Blair, 250.

CHAPTER 16

1. Forrestal, 51.
2. NWCA-M, 50, 161.
3. NWCA-M, 163.
4. Lord, 261.
5. Barde, 339.
6. NWCA-M, 233.
7. NWCA-M, 164.
8. Morison 1967, 148.
9. Forrestal, 52.
10. Barde, 341; Teluja, 192.
11. Fuchida, 212–13.
12. Morison 1967, 148.
13. NWCA-M, 163.
14. Hough, 229; Teluja, 190.
15. Morison 1967, 145.
16. Hough, 229.
17. Barde, 349–50.
18. Fuchida, 223.
19. NWCA-M, 163–64.
20. Smith, 137.
21. Smith, 138.
22. NWCA-M, 159–60.
23. Barde, 358.
24. Barde, 354–55; Buell 1974, 142.
25. NWCA-M, 164.
26. Fuchida, 222–23.
27. Lord, 270.
28. Fuchida, 199.
29. Lord, 270.
30. Smith, 138.
31. Adm 199/1302, 40; Barde, 351.
32. NWCA-M, 159–60, 164.
33. Buell 1974, 143.
34. Barde, 361; Teluja, 193.
35. Lord, 268–69.
36. Fuchida, 222.
37. Fuchida, 224.
38. NWCA-M, 161.
39. Frank, 225.
40. Lord, 265.
41. Dull, 162.
42. NWCA-M 52, 160–61.
43. NWCA-M 51, 179.
44. Forrestal, 54.
45. Morison 1967, 149–50.
46. Dull, 322.

47. Barde, 372–73.
48. Smith, 144.
49. Barde, 372–73.
50. Barde, 374.
51. Dull, 165.
52. Barde, 376–77.
53. NWCA-M, 176; Barde, 377.
54. Smith, 145.
55. Teluja, 194.
56. Dull, 166.
57. Fuchida, 226.
58. Lord, 272.
59. Teluja, 195.
60. Teluja, 197.
61. Fuchida, 227.
62. Toyama.
63. Dull, 171.
64. NWCA-M, 183–84.
65. Potter, 102.
66. Barde, 399.
67. Forrestal, 53.
68. Forrestal, 54.
69. Forrestal, 54.
70. NWCA-M, 185.
71. Blair, 239.
72. NWCA-M, 185.
73. NWCA-M, 185.
74. Teluja, 198.
75. Frank, 224.
76. Teluga, 200.
77. Barde, 346.
78. Barde, 347, 382; Morison 1967, 154.
79. Teluja, 192.
80. Barde, 384.
81. Lord, 266.
82. Smith, 150.
83. Frank, 228–30.
84. Frank, 231–33; Barde, 386–87.
85. Potter, 103.
86. Fuchida, 221.
87. Smith, 234, 236.
88. Teluja, 203.
89. Barde, 393.
90. Smith, 152–53.
91. Frank, 237.
92. Actually only two destroyers headed back to Pearl Harbor immediately after the *Yorktown* sank. The others headed for the rendezvous with Task Group 11.1 and then with the meeting of Task Groups 16 and 17 (NWCA-M, 186).

CHAPTER 17

1. Prem 3/163/6, 66–68; Churchill to Curtin, 5 April 1942.
2. Prem 3/151/4, 67–71; Curtin to Evatt, 13 May 1952.
3. Dull, 166.
4. Morton 1962, 125.

APPENDIX B

1. Cab 84/38/1045S.
2. Cab 84/40/4.
3. Cab 84/44/395.
4. Cab 84/42/144, 147.
5. Ismay II/3/137/3a.

Bibliography

PRIMARY SOURCES

Correspondence

Akagi: from Kanji Akagi to the author, 8 April 1983
Jacob: from Lt. Gen. Sir Ian Jacob to the author, 11 January, 23 February, 25 May, and 14 June 1983
Lundstrom 1: from John B. Lundstrom to the author, 18 May 1982
Lundstrom 2: from Lundstrom to the author, 7 December 1982
Toyama: from Saburo Toyama to the author, 10 July 1980
Yoshida 1: from Akihiko Yoshida to D. O. Caton, 24 December 1981
Yoshida 2: from Yoshida to the author, 16 February 1982
Yoshida 3: from Yoshida to the author, 5 April 1982
Yoshida 4: from Yoshida to the author, 27 May 1982
Yoshida 5: from Yoshida to the author, 2 October 1982
Yoshida 6: from Yoshida to the author, 1 March 1983
Zwitzer: from Hans Zwitzer to the author, 11 June 1982

Public Documents

The Public Record Office, London:

Adm 199: War History Cases and Papers
Adm 205: First Sea Lord's Papers
Adm 223: Admiralty Intelligence Papers
Cab 65, 66: War Cabinet Minutes and Memoranda
Cab 79, 80: Chiefs of Staff Committee Minutes and Memoranda
Cab 81: Chiefs of Staff Committees and Subcommittees
Cab 84: War Cabinet: Joint Planning Committees
Cab 88: Combined Chiefs of Staff Committees and Subcommittees
Cab 96: War Cabinet: Committees on the Far East
Prem 3/63: Papers relating to Australian and New Zealand forces

Prem 3/145: Papers relating to the Anzac area
Prem 3/151: Papers relating to the defense of Australia and New Zealand
Prem 3/154: Papers relating to convoys in and reinforcements for the Far East
Prem 3/163: Papers relating to the naval situation in the Far East
Prem 3/165: Papers relating to the Pacific
Prem 3/470: Exchange of telegrams between Churchill and Roosevelt

King's College, London

The Ismay Papers

Interviews

Jacob, Lt. Gen. Sir Ian. Interview with the author. Woodbridge, Suffolk. 14 April 1983.
The United States Strategic Bombing Survey: The Pacific Survey. Naval Analysis Division. Interrogation of Japanese Officials. Vols. 1 and 2 (N 27.2: J 27/v, p. 1, 2). The Campaigns of the Pacific War (N 27.2, p. 11).

Monographs

U.S. Army, Headquarters Far East Command, Military History Section. *Japanese Monographs*.
No. 22. "Seventeenth Area Army Operations, 1941–45."
No. 26. "Borneo Operations, 1941–45."
No. 37. "Eighteenth Army Operations." Vol. 1.
No. 45. "History of Imperial General Headquarters, Army Section, 1941–45."
No. 96. "Eastern New Guinea Invasion Operations, March–September, 1942."
No. 105. "General Summary of Naval Operations, Southern Force."
No. 120. "Outline of Southeast Area Naval Air Operations, December, 1941–August, 1942." Part 1.
No. 156. "Historical Review of Landing Operations of the Japanese Forces."
No. 169. "Outline of Naval Armament and Preparations for War." Part 4.

SECONDARY SOURCES

Unpublished Sources

Adjutant General's Office, War Department. "Strength of the Army." Center of Military History, U.S. Department of the Army.
Barde, Robert Elmer. "The Battle of Midway: A Study in Command." Ph.D. diss., University of Maryland, 1971.
Harkness, Albert. "Command History, U.S. Naval Forces in the Southwest Pacific Area in World War II: Part 1: Retreat in the Southwest Pacific." Operational Classified Archives.
Naval Historical Center, U.S. Department of the Navy. Ships' Histories Section. Individual histories of U.S. warships.
Naval War College. "Strategical and Tactical Analysis: The Battle of the Coral Sea, May 1 to May 11 inclusive 1942." Navpers 91050. Newport, 1947.

————. "Strategical and Tactical Analysis: The Battle of Midway Including the Aleutians Phase, June 3 to June 14, 1942." Navpers 91067. Newport, 1948.

Office of Naval Intelligence. "The Japanese Story of the Battle of Midway: A Translation." Division of Naval History, U.S. Department of the Navy, 1947.

Rosien, Arthur, et al. "The Official History of the Alaskan Department." Center of Military History, U.S. Department of the Army. Historical Section, Alaskan Department, n.d.

U.S. Military Academy, West Point. "The War with Japan." Part 1. Department of Military Art and Engineering, 1945.

Wenzel, Jon. "The Japanese Decision for War and the Genesis of the Three Phase Operational Concept." An as-yet unsubmitted and unpublished Ph.D. thesis.

Official Histories

Butler, J. R. M. *History of the Second World War: Grand Strategy, June 1941–August 1942*. Vol. 3, part 2. United Kingdom Military Series. London: Her Majesty's Stationers Office, 1964.

Cline, R. S. *The United States Army in World War Two: The War Department, Washington Command Post: The Operations Division*. Washington: Department of the Army, 1951.

Coakley, R. W., and R. M. Leighton. *The United States Army in World War Two: The War Department, Global Logistics and Strategy, 1943–1945*. Washington: Department of the Army, 1968.

Conn, Stetson, Rose C. Engelman, and Byron Fairchild. *The United States Army in World War Two: The Western Hemisphere: Guarding the United States and Its Outposts*. Washington: Department of the Army, 1964.

Conn, Stetson, and Byron Fairchild. *The United States Army in World War Two: The Western Hemisphere: The Framework of Hemisphere Defense*. Washington: Department of the Army, 1960.

Craven, N.F., and J. L. Cate, eds. *The Army Air Forces in World War Two: Plans and Early Operations, January 1939–August 1942*. Vol. 1. Chicago: University of Chicago Press, 1948.

Dziuban, Stanley W. *The United States Army in World War Two: Special Studies, Military Relations Between the United States and Canada, 1939–1945*. Washington: Department of the Army, 1954.

Gill, G. Hermon. *Australia in the War of 1939–1945. Series 2: Navy. Royal Australian Navy, 1939–1942*. Vol. 1. Canberra, Australia: Australian War Memorial, 1957.

————. *Australia in the War of 1939–1945. Series 2: Navy. Royal Australian Navy, 1942–1945*. Vol 2. Canberra, Australia: Australian War Memorial, 1968.

Gillespie, O. A. *New Zealand in the Second World War: The Pacific*. Wellington, New Zealand: Department of Internal Affairs, 1952.

Gillison, D. *Australia in the War of 1939–1945. Series 3: Air. Royal Australian Air Force, 1939–1942*. Vol. 1. Canberra, Australia: Australian War Memorial, 1962.

Greenfield, K. R. *The United States Army in World War Two: Command Decisions*. Washington: Department of the Army, 1960.

Greenfield, K. R., R. R. Palmer, and B. I. Wiley. *The United States Army in World War Two: The Army Ground Forces: The Organization of Ground Combat Troops*. Washington: Department of the Army, 1947.

Gwyer, J. M. A. *History of the Second World War: Grand Strategy, June 1941–August 1942.* Vol. 3, part 1. United Kingdom Military Series. London: Her Majesty's Stationers Office, 1964.

Hayes, Grace. *History of the Joint Chiefs of Staff in World War Two.* Annapolis, Naval Institute Press, 1982.

Heinl, Robert D. *Marines at Midway.* Washington: Department of the Navy, 1948.

Hoogenband, C. van den, and L. Schotborgh. *Nederlands-Indie contra Japan.* Vol. 2. The Hague, Netherlands: Department of Defense, 1949.

Hough, Frank O., Verle E. Ludwig, and Henry I. Shaw. *History of U.S. Marine Corps Operations in World War Two: Pearl Harbor to Guadalcanal.* Vol. 1. Washington: Department of the Navy, 1958.

Japanese Self-Defense Agency, War History Office. *Senshi Sosho. Middowe Kaisen.* No. 43. Tokyo: Asagumo Shimbun.

Kirby, S. Woodburn. *History of the Second World War: The War Against Japan, The Loss of Singapore.* Vol. 1. United Kingdom Military Series. London: Her Majesty's Stationers Office, 1957.

———. *History of the Second World War: The War Against Japan: India's Most Dangerous Hour.* Vol. 2. United Kingdom Military Series. London: Her Majesty's Stationers Office, 1958.

Leighton, R. M., and R. W. Coakley. *The United States Army in World War Two: The War Department, Global Logistics and Strategy.* Washington: Department of the Army, 1940–43.

McCarthy, Dudley. *Australia in the War of 1939–1945. Series 1: Army. The South West Pacific Area: First Year, Kokoda to Wau.* Vol. 5. Canberra, Australia: Australian War Memorial, 1959.

Matloff, Maurice, and Edwin M. Snell. *The United States Army in World War Two: The War Department, Strategic Planning for Coalition Warfare, 1941–1942.* Washington: Department of the Army, 1953.

Miller, John. *The United States Army in World War Two: The War in the Pacific, Guadalcanal: The First Offensive.* Washington: Department of the Army, 1949.

Milner, Samuel. *The United States Army in World War Two: The War in the Pacific; Victory in Papua.* Washington: Department of the Army, 1957.

Morton, L. *The United States Army in World War Two: Strategy and Command.* Washington: Department of the Army, 1962.

———. *The United States Army in World War Two: The War in the Pacific, The Fall of the Philippines.* Washington: Department of the Army, 1951.

Roskill, S. W. *History of the Second World War: The War at Sea; The Period of Balance.* Vol. 2. United Kingdom Military Series. London: Her Majesty's Stationers Office, 1957.

Stacey, C. P. *The Official History of the Canadian Army in the Second World War. Vol. 1. Six Years of War: The Army in Canada, Britain and the Pacific.* Ottowa: Ministry of National Defence, 1955.

Watson, M. S. *The United States Army in World War Two: The War Department, Chief of Staff: Plans and Preparations.* Washington: Department of the Army, 1950.

Wigmore, L. *Australia in the War of 1939–1945. Series 1: Army. The Japanese Thrust.* Vol. 4. Canberra: Australian War Memorial, 1957.

Books

Agawa, Hiroyuki. *The Reluctant Admiral: Yamamoto and the Imperial Navy*. Annapolis: Naval Institute Press, 1979. Tokyo: Kodansha International, 1979.

Argyle, Christopher J. *Japan at War*. London: Barker, 1976.

Barker, A. J. *Midway: The Turning Point*. London: Macdonald, 1971.

Belote, James H., and William M. Belote. *Titans of the Seas: The Development and Operations of Japanese and American Carrier Task Forces During World War II*. New York: Harper and Row, 1975.

Blair, Clay. *Silent Victory: The U.S. Submarine War Against Japan*. Philadelphia: Lippincott, 1975.

Blythe, Ronald. *The Age of Illusion: England in the Twenties and Thirties, 1919–1940*. London: Penguin, 1940.

Brown, David. *Carrier Operations of World War II: The Pacific Navies, December 1941–February 1943*. Vol. 2. London: Allen, 1974.

Browne, Courtney. *Tojo: The Last Banzai*. London: Corgi, 1969.

Bruce, George. *Sea Battles of the Twentieth Century*. London: Hamlyn, 1973.

Buell, Thomas B. *Master of Sea Power: A Biography of Fleet Admiral Ernest J. King*. Boston: Little, Brown, 1974.

———. *The Quiet Warrior: A Biography of Admiral Raymond A. Spruance*. Boston: Little, Brown, 1974.

Chandler, Alfred D., ed. *The Papers of Dwight D. Eisenhower: The War Years*. Vol. 1. Baltimore: Johns Hopkins University Press, 1970.

Churchill, Winston S. *The Second World War: The Hinge of Fate*. Vol. 4. London: Cassell, 1951.

Clausewitz, K. M. von. *On War*. London: Penguin, 1968.

Compton-Hall, R. *The Underwater War, 1939–1945*. Poole: Blandford, 1982.

Connell, John. *Wavell: Supreme Commander*. Edited and completed by M. Roberts. London: Collins, 1969.

Costello, John, *The Pacific War*. London: Collins, 1981.

d'Albas, Andrieu. *Death of a Navy: Japanese Sea Power in the Second World War*. London: Hale, 1957.

Deacon, Richard. *A History of the Japanese Secret Service*. London: Muller, 1982.

Dull, Paul S. *A Battle History of the Imperial Japanese Navy (1941–1945)*. Annapolis: Naval Institute Press, 1978. Cambridge: Patrick Stephens, 1978.

Dyer, George C. *The Amphibians Came to Conquer: The Story of Admiral Richmond Kelly Turner*. Vol. 1. Washington: Department of the Navy, 1971.

Feldt, E. *The Coast Watchers*. Melbourne: Oxford University Press, 1946.

Forrestal, E. P. *Admiral Raymond A. Spruance, USN: A Study in Command*. Washington: Department of the Navy, 1966.

Frank, Pat, and Joseph D. Harrington. *Rendezvous at Midway: U.S.S.* Yorktown *and the Japanese Carrier Fleet*. New York: Day, 1967.

Fuchida, Mitsuo, and Masatake Okumiya. *Midway: The Battle That Doomed Japan*. Annapolis: Naval Institute Press, 1955. London: Hutchinson, 1957.

Garfield, Brian. *The Thousand Mile War: World War II in Alaska and the Aleutians*. New York: Ballantine, 1978.

Glines, C. V. *Doolittle's Tokyo Raiders*. Princeton: Van Nostrand, 1964.

Hagan, Kenneth J., ed. *In Peace and War: Interpretations of American Naval History, 1775–1978*. Westport, Conn.: Greenwood, 1978.

Halsey, William F., and J. Bryan. *Admiral Halsey's Story*. New York: Whittlesey House, 1947.

Hayashi, Saburo, and Alvin D. Coox. *Kogun: The Japanese Army in the Pacific War*. Westport, Conn.: Greenwood, 1978.

Hezlett, Arthur. *The Aircraft and Sea Power*. London: Davies, 1970.

Hoehling, A. A. *The Lexington Goes Down: The Last Seven Hours of a Fighting Lady*. Englewood Cliffs, N.J.: Prentice Hall, 1971.

Hough, Richard. *The Fleet That Had to Die*. London: Chatto and Windus, 1963.

Hoyt, Edwin P. *How They Won the War in the Pacific: Nimitz and His Admirals*. New York: Weybridge and Talley, 1970.

Ito, Masanori. *The End of the Imperial Navy*. London: Weidenfeld and Nicolson, 1956.

Kahn, David. *The Code Breakers: The Story of Secret Writing*. London: Weidenfeld and Nicolson, 1966. New York: Macmillan, 1967.

King, Ernest J., and W. M. Whitehill. *Fleet Admiral King: A Naval Record*. London: Eyre and Spottiswoode, 1953.

Kiralfy, Alexander. "Japanese Naval Strategy." In *The Makers of Modern Strategy: Military Thought from Machiavelli to Hitler*, edited by Edward Mead Earle. Princeton: Princeton University Press, 1968.

Lewin, Ronald. *The Other Ultra: Codes, Ciphers and the Defeat of Japan*. London: Hutchinson, 1982.

Lord, Walter. *Incredible Victory*. London: Hamish Hamilton, 1968.

Lundstrom, John B. *The First South Pacific Campaign: Pacific Fleet Strategy, December 1941–June 1942*. Annapolis: Naval Institute Press, 1976.

Macintyre, Donald. *Battle for the Mediterranean*. London: Pan, 1970.

———. *Battle for the Pacific*. London: Batsford, 1966.

Manchester, William. *American Caesar: Douglas MacArthur, 1880–1964*. London: Hutchinson, 1979.

Marder, Arthur J. *Old Friends, New Enemies: The Royal Navy and the Imperial Japanese Navy, Strategic Illusions, 1939–1941*. Oxford: Clarendon, 1981.

Merril, James M. *A Sailor's Admiral: A Biography of William F. Halsey*. New York: Crowell, 1976.

Millot, Bernard A. *The Battle of the Coral Sea*. London: Allan, 1974.

Morison, S. E., *History of U.S. Naval Operations in World War Two: The Battle of the Atlantic, September 1939–May 1943*. London: Oxford University Press, 1948.

———. *History of U.S. Naval Operations in World War Two: Coral Sea, Midway and Submarine Actions, May 1942–August 1942*. Vol. 4. Boston: Little, Brown, 1967.

———. *History of U.S. Naval Operations in World War Two: The Rising Sun in the Pacific, 1931–April 1942*. Vol. 3. Boston: Little, Brown, 1968.

Muggenthaler, August Karl. *German Raiders of World War Two*. London: Pan, 1980.

O'Connor, Raymond. *The Japanese Navy in World War II*. Annapolis: Naval Institute Press, 1969.

Okumiya, Masatake, Jiro Horikoshi, and Martin Caidin. *Zero! The Story of the Japanese Navy Air Force, 1937–1945*. London; Cassell, 1957.

Paull, R. *Retreat from Kokoda: The Australian Campaign in New Guinea, 1942*. London: Secker and Warburg, 1983.

Pelz, Stephen E. *Race to Pearl Harbor: The Failure of the Second London Naval Conference and the Onset of World War II*. Cambridge, Mass.: Harvard University Press, 1974.

Pogue, Forrest C. *George C. Marshall: Ordeal and Hope, 1939–1942*. London: Mac-Gibbon and Kee, 1968.

Polmar, Norman. *Aircraft Carriers: A Graphic History of Carrier Aviation and Its Influence on World Events*. Garden City, N.Y.: Doubleday, 1969.

Potter, E. B. *Nimitz*. Annapolis: Naval Institute Press, 1976.

Prange, Gordon W. *At Dawn We Slept: The Untold Story of Pearl Harbor*. London: Joseph, 1982.

Preston, Anthony. *U-boats*. London: Excalibur, 1978.

Reynolds, Clark G. *Command of the Sea: The History and Strategy of Maritime Empires*. London: Hale, 1976.

Rhoer, Edward van der. *Deadly Magic: Communications Intelligence in World War Two in the Pacific*. London: Hale, 1978.

Rohwer, T., and G. Hammelchen. *Chronology of the War at Sea, 1939–1942*. Vol. 1. London: Allen, 1972.

Rosinski, Herbert. *The Development of Naval Thought*. Newport, R.I.: Naval War College, 1977.

Sadao, Asada. "Japanese Admirals and the Politics of Naval Limitation: Kato Tamosaburo against Kato Kanji." In *Naval Warfare in the Twentieth Century, 1900–1945*, edited by Gerald Jordan. London: Croom Helm, 1977.

Slim, William. *Defeat into Victory*. London: Cassell, 1957.

Smith, William Ward. *Midway: Turning Point of the Pacific*. New York: Crowell, 1966.

Spurr, Russell. *A Glorious Way to Die: The Kamikaze Mission of the Battleship* Yamato, *April 1945*. London: Sidgwick and Jackson, 1982.

Storry, Richard. *A History of Modern Japan*. New York: Penguin, 1960.

Thorn, Christopher. *Allies of a Kind: The United States, Britain and the War Against Japan, 1941–1945*. London: Hamish Hamilton, 1978.

Toland, John. *But Not In Shame: The Six Months After Pearl Harbor*. New York: Random House, 1961.

———. *The Rising Sun: The Decline and Fall of the Japanese Empire, 1936–1945*. New York: Random House, 1970.

Tomlinson, Michael. *The Most Dangerous Moment*. London: Kimber, 1976.

Tuleja, Thaddeus V. *Climax at Midway*. London: Dent, 1960.

Turner, L. C. F., H. R. Gordon-Cumming, and J. E. Betzler. *War in the Southern Oceans*. Cape Town: Oxford University Press, 1961.

Warner, Denis, and Peggy Warner. *The Tide at Sunrise: A History of the Russo-Japanese War, 1904–1905*. London: Angus and Robertson, 1975.

Werstein, Irving. *The Battle of Midway*. New York: Crowell, 1961.

Willmott, H. P. *B-17 Flying Fortress*. London: Arms and Armour, 1980.

———. *Empires in the Balance: Japanese and Allied Pacific Strategies to April 1942*. Annapolis: Naval Institute Press, 1982. London: Orbis, 1982.

————. *Pearl Harbor*. London: Bison, 1981.

————. *Sea Warfare: Weapons, Tactics and Strategy*. Chichester: Bird, 1981.

————. *Zero A6M*. London: Arms and Armour, 1980.

Winton, John. *The War in the Pacific: Pearl Harbor to Tokyo Bay*. London: Sidgwick and Jackson, 1978.

Periodicals

Cook, Charles O., Jr. "The Pacific Command Divided: The Most Unexplainable Decision." U.S. Naval Institute *Proceedings* 104, no. 9 (September 1978): 55–61.

————. "The Strange Case of Rainbow 5." U.S. Naval Institute *Proceedings* 104, no. 8 (August 1978): 66–73.

Fukaya, Hajime. "Japanese Wartime Carrier Construction." U.S. Naval Institute *Proceedings* 81, no. 9 (September 1955): 131–43.

Morgan, John G. "The Changing Nature of Modern Naval Leadership." U.S. Naval Institute *Proceedings* 104, no. 8 (August 1978): 76-79.

Peattie, Mark R. "Akiyama Saneyuki and the Emergence of Modern Japanese Naval Doctrine." U.S. Naval Institute *Proceedings* 103, no. 1 (January 1977): 60–69.

Toyama Saburo. "Years of Transition: Japan's Naval Strategy from 1894 to 1945." *Revue Internationale d'Histoire Militaire*, 1978, no. 38: 162–82.

Wilds, Thomas. "How Japan Fortified the Mandated Islands." U.S. Naval Institute *Proceedings* 81, no. 4 (April 1955): 401–7.

Technical and Reference

Bagnasco, E. *Submarines of World War Two*. London: Arms and Armour, 1977.

Brown, David. *Aircraft Carriers*. London: Macdonald and Jane's, 1977.

Bueschel, Richard M. *Mitsubishi A6M1/2/-2N Zero-sen*. London: Osprey, 1970.

Chihaya, Masataka. *I.J.N. Yamato and Musashi*. Windsor: Profile, 1973.

Chihaya, Masataka, and Yasuo Abe. *I.J.N. Kongo*. Windsor: Profile, 1971.

————. *I.J.N. Yukikaze*. Windsor: Profile, 1972.

Dictionary of American Fighting Ships. Vols. 1–8. Washington: Naval History Center, Department of the Navy, 1959–81.

Dulin, Robert O., and William H. Garzke. *Battleships: United States Battleships in World War II*. London: Macdonald and Jane's, 1976.

Francillon, R. J. *Japanese Aircraft of the Pacific War*. New York: Putnam, 1970.

————. *Japanese Carrier Air Groups, 1941–1945*. London: Osprey, 1979.

————. *U.S. Navy Carrier Air Groups: Pacific, 1941–1945*. London: Osprey, 1978.

Gunston, Bill. *The Encyclopedia of the World's Combat Aircraft*. London: Salamander, 1976.

Jentschura, Hansgeorg, Jung Dieter, and Peter Mickel. *Warships of the Imperial Japanese Navy, 1868–1945*. Annapolis: Naval Institute Press, 1977. London: Arms and Armour, 1977.

Lenton, H. T., and J. J. Colledge. *Warships of World War II*. London: Allen, 1964.

Parkes, Oscar. *British Battleships, 1860–1960*. London: Seeley, Service, 1966.

Silverstone, Paul H. *U.S. Warships of World War II*. London: Allen, 1965.

Watts, Anthony J., and Brian G. Gordon. *The Imperial Japanese Navy*. London: Macdonald, 1971.

General Index

Index of Ships